FROM PHILO TO ORIGEN

Program in Judaic Studies
Brown University
BROWN JUDAIC STUDIES
Edited by
Jacob Neusner,
Wendell S. Dietrich, Ernest S. Frerichs,
Calvin Goldscheider, Alan Zuckerman

Project Editors (Project)

David Blumenthal, Emory University (Approaches to Medieval Judaism)
William Brinner (Studies in Judaism and Islam)
Ernest S. Frerichs, Brown University (Dissertations and Monographs)
Lenn Evan Goodman, University of Hawaii (Studies in Medieval Judaism) (Studies in Judaism and Islam)
William Scott Green, University of Rochester (Approaches to Ancient Judaism)
Ivan Marcus, Jewish Theological Seminary of Americas
(Texts and Studies in Medieval Judaism)
Marc L. Raphael, Ohio State University (Approaches to Judaism in Modern Times)
Jonathan Z. Smith, University of Chicago (Studia Philonica)

Number 69
FROM JPHILO TO ORIGEN
Middle Platonism in Tradition

by
Robert M. Berchman

FROM PHILO TO ORIGEN
Middle Platonism in Transition

by
Robert M. Berchman

UNITY SCHOOL LIBRARY
UNITY VILLAGE, MISSOURI 6406

Scholars Press
Chico, California

FROM PHILO TO ORIGEN
Middle Platonism in Tradition

by
Robert M. Berchman

© 1984
Brown University

Support for the publication of this book in part from the Alperin family foundation of Rhode Island.

Library of Congress Cataloging in Publication Data

Berchman, Robert M.
  From Philo to Origen.

  (Brown Judaic studies ; no. 69)
  Bibliography: p.
  Includes indexes.
  1. Neoplatonism. 2. Philo, of Alexandria. 3. Origen.
I. Title. II. Series
B645.B47 1984   186'.4   84–10487
ISBN 0-89130-750-8 (pbk.)

Printed in the United States of America
on acid-free paper

C.1

For Eugen Kullmann

TABLE OF CONTENTS

ACKNOWLEDGEMENTS

I would like to dedicate this work to two teachers and friends who guided me in the years of my studies from Gambier to Providence.

Professor Eugen Kullmann of Kenyon College introduced me to Greek, Latin, and ancient philosophy. He taught me reverence for the languages and ideas of the ancients, and discussed with me the perennial issues of philosophy. From him I learned the meaning of the humanistic study of philosophy and religion. In this his retirement year I dedicate this work to him.

I wish to express a very special thanks to Professor Jacob Neusner of Brown University for his encouragement of this study. He offered the friendly hand and collegial support that every young scholar needs to pursue goals and realize them. For his sharing of these qualities I shall always be grateful.

Professor Horst Moehring provided the necessary milieu and continuous support for my first scholarly project. This work arose out of the fruitful seminars under his aegis, was initially expressed in my doctoral dissertation written under his guidance, and was consummated in my year as his colleague at Brown University. He taught me much about the intellectual culture of late antiquity and the values it proclaimed. From him I learned the manifold richness of Judaism and Christianity in their formative ages.

Through the years of researching and writing this work I always had the support of my parents Professor John Berchman and Mrs. Stella Berchman. My appreciation to both of them for their steady presence at my side in these years. I offer special thanks to Lynda Dykstra whose assistance in the editing of this work will always be appreciated. Finally, my affection to Mephistopheles, who reminded me daily of our afternoon constitutional, thereby providing the sojourns whereby we both came to know Providence.

Robert Michael Berchman
Providence, Rhode Island
31 August 1984

PREFACE

I.

This book is about the emergence of the Jewish and Christian Platonic philosophies in the formative period of Judaism and Christianity at Alexandria. These are the Jewish Middle Platonism of Philo, and the Christian Middle Platonisms of Clement and Origen. They are described within the context of the Middle Academy, and analyzed as expressions of the Platonic conceptual world during the early Imperium Romanum.

There are two stages in historical inquiry. The first is to uncover the site; the second is to restore it. The analogy of archaeology is an apt one. These stages must be kept separate, so that the artifacts may be studied, and then brought back together again. My goal is to bring the artifacts of Jewish and Christian Middle Platonism in a state close to their original and living condition. This is why they are examined first in relation to the Academic options they were contemporary with, and a part of, in the first three centuries of the common era. In this work the reader encounters the reconstruction of our site, not its uncovering. What one views is the reconstruction of an ancient city restored according to the central issues and problematics of its original construction. In this work we take a different tack.

In constructing a thesis one combs the sources for supporting evidence, in the orthodox modern way, and emerges with an ample array of data to support a stand. However, it is often the case with ancient sources that testimonies do not yield the type of coherency which support a thesis. Thus conventional solutions are either to excise statements as non-authentic, according to the critical methods of the nineteenth century, or explain them away as pre-critical phases in the development of an author's thought according to the critical methods of the twentieth century. Thesis construction has a limited justification. It creates good dissertations and monographs, and fuels the dim fires of learned discourse.

We do not approach these expressions of Academic thinking with a preconceived thesis, or view them exclusively within the context of "Judaism," "Christianity," "Jewish Philosophy," or "Patristic Philosophy." If we have a preconceived thesis based upon these categories of analysis we court disaster; first, by distorting the historical context of their expression, and second by treating Judaism and Christianity as monolithic and conceptually distinct conceptual systems.

The philosophers we examine were neither thesis builders or literary critics. They were not products of the modern academy. They were interpreters of their teachers, and thinkers who attempted to solve questions posed to them by their teachers. They were products of the Middle Academy whose modes and methods of thinking and questioning were quite distinct from mediaeval and modern ones. Enveloped in their own procedures they had little patience for the viewpoints of peers, let alone the fellows of the mediaeval or modern university. They worked from and within the doctrines of their teachers, and understood philosophical wisdom through their eyes.

The student must approach the sources as a "hearer" (akroatês) in the manner akin to how these ancient philosophers approached their teachers.[1] This involves an act of humility, and a modern discomfort as well. It means bracketing, but not discarding, modern approaches to the study of texts, so that we may listen to the actual problems and difficulties these philosophers grappled with. This requires taking seriously what these thinkers took seriously. It means, at least initially, that we merely describe their metaphysical norms, problems and solutions, and then in the last phase analyze the meanings they yield. This approach calls for the historian's restraint in the anxious moments when the philosopher asks for quick solutions to the issues at hand. It requires the attitude of a hearer.

Such an attitude is attempted in this study. It involves unavoidable repetition, but it offers are acceptable approach if we are to comprehend what the first Jewish and Christian Platonists of Alexandria proposed as solutions to the perennial problems of Greek metaphysics. Accordingly great care is taken to keep medieval and modern viewpoints in abeyance when we examine Philo, Clement, and Origen. This is not to say we approach these thinkers uncritically with the attitude of scholastic Ludites or Know-nothings. Rather as hearers we approach these thinkers on their own terms, and attempt to understand them within their ancient contexts.

2.

The divisions of this work were based upon the nature of available information, and the major philosophical themes that emerge clearly from an examination of the sources. It will be useful to delineate them here, so that the reader will find it easier to follow them in the chapters in which they occur.

The first is the question of the nature of reality and the problematics associated with it given the assumptions of the Middle Platonic theoretic. We begin our study with the two principle trajectories in early Middle Platonic thought that are most important for the subsequent self-definitions of Jewish and Christian Middle Platonic physics. These are represented by Antiochus of Ascalon and Eudorus of Alexandria. The Judaic Platonism of Philo, and the Christian Platonisms of Clement and Origen, represent an attempt to harmonize the two divergent theoretical positions proposed by Antiochus and Eudorus.

The second is the question of the nature and function of knowledge. Theories of knowledge utilized in the early Middle Academy by Antiochus are examined. He lays the foundation for one of the central assumptions of Jewish and Christian Middle Platonic epistemology in this period. This is the theory of revelation as knowledge (pistis), and revelation as the first principle of all discursive knowledge (doxa, epistêmê, gnôsis). We trace the unfolding of this theory, and its contribution to the Middle Platonic doctrines of knowledge held by Philo, Clement, and Origen.

The third theme addressed is the function of dialectic, and the development of a theory of biblical and evangelical demonstration by Philo, Clement, and Origen. They used the rules and theorems of dialectic to deduce systems of first principles from their respective Bibles. This issue brings us into the realm of Middle Platonic dialectic, and the principles of logic and rhetoric used by Jewish and Christian Platonists to demonstrate the efficacy and truth of metaphysical and epistemological postulates. We conclude our study with an examination of how dialectic is practiced by Origen in his Periarchôn (De Principiis). This work is offered as an example of how scriptural demonstration works, and reveals the central role dialectic played in the demonstration of philosophical norms in formative Christian Platonism.

It is hoped that the reader will understand why this history of Jewish and Christian Middle Platonism at Alexandria is presented thematically. It would be impossible to present such diverse and complex writings in any other manner. The reader will not find it easy to read this work. He will find few final and definitive statements, and a large portion of conjecture, hypothesis, and post facto interpretation. Given the nature of our sources and the gaps in our historical understanding of the Middle Academy, conjecture multiplies, as indeed it must. We hope, however, that our conjecture is that of the ancients themselves.

Sequential and narrative history is not easily written, let alone a history of ideas. Yet here we begin the process of writing a history of Jewish and Christian Middle Platonism between Actium and Dobruja. Our plan is to synthesize existing knowledge of the subject and, at a number of points, to add to that synthesis. Nonetheless, we recognize that the reader may not find his task simple. Given the nature of the sources and the problematics they address this is not surprising. It is hoped that the reconstruction makes an obscure and difficult topic less obscure and less difficult.

ABBREVIATIONS

A.	= Albinus, Witt
AAWG	= Abhandlung der Akademie der Wiessenschaften in Göttingen
ABAW	= Abhandlungen der bayerischen Akademie der Wissenschaften
AEHE	= Annuaire de l'Ecole des Hautes Etudies
AG	= Der Aristotelismus beiden Griechen, Moraux
AGP	= Archiv für die Geschichte der Philosophie
AJP	= American Journal of Philology
AJSR	= American Jewish Studies Review
AJT	= American Journal of Theology
BPhW	= Berliner philologische Wochenschrift
C	= Clement, Lilla
CHLAEMP	= Cambridge History of Late Antique and Early Medieaval Philosophy
CNPT	= Christianity and Neoplatonic Thought
CP	= Classical Philology
CQ	= Classical Quarterly
DB	= Doctrine of Being, Owens
DG	= Doxographi Graeci, Diels
DThC	= Dictionnaire de Théologie catholique
Did.	= Didaskalikos, Hermann, Plato VI, 152
EFRL	= Elementary Forms of Religious Life, Durkheim
EP	= Der Einfless Philos, Heinisch
En	= Entretiens Hardt
Erk	= Erkenntnis
FN	= Forschung zum Neuplatonismus, Thieler
GCS	= Griechische Christliche Schrifsteller
GL	= Geschichte der Logik, Prantl
HE	= Historica Evangelica, Eusebius
HLB	= Harvard Library Bulletin
HSCP	= Harvard Studies in Classical Philology
IPRPA	= Les Idées Philosophiques et Religieuses de Philon d'Alexandre, Bréhier
ISP	= International Studies in Philosophy
JEA	= Journal of Eastern Archaeology
JP	= Journal of Philology
Koe	= Koetschan (GCS)
KrV	= Kritik der reinen Vernunft, Kant
LN	= Logos und Nomos, Andresen
ML	= Mathematische Monatschrift

MP	= Middle Platonists, Dillon
Mn	= Mnemosyne
MusHelv	= Museum Helveticum
NGA	= Nachrichten von der Akademie der Wissenschaften in Goettingen
NS	= The New Scholasticism
O	= Origène; Origen, de Faye, Trigg, Nauton, Daniélou
P	= Philo, Gfrörer, Wolfson, Siegfried
PAPA	= Proceedings of the American Philological Association
PCF	= Philosophy of the Church Fathers, Wolfson
PE	= Praeparatio Evangelica, Eusebius
PG	= Die Philosophie der Griechen, Zeller
PJ	= Philo Judaeus, Drummond
PM	= Das Problem der Materie, Bäumker
PNP	= From Platonism to Neoplatonism, Merlan
PP	= Pronoia and Pardeusis, Koch
PR	= Philosophical Review
QJS	= Quarterly Journal of Speech
RCS	= Religion as a Cultural System, Geertz
RE	= Paulys Real Encyclopädie der Classichen Wissenschaft
RheinMus	= Rheinisches Museum
S	= Scholastik; Die Stoa, Pohhenz; Speusippus, Taran
SAW	= Sächsiche Akademie der Wissenschaften zu Leipzig
SBLSP	= Society of Biblical Literature Seminar Papers
SL	= Studia Logika
SM	= Speech Monographs
SO	= Symbolae Osloenses
SRG	= Rhetores Graeci, ed. L. Spengel
SVF	= Stoicorum Veterum Fragmenta, von Arnim
TP	= Tijdschrift voor Philkosophie Erkenntnis
TTP	= Two Treatises of Philo of Alexandria, Winston-Dillon
TU	= Texte und Untersuchunger
U	= Untersuchungen zu Ciceros philosophischen Schriften, Hirzel
U	= Untersuchungen zur Logoschristologie, Oade
UCS	= University of Colorado Studies
UPPLW	= Untersuchung über Philons und Platons Lehre von Weltschöpfung, Horowitz
VC	= Vigiliae Christianae
VN	= Vorbereitung des Neuplatonismus, Theiler
WRG	= Rhetores Graeci, ed. C. Walz.
Z	= Zetemata
ZNTW	= Zeitschrift für die neutestamenliche Wissenschaft
ZP	= Zeitschrift für Philosophie

N.B.   Titles of books and papers are usually in the footnotes with the name of the author immediately preceeding, and the indication of the page following. In the case of two or more works by the same author the title of the book or paper is partially reproduced according to the <u>sigla</u> listed above. Abbreviations of the works of individual ancient authors will be given when they are introduced. We have adopted longer or shorter abbreviations of works at different points in the book, e.g., Philo, <u>De Opificio Mundi</u> = <u>Opf.</u>; Clement, <u>Stomateis</u> = <u>Strom.</u>; Origen, <u>Contra Celsum</u> = <u>C. Cels.</u>; Cicero, <u>Tusculan Disputations</u> = <u>Tusc. Dispt.</u>; Sextus Empiricus, <u>Adversus Mathematikos</u> = <u>Adv. Math.</u>; Aristotle, <u>Metaphysica</u> = <u>Metaphys.</u>; or <u>Met.</u>, and so on.

INTRODUCTION

The Historical Interpretation of Philosophical Traditions:
Its Methodological Problems as
Exemplified in Middle Platonism

1.

The formation of Jewish and Christian Platonism from Philo to Origen is the subject of this study. Two dates within which it could be conveniently framed are the establishment of the princeps under Octavian in 28-27 B.C., and the death of Decius at the hands of the Goths in 251 A.D. The first date signals the onset of Roman hegemony in the eastern Mediterranean and the establishment of the Roman Imperium. The second date signals the beginning of some sixty years of political and social upheaval that culminates in the ascension of Constantine as Emperor, and the establishment of the Christian Imperium.

The later years of the Roman Republic and the first years of the Empire marked a renaissance in the Platonic philosophy. Plato's dialogues were recovered and reinterpreted from a variety of angles. In this period they were made the object of scholarly treatment and critical discussion associated with the names of Antiochus of Ascalon, Aryius Didymus, Archytas, Eudorus of Alexandria, and Cicero. In the early decades of the Roman Empire, Seneca and Philo of Alexandria continued the interpretations of Antiochus and Eudorus in their own reflections upon the teachings of Plato, Aristotle, and the Stoa. In the second century evidence appears of the scholarly work done by these early Middle Platonists in the writings and reflections of Clement, Albinus, and Ammonius Saccas. The first two figures wrote handbooks and monographs on a variety of philosophical themes. Finally, in the third century Origen concludes the significant contribution of this academic tradition.

In the first through the third centuries A.D. a great deal of debate went on among Platonists, Peripatetics, and Stoics. As a result, norms originally situated in one school tradition were adapted by others. In addition, Jewish and Christian thinkers added the wisdom of their sacred scriptures to the cacophony of philosophical discourse, and in so doing proposed new varieties of Platonism called Jewish and Christian. The figures we associate with this activity are Plutarch, Philo, Celsus, Clement, and Albinus. In the first decades of the third century, Origen enters into this dialogue and hammers out a synthesis intensely Christian and Platonic.

This study principally focuses upon one stream of Platonic thought -- the one that arises with Philo and ends with Origen. This permits us to study the Middle Academy diachronically, in the writings of these early Jewish and Christian Platonists, and also synchronically by comparing and contrasting their thought with the Hellenic Platonists.

This historical approach permits us to focus upon the central philosophical issues Middle Platonists addressed, and to bracket the questions of continuity, orthodoxy, and heresy that these thinkers share with the Neo Platonic Jewish and Christian philosophical traditions of late antiquity and the middle ages.

These years are framed in two events of very unequal importance in the public eye, but not so unequally matched in their results. First, was the battle of Actium (31 B.C.). Second, was the battle of Dobruja (251 A.D.). With the former the pax romana was established, and with the latter the conditions for the victoria christiana laid. At the beginning of the "Roman peace" Philo began his philosophical activity. In the period before the "Christian Victory" Origen concluded his philosophical activity.

We cannot allow more than a symbolic importance to the dates 28-27 B.C., and 251 A.D., and at times in this study we overstep these limits. The reason for this is that Jewish and Christian Middle Platonism can only be understood by taking the wide view chronologically, examining these Platonic philosophies as expressions of Hellenistic Platonism as a whole. Philo, Clement, and Origen inherit, and contribute to, a constellation of Platonic apriora and aporia which stretches backward to Plato, Xenocrates and Speusippus, and forward to Plotinus and Porphyry.

The events at Actium (31 B.C.) and Dobruja (251 A.D.) would prove not to have as strong a hold on later popular imaginations as the death of Jesus (31 A.D.), the destruction of Jerusalem (70 A.D.), or the vision at the pons mulvius (312 A.D.). But the first two dates frame the last three. If the former did not hold the imagination as the latter did, it is partly because of a transition in thinking to which we are heirs. An event would occur which was bigger, more subtle, and more complicated for our era than for the era which preceded it. This was the transformation of Dea Romana in the fourth century, into a new oikumenê with the Deus Christus at its head.

These historical facts will shadow us through the course of this study. We will describe, analyze, and formulate the central ideas and proposals of Philo, Clement, and Origen within the context of their own centuries. Almost two millennia of change in human thought and culture has intervened since the formative age of Jewish and Christian Middle Platonism at Alexandria. These changes have played their role only too effectively. These thinkers did not deal with the same constellation of issues as the later Patristic, mediaeval Jewish and Christian, or the modern philosopher. In the case of late antique and mediaeval philosophy it is true that they asked similar questions and faced the same aporia: of the universal and the particular, of the necessary and the contingent, of sensation and knowledge. However, they did not do so dogmatically. In the case of the modern philosopher their asking of philosophical questions, and the formulation of answers, differs so radically that we have lost the original context of their thought. Hence, the study of Middle Platonism from Philo to Origen is the study, principally, of hellenistic philosophy between Actium and Dobruja, and the Judaic and Christian Platonisms proposed at Alexandria in this period.

2.

This work has set for itself the ambitious goal of understanding Jewish and Christian Middle Platonism, and the transitional moments in its self-definition from Philo to Origen. To properly grasp these initial attempts at Jewish and Christian philosophical expression we must approach them on their own terms. This means that we cannot impose upon these thinkers issues and problems that were not their own. Questions of whether or not Philo's Judaic Platonism stands as a "normative" expression of Judaism, or Clement's and Origen's Christian Platonism fits the definition of Christian "orthodoxy or heresy" are not our concern. Our concern is what we perceive to be their concern. We examine these thinkers within the context of ancient philosophy, and the philosophical problematics they engaged in. Specifically, what is the relation of God to the universe, how are both known, to what extent does biblical revelation and philosophical wisdom agree, and how is a reality system deduced from sacred scripture?

These questions were first asked in a systematic way in formative Judaism and Christianity by the Jewish and Christian Platonists of Alexandria. It was at Alexandria in the first three centuries of the Common Era that a series of ontological, epistemological, and dialectical norms were postulated and refined which answered these questions. This study represents an attempt to describe, analyze and formulate how these central trends in formative Jewish and Christian Platonism emerged and defined themselves.

Inquiry into these philosophical options and problematics is vital for two distinct reasons. Only when we know who is talking to whom, and where a given inquiry begins and ends, shall we have an intelligible account of Jewish and Christian Platonism in its formative age. Once we grasp these first principles we begin to understand how two varieties of Judaism and Christianity expressed themselves within the trajectory of Hellenistic thought called Middle Platonism. This comprehension leads us to an appreciation of how philosophical exponents of Judaism and Christianity at Alexandria reflect the paideia of their age, and define their biblical teachings in the language of Greek metaphysics. Jewish and Christian Middle Platonism, in the formative age of Judaism and Christianity, reflects the deepest premises of Hellenistic culture. Hence, when we study the works of Philo, Clement and Origen not only do we encounter Judaic and Christian Platonists, thinkers who translated biblical revelation into Platonic wisdom, we also meet varieties of Judaism and Christianity which are wholly Platonic, and fully in accord with the philosophical culture of late antiquity.

Since our interest is in the analysis of Middle Platonic Judaism and Christianity, and not merely a restatement in modern language of its inherited assertions about itself, we resort to a different aesthetics and rhetoric from the ones appropriate in that context of discourse. Our attitude is that of the Middle Platonist who views himself as the repository of a millenium of philosophical culture, and the Jew and Christian who values the biblical revelation he holds as the archê and telos of this culture. Thinking dialogically we enter into the conceptual system of Philo, Clement, Origen, Antiochus, Eudorus and Albinus. In doing so we describe and analyze what is appropriate in their context of discourse, and reconstruct the concepts and problems these thinkers grappled with within the context of the Middle Platonic philosophy.

The emphasis in this study is to point out what is general to these Platonisms, rather than what is particular. The philosophical presuppositions each type of Platonism holds provide us with the taxa for the contrast and comparison of types of Platonism. What unites and differentiates the Middle Platonists from one another is not that they are Jewish, Christian or Pagan, but whether or not they maintain a Pythagorean or Peripatetic theoretic, or an Academic or Stoic physics. It is upon these considerations that formative Jewish and Christian Platonism faced problems and answered questions. In many cases a Philo had closer affinities to an Eudorus than to an Origen, and Clement was closer to an Albinus than to an Antiochus. Philo creatively interpreted Pythagorean Platonism to hammer out his own distinctive Jewish Platonism, and Clement utilized the writings of Philo and unknown Peripatetics to propose his unique Christian Platonism. Origen wedded together the metaphysical principles of Philo, Clement, the Neo Pythagoreans, and the Peripatetics to present the final expression of Christian Middle Platonism.

3.

There are a variety of analytical procedures to be utilized in the study of the philosophy of late antiquity. Historically, we focus upon one school tradition, then diachronically and synchronically study the different trajectories within this tradition. The structures of their conceptual system and the content of their conceptual norms are described and analyzed. This yields a picture of the similarity they share in conceptual structures, and the diversity they share in conceptual norms. Phenomenologically, we focus upon the constellation of problematics that this scheme and its norms present to those who share them. Description and analysis focus upon how philosophers pose questions, and how they answer them. Finally, we employ literacy analysis to focus upon the different genres of writing and rhetoric used for the presentation of philosophical ideas. Description and analysis pay attention to the form and structure of philosophical discourse. A recognition of the literary and rhetorical aspects of composition informs us about literacy intention of discourse, and the questions we can and cannot ask of a text.

While these approaches have been applied in the study of the works of the Hellenic Platonists, they have not been widely utilized for the study of the writings of Jewish and Christian Platonists. Modern scholars have traditionally focused their attention upon the place of Philo, Clement, and Origen in the unfolding of Jewish and Christian philosophy,[1] have asked about the orthodoxy or heresy of their theological proposals,[2] and have assessed their ideas within the context of their own normative theological standards for Judaism and Christianity.[3] Still others, whose focus is upon pagan philosophy, merely utilize these thinkers as a quarry, and their writings as _fontes_ for the study of late antique and early medieval philosophy.[4] The goal of this work is to apply the modes of analysis which have been traditionally applied to the Hellenic writings from the Middle Academy to Jewish and Christian Middle Platonic writings . This means that we approach the philosophies of Philo, Clement, and Origen as expressions of Middle Platonic thinking, and writing. First, we shall turn to the analytical paradigm employed for the examination of their concepts. Second, we turn to the analytical paradigm utilized in the examination of their literatures.

The study of Jewish and Christian Middle Platonism is problematic first of all in terms of methodology. How do we approach these thinkers? What questions do we ask of them?

We propose that we focus upon the conceptual system and norms proposed by these philosophers. This means we can identify the conceptual system which was Academic thinking in the late Republic and the early Empire, and delineate the stages of transition in Academic norms about reality, knowledge, and dialectic. Before we do this, however, we must enter into a preliminary discussion. What do we mean by conceptual systems and norms? To answer this question we have to turn to a scholarly tradition beginning with Kant, Hegel, and Durkheim that proposed the metaphor that knowledge, philosophy, and religions serve as conceptual frameworks that organize our experience of the world.

4.

The distinction between neutral content and active synthesizing forms of thought has been one of the postulates of epistemology ever since Kant's Kritik der reinen Vernunft. Hegel's historicist reading of Kant resulted in Kant's maxim being pushed from epistemology proper to metaphysics as a whole. The claim was that philosophical systems offer conceptual systems and theoretical schemes which organize and explain reality. This metaphor was later applied by Durkheim to religions. The Kantian maxim was modified such that it was said of religions that they organize the practitioner's experience of the world. Religions are the cognitive forms into which otherwise unstructured experience is poured. "It is... the function of the categories to dominate and develop all other concepts; they are the permanent molds for the mental life" (EFRL., 488). For Durkheim, "the principle categories... are born in religion and of religion; they are the product of religious thought" (22). The interpretive grid is something that is brought to experience by religions themselves.

This idea was institutionalized later by Geertz who expressed it in terms of religious conceptual frameworks that organize experience. He takes the notion a step beyond Durkheim by claiming "religious concepts spread beyond their specifically metaphysical concepts to provide a framework of general ideas in terms of which a wide range of experience -- intellectual, emotional, moral -- can be given meaningful form" (RCS., 120). Religions offer symbol systems that perform an invaluable service... in rendering the believer's presumably unformed and meaning-less experience "graspable" (24). For Geertz religious conceptual frameworks function as Kant's Anschauungen as the principle and primary forms of organizing experience. Hence, whether under the expression of "content and form", "conceptual systems", "systems of symbols", or "theoretical schemes", philosophy and religion function as interpretive grids which dictate the scope(s) of the thinkable.

This scholarly tradition has gained wide acceptance among those who study religions. It has found a lesser audience among those who study the history of philosophy.

For anthropologists, sociologists and psychologists, this paradigm has resulted in new questions being raised and new frontiers being probed in the study of religion. For historians the paradigm has provided new opportunities for exploring different religious traditions within given historical epochs. Let us apply this paradigm in the study of the history of philosophy. Let us examine one philosophical tradition, the Middle Platonic, in one period of time, from the first century B.C. to the third century A.D.

The first three centuries A.D. were the formative ages of Judaism and Christianity. During this period two religious traditions developed a variety of philosophical options which interpreted and dictated the scope of the thinkable. The most important of these philosophical options was the Platonic represented in the figures of Philo, Clement, and Origen of Alexandria.[6]

5.

Our study of formative Jewish and Christian Platonism works from the dual assumptions of common constructs and diverse norms. In reconstructing the philosophical thought of Philo, Clement, and Origen, we make a balanced comparison based upon analogy and contrast. This entails not only comparison between these Jewish and Christian Platonisms, but among the variety of Hellenic Platonisms as well. Comparative procedures take two directions. They can be utilized to help establish what is a typical formative Jewish and Christian philosophy. This is done by analyzing the differences with the surrounding philosophical culture. Comparative procedures can also be done to identify those characteristics which Jewish and Christian Middle Platonism share with other Middle Platonic options. In the first instance a taxa is built upon contrast, in the second a taxa is built upon analogy. The goal is to make a balanced comparison. An analysis marked by absolute divergence or identity would make no sense. This approach has plagued many a study on the Jewish and Christian Middle Platonists of Alexandria. We follow a procedure that turns on contrast and analogy between metaphysical options. Through contrast and analogy we reconstruct the conceptual system proposed by these thinkers, and trace the relationships among their norms.

Analogy and contrast focus upon which norms are stressed by a thinker. This aids in the determination of the transition that occurs between thinkers. Norms, problematics, and answers are defined, addressed and postulated on the basis of what teachings are stressed and attacked. The disadvantage of a procedure that relies on analogy and contrast is a lack of precision. No phenomenon corresponds or contrasts with another exactly, and no philosophical option can be reduced to or explained by another. The advantage is that once informed of analogies and contrasts we are able to reconstruct norms, problematics, and answers more precisely, and trace transitional moments more fully rather than relying solely on one procedure or an other in isolation, with no comparative reference whatsoever.

Within these sets of culturally conditioned conceptual frameworks there are a variety of divergent norms. Norms are metaphysical, epistemological, and dialectical regulations and are the philosophical assumptions that make up conceptual constructs.

They are generally explicit such as definitions of God, the world, the nature of knowledge and its function, and theorems of logic and rhetorical syllogistic. Each Platonic conceptual framework varies in its norms from others. Some norms arise from a Neo Pythagorean matrix, and still others from Peripatetic and Stoic matrices.

Norms are philosophical assumptions. They function as philosophical facts. They are the basic formulations that any philosopher employs to state what reality is, how it is known, and how it is defined and demonstrated.[7] Norms are not constant. They change as answers to problematics change. Once we identify a norm we can trace transitions which occur in it. In assembling a constellation of norms we can answer the types of questions such as those posed above, and trace the analogies and contrasts between norms synchronically and diachronically.

The nonconstancy of norms does not contradict the claim of a constancy of conceptual frameworks in Middle Platonism. A variety of norms are to be expected within any conceptual system. They are also extant in the Academic scheme of interpreting reality. Indeed, the Platonic conceptual system organizes diverse norms and adjudicates among them. The synchronic and diachronic analysis of norms permits us to trace the transitional moments in the unfolding of this Middle Academic conceptual framework.

The raw materials of Philo, Clement & Origen's intellectual experience were contained in their Bibles, and the symbolic systems used to organize and make sense of these, were Platonic. Platonism(s) provided the interpretive grid and symbolic system whereby they grasped and made comprehensible their scriptures. The Platonic philosophy provided the active synthesizing forms of thought for the neutral content, at least philosophically of divine revelation, and thereby provided the primary forms of organizing doctrines of being, how it is known, and how this knowledge correlates to revelation dialectically.

Besides organizing experience, as religious frameworks do, philosophical frameworks organize the world of the believer. To the extent that Jew, Christian, and Hellene share a common cultural experience and mode of organizing it, we have a single world that is organized in similar ways ontologically, epistemologically, and dialectically. It is this constructed entity, in its philosophical dimensions, that we shall examine in this study.

This common picture of a single world is organized through Platonic constructs. This one world is seen through a variety of perspectives which are dependent upon the type of Platonic framework utilized, and the understandings of biblical scripture proposed on the basis of these frameworks (this applies only to Jewish and Christian Platonism). Since the categories comprising formative Jewish and Christian conceptual systems are translations of philosophical states, they yield knowledge of the intellectual realms and frontiers of the philosophical options proposed in the formative periods of Judaism and Christianity.

These categories translate intellectual states which these thinkers maintain constitute the inner meaning of scripture. Hence, scripture must be read allegorically to understand these states, and scripture must be utilized as the premise for all philosophical frameworks proposed. According to these Platonic philosophers the ontological and epistemological postulates they advocate are contained in their sacred writings. They demonstrate these, dialectically, from the premises of scripture utilizing the rules and formulae of logic and rhetoric. What they proposed, then, is not only a single world organized and known through Platonic philosophical constructs. The knowable is demonstrated from scripture itself. Hence, we encounter an <u>apodeixis biblikê</u> and <u>euaggelikê</u> whose function is to legitimatize the philosophical postulates proposed as authentically Jewish and Christian. It is this demonstrative mechanism, in its logical and rhetorical dimensions, that we shall examine in this study.

In their conceptual capacities, these exponents of Jewish and Christian Platonism offer diverse webs of interpretation, encompassing things as a definition of God, his relation to the universe, the relation of the degrees of reality to one another, how God and the universe are known, and how philosophical wisdom and biblical knowledge correlate to one another, with the former being deduced from the latter.

Jewish and Christian Platonism in the first three centuries A.D. are kindred conceptual frameworks which can be compared to Hellenic Platonism in the same period. They share a common conceptual framework which organizes and filters the world and the experience of the world, through synthesizing forms of thought that are elemental components of Graeco-Roman civilization. Thus, the conceptual frameworks utilized by Philo, Clement, and Origen to organize the world, and the experience of the world, arise from a framework of general ideas that form the cultural system of Hellenistic <u>paideia</u> in general and the Platonic <u>philosophia</u> in particular.

The study of Jewish and Christian Platonism in the formative age of Judaism and Christianity permits us to compare these diverse philosophical constructs to one another, and to Hellenic Platonic constructs. Hence, although there is a diversity in how a Philo, Clement, Origen and Albinus define reality and knowledge of it, they share a common nexus of conceptual frameworks and norms whereby they organize and explain reality and how it is known. In this sense, when we study Jewish, Christian, and Hellenic Platonism in the first three centuries A.D., we must be aware of a conceptual relativism that nonetheless offers holistic diversity.

In summary, this study of formative Jewish and Christian Platonism is based on contrast and analogy. The goal is to make a balanced comparison of conceptual systems and norms. There are no alien conceptual frameworks or massive conceptual disparities in the Platonic philosophies we study in this work. Even the philosophical options rejected by the Middle Platonists under examination, such as Stoic, Peripatetic and Gnostic proposals, are argued against within the context of common conceptual frameworks. This is an important point to recognize because the variety of conceptual frameworks we encounter in the Judaisms and Christianities of late antiquity are rooted in a constellation of active synthesizing forms of thought grounded in a common cultural milieu. Thus, most of the options proposed in late antiquity are translatable. Furthermore, they arise from, and are translated through the familiar literary idioms of Graeco-Roman philosophy and rhetoric.

6.

Literary studies of the writings of Philo, Clement, and Origen are still in their infancy. The most substantial work has been done on the works of Philo[8] and Origen.[9] This research is important because it shows that the Jewish and Christian Platonists of Alexandria utilized the same genres of literary and rhetorical composition as their Hellenic peers. This means that we do not encounter in Philo, Clement, and Origen a particular type of literature, specifically Jewish or Christian; and reflects the same fact we encountered in the analysis of conceptual systems and norms.

The writings of Philo, Clement, and Origen fall under the genres of monographs (syggrammata) and commentaries (hyponêmmata). The former type of writing was principally used for the defense of philosophical positions and the latter for exegesis of biblical works. None of these writers composed technical philosophical commentaries on the Categories or paraphrases of the Timaeus, as Taurus, Atticus, Severus, and Adrastus did. When they wrote commentaries, the commentaries were generally upon biblical works and themes; and when they wrote monographs they were to defend their biblically grounded philosophical norms and attack their opponents.

These paraphrastic commentaries on biblical works and these monographs on metaphysical themes were written according to recognizable literary genre, and argued in accordance with the rules and theorems of Hellenistic rhetoric. From the results of the literary critics we can claim that it was not the aim of these philosophers to present theological tractates on the models of Maimonides, Aquinas, and Luther. Rather they composed writings on biblical and philosophical themes that reflected the works of a Salutius or an Alexander Aphrodisias.

The texts composed by these philosophers are highly stylized products. We can distinguish three elements common to both monographs and commentaries. First, there is an elucidation of a theme, or a primary text, and a basic gloss on it. The authors give evidence of having consulted several sources to establish postulates, and interpretations. They usually utilize the works of contemporaries or immediate predecessors. Second, there is a more expansive paraphrase (auxêsis) that is offered particularly where a postulate is being defended, or where the meaning of a text is controversial. Third, there is the introduction, indirectly, of parallel interpretations from other philosophical schools. This is because their doctrines have relevance to the issue under discussion.

Commentaries (hyponêmmata) are principally exegetical, and monographs (syggrammata) are strongly polemical. Philo's main opponents are other Jewish philosophical interpretations -- Platonic, Peripatetic, and Stoic. Clement's monographs exhibit the same strategy, but a different situation. His audience is Christian. Origen's works are akin to those of Philo and Clement. His writings are polemical and all directed against Christians (Gnostic and Stoic), Platonists, and Stoics. In this study we shall focus upon one of Origen's monographs, the Periarchôn (De Principiis). It is an example of how a Christian Platonist demonstrates metaphysical norms from the premises of biblical scripture. The work illustrates how a Christian debated philosophically in the period under study.

It is appropriate to briefly outline the method followed in handling Platonic sources for the reconstruction of the central concepts and problems of Jewish and Christian Middle Platonism. First, whenever possible sources are utilized from the period of the first century B.C. through the third century A.D. to illuminate and clarify the conceptual schemes proposed by Philo, Clement, and Origen. Those figures which have the most influence upon a philosopher's thought are utilized extensively to explain the norms and problematics addressed in this study. For example, the writings of Eudorus and the testimonies ascribed to Antiochus are used when we reconstruct Philo's metaphysic. Second, earlier Platonic sources from the period of the Old and New Academies are drawn upon only to supplement Middle Platonic sources, or when lacuna are so severe we must rely on them for information concerning conceptual schemes and norms. For example, the writings, testimonies, and fragments of Plato, Speusippus, and Xenocrates are used to flesh out the doctrines of the ideas and the categories and their function in the Old Academy. This permits a comparison between these doctrines and those which appear in the Middle Academy in Philo, Clement, Albinus, and Origen.

Although it is clear that these writings serve as fontes for the Jewish and Christian Middle Platonists of Alexandria no attempt is made to trace sources in the manner of a Quellenforschung. We cannot state that Philo used an Antiochean source, or that Origen used a specific statement of Albinus or Numenius. This is due to the nature of our sources and the fact that these thinkers did not use sources in the manner of a modern academic. All that is noted is that discernible conceptual schemes and norms unite sources, and that by examining one within the context of others we are aided in reconstructing the content of a thinker's world.

In the case of the concepts and doctrines of the Peripatetics and Stoics, the limitations on their use are even more severe. Here the testimonia serve, at best, as loci paralleli, and assist the researcher in illuminating the recesses of Philo, Clement, and Origen's philosophical and rhetorical worlds. Peripatetic and Stoic doctrines did not come to these Platonists in 'pure' form, but through earlier Platonic intermediaries. They were then reformulated by these thinkers within the context of their Platonic philosophies. These doctrines are the brooks which feed a Middle Platonic stream in the distant hills beyond sight. We know these waters mingled with the Platonic, but it is difficult to determine when they entered Platonic thought beyond probable guesses. All that can be said is that these waters co-mingled in our stream in the dim periods of the Old and New Academics, and emerged in a variety of Middle Platonic metaphysical proposals. Our goal is to reconstruct their forms in the Platonic traditions of the Middle Academy as represented in the writings of Philo, Clement, and Origen.

The doxographies on rhetorical theory authored by philosophers and rhetors in the first centuries A.D. provide the evidence for the reconstruction of Philo, Clement and Origen's rhetorical ideas. Like most philosophers of the Middle Academy these men viewed rhetoric as a kind of rhetorical logic, and crafted arguments according to the rules and theorems proposed in the handbooks of their age. They argue their philosophical ideas rhetorically. They attempt to demonstrate the cogency of philosophical doctrines through the rules and theorems of rhetoric. Since this aspect of Middle Platonic thought has been almost completely ignored we have chosen to analyze Origen's knowledge and practice of rhetorical theory, and attempt to reconstruct his technê through a form-cri- tical analysis of the Praefatio 1-4 and De Deo I, 1, 1-9 of the Periarchôn (De Principiis).

As a word of caution, it must be mentioned that the writings of these Platonic thinkers are often conceptually unsystematic and fragmentary. Thus, given the nature of our sources it is difficult, if not impossible, to demonstrate that specific testimonia and fontes were known to Philo, Clement, and Origen. Is it not the purpose of this work to identify literary dependency between writings in the realm of philosophical doctrines, or to show that in the area of rhetorical theory there is a literary dependency upon the writings of the Hellenistic and Roman rhetoricians. We merely describe the theoretics, epistemologies, and dialectical-rhetorical theories of these thinkers, and explain how the confluence of these streams emerge in the demonstration of philosophical theses.

7.

This work directs itself toward understanding the principle concepts and problems of Jewish and Christian Middle Platonism in the formative ages of Judaism and Christianity in late antiquity. The goal of this study is to describe, analyze and formulate how reality was known, and how it was demonstrated from the premises of biblical scripture by the Jewish and Christian Platonists of Alexandria from Philo to Origen. The aim of this study is principally to uncover the universal philosophical norms and the language of philo- sophical discourse utilized by the Jewish and Christian Platonists of the early Empire. In so doing we shall grasp the issues which were at the center of philosophical thinking in the period when Judaism and Christianity were hammering out a philosophical culture of their own at Alexandria.

The value of such research is that it places Jewish and Christian Middle Platonism in its proper context, and aids us in better comprehending the philosophical options proposed by these religious traditions. Philo, Clement, and Origen are not distinguished so much by their Judaism and Christianity as they are by their allegiance to Platonism and the particular world-view it professes. The Platonic nexus unites them not only to one another but to the rich tradition of Hellenism to which they are heir. Hence in the first to the third century A.D. varieties of Judaism and Christianity emerged which were intensely modern and scientific and fully integrated into the Graeco-Roman culture of their time.

This datum is an important one to consider because it reflects the entrance of these religious traditions into the mainstream of Hellenistic culture, and helps explain the successful assimilation of its intelligentsia with those of the school Platonisms of the early Empire. Philo, Clement, and Origen translate revelation into knowledge and in doing so set up the conditions for the possibility of the monumental dialogue between Platonism and biblical thought which dominates the last centuries of antiquity.

More significant for the historian of religions and philosophy is the opportunity that Jewish and Christian Middle Platonism yields for the study of how two religious traditions philosophically defined themselves at Alexandria in the first three centuries of the common era, and the data this yields for the reconstruction of two varieties of Judaism and Christianity within the context of their Graeco-Roman milieu. The interaction between Jewish, Christian, and Hellenic thinkers shaped the normative outlines of later Judaism and Christianity in the Hellenistic east of the Empire. Out of the diversity of philosophical options open in these first centuries the ability of Philo, Clement and Origen to define and translate the central concepts of their religious traditions set the metron of all subsequent Jewish and Christian philosophical thought in late antiquity, Rabbinic as well as Patristic.[10]

I. PHILO OF ALEXANDRIA

1. Introduction: The Early Middle Academy: Antiochus and Eudorus

1.1   To begin a reconstruction of the theoretic of Philo we cannot preface it with a reconstruction of the theoretics of Antiochus and Eudorus. Fortunately the works of Dodds, Dörrie,[1] and Dillon[2] on the history of the Platonism of this period, and those of Thesleff and Burkett on the Neo-Pythagorean movement in the first century B.C. permit us to forego this exercise. Working from their results we can better reconstruct the subtleness of Philo's Judaic Platonism.

If we are to properly understand the philosophical context of Philo's thought we have to examine his theoretic within the parameters of the early Middle Platonisms of Antiochus of Ascalon, Archytas, and Eudorus of Alexandria. Given the complexity of the sources and the diverse themes addressed by the philosophers of the fifth Academy we shall enter into Philo's metaphysic through the doctrine that is central to it, and examine how this doctrine was framed by his predecessors Antiochus, Archytas, and Eudorus.

The doctrine we shall focus upon is the doctrine of the categories, not because it stands out as a special concern of Philo's, but because by means of it we can enter into the theology and physics of Philo's theory of first principles. It was upon the interpretation and use of the categories that Middle Platonists divided, and it was how one interpreted and used the categories that a theoretic could be defined, within a Platonic context, as Stoic-Peripatetic or Pythagorean.[3]

The contribution of Philo to the history of Platonic thought bequeathed to his heirs Clement and Origen, was his categorical doctrine, and the philosophical theology and physics which complemented it. This doctrine had its origins in the debates concerning the categories in the generation before Philo. Hence in order to appreciate Philo's proposal we turn to Eudorus and Antiochus. In so doing we gradually enter into the labyrinth of Philo's theoretic.

The doctrines of categories developed in the Academy, Lyceum, and Stoa were conceptually and functionally diverse due to the different physical theories that they complemented. It is not possible to trace the history of categorical doctrine between these school traditions, nor is it possible to explain how the Platonists before the Middle Academy adopted the Peripatetic and Stoic categories as their own. Both can be explained, however inadequately, in our discussion of categorical doctrine in the early Middle Academy.

Three centuries separate Philo of Alexandria from the Old Academy. In the centuries between the first and fifth Academics the teachings of Plato were interpreted, criticized, and reinterpreted again. All the while Plato's works remained in high repute, forming the basis of a philosophical culture. We are at a disadvantage when we enter into this interpretative process with so late a figure as Philo, but it is with this figure that we begin. Accordingly, in the subsequent chapter, Philo's writings will be examined with an eye on how his doctrines are related with the Platonic interpretations of the so-called fifth Academy. This is done so that we can grasp where Philo's Platonism came from and assess where it leads in relation to the Platonic interpretations of the Middle Academy.

In many ways, Philo of Alexandria occupies a unique position in the history of Platonism. He stands at the beginning of a phase of Platonic thought called Middle Platonism, as one of its first articulators. He also is the founder of a tradition of Platonic interpretation that is Jewish and later Christian. Philo stands as his Logos. He is the creator and sustainer of a Platonic and Biblical world.

This fact is of no little importance to our study. The studia philonica has reached a turning point. General dogmatic assertions and generalizations are no longer acceptable or even possible. Philo is a philosopher in the tradition of the Platonic Academy. If we listen we hear a voice in which what is Hellenistic and Jewish are one. To separate one from the other is to misinterpret Philo's world.

In this section no attempt is made to cover every facet of Philo's thought. The theses addressed are limited in scope, and represent no more than a small contribution to the multi-dimensional picture that is Philo. We have chosen to deal with what is perhaps the major problematic of his metaphysic, the relation of God to the Universe. Philo's theological and ontological postulates raised this problem for him, and the history of Jewish and Christian Middle Platonism is a response to this problem. Even Philo responds to Philo on this point. It is this basic theme that we propose to examine beginning with Philo. His theoretic will be studied in the context of the past so that we may comprehend his present, and grasp the present he bequeathed to the future.

1.2   The doctrine of the existence of two ontologically distinct realms of being, the authentic and the image, goes back to Plato's Timaeus. The epistemological distinction between the opinion (doxa) and knowledge (epistêmê) provided the basis upon which Plato based the ontological distinction between the sensible and intelligible worlds (Tim., 27d-28e). In the mythos we are told that the two realms are relative as original or pattern (paradeigma) to its image or imitation (eikôn: Tim., 29b; 48e). However, in none of the dialogues did Plato precisely explain: 1) how the sensibles relate to the intelligibles; 2) how the intelligibles are related to each other; or 3) what is the first unifying principle(s) of all things. Indeed, he remarks no one has the right to undertake so great a task (Tim., 48c-d). The five genera or kinds of forms introduced in the Sophist (254-255e) were not utilized by any Platonist before Plotinus to solve these problems. Hence, in the history of Platonic thought, at least until Plotinus, the vexing hydra faced by any Platonist was the answering of these problematics.

If there is a generative problematic in Middle Platonism it is the one enunciated above. If there is a constellation of doctrines used to overcome this vexing hydra it principally contains the Logos doctrine, the doctrine of ideas, and the doctrine of the categories. We shall unpack the first two doctrines and begin our journey with a discussion of the third doctrine.

It is within the context of the categories that Philo presents his doctrines of the Logos and the ideas.

Ever since the edition of the Aristotelian corpus prepared by Andronicus of Rhodes in the first century B.C. the Categories has been the subject of numerous commentaries and debates among Platonists, Pythagoreans, Peripatetics, and Stoics. These debates were philosophically important because the categories were utilized to solve a series of metaphysical problems. Philo was an early participant in these debates after "Archytas" and Eudorus, although he prepared no technical commentary upon the categories.[4]

Philo's use of the categories did not arise from the problem of their efficacy. Rather, it arose as a solution to the problems his own philosophical theology raised. Philo's metaphysic is built, and then totters upon, the distinction between unqualified, and qualified existence, i.e., between hyparxis and poiotês. The distinction is not Philo's. It reaches back to the ontological dualism of the Old Academy and the New Pythagorean metaphysic that was formulated by "Archytas" and Eudorus in the period of the fifth or Middle Academy.[5]

The theory of ontological diairesis begins with Plato and the Old Academy. By the time of the Middle Academy the division of reality into two spheres was Platonic dogma.[6] Plato's epistemological distinction between true opinion (doxa alêthês) and knowledge (epistêmê) provided the grounds upon which he based the ontological distinction between the sensible and intelligible worlds (Tim., 27d-28e; 29b, 48e). Plato's epistemological division was made an ontological one by Xenocrates (fr. 12 Heinze). In mainstream Platonism the division was between the sensible and intelligible worlds.

In some traditions of Platonism the categories were excluded from the intelligible world altogether, and had referential efficacy only for the sensible world. The Neo Pythagorean trajectory maintained this orthodox Platonic interpretation. "Archytas" and Eudorus give us examples of this traditional viewpoint (Stobaeus, Anth., i, 41, 2; Simpl., In Phys., 181, 10ff.). In the new Academic tradition represented by Antiochus, however, the ten Peripatetic categories were subsumed under the two Academic categories (Cicero, Ac. Post., 27ff. cf. Part. Or., 139). Antiochus' Platonic interpretation is not unorthodox, but it is distinct from the theory advanced in the Old Academy, and among the Neo Pythagoreans. These doctrines of diairesis and the categories are significant within the context of the respective philosophical theologies of Eudorus and Antiochus.

Among the Neo Pythagoreans there emerged a theory of a first "One" who is Nous, but something superior to Nous (cf. Archytas, in Stob. Anth., i, 41, 2). This first intellect is above two lower ones called substance or matter (ôsia) and form (morphô). Eudorus also follows a system which he attributes to the Pythagoreans. It has three principles. There is a supreme principle called the One, who is above a pair of opposites called a Monad and a Dyad (Simpl. In Phys., 181, 19ff.). The One is above all qualification, while the Monad represents form, and the Dyad matter. In this tradition of interpretation the categories do not apply to the first principle, who is above the Pythagorean table of opposites, but they apply to the other principles. According to the new Pythagoreans diairesis is between an unqualified first noetic One, and qualified form and matter. Real Being is limited to the first one alone. The Monad and Dyad are less than real.

This formula proposes two spheres of Being, and a sphere of non-Being. Being per se is unqualified existence, and Being per accidens is qualified existence (form-monad). Non-being (mê on) is unqualified existence (substance-matter-dyad: cf. Moderatus, in Simpl. In Phys., 230, 34ff.; Numenius, Simpl. In Phys., 230, 34ff.; Numenius, Simpl. In Phys., 231, 4-5). Being per se does not extend to the intelligibles or to sensibles. The intelligibles and sensibles are part of being per accidens.

The categorical dimensions of this reformulation are important as well. The categories have referential efficacy only for things in nature. Eudorus adopts the Academic categories of Absolute and Relative (Simpl. In. Phys., 248, 2ff.), and then states that the Peripatetic categories are concerned only with the physical world (Simpl. In Phys., 206, 10ff.). They have no relevance to the intelligible world where true being resides. "Archytas" takes it for granted that the categories concern only the sensible world (cf. Szlezak, Pseudo-Archytas, 22, 31; 31, 5).

The Neo Pythagorean doctrines of the categories, must be seen in the context of their metaphysics (Simpl. In Phys., 206, 10ff.; 230, 41ff.). Where the categories have efficacy we encounter Being per accidens. Where they do not we encounter Being per se. Hence, in the Neo Pythagorean theology, and corresponding ontology, God is radically separated from all other entities. Being per se is limited to the first One and Nous alone. The second intellect is called a Monad and Form, and is being per accidens. The third principle is called a Dyad, Matter, and Substance, and is non-being (mê on). The dividing line between real being and relative being is the distinction between unqualified and qualified existence. The One is "bare existence," the Monad is "qualified existence" (poiotês), the material realm is made up of "qualified forms" (poia eidê), a combination of immanent ideas and matter, and matter is unqualified substance (ôsia). In sum: diairesis separates essential existence, which belongs to the first One-Nous, from accidental existence, which belongs to the Monad-Form. The Dyad-Substance-Matter falls below accidental existence, and is a type of non-being.

In the fifth Academy there emerged another categorical theory. Antiochus maintained there was no possibility of anything immaterial, transcendent, or external to the material universe. God was a substance, a kind of Stoic fire in its most refined form, and the Logos (demiurge) and world-soul were refined material forces immanent in the world (Cicero, Ac. Post., 27 ff., 39; Fin., iv, 12, 36). For Antiochus God, Logos, and Soul were material because nothing incorporeal was capable of acting or being acted upon (Cicero, Ac. Post., 39). Indeed, if the first principles were not material they could not form a world (Cicero, Ac. Post., 27 ff.).

According to Antiochus God and the Logos-Soul, qualified are (poiotês). Further-more, there exists no distinction between qualified and unqualified existence or Being per se and per accidens. Only matter (hylê) is unqualified, but it is not non-Being (mê on). Given this it appears that the categories have referential efficacy to all things in the universe. There is nothing that does not participate in the categories.

Although Antiochus does not explicitly state it, it appears that the four Stoic categories have referential efficacy to the universe. These categories are "substratum" (hypokeimenon) or "substance" (ousia), "quality" (poion), "changing states' (pôs echon), and "varied relation" (pros ti pôs echon: SVF II, 369-375). The reconstruction of Antiochus categorical theory looks like this. At the apex of Antiochus' universe is God, or rarefied substance, and at the bottom is matter. In between are quality, perhaps the Logos-Soul, and the qualified existants in changing states and in relation to each other. All things, save matter, are in some sense qualified.

In summary, Antiochus does not structure Being upon a distinction between unqualified and qualified. He structures Being upon the correlation between activity and passivity, quality and want of quality. With Antiochus the Platonic distinction between Being and Becoming is reduced to the Stoic distinction between that which is active, and that which is passive. God is the active principle in the cosmos, and matter is the passive principle. There is no distinction between sensible and intelligible, corporeal and incorporeal. In this tradition there is no ontological dualism, only a modified ontological monism.

In the half-century before Philo we encounter two radically distinct theologies, ontologies, and doctrines of the categories. Philo was acquainted with both Platonic options. Whereas the Pythagorean trajectory emerges in his theology, the Antiochean emerges in his physics. Indeed, Philo's theology, doctrines of the ideas and the categories offer a critical synthesis of these traditions of Platonic interpretation.

2. First Principles: God and the Logos.

2.1   To present a systematic outline of the theoretic of a thinker as unsystematic as Philo is hazardous. However, with caution, it is possible to reconstruct the central doctrines of his metaphysics. Dillon is correct (MP, 128, 138; TTP., 217-219) that it is principally through Eudorus that Philo gains knowledge of Neo Pythagorean theories, and that Eudorus' doctrines were formative for the development of Philo's own metaphysic. However, Philo did not merely take over Eudorus' doctrines. He critically evaluated them, taking that which was useful and discarding that which was not. He culled his theological definitions from Eudorus' philosophical theology and affirmed the radical transcendence of the biblical God. However, he rejected the radical ontological dualism of Eudorius' theoretic. It was here that his own reflections on the Timaeus and the physics of Antiochus aided him in affirming God's relation to the universe.

Philo's first principles represent a reaction against, and an adoption of, theories of first principles articulated in the first century B.C. Neo Pythagorean schools, and in the fifth Academy. The leading exponent of the latter position was Antiochus of Ascalon. The leading exponent of the former position was Eudorus of Alexandria. It would not be correct to characterize Philo as directly responding to Antiochus and Eudorus, but we can say that he was conversant in the metaphysical theories of the school traditions they were associated with, and established a third school tradition out of elements of both. We know this because Philo's theoretic combines an Antiochian physics, and a Eudorean first principles. In this section we shall reconstruct the underlying principles of Philo's theoretic.

Philo's philosophical theology stands quite close to Eudorus', and thus in opposition to Antiochus'. In this section we shall unpack Philo's philosophical theology by examinng his doctrines of God and the Logos.

Philo postulates two "Ones." He identifies the first One with God, and the second One with the Logos.[7] The ideas, also identified with numbers and powers, are the products of divine contemplation. He defines the Father as an on and a nous, and characterizes him as an hyparxis (QD., 62). He defines the Logos in two stages: first, as an antemundane entity, and second as a mundane entity. In its antemundane stage it is defined as a to genikôtaton and ti (Leg. Alleg., ii, 86; iii, 175; Det., 118). He is the typos of the ideas (QD., 57; Leg. Alleg., iii, 96; Cher., 127; Prov., i, 23). In its mundane stage it is also the law of the universe that holds the physical things together (Fug., 20, 110, 112; QE., 68; Heres 38, 188; 24, 119; 26, 130).[8]

It would be hasty to assert that Philo merely reproduces a Neo Pythagorean first principles. What he does is adopt the Eudorean distinction between a first God who is wholly unqualified, and all else that is, in varying degrees qualified. Philo's God is based on the first hypotheses of Plato's Parmenides, and of his Logos is based on the second hypotheses of the Parmenides. God is an utterly transcendent entity while his Logos is both transcendent and immanent in the universe. God is bare being and existence (on; hyparxis: QD., 62), while his Logos is the most generic something of the universe (to genikôtaton; ti: Leg. Alleg., ii.86; iii.175; Det., 118).

In summary, from the technical terminology employed it is clear that Philo conceived of God in the manner of the Neo Pythagorean One, and his Logos in the manner of a second One above and within the universe.

2.2   To explain the Philonic theology we must turn to his first principles, and explain how Philo relates God to the Logos and the ideas. This entails an examination of his doctrines of God, the Logos, and the ideas.

Philo's philosophical theology contains two doctrines that are bonded together. God is a Pythagorean Nous and the Logos is the Pythagorean Monad. God is a Nous above all material qualification, and the Logos is a demiurgic Mind that is both above material qualification, and a world soul who is materially qualified. Philo's God is the radically transcendent first mind of the Pythagorean philosophical theology, and the Logos is the transcendent mind and world-soul of the Platonic and Stoic philosophical theologies. The distinction is between God, who is an unqualified existence, being and intellect, and the Logos who is a qualified existence, being and intellect. Upon this fault line Philo constructs his metaphysic.

Philo maintains that God is an intellect above all qualification. God has no distinction of genus, species and differentia (QD, 62). Dillon (TTP., 217) is correct that God is not a countable unit, and has not intelligible or material distinction. This bare existence and being stands alone as the first principle of Philo's universe.[9] Philo's Logos is an intellect that is the most generic something (Leg. Alleg., ii, 86; ii, 175; Det., 118). The Logos is the most generic principle in Philo's universe. He is a countable unit, and has intelligible, but no material distinctions.[10]

The background to the theory of ideas in the later Platonic philosophy has been much discussed (cf. R.M. Jones, CP., 21, 317-326; Theiler, VN., 18-19; Witt., A., 70-75; Dillon, MP., 91-96; 128-129). As noted the origins of this theory can be traced back to Xenocrates. Xenocrates called the ideas mathêmatika derived from the divine intellect (nous-monas). He regarded the Dyad or world-soul, which he separated from the supreme monad, as the number in which the ideas (mathêmatika) are contained (fr. 60 Heinze).

2.3   Xenocrates identified the ideas with the numbers, postulated a first One as the first principle of all things, and identified the Indefinite Dyad with the second principle of his theoretic (fr. 15, 18; cf. Cherniss, PM., xiii, i, 92, n.a.; fr. 28, 62, 64, 68; Cherniss, I, n. 176, 480-481, 484-485). This second principle was probably identified with matter, multiplicity, and the overflowing (fr. 28, 68). Unlike Speusippus, Xenocrates declared that the One-Monad is a Nous (fr. 16), from which the universe is derived (Theoph., Metaphys., 6a23ff.; fr. 15). The One is both a transcendent and immanent principle (fr. 16-18), and immaterial (fr. 67). The Dyad is identified with matter and perhaps the world-soul. It is a principle in opposition to the One, and is likely a disorderly and evil principle. If the Dyad is not the world-soul then the world-soul is formed from the Monad and Dyad, and exhibits qualities of both principles (cf. Plutarch, Proc. An., 101de).

Although there is no direct evidence, it is likely that Xenocrates was the first to place the ideas within the supreme Intellect-Monad. In Plato and Speusippus the ideas and numbers are separate entities that exist independently of any mind as separate existants. In Xenocrates this Intellect contemplates the ideas-numbers, and they may be the contents of this self-contemplating Nous. Thus, it is likely that Xenocrates' One contemplates the sum-total of the ideas-numbers, and they form the content of his mind. Xenocrates is the first to propose a conceptualist theory of the ideas. The ideas are objects of thought for a contemplating mind, and are placed within this contemplating mind. He also proposed a thinking first principle and identified it with One. These two theories become significant for later Platonism. Since Xenocrates called both the monad and dyad Gods he held that the ideas were contained in God. From this formulation the metaphysical structures of subsequent doctrines of the ideas take their start. Xenocrates' system had no use for Speusippus' mathematicals He identified the ideas with the numbers (Arist, Metaphys., 1028b24ff.= fr. 34), and maintained that the mathematicals were the cause of the sensible particulars. The idea is the paradigmatic cause of natural phenomena (fr. 30) and is the source of lines, planes, and solids, or the geometrical entities (Arist., Metaphys., 1085a7ff.). The mathematicals produce the geometricals, and the species (genê) of the Great and Small.

The immediate background to Philo's theory lies in the fifth Academy with Antiochus and his interpreters Varro and Arius Didymus. This trajectory conceives of the ideas in a Stoic manner (cf., Aug, CD., vii, 27). Varro identifies the ideas with Minerva, and calls the ideas God's indwelling wisdom. The Stoic formulation is extant in (SVF II 908). For Varro the ideas are wholly corporeal and situated in the mind of God (Aug, CD., vii, 16; iv, 10).

The corporeality of the ideas is clear from (Ac. Post., 30ff.). Cicero calls the ideas notiones (ennoiai) and rationes (logismoi). These terms are Stoic in origin. Hence, the ideas are thoughts which the divine mind beholds. They are wholly material, and have no transcendent dimension. They are the logoi spermatikoi contained in the Logos, and the patterns upon which the Demiurge-World-Soul creates the world (Cicero, Or., 8ff.).

If Antiochus received a theory of the ideas as thoughts of God, it is not from the Old Academy, but through some Stoic intermediary. His theory is summed up by Seneca (Ep., 58, 16-22). The ideas are called: "est eorum quae natura fiunt exeplum aeternum". This is close to Xenocrates' definition (fr. 30 Heinze), but it is formulated in a Stoic manner. The ideas are logoi spermatikoi, seminal reason principles, in the mind of God and the formative principles of the universe.

Philo reformulates Antiochus' doctrine in two ways. First, since his God and Logos are immaterial, the ideas they think are immaterial. Second, since he maintains a degree of reality metaphysic, the ideas have a transcendent as well as immanent aspect. There are transcendent immaterial ideas in the mind of God and immanent immaterial ideas in the mind of the mundane Logos.

The immediate background to Philo's reformulation lies in first century B.C. Neo Pythagorean criticism of the Antiochean formula (cf. Dillon, MP., 128). Eudorus saw the ideas as numbers and as immaterial. It is the working of the Monad on the Dyad that produces the world of ideas (logoi).

The relation of the ideas to the divine intellect is two-fold. They are God's thoughts (Opf., 17-19), and their place is the Logos of God (Cher., 49; Opf., 20). They are the objects of God's contemplation, and are contained in the Logos, or the mind of God in its mundane phase (Heres, 188 Fuga, 110; 112). The ideas constitute an intelligible universe that is comprehended and placed in the mind of God. They also constitute a sensible universe thought by the mundane Logos (Ling., 137). Hence, God's Logos is identical with the sum total of the ideas.

In summary, the ideas are: 1) the objects of God's thought; 2) contained in God's Logos; 3) the Logos, the ideas, and the intelligible world (Opf., 24, 25; Sacr., 83; Ling., 172; Somn., i, 62); and 4) defined in relation to God, to God's Logos, to the sensible world, and to matter. Although Philo accepts the theory that the ideas are divine concepts and exemplars used in the creation of the physical world, in the manner that Antiochus says, he dematerializes the ideas, and gives them a transcendent dimension. He must have formulated this following the teachings of Eudorus.

2.4   Philo's doctrine of first principles is further refined by his distinction of stages in the existence of the Logos, and phases within each stage.

In its antemundane stage the Logos is called the Mind of God and this Mind has two phases. In its first phase the Logos is an intellect at rest fully identical with God's intellect (Opf., 20). In its second phase the Logos is the place of the ideas, and the active demiurgic principle of creation (Opf., 24, 25; Conf., 172; Somn., i, 62).[10] In both phases the Logos is the most generic entity (Leg. Alleg., ii, 86; iii, 175; Det., 118).

Philo calls the Logos the generic Mind in which the ideas exist. They function as objects of God's thought (Opf., 17-19), and as patterns for the creation of the sensible world (QD., 57; Leg. Alleg., iii, 96; Cher., 127; Prov., i, 23). From this we can infer that the generic Logos is also a demiurgic Mind that uses ideas to create the physical world (Opf., 16; Heres 156). The generic and demiurgic Logos are not distinguishable. The Logos is one and the same thing with the mind of God containing God's thoughts. He is also a demiurgic who uses the ideas in the creation of the universe (Cher., 49; Opf. 20).

In its mundane stage the Logos is a distinct entity from God as the reason-principle of the universe (Leg. Alleg., iii, 150; Heres 119). In this phase the Logos is a divine intellect active in the cosmos. It is the principle that holds the material universe together. The Logos, as supreme Nomos, binds the created universe together by the law of opposites, by the law of the harmony of opposites, and by the law of the perpetuity of the species.

Philo's favorite metaphor for the Logos is as the "divider" (tomeus). He divides things into equal opposites, binds the opposites into a harmony, thereby guaranteeing that the "seminal essences" of things may be perpetuated indefinitely (Heres 26, 130). Philo calls the Logos the "seminal and craftsmanlike Logos" (spermatikos kai technikos logos: Heres 24, 119; Act., 17, 85), who sets the "seeds" (spermata) of all things and nurtures them (QE., 68). Philo calls these seeds "bonds" (desmoi), and the "powers" of God (dynameis). He infers that it is through the divine ideas that the Logos rules the sensible universe (Fug., 20, 112; Heres 38, 188).

Philo refers to the Logos as wisdom, and the first born or created being (Abr., 151; Ling., 46; Somn., i.215). The identification of the Logos with wisdom is an idea Philo borrowed from the wisdom literature of his bible. The Logos and Wisdom are one and the same thing for Philo (Leg. Alleg., i.65). Philo draws heavily from Prov. 8:22 and the Wisdom of Solomon 9:9 to express the notion that the wisdom of God assists God during creation. Hence, the Logos is the expression of God's wisdom and the principle who is God's instrument in the creation of the sensible world. Hegermann (TU 82 1961, 93-99) notes that this assimilation of the Logos and wisdom enters Christianity at the earliest stages of its expression as well. However, we are indebted to Philo for expressing this concept metaphysically, and thus presenting a norm which becomes commonplace in the later Christian Platonisms of Clement and Origen, as well as the Stoicized Platonism of Justim Martyr (Dial., 61; Apol., i.23; ii.6).

2.5   Now that we have reconstructed the major elements in Philo's first principles we now turn to the important question of how he understood the relation between God, the Logos, and the ideas, and thus the noetic and material realms. In order to do this we have to clear the decks of relational interpretation offered by Drummond and Wolfson. We do not propose to critique the whole of the Drummond-Wolfson reconstruction of Philo's theoretic, but since several interpretations of Philo's first principles hinge upon their reconstruction, we must review them.

Philo's philosophical theology has been extensively studied. The flash point of interpretation is whether or not Philo postulates an existentially distinct phase of the Logos before the creation of the world.

Wolfson maintains (P., i.239f.) that Philo proposed a three stage doctrine of the Logos. It has two antemundane phases and a mundane phase. In its first antemundane phase it is existentially one with God, and in its second it is existentially distinct. In its mundane phase the Logos is also existentially distinct from God. Coupled to these disparate existential phases of the Logos Wolfson holds that the relation of God to the Logos is both logical and generative. God and the Logos are logically one in the antemundane phases of the Logos, and distinct in the Logos' mundane phase. The conclusion is that the antemundane Logos exists logically and generatively intra mentem dei, and the mundane Logos exists extra mentem dei.

Wolfson's thesis was offered as a response to the two stage doctrine of the Logos proposed by Dähne (P., i.208-212), Gförer (P., i.176-179), Zeller (PG., iii.214ff.), Heinze (LL., 255), Drummond (PJ., ii.174) and Bréhier (IR., 154). This interpretation maintains that Philo proposed a logical and existential unity between God and the antemundane Logos. The ground for this is that Philo did not explicitly state that the antemundane Logos is generated by God. Only the mundane Logos is generated. Hence, the ante-mundane Logos exists logically, intra mentem dei, but exists generatively, extra mentem dei.

The evidence suggests that Wolfson's interpretation is not the correct one. No where does Philo state that the antemundane Logos is generated or even emerges from the mind of God as an existentially distinct being. It appears that Wolfson has read into Philo Clement's notion of a hypostatic Logos that "comes out" (proelthon) of the mind of God (Strom., v.16.2; iii.336.5ff.). Moreover, Philo clearly identifies the antemundane Logos as the mind of God and no more than that (Opf., 20). The Logos is the object of divine contemplation, and the place of the ideas (Opf., 24-25; Sacr., 83; Ling., 172; Somn., i.62; Opf., 36, 129; Heres, 280; Plant., 50; Ebr., 133; Ling., 172). To assert that the antemundane Logos exists as a distinct and generated Logos apart from God is a misrepresentation of Philo's writings. This is important to note because Philo proposes a categorical scheme to link God to the Logos, and God to the universe.

2.6   Philo calls God being and bare existence (on; hyparxis: QD., 62), and the Logos being and generic something (on; ti: Leg. Alleg., ii.86;iii.175; Det., 118). God and the Logos both are Absolute Being, but God exists unqualified, the Logos exists qualified. The distinction is between that which is hyparxis and that which is poiotês. To unpack this we must turn to the background of Philo's doctrine of the categories.

It is upon the fault-line between "unqualified" (apoios), and qualified (poiotês) that Philo's metaphysics rests.[11] Yet, in maintaining the radical transcendence of God he jeopardizes the unity he claims exists between God and the universe. To assert this unity Philo defines both God and the Logos as being. The former is characterized by bare, unqualified existence, and the latter as generic and qualified existence.[12] God is above genus, species, and difference, and the Logos is the most generic something who contains the intelligible and sensible worlds within itself.

For the student who is interested in the history of Middle Platonic philosophical theology, and the history of the categorical formulation in Middle Platonism Philo's formulations are important. Philo's metaphysical dilemma is determined by two basic postulates: 1) the Neo Pythagorean distinction between a first intellect, or really real existant, and all other existants, the chôrismos between hyparxis and poiotêtes; and 2) the Platonic distinction between intelligible and sensible worlds. This is the kosmos noêtos and kosmos aisthêtos. The first distinction arises from Philo's acceptance of the basic tenets of the Neo Pythagorean philosophical theology.[13] The second distinction he inherited from the Middle Academic view of reality. Let us turn to the first distinction and the problematic associated with it.

Philo's goal is to overcome the chôrismos between God and the universe, and also to maintain the integrity of God. This means that the model proposed by Antiochus, and the trajectory of Middle Platonic theoretic he represents, is not accepted as the viable solution to Philo's problem. In its place Philo falls back on two Platonic doctrines. First is the old doctrine of imitation. Second is the new doctrine of the categories. We shall examine this second doctrine because Philo's categorical theory constitutes an original contribution to Middle Platonic metaphysics.

The Platonists of the Old Academy postulated two fundamental categories. These were the Absolute (kath'hauto) and the Relative (pros ti: Xenocrates, fr. 12 Heinze). Under the first the intelligible world was subsumed and under the second the sensible world was subsumed. This doctrine had its origins in Plato's theory of diairesis presented in the Sophist, the Politikos, and the Philebus, and was applied to solve the problem of the relation of the intelligible and sensible realms encountered in the Timaeus.[14]

In addition to these two Academic categories we have mention of a third ascribed by Simplicius to Plato's pupil Hermodorus (Simp, In. Cat., 248,2ff). Plato is recorded by Hermodorus to have made a distinction within a category of Alio-relative (pros hetera) between contrary and simple relative of (cf. Plato, Soph., 255c). Whether or not Plato postulated such a division in the manner Hermodorus says is not possible to ascertain (cf. Heinze, Xenocrates, 37f.). By the first century B.C. dochotomic division is known by Eudorus, and commented upon in Neo Pythagorean circles by Callicratidas (De Dom. Fel., 103, 12-13). Later Sextus Empiricus refers to this concept (Adv. Math., ii, between absolutes, contraries, and relatives.

Heinze notes that in the Old Academy Xenocrates differentiated between the categories of the Absolute (kath'hauto) and Relative (pros ti: fr. 12). This division of being is Platonic dogma by the first century B.C. Eudorus (Simp, In. Cat., 174,14ff.) shows that he adopts Xenocrates' Academic categories in his criticism of the Aristotelian categories.

By the first century B.C. Platonists as divergent as Antiochus (Cicero, Luc., 46) and Eudorus (Stobaeus, Anth., i.41.2; Simplicius, In Phys., 181,10ff.) accepted this diairesis of reality as Platonic dogma. Antiochus even goes so far as to accept that Peripatetic diairesis as a component of Platonic diairetical theory (Cicero, Part. Or., 139; Luc., 46; Cicero, Fin., v. 16). This represents a new addition to Platonic diairetical and categorical theory.

The type of diairesis utilized by Antiochus was neglected by Aristotle (An. Pr.,
46a33) and the Old Lyceum (Boethius, Div., lxiv, 891-892 Migne). What Antiochus did was
combine Academic and Peripatetic division. Mention of Antiochean diairesis is in
Cicero's Topica. He states:

> In partitione quasi membra sunt, ut corporis caput humeri manus latera crura
> pedes et cetera; in divisione formae sunt quas Graeci eide vocant.
>
> (Top. 30)

2.7   Philo's doctrine of the categories and his theories of division have their origin
in the debates over both by Eudorus and Antiochus. Following Eudorus Philo postulates a
division between two distinct orders of reality. Following Antiochus he asserts that there
is a fundamental relationship between God and the universe. Under the category of the
Absolute Philo subsumes God, the Logos, and the ideas. Under the category of the
Relative he places the material world.

As this sketch suggests there is a continuity between Philo's ontological and
theological doctrines, and this is expressed by Philo in his categorical theory. The
significance of this theory, and its relation to his philosophical theology and ontology has
largely been ignored by modern scholarship.[15] This is a lamentable lacuna because it is
categorically that Philo relates his radically transcendent God to the Logos and the
universe. It is categorically that Philo overcomes the chôrismos between God, who is
hyparxis, and the world, which is poiotês.

The Logos and the ideas constitute the intelligible world, and the physicals
constitute the sensible world. The relationship between these world is maintained by the
Logos.[16] He contains the intelligible world within himself (Opf., 20; Cher.,49),[17] makes
the sensible world in the image of this intelligible world (Opf., 16,32,129;Heres, 280;
Plant., 50; Ebr., 133; Ling., 172), and is the power of God extended from the center to the
extremes of the material[18] universe comprehending it in himself (Fuga, 110, 112; Plant.,
9; Ling., 137).

The Logos has the designation of the most generic something of the universe (to
genikôtaton; ti: Leg. Alleg., ii.86,iii.175;Det., 118). He is the immaterial bond of the
universe (Somn., i.62; Plant.,9), and the place of the ideas (Cher., 149). He is the most
generic of entities of both the intelligible and sensible worlds. The ideas he contains
within himself are the transcendent source of all the shapes and figures of things in the
sensible world (Opf., 32,97). The Logos and the ideas are the source of all quality and
relation in the sensible world, and are the generic figures for all the genera, species, and
differentia extant in the material realm.

We noted that Philo calls both God and the Logos being. God is termed (on), and the
Logos termed (ti: QD.,62; Leg. Alleg.,ii.86;iii.75; Det., 118). The first term refers to that
which is unqualified and above genus, species, and differentia. The second term refers to
that which is the most generic of all things, and hence that which contains within himself
all the genera, species, and differentia of the universe. If by means of these terms Philo

relates God and the Logos, then it is by means of the categories that Philo relates Absolute and Relative reality to one another, and thus the universe, in toto, to God. To see how Philo extends God's being to the world, and overcomes the fault-line endemic to the Neo Pythagorean theoretic we turn to an examination of his doctrine of the categories.

The evidence we have suggests a sharp series of debates upon the central issues and problems of the Platonic metaphysics in this transition period between the Republic and the Empire. Ariston, the student of Antiochus and his contemporary Dion, wrote treatises on the Categories and related topics in hellenistic philosophy, and the latter carried them to Alexandria. Eudorus under the influence of the Neo Pythagorean renaissance of his times raced vigorously to the Antiochean Platonism of these thinkers. His works were well known by his contemporaries. The most important among these contemporaries were Arius Didymus (Stobaeus, Ecl., ii. 42, 7ff.), and Plutarch (IQ., 369e). Philo fully absorbed these materials and offered his own response to them.

3. The Categories of Being.

3.1   Before Philo, Academics and Peripatetics agreed that the categories had referential efficacy only to material things.[19] An early Middle Platonist such as Eudorus stated that the categories applied only to the material realm, and not to God. Antiochus, viewing God and the universe in a materialist's manner, thought that the categories had referential efficacy to both the universe and God. With Philo we see a shift in the view that the categories apply only to things material, but not to things immaterial. He postulates that they have referential efficacy to both intelligibles and sensibles.

Philo divides reality into the two Academic categories of the Absolute (kath'hauto) and the Relative (pros ti). This division can be inferred from his distinction between the intelligible and sensible worlds extant in his discussion of double creation (e.g., Opf., 16), and from his understanding of the Logos as divider (Heres, 133-226, esp., 152;221-223). To these two principle categories he may have added a third category called the Alio-relative. This category is between the Absolute (simple) and the Relative (contrary) relative. Each division of reality has its own set of categories. They are four in number (Philo subsumes the ten Aristotelian categories under the four Stoic categories.)

This diairesis of Being may be illustrated in the following way:

	God
Absolute:(kosmos noêtos)	Logos (Ideas)
	Logos (Ideas)
Relative:(kosmos aisthêtos)	Sensibles
	Matter

The categories applicable are:

Simple: being, relation, place, quality

Contrary: quality, relation, changing states, quantity substance,
                                        quality, quantity, state, position, place, time, passivity,
                                        action

The categories applicable to both are:

Alio-relative: being (ti), quality and relation, quantity

        The Simple categories include the Academic-Stoic category of being and the new
Academic categories of relation, place, and quality. The Contrary categories are the four
Stoic and ten Peripatetic categories. This list reflects a conflation of reshuffling of the
Aristotelian categories. Philo identifies time and place with when and where and
subsumes them under quality. The category missing is date, but he may have considered
this as an aspect of time. The Alio-relative categories are being, quality, and quantity.
Being is the Stoic category (ti) which Philo identifies with the Logos. Quality is this
Logos immanent in the world, and quantity is matter. The categories of quality and
quantity are the Neo Pythgorean categories with the former being equivalent to form and
the latter to matter.

        The key term in Philo's scheme is relation (pros), which he defines in two ways:
first, in the Academic sense of the relation of copy to paradigm (Opf., 16,36,129; Heres,
280; Plant., 50; Ebr., 133; Ling., 172); and second, in the Neo Pythagorean sense of the
relation of absolutes to each other, contraries to each other, and alio-relatives to each
other. It is this second usage that is instructive. Here the Logos is equivalent to relation
and quality.

        We cannot say with any certainty that Philo adopted this third distinction.
However, he knew of Eudorus' writings, and those of several Pythagorean authors. Thus,
it is possible that he knew of this third category, and utilized it. If he did hold to a
tripartite theory of the relative it would have the following scheme: 1) Simple relative
would apply where even is the nature of the Absolute; 2) Contrary relative would apply
where odd is the nature of the Relative, and 3) Alio-relative would apply where the
Absolute and the Relative are related to each other. This tripartite theory would then be
applied to define the relation of the intelligibles to each other; the sensibles to each
other, and the relation of the intelligibles to the sensibles.

        The simple relative would define the entities within the Absolute category of being.
The categories employed for definition would be those of being, quality, place, and
relation. The contrary relative would define the things within the Relative category of
being. The categories used for definition would be substance, quality, quantity, time, and
space, or those categories concerned with the physical world (Dec., 30ff.). The
Alio-relative would define the relation between Absolutes and Relatives. The categories
employed here are something, quality, relation, and quantity. The logical something and
the formative quality refer to the antemundane and mundane aspects of the Logos.
Quality refers to matter. As the most generic entity the Logos mediates between the two

realms of being (Leg. Alleg., iii ,175). Hence, in addition to the categories that have referential efficacy to the intelligible and sensible worlds (the categories of simple and contrary relation), we have a set of categories that are Alio-relative as well.

3.2 As we have seen Philo defined the Logos as a most generic something and the ideas-numbers as the generic figures and forms of things. Implied in these statements is the notion that both the Logos and the ideas are qualified. If they are qualified, then they can be defined categorically. To grasp what Philo means let us examine what "qualified" signifies.

Philo postulates two first principles. God is being above qualification, and the Logos is the most general being. While no category is applicable to God, who is above genus, species, and differentia, a set of categories have referential efficacy to generic being, or the Logos. God is unqualified (Leg. Alleg., i.15,51; iii.73,206). He is called bare existence (hyparxis) (QD.,62). The Logos and the ideas, however, are qualified as the most generic something and the generic figures and forms of things (Leg. Alleg., ii.28; iii.175; Det., 118; Opf., 32,97). The question is how are they qualified, and when Philo asserts this does he mean qualified in a different manner than he does when he refers to the sensibles?

Philo's theory has its probable origins in the early Middle Academic notion of different modes of being (cf. Seneca Ep. 58). Seneca tells us that the distinction between God and the Logos is a distinction between esse pereminentiam (being), and esse ea quae proprie sunt (being itself: Ep., 58, 16f.). The distinction between Philo and Seneca's formulations are that Philo's God is beyond qualified Being as a first Neo Phythagorean One, and the Logos is a most generic Being, as a second Neo Phythagorean One. Hence, Philo's God is more transcendent than Seneca's esse pereminentiam, and his Logos is an entity that exhibits characteristics of both Seneca's esse pereminentiam and ea quae proprie sunt. While the Logos is the highest qualified entity, God is not bound by any qualification. The dividing line is between (hyparxis) and (poiotês). God is being (on), and the Logos is something (ti).

The category of being (on; ti) is the linchpin of Philo's categorical theory. The reasons for this are: 1) God, who is above genus, species, and differentia is called being (on: Deus 11; Heres 187); and 2) The Logos, who is the primary genus, is also called being (ti). Philo borrows the term and category (ti) from the Stoics. In Stoic categorical theory the indefinite something is identified with being (ti=on cf. Seneca, Ep., 58,8; Alex. Aph., In Top. 155; Diog. Laer. V., 61; Plot., Enn., vi,1,25). Philo further qualifies the Logos by calling him "the most generic" (to genikôtaton) something (Leg. Alleg., ii,28; iii, 175; Det., 118). Hence, being (on; ti) is the highest category and all other categories are subsumed under it. Quality,relation, and place are subsumed under this most generic category, and (ti) is placed beneath the wholly unqualified God, or (on).

The first category subsumed under something (ti) is quality (poion). Quality refers to the generic figure, who is the Logos, and to the generic figures which are contained in the Logos. The ideas, the source of all material qualities, are located in the most generic Logos. (Opf., 32, 97; cf. Opf., 17-19). The quality of the Logos is expressed by the term to genikôtaton (Leg. Alleg., ii,28; iii, 175; Det., 118). Quality also refers to the ideas.

Quality is expressed by a variety of terms (Opf., 32, 97). They define the different species of figures which the ideas constitute, and the specific differences among the species of figures which the ideas are sources of (Opf., 32, 97). Thus, quality has referential efficacy to the Logos and the ideas, and by means of this category Philo defines the incorporeal attributes of the intelligibles.

The second and third categories subsumed under something (ti) is relation and place, (chôra, topos, pros). Relation is expressed in a variety of ways. God is in relation to the Logos, who is the sum-total and place of the ideas (Opf., 20; Cher., 49). The Logos is in relation to God as the object and place of his thoughts (Opf., 20: oud'ho ek tôn ideôn kosmos allôn an echoi topon e ton theon logon.) The Logos is in relation to the ideas (Opf., 24,25). The Logos and ideas, as primary and secondary intelligibles, are related to the sensible universe as its paradigm(s) (Opf., 20; Cher., 179; cf. Opf., 29,36,129: Heres 280; Plant., 50; Ebr., 133; Ling., 172,146; Leg. Alleg., i,19,21).

In summary, Philo postulates a set of categories that have referential efficacy to the intelligible world alone. They are the categories of being, relation, place, and quality. They serve to qualify the existants in the noetic world just as the material categories qualify the things in the material world.

3.3   Wolfson is correct (P., ii,106) that for Philo, the sensible categories are the Stoic categories of substance, quality, and changing status (hypokeimenon-ousia, poion, pôs echon: SVF II 369-375). The term substance is employed, as is judged from Philo's use of body in the same passage, in the Stoic sense of substance. Substance and matter are identical terms. Philo repeats this definition at (Post., 48,168) and (Abr., 31, 163). Philo lists the categories which are applicable to the sensible world, and those which are used to define the sensibles at (Spec. Leg., iii,73,206). He does this indirectly by affirming that substance (ousia), quality (poiotês), state (schêsêôs), and motion (kinêsis) do not apply to God. These categories are the ones he states are 'in nature' in (Dec., 30ff.).

From this brief sketch it would appear that by qualities (poiotês) Philo means physical or accidental qualities, and that the sensible categories have referential efficacy only to the sensible realm. If this is the case, then Philo merely reproduces a standard Middle Platonic categorical doctrine. Substance (ousia) refers to matter (hylê) and the remaining categories are relevant only to define the accidental qualities and states of material things. Let us examine how he defines the term quality in the sensible realm, and the categorical theory which complements his meaning of accidental quality.

First, quality refers to one or more of the categories and denotes an accident inherent in a material thing. Second, it refers to genus, species, and differentia. Third, it means form as contrasted with matter.[20] Fourth, it means form. Now let us turn to examples of each.

In (Leg. Alleg., i,13,36) Philo speaks of the difference between the shape (morphê) and the qualities (poiotês) of a man. Shape refers to the material thing and the qualities to the accidents that determine the shape of a material thing. In (Immut.,ii.55-56) God is denied of all qualities by asserting that he is shapeless (morphosantês). By this Philo means that God is not characterized with qualities applicable to sensible things. What he means by both references is clarified in (Cher., 21,67). When Philo denies qualities of God the example he gives is that of a white man. The quality is the man's whiteness, and by poiotês Philo means accidental quality, viz., whiteness.

In (Opf., 32,97) Philo states that the right-angled triangle is the starting point of qualities (poiotêton). It is called the source of every figure (schêmatos) and quality (poiotêtos). In this sense the right-angled triangle functions as the generic source of all qualities. Hence, we must assume that there are species of this right-angled triangle with specific differentia in the world which exhibit definitive qualities that make up every figure. The different species are definable by noting their different qualities.

At (Aet., 16,79,81) Philo refers to the quality of the physical world. By this he means the qualities of things patterned after the ideas (Spec., 8,47,60,327,329), which are the qualities created by God in things (Spec., 60,328). These are embodied qualities or the instantiation of form in matter (Post., 48,168; Abr., 31,163; Opf., 18,45,46,49,57,131, 134,141; Immut., 13,62; Deter., 6,15; Agr., 3,13; Plant., 32,133; Conf., 37,185-187; Heres, 50,247; Fuga, 2,13; Somn., i.5,27).

At (Heres, 188; Fuga, 110) Philo maintains that the Logos is the formative power of the universe and that principle which holds the sensible world together. By this Philo means that the Logos is the immaterial form that holds together material things much like the immanent ideas are the forms that hold together matter.

From these examples we suggest that Philo understands quality to signify the accidental qualities of physical things. Accidents are defined by dividing a genus into its species, and a species into its individual members. In defining accidental qualities one contrasts form from matter. Finally, since the Logos is coextensive with the material universe, and is the formative power of the sensible world, the qualities exhibited by matter are due to the formative power of the Logos (Spec. Leg., iv.,42,231). Thus, we infer that the species of sensible things are formed to their predetermined genera by the Logos who uses the ideas as the generic source for every quality. This means that each corporeal object is defined by its accidents, and classified according to its accidents. For example, Philo refers to the heavens as "qualified forms" (poia eidê: QD., 62).

The categories which have referential efficacy to things in nature are the four Stoic categories listed above as substance, quality, changing states, and quantity. It is likely that Philo also claimed that the ten Peripatetic categories applied to things in nature. This is inferred by his discussion of the categories in (Dec.,30ff.). Thus, Philo's categorical doctrine, at least as it applies to the sensible world, contains a mixture of Stoic and Peripatetic elements. Since he sees both the Stoic and Aristotelian categories as categories to be used in the definition of material things, his employment of both sets, at least for Philo, is not inconsistent.[21]

3.4   From our examination of Philo's categorical doctrine it would appear that he divides reality into two spheres, and defines the intelligibles and sensibles according to the categories applicable to them. The motivation behind Philo's categorical theory is to establish a relationship between Absolutes and Contraries. The intelligible categories relate God, the Logos, and the ideas, and the sensible categories relate the Logos and the ideas to the sensibles, which are a combination of form and matter.

Although Philo has presented a scheme whereby Absolutes are related to one another, and Contraries are related to one another, we still have to unpack how he relates the Absolutes and Contraries to each other. In our discussion of Philo's sets of categories we have been indirectly introduced how he relates Absolutes and Contraries. As noted the categories of being (ti), quality (poiotês), and relation (pros) have referential efficacy to the Logos. These categories thus are part of Philo's third set of categories, he Alio-Relative. To them we must add a third category. This is quantity (poson), and Philo generally associates it with matter (hylê-ousia). By means of the categories of being, relation, and quantity Philo completes his categorical doctrine, and explains how the intelligibles are related to the sensibles.

Quality and relation is equivalent to the Logos imminent in the world and quantity is the matter formed by the Logos in his role as divider (tomeus: Heres, 133-236). Indeed, in diairesis the Logos shapes the undifferentiated substance of the world. He is responsible for arithmetical and proportional equality in the physical world (Heres, 221-223). The instruments he employs to effect equality out of quantity are the ideas. They are the source of all the forms and shapes matter takes on once it is qualified by the Logos. Relation corresponds to the Logos imminent in the world.

The background to Philo's doctrine of the Alio-Relative categories is difficult to ascertain.[22] Dillon (MP.,135;180) suggests its origins in his categorical theories of Archytas and Eudorus. The former wrote a treatise which dealt with diairesis is his On Opposites, and the latter wrote a critique of the Aristotelian categories in his Categories. Although the work by Archytas is lost, Eudorus' is not. He calls the One substance, the Monad quality, and the Dyad quantity. Quality is equivalent to form, or the Logos, who imposes himself on quantity to create the idea-numbers, and thus the world.

If the Absolute categories function to relate the intelligibles to one another,and the Contrary categories to relate the sensibles to one another, then the Alio-Relative categories serve to relate the intelligibles and sensibles to one another. These categories mediate between Absolute and Relative reality, an relate these two realms to each other.

This third category can be traced back to Plato's unwritten doctrines as reported by Hermodorus (Simpl. In Phys.,248,2ff.). Plato was reported to have made a distinction within a category of alio-relative (pros hetera) between contrary and simple relative (cf.Heinze, Xen.,37f.). Whether or not Plato actually asserted this is impossible to ascertain, but the claim was reasserted in Neo Pythagorean circles. Callicratidas (De Dom. Fel., 103,12-13 Thesleff) makes use of the Platonic categories,and Sextus Empiricus says that the Neo Pythagoreans made a distinction between Absolutes, Contraries, and Relatives. Dillon notes (MP.,134) it is tempting to see Eudorus as an intermediary here. It is equally tempting to see Philo working off this intermediary.

If Philo postulates a theory of the categories as we have described, then we see a categorical option that bridges both Neo Pythagorean and Aristotelian doctrines. Following the former he asserts that the Aristotelian and Stoic categories have referential efficacy only to the sensible realm. Following the latter he accepts the notion that categories do have referential efficacy to the intelligibles as well. Since these categories cannot be the sensible categories, he postulates a set of intelligible categories. Finally, he takes the radical step of claiming a set of categories which have referential efficacy to both divisions of reality. Indeed, the radicality of his proposal is profound. Simple relation and the categories which qualify simple relations are the Absolute categories. Contrary relation and the categories which qualify contrary relations are the Contrary categories. Alio-relative relation and the categories which qualify alio-relative relations are the Alio-Relative categories. Whereas the first two sets of categories are limited to Absolute and Relative reality respectively, the third set applies to both divisions of reality.

The significance of Philo's formulation is that he can categorically relate the intelligibles to each other, the sensibles to each other, and the intelligibles to the sensibles. Furthermore, since the Logos is an extension of God's intellect and power in the universe Philo can now link God to the universe categorically as well as paradigmatically, and yet maintain the radical distinction between God and the universe.

In summary, Philo sets up a division of Being, and proposes that Being can be defined categorically. The intelligible world is classified and defined by one set of categories, and the sensible world by another. Both worlds, and their categories, are subsumed under the Logos, who is the primary genus of the intelligible and sensible worlds, and the most generic category.

The categories provide Philo with a tool to correlate the two spheres of reality to each other, and to define the existents in each sphere. Thus, in addition to the traditional Academic theory of paradigmatic relation, Philo adds the theory of categorical relation. By means of both theories he relates: 1) the sensibles to the intelligibles, 2) the intelligibles to each other, and 3) God to all things.

The Platonic philosophy, at the end of the first century B.C., offered either the ontological dualism of the Phythagorean Platonism of Eudorus, or the onotological monism of the Stoicized Platonism of Antiochus. Both Platonic interpretations had radically altered or wholly eliminated the older Platonic distinction between Being and Becoming. It is within this context that Philo hammers out his own theoretic. First, he adopts the radically transcendent One of the Phythagoreans and places him at the head of reality. Second, he adopts the transcendent One of the Phythagoreans and makes him the primary genus of the intelligible world. Third, he postulates a world-soul as the immanent power of the universe, and makes him the primary genus of the material world. The first intellect Philo calls God; the second and third he calls God's Logos.

Philo's categorical doctrine differs from antecedent theories in that he affirms that a set of categories has referential efficacy to the intelligible realm just as a set has referential efficacy to the sensible realm. He asserts this because he defines the Logos as the most generic something under which all the categories are subsumed.

In his attempt to maintain the 'integrity' of God, Philo postulates a radically transcendent God that is wholly unqualified. This unqualified God is distinguished from all qualified things. In his attempt to maintain the 'integrity' of the universe Philo presents a theoretic whereby God's power and being is extended through the whole universe (sensible and intelligible).

Philo walks a middle-path between Eudorus and Antiochus. He maintains a distinction between God and the universe, and thus avoids the ontological monism of Antiochus' metaphysic. He proposes a relation between God and the universe that avoids the ontological dualism of Eudorus' metaphysic. In short, Philo offers a degree of reality metaphysic that redefines, in a fresh way, the Platonic distinction and relation between paradigm, copy, and image. Now that we have sketched Philo's doctrines of first principles and the categories we turn to how Philo applies these doctrines to define the intelligible and sensible worlds.

4. The Noetic Realm: God and the Antemundane Logos.

4.1   At the acme of Philo's theoretic stands God, the Logos, and the ideas, which are situated in the Logos of God. These entities stand in a hierarchical relationship to one another, and are conceived in terms of the Neo Pythgorean doctrine of the two Ones based upon the first two Hypotheses of Plato's Parmenides.[23]

God is called the One, the Monad, and the really existant (QE., 11; Heres, 187). He is a simple One and to distinguish God from the Logos Philo refers to him as more primordial than the Monad, sic. the Logos (QE., 11.68; Leg., 6). The Logos is also called the One and the Monad but he is no simple One. As the divine reason principle and the active element of divine reason the Logos is the place of the ideas. The unity in plurality which is the Logos is reflected in Philo's definition of the transcendent Logos as the Hebdomad (Opf., 100; Heres, 216; Spec. Leg., ii.58ff), and the immanent Logos as spermatikos (the sum-total of the logoi spermatikoi: Leg. Alleg., iii.150; Heres, 119).

God, thus, is above the Logos and the ideas, but the latter are wholly within the mind of God, at least as they exist in the intelligible world. God is a simple One, and the Logos a unity containing the ideas. The Logos is the most generic something of the universe (Leg. Alleg., ii.86; iii.175; Det., 118), who contains the ideas. In thinking God creates the noetic realm, and upon this paradigm his Logos creates the material realm (Opf., 16; Leg. Alleg., iii.96). God's Logos is an image (eikôn) of God as archetype (paradeigma), and is itself an archetype to all other things, which are its images.

Just as God is above the Logos and is the origin of the Logos and the intelligible world, the Logos is above the sensible world and is the origin of the sensible world (Cont., 2; Praem., 40; Leg. Alleg., i.19; iii.96; Ling., 146; Cher., 127; Sacr., 8; QD., 57; Fuga, 95; Prov., i.23). The Logos is the totality of the powers which are identical with the ideas of God (Opf., 24-25; Sacr., 83; Ling., 172; Somn., i.62). Given this, we can infer that God is indivisible unity (Gig., ii.52), and the Logos is generic unity (Leg. Alleg., ii.86; ii.26; Det., 188).

Philo works out this relationship on the basis of his different definitions of the term Unity (monas)[24]. God is an indivisible unity (Gig., 11.52), and the Logos a divisible and generic unity (Leg. Alleg., ii.21,86; iii,49,169). Existentially God is bare existence (hyparxis: QD., 62), and the Logos is qualified existence (Leg. Alleg., ii.86; iii.175; Det.,

118). Thus, although they share the common designation of being (on), God and the Logos exist differently. God exists as an indivisible unity and is wholly unqualified, and the Logos exists as a generic unity, and is qualified. By means of this schema Philo maintains the radical transcendence of God, but insures that God is in a fundamental relationship to the universe through the Logos. Within the context of early Middle Platonism, Philo stands between Eudorus, on the one hand, and Antiochus, on the other.

It is clear from Philo's writings that God thinks the ideas. The place of this doctrine in the history of Platonism goes back as far as Xenocrates in the Old Academy (fr.60 Heinze).[25] The probable origin of Philo's variation of this doctrine goes back to Antiochus and his followers Varro and Arius Didymus (Augustine, CD., vii.28; Seneca, Ep., 65). In both sources the ideas are defined as thoughts of God, and presumably they exist in the mind of God (cf. Cicero, Or., 8).[26]

Philo calls the ideas, in the Stoicized manner of the fifth Academy, seminal reason principles (logoi spermatikoi: Leg., 55). However, the ideas have a transcendent as well as immanent aspect (Opf., 20), and are not thought of by Philo as in any sense corporeal in either phase of their existence. This shift in understanding the ideas may be Philo's original contribution to Middle Platonism. Thus, the ideas are the incorporeal powers of God that exist in the transcendent Logos and in the world (Opf., 19-20; 24-25; Ling., 172; Somn., i.62).[27]

The relation of the ideas to God is simplified by Philo in that he conceives of the Logos as the totality of the ideas and powers of God (Opf., 24-24; Somn., i.62; cf. Opf., 17-19). Hence, the relationship of the ideas to God is identical with the relationship of the Logos to God. The ideas are a generic unity identified with the Logos (Opf., 24,24; Jacr.,83), and they are qualified (Opf., 32,97).

In summary, Philo's picture of the noetic realm, the kosmos noêtos, consists of God, the Logos and the ideas. God is the thinker, and hence the creator of this world. He is its origin (archê: Opf., 17-19). God is the indivisible simple monas (Gig., ii.52), and the Logos the divisible and generic monas (Leg. Alleg., ii.86; iii.175; Det., 118; Opf., 15,35). In this sense God is above the Logos and the ideas, God is a monas above the monas (Cont., 2; Praem., 40).

4.2   In relating God to the intelligible world in such a manner Philo attempts to temper the Neo Pythagorean elements in his theoretic. This is done to overcome the absolute chôrismos between God and the universe that is endemic to a Neo Pythagorean theoretic. Philo further glosses over this gap by introducing the distinction between a God who is unqualified (apoios) and a Logos who is qualified (poiotês). Although this appears as a reassertion of the Neo Pythagorean position as proposed by Eudorus it really represents something quite different. He understands this distinction within the context of a categorical doctrine that asserts their fundamental unity. Let me explain.

The relationship between the intelligibles of the noetic realm is a simple relation. God, the Logos, and ideas are defined, categorically, as being. These beings are unqualified (God), and qualified (the Logos and the ideas). Qualified being is defined in terms of relation and place. Unqualified being cannot be defined at all.

God stands at the head of this relationship, and below him are the Logos and the ideas. God is an indivisible unity (Gig., ii.52), and the Logos is a most generic unity (Leg. Alleg., ii.86; iii.175; Det., 188). This distinction is between a simple and complex One, between an unqualified unity and a qualified unity. The relation between them is understood categorically in the distinction between God, who is being as on, and the Logos, who is being as ti. This in turn, hinges upon the cognate distinction between that which is hyparxis and that which is to genikôtaton (QD., 62; Leg. Alleg., ii.21,86; iii.49,169).

Since God is unqualified, and neither genus, species, or differentia none of the categories have referential efficacy to him. Since the Logos is generically qualified the categories of quality, relation, and place have referential efficacy to him and the ideas. Philo's use of the terms on for God (QD., 62), and genikon (Leg. Alleg., i.9,23) for the Logos suggests the distinction between the two he means. God is non-generic being and the Logos is generic being. As the most generic something the Logos is qualified by the categories of being which have referential efficacy to the intelligible realm.

The Logos is qualified in the most general way possible. He is a something (ti), and the most generic entity (to genikôtaton), who is the place of the ideas (chôra, typos). The relation of the Logos to God is the simple relation, to use Neo Pythagorean language, of the unqualified first One to the most generally qualified Second One. The ideas are qualified both in relation to God and in relation to his Logos, and to matter. The ideas are generic forms (eidê) which are the source of the variety of species of ideas (species) that exist in the mind of God's Logos (chôra, topos). The relation of the ideas to the Logos of God is the simple relation of the most generic thoughts to their thinker.

Philo's Neotic (Absolute) realm has the following structure:

God (on, hyparxis)
Logos (ti, genikôtaton, monas)
Ideas (genê)

The categorical structure of Absolute being is the following:

God (apoios)
Logos (pros, topos, chôra)
Ideas (pros, topos, chôra)

Philo's doctrine of the categories is an attempt to bridge the chasm between an absolutely transcendent God, and a transcendent Logos, and intelligible world, and the sensible world.

The fault-line in the Neo Pythagorean theoretic Philo inherits and reacts to is between Being per se, which is limited to God alone, and being per accidens, which is the intelligible and sensible worlds. Although Philo guarantees the radical transcendence of God by keeping this categorical distinction, he alters the division between essential and accidental being to the older Platonic distinction between absolute (kath'hauto) and

Relative (pros ti) being. Under the first category he subsumes the intelligible world,and under the second he places the sensible world.

5. The Material Realm: God and the Mundane Logos.

5.1 In the last section we postulated the thesis that Philo employs three definitions of relation, and uses the notion of simple relation to define the relationship between God, the Logos, and the ideas. In this section we shall pursue the thesis that he uses the second concept of relation, that of contrary relation, to define the relationship between the sensibles, and the third concept, that of alio-relation, to define the relationship between the intelligibles and the sensibles. To adequately show that Philo utilizes these last two notions of relation we have to enter into Philo's physics proper, and sketch his doctrines of creation, the mundane Logos, the immanent ideas, and matter. As we enter into this phase of our reconstruction we must note that Philo relies on two sacred texts, Genesis and the Timaeus.

For Philo Genesis deals with the origin of the world only from 1:6 on.[28] The stereôma which is mentioned in this pericope hints at the corporeal world, which is stereon by its own nature. Upon this Philo explains creation (Opf., 36). The Timaeus represents the starting point of Philo's interpretation of Genesis. Working from both accounts of creation Philo postulates a doctrine of double creation. God creates the intelligible world, and then the demiurge creates a sensible world as an image of the intelligible world (Opf., 16). The sensible world is an image (eikôn) of the intelligible world, which is its model and pattern (Opf., 36, 129: Heres, 280; Plant., 50; Ebr., 133; Ling., 172). In these passages Philo reproduces the Academic doctrine that the sensible world was patterned on the intelligible world, and that the sensible world was created by the demiurgic Logos (Leg. Alleg., i.19; Ling., 146; Cher., 127; Sacr., 8; QD., 57; Fuga, 95; Prov., i.28; fg. Leg. Alleg. III.96)

Philo understands the relation between a copy and its model, not as a Neo Pythagorean would, as the relation between contrary orders of existence. Rather he understands relation as a Platonist reading Genesis through the prism of the Timaeus would, as the relation between kindred orders of existence. The opposite or contrary of God and the intelligible world is matter and the unformed mass of the material substrate. The sensible world is created from matter in the image of the intelligible world, and not in opposition to either. Just as the sensible world is created by the demiurgic Logos it is sustained by the five powers of the Logos.

5.2 Philo defines the Logos as the 'first-born son' of God, who is the 'commander' of the universe (Agr., 51). He is one of the two chief powers that proceeds from God and Sophia (Fuga, 109; Cher., 27ff; QE., ii, 68). The Logos is filled with the powers of God (Somn., i, 62) and is the charioteer of God's immaterial powers (Fuga, 101).

There are Stoic as well as Peripatetic elements to Philo's model, and they come out most clearly in (QE., ii, 68). The five powers of God are arranged as: creative, regal, merciful, legislative, and forbidding, and they are all subsumed under the Logos. The first three dynameis may be translated as 'potentialities,' and the last two are two aspects of the Stoic nomos kata physin (SVF III 314).[29]

As the power of God the Logos (as the sum-total of all logoi in the world) is the "creative" and "regal" power of God, and rules his creation (poiêtikê: basilikê dynamis). This definition is not without significance. If dynamis means 'potentiality,' which proceeds to energeia or 'actuality' in the physical world, then we have an example of a Peripatetic ontological theory adapted to a Platonic cosmological theory. Most likely, however, Philo interprets dynamis in the Stoic sense, as Antiochus did, as an aspect of the Supreme God mediated through the Logos in the universe. That is, the Logos is the formative power of God in the universe.

The Logos is not only the transcendent kosmos noêtos which is the model of the sensible world. In its mundane phase it is the law and harmony of the universe (Heres, 188; Fuga, 110, 112; Plant., 9). It is the formative principle of the physical universe that stretches from the center up to the extremities of the world comprehending it in itself (Ling., 137; Migr., 182; Sobr., 63; Somn., i, 63). The Logos is in the universe as an intelligent and rational nature (Heres, 48), and when impressed upon matter as its reason principle, it becomes coextensive with the physical world (Heres, 44). Coextensive with the physical world, the mundane Logos is the third power within Philo's universe as the ruler of the sensible world (QG., iv,8; Abr., 120ff.).

Philo's theory of powers complements his theory of the division of being into two parts, and his postulate that each sphere of being has its own causal principle, which is its sustainer or power. Philo calls the antemundane Logos the creative power (poiêtike dynamis), and the mundane Logos the ruling power (basilikê dynamis) of the universe. Above these powers stands God, who is the source of power, but is not himself a power.

Philo also calls the mundane Logos, who is the ruling power of the sensible universe, the supreme planter (Plan., 2-3). This term and its function has meaning within the context of Philo's theory of matter. Once the universe has been created the mundane Logos is the law that holds it together (Heres, 188; Fuga, 110; 112; Plant., 9). The ideas are the powers of God (his Logos) spread throughout the universe giving matter form, and hence quality to the bodies (sômata) that make up the sensible world.

5.3   Before we enter into an examination of matter we must define Philo's theory of elements, and whether or not he maintains a notion of creatio ex nihilo.

The elements or types of material substance constitute matter (hylê) and matter is formed into qualities (i.e., poia eidê: QG., 62). All the elements regardless of their qualifications are unqualified prior to the creation of the sensible world. Indeed, matter is unstructured and unqualified until the act of creation (Fuga, 9; Spec. Leg., i,328).

It is not fully clear whether Philo maintains a five or four element universe. In (Plan., 1-8) he vacillates on this question, in (QG., iv,8; 111,3) he affirms a five element scheme, and in (Heres, 152-153) he proposes a four element universe. Dillon maintains (MP., 170) that Philo does not treat either as a fifth material substance, but rather as the purest form of fire which is not subject to growth and decay, and moves eternally in a circle. If Dillon is correct then Philo divides the universe into three tiers. There is earth, heaven, and an area between aether and earth called (metarsia). Given the fact that the intelligible world is divided into three spheres, it would be cogent if Philo divided the sensible world into three spheres as well. Hence, it is likely that Philo held to the theory of a four element universe.

This points to the conclusion that Philo did not propose, as Wolfson maintained (P., i,308ff.), a doctrine of creatio ex nihilo.[30] This is an important conclusion to consider because it impacts upon the whole question of the nature of Philo's physics, and how he understood the sensible world, and matter. Let me explain the reasons for this conclusion.

The reconstruction of Philo's doctrine of creatio ex nihilo is based upon a fragment from the De Providentia preserved in Eusebius' Praeparatio Evangelica (vii,21), and a reference in the (Somn., i,76). Both testimonies present the term "to create" (ktizein) in a manner which suggests creation ex nihilo. To this may be added a statement from (Spec. Leg., ii,2) that before creation nothing was ranked with God.

Instead of viewing Philo as the originator of the doctrine of the creation of matter out of nothing, which is the position commonly accepted by modern scholars (Dähne, GD., 328ff.; Siegfried, 232ff.; Soulier, 22f.; Drummond, i,297-310; Baeumker, 384, Zeller, iii.2.436; Heinisch, 152; Bréhier, 80-82; Frank, 75 n.10; Weiss, 31-33; Wolfson, i,308ff.), we should examine the possibility that the demiurgic Logos creates the sensible world out of a pre-existing, formless matter.[31] The basis for accepting this interpretation rests upon two grounds. First, of all the Platonic schools of the first century B.C./A.D. only the Neo Pythagorean tradition, represented by Eudorus, claimed that matter was created (Simpl, In Phys., 181,10ff.). However, Philo had an animus against the Neo Pythagorean physics (Heres, 160). Second, the evidence suggests that Philo proposed a doctrine of creation based on an allegorical interpretation of the Timaeus.[32]

Philo uses the terms (ktistês, ktizein) to designate 'creation' and 'to create' in (Somn., i.76). Weiss notes these terms generally refer to the creation of the intelligible and the sensible worlds not matter (UKJ., 55-56-59). This interpretation is correct. Although the world is created, matter is not. Matter is eternal. There is no reason to believe that for Philo 'creation' and 'to create' refer to the creation of either the world or matter out of nothing.

Philo states in (Heres, 160) that matter existed prior to the creation of the world. This view brings the fragment from the De Providentia into question, which begins with the words:

peri de tou posou tês ousias, ei gegone ontôs. (Mras, i.403,20) (De Prov., ii,49)
it continues:

quia non solum creare et edere materiam proprium
et providentiae. (Aucher).

The question is how did Philo understand the terms gegone and creare et edere? Is Philo referring to the creation of matter out of nothing? Or is he referring to the formation of matter into bodies?.

The terms creation, and to create refer to the creation of the intelligible and sensible worlds, and not to the creation of matter. This is clear from (Opf., 29). Here, Philo does not: 1) identify body (sôma) and place (chôra) with matter (hylê); 2) or identify the substrate (hypodochê) with matter (hylê); 3) or the void (kenos) as that from which the substrate (hypodochê) is created. In (Ling., 136) this view is further underscored. Hence, Philo does not: 1) identify body (sôma) with matter (hylê); nor 2) does he identify place (chôra) with matter (hylê). Finally, for Philo a body (sôma) is a compound of form (eidos) and matter (hylê), and place (chôra) is identified with the Logos not with either the substrate (hypodochê) or matter (hylê). Thus creation pertains to the intelligible and sensible worlds, not to matter which is eternal. When Philo, in the (De Prov., i,403,20; ii,49) and in the (Somn., i,76), refers to creation (gegone, creare, ktistês) he means the creation (formation) of the universe, not the creation of matter. The created things have form and shape. Matter is uncreated, formless, shapeless, and eternal until the creation of the world (Fuga, 9; Spec. Leg., i,328).

The statement Philo makes at (Leg. Alleg., ii ,2) that neither before creation was anything to be ranked with him, supports this interpretation. God is not associated with matter until it is formed by the Logos. No bond exists between God and matter before creation. It is only when matter is created into the qualified forms that there is an association between God and matter. This is why nothing was ranked with God before creation. Before creation, matter is merely matter (ousia=hylê: cf. De Prov., i, 403, 20). Once created (formed) it is being (onta).

On the question of the creation of the universe Philo partially follows the teaching of Plato in the Timaeus. The universe was created at a certain point in time by the Demiurge out of a matter both eternal and unformed. According to Philo, Moses proclaimed this same doctrine in Genesis (Aet., 15; 13: Decal., 58; Prov., i, 7: cf. Tim., 2828b). The universe has a beginning and is created (genêtos), but matter is eternal and uncreated. The evidence suggests that Philo takes the account of Genesis literally and the account in the Timaeus allegorically. According to Philo the origin of time is closely dependent on the origin of the world and not prior to it (Opf., 26-28; Leg. Alleg., i, 2, 20). Before the origin of time and the world there existed eternal matter. Philo, concerning the eternity of matter, adopted the Aristotelian view of the origin of the world (De Caelo), ii, 283b 26-30); cf. Aet., 10, 14), and the allegorical interpretation of (Tim., 28b), which in the Old Academy was the cosmological proof-text of Xenocrates and Crantor (Xenocrates, fr. 54 Heinze; cf. Ioh. Phil, Aet., vi, 8, 146, 15-24). Although Philo makes it clear that the universe was generated and had a beginning, he also lays emphasis on the fact that its origin did not take place in time, (Strom., vi, 145, 4-5; 11:506-19).

In summary, Philo postulates the creation of the intelligible and sensible worlds, but not the creation of matter. By the term creation Philo means the generation and creation of the physical world by the Logos, and the intelligible world by God. Matter is eternal and constitutes the stuff of the sensible world, the substratum out of which are formed bodies, and hence sensible things.

5.4   In (Ep., 65) Seneca presents the Antiochean 'metaphysic of prepositions.' This theory forms the basis of Philo's doctrine of creation.

According to Philo the Logos of God is the instrument in the creation of the world (Leg. Alleg., iii, 96). Philo expresses this notion prepositionally. The Logos is that "through which" (di'hou) the world is created (Cher., 125ff.). Philo's use of this prepositional construct reveals the origin of his doctrine. Its origin is in the Antiochean physics as presented in the writings of Seneca (Ep., 65).[33] In addition, Philo's doctrine of causation is closely linked to his doctrine of the Logos as creative and regal power of the universe, and God as the first cause of all things. This link becomes clear if we examine the position of Seneca, and compare it with Philo's.

Seneca presents the doctrine in terms of the two causes of the Stoics, the four of the Peripatetics, and the one cause of the Platonists (Ep., 65, 4ff.). Seneca understands Platonic cause to be the ideas, numerical and geometrical entities (Ep., 65, 8). Seneca's list of prepositional causes are five: from which, by which, that in which, that towards which, and that for the sake of which (Ep., 65, 8). They correspond to matter agent (Demiurge, Logos), immanent form, paradigm, and final cause.[34] For Philo the Logos is the image (eikōn) of God, who is its archetype, and itself (the Logos) is the archetype to all other things, which are its images (Leg. Alleg., iii, 96). At (Cher., 125ff.) the Logos is described prepositionally as the organon of God. In these passages we encounter the notion that the Logos is the paradigmatic and instrumental cause of the universe. Since the ideas, numbers, and geometrical entities exist in the mind of God it is clear that they function as paradigmas, and as instruments used by the Logos in the creation of the world (Opf., 29; 16, 36, 129; Heres, 280; Plan., 50; Ebr., 133; Ling., 172). In summary, Philo conceives of intelligible and sensible creation in an orthodox Middle Platonic fashion. He identifies paradigmatic cause with God, the Logos, and the ideas, efficient cause with the Logos, instrumental cause with the Logos, final cause with God, the Logos, and the ideas. Matter is not caused, but is created and held together by the Logos, and his powers or immanent ideas. The mundane Logos, and the immanent ideas are the immanent form of the sensible universe. The Logos and ideas are what Seneca calls the "that in which." Let us examine Philo's conception of the mundane Logos, and the immanent ideas as the immanent form of the sensible universe.

The Logos for Philo is the sum-total of the divine ideas in activity in the world. They are the creative principles of the material world (Opf., 20). Philo's doctrine of the immanent ideas has close affinities to that ascribed to Antiochus (Augustine, CD., vii. 28). The principle difference between the Philonic and Antiochean doctrines is that Philo maintained that the immanent ideas were immaterial (Ebr., 25; 33; VM., iii. 3; Dec., 21) while Antiochus held they were material (Cicero, Ac. Post. 30ff.).[35] The similarity between the doctrines is that Philo understood the immanent ideas as seminal reason principles (Leg., 55) who together constitute the seminal Logos (Leg., iii. 150; Heres, 119). The technical terminology utilized by both is of Stoic provenance both in terms of the ideas (logoi spermatikoi; rationes), and the Logos (logos spermatikos). This reflects the adoption by the early Middle Academy of Stoic physical theory as fully "Platonic."

We shall now examine how Philo fits his 'metaphysic of prepositions,' and his doctrines of mundane Logos and the immanent ideas into his doctrine of being. To accomplish this we return to his diairetical and categorical doctrines.

_5.6_   Philo's Logos practices Academic diairesis (Heres, 133-236). First, he divides matter in two. Second, he defines the sensibles into their genus, species, and differentia (Mon., 1.6). The origin of Philo's doctrine of division can be traced back to Antiochus (Cicero, Luc., 43; Part. Or., 139). Although Antiochus focused upon the categories of speech, Philo makes it clear that the categories refer to speech and reality (Dec., 30ff.). In terms of material reality, the ideas or powers of God act upon matter so that suitable form might engage each genus (Sacr., 13; Deus 21), and through the use of analysis each sensible thing can be defined and classified.

Philo divides the transcendent ideas into genus, species, and differentia (Opf., 32, 97), and each idea into its accidents (Mut., 21, 121-123). Philo divides the immanent ideas in similar fashion, and in defining the sensibles he distinguishes between the everlasting, active, and perfect "habit" (hexis) and its accidents. The term habit refers to the quality (poiotês) a sensible possesses. A sensible possesses qualities because of the form (eidos) it is molded into in accordance with its transcendent pattern. Each genus has its species, and each exhibits accidents that permit the definition of the quality each particular possesses (Leg. Alleg., 11, 4, 13; cf. Somn., i, 32; VM., iii, 13; Gig., 13). For example, there is music and musician, medicine and doctor. The Logos is the articulator by the process of division of the undifferentiated material substance of the world (Heres, 133-236; cf152ff,; 221-223). In this capacity the Logos is the instrument of God in the creation of the world (Leg.Alleg., iii.96; Cher., 125ff.).

Philo defines the things of the sensible world through the categories. In this way he begins the extensive classification which is necessary for determining the properties of, and relations between sensible things. Philo's Logos practices dichotomic diairesis (Heres, 133-236)[36] and defines the sensible things categorically.

In (Mon., i, 6) Philo shows us how classification works, and indirectly how definition commences upon the formation of matter into bodies by the power of the ideas immanent in matter. When this statement is viewed within the context of (Heres, 133-236), we see that the Logos divides the material substance of the world, and that the ideas give material substance its form.

God replying to Moses states:

> As among you, seals, whenever wax or any similar material is applied to them, make innumerable impressions, not suffering the loss of any part, but remaining as they were, such you must suppose the powers around me to be, applying quality to things without quality, and forms to the formless, while they experience no change or diminution in their eternal nature. But some among you call them very appropriately ideas, since they give ideal form to each thing, arranging the unarranged, and communicating determinate limits and definition and shape to the indeterminate, and indefinite, and shapeless...

The immanent ideas assign a distinctive set of qualities to each species of material things (Heres, 61-62). They constitute the powers of God in the sensible universe, and the means by which the Logos brings order to matter by giving matter form and structure (Norm., 23; cf. Somn., ii, 6). The Logos and the ideas are the measures (metra) of the universe, and the standards upon which matter is formed into bodies (Sacr., 15; QG., iv, 8; Opf., 4-5; Sacr., 13).

According to Philo the sensible world is a vast cosmos in which the ideas stand to one another in relations arranged according to genera and species (Leg. Alleg., ii, 7). These powers which are the thoughts of God held together by the mundane Logos, constrain and form the multiplicity of phenomena into a unity (Spec. Leg., ii, 34).

The material substrate is divided and formed by the Logos. Since the Logos is the most generic category or something (ti; to genikon; to genikôtaton: Leg. Alleg., ii. 86; i. 9, 23; iii. 175; Det., 118), and matter (hylê), is substance (ousia), the matter formed by the generic Logos is qualified substance (poia eidê: QD., 62). All qualified material substance is characterized by quality, quantity, time, and place (Dec., 30).

In summary, Philo's dialectical schema reflects objective ontological relations and not merely conceptual ones. The Logos divides and forms the world dichotomically. As divider the Logos functions as the instrument of God in the creation of the world, and the archetype of all things in the world, which are its images. Thus, Philo's conception of diairesis, and of genus, species and differentia, suggests a diairectical schema, in which the relation of the general to the particular reflects the objective ontological relation of model to copy, and form to matter.

Since Philo admitted both essential and accidental attributes in his classifications and definitions it appears that he does not reproduce the Aristotelian conception of genus, species, and differentia. Although he uses the words eidos and genos, to refer to less general and more general classes, he did not use them in the technical Aristotelian sense. Aristotle's genera and species are established on the basis of essential attributes only, and his notion that the species are the actualization of the genus in the final differentiae is incompatible with Philo's conception of an entity as the focus of all its relations to every other entity and to the whole. The Philonic classes are established by the similarity and relation there is among the members of each class. Imitation and variety of relation is the unifying bond between two worlds.

Philo was trying to establish a natural classification of things on the basis of genera and species that are subsumed under the primary genus, the Logos. In this way he could determine the sum-total of the relations of each class with respect to every other class, and to the whole. Given his assumptions, he has to admit accidental attributes with all the consequences that entails. Thus, Philonic diairesis, rests upon the notion that each thing is the focus of all its relations in respect to everything else, and to the whole, and that these relations are defined categorically.

5.7   As noted previously the Logos is identified with quality and relation (the immanent ideas are identified with quality, relation, and place), and matter with quantity as the material substrate (hylê). Hence, categorically, Philo's sensible universe has the following structure:

Logos (<u>poiotês</u>, <u>pros</u>)
Ideas (<u>poiotês</u>, <u>pros-ti</u>, <u>topos</u>)
Matter (<u>poson-posotês</u>, <u>hylê</u>).

Since the mundane Logos is an aspect of the antemundane Logos, he is also the most generic something of the sensible universe (<u>genikôtatos</u>, <u>ti</u>) who contains within himself the immanent ideas The mundane Logos and the immanent ideas have the following structure:

Logos (<u>genikôtatos</u>, <u>ti</u>; <u>poiotês</u>, <u>pros</u>, <u>topos</u>)   Intelligible world
Ideas (<u>poiotês</u>, <u>pros-ti</u>, <u>topos</u>)

Together the intelligible and sensible worlds have the following structure:

Logos (<u>genikôtatos</u>, <u>ti</u>; <u>poiotês</u>, <u>pros</u>, <u>topos</u>)   Sensible world
Ideas (<u>poiotês</u>, <u>pros-ti</u>, <u>topos</u>)

Logos (<u>genikôtatos</u>, <u>poiotês</u>, <u>pros</u>, <u>topos</u>)
Ideas (<u>poiotês</u>, <u>pros-ti</u>, <u>topos</u>)
Bodies (<u>poiotês</u>, and the four Stoic and/or ten Peripatetic categories)
Matter (<u>poson-posotês</u>, <u>ousia-hylê</u>).

Philo's theoretic or physics is fully Middle Platonic and his norms are wholly consistent with those of the two dominant trajectories of Academic thought in first century Middle Platonism. Philo's Judaic Platonism represents a new trajectory in Middle Platonic speculation at Alexandria insofar as it is representative of a fruitful synthesis of the theoretics of Eudorus and Antiochus.[37]

To fully appreciate the Middle Platonic option Philo proposes and the conceptual system he offers based upon early Middle Academic norms, his theoretic must be examined within the context of these Platonic trajectories. Philo walked a middle-path between Eudorus and Antiochus, and offered a metaphysic which combined elements from both. It is difficult to assess what criteria he used to determine which aspects of each theoretic he found compatible with his Bible, but it is clear that he saw his Platonism fully congruent with the teachings of scripture. The resulting synthesis of the Platonic and the Biblical was his Jewish Platonism.

Philo's part in the intellectual formation of late antiquity is miniscule. In this formative period of Judaism his writings were unknown by his Graeco-Roman contemporaries, as far as we know. Nonetheless, his vision of Judaism in the mantel of Plato illustrated the common foundations he shared with the Hellenism of his time. This Judaic Platonism was a product of the intellectual life of Alexandria, and a reflection of the rich variety of Judaism born in its academy.

In the century which would follow upon his own, Philo's works would become authoritative for Christian Platonists at Alexandria. In the formative period of Christianity his writings formed the basis for the Christian Platonisms of principally Clement, and then Origen. Philo's vision of Moses and Plato was complemented by that of Jesus. This Christian Platonism, like the Jewish that preceded it, was steeped in the foundations of Hellenism and represented the might and learning of Alexandrian Platonism.

Philo's achievement was to become the first result in the formation of a philosophy based upon the twin pillars of the Bible and Platonic scripture. The way was prepared for the triumph of Plato in Christian philosophical teaching. Let us turn to this prospect, and its initial expression in Clement.

II. CLEMENT OF ALEXANDRIA

Introduction

We have tried to describe, analyze, and interpret the originality of Philo's contribution to Middle Platonic metaphysics. It remains to inquire how much originality may be ascribed to his heir, Clement. The question may be put in this way. Which probable results can be achieved by the study of Clement's thought within the context of Middle Platonism? How does he expand upon the norms established by Philo? Where does Clement offer new norms and in what sense are they original contributions to the solution of our series of metaphysical postulates?

Clement accepted and expanded upon two doctrines central to Philo's theoretic. These are the Logos doctrine and the doctrine of the categories. In each case the broad outlines of Clement's theories agree with Philo's, and yet they also differ. Clement postulates two distinct phases of the antemundane Logos rather than one. He asserts that a single set of categories have referential efficacy to both the intelligible and sensible worlds,[38] and in an attempt to link together God and the Logos he introduces the concept of referential equivocity.

These additions offered by Clement must be seen within the context of the metaphysical problem Philo addressed and attempted to answer. This was the nature of the relation between God and the universe. In the wake of Philo's Logos and categorical doctrines, Clement offers his own, and by means of them he attempts to bridge the ontological gap between God, the Logos and the universe.

Clement's activity is directed toward a reformulation of Philo's doctrines and his answers to these problems. Central to his enterprise is a redefinition of the Neo Pythagorean doctrine of the two "Ones" based upon the first two hypotheses of Plato's Parmenides. Here he offers a new theory, at least for Alexandrian Middle Platonism, based upon the notions of identity, similarity, and difference.

Clement senses the unstable nature of a theoretic that fails to solve the problem of the chôrismos between a God who is hyparxis and a Logos and universe that is in varying degrees poiotês. In his attempt to overcome this ontological gap he proposes three distinct stages of the Logos, a new categorical doctrine, and attempts to relate God, the Logos, and the world through the notions of identity, similarity, and difference. In the wake of these reformulations he establishes for Christian Middle Platonism a definition of God and the universe that devalues the radical transcendence of God proposed in Jewish Middle Platonism. This reformulation, in turn, points toward the shift in Middle Platonic metaphysics from the Neo Pythagorean-Platonic axis of early Middle Platonic thought to the Aristotelian-Platonic axis of later Middle Platonic thought.

That Clement approaches reality and defines it in a manner that reminds us of Philo need not surprise us.[39] His first principles echo the refrain of a God above the One, and a Logos identified as the One. His physics reflects an understanding of the universe wherein the Logos is the sum-total of the intelligible world, and the creator and sustainer of the sensible world. In his attempt to overcome the philosophical problems that face a Platonist he utilizes doctrines of the divine intellect and the categories.

Despite these similarities between Clement and his teacher Philo, certain dissimilarities need be mentioned at the outset. Clement's Logos and categorical doctrines differ from Philo's. They reflect the tendency in second century Platonism to integrate the teachings of Aristotle with those of Plato. These subtle changes emerge in Clement's technical terminology and in his understandings of the Logos and the categories.

In the second century, Middle Platonism shifts its epic center away from its earlier emphasis on the separation of God and the universe based upon Neo Pythagorean principles toward the unification of God and the universe based upon Peripatetic principles. With Clement we witness one of the first examples of this change in Platonic thinking. He institutionalizes many of the metaphysical norms postulated by Philo, and introduces a variety of his own. His importance for our study cannot be underestimated. Clement carries into early Christian Platonism a philosophical interpretation first articulated in the Judaic Platonism of Philo. Furthermore, he hammers out a metaphysical system that becomes paradigmatic for later Christian Middle Platonism in the Empire.

Clement's Platonism has close affinities to those of Antiochus and Philo, but it also has strikingly dissimilar features as well. Among these are a move toward a Nous theology, and a Peripatetic categorical theory. It is difficult to judge if Clement's Platonism represents a break with earlier Middle Platonism, but it certainly represents a transitional moment. Clement extends Middle Platonic theory to encompass a series of Speusippian and Aristotelian norms. Indeed, he combines a series of Platonic and Peripatetic norms that had not been placed together earlier. Finally, he institutionalizes the norms of Jewish Middle Platonism, as represented in Philo, and sets them up as Christian Middle Platonism's own.

Clement's theoretic contains a number of varied elements. His theology maintains the Neo Pythagorean dimensions extant in Philo, but tempers the radical transcendence of God by relating him through a Peripatetic doctrine of equivocals to the Logos and the universe. His ontology is Academic in the manner that Philo's is, and his physics continues the Peripatetic model found in Antiochus and Philo. His cosmology and physics serve to further these ontological ends by linking God and the universe in a more solid fashion than the older Platonic notions of imitation and participation.

Clement's Platonism is the first systematic expression of Christian Middle Platonism in the formative age of Christianity. Distinctly Christian and Platonic, Clement's theoretic reflects in large measure the Platonic norms of Jewish Platonism proposed by Philo.

As the first articulator of a systematic Christian philosophy based upon Platonic principles, Clement establishes Christian Platonism as another philosophical option among the variety of school Platonisms. He presents the teachings of his scriptures in a scientific manner, and offers the wisdom of his testaments as the consummation of Greek philosophical thinking itself. It is largely due to his efforts that Origen's philosophy takes on the form it does, and that Christian Platonism becomes recognized as a philosophy by its opponents Galen, Celsus, and later Porphyry. Clement's place in the history of Platonism is important within the context of Jewish and Christian Platonism in particular, and hellenistic Platonism in general. Hence, within the context of our study, Clement's philosophy constitutes a transition in Platonic thinking that is important for the subsequent Christian Platonism, and a transition that reflects the philosophical culture of Platonism as a whole. Clement's thought reflects a conscious attempt to reconcile Plato, Aristotle, and Pythagoras.

1. First Principles: God and the Antemundane Logos

1.1   Clement posited two separately existing Neo Pythagorean "Ones."[40]   God is above the _monas_, and the Logos is both _monas_ and _panta hen_. To understand Clement's theology, we shall first discuss the two principles _tout court_.

Clement maintains the Philonic theological hierarchy. God stands at the head of this hierarchy, and the Logos is subsumed under him. God is above genus, species, and differentia (Strom.., (v. 12. 81: ii. 380. 18f.). By this Clement means God is not a countable unit, and he is above the _monas_ (Strom., v. 81. 5-6 (iii. 380. 18-22). The parallels with Philo's formulations are clear (QD., 62; Cont., 2). For both, God is "unqualified," and radically distinct from all that is "qualified" (Strom., ii. 16. 1 (ii. 116. 33f.' vi. 71. 5 (ii. 374. 18-20).

The absolute transcendence of God is expressed in two ways by Clement; first, ontologically and second, epistemologically. Clement maintains that God is above space and time, and cannot be situated in a determined physical place (Strom., vi, 71. 5 (ii. 374. 18-20); v. 81. 5-6 (ii. 380. 18-22). He cannot be defined by the categories. Clement also holds that God is beyond thought (Strom., ii. 6. 1 (ii. 115. 27-28); iv. 156. 1 (ii. 317. 21-22); v. 65. 2 (ii. 369. 26); v. 71. 5 (ii. 374. 19-20); v. 81. 4 (ii. 380. 16-17); v. 82. 4 (ii. 381. 8).[41] Categorical definition involves distinctions between genus, species, and differentia. Since God cannot be defined categorically it follows that he cannot be known. Nothing can be directly known of God because such determinations are applicable only to qualified things. God is wholly unqualified.

Below this absolutely transcendent God stands the Logos. The antemundane Logos has two phases. First, it is identified with the intellect of God, and exists _intra mentem dei_. Second, it is called an _hypostasis_ distinct from God, and it exists _extra mentem dei_.[41] In the former sense the Logos is a mind at rest and the place of the ideas. In the latter sense the Logos is an active mind who thinks the ideas.

The Logos, as the intellect of God (Strom., iv. 155. 2 (ii. 317. 11); v. 73. 3 (ii. 375. 18-19), is the "place" (chôra) of the ideas of God (Strom., v. 16. 3 (iii. 336. 8). Clement defines this manifestation of the Logos as Philo does, and uses the doctrine of ideas postulated by Philo to affirm that the Logos is the place of the ideas (cf. Opf., 20; Cher., 49; Strom., v. 16. 3 (iii. 336. 8): Opf., 17-19). The terminology Clement uses, however, is novel. The <u>logos tou theou</u> of the last passage is one and the same thing with the <u>patrikos</u> <u>logos</u> of the <u>Hypotupôseis</u> (Stählin, <u>GCS</u>., iii. 202). Clement calls the <u>logos</u> of the Father <u>nous</u> (<u>Strom</u>., iv. 155.2 (ii. 317. 11), whereas Philo does not refer to God or the Logos as <u>nous</u>. This is a Neo Pythagorean term (e.g., Eudorus; Simpl., <u>In Phys</u>, 181, 10ff.) employed by second century Platonists such as Albinus (<u>Did</u>., 163, 12-13; 163, 27-30) and Neo Pythagoreans such as Numenius (ff. 12, 15 des Places) to define the divine intellect(s). This turn to a Nous theology we shall discuss later, when we examine Albinus and Numenius' theoretics.

Clement's doctrine of ideas closely parallels Philo's. The theory can be traced at least as far back as Antiochus (Cicero, <u>Or</u>., 8; Aug, <u>CD</u>., vii. 28), if not to the Old Academy (cf. R.M. Jones, <u>CPh</u>., 21 (1926), 324-325; A.N.M. Rich, <u>Mnen</u>., iv, 7 (1954), 126; Xenocrates, fr. 15, 34). Philo worked off the Antiochean formulation (cf. Theiler, <u>VN</u>., 15-16; Loenen, <u>Mnen</u>., iv, 10 (1957), 44-45; Merlan, <u>CH</u>., 55) and it was from this source mediated through Philo that Clement most likely received the doctrine. The major distinction between Clement's doctrine and Philo's is in the use of terminology. Clement's use of terms such as <u>noêsis</u>, <u>noêma</u>, and <u>nous</u> suggest a context of understanding that is close to Albinus' formulation. Hence, while Clement's Logos, in Philonic manner, is identical with the mind of God, and the ideas which are its thoughts (<u>Strom</u>., v. 16. 3 (iii. 336. 8): <u>Opf</u>., 17-20) how the Logos thinks the ideas differs from Philo's description. These distinctions in terminology will be explored in greater depth later.

<u>1.2</u>   Clement also calls the Logos the wisdom of God and identifies the Logos, at least in its first antemundane phase, with the mind of God. To fully appreciate Clement's Logos doctrine and the role it plays in his theoretic, let us examine what Clement means by calling the Logos the Sophia of God.

The Logos is called divine wisdom (<u>sophia</u>) by Clement, and is seen as the first of the beings created by God (<u>Strom</u>., vii. 7. 4: (iii. 7. 0-13); v. 89. 4 (ii. 385. 4).[42] The source of this interpretation is Philo who identifies the Logos with wisdom (<u>Leg. Alleg</u>.., i, 65; <u>Abr</u>., 51; <u>Conf</u>., 46; <u>Somn</u>., i, 215). There is an immanent, as well as transcendent aspect, of Clement's notion of the identification of the Logos with wisdom. First, Clement identifies the Logos as second hypostasis with wisdom, and Logos-Wisdom is called the principle of created things. Second, Clement calls the Logos the power of God (<u>Strom</u>., vii. 7. 4 (iii. 7. 9-13). In the first case, wisdom is identified at least partially, with the immanent Logos. The mundane Logos is the power which holds the sensible universe together (<u>Protr</u>., 5. 2 (i. 6. 7-9); <u>Strom</u>., v. 104. 4: (ii. 396. 16); vii. 5. 4 (iii. 5. 22ff.); vii. 9. 2 (iii. 8. 14-15). The coupling of the terms Logos and powers brings us back to a doctrine encountered in Philo.

As the power of God, the Logos contains both the intelligible and sensible worlds within itself (<u>Strom</u>., i. 156. 2; (ii. 317. 24-318. 2); <u>Strom</u>., ii. 5. 4 (ii. 115. 23-24). The power of the Logos is his capacity to comprehend the universe, to order it, and to form it in accordance with the divine ideas, who are the formative principles of the cosmos. Although Clement does not reproduce the extensive doctrine of power encountered in Philo it is clear that the power of the antemundane Logos, or <u>patrikos logos</u> (Stählin, iii.

202; cf. Strom., iv. 155. 2), and mundane Logos (Strom., vii. 5. 4; v. 104. 4; Protr., 5.2) are correlate powers that reflect Clement's division of Being. The intelligible and sensible worlds are ruled by different aspects of the power of the Logos. Hence, through the power of the Logos, God's wisdom is creator and sustainer of the universe. As the immanent form of the sensible universe, the Logos is conceived of as the immaterial law or harmony of the physical world. The mundane Logos holds the cosmos together, and administers it insofar as he penetrates it from one extremity to the other (Protr., 5. 2 (i. 6. 7-9); Strom., v. 104. 4 (ii. 396. 16); vii. 5. 4 (iii. 5. 22ff.); vii. 9. 2 (iii. 8. 14-15).

The mundane Logos comprehends the universe in itself (Strom., ii. 5. 4 (ii. 115. 23-24); ii. 6. 2 (ii. 116. 4-5); v. 73. 3 (ii. 373. 20-21); v. 81. 3 (ii. 380. 13-14). The power of comprehension is the agency of the formative power of the Logos, and this power is the harmony or law of the physical world. In this sense the mundane Logos is the formative power of the universe, who by means of the immanent ideas (powers) forms matter into its prescribed genera and species on the model of the transcendent ideas.

The mundane Logos is coextensive with the universe as the law and harmony of the sensible world (Strom., v. 104. 4 (ii. 396. 16); vii. 5. 4 (iii. 5. 22); vii. 9. 2 (iii. 8. 14-15); Protr., 5. 2 (i. 6. 7-9). In all respects Clement's mundane Logos, as a metaphysical principle, is identical to Philo's (Heres, 188; Fuga 110, 112; Plan., 9; Ling., 137).

The mundane Logos is not a material entity, but the incorporeal power that holds the physical world together penetrating it from one extremity to the other. It exists outside the mind of God as the place (chôra) of the world, but is not identified with matter (hylê) or the receptacle (hypodochê). Pohlenz (S., i, 417-418) proposed that Clement's Logos was a Stoic Logos, but there is not much doubt that Lilla (C., 210) is right that this is not the case. First, it would be inconsistent with the inner logic of Clement's theoretic for Clement to propose a material Logos as a third principle. Second, Clement's dependency upon Philo for his doctrine of the mundane Logos is quite clear (Plan., 9; Fuga, 110, 112; Heres, 188; cf. Ling., 137). Third, Clement's Logos is akin to other Middle Platonic doctrines of the Soul of the world. It is close to Albinus' (Did., 165, 3-4; 170, 3-6), and has affinities to Plutarch's (QP., 1001b; IO., 373d; In Tim., 1026c.). It is clear that this 'helmsman' (oiakizon) is like Numenius' (Strom., vii. 5. 4; Eusebius, PE., xv. 12. 3). It is immaterial.

The first phase of the antemundane Logos is distinguished from the second by Clement. The distinction is between the reason of God, and the Logos generated by god as a distinct being, Son, and second hypostasis (Photius, Bibl. God., 109: Stählin, GCF., iii. 202. 16-22).

Zahn (FG., 144-145), Wolfson (PCF., 211), and Lilla (C., 200 n. 1) are correct that the Logos "proceeds" (proêlthon) from the Father and exists as a distinct entity (Strom., v. 16. 5 (ii. 336. 12-13)[43] in itself. In this second antemundane phase the Logos is represented as the totality of the ideas and powers of god, or monas, that make up the intelligible world, or kosmos noêtos. As the image of God the Logos functions as the first creative principle (archê) of all things, and the wisdom (sophia) of God. Evidence for the first postulate is extant at (Strom., iv. 156. 1-2 (ii. 317. 24-318. 2). The Logos is the unity (panta hen) that comprehends everything in itself (Strom., iv. 156. 2).[44]

Although there are parallels between Clement's formulation and Philo's (Opf., 24, 24; Sacr., 83; Ling., 172; Somn., i. 62) we must be careful not to assert that the two thinkers propose the same doctrine (cf. Lilla, C., 204-205). First, Clement's Logos is a distinct entity apart from God. Second, Clement calls the hypostatic Logos a Nous, and compares the Logos to a circle, who comprehends the totality of the divine ideas in itself (Strom., iv. 155. 2; iv. 156. 1-2). Third, Clement does not call the Logos a "most generic something" (cf. Leg. Alleg., ii, 86; iii. 175). Fourth, although based upon the second hypotheses of the Parmenides, Clement's Logos is a One conceived in terms of a second Nous that comprehends the intelligible world in its own right. Clement's Logos is not merely the place of ideas and the extension of God's intellect. The Logos is an active intellect distinct from God, who thinks the ideas.

Although Clement's formulation of the mundane Logos is not distinct from Philo's and other Middle Platonic definitions, one aspect of his theory is. Clement distinguishes between two phases of the antemundane Logos, which correspond to the two Ones of the Neo Pythagorean interpretation of the first two hypotheses of Plato's Parmeides. In making this distinction between the mind of God and a separately existing hypostasis, Clement altered the structure of the Philonic theology.[45] God and the non-hypostatic Logos stand together as a unity. The hypostatic Logos has two distinct phases, one transcendent, and the other immanent. The antemundane and mundane Logos stand as distinct, and yet inter-related, divine principles. This reformulation is not without significance. We shall have the opportunity to discuss it later.

The parallels between Clement's Logos concept and Philo's have been pointed out by many scholars (e.g., Redepenning, Vacherot, Preische, Merk, Gall, de Feye, Daskalikis, Bigg, Wolfson, Lilla). However, there are also some important differences. There is little doubt that the Logos for Clement has three stages of existence.

For Philo it has only two. Thus, against Wolfson's view (PCF., 204-217; 266-270), the continuity between Philo and Clement ceases on this important point. For Philo the first two stages of the Logos are intra-mentem dei, and only the third extra-mentem dei. For Clement the Logos has three stages: 1) identified with the mind of God (Strom. iv. 155. 2 [ii. 317. 11]; v. 73.3 [ii. 375. 18-19]), i.e., it exists intra-mentem dei; 2) as a separate mind or hypostasis, it exists extra-mentem dei (Photius, Bibl. Codex 109 = Stählin, iii. 202. 16-22; cf. Cassiodorus, Ep. S. Jn., = Stählin iii. 209-210); and 3) as the supreme mind of the world, i.e., it exists extra-mentem dei.

Wolfson is right to say that the Logos is subordinated to God, in his second and third stages (PCF., pp. 204-207). Yet in his first stage (as one and the same thing with the mind of God and the place of God's ideas), Pade is correct that the Logos is not subordinate to God (Pade, U., p. 148-160). Hence, the interpretations of Wolfson and Pade are not contradictory. The correct interpretation is that in phase one (1) they are equal, e.g., there is no distinction between God and his intellect (Logos), and in phase two (2) and three (3) they are subordinate to God.

The discontinuity between the Logos doctrines of Philo and Clement on these points has been noted by Wolfson and Zahn. There is a distinction between the Logos which is the reason of God, and the generated antemundane Logos which is a distinct being as God's Son and hypostasis. (Wolfson, PCF, p. 204-217; 269; Zahn, F, p. 144-5; 134 n. 2; cf. Casey, JTS 25 (1924), p. 43-56). We assert, against Pade (U., p. 148-160), that unlike Philo, Clement held a two-stage rather than a one-stage antemundane Logos theory. We shall focus upon the antemundane Logos in this section, and discuss the mundane Logos later.

This conclusion is based on two hypotheses. First, that Clement borrowed almost in toto the structure of Philo's doctrine of the Logos. Second, he transformed it. The structure of Clement's theology is Philonic. The Logos exists in three stages. The transformation is that in each of the stages the Logos has three distinct types of existence. In stage one of the antemundane stage he is identical with the mind of God and exists noetically. The Logos is intra mentem dei. In stage two he is a separate entity from God as an hypostasis and exists as the transcendent mind of the world. The Logos is extra mentem dei. In its mundane phase the Logos is a separate hypostasis who exists in the world as the mind of the world. Again the Logos exists extra mentem dei.

The central problem Clement faces is that of the relation of God to the universe, and the corollary problems of the relation of the sensibles to the intelligibles and the intelligibles to each other. The older Platonic solution to this problem was the imitation theory based upon the doctrine of the ideas. The ideas are viewed as the thoughts of God contained in the antemundane Logos. The Logos and the ideas he contains within himself constitute the intelligible world. The sensible world is created by the Logos on the patterns of the divine ideas. Thus the sensible world imitates the intelligible world which is in the mind of God's Logos.

Although this doctrine links God to the physical world, through the intermediaries of the Logos and the ideas, it does not overcome the gap that exists between God and the universe. To complement it Philo proposed two additional doctrines to bridge the fundamental ontological gap of Platonic metaphysics. These were the doctrines of the mundane Logos, and the doctrine of the categories. Clement builds upon Philo's theories by offering a two-stage doctrine of the Logos, and a categorical doctrine that affirms the referential efficacy of a single set of categories for both the intelligible and sensible realms. By means of the first he proposes an identity between God and the Logos, and by means of the second he offers a notion of similarity between the degrees of reality which complement the imitation theory based upon the doctrine of ideas.

Clement 's distinction between two phases of the antemundane Logos represents a major transition from the one phase antemundane Logos of Philo, and reflects a second century Platonic tendency to hypostasize the second intellect. To appreciate the full dimensions of Clement's reformulation we must view it as a continuance of the Philonic conception of antemundane Logos, and the addition of a hypostatic conception of the antemundane Logos as well.

1.3   Clement's new theological norm is based on his reinterpretation of the Neo Pythagorean interpretation of the first two hypotheses of Plato's Parmenides. Clement calls his Logos a nous (Strom., iv. 155. 2; cf. Photius, Bibl. Codex, 109: GCS., iii. 202.

16-22). This is reminiscent of the definitions proposed by "Archytas" and Eudorus (Stobaeus, Anth., i. 41. 2; Simpl., In Phys., 181, 10ff.), and is analogous to the definition of the nous proposed by Numenius (Eusebius, PE., xi, 18, 22). As a first One the Logos is identical with the mind of god and with the ideas, which are its thoughts, and still immanent in it (Strom., v. 16. 3). The Logos is the intellect (nous) and place (chôra) of the ideas as the intellect (nous) of God (Strom., iv. 155. 2 (ii. 317. 11); cf. v. 73. 3 (ii. 375. 18-19). When the Logos actively thinks the ideas (Strom., v. 16. 3) as the second One (monas: Strom., v. 93. 4) and Unity (panta hen: Strom., iv. 156. 2), the Logos is the ousion hen and nous of the universe.

If we examine Clement's philosophical theology closely it becomes clear that the radical distinction Philo maintained between God and the antemundane Logos is blurred. This is also true for the distinction Philo maintained between the antemundane and mundane Logos.

The Neo Pythagorean Ones are reformulated to constitute the two phases of the antemundane Logos by Philo. Above both "Ones" stands God absolutely transcendent and without attributes. At initial glance it would appear that Clement has widened the Middle Platonic chôrismos between God and the universe. How does the postulate of a hypostatic Logos overcome the ontological gap between unqualified (apoios) and qualified (poiotês) existence? Does not Clement return to the radical dualism of the Neo Pythagorean theoretic which Philo attempted to overcome? These questions are important to consider, and we shall discuss them once we examine Clement's doctrines of Being and the categories.

In summary, Clement's first two principles are defined in a manner that exhibits affinities to formulations proposed by Eudorus, Philo, and Numenius. Clement's philosophical theology reflects his critical appraisal of these earlier Academic (Neo Pythagorean) interpretations of the first two hypotheses of the Parmenides.[46]

Clement maintains the central features of Philo's philosophical theology. His God is a Philonic God; the relation of God to the Logos, at least in the first phase of the antemundane Logos, is also Philonic in inspiration. However, Clement's hypostatic Logos is not a Philonic Logos, but something quite different. It is a Logos-Nous that has affinities to the Nous of Albinus. Finally, Clement's doctrine of ideas exhibits parallels to the doctrines of Philo and Albinus. The ideas are thoughts of God placed in the Logos, and the ideas are actively thought and apprehended by the Logos. Hence, in three areas, the doctrine of God, the Logos and the ideas, Clement proposes a series of changes. Each reformulation stands as a new norm in Middle Platonic metaphysics.

To fully appreciate the complexity of Clement's proposal we must examine antecedent theories of identity, similarity, difference, and equivocity.[47] In the following pages we shall examine these doctrines in Aristotle, Speusippus, and the early Middle Academy. This overview will provide us with the proper context to grasp the nature of the relation of God to the Logos, and the relation of the noetic and material worlds to God and the Logos in Clement's theoretic. These theories lie at the heart of Clement's solution to the multi-faceted problem of the relation of God and the universe.

2. The Categories of Being

2.1   Clement's categorical doctrine is difficult to reconstruct.[48] He did not write a commentary on the Categories. He merely reproduced a doxographical account of Middle Platonic categorical doctrine (Strom., viii. 8. 23 (iii. 94. 25-95. 26).[49] He linked this theory with his own version of the metaphysic of prepositions (Strom., vii. 9. 2f. iii. 9f. 12ff.). This tells us something about the context of Clement's categorical doctrine, and its affinities with the doctrine proposed by Philo.

The outlines of Clement's theory are extant in his philosophical theology. Working off his reformulation of the Neo Pythagorean interpretations of the first two hypotheses of Plato's Parmenides Clement defines his antemundane Logos as two Ones. The first One is identical with the mind of God, and the second One is a distinct hypostasis separate from God. The hypostatic Logos has two phases. He is transcendent, and constitutes the intelligible universe, and he is immanent in the sensible universe as the law which holds it together.

It is the second One, or hypostatic Logos, that mediates between what is Absolute (kath'hauto) and what is Relative (pros ti). The mundane phase of the second One is defined within the context of Philo's immanent Logos, while the antemundane phase of the second One must be seen within the context of Clement's own reformulation of Philo's antemundane Logos, and the tendency among second century Middle Platonists to hypostasize the second intellect of their philosophical theologies.

If the Parmenides of Plato affords the backdrop to Clement's theology, then Philo's categorical theory sets the context within which to comprehend Clement's doctrine of categories. Clement fine tunes Philo's theory with the aid of Peripatetic theories. Witt (A., 39) maintains that Clement's other fontes are the Peripatetic commentators of the first century A.D., principally Andronicus, who had as his source Boetheus of Sidon (cf. Moraux, AG., 144-164). Let us now turn to an examination of Clement's ontology, and the categorical doctrine that accompanies it.

Theiler (VN., 6ff.) and Witt (A., 38f.) note that Clement rejected the notion, proposed by Eudorus, that Aristotle's ousia must be rejected on the ground that sensible and intelligible reality cannot be subsumed under a single genus. The ground for this assessment is that Clement combines the ten Peripatetic categories, and subsumes them under the two Academic categories (Strom., viii, 24. 1 (iii. 95. 4ff.). If this is indeed Clement's view, then we have witnessed a major transition in Middle Platonic categorical thinking, at least in its Alexandrian trajectory.

Although Philo subsumed sensible and intelligible reality under a most generic entity, he did not propose that the Logos was a substance (ousia). The category substance was a material category (ousia=hylê: Dec., 30ff.). In this sense Philo followed standard Neo Pythagorean procedure in respect to substance (ousia). It is material (cf. Eudorus, Simpl. In Phys., 181, 10ff.). The sensibles and intelligibles were subsumed under a category, but this was the most general category or something (ti). Philo's adherence to Neo Pythagorean doctrine, at least on this point, forced him to propose a whole new set of categories applicable to the intelligible realm while keeping those that had referential efficacy to the sensible realm.

Clement rejected this proposal. He assumed that the ten categories had referential efficacy to both the intelligible and sensible worlds. If (Strom., viii. 24. 1 (iii. 94. 25-95. 26) is to be taken seriously, then we must suppose that Clement, like Adronicus and Antiochus, subsumes the ten Aristotelian categories under those of Platonism, by regarding the last nine as pros ti or symbebêkota as well as kath'hauta.[50]

The probable background to Clement's reformulation can be traced to Andronicus, who following Xenocrates (fr. 12), made the Absolute (kath'hauto) and the Relative (pros ti) his ultimate categories. He placed thermon in the category of poia (the Stoic term is pôs echônta), but thermantikon in that of poiêtika or pros ti. Boetheus of Sidon who was indirectly dependent on Andronicus (cf. Prantl, GL., 542-543), found the latter category in Plato's (Sophist 255c) and the (Republic 438a). Clement, who reproduces Boetheus' diairesis in (Strom., viii. 24, 1, 5; cf. Prantl, GL., 547; Witt, A., 36ff.; 60ff.), adopts the same model as that of Andronicus, Boetheus, and Antiochus (Cicero, Fin., v. 16).[51]

The additional link to Speusippus is an important component in understanding Clement's theory. Speusippus maintained that through diairesis one classifies sensibles (Arist. An. Post., 97a6-22; Anonymous, In An. Post., 584, 17-585, 2; Arist, Metaphys., 1044a5-9; 1045a12-14; Part. An., 642b 5-644a11).[51] He proposed an exhaustive classification of the whole of existence, based on the notions of identity, difference, and similarity of each thing in respect to every other thing, and to the whole. Speusippus' conception is that any entity is like a point, and that knowledge of each thing requires knowledge of all the differentiae. The differentiae are defined by means of the notions of identity, difference, and similarity. It is the task of diairesis to determine the relation of the sensibles to each other and to the whole.[52]

It is likely that Clement conceived of diairesis in a similar fashion (Strom., viii. 19. 1-8 (iii. 91. 27ff.) as Antiochus (Cicero, Fin., i, 22; ii, 30; iii, 40; cf. Tusc., v, 72; Top., 30). When Clement speaks of division of genus into species and definition as the stating of essential attributes reached at the exclusion, at every stage, of members of co-ordinate species, he is referring to sensible things. However, since he subsumes the ten categories under both Academic categories it is possible that division and definition refer to intelligible things as well. Identity, difference, and similarity refer to all things subsumed under a single genus.

For Clement the Logos is the archê of all division and definition. In (Strom., iv. 156. 2 (ii. 317. 24-318. 2) Clement calls the hypostatic antemundane Logos the circle of all powers bound into one point. The powers are represented as the radii of the circle, which all meet in its center. This is reminiscent of Speusippus' conception that any entity is like a point (Arist, Metaphys., 1044a 5-9). Granted, Clement refers to the Logos, and Speusippus to a sensible, but the principle is the same. The second One is like a point to which the identification of any intelligible with its differentiae is made. The differentiae are established by means of identity, difference, and similarity. The Logos is the focus of all the relations, and the basis for an exhaustive classification of the whole of existence.

Clement is able to assert such an hypothesis because the Logos has a separate existence as a hypostatic entity (Strom., v. 16. 5 (ii. 336. 12-13). It does not exist as a primary genus as the Logos of Philo. Clement's universe is a system of relations which ultimately depend upon, and take their meaning from, the Logos and his powers (ideas). All things have a bond of similarity with the Logos-point. There is an ontological order of substances -- the Logos, ideas, numbers, magnitudes, soul, and sensibles. It is the task of diairesis to determine these relations. This is done by classifying the identity, similarity and difference, among all entities related to the Logos.

2.2   There is a bond of similarity among the classes (S1) in Clement's conception of imitation.[53]   This is the aspect of Clement's thought that is Platonic. However, Clement's concept differs from Plato's as well. For Plato the essence of a particular consists in similarity with the corresponding idea. A tree is a tree because it participates in, or imitates, the idea of tree. For Clement the essence of any entity is not merely its similarity to an idea. Similarity is only one of several relations, the sum-total of which is a thing's essence. Identity and difference appear also in Plato, but in Plato they are substantial ideas that communicate with each other and all the other ideas. For Clement they, with similarity, are the most general notions with which to work.

Clement's classes are established by the similarity there is among members of each class (S2). This similarity, unlike that which is the unifying bond among the classes (S1) is a symmetrical relation as a circle, or the radii of a circle bound and united in one point (Strom., iv. 156. 2). Clement divides properties into individual and common (Strom., viii. 24, 1, 5). In establishing the former the notion of difference is operative. In establishing the latter, similarity in its two aspects is operative (S1 and S2). In each case similarities are established by discovery of the element common to two or more things. The result of this conception of similarity is a real unifying bond among the classes and within the classes. This unity of all things represents the order of being. The essence of any entity, be it essential (Absolute) or accidental (Relative), has a relation to every other entity, and to the Logos. These relations are identity, difference, and similarity.

2.3   At the top of Clement's structure of Being is a first principle (archê) and intelligent (nous) called God (Protr., x. 98. 4; (Strom., iv. 25. 162, 5; v. 12. 82, 1). This God is the good (agathon), measure (metron) and number (arithmôs) of all things (tôn holôn: Protr., vi. 69. 2). His is called a One (hen: Paed., i. 8; 71, 1; 74, 1; ii. 8. 75, 2; Strom., vii. 17; 107, 4), which is beyond unity and the monad (Paed., i. 8. 71, 1; cf. Strom., v. 12. 82; 1; v. 6; 38, 6). Below God is the Logos and the intelligible world contained in the Logos (Strom., v. 14; 94. 1; cf. iv. 25; 155. 2; v. 3; 16. 3; v. 11; 73. 3). The ideas are called genera (genê), and are the models of all the species of the sensible world. The Logos, who contains the intelligible world in itself, is also called the paradigmatic monad (Strom., v. 14. 93, 4f. cf. iv. 25; 156. 1ff.), which stands in a similar relation to the sensible world, and to matter (Protr., ix. 88. 2; Strom., iv. 23; 151, 3; 152, 1; iv. 25; 175, 2).

The structure of Being according to Clement is the following:

God (hen)

Logos-Monas (kosmos noêtos)

Ideas (ideai-genê)

Logos-Monas (kosmos aisthêtos)
Ideas (logoi-species)

Dyas-Hexas (hylê)

Clement maintains that there is an absolute difference between God and all other things. In the intelligible realm this distinction is between an unqualified, absolutely transcendent God, and the hypostatic Logos and the ideas. Clement's radical distinction between God and the other existants is based upon the Neo Pythagorean and Philonic distinction between bare and unqualified existence, and qualified existence.

Clement's identification of God and the first phase antemundane Logos and the ideas, is based upon the logical identity between the divine mind and his thoughts. Noetic identity between God, the Logos, and the ideas is evident in Clement's use of the term mind (nous) to define God and the Logos, and the term noêma to designate the ideas. Existential difference between God, the Logos, and the ideas is evident in Clement's distinction between God as the first One (hen), and the Logos as second One (monas) who contains the ideas within himself. Finally, it must be noted that Clement also employs the notion of similarity to characterize the relation between God and the Logos. The Logos is the image of God the Father, and thus similar to him.

The notions of identity and similarity are also employed by Clement to relate the intelligible world to the sensible world, and the antemundane and mundane Logos. Difference is also operative in that there is an ontological distinction between intelligibles, sensibles, and matter. The first two are in varying degrees being, and the third is non-being.

Clement divides and classifies reality on the basis of identity, similarity, and difference. This classification of things based upon diairesis has the following structure:

God (apoios, hen)

Difference:

———————————

Logos poiotês, monas)
Ideas (poiotês)
Cosmos (poiotês)

Identity:

God (nous): Logos (nous); Ideas (noêma)

Similarity:

God (paradigma: Logos (eikôn)
(kosmos noêtos): (kosmos aisthêtos)
Ideas (ideai): Ideas (eidê)

In summary, by means of the notions of identity, difference, and similarity, and by the use of the categories, Clement maintained that the mind establishes a classification of intelligibles and sensibles which is the necessary condition of knowledge and definition. After determining the properties of, and relations between, ideas, which are centered in a point called the Logos, the mind proceeds to an investigation of the sensibles. Knowledge of each thing requires knowledge of its differentiae in respect to everything else. Definition states the attributes of a thing, which are reached by exclusion of members of co-ordinate species, at every stage (Strom., viii. 6. 19. 1-8). Clement links the traditional Academic diairesis with the Aristotelian theory of definition by the aid of demonstration (Strom., viii. 6. 17, 1). Division and definition are carried out by means of the notions of identity, difference, and similarity (Strom., viii. 8. 24, 1, 5).[54]

2.4   The first step in diairesis consists in the application of the question whether things are identical, similar, or different. The goal is to establish classes of things which are identical. The principles of similarity and difference are also operative in division, and these result in the establishment of further classes of things. This understanding of diairesis is an important component of Clement's theoretic. Identity, similarity, and difference are the notions upon which the unity of each substance within a particular class of things are to be first principle or principles. Let me explain.

God is called the measure and number of all things (Protr., vi. 69. 2). By metron and arithmos Clement means that God is the point of focus of all relations within the cosmos. The Logos is called the circle in which all the powers in the universe are bound together into one point (Strom., iv. 156. 2). By panta hen Clement means that the Logos is also a point or focus of all relations within the cosmos. These two principles are the ground for the division and classification of all things in the universe.

Clement utilizes dichotomic division to define the relation of the Absolute (kath'hauto) and the Relative (pros ti). First, he maintains that the intelligible and sensible worlds are different. Second, he relates the two on the basis of similarity. Clement is Platonic in this sense. This is outlined as:

Absolute (kath'hauto)

Difference:

Relative (pros ti)

Similarity:

Intelligible World (kosmos noêtos)

Sensible World (kosmos aisthêtos)

The difference between the two realms is based upon the Platonic postulate of different degrees of reality. The sensible world is a copy of the intelligible world. It is not identical to it. The categories play a central role for Clement in defining the differences and similarities between these two worlds, as well as classifying the different entities common to each.

Since God is neither genus, species, or differentia, none of the categories have referential efficacy to him (Strom., v. 12. 81, 5f.: (ii. 380. 19f). However, this is not the case with the Logos. The categories have referential efficacy to the Logos. The categories of substance, quality, place and relation are relevant to the antemundane Logos, and these categories plus the remaining six are relevant to the mundane Logos.

In the intelligible world entities are classified into two groups: the Logos and the ideas. The categories that have referential efficacy to the Logos and the ideas are being (substance), relation, place and quality. The ideas are situated in the Logos. He is their place (chôra: Strom., iv. 155. 2 (ii. 317. 11); v. 73. 3 (ii. 375. 18-19). They are in relation to the Logos (Strom., v. 16. 3 (iii. 336. 8); iv. 155. 2); iv. 156. 2), and they are qualified as a unit (Strom., iv. 156. 2; v. 93. 4). We shall have the opportunity to discuss this when we examine Clement's physics.

In the sensible world, bodies are classified into many groups insofar as every sensible is a copy of the ideas and a combination of form and matter held together by the immanent ideas. All ten Peripatetic categories have referential efficacy in this realm. We shall also have an opportunity to discuss this when we examine Clement's physics.

Clement uses the categories to define the exact nature of the relation between existants based upon these three notions. Save God the Father, all existants are characterized by one or more of the categories.

The categorical structure of Absolute and Relative Being is the following:

Antemundane Logos   (ousia, poios, pros, pou)

Mundane Logos   (ouisa, poios, pros, pou, pote, keisthai, echein, poiein, paschein

3. God and the Antemundane Logos: The Intelligible Realm

We had mentioned earlier that Clement's postulate of a hypostatic Logos (Strom., v. 16. 5 (ii. 336. 12-13), was a necessary step to separate God and the Logos, and affirm them as separate identities. The primary difference between God and the Logos is that the Logos is generated and God in ungenerated. However, the Logos is also one and the same thing with the mind (nous) of God (Strom., v. 16. 3 (iii. 336. 8). Thus, unification is expressed through the notion of similarity. The issue we examine next is how are God and the Logos identical and different? The first is presented through the doctrine of equivocals.

Clement knew of the notions of equivocals, univocals, and paronyms (Strom., viii. 8. 24, 1, 5 (iii. 95. 4ff.). These terms are mentioned in connection with his categorical theory. This conflation can be traced back to Boetheus of Sidon and Antiochus (cf. Prantl, GL., 547; Witt, A., 38). It is from this trajectory of Platonic reflection, mediated perhaps through Philo, that Clement receives this doctrine. The original Antiochean context of these notions was the treatment of the Aristotelian universal and the Platonic ideas.

3.1 Cornford notes (PP., 110-111; 160-161; 245) that the original context of the discussion of equivocals was within the discussion of the hypotheses of Plato's Parmenides. The Middle Platonic context follows in the footsteps of this original discussion. The relation of the Aristotelian universal and Platonic idea fits within the context of the first two hypotheses of the Parmenides. Could it be that Clement critically reflected upon this problem, and offered a proposal of his own? If so, we must examine the background of the discussion of equivocals in the old Lyceum, by Aristotle and its expression in the Middle Academy by Clement.

Cornford shows that the question of equivocals arose from Plato's use of pollachôs, and that the school discussions focused upon the way in which slight changes in the meaning of words can wreak havoc in a sequence of otherwise valid arguments. Difficulties arise in the case of things which are in one way the same, but in other ways are different. When the unity is evident, but the differences are liable to escape attention, problems arise.

Aristotle, in the opening lines of the Categories, gives us an illustration of this.

Things are called equivocal whose name alone is common, the definition as denoted by the name being in each case different. For example, a man and a painting are both called a Zôon. With these the name is common, while the definition as denoted by the name is in each case different. For if one should explain what is the nature of Zôon in the one and the other case, he would give the proper definition of each. (Cat., I, 1a 1-6)

Equivocals are things which have one name in common, but different definitions are denoted by this name. Univocals are things which have a common name and definition (Cat., I, 1a 6-12). Thus, zôon or animal has the same definition as found in man and ox.

Paronyms are things which are denominated with different case endings, from one of the instances. A grammarian receives his designation from 'grammar,' and the brave are named from 'bravery' (Cat. I, 1a 12-15).

Elsewhere Aristotle says that equivocal things and univocal things are paronyms (Top., I, 15, 106b 29 -- 107a 2). Hence paronyms cut across the classes of equivocals and univocals, and are differentiated by grammatical and metaphysical criteria. The point Aristotle makes is that equivocals, universals, and paronyms are expressed, grammatically and metaphysically by the categories.

Owens (D., 51) is correct that the Greek words rendered by 'equivocal' and 'univocal' designate things, and that with Aristotle things as well as terms are equivocal. Indeed, in (Metaphys. IV) things are the primary concern of Aristotle's investigations (cf. Owens, D 52-53). Aristotle says that the term thing may denote any of the categories, and that things are denominated by the same term in different ways according to differences in form that are expressed by the categories.

The goal of investigation is to define and distinguish the different manners in which things are expressed in various ways. For example, in the Topics (I, 15, 106a 1-8), the Good is described as a unit containing both qualities and things which yield a result. The results are things with different natures -- or forms -- and different definitions since they belong to different categories. This is further unpacked by Aristotle at (NE I, 4, 1096b 23-29). Various things are good because of: 1) a common origin (aph henos); or 2) a reference (pros hen). Hence, things are denominated from the source whence they spring, and they have reference to that source insofar as they proceed from it. Finally, in treating the good, Aristotle proposes another possibility: by chance (NE V, 2, 1129a 30; Top., I, 15, 107a 19-21). This possibility is expressly ruled out for consideration as a full equivocal (e.g., Metaphys., III, 2, 1003a 34; 4, 1006b 18-20).

Aristotle proposes three subdivisions of equivocals: 1) by chance; 2) by reference; 3) by analogy. Only two (2) and three (3) designate equivocity in the full sense of the term. We shall examine the referential and analogous equivocals more closely.

According to Owens Aristotle explains the "by reference" (pros hen) equivocals in his (Metaphys. (K, 3, 1060b 36-1061a 7). In speaking of Being he focuses on the expressions 'medical,' and 'healthy.' Things are 'healthy' or 'medical' through reference to some one thing. This is 'health' in the former case and 'medical science' in the latter. 'Health' is a form or nature which is found in the disposition of the bodily organism. The form 'health' is not in the color or medicine, nor is the habit 'medical science' in the treatise or knife. These secondary instances, viz., color, medicine, treatise, knife, all have their own proper forms, but are of such a nature as to have some reference to health and medical science (Metaphys., 2, 1003a 34-55). The nature expressed in each case is found only in one of the instances. All the others have different natures, but with a reference to the nature of the primary instance. Hence, equivocity may be derived from things to definitions (Top. I, 15, 107b 6-12).

The question arises: "In what sense can terms and concepts and things be expressed by the word 'equivocal'?" Equivocal relation is that of sign to the thing signified (Top. V, 2, 130a 1-4). Thus, definitions and terms signify things or they are signs of the things signified. Definitions and terms are also denominations of things they signify, e.g., color is healthy because it signifies the health of the body. The definition is the conceptual expression of the entity of the thing (Top., VI, 3, 140a 34-37: ho logos tês ousias). Equivocity is in things, but is defined by reference in concepts and terms. This is what is meant to be equivocal "by reference" (pros hen).

The third division of equivocals is the type "by analogy." Bonitz shows that type is mentioned throughout the writings of Aristotle (Ind. Arist., 47b 41-48b 4). Stewart states that for Aristotle analogy is a type of mathematical relation (Notes on the Nic. Ethics, pp. 424-428). For example, arithmetical proportion is quantitative, and geometrical is qualitative (NE V, 5, 1131a 30 -- b 4). Analogy, thus, is both quantitative and qualitative. The requirement for analogy is that analogy consists of four terms having an equality or similarity of proportions between each pair. Analogy is located in things themselves "for in every category of Being the analogous is present" (Metaphys. 1093b 18-21). This notion permits Aristotle to state that the analogous constitutes classes of things wider than the generic types (Top., I, 17, 108a 7-12). Indeed, as Trendelenburg states (K, pp. 151-157) things that differ in genus can be one by analogy (Metaphys. IV, 6, 1016b 31 1017a 3; cf. 9, 1018a 13).

This notion means that the analogous is wider than a generic class.[55] Aristotle tells us analogy may be used as a means of obtaining knowledge of things we do not immediately perceive (cf. Phys. I, 7, 191a 7-12). The referential, however, is not wider than a generic class. There are only two terms in relation. This is the relation of a secondary instance to the primary instance. Thus, the analogous and the referential are two distinct types of equivocals (D., 56-59). The important point is that equivocity by reference is not used for classification, but equivocity by analogy is. Nonetheless, "by reference" (pros hen) plays an important role in Aristotle's Primary Philosophy. This distinction, as Brentano shows, does not apply in the later Lyceum (BS, pp. 91-98). In the Peripatetic Schools "by reference" and "by analogy" are combined.[56]

What does all this mean within the context of Middle Platonism, and Clement? We must remember the original context of the question of equivocals in the Old Academy. This was a question that arose from reflections upon the hypotheses of Plato's Parmenides. We must also remember that these hypotheses were utilized in the Middle Academy, and by Clement, to articulate a philosophical theology. The two "Ones" of the Parmenides were proclaimed as the ground not of any particular type of being, but of all being without exception. They were viewed as first principles by reason of their very nature. In this sense they were the universal principles that extended necessarily to all things. Their extension was an analogical, not a univocal or equivocal one. Things are denominated from the source whence they spring. The problem faced by Middle Platonists who worked off the hypotheses of the Parmenides was the nature of the relation between the first principles associated with each.[57]

3.2   There are three uses of the equivocal doctrine by Clement to relate God to the Logos and the Logos to itself. God and the first phase of the antemundane Logos are equivocal terminologically. The Logos is the nous of God, and is one and the same with the mind of God which contains his thoughts or ideas (Strom., iv. 155. 2 (ii. 317. 11); v. 73. 3 (ii. 375. 18-19). The Logos is identical with God "as the same from the same" (apo tou autou kai pros tou autou: Strom., viii. 8. 24, 8-9 (iii. 95. 18ff.) From the identity of the term nous, Clement postulates the analogical identity of God and the Logos. This formulation is different from Philo's. Although Philo postulates that the Logos is the place (chôra) of the ideas, and that the divine mind (theios logos) is the reason or mind of God (cf. Wolfson, P., i, 230), Philo never states that God and the Logos are equivocal, analogice.

The first and second antemundane Logos are equivocal terminologically and analogically. Clement's use of the term "proceeds" (proelthôn) to describe how the Logos emerges from the first stage of its existence and enters upon its second stage is kindred to the expression "from the same to the same" (apo tou autou kai pros tou autou: Strom., viii. 8. 24, 8-9 (iii. 95. 18ff.) From the identity of the term Logos, Clement postulates the analogical identity of the two phases of the antemundane Logos, even if they exist differently.

God and the Logos are also equivocal from resemblance (homioteta: Strom., viii. 8. 24, 8 (iii. 95. 20). The Logos is the image (eikon) of God. In this case the resemblance is between the hypostatic Logos and God. Hence, it does not refer to the equivocal relationship between the Logos when the Logos is the nous of God.

The antemundane Logos and the mundane Logos are equivocal from resemblance as well. They share the same term, and function. The antemundane Logos contains the ideas and powers within himself as a transcendent entity, and the mundane Logos contains the immanent ideas and powers within himself as the universal world-reason (Strom., iv. 156. 2 (ii. 336. 12-13); Strom., ii. 5. 4 (ii. 115. 23-24).

By means of the notions of identity, analogy, and resemblance, Clement attempts to relate God to the Logos. God stands as the focus of all relations between things intelligible and sensible, since he is in relation to the Logos.

Clement's theory constitutes a transitional moment in Middle Platonic metaphysical thinking.[58] He is a participant in the shift of the Middle Platonic theoretic from the Neo Pythagorean matrix of the early Middle Academy to the Peripatetic matrix of the Academy in its middle period. Clement has taken the postulates of Hellenic Neo Pythagoreanism and Judaic Platonism and fine-tuned them to propose a set of norms that form the basis of an emerging Christian Platonism.[59]

In summary, Clement proposes a new mode of presenting the structure of Absolute being. Working from the notions of identity, similarity, and difference, he defines the series of relations among different classes of intelligible and sensible things. Integral to this process of classification is the use of theories of equivocity by which he relates God and the Logos, and the categories whereby he relates all entities to each other.

The use of this fresh approach to define the structure of Being allows Clement to address and answer the three problems that faced Philo, but in a new way. These questions are: (1) How are the sensibles related to the intelligibles?, (2) How are the intelligibles related to each other?, and (3) How is God the first principle of all things? Through the notions of similarity and identity he answers the first two issues. The question that remains to be addressed is his answer to the third problematic. To answer this we turn to an examination of Clement's physics.

4. The Material Realm: God and the Mundane Logos

4.1   As we have noted, two principle trajectories of thought dominated early Middle Platonism. On one side was the Stoic Platonism of Antiochus of Ascalon, and on the other was the Pythagorean Platonism of Eudorus of Alexandria. Jewish Middle Platonism, represented by Philo of Alexandria, offered a type of Platonic speculation which combined the first principles of the Eudorean metaphysic with the physics of the Antiochean metaphysic. To appreciate Clement's place within the context of the Platonic philosophy of the early Empire we must view him as the philosopher who continues the Philonic synthesis in modified form in his Christian Platonism.

Clement's physics is not merely a reduplication of previous theories about the origin and nature of the material world. It offers a novel interpretation as well. Clement introduces a decidedly Speusippian and Aristotelian coloring to Middle Platonic physics. The notions of identity and similarity anchor his formulations concerning the relation of God to the Logos and the ideas. His use of the ten Peripatetic categories illustrates his attempt to relate the noetic and material worlds to one another.

Clement introduces us to these doctrines in (Strom., viii. 6. 17: (ii. 90. 9ff.; viii. 7. 24: (ii. 95. 4ff.). Although Clement reproduces these doctrines from doxographical sources, we have no reason to assume that he has no creative use for them. He uses these doctrines to describe and define the value, order, and structure of the material world, and to complement the paradigmatic ontology traditionally employed by Platonists to relate the physical and noetic worlds to each other. However, before we examine Clement's contributions to the Middle Platonic physics of the second century, we shall examine his doctrines of the mundane Logos, the ideas, and creation.

4.2   The Logos doctrine is one of the central components of Clement's theoretic. The Logos is the only entity which exists in both the intelligible and sensible worlds, as well as in the mind of God the Father. The identity of the Logos in all its aspects permits Clement to affirm a similarity between the intelligible and sensible worlds.

Working from the premise of an equivocal relation between the two phases of the antemundane Logos and the mundane Logos, Clement asserts that the sensible and intelligible worlds are not different, but similar. As a mind comprehending its thoughts, the Logos comprehends the universe in its transcendent as well as immanent moments (Strom., iv. 156. 2 (ii. 317. 24-318. 2); ii. 5. 4 (ii. 115. 23-24). In addition the Logos functions as the point upon which all created things have reference, and are defined. As the point and source of all things in the universe the Logos stands as the fulcrum of Clement's universe. To appreciate this notion let us turn again to Clement's doctrine of ideas.

4.3   The ideas are defined by Clement as thoughts of God contained in the Logos (Strom., iv. 155. 2 (ii. 317. 11); v. 73. 3 (ii. 375. 18-19); iv. 156. 1-2 (ii. 317. 24-318. 2); v. 93. 4 (ii. 387. 21).[60] Clement maintains that the ideas are contained in the Logos in both its antemundane phases. The ideas themselves, however, are the result of the act of thinking by God. They are his thoughts (Strom., v. 16. 3 (iii. 336. 8). In the first phase of the antemundane Logos they are in the Logos. He is their place (chôra). In the second phase of the antemundane Logos, the Logos itself is the totality of the ideas or powers of God, which together form the intelligible world as monas (Strom., v. 93. 4).

The ideas have importance in Clement's theoretic as the intelligible pattern of the sensible world (Strom., v. 94. 5 (ii. 388. 2-5); v. 94. 1 (ii. 388. 5-6); v. 93. 4 (ii. 387. 21-23). The Logos, as the demiurgic principle of creation (Strom., v. 16. 5 (ii. 336. 12-13) utilizes them to create the sensible world.

Clement's language is not fully consistent, but the ideas contained within the Logos are called dynameis, and the Logos as the sum-total of the ideas, is referred to as dynamis. Although the translation of these terms can be rendered 'power' it is also possible that Clement understands them as 'potentialities' and 'potentiality.' If Clement conceives of the ideas and the Logos in the latter sense, then we may be encountering a transition in Middle Platonic thought to a Peripatetic conception of the relation between God and the Logos, and the ideas. If this assessment is correct, then God, as actuality, would be the cause of the Logos and ideas, and the entity which brings them from potentiality to actuality. First, the cosmos is generated extra-temporally as an intelligible world, and then temporally as a sensible world. The cause of this generation of the universe in the Logos is a transcendent God, who is a kind of nous akinêtos. The thoughts of God are first the thoughts of God's Logos, then they are the thoughts of a distinct transcendent intellect, and finally they are the thoughts of an intellect in the cosmos.

Clement uses the term ennoêma to describe the ideas thought by God. As the thoughts of the antemundane (second phase) and mundane Logos, the ideas are potential. Clement uses the term dynamis to describe the ideas thought and contained in the Logos (Strom., v. 16. 3 (iii. 336. 8); Strom., iv. 156. 102 (ii. 317. 24-318. 2); Strom., ii. 5. 4 (ii. 115. 23-24). The relation of the ideas to God and the Logos are the relation between the ideas of a nous akinêtos and a nous kinêtos, of ideas in actuality and in potentiality.

This formulation is important because it points to Albinus' theory of the relation of the ideas to the divine intellect.[61] Lilla (C., 202) is correct that there is a correspondence between Clement and Albinus here (cf. Did., 163, 12-13, 27-30). However, the correspondence is much more profound than merely a reduplication of the notion of the ideas as thoughts of God, as originally proposed by Antiochus and Philo. Clement's formulation must be seen within the context of second century Platonism's move toward a Peripatetic metaphysic and its Nous theology.

Clement's theory of ideas differs from Philo's in only one aspect. The ideas are thought not only by God, but also by the Logos. The reason for this is that Clement's Logos exists as a distinct entity from God, and in this capacity it thinks the ideas in its own right. In Clement's scheme, the ideas are identical with the mind of God and the Logos as the objects of thought for both. Clement uses the notion of identity to characterize the relation of the ideas to God and the Logos.

This notion is important. Clement says that the Logos is identical with the ideas as the circle of all powers being bound in one point (Strom., iv. 156. 1-2: (ii. 317. 24-318. 2). The Logos, as the sum-total of the ideas, is the point upon which the whole series of relations among things in the universe is grounded. This is what Clement means when he states that the Logos is the ground (archê) of all things. The Logos is the logical as well as cosmological principle of all things (Strom., v. 16. 5 (ii. 336. 12-13). Hence, all identity, similarity, and difference in the universe has it point of convergence in the Logos.[62]

Clement's doctrine, in its transcendent form, is expressed in Philo (Opf., 17-20; Cher., 49). Clement's reformulation, in its immanent form, existed in the well known passages in Varro and Seneca (Aug, CD., vii. 28; Seneca, Ep., 65, 7). Theiler has shown (VN., 18-19, 40, 119) that this doctrine can be found in Antiochus, and Luck's treatment makes Theiler's evaluation conclusive (Luck, 21; fr. 8; 56; 60). The ideas are identified with the Stoic logoi spermatikoi, and placed within the Logos-Soul. Clement combines the two interpretations, and adds to it a hypostatic transcendent Logos that thinks the ideas as well. Finally, he offers a novel notion to explain how the ideas are transferred from God to the antemundane and mundane Logos. Thus, what is self-evident in Albinus, as Rich and Loenen observe (129; 43ff.), is proposed implicitly by Clement. There is no direct connection between Clement and Albinus. Albinus formulates his own version independently from Clement. He probably worked off the Aristotelian theology adopted by Maximus and Antiochus.[63] Let us now turn to the function of the ideas in Clement's physics proper.

4.3   Clement utilizes two principle texts as the basis for his physics. They are Genesis and the Timaeus. The ideas are paradigms for the sensible things patterned after them. The sensible world is an image (eikôn) of the intelligible world (Strom., v. 93. 4 (ii. 387. 21-23). This is clear from Clement's exegesis of Genesis 1:1-3 extant in (Strom., v. 95. 4 (ii. 388. 2-5). The heaven, earth, and light mentioned in Genesis are not the sensible heaven, earth, and light, but their intelligible patterns, or the ideas (Strom., v. 94. 5 (ii. 388. 1-2). To this extent his position is identical to Philo's.[64] Working from these accounts, Clement postulates a double creation. God thinks the intelligible world and the Logos (Strom., v. 16. 5: (ii. 336. 12-13), and the Logos in turn fashions the sensible world on the divine ideas (Strom., v. 94. 1: (ii. 388. 5-6); v. 93. 4 (ii. 387. 21-23; v. 94.5 (ii. 388. 2-5).

This doctrine of a double creation is based upon the traditional Platonic theory of imitation, but it also contains some new theories as well. Clement would not deny that the sensible world is a copy of the intelligible world, or that the Logos is an image of the Father. These notions are basic to his physics. However, it is how he defines the copy-model theory that is new. The notions of similarity, identity, and difference as well as the doctrine of the categories alter how Clement defines double creation as well as the value, order, and structure of the material realm. It is Clement's use of these theories that constitutes his original contribution to Middle Platonic physics. Imitation can be expressed in three different ways, and defined according to ten categories.

As the creative principle of all things the Logos is the instrument of God in creation of the world (Strom., v. 38. 7 (ii. 353. 1-3); vi. 58. 1 (ii. 461. 6-8); vi. 145. 5 (ii. 506. 19-21). Clement expresses this notion through the now familiar metaphysics of prepositions' (Strom., viii. 9. 27, 3ff. (iii. 97. 10ff.). The pedigree of the construct can be traced back to Philo and Antiochus.[65] Although Clement presents a doctrine of causality (Strom., viii. 9. 25 (iii. 95. 27-97. 23), the exact nature of God's causality is obliquely presented. Its vague character may result because Clement cannot describe the causality of God in traditional terms.

God is both the final and efficient cause of the universe. God is father and maker of the universe. Although God is the father and the maker of the cosmos, he is not its demiurge. The Logos is the demiurge. God imparts the ideas to the Logos, who then makes a sensible world based on the model of the intelligible world. Hence, the Logos, or nous (Strom., iv. 155. 2 (ii. 317. 11); cf. Stählin, iii. 202), is the efficient and instrumental cause of the sensible world.

In Clement we encounter a conflation of the philosophical theology of Eudorus and Philo, and the causal doctrines of Antiochus and Philo. Given this it appears that God is a nous akinêtos (cf. Stählin, iii. 202), who creates the intelligible world, the Logos and the ideas. He is the final and efficient cause of the world. The demiurge, or Logos, is a nous kinêtos, who creates the sensible world, as the efficient and instrumental cause of the world. God thinks the ideas and places them in his Logos. The Logos thinks the ideas and creates a world in their image. Since Clement identifies God and the first phase of the antemundane Logos, and the first phase of the antemundane Logos with the second, efficient cause is identified with both God and the antemundane Logos.

Finally, not only is the Logos the organon of God in the creation of the world, he is also the immanent form of the physical cosmos (Strom., viii. 9. 27, 3 (iii. 97. 15). Thus, not only is the Logos the efficient and paradigmatic cause of the universe in its antemundane phase, he is also that which gives it form, as its immanent Idea, in its mundane phase.

4.4   The relation of the intelligible and the sensible worlds is that of a model to its copy (Strom., v.93.4 (ii.387.21-23); v.94.5 (ii.388.1-2); cf. v.94.5 (ii.388.2-5). Although it is clear that Clement understands similarity in the standard Platonic manner of imitation, it is also apparent that similarity means to Clement, as it did to Speusippus, a bond of similarity among the classes (Iamblichus, Theol. Arith., 82, 8-9; 43-60; Arist, Metaphys., 1028b15-27). Whereas Speusippus' basis for similarity among classes is based upon numbers, for Clement the basis for similarity is based upon ideas. Despite this difference, Clement, like Speusippus, maintains that there are similarities among classes of intelligibles, sensibles, and their principles (archai). There are also similarities within classes themselves.

The similarity is one of correspondence and analogy. It is the task of diairesis to determine the relations of the sensibles to each other, and to the intelligibles. This is why he subsumes the ten Peripatetic categories under the two Academic (Strom., viii.7.24,1,5), and why he discusses the notions of similarity, difference, and identity within the context of this combination. Clement discusses the types of definition at (Strom., viii.6,18,2,7).

Clement makes the Absolute (kath'hauto) and the Relative (pros ti) his two ultimate categories, and makes the Logos the principle who mediates between these categories of being. The intelligible universe falls under the category of the Absolute, and the sensible universe under the category of the Relative. The Logos is the archê of both divisions of being (ousia). Indeed, the Logos is in relation to the intelligible world as its sum-total, and to the sensible world as its product and correlate.

The early Middle Platonists within the Pythagorean trajectory, such as Eudorus and Philo, were hesitant to subsume the Peripatetic categories under those of Platonism. If (Strom., viii.8.24,1,5) is to be taken seriously, then we must suppose that Clement subsumes the ten Aristotelian categories under those of Platonism. This is a significant transition in metaphysical thinking because it assumes that sensibles and intelligibles can be subsumed under a single (ousia) with a common set of categories having referential efficacy to each.

We noted earlier that Clement postulated an identity between the antemundane and mundane Logos. In (Strom., viii.7.24.5) he mentions heteronyms, specific heteronyms, polynyms, and paronyms. He chooses an example to illustrate a homonym derived from similarity of function. This example is pous. Other examples of equivocal terms are listed at (24.8-9). I think we can expand Clement's notion of equivocal function to explain how he conceived the relation of the antemundane Logos and transcendent ideas, and the mundane Logos and the immanent ideas. The mundane Logos functions as the antemundane Logos does. It is the point of reference for the ideas, and the basis upon which all division and definition proceed. They share a similarity of function. By means of this construct Clement asserts that the same procedure of division and definition that applies to the intelligible world applies to the sensible as well. As such the sensibles and the intelligibles are subsumed under a single ousia, the Logos, and the same set of categories have referential efficacy to both entities.

The Logos and the ideas are the formative principles of the physical universe (Protr., 5.2 (i.6.7-9); Strom., v.104.4 (ii.396.16). They are the powers that qualify matter, and the extent to which matter presents itself as a qualified form is defined categorically. The categories used to define the relation of the ideas to matter are the ten Peripatetic categories.

Witt (A., 38) proposes that the origin of Clement's categorical doctrine can be traced back to Antiochus (Cicero, Fin., v.16). The subsequent transmission of the doctrine went in at least two directions. These were the Neo Pythagorean trajectory represented in Eudorus, and the Peripatetic trajectory represented in Ariston, Andronicus, Adrastus, and Boetheus of Sidon (cf. Witt, A., 66-67). If Witt's thesis is correct then we must place Clement's theory in the latter trajectory. This is not without significance. First, Clement's formulation points toward second century Platonism's adaption of Peripatetic categorical norms. We find evidence of this in Albinus as well. Second, it establishes a norm that becomes orthodox in Christian Middle Platonism. We find that Origen of Alexandria utilizes the same doctrine as Clement and Albinus.

Categorically Clement's sensible universe has the following structure: The mundane Logos is identified with quality and relation; the immanent ideas are identified with quality, relation and place. Matter is identified with quantity as the material substrate (hylê). The sensibles which are a combination of form and matter take on characteristics which are defined through the ten Peripatetic categories. The structure of the material realm is:

Logos (poiotês, pros)
Ideas (poiotês, pros, topos)
Sensibles (poiotês, the ten categories
Matter (poson-posôtês)

The mundane Logos is the place of the ideas. He holds together all the qualified forms in the sensible universe categorically. There is nothing in the sensible realm that does not participate in, and hence is not definable by the categories. Thus, the structure of Relative Being is defined by categorical analysis as are each of the sensible things.

It is the task of diairesis to determine the relation of both intelligibles and sensibles to each other, between one another, and to the whole. Since Clement admitted both essential and accidental attributes in his classification, and in his definitions, he did not use the Aristotelian conception of genus and species in his system. In this sense he follows Philo.

The central category is relation. Clement understands relation in three ways: (1) in terms of identity, similarity, and difference, (2) in terms of imitation or participation, and (3) in terms of variety of relation. Clement relates the sensibles to each other, and classifies them according to different genera and species through the category of relation.

His diairetical scheme for the sensible realm is close to the scheme he employs for the intelligible realm. The same categories apply to each although more of the categories have relevance to the physical world because of the nature of the material substrate. This is an important shift in Middle Platonic categorical thinking, at least in the trajectory of Platonic thought in which Clement was situated. The categories are not restricted to sensibles alone, but also have referential efficacy to the intelligibles. They are ontological entities that permit the philosopher to define the nature of Being in its entirety.

In summary, Clement's diairesis and orders of Being, are established by the similarity there is among the members of each class and each order of Being. The origin of Clement's theory is extant in Philo, Boetheus of Sidon, Antiochus, and perhaps it can be traced back to Speusippus. By means of the notions of identity, difference, and similarity, he offers an exhaustive classification of the properties, and the relation between the intelligibles and the sensibles. This classification of things is defined through the categories. By means of the categories he defines the exact nature of the similarity, difference, and identity among sensible things, and classes of sensible things.

Clement does not present a systematic classification of sensible things. However, he does classify sensibles according to the genera and species of the ideas they fall under. In this way he determines the sum-total of the relations of each class to every other class of sensible things, and to the whole.

Clement's theoretic does not assert an ontological chôrismos between Being and Becoming nor does it affirm that an ontological fault-line exists between that which is hyparxis and poiotês. Instead Clement maintains a relative ontological distinction between two kindred spheres of Being, and an identity and similarity between God, the Logos, and the sensible world. This transition which begins with Philo accelerates in a series of cognate theories proposed by Clement. Central among them were a redefinition of the structure of Being through the notions of identity, similarity, and difference, and the proposal that a common set of categories has referential efficacy to both the Absolute and Relative categories of Being.

Now that we have outlined Clement's doctrines of God, the Logos, the ideas, and the categories as they pertain to the material realm, let us turn to his cosmological doctrine, and his doctrine of matter. This assessment will permit us to conclude our study of Clement's physics.

4.5   To make the sensible world, God had to create it on the pattern of the divine ideas (Strom., v. 94. 1 (ii. 388. 5-6); v. 93. 4 (ii. 387. 21-23). In addition, he had to create it from something. This something is matter (hylê). Although the sensible world is created out of matter, matter itself is eternal, and non-created (Strom., v. 89. 5-6).[66] Like Philo, Clement also views matter as something devoid of quality and form. Furthermore, he asserts that matter is a kind of non-being (mê on). Once formed, or created by the Logos, matter attains the status, ontologically, of being (ousia).

Lilla (C., 195) is correct that Clement did not offer a theory of creatio ex nihilo.[67] This is clear from Clement's terminology. The substantive creation (ktistês), and the verb (ktizein) refer to the origin of the intelligible and sensible worlds, not to the origin of matter (cf. Lilla, C., 194 n. 3). This is important to note for at least two reasons. First, it shows that the Logos creates the sensible world by introducing form (eidos) into matter (hylê). Second, it illustrates how Clement conceived the role of the mundane Logos and the immanent ideas in his physics. The mundane Logos holds matter together by thinking the ideas, which are immanent in the universe.

According to Clement the sensible universe had a beginning (Strom., v. 92. 2), but this beginning did not take place in time (Strom., vi. 145. 4). The proof-texts are (Tim., 28b and Gen., 2:4). For the first notion Clement depends upon Philo (Opf., 26-28; Leg. Alleg., i, 2), and the second is a reflection of Middle Platonic dogma (Plutarch, In Tim., 1014a; cf. Proculus, In Tim., i. 381; Philo, Aet., 13, 15; Prov., i, 7; Decal., 58).[68]

Clement views the creation of bodies (sômata) from the combination of opposites, form (eidos) and matter (hylê). This tells us that he conceived of the relation of the Logos and ideas to matter as a relation of contraries. Thus, contrary relation is the nature of all relation in the Relative category of Being. The basis for this interpretation is that Clement views matter as the contrary of God and the intelligible world (the Logos and the ideas). Matter is the unqualified, unformed, material substrate the Logos forms to create the physical world.

There are four elements in Clement's universe. They are fire, air, earth, and water. Matter is the substratum of these elements. Clement's definition of matter is based on the account of the (Tim., 49e-50a, 50b-c, 50d-3). It is formless and identified with the receptacle (hypodochê) of the (Tim., 50d-e). This correlation goes back at least to Aristotle, who identified the receptacle of the Timaeus with matter (Arist., Phys., iv.209b 11-13; De Caelo, iii.306b17-19; Phys., i.191a 8-12).[69] This doctrine was Platonic by the time of Antiochus (Cicero, Ac. Post., 26-27ff.), and Philo (Fuga, 9; Spec. Leg., i, 328).

To understand Clement's doctrine of matter and its creation, it is necessary to view it within the context of the doctrines of Antiochus and Philo. In (Strom., v. 89. 5-6 cf. Photius, Stählin, iii. 202. 10-11) Clement affirms the formlessness and unstructuredness of matter prior to its creation or formation into bodies. Material things are called poia, and the Logos is equated with the world-soul that contains these forms. The poia are the formative power of the immanent ideas, who become the formative power of the cosmos in the Logos (Prot., 5.2 (i.6.7-9); Strom., v.104.4 (ii.396.16); vii.5.4 (ii.5.22ff.); vii.9.2 (iii.8.14-15). The Logos, the divine reason-principle, is the active element of God's creative thought. The ideas are seminal-reason principles, and serve as the creative principles of the physical world. The mundane Logos is the instrument of God in the formation of the world. On the logical and the cosmological level the Logos divides and forms the undifferentiated material substance of the world into a cosmos.

4.6   Clement's conceptual system and metaphysical norms reflect the Middle Academy of which he was a participant.[70] Working off the trajectories of Judaic and Hellenic Platonism, of which he was heir, Clement proposed the first expression of Christian Platonism at Alexandria.

His theoretic mirrored the changing face of second century Platonism. Adhering to the Neo Pythagorean theological norms, which were now dogma in the Middle Academy, he nonetheless modified the radical transcendence of God by proposing a new categorical relationship between God, the Logos, and the universe, and a new way of defining the relationship between the first and second intellects of his theoretic. These modifications were accomplished with the aid of Peripatetic doctrines, and resulted in one of the earliest examples of the shift in Academic thinking from the Neo Pythagorean matrix of the first centuries B.C./A.D. to the Aristotelian matrix of the second and third centuries A.D.

The motivation for this reassessment of early Middle Platonic theological norms is difficult to assess. However, at least with Clement, it is likely that he was compelled to overcome the lacuna between God and the universe that was endemic to the Neo Pythagorean theoretic. This goal he shared with Philo, and by following his lead institutionalized the norms of Jewish Platonism in Christian Platonism.

Clement's metaphysic is important not only for its acceptance and legitimization of the Philonic metaphysic. It is also important in its own right as the first systematic expression of Christian Platonism in the early Empire. His norms became the bed-rock for all subsequent Christian Platonisms in the hellenistic east. Within the context of the Middle Academy Clement's theoretic is significant because it foreshadows a series of changes in the Platonic thinking of the second and third centuries. Although his works were not a direct fons for Albinus' metaphysic they reflect the Peripateticizing temper of the Platonism which Albinus represents. Thus, not only is Clement important within the context of Jewish and Christian Middle Platonism in its formative periods. He is also a barometer of the epic changes that would occur in the last phase of Middle Platonism at Alexandria under the aegis of Ammonius Saccas, and his student Origen, the Christian Platonist.

In summary, Clement is a central figure in the formative period of Christian Platonism. His vision of Christianity in the mantel of Plato illustrated the common foundations he shared with the Hellenism of his time. His Christian Platonism was the product of the intellectual climate of Alexandria, and was a reflection of the rich variety of Christianity emerging from its schools. With Clement we see no distinction between Hellenism and Christianity, Platonism and Christianity. He forges a thoroughly hellenized and Platonized Christianity that affirms the teachings of Jesus as the consummation of Platonic wisdom.

Clement's philosophy is representative of a fruitful synthesis of the theoretics of Eudorus and Antiochus mediated through Philo and unknown Peripateticizing Platonists. He is fully conversant in these variety of school traditions. The evidence we possess suggests that he entered into the issues and problems of the Middle Academic metaphysics, and proposed his own response to them. His philosophy, like Philo's, was built upon the twin pillars of biblical and Platonic authority. His theoretic, although similar to the Philonic, also differed. Just as Philo's Platonism reflected the tenor of Pythagorean thought, his reflected the tenor of Peripatetic thought. Just as Philo's theoretic reflected first century Middle Platonic norms, his reflected the norms of second century Platonism.

If the transition in Middle Platonic thinking at Alexandria in the first two centuries of the Empire reflects a movement from Pythagoras to Aristotle, we must examine the appearance of the mature expression of this transition. This is necessary because the consummation of the trajectory of Platonism we study appears in the figure of Origen of Alexandria, and his Middle Platonic proposal was built upon the bed-rock of an Academic-Peripatetic synthesis. It is impossible in such a study to trace the history of second century Platonism in toto to explain this change in Academic thinking. However, we can turn to one figure as an example of this transition. He stood between Clement and Origen, and was indirectly linked to both. Let us now turn to the philosophy of Albinus.

III. ALBINUS

1. Introduction

Albinus stands at the center of an evaluation of Jewish and Christian Middle
Platonism at Alexandria for at least three reasons: First, as Witt has shown (A., 32-41),
one of the sources of Albinus' metaphysic was Clement. Second, as Koch noted (PP.,
243-268), Albinus provided a paradigm for Origen's metaphysic, and set up the schemata
for Origen's evaluation and understanding of the earlier theoretics taught Origen by his
teacher, Ammonius Saccas at Alexandria. Third, Albinus proposed a thoroughly
Peripateticized Platonic theoretic, which at least in the case of Origen, resulted in the
final shift of Christian Middle Platonism from the Pythagorean-Platonic axis of Philo to
the Aristotelian-Platonic axis of Origen.

The Hellenistic philosophers of the early Empire, located in the Platonic tradition of
metaphysical speculation, had defined the agenda they wished to address, and had
proposed a series of answers to the central problems of their age. Our concern is to
describe the constellation of issues raised by the Middle Platonists, and the shifts that
occur in their philosophical reflections. In our study we have focused upon the original
contributions made to the Middle Platonic philosophy by Philo and Clement. Now we turn
to Albinus, and probe his Didaskalikos for the originality of its postulates. Two theories
stand at the forefront in our quest. They are his Nous theology and categorical
ontology.[71]

Central to this shift in metaphysical thinking were Albinus' Nous theology and
categorical ontology. By means of these doctrines a Platonist reformulates the variety of
early Middle Platonic answers to the question of the relation of God to the universe, and
the problematics of the relation of the sensibles to the intelligibles, the intelligibles to
each other, and God as the first principle of all things. Just as Clement formulated his
theoretic within the context of Philo's, Origen develops his within the context of Albinus',
and interprets the doctrines of Clement and Philo under the partial influence of Albinus'
Peripateticized Middle Platonism.

1.1 For the student interested in the history of Middle Platonic metaphysics
Albinus is important for at least three reasons. First, Albinus is the first Middle Platonist
to define the theologicals as intellects on the Peripatetic model. Second, his analysis of
the relation of the theologicals to one another and the universe through the use of the
categories shifts Middle Platonic thinking away from the Neo Pythagorean understanding
of the structure of Being. Third, both the Nous theology and categorical ontology
proposed by Albinus form the core of the later Platonic theoretics of Christian Middle
Platonism in Origen of Alexandria,[72] and Hellenic Neo Platonism in Origen, and
Hierokles.[73]

- 83 -

Since Albinus is important for Platonic self-definition in the late second and early third centuries, his contribution to Christian Middle Platonism, although indirect, is substantial. Leonen is correct that Albinus did not merely offer a summation of Platonic dogma (Mn., iv,9 (1956), 296-319.[74] He was at the center of a critical rethinking and reformulation of the basic principles of Middle Platonic metaphysics.

His contributions are best exemplified in his use of the Peripatetic doctrine of the divine intellect (nous). As Armstrong notes, this brought with it a change in not only Platonic understandings of the divine intellect, but also in the divine ideas (En., v, (1960), 402-403). Another significant contribution lies in his categorical doctrine (Witt, A., 66-67). We must view these two doctrines as closely tied together. It is no coincidence that both reflect a Peripatetic pedigree, and Albinus' use of them reflects the extent to which the thought of Aristotle lies at the center of second century Middle Platonic reflection. Only by harmonizing the teachings of Plato and Aristotle could the chôrismos between God and the universe be overcome.

The first question to be asked is: What significance and contribution does Albinus make to Jewish and Christian Middle Platonism at Alexandria? There is no indication that Albinus knew of Philo, and what he did know of Clement is modest indeed. Hence, what is the value of examining Albinus within the context of Jewish and Christian Middle Platonism at all?

The study of Albinus is important for at least two reasons: First, he provides us with an example of Hellenic Middle Platonic thinking in the second century. The concepts and problems he deals with are analogous to those faced by his second century Christian contemporary Clement. Second, the Peripaticizing tendency we encountered in earlier Middle Platonists expresses itself forcefully in the Didaskalikos. Many of the doctrines and reformulations proposed by Albinus offer later Middle Platonism, and non-Plotinian varieties of Neo Platonism, new norms and solutions of significance. Indeed, in the third century the two Origens and Hierokles represent the consummation of this trajectory of second century Middle Platonic thought.

Albinus walks a thin line between what earlier Platonists would perceive as Antiochus' ontological monism, and the Neo Pythagorean ontological dualism of Eudorus and Nichomachus. He affirms a distinction between levels of reality and the existants that populate them, and at the same time affirms a referential connection among the noetic and sensible realms. Not only are the two divisions of reality related to one another by imitation as model to copy, but both realms share a common first principle and set of categories. Although such notions were extant in Clement, and to a limited extent in Philo, Plutarch, and Atticus, Albinus is the first Middle Platonist to express these ideas in the language of a coherently developed Peripatetic-Platonic doctrine of Being.

The originality of Albinus' metaphysic is that it overcomes the chôrismos between God and the universe evident in earlier Middle Platonic theoretics. The Nous theology provided Albinus with a doctrine of the divine intellect that stresses a noetic continuity, rather than discontinuity, between God, Nous (Logos), and Soul (Logos). The categories provided him with the ontological thread whereby he could link the different existants and degrees of reality to one another, and yet maintain their distinctness.

2. First Principles: God, Idea, Matter

2.1 There are two novel notions Albinus introduces into Middle Platonic speculation about the first principles of things. These are the distinction between actuality and potentiality, and the difference between the essential and the accidental. By means of these two concepts Albinus argues that only God is eternally active. He thereby saves for God a special place in the Platonic metaphysic.

He also asserts that all potential things are accidental, but upon actualization they become essential. Thus, once actualized the whole intelligible world is essential, and in an immediate relation to God.

The sensible world is eternally potential, and always accidental. Nonetheless, since it is created and sustained by God, through the agency of the Nous and the Soul, it is in a mediate relation to God, and partakes of being. God is the archê and the telos of the sensible world. He creates it, sustains it, and directs it towards himself. Once formed into a cosmos the sensible world is constituted of simple and intelligible matter fully contingent upon a God who is its necessary starting point and end point, and the Idea which is its paradigm. However, first things first. Let us examine Albinus' doctrine of first principles; God, the Idea, and Matter, and his third archê, God, Nous, and Soul.

We shall commence with a description and analysis of Albinus' theology, move on to his discussion of the Idea, and conclude with his theory of Matter. This scheme permits us to examine Albinus' thought in the wider context of our study. First, we unpack his description of the theologicals, intelligibles, and sensibles. Second, we analyze how Albinus proposes to solve the relational problems involved in his Platonic theoretic. Third, we can move on to a description and analysis of his physics proper and the theories of creation and matter he proposed.

2.2 Albinus argues for the existence of a supreme God on the ground that where there is a better there is a best. Better than Soul is Nous, better than Nous in potentiality is Nous in actuality, and better than this is the cause of both an eternally active first Nous, or God (Did., 164, 6ff.).

The startling aspect of Chapter X is its technical terminology. It resembles little that we have seen in a Middle Platonic context previously. This is not to say that Albinus was the first to use these terms as a Platonist. Witt notes (A., 125) earlier Platonists such as Maximus, Plutarch, and Arius utilized them. To this group we may add Clement. However, these thinkers limited their program to the use of the term nous to describe the divine intellect. Wholly absent from their discussions is the added dimension of actuality and potentiality. To find such a notion we have to go back to Antiochus, but the context of his remarks are quite different from Albinus'. For Albinus God is not regarded as organic with the universe (cf. Cicero, Ac. Post., 28).

Albinus' formulation does not have its origins and link to the Stoicized theologies of Antiochus or Arius, nor can it be linked to the Neo Pythagorean theology of Eudorus (cf. Alex. Aph., In Met., 59,7).[75] Rather it represents something quite new which is the introduction into a Platonic context of a Peripatetic theological norm. It is here that we hit upon the originality of Albinus' contribution to Middle Platonic theoretic. Let me explain.

Albinus presents us with three entities in descending order of value: God, Nous, and Soul. These entities constitute the theologicals of Albinus' theoretic. God is distinct from the Nous and Soul as the only eternally active intellect. The others are potential intellects until actualized by God (Did., 164, 21ff., 36ff.). God orders the cosmic mind and world soul in accordance with himself. He is the principle which energizes and awakens the others. He is the first cause of the mind of the Nous-Soul.

This notion stands as the fulcrum of Albinus' theoretic. Upon it he builds his doctrine of the structure, order, and value of reality. God is the principle which actualizes the Nous and Soul, who in turn, create and sustain a world. What we encounter in Albinus' theoretic is a picture of a dynamic process whereby all entities and things, save God, move from potentiality to actuality, from existence per accidens to existence per se. This represents a considerable shift from earlier Middle Platonic theoretics where we encounter the pictures of a static creation of a Logos and the world based upon the notions of identity, similarity, difference, and imitation. Entities and things exist per se and per accidens in these theoretics, but there is no notion of the movement, organization, and creation of a world from potentiality and accidentality to actuality and essentiality as there is with Albinus. Let me explain.

Albinus sets a first intellect, God, above the demiurgic mind and soul of the world. He calls this first intellect Father because he is the cause of all things. He does not maintain that there is a distinction, hypostatically, between the cosmic mind and world soul.[76] They are two aspects of Albinus' second divine intellect which are logically moved from potentiality to actuality by the first intellect. This is what Albinus means when he states that God is the cause of its mind and the awakener of its soul (Did., 164, 21ff.; 36ff.). Once actualized the Nous forms the universe in the now ordered Soul by bringing measure to matter on the model of the divine ideas (Did., 163, 28f.). The second intellect is the organon of the first intellect's mind and will.

Albinus postulates a first intellect, whose essence is activity, who is the object of his own thought, and who is the unmoved mover and first cause of all things. The second intellect has two aspects as Nous and Soul. He is actualized by God and this results in the awakening of his Soul, and the creation of the world. Actualization is the apprehension of God and his ideas.[77] Apprehension results in the formation and creation of the intelligible and sensible worlds.

In summary, God is a nous akinêtos whose essence is pure activity. He arouses and attracts to himself the cosmos intelligence and the world soul. Through the second intellect he takes possession of matter, and reduces it to order in its soul. God is absolute perfection and the actuality of all things. All other entities are neither perfect or actual. The Nous and Soul are moved to actuality from potentiality, and to perfection in the apperception of the ideas of God.

The ghost of the earlier Middle Platonic philosophical theology casts a shadow upon Albinus' theological proposal. Previously the fault-line which ran through the Academic theoretic was the distinction between "unqualified" and "qualified." Now the line is defined in terms of the distinction between "actuality" and "potentiality." This distinction is the leit-motif of Albinus' metaphysic, and reflects the dynamic molds of his view of reality. From Nous and Soul to Matter the cosmos is in a process of actualization.

2.3   Albinus' second principle is the Idea. Just as he offers a new wrinkle to the Middle Platonic philosophical theology so he proposes a new version of the doctrine of the ideas.[78]   Since Albinus' first God is an Aristotelian Nous the ideas he thinks are the sum-total of his divine intellection. In relation to God the idea is designated by the term intellection (noêsis: Did., 163, 13; 164, 27, 37). In relation to all other intellects, man, matter, and the sensible world the Idea(s) is designated by the terms thought (noêton), first (prôton), measure (metron), and paradigm (paradeigma: Did ., 163, 13-16). Let us unpack Albinus' doctrine of the Idea.

Witt claims (A., 124-127; cf. 70-75) that Albinus' theory represents a conflation of two doctrines. These are the doctrines of the divine ideas hammered out in the Middle Academy, and the Peripatetic doctrine of the divine intellect. Armstrong claims (En., v. 404) that Albinus is offering something more than the conflation of two distinct doctrines. He argues that Albinus proposes a new version of the doctrine of ideas based upon his understanding of God as Nous. The evidence suggests that Armstong's assessment of Albinus' theory is on firm ground.

According to Albinus God does not think the ideas as objective realities, but as subjective concepts. The former are objects of the intellects that think them. The latter are products of the divine intellect itself. Therefore, the divine ideas are thought by God who thinks himself and they are interior to his intellect. This represents Albinus' conceptualist theory of the ideas. The divine ideas thought by the Nous, Soul, and the human intellect are exterior to these intellects. They constitute the ground of knowledge and being. This represents Albinus' realist theory of the ideas.

The conceptualist position has its origins both in the Middle Academy's theory of the divine ideas, and in the Peripatetic attack upon the doctrine of ideas as originally articulated by Plato.[79]   For Albinus the ideas are products of divine contemplation which to their thinking are not real objective entities, but mere concepts. The realist position is a restatement of the older Platonic doctrine of ideas proposed by Plato and in the Old Academy.[80]   For Albinus the ideas are for every intellect, save God's, objective realities. They are the basis for the structure, order, and value of all knowledge and being.

This double theory allows Albinus to maintain the integrity of the divine intellect. God thinks the ideas. They are derivative concepts thought by God when he contemplates himself. It also permits him to reassert the primacy of the ideas in the Platonic metaphysic and epistemology. They are not derivative to any other intellect except God's. Thus, they are objective realities that are grasped by the Nous and utilized to create a world, thought by the Soul so that this world is sustained, and perceived and contemplated by the human intellect who upon knowing them ascends, eventually, to a knowledge of their thinker. This brief excursus into Albinus' theory of the ideas is necessary for a proper understanding of the second principle in his metaphysic which is the Idea. The Idea is a product of God's intellect as well as the final and efficient cause of creation.

Albinus defines the Idea in five different ways. Albinus' Idea is in relation to God, Man, Matter, and the sensible world (hôs pros ti). It is respectively noêsis, noêton, prôton, metron, and paradeigma. Regarded per se (hôs pros autên) it is ousia (Did., 163, 13-16). The term Albinus uses to designate the Idea in relation to God is noêsis. This is the conceptualist part of his theory. He uses a variety of other terms, noêton, prôton, metron, paradeigma, to designate their relation to all other intellects. These terms represent the realist part of his theory. The first designation underscores that the Idea is a product of divine intellection. The other designations assert that the Idea is an objective object of thought, the measure of all thought, and the model for all things in the sensible world.

It is in its relation to matter and the sensible world that the Idea functions as a first principle. It is the measure of matter and the model for the sensible world. First, we shall examine how the Idea is viewed as final, efficient, and paradigmatic cause of the universe. Then, we shall address Albinus' understanding of the Idea as the measure of matter.

The Idea functions as a final, efficient, and paradigmatic cause in Albinus' metaphysic.[81] It is both an eidos and a paradeigma (Did., 164, 15). As the noêsis theou in the mind of God the Idea is the final and efficient cause of the universe. As the paradeigma ta kata physin it is the paradigmatic cause of the universe.

The background to Albinus' formulation is extant in Seneca (cf. Theiler, VN., 16; cf. Witt, A., 75-76). In (Ep., 58,19;65,7) Seneca added the Idea as a 'fifth' cause to the four of Aristotle. Albinus modifies this teaching by not making a distinction between separate causes, but between two aspects of the same cause. It is not that the Idea is a 'fifth' cause in Albinus' formulation. Rather, Albinus combines the final, efficient, and paradigmatic causes together into one cause, the Idea, and the Idea along with God and Matter become the three causes in his theoretic. This reformulation may not be original to Albinus (cf. Witt, A., 75-76; Dillon, MP., 281), but goes back to Arius Didymus (Theiler, VN., 16). That this is the case is likely because by the second century if not earlier (Diels, Dox. Gr., 485; Cicero, Luc., 118) the doctrine of three causes had become Platonic dogma (Diog. Laer, V., iii,69)

This so-called cleaning up and clarification of the concept of cause in the context of the Idea was motivated by the Nous theology of this trajectory of Middle Platonic speculation. As the 'unmoved mover', God is the cause of all things, he orders the cosmic Nous and the world soul in accordance with himself and his thoughts. By his will God filled all things with himself, roused up the world soul, and turning it toward himself became the cause of its mind. The world soul set in order by the first God then sets in order the whole of nature within this world (Did., 164,35-165,3).

The process of causing the Nous and Soul to move from potentiality to actuality by God ordering them in accordance with himself and his thoughts (sic. the Idea) lies at the basis of Albinus' doctrine (Did., 164,166ff.; 164,35ff.). Once actualized, and in harmony with God and his thoughts, the Nous imparts the ideas to the now organized world soul, who imparts them or instantiates them in matter, thereby forming a world. The actualized Nous and World Soul apprehended, become the paradeigma and eidos of the universe.

The results of this reformulation, whether or not it is original to Albinus, is that the cumbersome 'metaphysic of prepositions' common to Seneca, Philo, and Clement, no longer need be utilized to explain how the universe is created.[82] More significantly the five-fold relation of the Idea to God, Man, Matter, and the Sensible World permits a new relational context to be formulated that links God, through his Idea, per se to the intelligible world, and per accidens to the sensible world. That which is essential is actualized in accordance with God and his thoughts, and that which is accidental is in a state of potentiality striving toward an accordance with God and his thoughts. We shall have the opportunity to discuss this later.

Just as the Idea serves as the final cause for the intelligible realm as its telos in the mind of God, it also serves as the final and efficient cause for the sensible world as its paradigma and eidos. Albinus' conception of the Idea in its relation to the sensible world is not novel. It is the paradigmatic cause of the sensible world in that it serves as the model for this world. It is the immanent form of this world in so far as the ideas are the formative principles in the material realm. This is what Albinus means when he calls the Idea the paradeigmatikê archê and the paradeigma ton kata physin aiônion. This formulation reflects the doctrine of the transcendent and immanent ideas encountered in earlier Middle Platonists who recognized both aspects of the ideas, and utilized both in their theoretic or physics.

In summary, the originality of Albinus doctrine of ideas lies in two principle parts. First, is the manner in which the Idea is related to God, Man, Matter, and the Sensible World. Second, is the way in which these relations are expressed in terms of actuality, potentiality, essentiality, and accidentality. As noêsis tou theou the Idea is the actuality of divine consciousness. As noêton, prôton, metron, and paradigma the Idea is the object of consciousness, the measure of matter, and the model of all sensible things. By defining the interrelationship between God's Idea, the intelligibles, and the sensibles in this manner Albinus offers a new model for defining the relationship of the sensible to the intelligibles, the intelligibles to one another, and how a Platonist should view the notion that God is the first principle of all things. Albinus' universe is a dynamic one, not a static one.

Albinus' doctrine of the Idea points toward to a development in Middle Platonic categorical theory and the definition of Being which is very significant. However, before we can discuss this aspect of Albinus' thought we must examine his third first principle, Matter.

2.4   Albinus defines matter "as not body... but potential body (Did., 163,7). Matter (hylê), is the material substrate (hypokeimenon), which has the potential to receive the idiotêta impressed upon it by the immanent ideas. As the place (chôra) and receptacle (hypodochê) of the universe it is devoid of all form and structure until formed into bodies (Did., 163,3-7). Matter is the eternal 'stuff' out of which the sensible world is formed.

Matter functions as a first principle in the following way. The second intellect creates the sensibles out of matter by shaping matter in accordance with the thoughts of

God which it has apprehended upon being actualized (Did., 162,35ff.; 163,3-7). Since matter is eternal and the cosmos created, it is clear that Albinus does not maintain a doctrine of creation ex nihilo.[83] Matter exists eternally and prior to the creation of the world. Hence, the term create (genitôs) means: (1) that the universe is always in the process of generation, and (2) that by eternally being in the process of generation the Nous creates (katakosmei) or brings into order eternal matter into bodies. Albinus' formulation reflects an Aristotelian view of matter and the origin of the world coupled to an allegorical interpretation of (Tim., 28b).[84] Matter is not created out of nothing nor at a point in time. It is an eternal process of generation by the cosmic Nous.

The Aristotelian dimensions of Albinus' understanding of matter, and how matter moves from potentiality, as matter, to a kind of actuality, as body, is not a novel contribution to Middle Platonic theories on matter. Like earlier Middle Platonists he maintains that matter is eternal, unqualified (apoios) and unstructured (aschêmatos: Did., 163,3-7). Once formed it takes on specific qualities and structures. In this regard Albinus offers little that is new to Middle Platonic physics.

What he proposes that is new, however, is the potentiality-actuality hypothesis to explain how matter becomes a body (Did., 163-f). In proposing this Albinus shifts the focus away from the static view of the universe common to Academic views on this subject. Both his definition of matter and the function it serves as one of the first principles of his theoretic explains why he refused to associate matter with evil as did Plutarch (An. Pr., vi), Atticus (Proclus, In Tim., i.391,10), and Numenius (Proclus, In Tim., 196,16).

Albinus shares an important point of continuity with Philo and Clement in his doctrine of matter.[85] God is not excluded from the material universe. He is its orderer. However, how Albinus conceives of God as orderer of the universe is different from these earlier Middle Platonists. Matter is roused from its unstructured state into bodies by a Nous who actualizes it to the extent that matter can be actualized. God's power to create is a dynamic one that stretches through the whole of the universe, not a static one whereby he merely forms a world on the pattern of the ideas (although Albinus employs this imagery as well). This view of matter and creation has a profound impact upon the Platonic imagination, and reappears in the Christian Middle Platonic theories of Origen.

Finally, Albinus' doctrine of matter and creation explain why he does not call matter 'non-being' (mêton). As we have noted, this term means different things to a variety of Middle Platonists. For Numenius (Proclus, In Tim., 196,16), and Moderatus (Simpl. In Phys., 230,34ff.) it means the absence of being all together and hence the association of matter with evil. For Clement it reflects the state of something unqualified and unformed which upon being created or formed becomes being (Strom., v.89.6). For Albinus, on the contrary, matter cannot be non-being because when in its unformed state it is potentially being, not something devoid of being. This notion of matter as in potentiality (dynamei: Did., 163,3-7) becomes a postulate of later Platonic thinking, and is utilized by Christian Platonists in their debates with Platonic and Gnostic adversaries who argue that God is excluded from the material universe (cf. Origen C. Cels., iv.65).

In summary, Albinus' first principles contain a series of new proposals that aid in redefining the face of Middle Platonic theoretical physics. Within the context of Christian Middle Platonism Albinus' reformulations have a profound impact upon the thought of Origen. In particular, it is Albinus' notions of potentiality and actuality and his definition of matter in the context of this concept that aid Origen in proposing a Christian Platonic option on the basis of the Nous theology.

A major contribution that Albinus makes to the Middle Platonic philosophy is the doctrine of Being he proposes and the categorical doctrine that is associated with it. By means of his categorical theory he further strengthens the bond between God and the universe, and solves the relational problematics that confront the Middle Platonic theoretic. Let us turn now to his doctrine of being.

3. The Categories of Being

3.1 Witt (A., 118) notes Albinus' use of the Peripatetic doctrine of the categories and claims that Albinus accepted the doctrine in its entirety. This assessment is no doubt correct and has important ramifications for how Albinus viewed Being and the place of the categories in this understanding of reality.

Albinus, following Antiochus, Philo, Clement, and the Theaetetus-Commentor, does not criticize the Aristotelian doctrine of the categories. Like Arius Didymus (Stobaeus, ii,137,8-12), he employs the categories to underscore the postulate that sensible and intelligible reality can be subsumed under a single genus insofar as ousia is common to both realms. This we shall have opportunity to discuss later.

Albinus, following a practice that had long been Platonic dogma, divides reality into two spheres. They are Absolute (pros auto) and Relative (pros ti) Being.[86] The Absolute realm is populated by God, Nous, Soul, and Idea, and the Relative realm is populated by the sensibles. Under these two categories of being Albinus subsumes the ten Peripatetic categories (Did., 156,23).

It appears that Albinus practices Academic as well as Peripatetic diairesis.[87] He divides reality into its parts, and defines the entities in each realm categorically. The basic principle of dialectic is to define the substance of each thing and then its accidents (Did., 156,21ff.). There are five types of dialectical examination. Three are concerned with substances, and two with accidents. One defines a substance and its accidents by descending (a priori) through division and definition, or by ascending (a posteriori) by analysis.

Through division and definition Albinus defines the entities of the two realms of being. He defines substance in its essential as well as accidental manifestations dialectically.

3.2 Albinus claims the categories for Plato (Did., 159,34f.), with a reference to their being found in the Parmenides and elsewhere. The Theaetetus-Commentary written by an early contemporary of Albinus finds the categories employed at (Theat.,152d: cf.

TC., 68,1ff.)[88] The question arises as to the origin of Albinus' discovery of the categories in the Platonic dialogues, and once discovered to what entities do they have referential efficacy? As to the first question, the Peripatetic categories are ascribed to Plato by earlier Middle Platonists as well. Among these are Plutarch, Clement of Alexandria, and the Theaetetus-Commentator. Hence, by the time of Albinus such a view was common place among many Platonists and Peripatetics (cf. Witt, A., 12,38,66-67). As to the second question, Dillon (MP., 279) illustrates where they would be found by Middle Platonists reading the Parmenides as Albinus would. Dillon's reconstruction is most informative, and illustrates how Albinus might have used the categories. Some of the categories are in the first hypothesis (1370-142a) to be denied of the One. This would explain why Albinus maintains that the primal God is neither genus, species, or difference (Did., 165,5ff.). They are also in the second hypothesis (142a-155e), and are asserted of it. The categories asserted are quantity (150b), quality (137d,144b), relation (146b), place (138a,145e), time (141a), position (140a), state (139b), and activity and passivity (139b).

Since the second hypothesis refers to, at least in Albinus' scheme, the cosmic Nous and the world soul it would appear that quality, relation, and place have referential efficacy to the Nous; while quantity, state, activity, and passivity along with the others have referential efficacy to the Soul. The ground for this conclusion rests on the fact that the Nous, in potentiality, is characterized by these categories plus substance, and the Soul, in potentiality, is characterized by the same categories as the sensible world.

Albinus' division and definition of the third archê is not a radically new development. Although the primal God is beyond genus, species, and differentia, and thus cannot be defined, he is defined negatively through three adjectival and five substantial epithets. God is essential as the three epithets ending in teles suggest (Did., 164,28ff.). God is also characterized by divinity, substantiality (ousiotês), truth, symmetry, and the good. The Nous-Soul is not beyond genus, species, and differentia and is defined through the ten categories of being.

Albinus' definitions of God, Nous, and Soul reflect that either as substantiality or substance these entities are essential. However, they are essential in different ways. God's essentiality cannot be defined categorically whereas the essence of the Nous and Soul can. In this manner Albinus affirms the distinction between God and the Nous-Soul, and yet underscores that all three entities share a common constellation of characteristics.

The sensibles are also defined by the ten categories. However, the sensibles are characterized by accidentality not essentiality. Albinus infers this when he defines the Idea as hôs pros ti to the sensible world, which is its product and correlate (Did., 163,13). This also is evidenced when he states that the goal of dialectic is to define a substance and its accidents (Did., 156,21ff.). He can only be referring to the sensibles in this context.

In summary, Albinus maintains that a common set of categories have referential efficacy to Absolute and Relative being. He also affirms that the entities of both realms can be defined categorically. His application of this principle to God, Nous, and Soul is not a radically new development although many more categories have referential efficacy to the Nous-Soul in Albinus' theoretic than in the others we have examined.

3.3   God, Nous, Soul, and the Idea constitute Absolute being. However, only God and his Idea actually exist per se. The Nous and Soul only potentially exist per se. Once they are actualized by God, and become one with God and his Idea, they exist per se. This does not mean that they exist per accidens. It merely means that they move from a potential state of essential existence to an actual state of essential existence. This is why when in potentia the Nous and Soul are characterized by substance plus the other categories, and in actu they are characterized by substance alone.

Albinus expresses this transition from potentiality to actuality in two ways. First, the intelligible world, once actualized, becomes being per se (pros auto). Matter, once actualized, becomes being per accidens (pros ti: kata symbêbekos). Second, the exact nature of this actualization can be expressed according to the categories. The category of substance characterizes the intelligible realm, and the remaining nine plus substance characterize the sensible realm.

This scheme permits Albinus to assert that a series of referential states exist between an intelligible world in potentia and a God eternally in actu, without worrying whether or not this universe falls within the category of pros ti before it is actualized. This represents a significant advance over antecedent Middle Platonic theories. It also allows him to effectively deal with the problem of matter. In potentia matter is devoid of all form and structure, but it has the potential to be formed and structured. Once God actualizes the cosmic nous, and the cosmic nous the world soul, matter becomes actualized. In actu it forms a sensible world. In order to explain how this could occur he postulates that matter is under God's domination and is eternally generated when it is in potentia (Did., 162,25ff.). In actu matter continues in eternal generation (Did., 169,26-30), but now, presumably, in accordance with the Idea, which is ta kata physin (Did., 163,10ff.; 21). In actu matter takes on shape and form, and falls under the category of pros ti.

The intelligible and sensible worlds have referential efficacy to one another categorically. The same categories that characterize the noetic realm also characterize the material realm. First, we shall sketch the structure of Being according to Albinus. Second, we shall view the relation of the categories to Absolute and Relative Being.

Albinus structures reality in the following manner:

	God (oute apoios...poios); Idea
Absolute:	Nous (poiotês)
	Soul (poiotês)
Relative:	Bodies (poiotês)
	Matter (apoios)

The categories of Being are arranged in a two-fold manner. First, Albinus presents them in terms of reality in potentia. Second, he presents them in terms of reality in actu.

God (oute genos...oute eidos...oute diaphora); Idea (substance)

In Potentia: Nous (quality, relation, place, substance)

Soul (quality, relation, place, substance, quantity, state, activity, passivity)

In Potentia: Matter (apoios)

God (oute genos...oute eidos...oute diaphora); Idea (substance)

In Actu: Nous (substance (ousia)

Soul(substance (ousia)

Sensibles (quantity, quality, quality, relation, place time, position, state, activity, Passivity):

Along with this Academic division of reality and the Peripatetic definition of reality Albinus also reintroduces the paradigmatic ontology of the Idea(s). The Idea, in potentia, is in an essential relation to God, who thinks the Idea, and to the Nous and the Soul who have not as yet apprehended God and his thoughts. The Idea, in actu, is in an essential relation to God, the Nous, and the Soul, when the latter have apprehended God and are one with his thoughts. The Idea has no relation to matter in potentia, but only once the Nous and Soul are actualized and a world is formed upon the pattern of the Idea(s). The Idea's relation to this world, in actu, is an accidental one. Thus, when both worlds are actualized, the Idea is per se to the noetic realm, and per accidens to the material realm. When both worlds are potential worlds the Idea is per se to itself, its thinker, to the Nous and a Soul. It has no relation whatsoever to matter until matter is actualized.

4. God, Nous, Soul, and the Idea: The Noetic Realm

4.1   Albinus' doctrines of first principles and the categories illustrate how he views the order and structure of being. In this section we shall examine how Albinus defines the noetic realm. We shall begin with an examination of Albinus' theology, and end by briefly studying his doctrine of the Idea.

Albinus maintains that God, as first intellect, is neither genus, species, nor differentia (Did., 165,6ff.). The Nous, as second intellect, is not called a 'most generic something,' or conceived as a primary genus which contains genera and species. The Soul, which is an aspect of the Nous, functions to hold together (Did., 170,3-6), and order the universe (Did., 165,3-4).

Although there are similarities between Albinus' theologicals and those of Philo and Clement, there are dissimilarities as well.[89] Albinus conceives of God as activity, for otherwise he could not postulate an eternal substance (ousiotês: Did., 164,32) which would be necessarily everlasting. This first God, who is activity, moves without being moved, and causes motion in a non-physical way, by being an object of all that he moves (Did., 164,16ff.; 164,36ff.). God, for Albinus, is both the final and efficient cause of things. He is the efficient cause by being the final cause. He is an eternal entity whose influence radiates through the entire universe through his Nous and Soul.

Albinus' Nous has three aspects. God is eternal activity and the unmoved mover. The Nous moves the Soul who in turn orders the universe. What Aristotle called movement (kinêsis) Albinus calls intellection (noêsis) and will (boulêsis), and both are conceived of in terms of 'ends.' This is why Albinus uses the epithets ending in teles to describe God (autotelês, aeitelês, pantelês: Did., 164,30ff.). Nous and Soul are caused in that God is the object of their thought. The prime mover by activating them activates an entire universe.

Since God is immaterial, Albinus ascribes to it only mental activity, viz., knowledge. God is the only intellect that involves no process, no transition from premises to conclusion, but is direct and intuitive. God is prime mover, an actual and eternal mind. The term substantiality (ousiotês: Did., 164,32), which has hitherto not appeared in Middle Platonic theological lexica, is applied to God. It follows then that the object of divine knowledge is God himself. Like Aristotle, Albinus ascribes to God knowledge which has only itself for its object. Unlike Aristotle, he also claims that God has his ideas as the objects of his thought. However, these ideas are not distinct from the mind of God, but are one with it.

Albinus' formulation is not of the old Lyceum. His God is not Aristotle's noêsis noêseôs (Metaphys., 1074b22) where self-knowledge is not knowledge of other things. It is a product of the Middle Academy and the New Lyceum. God has a self-knowledge which is knowledge of the universe. God forms this universe as an act of will.

God has an influence on the universe that flows from his knowledge. He activates the Nous and Soul noetically, and a universe is patterned on his divine ideas. In this way Albinus asserts God's creative activity in the universe, and a knowledge of the laws of the universe since he knows the world soul, who is the law and harmony of the universe (Did., 170,3-6). This theistic rendering of Aristotle's Nous allows for theories of divine creation and divine providence. The first Nous through the agency of the second Nous and the world soul creates and sustains the world. Even matter, which is eternal and without form or shape, is throughout eternity maintained in existence by God.

According to Albinus, then, God is essential as first cause and first substance. The order, structure, and value of all things are based on God. Indeed, one of the most conspicuous features of Albinus' view of the universe is its thorough-going teleology. All that exists exists for an end. In the noetic realm there is a conscious working towards ends. The Nous and Soul, for example, work toward a knowledge of God and his thoughts. All that exists in the material realm, if it possesses intellect, strives towards divine knowledge as well. Even nature exhibits an unconscious striving towards ends. Albinus postulates providential activity, so far as maintenance of the world is concerned.

The teleological idea plays an important role in Albinus' attempt to relate God to the universe, and the different degrees of reality to one another. Most significantly it assists in overcoming the lacuna that exists in previous Middle Platonic theologies between the first and second intellects. The second intellect is neither a divine thought nor an entity created in the image of its Father, as it proceeds from its Father. The Nous is an eternally existing entity who is caused and ordered by God in accordance with himself and his thoughts. The Soul, like the Nous, is not an aspect of the first intellect, or made in the image of the second intellect. It is an eternally existing entity caused, or aroused into order by its Nous, who turns it towards God and his thoughts.

4.2   This way of defining how God causes first an intelligible cosmos, and then a sensible one, permits Albinus to radically devalue the paradigmatic theology of earlier Middle Platonism and the imitation doctrine that accompanies it. It is not that he does away with it. On the contrary, the doctrine of ideas plays a role in his cosmology. However, how the ideas function differs in Albinus' scheme. They are not merely the efficient cause of the world. They are also the final cause of the universe. The intelligibles strive to reach their end in striving toward a fulfillment of the forms they are patterned upon and which are immanent in matter. The ideas function less as paradigms, and more as ends, for non-material as well as material things.

God, as first and unmoved mover-intellect, causes the universe to order itself by being an object of desire. He operates directly on the Nous and Soul, and indirectly through them and the Ideas upon matter. The first activity produces an intelligible world, and the second a sensible world. God is the efficient cause by being the final cause of all things. Since the Idea is God's self-reflection, it too is the efficient and final cause of all things.

The telelogical dimension of Albinus' theoretic allows him to explain in cogent fashion how radically transcendent God is the first principle of all things. It also solves the issue of the relation of the intelligibles to one another, and the sensibles to the intelligibles. All things in the universe are related to one another in that they strive to reach their full potentialities. The essential entities find their telos in God and his thoughts, and the accidental things find their telos in approximating the ideas of God both at the hands of the demiurgic Nous and as they are instantiated in matter. The universe finds it ends in God, and its paradigm. This dynamic conception of a universe striving to fulfill itself replaces the static notion of a universe duplicated in the image of something else.

5. The World Soul and the Ideas: The Material Realm

5.1   Although Albinus' philosophical theology and categorical ontology represent new norms in Middle Platonic metaphysical thinking, his physics offers little that is new.[90] Apart from adjusting the traditional definition of matter from the Middle Platonic chôra-hypodochê-hylê to the Aristotelian definition of hylê as dynamei... sôma (Did., 163,7) what we encounter is a doxographical account of a Middle Platonic doctrine of matter.[91]

The Peripatetic provenance of the physics of the Didaskalikos is due to its reliance upon the Epitome of Arius Didymus. This further suggests that the philosophical structure of Albinus' physics is mainly dependent upon the physics of Antiochus (cf. Witt, A., 95-103; e.g., Diels, DG., 72: "At est ubi cum Antiocho pungent," the view of Arius).

The probable reasons for the unoriginality of Albinus' physics are that the doctrines of matter and the immanent ideas, which are central components of Middle Platonic physics, had a strong Peripatetic and Stoic hue as early as Antiochus and Philo. Hence, there was no need to adjust theories of the sensible world as there was for those concerning the intelligible world.

To this extent the physics of Albinus has close affinities to those of Philo and Clement of Alexandria insofar as both thinkers describe and define the material realm in a manner akin to Antiochus as well. The conflation of Stoic and Peripatetic principles need not concern us as this characterized the physical doctrines of all the schools of this period (cf. Witt., A., 96). Let us now turn to Albinus' definition of the material world.

The principle doctrines that constitute Albinus' physics are those of matter, the Idea, and causes, which include theories of the ideas and first principles. Insofar as we have discussed these in detail previously, we shall focus upon how Albinus explains the eternal formation of the material world by the Nous in its demiurgic capacity, and its maintenance by the Soul.

God orders the world soul and in doing so creates the sensible world (Did., 164,36ff.; 169,26ff.; cf. 164, 16ff.). The creation of the world did not occur at a point in time, but is in a constant state of coming to be. The world soul is not created by God. It exists eternally and is brought into order (katakosmei: Did., 269,31). By create (genetôs), Albinus means a process of continual generation.[92] Since the sensible world is dependent upon an outside source, God, for its existence, this cosmos is said by Albinus to be created. However, we should not assume a temporal creation for the sensible world, nor ascribe to Albinus the doctrine of a creatio ex nihilo. As Lilla (C., 193-198) and Dillon (MP., 286-287) note, Albinus' doctrine is a classic example of Middle Platonic theories of matter and creation, and reflects no inconsistency in his thinking as Witt (A., 120) has claimed.

5.2   The structure of the sensible world offered by Albinus represents little that is new. On the question of whether or not the world is comprised by four or five elements Albinus opts for the latter position. He postulates the four Platonic elements (Did., 168, 9f.), and appears to recognize the 'heavens' as a fifth element in the manner of the Peripatetics (Did., 168,34ff.). He states that the daimonês inhabit all the elements except earth, and lists the elements as aether, fire, air, and water. Here we have the four element universe. Later, at the end of chapter XV, he refers to aether as the outermost element divided into the sphere of the fixed stars and the planets (Did., 171,30ff.). After this comes air and earth. This aether would be the fifth element although he does not state that this element exists, as it would in a five element universe, with fire between aether and air. However, his mention of the heavens in (Did., 168,34) could be interpreted as this fifth element. Dillon (MP., 315) notes that this is what Apuleius maintained on these matters (cf. Howald, Herm., (1920), 75). Witt, on the other hand (A., 98), suggests that Albinus maintained a five element universe. In any case, we have seen this kind of ambiguity before in the physics of Philo of Alexandria (VM., ii.148; Det., 154; Plant., 1-8).

The problem confronted by Albinus, like Philo and Apuleius, is how to fit aether into the four element universe postulated in the Timaeus. If one takes the heavens of (Tim., 55c) as this extra element, it is possible to fit it in. Nonetheless, a certain sleight of hand is required to reconcile the Platonic and Aristotelian universes (cf. Dillon, MP., 171,186,315). If these thinkers were not doing this then we have to assume that they understood aether in the Stoic sense as the purest form of fire. This may have been the case with Philo, but Albinus' interpretation must be viewed within the context of his theoretic. God is the first mover, who orders the world soul, and thereby creates a world. It is likely that he took aether in the Aristotelian sense as having a circular motion and being the stuff out of which the stars are formed. In such a manner he could conflate the two theories into one, and link both to his interpretation of the Timaeus.[93]

Albinus connects 'to make' (poiein) with 'quality' (poiotês). He argues that if the creator is incorporeal, then the qualities used in creation must also be incorporeal. This postulate infers that the 'creative elements' of the universe (ta poiounta) are immaterial. Dillon notes (MP., 285) that this etymological connection was utilized by Antiochus, or at least Cicero's Antiochus (Ac. Post., 27ff.). This is an important observation because it tells us that Albinus thought of the qualities (poiotês) as forms immanent in matter, or the logoi spermatikoi. They are the immaterial immanent ideas.

The poiotês play a central role in Albinus' physics. The awakened world soul extends from the center up to the extremities of the universe. Its Nous comprehends the universe in itself, as Soul it holds it together (Did., 170,3-6). We have to assume that which it comprehends are the immanent ideas, and in comprehending them the order of the sensible universe is caused (Did., 165,3-4).[94]

5.3   The poiotês immanent in matter are created by the world soul to form matter into bodies, and thereby create a sensible world. Let us examine how the formation of this world is explained by Albinus.

This activity of forming the world is common to all five elements insofar as all the levels of the material realm are more or less corporeal and reflect the instantiation of the immanent forms (ideas) in matter. These creative-elements constitute the "qualities" (poitêtes) of material things, such as color or whiteness, and are distinguished from the "embodied qualities" (poia) of material things (sômata). Albinus spells this out within the context of how we know the sensible things in chapter IV. The creative-elements present themselves to the mind as "forms-in-matter" (eidê), or secondary intelligibles (Did., 154, 22ff). Each material thing has two dimensions: qualities (poiotêtes), and embodied qualities (poia). Both are aspects of a "composite body" (athrôisma), or the combination of "form" (eidê) and "matter" (hylê) (Did., 155, 32ff).

The distinction is between the two aspects which make up any material thing, viz., its universal "qualities," that it shares with other physicals. An example is whiteness or color. Its "embodied individual qualities" are particular to it alone. Hence, the same "qualities" are found in a variety of individual things, but they are "embodied" differently in each individual thing. This is why Albinus refers to "embodied qualities" (poia) as "accidents" (ta kata symbêbekos Did., 155, 37-156, 1). Both aspects of the phenomenon are the result of the dispersion of "qualities" (poiotêtes), as "creative elements" (ta poiunta), into matter (Did., 166, 25ff, cf. 162, 25ff; 163, 3-7).

God causes and sustains the universe. His poiotês are incorporeal and are the creative elements of the universe. The poiotêtes are the forms immanent in matter that are instantiated in the universe by the cosmic mind (Did., 166, 25ff; 164, 36ff). The soul of the world is the cosmic-orderer and the reason of the universe (Did., 169, 31ff; cf. 164, 36ff). The sensible world is the copy of the Idea (Did., 163, 21); and 2) and is a world actualizing itself in relation (reference) to God's Idea which is its final and efficient cause (Did., 163, 12-15). The relation of the sensibles to the intelligibles is that of copy formed in the image of its model, and the relation of that which is acted upon to its act.

It would be incorrect to assert that these transitions in Middle Platonic metaphysical thought were solely due to Albinus. The utilization of Aristotelian theories were common to Philo, Clement, and as we shall see, even some Pythagorean Middle Platonists as well. Nonetheless, Albinus is the first to explicitly propose a series of Peripatetic solutions to the problematics of the Middle Platonic metaphysics in the period we are studying. Albinus, and the paradigm shift he proposed, are important because they defined the metaphysical direction of later Hellenic and Christian Middle Platonism. The first principles and doctrine of being he hammered out emerged in Origen. Indeed with Origen we encounter a Middle Platonic option that is strongly Peripatetic. The Pythagorean elements of the earlier Jewish and Christian theoretics are domesticated through the adoption of central Aristotelian doctrines by Origen.

5.4   This transition in second century Middle Platonic metaphysics has led many scholars to assert that the origins of Neo Platonism can be traced back to the early second century and to Albinus. This interpretation is rejected on three grounds. First, the central problematics of Middle Platonic metaphysics differ from the Neo Platonic. Second, the Middle Platonic philosophical theology and doctrine of Being are distinct from the Neo Platonic. Third, Neo Platonism rejects many of the Aristotelian postulates of this later Middle Platonic metaphysics. Indeed, with Plotinus we encounter the Neo Platonic reaction against a series of Middle Platonic proposals. Specifically, there is a rejection of the Nous theology of later Middle Platonism, and the doctrine of categories that was associated with it.

This is not to say that some of these Middle Platonic proposals were not continued in fourth century Neo Platonism. Hierokles, and Origen the Neo Platonist, continued the profound synthesis of Plato and Aristotle proposed by Albinus, Origen of Alexandria, and Ammonius Saccas.[95] However, the criteria articulated by Plotinus and institutionalized by Porphyry constituted Neo Platonic orthodoxy. Their victory was so complete that Proclus affirmed the Plotinian triumph by criticizing those interpreters of Plato who refused to place the 'one' above the Nous, and for considering the Nous itself as the highest being (In Plat. Theol., 2, 4=fr. 7 Weber). It is precisely the distinction between Middle Platonism and normative Neo Platonism, which must be discussed before we enter into an analysis of the final phase of Middle Platonic metaphysics.

6. Albinus and Origen

6.1   Albinus' theoretic or physics represents, or is representative of, a water-shed in Middle Platonic metaphysical thinking. It had a profound impact upon Origen of Alexandria (cf. Koch, PP., 243-268), and forms the basis for Origen's reformulations of the metaphysical postulates of Clement and Philo of Alexandria.

Origen walks a thin line between the authoritative norms of his teacher, Clement, and the formative norms of the 'new' Peripatetic Platonism of the late second and early third centuries exemplified by Albinus. In Origen, we encounter a metaphysic which reminds us of the early Jewish and Christian Middle Platonisms of Clement and Philo, and at the same time we are aware that we encounter something quite different as well. In this sense Origen represents a pivotal figure in the history of formative Christian Platonism. He represents a break with the older theoretics of early Jewish and Christian Middle Platonism. However, we must be cautious in our assessment of Origen. His theoretic, and his definition of the structure of Being, is principally Middle Platonic. It principally reflects the intensely Peripatetic Platonism of the school activity around Ammonius Saccas. Origen's thought represents the consummation of Middle Platonic thought, not the initiation of a new phase in Platonic thinking itself.

To adequately assess Origen we must clear the decks, so to speak, and address a preliminary question. Is Origen's theoretic Middle Platonic or Neo Platonic? The answering of this question is important because we maintain that Origen's thought has largely been misrepresented by the reading of later Neo Platonic norms back in to Origen. The reasons for this are varied. First, his central work, the Periarchôn, is extant principally in redacted form in Rufinus' De Principiis.[96] In this work Rufinus ascribes to Origen a number of doctrines that better reflect the Platonism of Rufinus' time, not Origen's. This becomes clear when we examine the works from Origen's own hand and compare them with this redaction. Second, many of the evaluations of Origen's philosophy are mediated through the fifth through sixth century assessments of his theology.[97] Again we encounter a 'reading-back' into Origen of doctrines that were not his own. Third, modern scholarship upon Origen has principally been concerned with the 'orthodoxy' or 'heresy' of Origen's thought, and has evaluated it through the metron of later Christian Neo Platonism, and the decisions of the church councils.[98] In this sense they replay the Origenist controversy debated by Jerome and Rufinus, and add to an already distorted Patristic evaluation of Origen, a Neopatristic evaluation.

Our goal is to describe and analyze Origen's Platonism within the context of the variety of Platonic options in the first three centuries. In this respect our analysis is principally historical, and descriptive, not theological and evaluative.[99] To begin our study let us address the question of the distinction between Middle and Neo Platonism, and why we propose that Origen belongs to the former phase of Platonic thought, and not the latter.

6.2   A major debate among those who study the philosophy in late antiquity is the question whether or not a thinker is a Middle Platonist or Neo Platonist. This distinction among the Platonisms of late antiquity was initially introduced by Eduard Zeller in his Die

Philosophie der Griechen.[100] It is clear that such a distinction was not held by ancient Platonists, and thus it serves as a distinction which the modern student employs for purposes of classification and definition. As a means to this end it is a useful tool, but it should be seen for what it is, viz. a means through which we can trace similarities and dissimilarities between different Platonic thinkers in a continuous philosophical tradition.

A fundamental problem has always beset this classification of Platonisms. What are the criteria utilized whereby distinctions are made between Platonic thinkers? This is a difficult question to answer. In the remainder of this chapter the attempt will be made to answer this question.

In the nineteenth century the question asked was how close are Platonism and Neo Platonism? Initially the judgement was that Platonism and Neo Platonism were completely different. Plotinus was not a mere interpreter of Plato, but proposed a radically different philosophical option. Since so-called Middle Platonism was the forerunner to Neo Platonism it too represented a different philosophical option than originally proposed in the Old Academy.

In the twentieth century there was a reaction against this view and the argument was made that all later Platonists were interpreters of Plato, and that the philosophical options they proposed (with the aid of certain Peripatetic and Stoic metaphysical principles) were essentially Platonic. As such the later Platonisms represented an interpretation of Plato. Scholarship occupied itself with the diverse meanings of these later interpretations of Plato, and evaluated the historical accuracy of these interpretations. This step back from the radical separation of the thought of Plato from that of his heirs has demonstrated to be a correct one.

In the aftermath of this debate there resulted the increasing awareness of the differences as well as similarities between Middle Platonism and Neo Platonism. Hence, there ensued a new debate on the lines of the old one. How close are Middle Platonism and Neo Platonism?

Initially the judgement was that the two Platonisms were almost identical. This trajectory of scholarship was represented by figures such as Merlan, Armstrong, Wolfson, Henry, Schwyzer, Harder, and Theiler.[101] They decreed that the seeds, if not the fundamental principles of Neo Platonism, could be traced back to the Old Academy and the first generation of Plato's pupils or at least to the New and Middle Academies. Hence the metaphysical doctrines of Philo, Albinus, Clement, and Origen were proto-Neo Platonic. Their systems were representative of a partial, not fully developed, Neo Platonism. Origen's philosophy was represented as the first developed system of Neo Platonism, that would be fully articulated in Plotinus, and codified in the Neo Platonic schools.

In the last quarter century a group of scholars working from the seminal insights of Dodds have backed away from the conclusions arrived at by these Neo Platonic scholars. This trajectory of scholarship, represented by Loenen, Lilla, Dillon, Andresen, de Faye and Koch, took Middle Platonism as a distinct type of Platonic thinking that must be understood within its own context.[102] Recognizing that Middle Platonists worked with a set of Platonic apriora, and aporia that were connected with those which precede and follow their own, they argued that how they were addressed and interpreted permits us to define Middle Platonism on its own terms.

Now, the difficult question must be asked: "What are the criteria employed that distinguish Middle Platonism from Neo Platonism? How do we define either? First we must ask: Did the ancients provide clear-cut criteria for differentiating the two?" Unfortunately, no criteria are explicitly outlined. Second, we must ask: How do we define the differences if the ancients explicitly listed none? Fortunately, they are implicit in the sources. Hence, they can be reconstructed from the sources themselves. A taxa can be set up with six categories applicable to both types of Platonism. Middle Platonism holds:

1.   Two and no more than three spheres of being subordinated to one another, so that we have degrees of reality, viz. intelligible-sensible; or theological; intelligible; sensible, which represent higher and lower degrees of being. All the spheres are characterized by essence. There is no unreal sphere of being. All spheres of being can be defined categorically.

2.   The generation-creation of each inferior sphere of being from its superior. This generation has two phases: mental (logical) implication and causal (spatio-temporal).

3.   The supreme principle of the first sphere of being is an intellect. He is above genus, species, and differentia and cannot be qualified or known except analogically. He is the most universal concept, yet fully limited. He is not indeterminate but determinate.

4.   The description of this determinate is generally nous. He is above the monas and dyas and is complete simplicity.

5.   There is increasing multiplicity in each subsequent sphere of being which designate not only a greater number of entities in each subsequent sphere, but also the increasing indetermination of each entity, until we arrive at spatio-temporal determination.

6.   The knowledge appropriate to the supreme principle is different from the knowledge of any other object. The entities of the intelligible and the sensible worlds can be known by their attributes. Only through the negative process of the elimination of attributes may the first principle be known.

Merlan presents the following assumptions which are among those characteristics of Neo Platonism:[103]

1.   A plurality of spheres of being strictly subordinated to one another, so that we have a series the single terms which represent higher and lower degrees of being -- with the last, most unreal sphere of being comprising what is usually called perceptible being, i.e. being in time and space.

2.   The derivation of each inferior sphere of being from its superior, this derivation not being a process in time or space and therefore comparable to a mental (logical) implication rather than to a causal (spatio-temporal) relation,

thus the "causality" of all spheres with regard to each other not being of the type of efficient causality.

3. The derivation of the supreme sphere of being from a principle which as the source of all being cannot be described as being -- it is above being and therefore fully indeterminate, this indeterminateness being not the indeterminateness of a most universal concept, but an ontic indeterminateness, i.e. fullest "being" precisely because it is not limited to being this or that.

4. The description of this inderminateness also by saying that the supreme principle is One, this oneness expressing not only its uniqueness but also its complete simplicity, i.e. the lack of any determination. "One" designating not some kind of adjectival description, but rather the positive expression of the supreme principle being neither this nor that.

5. The increasing multiplicity in each subsequent sphere of being, greater multiplicity designating not only the greater number of entities in each subsequent sphere, but also increasing determination (limitation) of each entity, until we arrive at spatio-temporal determination and therefore at the minimum of oneness.

6. The knowledge appropriate to the supreme principle as being radically different from the knowledge of any other object in that the former in view of the strictly indeterminate character of the supreme principle cannot be predicative knowledge, which is appropriate only to beings exhibiting some determination.

And the most fundamental difficulty characteristic of what is called Neo-Platonism is the explanation and justification of the why and how of the passage from the One to the multitude, with the principle of matter playing an important role in this process.

If we take these assumptions as characteristic of Neo-Platonism we have to conclude that Middle Platonism, while anticipating some of these doctrines, did not present them in the same manner or as systematically as Neo Platonism. The reason for this is that in many respects the Middle Platonic metaphysical agenda differed from the Neo Platonic.[104]

Indeed, it is not the apriora as much as it is the aporia addressed, and the manner of their solutions, that distinguishes Middle and Neo Platonism. Indeed the examination of our three problematics illustrates how these two types of Platonism differed in their solutions about the nature of God, his relation to the universe, and the structure of Being. Middle Platonists often employed "Peripatetic" and "Platonic" doctrines, in unison, to solve the problematics they were concerned with:[105] Neo Platonists also employed these doctrines to solve the same problems, but did so in radically different ways.

In the next section we shall reconstruct how Origen the Middle Platonist approaches these problems and solves them. Before we undertake this, however, we shall briefly examine the Neo Pythagoreans, Moderatus, Nichomachus and Numenius. This is done for two reasons. First, Origen's theoretic critically uses the doctrines of this Platonic tradition. Hence, it is imperative to review them. Second, an analysis of the Neo Pythagoreans provides us with a synopsis, looking backwards and forwards, of Middle Platonism in transition.

IV. MODERATUS, NICHOMACHUS, AND NUMENIUS

The final transition in Middle Platonic philosophical theology and ontology, initially proposed in the writings of Philo and Clement and worked out in the Didaskalikos of Albinus, reaches its culmination in Origen. At the dawn of the third century Middle Platonic metaphysics reaches the acme of its development in Christian Middle Platonism.

The midwives to this process were the Neo Pythagorean Platonisms of Moderatus, Nichomachus, and Numenius. Another agent in this transition was the Peripatetic philosophy of the last decades of the second century proposed by Alexander of Aprodisias.

The environment in which these elements were mixed and harmonized was the school of Ammonius Saccas. The first thinker to propose a series of final solutions, and, hence new norms for the central problematics of Middle Platonic metaphysics, was one of the earliest students of Ammonius -- Origen of Alexandria. His answers and reformulations constitute the final chapter in the history of Middle Platonic thought.

As a prolegommenon to Origen it is necessary to sketch certain Middle Platonic-Neo Pythagorean proposals. Hence, we shall examine the theoretics of Moderatus, Nichomachus, and Numenius. This section serves a two-fold function: First, it permits us to review certain transitional moments in the philosophies of Philo, Clement, and Albinus. Second, the Neo Pythagoreans suggested some seminal norms. Among these were: 1) a hierarchy of divine hypostasis; 2) a dynamic relationship between the divine hypostases and the universe they create and sustain; 3) the theory that not only are there three hypostases, but also three moments of a supreme hypostasis; and 4) that every productive cause is superior to that which produced it.

1. Moderatus

Moderatus divides Being into the categories of the Absolute and the Relative. The distinction is between the intelligible and the sensible worlds. It appears that each realm has two aspects. The Absolute realm consists of a First and Second One, and the Relative realm of a Third One and Nature (which is the non-rational aspect of the Third One, cf. Simpl. In Phys, 230, 34ff.).

This norm is presented by Moderatus, according to Porphyry, in the following way (Porphyry, VP., 48). Being is immaterial, immutable, and eternal. Becoming is material, mutable, and changeable. This is inferred from Moderatus' distinctions between Unity, Sameness, and Equality, on the one hand, and Otherness and Inequality which suggests Plurality, on the other. From Porphyry's testimony it appears that Moderatus holds an opposing pair of supreme principles called the One and the Other (VP 48). From Simplicius' testimony it appears that Moderatus holds a system of related hypostases. It is likely that Moderatus postulates two distinct realms of reality each related to the other through the three hypostases. Hence, Porphyry and Simplicius present complementary evidence. Porphyry's testimony focuses upon Moderatus' division of reality, and Simplicius' testimony focuses upon the nature of the hypostasis proposed by Moderatus.

Simplicius reports that Moderatus conceived of three Ones (Simpl. In Phys., 230, 34ff.). Dodds is correct that the importance of Moderatus for subsequent Platonic thought is his adaption of the three hypotheses of the Parmenides for his presentation of first principles (CQ 22 (1928) 129-142). Dillon is right that Moderatus' scheme is best explained as a system of hypostases (MP., 347). He postulates a First One above Being and Essence; a Second One called the "truly existent" (ontôs on), who is the object of "intellection" (noêton) since he contains the Forms; and a Third One, or world-soul (psychikon). The third hypostasis "participates" (methechei) in the second hypostasis.

The first hypostasis on First One is above Being, and is akin to the One of Eudorus and Archytas (Eudorus, cf. Simpl., In Phys., 181, 10ff.; Archytas, cf. Stob., Anth. I, 41, 2). It has close affinities to the God of Philo (e.g. QD., 62; Leg Alleg., III, 206), and the God of Clement (e.g., Strom., V. 81. 5-6 [ii. 380. 18-22]; ii. 6.1 [ii. 116.2ff.]; vi. 71.5 [ii. 37ff. 18-20]. Moderatus' First One is a Nous, but a nous above all qualification, i.e. poson.

The second hypostasis is the truly existent One, the paradigmatic Nous who is the realm of the ideas. It is akin to the Monad of Eudorus and the Form (logikos-rhêtos) of Archytas (cf. Eudorus, cf. Simpl., In Phys., 181, 10ff.; Archytas, cf. Simpl., Anth., I, 41, 2). This Second One has parallels to the first-stage Logos of Philo (e.g., Opf., 24, 25; Sacr. Ab., 83, Conf., 172; Somn., 1-62), but is closest to Clement's second hypostasis in the second stage of its existence (e.g., Strom., IV. 156.1-2 [ii. 317.24-318.2]).

Dillon asserts (MP., 348) that it is not clear if Moderatus distinguishes between a Logos subordinated to the first One (the first-stage Logos of Philo and the second-stage Logos of Clement), or whether the Logos is identical to the first One as the active aspect of his noêsis. Simplicius' reconstruction aids us on this problem. Simplicius reports that the First One "wishes to produce from itself the generation of things." Hence, we can assume that Moderatus' Second One is similar to Clement's Logos-hypostasis. Clement's Logos, "proceeds" (proelthon) from the supreme intellect (Strom., V. 16.5 [ii. 336.12-13]; Simpl., In Phys., 230, 34ff.), and is its first product. Moderatus' Second One most likely is generated by the first one.

At the level of the Second One Moderatus postulates that matter comes into existence in the form of posotês. Dillon (MP., 345) is right to claim that Moderatus' Second One has its source in the Indefinite Dyad of Eudorus (Simpl., In Phys., 181, 10ff). Hence, in Moderatus' universe, there is an opposition between a Monad and Dyad with the Second One imposing form on quantity (Monad = form; Dyad = quantity) thereby producing matter.

The Third One is the Soul, and it participates in the Second and First Ones. It resembles the world-soul of Philo (e.g., Heres 188 Plant. 9; Fuga 110, 112), and Clement (e.g., Protr., 5.2 [i. 6.7-8]; Strom., V. 104.4 [ii. 396.16]; vii. 5.4 [iii. 5.22ff.]; vii. 9.2 [iii. 8.14-15]). It is the supreme law of the universe, it is immanent in the sensible world, and holds it together. Unlike Philo and Clement, but like Numenius (fr. 22 de Places) and Albinus (Did., 164, 36ff.), Moderatus postulates that the third hypostasis has a non-rational aspect. The difference, which is significant, is that for Moderatus the non-rational soul is a reflection of the rational one, not the rational soul in potentia. Moderatus views the sensible world as a shadow of intelligible matter (posotês), which is the Indefinite Dyad manifesting itself at the level of the Second One. Matter is not found merely at the lowest level of the universe, but it has its archetype at the second level of the Absolute realm. This again is an interpretation of the early Neo Pythagorean first principles postulated by Archytas and Eudorus.

The significance of Moderatus' formulations are considerable. He presents the first systematic harmonization of the Pythagorean first principles articulated in Archytas and Eudorus. He presents them in a system of three distinct hypostases linked by participation with a fourth entity Nature reflecting (emphasis) the Third One. In addition he presents 'Quantity' as the intelligible archetype of matter. Finally, he offers the first coherent attempt to relate the two hypotheses of the Parmenides to each other on the models of a hyperousion hen, and ousion hen. These theories present themselves again in Philo and Clement with striking parallels.

There is little indication that Moderatus proposed a coherent theory of the categories built upon the proposals of Archytas and Eudorus. He posits the First One to be above all attributes, the Second One to be Form, and the Third One to be Quality; and Nature to be material substance. The Dyad introduced at the level of the Second One is Quantity. The Second One as Form orders the Otherness and Inequality of the Quantity or the Dyad. The result is the generation of the beings that make up the Third One or world-soul. It is in this sense that matter is the reflection of the third hypostasis as Nature.

In this categorical scheme there is no evidence that Moderatus held a different opinion of the ten categories of the Peripatetics than did Eudorus. They do not apply to the Absolute Realm at all, only to the Relative (Simpl., In Cat., 174, 14ff.). Substance refers only to material substance, and the rest of Aristotle's categories apply only to the physical world. They have no relation to the intelligible world where true Being resides. In the case of the Pythagorean categories, however, Moderatus offers an explanation consistent with Eudorus: the First One = Substance; the Second One = Quality; the Dyad = Quantity; Relation = the logos immanent in the world, or the Third One, who is the sum-total of these immanent ideas.

Finally, there is no hint in Moderatus of what we find in the later Pythagorean Middle Platonists Numenius and Nichomachus, that there is a relation of actuality and potentiality in the universe starting from the First One and spreading down to created matter. The relation of the sensibles to the intelligibles, the intelligibles to each other, and God to each is based on the model-copy-image theory of the Platonic school traditions. For the first move beyond this static Platonic model to the dynamic Aristotelian model we have to wait for the dramatic transformation in Middle Platonic thought with the second century Peripatetic Middle Platonists Albinus and Origen.

2. Nichomachus

Nichomachus presents a division of Being according to the Academic distinction of Being and Becoming (Intr. Arith., I, 2, 1). Being is immaterial, eternal, and immutable. Becoming is material, changeable, and mutable. Becoming is of its own nature "not really existent" (ouk ontôs onta).

In addition to this Academic division between Being and Becoming, Nichomachus makes a second Pythagorean distinction between Even and Odd/Limit and Limitlessness (Intr. Arith., II, 18, 4). This distinction is followed by a third one. Working from (Tim., 35a) Nichomachus notes a distinction between the Same and Other. He states that it is a distinction between an essence which is indivisible and always the same, and an essence which is divided. Quoting Philolaus he states that existent things must all be either limited or limitlessness, or limited and limitlessness at the same time. Existent things are made after the image of number (the ideas-numbers), that are composed from the Monad (even) and Dyad (odd).

Upon these postulates Nichomachus sets up a two-fold model to explain the creation of the sensible world. The first is that the ideas or numbers are placed in the mind of the demiurgic intellect who uses them for the creation of the world. The second is that God is equated with the Monad (Theol. Arith., 3, 1ff. de Falco). He is seminally in all things within both realms, and comprehends potentially (dynamei) all actualities. He is called the principle of unity, the knowledge of all things, the potentiality of all actualities. The first proposal reflects the standard Middle Platonic theories of Philo and Clement. The second proposal reflects a later notion in Middle Platonic metaphysics, and has parallels to theories proposed by Albinus, Numenius, and Origen.

Nichomachus' God is both a Nous and a Demiurge (Theol. Arith., 4, 3ff.). Dillon is correct that he seems to make no distinction between the two (MP., 355). Nichomachus defines this demiurge intellect as a technikos logos (Theol. Arith., 4, 6), or if we are to take Photius' testimony as well, a spermeitîtês logos (Plotius, Bibl. Codex., 119). He is the active principle which creates the physical world. This supreme Nous or Monad also creates the Dyad (matter or hylê) by self-doubling (diphorêtheisa). He is also the sum-total of the logoi. In this aspect he is not hylê, but the structure of hylê, the all-receiver. The Dyad is the "outer limit" (kampstêr) in the flow of existence from the Monad, who is both starting-mark, and finishing-line (Theol. Arith., 9, 4ff.). Hence, God is the beginning and the end of all things. Dillon is right that this suggests a theory of Procession and Return (MP., 355). This idea is repeated again at (Theol. Arith., 19, 5ff.).

Here, however, we encounter a triadic division of the material universe with the Triad or Logos in the world being equated with an intellect. The world-soul is its projection and rational aspect (cf. The Hexad. Theol. Arith., 48, 18). This intellect is called the "form" (eidos) of the universe, which gives definition and shape to matter by means of the powers of all the qualities, and is equated with Number (Theol. Arith., 17, 19ff.). This is a description of the Logos as the formative principle of the world. This world-soul is called "form of forms" (eidos eidôn: Theol. Arch., 45, 6). It receives forms (ideas-numbers) from the Logos and projects them upon matter thereby forming it as harmony and number. As the Hexad it is called cosmos (Theol. Arith., 48, 18).

Nichomachus presents his God as consisting of three entities in descending order of importance: 1) a First God, or first One on the Kosmopoios Theos, viz., the highest good, the Nous; 2) a Second God, or second One, viz., the first-born One, demiurgic Logos, or technikos nous and 3) the Logos of the world (and world-soul), the spermatikos nous (Theol. Arith., 4, 3ff.; 4, 6ff.; 57, 20ff.; 79, 5ff; 45, 6; 45, 13; 48, 18). Hence, we have a hyperousion hen, an ousion hen, and a third principle with two aspects, viz., the Triad-Logos and the world-soul, its projection.

This presentation may appear as too schematic given the obliqueness of Nichomachus' presentation. Nonetheless, it appears a defensible interpretation on two grounds. First, we must keep in mind Nichomachus' distinction between the Same and Other, viz., the distinction between the essence which is indivisible and always the same, and the essence which is divided. Second, we must remember Nichomachus' notion of God, the first One, as the potentiality of all actualities. The First God is the Same, the essence which is indivisible, the Mind, who is the potentiality of other divine actualities, viz., the second demiurgic Logos, and the third immanent Logos, and its projection the world-soul. Nichomachus is not presenting three distinct hypostases, rather he is presenting three moments of the hypostasis of the Nous, the first One: as Being, Intelligence, and Life.

3. Numenius

The theology of Numenius is strikingly similar to that of Albinus and Nichomachus. It has a triadic scheme. This scheme is presented as a hierarchy. There is a parallelism between the three divine entities which is roughly but succinctly described by Proclus (In Tim., I, 303, 27ff. = fr. 21).

There is a supreme God above all attributes. He is the Good (fr. 16), the One (fr. 19), and has all the characteristics of the first hypothesis of the Parmenides (fr. 11, 5). The first God is called an intellect (fr. 16), a primal intellect who is identical with "essential being" (fr. 17). He thinks only by utilizing the second intellect, and the third intellect (which is as we noted the lower aspect of the second) is "that which determines" (ho dianooumenos), or noetically holds together the cosmos. He is exempt from all activity (fr. 12), and is called a God at rest (fr. 15). Numenius asserts that the first intellect is a kind of "innate motion" (kinêsin sumphuton) from which derives order, permanence, and preservation of the cosmos (fr. 15). Dillon is correct that he is the 'motionless motion' and hence the energy which produces the stability and order of everything else (MP., 369).

The second God and the third God are one (fr. 11). Numenius appears to be making a distinction we encountered in Albinus, viz., a distinction between two aspects of the active nous (Did., 164, 36ff.), but with one important difference. For Numenius, the second and third God are a cosmic mind and world-soul respectively. The former is a demiurgic intellect, and the latter a Mind, which becomes ordered, once it has been ministered by the second intellect (fr. 11).

The world-soul has two aspects, one irrational, the other rational. Hence, it is an entity which requires ordering. Once drawn up into the character of the second God it is ordered. In this stage the second and third Gods are essentially one entity. In this sense the second intellect is called a helmsman who binds matter together in a harmony (fr. 18).

Numenius equates the first God with the Absolute Living Creature, viz., the world "formed" by the second God, which constitutes the third God (fr. 22). Hence, the second God is the extension of the first God's intelligizing into the world-soul itself. In this sense, like Albinus' primal God, Numenius' is not absolutely transcendent. Dillon is correct (MP, 372) that the first God is only an active intellect insofar as he communes with the second, and the second is only actively demiurgic insofar as he communes with the third (fr. 22). Yet at the same time the first God is distinct from the second (fr. 2). Hence, Numenius' first God is ineffable and comprehensible only by the second intellect. Like Albinus' God, he is neither qualified nor unqualified (Did., 165, 4ff.).

The second God is an active intellect, or better said a mind in motion (fr. 15). He is not like the first God, who is stasis. He is the "imitator" (mimetês) of the first God or principle of Being (fr. 16). The God of generation, he is divine only by participation in the "first Being" (prôtos on: fr. 16, 19, 20) [following Dodds (SP, 48-52) and Dillon (MP., 363)]. He is also sent down through the spheres and participates with those beings who are ready to participate with him (fr. 12). As we shall see, the similarity between the Numenius' nous-kuthernêtês and Origen's Pneuma is a striking one.

Numenius posits three divine intellects. First, a mind at rest who is the ground of all Being. Second, a mind in motion who creates the physical world. Third, a world-soul who is the bond of the universe. The relation of these three entities to one another is presented in two ways. The first God is called the Good, a One, who is the father of the creator God. The second God is an imitation of the Father, and hence participates in the essence of the Father. The Third God has two phases, a non-rational and a rational one. Once it becomes rational the world-soul constitutes the ordered universe. The first God is also called an intellect identical with essential Being. He is an intellect at rest which activates itself by utilizing the intellect of the second God. The Third God, in turn, is the extension of this intelligizing power into the universe.

While the first scheme is Platonic in expression, the second is Peripatetic. The nature of the relation between the first God, and the second and third gods is: 1) that of model and copy; the third God participates in the second God, and the second God in the first God; and 2) that of a "motionless motion" (sic. unmoved mover), or first contemplative intellect who is the energy which produces the second intellect. The second intellect, in turn, produces the stability and order of the world-soul or cosmic intellect.

Unlike Albinus there is no indication that Numenius attempted a way of harmonizing these two distinct metaphysical formulas. Both stand irreconcilably side by side in his theoretic.

To summarize: Numenius represents a second century figure who offers new structural and conceptual norms within the Middle Platonic-Neo Pythagorean trajectory represented by Archytas, Eudorus, Philo, and Clement. First, he defines the first God as a nous. This is the first explicit definition of the Father as a nous in this trajectory of Middle Platonic thought. God the Father is an intellect at rest, not an active intellect. He is identical with essential Being. Second, the second God is called an active intellect (kinoumenos). Although this is not the first example of this definition in this tradition of thought (cf. Nichomachus, Iamblichus, TA., 79, 5ff.), Numenius is the first to propose a triadic hierarchy of the first, second and third intellects (if we take the third God as the lower aspect of the second). Third, Numenius' notion of the second intellect as a helmsman progressing through the spheres of the cosmos is an important idea. This nous is sent down by the first God for those who would like to participate in it. The formula is very close to that proposed by Origen concerning the pneuma.

The Neo Pythagorean theoretic, principally as exemplified by Numenius, recurs in the theoretics of Origen of Alexandria and Plotinus. Heinemann and Langerbeck (H, 61 [1926], 1-27; JHS., 77 [1957], 67-74) maintain that the transmitter of these Pythagorean first principles was Ammonius Saccas. Seeberg and Dörrie (ZKG., 61, 136-170; H., 83, 439-478) concur with this assessment. However, since Ammonius either wrote nothing, or nothing survives which he composed, it is extremely difficult to unpack the content of Ammonius' transmission of the writings of Numenius, and examine what Ammonian doctrine was passed on to his pupils. These problems are nicely sketched by Dodds in his article on "Numenius and Ammonius" (EH., V, 1-32, cf. 24-32). Hence, we must be cautious in our assessment of the transmission of Neo Pythagorean doctrine by Ammonius to Origen and Plotinus.

Nonetheless, Koch (PP., 226-228), fully recognizing this problem, follows de Faye (O., II, 208ff.), and convincingly argues that Numenius was the major Neo Pythagorean source for Origen's philosophy, and that Origen received his knowledge of Numenius from Ammonius Saccas. The basis for this conclusion rests upon Origen's references to Numenius, and the Pythagorean elements basic to Origen's own first principles. Hence, although it is not possible to ascertain if Ammonius was a Pythagorean (cf. Dörrie, H., 83, 465) we can, with caution, affirm that Neo Pythagorean concepts were known and utilized by Origen, his pupil.

The important issue is how Origen used these Neo Pythagorean principles, not if he used them. We can make four positive assertions about Origen's utilization of Numenius' theoretic: 1) he adopted the Pythagorean schemata of the first two principles, and discarded the third principle; 2) he rooted his first principle in a Nous formulation even more firmly than Numenius did; 3) he maintained the Numenian doubleness of the second principle by defining it as a Mind (nous) and a demiurge (dēmiourgos); and 4) he had the function of each principle overlap by affirming Numenius' doctrine of proschrêsis.

If we are correct about these assertions then we can qualify Origen's use of these fontes even further. First, Origen does not merely reduplicate Neo Pythagorean doctrine. He reformulates it. Second, Origen's reformulations are undertaken within a specific context. This context is two-fold. The major influences upon Origen's theoretic are the early Middle Platonic doctrines of Philo and Clement, the middle Middle Platonic doctrines of Albinus, and the Peripatetic doctrines of perhaps Alexander of Aphrodisias.

Third, Origen's use of and knowledge of the Neo Pythagorean first principles has a wider context than merely Ammonius, and they are redefined within the framework of the Peripatetic tendencies of middle and late Middle Platonism. Hence, Origen did utilize Neo Pythagorean concepts, but what he used were reformulated within a Peripatetic context, and thus cannot be called simply Pythagorean.

These are important points to note because Origen's theoretic has been incorrectly defined as Pythagorean since the time of Justinian. There are Pythagorean elements in his first principles, but it would be incorrect to assume that they are principally Pythagorean. The Peripatetic element is much more profound in Origen's system than most have realized, and it is this aspect of Origen's theoretic that defines the meaning of the Pythagorean aspect of his thought.

In summary, as we move on to our analysis of Origen's theoretic we must keep in mind the Pythagorean thread in his thought, but also maintain an awareness of the Platonic and Peripatetic threads as well. Origen weaved a complex mosaic of concepts together, and the transitional stages we have traced up to this point in the Platonic theoretics of Philo, Clement and Albinus, in the Neo Pythagorean theoretics of Moderatus, Nichomachus and Numenius have their consummation in Origen. The catalyst in this final Middle Platonic synthesis, however, comes from another source, the Peripatetic. How Origen weaves all this together shall be the topic of our next section.

V. ORIGEN OF ALEXANDRIA

Introduction

Hal Koch's monograph published in 1932, is still the best general work on Origen's philosophy.[106] It is, however, mainly concerned with an investigation into the sources of Origen's Platonism, and a comparison of his doctrine with those of earlier Platonists, Stoics, and Peripatetics. It does not include an examination of the inner coherence of Origen's Middle Platonic theoretic. In the following pages the attempt will be made to see Origen's doctrines from the historian's primary point of view, which tries to understand a system from its central problematic point. This attempt at the reconstruction of Origen's philosophy will be undertaken with hardly a glance toward Plotinus. The attempt will be to understand Origen within the context of the Platonic and Peripatetic school traditions. It is not my intention to discuss the historical exactness of Origen's interpretation of Plato, or the orthodoxy and/or heresy of his theological formulations. This study is limited to the principle points of his philosophical theology and ontology. Origen's formulations lead to the solution of the three problematics which dominated the Platonic thought of this period: 1) the relation of the sensibles to the intelligibles; 2) the relation of the intelligibles to one another; and 3) a first principle as the unity of all things.

As we enter our examination of Origen's theoretic we are confronted with the task of interpreting his ideas out of sources which are largely corrupted. Our work is further hindered by Origen's own want of a consistent philosophical vocabulary, and the tendency of his writings to be less than clear and explicit concerning his fundamental philosophical principles.

Given the first problem the following ground-rules are observed. K.F. Schnitzer in his Origenes Über die Grundlehren Glaubenswissenschaft, Stuttgart: 1835, and P. Koetschau in his critical edition of the De Principiis, Leipzig: 1913 present us with a guide as to the use of sources. The most important texts for the reconstruction of Origen's thought from the evidence of the Periarchôn (De Principiis) are:

a.   the redaction of the Periarchôn (De Principiis) by Rufinus.

b.   the fragments of Hieronymus which are a re-presentation of Rufinus' work culled from Jerome's Ep. ad Av. (cf. Koetschau p. ixxxviiiff.).

c.   the letter of the emperor Justinian to Mennas wherein Origen's doctrines are presented (cf. Mansi, Sacr. concil, nova et ampl. collect. IX 524e-533a.; Koetschau, cvff.).

d.   the anathemas which are extant partly in Justinian's Ep. ad Men. (Mansi
     IX 533-537), and partly in the anathemas from the Synod of Con. (cf.
     Mansi IX 396-400.; Koetschau, cviis.; cxix, cxxi).

e.   the fragments from the writings of Antipater of Bostra, Leontius,
     Epiphanius' Haer., and Theophilus; Ep. synod. (cf. Koetschau, cxvff.).

f.   Basil and Gregory's Philokalia which are parallel fragments to those
     presented by Rufinus (cf. Koetschau, ciff.), and Photius's Bibl., ch. viii.

Origen's philosophical ideas, as presented in the Periarchôn (De Principiis), are
compared to those extant in his other writings, e.g. C. Cels.; Comm. in Jh.; Hom. in Num.;
Hom. in Sam. whenever possible.[107]   Although this is a most helpful guide to the accuracy
of what is ascribed to Origen in the fragments and redacted pericopae which constitute
the Periarchôn (De Principiis) it must also be used with caution. Some of Origen's
doctrines are redefined in these later writings, and they represent more the thinking of
the later Origen than the Origen of the Periarchôn (De Principiis). Therefore, these texts
are only cited in connection with the Periarchôn (De Principiis) both to test the veracity
of the later testimonies which are all we have left from the earlier work, and to note,
when appropriate, where the testimonies do not coincide.

Given the second problem the following ground-rule is observed. Whenever possible
the attempt will be made to reconstruct Origen's philosophical ideas as he presents them.
However, the text-problems are so immense and Origen's own vocabulary so imprecise,
that reconstructions are presented as a theses and nothing more. This als ob approach to
Origen's theoretic has its limitations, but it is the only course open to a student of the
history of philosophy who works upon Origen. The theses proposed, hopefully, can be
sustained from the sources themselves. At times the evidence is circumstantial, but it is
the type of evidence which must be presented if we are to venture to understand the
Christian Middle Platonic option Origen proposed.

Three errors in particular have prevented a proper appreciation of Origen's place in
the unfolding of Middle Platonic thought in general, and Christian Middle Platonism in
particular.[108]   There was the failure to recognize the Middle Platonic character of
Origen's theoretic, epistemology, and dialectic. This vitiates the work of many
interpreters from Redepenning down to Danielou. There was the belief that Origen was a
Christian theologian whose philosophical assumptions were of secondary importance. This
is the least pardonable of Danielou and Bardy's interpretation of Origen.[109]   There was
the ascription to Origen of later Neo Platonic notions. Although Heinemann and Cadiou's
identification of the Christian and Hellenic Origen has been corrected by Dörrie and
Langerbeck, this confusion has been perpetuated by the tendency to "neo-Platonize"
Origen in another guise.[110]   The thought of Origen was as a product of the school of
Ammonius Saccas, and thus a "source" for early Neo Platonism. Thus, Origen's doctrines
could be explained in terms of the writings of Plotinus and Porphry.[111]   This third error

is the most significant and explains why the first error has been perpetuated. It is this legacy of Origen scholarship which we shall now address.

Origen's Neo Platonism is "proved" in two ways. Origen was said by Porphry and Eusebius to have been in this circle of Platonic thinkers.[112] Add to this the fact that in many passages Origen spoke of three divine hypostases and a First Principle beyond intellect and being. These notions were also held by Plotinus, _ergo_ Origen presented a cogent, if incomplete Neo-Platonic philosophical theology which may be explained from the writings of the "fully" developed Neo Platonisms of Plotinus, Porphry, or even the Christian Neo Platonism of Gregory of Nyssa.

The second method of "proof" rests on negative evidence. Origen was a member of the school of Ammonius Saccas. As one of the earliest formulators of Neo-Platonic doctrine he was intimately familiar with its ideas. Although he was not a "creative" thinker in the mold of Plotinus, his works constitute a _fons_ for early or primitive Neo Platonic thought. Analyzed within the context of the writings of the developed Neo-Platonist Plotinus it is clear that the _residum_ of Origen's thought is important as a milestone on the road to Neo Platonism.

These are large assumptions, and if we are to avoid making them we must find convincing parallels between Origen's conceptual assumptions and those of antecedent Middle Platonists who we know were either directly or indirectly his _fontes_.[113]

Despite the tendency of earlier scholars to view Middle Platonism from the context of its culmination in Neo Platonism, the distinct character of Middle Platonic metaphysics has been recognized for sixty years. Jaeger, Theiler, Witt, Lilla, and Dillon have done much to illuminate the conceptual presuppositions of the various strands of Middle Platonic thought, and to bind them together.[114] Within the field of Origen studies the work of de Faye and Koch represented the first (and unfortunately the last) attempts to define Origen's place within this constellation of Platonic thought. It is, thus, from the work of these scholars and the Middle Platonic sources that our examination of Origen commences.

The results of scholarship upon Origen thus provide us with a vast _apparatus fontium_ from which to reconstruct the philosophy of Origen. According to de Faye, Koch and Andresen the works of Philo, Clement, and Albinus loom as the best parallels to be utilized. According to Langerbeck, Dörrie, and Theiler a second group of sources are the writings of the Aristotelian commentators, principally Alexander of Aphrodisias. Hence, in a study on Origen's philosophy the fontes to examine are those proposed by de Faye, Koch, Andresen, Langerbeck, Dörrie, and Theiler. The _loci paralleli_ best suited for this task are those extant in the writings of Platonists and Peripatetics from roughly 150 to 220 A.D.

The tendency of scholars until recently not to appreciate the high regard Middle Platonists held for Aristotle (and to a limited extent the teachings of the Stoa) resulted in the overlooking of the originality of this period of Platonic thinking. The results have been the desire to overemphasize the originality of the Neo Platonic thinkers by playing down the achievements of these Middle Platonists. This misunderstanding was engendered by a too-literal minded interpretation of key Middle Platonic concepts in the light of later Neo Platonic ones.[115] These misconceptions have resulted in a series of lacunae in respect to a proper understanding of Origen's philosophy. Thus, in order to accomplish this it is necessary to place Origen's thought within its correct philosophical matrix, viz., Middle Platonism, and the Peripatetic philosophy of the early Empire.[116]

Koch is correct (PP., 225-35; 243-280) that Origen is indebted to the tradition of Hellenic Middle Platonism represented by Albinus and Numenius and the tradition of Jewish and Christian Middle Platonism represented by Philo and Clement. Cadiou (JO., 242) is right in suggesting that the tradition of Aristotelian philosophy represented by Alexander of Aphrodisias is of seminal importance for a correct understanding of Origen's metaphysics. Origen hammered out a series of new metaphysical norms which redefine the Middle Platonic definition of the structure of Being. His sources were four: 1) the Jewish and Christian Middle Platonists of Alexandria; 2) the Hellenic Middle Platonists of the so-called Gaius-Atticus group; 3) the Neo Pythagoreans; and 4) the Peripatetic commentators.

Dörrie has shown (PM., 324-360) that these four tributaries merged in the school of Ammonius Saccas. It was in this milieu that Origen systematically harmonized the doctrines of Plato and Aristotle into his first principles. The results constituted the final phase in Middle Platonic metaphysics and set the stage for a new phase in the history of Platonic thought, the Neo Platonic.

For the purpose of the present chapter, we shall confine ourselves mainly to Origen's philosophical view illustrated by the Periarchôn (De Principiis) with references to the Contra Celsum and the exegetical-homiletical literatures. A proper account of Origen's philosophy as a whole must await a close analysis of the Peripatetic commentators from Andronicus to Alexander, and their reformulation of the Aristotelian doctrine of the categories; a comprehensive reconstruction of the Neo Pythagorean fragments of Moderatus, Nichomachus, and Numenius; and Chalcidius' redaction of Origen's lost work On Genesis. Hence, this reconstruction is principally a prolegommenon to future work on Origen's philosophy. It is descriptive in its goal, and brackets any attempt to offer a normative evaluation of Origen's thought.

Origen's conceptual system is an elaboration of Albinus' Platonism, strongly influenced by the Neo Pythagorean corpus and the writings of Clement and Philo. Through his teacher Ammonius, he was introduced to the writings of Alexander of Aphrodisias and the teachings of the New Lyceum. We find Origen making much use of the writings of "Aristotle" in his effort to present a Christian Middle Platonic proposal. He believed, with Albinus and Ammonius, that Aristotle was essentially a Platonist. Origen was not hostile to the Peripatetic philosophy.

Following on the new direction given to philosophy by Albinus and Ammonius, Origen proposes a series of scholastic elaborations of Middle Platonic metaphysical doctrine. The harmonizing method of philosophising favored by Middle Platonists is followed by Origen. His activity circles around the exegesis of Platonic, Aristotelian and the biblical scriptures. He composes essays on such ancient subjects as being and existence and the nature of God, and is fortified in his work by insights gained from contact with the revealed wisdom of the Bible.

Origen employs a great freedom of symbolic interpretation so as to make Plato agree, not just with Pythagoras or Aristotle, but with numerous statements from the Old and New Testaments. It becomes absolutely imperative that the philosophers are perceived as consistent with these inspired authorities, and with Origen himself. This last aspect had always been a necessity for Platonists, and it becomes much more paramount now. Origen holds that the whole of each biblical work is infused with philosophical significance. Indeed, on the authority of Origen a Middle Platonic metaphysical view is asserted for each biblical work and the verses of biblical scripture serve as the premises for philosophical truth.

Origen works from a number of sacred works and doctrines. The Dialogues of Plato, the Works of Aristotle, the cosmogony of Genesis, the theology of S. Paul and S. John, not to mention the teachings of a Moses or Samuel. Within the framework of this corpus Origen moves at will, interpreting, reinterpreting, refining and refuting concepts. The most damning accusation he could propose was that of being non-Apostolic and un-Platonic. Origen accuses unknown Stoic and Gnostic Christians of both intellectual crimes constantly. They all fail to make correct metaphysical interpretations, they confuse concepts, and they do not discriminate with any finesse the truths taught in these two sacred scriptures.

In this activity of dialectical warfare Origen is found in a curious position. On the one hand he frequently appears as a conservative, repudiating the innovations of his Gnostic opponents or the materialist metaphysics of the Stoics. On the other hand, it is plain that Origen devised in many ways a more elaborate Platonic-Peripatetic theology and metaphysics than either Clement of Alexandria or Albinus and in many important respects laid the foundations for the later Neo Platonic philosophy of Plotinus, and through him Porphyry, Hierokles, Origen, and Gregory of Nyssa. Origen's relation to Neo Platonism, however, is a matter for another treatise. Our concern here is with Origen's metaphysics as illustrated by second century Platonism and Peripateticism. It is in this sense we turn to his philosophy, and not in any other. Let us now turn to an analytical outline of the principal theories and doctrines which underly Origen's philosophy.

1. The Structure of Being: A Metaphysical Description
The Realm of the "Ones"

1.1   Origen's philosophical theology represents the mature synthesis of two currents in Middle Platonic thought. These are the Aristotelian and the Neo Pythagorean conceptions of God as an intellect (nous, noêsis, to nooumenon: De Princ. I,1,6 21,13; Cat. in Joann., 495,24), defined as a One and Unity (monas, henas: De Princ., i,1,6 21,13ff.) above all created intellect and being (C.Cels., VII,38 188,11; Coh. ad Mart., 47 43,8). Indeed, Origen's philosophical theology is the first mature expression of a Nous-Henas theology in Christian Middle Platonism.[117] With Origen we leave behind the demiurgic philosophical theologies of the early Middle Platonisms of Philo and Clement, and enter into a philosophical theology that reflects the later milieu of the late second century philosophical theology of Albinus, and the second century philosophical theology of Numenius.

Origen represents a major transitional moment in the history of Middle Platonic theoretic. His utilization of Peripatetic and Neo Pythagorean norms together alters the face of Christian Middle Platonic philosophical speculation, and represents the consummation of Middle Platonic theoretical reflection from Antiochus to Albinus. His doctrines of God and Being radically change a series of metaphysical norms in the areas of the ideas, the creation of the world, and the divine hypostases. Our goal in the pages to come is to describe and analyze Origen's theoretic.

Origen postulated two Ones, or first principles.[118] The first "One" is a transcendent monas and henas that is the ground of the whole noetic world.[119] Origen refers to this One as God the Father. The second "One" is a monada and henada that contains within himself the intelligible universe, and he presides actively over the generation of the sensible world. Origen refers to this second "One" as Son, Logos, Wisdom, and Christ.

The Father is the first element in the divine triad of hypostases, and as the begettor of the Logos-Son he is the necessary first principle of all things. The Logos-Son is the sufficient principle of all things, and functions as the agent for and demiurgic principle of the created world. Origen is clear that he envisaged two principles, but not three. Both "Ones" can be identified as subjects of the first and second hypostases of Plato's Parmenides.[120] In Origen these two Ones are merged with inevitable tensions.[121]

The realm of the One includes not only the first and second "Ones," but also a Pneuma, beneath the first and second "Ones." The Holy Spirit is not a principle as much as he is a soteriological agent for redemption. These two "Ones" and its "Holy Spirit" make the Realm of the One complete. It appears to have the following structure:

The First One
(Father)

The Second One
(Son, Logos, Christ, Wisdom)

+

The Holy Spirit

_____

1.2   Properly speaking the noetic (intelligible) world is part of the realm of the second "One." Within this realm are the Logos and the Holy Spirit. Origen postulates the necessity for the participation of the lower orders in the higher, but he also maintains that the realm of the "Ones" is pure and not characterized by any of the qualities of the lower orders.

Origen did not systematically employ the notion of process from the one to the many which characterized later Neo Platonic thought. He holds the Jewish and Christian Middle Platonic formula that the "Ones" create the lower realms on the analogy of procreation. Coupled to this concept is the notion of aspects or moments common to each hypostasis. God the Father, or first hypostasis, is defined as an eternal ungenerated Mind and Being "above" the Logos-Son, or second hypostasis. This second God is defined as an eternally generated Mind and Being which thinks and then creates the lower levels of being. The Holy Spirit, or third hypostasis, is defined as the first generated Mind and Being who works in the lower levels of being to save or bring the "saints" into the realm of the "Ones." Origen postulates that God the Father is the ruler of the noetic realm, that the Logos-Son is the primary intelligible and creator of the sensible realm, and that the Holy Spirit is the soteriological agent for the created minds that exist in both realms.

The noetic realm itself has two _momenta_. First, it exists "potentially" in the Mind of the Logos-Son. Second, it exists "actually" outside of the Mind of the Logos-Son. In its intradeical moment it is within the realm of the "Ones," and in its extradeical moment it is outside this realm existing in its own right. This doctrine is the most perplexing in Origen's system. It appears that he conflates two notions common to antecedent Middle Platonic thought. First, there is the idea of an eternally active Mind that thinks the world. Second, there is the notion of this Mind as the demiurge that creates the universe. This habit of referring to the Logos-Son and the created realms in different ways to suit different contexts is a feature of Origen's exegesis that is bewildering. In any case the noetic realm appears to have the following structure:

1)   The Second One
                      (Son, Logos, Christ, Wisdom)

                                   +

                (the genera and species of the noetic realm)

2)   The Second One
                      (Son, Logos, Christ, Wisdom)

                      —————————————————

                (the genera and species of the created realm)

1.3 The Created Realm

The created realm constitutes the _Zôa_ of the material realm. These are the corporeal genera and species of the sensible universe. The created realm has two moments of existence in the Mind of the Logos-Son. First it is prefigured, and exists _in potentia_. Second it is created, and exists _in actu_.

The created realm stands between the noetic realm and the material realm, and the beings that exist in this realm partake of characteristics common to both. To create the world, matter is given form by the Logos, whose _logoi_ penetrate it unceasingly. Indeed, the demiurgic Logos is the principle that introduces "differentiating quality" to the sensible world. Within this realm of being there are different levels of being descending from the rational creatures to the material substrate. The structure of the created realm is the following:

1)   The Second One
                                (Son, Logos, Christ, Wisdom)

                                            +

                        (the genera and species of the psychic realm)

2)   The Second One
                                (Son, Logos, Christ, Wisdom)

                        _____

                        (the genera and species of the material realm)

The beings that exist in this realm are the angels, "daimones," created minds, humans, animals, and plant-souls. All the entities in this realm are to a greater or lesser degree corporeal.

All noetic beings belong to the created realm insofar as all intellects have fallen from the divine realm. Hence, there is no sharp distinction made by Origen between the intelligible and sensible worlds. All rational creatures are to a greater or lesser extent corporeal. Nonetheless, it would not be correct to assert that Origen does away with this standard Middle Platonic division of being completely. He holds a degree of reality metaphysics. However, we can cautiously affirm that the sharp division between the intelligible and sensible worlds held by antecedent Middle Platonists has been reformulated by Origen.

1.4 The Material Realm

The material realm consists of the material substrate (hypokeimenon), which is eternal insofar as it is not created in time. This substrate is informed with qualities by the second intellect when he fashions it into the genera and species of the created orders. To create the world, matter is given form by the demiurge (Logos), whose logoi penetrate it unceasingly. This differentiating quality is proper to the whole cosmos. Hence, any ensouled creature belongs to this realm as well as to the created realms.

These subjects are only touched on in the redactions of Rufinus and Calcidius, but we can, with caution, say that Origen views the material substrate as a kind in "non-being" before its formation by the Logos, and relative being after the creation of matter into genera and species. However, Origen rejected, as did the general consensus of most Middle Platonists, the belief of Plutarch and Atticus in the non-being of the world, and the previous existence of an evil world-soul.

From Origen's doctrine of matter and his definition of the material realm we can see the breakdown of the earlier Middle Platonic division of being into two categories. The many varieties of created things exist in one or more realms, viz. the noetic, created, and material. In its place Origen is proposing both a radically simplified division of Being into essential and accidental being, and a multiplication of the degrees of being based upon distinctions between essential and accidental Being. In any case the structure of the material realm looks like the following:

Formed Matter (created genera and species)

+

Unformed Matter (hypokeimenon-substrate)

2. The Categories of Being

2.1 Origen's doctrine of the categories is difficult to reconstruct. In general he continues the trajectory of categorical theory that we encountered in Clement and Albinus. Following Clement he subsumes intelligible and sensible reality under a single ousia and affirms that all ten categories have referential efficacy to the sensible realm and at least three have referential efficacy to the intelligible realm. Following Albinus he identifies substance with the highest God, and incorporates into his categorical scheme notions of potentiality and actuality.

The ease with which Origen employs his categorical doctrine suggests that the immense struggle in the early Middle Academy over the efficacy of the categories has been resolved. The Neo Pythagorean bias against the Peripatetic categories exemplified in the pseudo-Archytas, Eudorus, and to a limited extent in Philo has been overcome. In its place we find a Peripatetic categorical doctrine existing comfortably within a Platonic metaphysic. The revolutionary proposals of Clement and Albinus are dogma by the time of Origen.

This shift in categorical thinking is not a minor event in the history of Middle Platonism. It represents an unequivocal rejection of the doctrine of being proposed in the early Middle Academy by Eudorus and Philo, and signifies the movement in later Middle Platonic thinking with the doctrine of being proposed in Platonic circles with affinities to the emerging Aristotelian philosophy of the middle second century. This trend will not be reversed in the Platonic schools until the middle of the third century with Plotinus.

To fully appreciate the dimensions of Origen's categorical doctrine we shall examine it indirectly through his cognate doctrines of necessity and contingency, essentiality and accidentality. It is in these doctrines that Origen implies, but admittedly never explicitly states, that God is being (ousia) per se, and all other entities from the Logos to ensouled creatures and material things are being (ousia) per accidens. This means that God is the only entity that is characterized, at least categorically, by being alone. All other entities are characterized by being plus one or more of the categories. This distinction between God and everything else is presented by Origen in terms of the difference between existing necessarily and contingently, and between being essentially and accidentally. God is the only being who exists necessarily and is essentially. Hence, he is characterized by being alone. Only at the end of time when God is all in all do all things become one with God the Father, and are thus characterized, categorically, like the Father.

Thus, as we move into Origen's theoretic we must remember that much of what it says is dependent upon the doctrine of being and the categories held by Origen. Without his views on these doctrines he could never have proposed the first principles he does in the Periarchôn (De Principiis) and the writings which follow upon it.

2.2 Origen uses the categories in his philosophical writings, although he does not always refer to them. Ever since the first edition of the Aristotelian corpus prepared by Andronicus of Rhodes in the first century B.C., the Categories has been a subject of debate among Peripatetics, Platonists, and Stoics alike. Dexippus summarized and explained the importance of this debate among philosophers in this period (CAG, IV,2,5, 16-24).

Origen did not write a technical commentary on the Categories, but he is in the long line of Middle Platonists who found Aristotle's categories acceptable. They are relevant and applicable to the realms of Being and Becoming because both intelligibles and sensibles may be subsumed under a common ousia. To this extent Origen agrees with Albinus and Clement that the Peripatetic categories are applicable to a Platonic metaphysic.

Origen employs the Peripatetic categories to define being in the three divisions of reality. His division of reality is into two main spheres, Being and Becoming. Within this general division he differentiates between two levels of Being, viz., the realm of the "Ones," and the noetic realm, one level of Becoming, viz., the material realm, and the psychic realm, and one level of Non-Being, viz., the material substrate. In drawing these definitions Origen asserts: 1) that reality is divided ontologically into two Academic categories, and 2) that Aristotle's categories apply to all levels of reality. They have no referential efficacy to the first theological, but they do to the second and third theological-mathematicals,[122] and all created things.

Substance applies to all levels of reality, but only God the Father is substance per se. All the other entities are substance plus one or more of the ten categories, and hence are substance per accidens. How substance exists is also determined through the categories with the same per se/per accidens characterization. The structure of Being proposed by Origen has the following outline:

God

(ousia)

The Noetic Realm

The Logos and Holy Spirit

(ousia, pros, poiotês)

The Material Realm

(ousia, pros ti, poson, poion, poiein, echein, keisthai, pou,

pote, paschein)

It appears that Origen interprets the categories as about beings or things. Thus, they refer to Being qua Being in its many variations. He uses the categories to define Being qua Being, and to show that all Being may be subsumed under one common ousia called God the Father. There is no hint of the later Plotinian reformulation of categorical doctrine. Origen still works within the framework of reference he inherited from the Middle Platonic and Peripatetic traditions he draws from.

The doctrine of the categories is one of the most important elements of Origen's metaphysics. How he defines and uses them shows the extent to which his theoretic or physics takes on a Peripatetic hue. The categories constitute the structural framework of his understanding of Being, and whenever he defines the divine hypostases, or the intelligibles, or the sensibles, the categories are his way of determining their Being. Hence, when we enter into a description of Origen's first principles and his theoretic, we must keep in mind his use of this central doctrine. By means of it he links the different degrees of reality to each other, and subsumes them under his primary substance -- God the Father.

This is our brief introduction to Origen's theology and metaphysics. In the following sections we shall unfold Origen's philosophical system in detail, attempt to clarify what he is saying, and define what new norms he offers to Middle Platonic theoretic and physics. We shall begin with a description of his metaphysics, and then move on to propose a thesis which analyzes how Origen defines the structure of being.

3. First Principles: God and the Logos

3.1 Origen posits two first principles and three hypostases: God the Father, the first intellect, and the Logos-Son, the second intellect, are his first principles. The Holy Spirit, the third intellect, is the third hypostasis in his system, but it serves a soteriological function. The Holy Spirit is not a metaphysical principle.

Our entrance into Origen's doctrine of hypostases will be approached from the Periarchôn (De Principiis) I, 3, 5 (55, 4-56, 8). The formulation is reconstructed from the testimonies of Justinian and Jerome, and the redaction of Rufinus. Two factors are apparent from the start: 1) There are three entities set out in ascending order of importance, Holy Spirit, Son, and Father, which suggests a hierarchy of Being;[123] and 2) this hierarchy of Being is defined in terms of the "energy" and "activity" (enargia, actus), as well as the "power" (dynamis, potens) of each entity. This formulation is a central one because it informs us, at least partially, of how Origen viewed the nature of the relationship between God and the generated and created things. It also provides us with an initial insight into how Origen understood the structure of Being.

The Father extends his energy and power to everything that exists; the Son extends his power to all rational and non-rational things, and the Holy Spirit to a select group, the "saints."[124] If we follow the testimony of Jerome, Origen asserted a subordination of the sensible to the intelligible world, and more significantly an essential subordination of the three hypostases to each other (Jerome, Ep. ad Av. 2 = Migne XXII 1061). If we follow the version provided by Justinian, Origen subordinated the sensible world to the intelligible world, and made a distinction only in the degree of power each hypostasis possesses (Just. Ep. ad. Men., IX 524). If we follow Rufinus' redaction we are presented with a distinction between sensible and intelligible things, and the subordination of the former to the latter. The activity of the Father and Son are equal in terms of extension. However, a distinction is made, in terms of extension of power, between the Father and Son on the one hand, and the Holy Spirit.

Taken together these versions all agree on one point. There are distinctions between the physical and noetic world, and the noetic and supranoetic world. The point they disagree on is the nature of the relationship between the first two hypostases. The third hypostasis, in all three testimonies, is subordinated to the first two. Hence, the question to be addressed is: does Origen propose a doctrine of essential subordinationism (Jerome), or a doctrine of equivocity (Rufinus) between the Father and Son?

3.2 God: The First One

Origen places a first intellect, God the Father, at the apex of being. Origen's doctrine of God is based on the following points:

1.   God is non-material, and without movement, yet he is an intellect.

2.   He is far away from the sensible world, above any kind of created qualification.

3.   He is a monas, a hen, and an arche. [125]

4.   He cannot be comprehended by the human mind; he is known only to his Son; he is ineffable.

5.   He is necessary being and existence.

That God can have neither shape nor body nor parts nor any kind of created quality is standard Middle Platonic doctrine. This is why it appears that Origen's definition of the Father is based upon the first hypothesis of Plato's Parmenides (137d, 138a). Origen's God, being an intellect (noêsis, nooumenon: Cat. in Jh., IV,495,24), is endowed with thought, and is characterized by noetic-bouletic activity (Cat. in Jh., IV,495,20; De Princ., II,9,1 164,5ff.).

Origen's God is without movement and is non-material (C. Cels., VI,64 16; De Princ., I,1,5 20,5f.). This is what Origen means when he says that God is "beyond being" (Coh. ad Martyr., 47,43), and "beyond the being and intellect of all things" (C. Cels., VIII,38 188,11ff.). All other intelligible beings either move and/or are material. This is an important concept to grasp. Origen's God is not a Plotinian "One" beyond all being and intellect. God for Origen is an intellect and a being, but a type of intellect and being radically different from all others. [126]

We know that God is far away from the sensible world because he is "beyond the intellect and being" which is corporeal and definable (C. Cels., VIII,38 188,11ff.; IV,14 284,27). Indeed, he cannot be qualified materially at all. He is beyond time and space, and all the qualifications of material things (De Princ., I,1,5 20,5f.; I,1,6 21,10ff.; I,1,7 24,1ff.).[127]

Origen calls God a monas and a henada (De Princ., I,1,6 21,13ff.), and he is the first principle of all things (C. Cels., I,24 75,16). Origen is careful to make quite clear that this "One" is a noetic "Unity" that is the "ground" of the whole noetic world. Origen defines God as:

...intellectualis natura simplex, nihil omnio in se adiunctiones admittens; uti ne maius aliquid et inferius in se habere credatur, sed ut six ex omni parte monas, et ut ita dicam henas, et mens ac fons ex quo initium totius intellectualis naturae vel mentis est.

(De Princ., I,1,6 21,13ff.)

God is not an agnostos theos for Origen. He is known to his Son, and to the Holy Spirit (De Princ., I,1,8 25,13ff.). God, however, cannot be known directly by the human mind. In this sense he is "ineffable" (C. Cels., VII,43 2,13ff.). However, Origen implies that God may be known to the human intellect through the medium of the Son, and the agency of the Holy Spirit (Comm. in Jh., II,10 64-65). He cannot be known through the agency of human intellection alone, which is a type of sensible intellection (aisthêsis). He can be known through divine agency, which is a kind of intelligible intellection (noêsis-gnôsis).

Origen defines God as a necessary being and existant (In Lib. I Sam., I,11 20,16-21,7). This is an important concept for Origen. No other entity is necessary. Indeed, it is upon this postulate that Origen distinguishes the being and intellect of the Father from all others. This doctrine constitutes the fundamental feature of Origen's theoretic.

Summary

Origen's doctrine of God is both similar and distinct from those proposed by Philo and Clement. God is incorporeal, but he is not formless and without any attribute. He is above the monas or henas, but he is a hen and monas. He is not unknown. He is known to the Son, and indirectly to the human intellect through the agency of the Son and Holy Spirit. God is necessary being.

Two features are discernable from Origen's formulation. First, Origen's God is not the radically transcendent God of the earlier Platonic-Pythagorean theologies. He is knowable at least to his Son. Second, Origen's God appears to be a different kind of being and intellect from the definitions of God postulated by the earlier Middle Platonists. Origen's definition of God has close parallels to those proposed by Numenius (fr. 5,15,16,17) and Albinus (Did., 153,37; 161,1; 164,7,21,26,28ff.), but unlike the first God of

Numenius and Albinus, Origen's God is not so radically transcendent or unknowable. It is as if the ontological distance between the first and second principles has been lessened, but an intensification of the difference between the type of being and existence that characterizes God and his creation has been postulated.[128]

3.3 The Logos: The Second One

Origen's Logos plays an important role in his metaphysics. The concept has been much studied, and its dependence on the concepts of Clement and Philo has been generally recognized. However, the link between Origen, Clement, and Philo, at least metaphysically, has been overemphasized. To understand Origen's Logos, as a metaphysical principle, we have to move out of the conventional taxa of analysis employed by students of Origen. The present section aims, therefore, at drawing attention to the close connections which exist between Origen's Logos concept, and the corresponding metaphysical principles of later Middle Platonism and Peripateticism.

Origen's Logos concept is based on the following points:

1.   The Logos is transcendent and incorporeal, but has attributes.

2.   He is above the sensible world, and yet the sum total of the genera and species of the material world; he is an _arché_; and an _idea ideôn_ and an _eidos eidôn_.

3.   He is a _monas_ and _henas_, and the demiurgic intellect of creation.

4.   He is of the same substance of the Father, but exists differently than the Father does.

The primary distinction between Origen's Logos concept, and those of Philo and Clement is that Origen's Logos does not have different stages of existence.

As the second intellect the Logos is incorporeal (De Princ., I,2,2 28,17ff.), but contains within himself:

...scilicet in semet ipsa universae creaturae vel initia, vel rationes, vel species.
(De Princ., I,2,2 30,7ff.)

The Logos is incorporeal, and contains all things in himself. The Logos (also called wisdom) is that which:

...species scilicet in se et rationes totius praeformans et continens creaturae...
(De Princ., I,2,2 30,10ff.)

The Logos is also the paradigmatic idea or "idea of ideas" (C. Cels, VI,64 ii,135), and the "form of forms" (C. Cels., VI,64 ii,135). By this Origen means that the Logos is the primary intelligible and generic entity that contains within himself the genera and species of the created order (Just. Ep. ad Men.=Mansi IX 528,489d), and is the formative principle of all things. As Origen states:

...en archê hen ho logos hina kata tên sophian kai tous typous tou systêmatos ton en auto noêmaton panta gignetai.

(Comm. in Jh., I,119 113)

The distinction between Origen's definition of the Logos, and the Logos of Clement and Philo, is that Origen's Logos is not identical with the mind of God. Furthermore, there is no hint that Origen calls the Logos the "place" (chôra) of the ideas.[129] Rather the Logos is conceived as an active intellect that thinks the genera and species of creation within his mind, and who creates them outside of his mind. To grasp Origen's reformulation we must turn to his critique of the Middle Platonic doctrine of the ideas.[130] First, however, we shall describe Origen's Hypostatic triad.

3.4 The Hypostatic Triad: The Realm of the Ones

Origen calls the Logos a henada and a monada according to the testimony of Justinian (Just. Ep. ad Men.=Mansi IX 536d). This is likely correct since Origen's Logos is defined in terms of the second hypothesis of Plato's Parmenides (145c 1-5). Origen's Logos is based on the Neo Pythagorean interpretation of the second hypothesis from this work. Like most Middle Platonists Origen maintained that the intelligible world was "one" (e.g., Albinus, Did., 167,33-34), and that the second principle constituted the sum total of the noetic world.

The Logos is of the same substance of the Father (De Princ., I,2,5 33,8; I,2,6 34,23ff.), although he is not tout court like the Father. He is merely an image of the Father. The Logos subsists like the Father (De Princ., I,2,2 28,13ff.), but does not exist like the Father (In Lib. I Sam. Hom., I,11 20,16ff.). Unlike the Father who exists necessarily, the Logos exists contingently (De Princ., I,2,2 29,11ff.). The Logos is an eternally generated intellect and being (De Princ., I,2,4 33,4ff.).

The Son is said to be the only entity who "by nature" is with the Father from the beginning (Comm. in Jh. II,10 p. 65). This statement, when viewed within the context of (De Princ., I,2,8 38,14-39,4), suggests that "by nature" Origen means that the Son is made in the "likeness" of the Father (De Princ. I,2,8 p. 39,4-11. cf. In Jerem Hom. X 7 iii. p. 77,9-12; Comm. in Jh. XX 18 iv. p. 350, 24). Hence, the likeness of the Son to the Father is a formal likeness. Hence, the Father is both the formal and paradigmatic cause of the Son. This is what Origen means when he states:

...quod exinaniens se filius, qui erat in forma dei...

(De Princ. I,2,8 p. 38,16f.)

Thus, the Father is the final cause of the Son insofar as he is the form upon which the Son finds his desired end (e.g. De Princ. I,2,8 p. 38,14-39,4). There exists the substance of the Father, and the image of this substance. Insofar as the goal of the Son is to be like the Father in every detail, the Son is the first of created things in relation to the Father.

The Father is also the efficient cause of the Son. At (De Princ. IV,4,1 p. 349,11f.) Origen states that the Son was begotten of the Father's will, as wisdom the first-born of all creation. Justinian asserts that the word egenêthe, and the designation of the Son as ktisma, suggests that the Son was made in the image of the Father (Just. Ep. ad Men.=fr. 32 Koe.=Mansi IX 525,489b). Origen indeed says this but with a qualification omitted by Justinian. Origen asserts that since the Son is a likeness of the Father there was no time when he did not exist (De Princ. IV,4,1 p. 349,15ff.). Indeed the Son is begotten (gennêma), but he is eternally begotten (cf. In Jerem. Hom. IX 4 iii p. 70.; Ep. ad Heb. Fragmentum Pamphili Apologia Lomm. v. p. 297). This is a central qualification in Origen's philosophical theology. The Son is not just another created Being. He is the first of created beings as the only eternally generated being. This fills in the background to Origen's claim that the Logos exists differently than God. The Son is created. The Father is eternal.

The causal relationship between the Father and the Son holds for the Holy Spirit as well (e.g. Comm. in Jh. II, 10 iv. p. 64-65; cf. De Princ. P 4 p. 11,3ff.). The Father is the final or formal cause of the Holy Spirit (In Num. Hom. II,8 Comm. X. p. 120). The Holy Spirit exists with the Father through the Logos-Son. In this sensè he is one in nature with the Father and Son (De Princ. I,3,5 p. 54,20-56,8), but exists differently than the Father and the Son (cf. De Princ. P 4 p. 11,3ff.; Just. Ep. ad Men. fr. 9 Koe.=Mansi IX 524).

The evidence shows that the Son is the intrumental cause of the Holy Spirit. The Holy Spirit was made through the Son, and is the first in rank of all the things that were made through the Logos (Comm. in Jh. fr. 1 Koe. iv. p. 483,19ff.; (Comm. in Jh. II,10 iv. p. 64-65); De Princ. I,2,3 p. 30,9-15). Like the Son, the Holy Spirit is something created or begotten (gennêma: Just Ep. ad Men.=Mansi IX 528, 489.; cf. Epiphan Haer. 64.5: kai to pneuma to hagion ktiston eisêgêsato); cf. Jerome, Ep. ad Av. 2 Migne XXII 1060.). Origen understands the nature of the Holy Spirit's "creation" as different from the creation of the lower created things. Hence, we must be cautious about Jerome and Justinian's testimonies concerning Origen's definition of the "createdness" of the Holy Spirit.

3.5   There is no world-soul in Origen's theoretic as there was in earlier Middle Platonic proposals. He never identifies the Logos or the Holy Spirit as an anima mundi.[131] The Logos is the supreme law and harmony of the universe, and his logoi hold together, administer, and penetrate matter. However, as the formative principle that orders matter, the Logos is itself non-corporeal and without soul.

Origen explicitly refuses to identify his pneuma (Holy Spirit) with the pneuma of the Stoics. The Holy Spirit, thus, is not a world-soul either. The Holy Spirit has no metaphysical function. He brings the knowledge of God to the saints so that they may return to the Father. Hence, the Holy Spirit has no ontological or cosmological role to play in Origen's metaphysics.

In summary, Origen stresses the transcendence of God and places the Logos and Spirit in a subordinate relationship to one another. Each member of the hypostatic triad exists separately and differently from the other, but they all share the same substance. Origen explains the existential differences between the Father, Son, and Spirit in generative terms. The Father is eternal and ungenerated, the Son is eternally generated, and the Spirit is generated. Generation indicates that the Son and Spirit share the same essential characteristics as the Father. This distinguishes them from all other beings.

There was no time when the Son did not exist, but it appears there was a time when the Spirit did not exist. This is clear from his use of the term "eternal." Since the Spirit is not eternally generated it is subordinate to the Son. The Logos is the cosmological principle in Origen's theoretic. We can see this in our brief discussion of its role in the creation of the Spirit. The Spirit has no metaphysical function whatsoever, and is thus not a metaphysical principle.

3.6 The Noetic Realm

An important distinction between Origen and all the Middle Platonists examined up to this point is that the doctrine of ideas plays no role in his theoretic or physics. Koch is correct when he states:

...für Origenes haben die Ideen keine Funktion; sie stehen da als ein überrest vom ursprünglichen Platonismus, welchem auszulassen men sich nicht hat bequemen können.

(PP., 256)

For Origen the ideas are mere phantasia mentis (De Princ., II,3,6 122,4) of the human mind. They are unworthy of being ascribed to the divine mind at all.

He calls them in a Peripatetic fashion teretismata (C. Cels., I,13 66.6f.; II,12 141,1.cf. Arist., Anal. Post., 83a 33). This is a significant transitional moment in the history of Middle Platonic theoretic because the ideas performed a central function in the earlier Middle Platonic cosmologies. They serve a central function cosmologically and epistemologically in these earlier Platonic metaphysics.[132] Thus, our question must be, if the doctrine of the ideas is not utilized by Origen why is this so? What doctrine is proposed to take its place? We shall attempt an answer below.

Origen is aware of the doctrine of ideas. His reformulation of the doctrine is a conscious one. He follows the distinction made by Albinus between the primary and secondary intelligibles (Did., 166,2ff.; 55,34). For Origen the primary intelligible is the Logos-Son. He is the idea ideôn (C. Cels., VI, 64, 11, 135). He does not deny the existence of the secondary intelligibles, at least as they were formulated up to his time among Alexandrian Platonists, but his ideai (Comm. in Jh., IV 35 268,24f. VIII 24.324,6f.), and logoi (C. Cels., V 39.43, 24) are conceived as they prefigurations of all the genera and species of the sensible world. However, these prefigurations are not imaginary forms. They are the real genera and species of creation, not the imaginary forms the Greeks call ideas (De Princ., II,3,6). Let us unpack Origen's theory.

The Logos is the primary intelligible or the "idea of ideas" (C. Cels. VI 64 II, 135). The Logos, as primary intelligible, is also called the "being of beings" and "form of forms" (C. Cels. III 64 II 135). Indeed the Logos is a praefiguratio, of...

> panta ta genê kai ta eidê synaidia este...
>
> (Just. Ep. ad Men., = Mansi IX 528, 489d)

The ideas are that which are contained:

> kata tên sophiou kai tous typous tou systêmatos ton en auto noêmaton.
>
> (Comm. in Jh., I, 24, 1f.)

The Logos-Son is the primary intelligible, who contains within himself the secondary intelligibles which are the eternal genera and species of creation.

Origen's definition of the Logos-Son as an idea ideôn and as an ousia ousiôn cannot be separated (C. Cels., VI, 64 II 135). As the idea of ideas the Logos is the primary form of all created things. As the substance of substances the Logos is the principle which gives substantial existence to all created things (De Princ., I, IV,5,68,10ff.).

The logoi are "things according to nature" (ta kata physin: C. Cels., V 39. 43, 24), and exist within the mind of the second hypostasis as a prefiguration of the intelligible and sensible worlds (C. Cels., VI 63 135, 10); Comm. in Jh., XIX 22 324, 7; De Princ. I, 4, 4 67, 12). By logoi Origen presumably means the immanent ideas or logoi spermatikoi. He also calls them eidê. In both cases these are ideas or forms-in-matter, and nature is prefigured according to the eternal genera and species situated in the divine intellect. Since, the Logos is the being of beings and the ground of all things (De Princ., I, 4, 5 68, 10ff. cf. C. Cels VI, 64 ii, 135). He thinks the ideas, which exist in God's wisdom (De Princ., I, 4, 4 67, 12; Comm. in Jh., VIII 24 324, 7). However, the sensible world is not made in the image of transcendent ideas in the mind of God. Rather:

> Et si utique in sapientia omnia facta sunt, cum sapientia semper fuerit, secundum preafigurationem semper erant "in sapientia" ea, quae protinus etiam substantialiter facta sunt.
>
> (De Princ., I, 4, 5 68, 1ff.)

Hence, the universe and its creation are eternal. Both are prefigured in the divine mind and brought into existence through the agency of the Logos.

As an archikê dynamis, the Son contains the ideas in his mind, as a prefiguration (De Princ., I, 2, 30, 7f.; I, 4, 3 65, 9-12; cf. I, 4, 5 67, 19-68, 15). As an energeias, the Logos creates these prefigurations by instantiating in matter the beginnings, causes, and species of creation (De Princ., I, 2, 12 45, 10f.).

Origen employs the standard Middle Platonic metaphysic of prepositions (cf. Theiler, VN., 18f.)[133] to explain physical creation. The Logos is the efficient and material cause of creation (Comm. in Jh. II.10 iv 64-65). Koch is correct (PP., 255) that it is in the terms to ex ou, which is "matter" (hylê), and to'kath'ho, which is "form" (eidos), that we gather clues which explain Origen's theory of physical creation (Comm. in Jh. I,1 20ff.; cf. 24,9). Matter is formed into bodies (sômata) by a demiurgic agent, viz., the Logos-Son.

Koch is also right that Origen's doctrine of creation has a Peripatetic dimension (PP., 252,255). Koch notes that Origen utilizes the Aristotelian hylê eidos-concept and that it starts at the center of his understanding of creation. Matter is created (formed) by the demiurgic intellect. He forms matter into bodies, and thereby creates a sensible world (C. Cels., IV 54 327,21) in accordance with the eternal prefigurations of divine wisdom (De Princ., I,4,5,67,19-68.15). Hence, it is by means of these two models that Origen explains creation.

In summary, the noetic realm is made up of the Logos, and presumably the Spirit. As the primary intelligible, and the prefiguration of the sensible world, he eternally contains within his intellect the genera and species of this word. Once the Logos forms matter in accordance with these logoi a world is created. Central to this aspect of his physics is the notion of the Logos as efficient and instrumental cause. The Logos forms matter into bodies in the process of creating the world. The actualization of his prefigurations in matter results in the formation of a world. They do not exist in the divine mind prior to their actualization in matter, and once they are in nature, they are called logoi and ideai.

3.7 The Material Realm

If we couple Origen's doctrine of matter, and his doctrine of the actualization of the eidê-logoi in the sensible world through the agency of the demiurgic intellect, we can reconstruct Origen's physics.

The relation of material things to intelligible things is the relation of noetic act to the potentiality of matter to be acted upon. The agency or instrument of this relation of cause and effect is the Logos (Comm. in Jh., fr. 1 = 483-485). The Logos is the efficient and instrumental cause of the universe (Comm. in Jh., fr. 1 484, 12ff.). He is the creator who causes the heaven and earth's coming into being. He is the cause of being and existence of the intelligibles and the sensibles (Comm. in Jh., fr. 1, 495, 2ff.).

The relation of the sensibles to the intelligibles is the relation of material things to the primary intelligible, the Logos, who causes the material things to exist by the instantiation of his eidê-logoi into matter. The relation of the sensibles to the intelligibles is not that of copy to model, the Platonic thesis, but that of matter to form, the Peripatetic thesis.

The material substrate is the raw material of potential bodies for Origen, and the sensibles are the combination of hylê and eidê (hypokeimenon and logoi). The material substrate is fashioned into bodies when it is created by the Logos according to the logoi which are ta kata physin (C. Cels., V. 39 43, 24f.). Once created into bodies matter constitutes Relative Being (Comm. in Jh., I, 1 24, 7ff.).

Origen's theory is very close to Albinus' (Did., 162, 25ff.; 163, 21f.).[134] However, the copy-model theory, which plays a role in Albinus' explanation of the creation of matter into bodies, is toned down considerably by Origen. For Origen, matter is formless and without quality before its formation or creation. It is a kind of "non-being" (Comm. in Jh., I. 17 22, 16f.). Matter becomes Being by an act of the Logos who orders it as its efficient and instrumental cause.

The created realm, and the sensibles within it exist in two stages. First, the Logos contains, all the eidê and genê of the sensible world in potentia and intra-mentem (De Princ., I, 2, 2 30, 7f.). Second, the eidê and genê are then instantiated in matter (e.g., Comm. in Jh., XIII. 21 245, 1ff.). The creative activity of the Logos, in actu, causes bodies to exist extra mentem, in the universe (e.g. C. Cels., IV. 57 329, 25; De Princ., III, 6, 6 329, 8ff.). Again with Origen there are no divine ideas which function as the paradigms for sensible creation as in earlier Middle Platonic doctrine. The ideas cease to have any significant cosmological function. They are no longer the paradigms of the material world. They are the potential genera and species of an actual world to be created by the Logos.

This is clear if we examine Origen's use of what Theiler called the 'metaphysics of prepositions' (VN., 18f.). Origen speaks of (material) things that have the cause of their movement, that are moved from without, and that are moved through themselves (De Princ., III, 1, 2 196, 16ff.; Orat., VI,1 311,16ff.). The prepositions are: "from within" (apo); "out of" (ex); and "through" (dia). It is clear that all movement of bodies is due to an efficient and instrumental cause. The efficient-instrumental cause of all physical things is the Logos. He is "that through which" (to dia), and "that in which" (to eu: Comm. in Jh., I.10 63-64) matter is formed. The movement "from within," "out of," and "through" refers to instrumental cause or the Logos to dia. The Logos is also cause as the Immanent Form, or (to eu), insofar as matter ensouled is held together by form and characterized by qualities. The Logos is not referred to as a Paradigmatic cause, or "that towards which" (to ept'ho: cf. Seneca, Ep., 65,4ff.). This prepositional cause has dropped out of Origen's vocabulary. Origen had discarded the notion of the transcendent idea (ideas) as paradigmatic cause. Origen's formulation represents a shift in Platonic thinking.

The concept of Paradigmatic cause was utilized by Seneca (Ep., 65,4ff.), Potamon of Alexandria (Diog. Laert., P 17), Philo (e.g., Prov., 102f.; Cher., 125ff.), Clement (Strom., ii.20.110 [ii.173.17ff.]), and Albinus (Did., 163,35ff.) to explain physical creation. Origen could have presented the Logos as the Paradigmatic cause of creation, but he avoids employing this causal concept. The notion of paradigmatic cause is only used when he explains the creation by God of the Logos-Son (C. Cels., VI 64 II 135; De Princ., IV,4 1 349,11).

In summary, the created realm includes all those things formed from the material substrate. For Origen's scheme the Logos potentially comprehends all actualities, and then actualizes them thereby creating a world. Hence, Origen's Logos is both an intellect and a demiurge like Nichomachus' Technikos logos (Theol. Arith., 4,6). Like Numenius' second God, Origen's Logos is an "image" or "imitation" of the first God and first principle of Being (fr. 16 des Places), who creates a world of corporeal things.

3.7 The greatest dissimilarity between the philosophical theology of Origen and those of antecedent Middle Platonists is that Origen's third hypostasis is not a world-soul, but a Holy Spirit. We cannot agree with Koch (PP., 254) that Origen's reluctance to identify the Logos or Holy Spirit with the world-soul is the result of his Christian background. Philo and Clement, as noted, identify the Logos with the world-soul in their theoretics. In order to understand why Origen took this metaphysical step it is necessary to describe his doctrine of matter.

3.8 Origen denied the existence of an original matter, but he did not support a theory of creatio ex nihilo. The evidence suggests that Koch is right (PP., 253). Origen holds a theory of matter akin to Albinus' (Did., 162,25ff.). For Origen matter is "without quality" (apoios: De Princ., IV,4,7 357,29ff. cf. II,1,4 109-111). It is treptê and allolôtê (De Princ., II,1,4 109,22 cf. notes by Koe.). Once formed matter has qualities and constitutes a cosmos.

For Origen, the material substrate has an independent existence and was not created in time.[135] Furthermore, matter is without quality and has no specific structure (Orat., 27,8. 367,16). It has a kind of "non-existence" as the formless stuff of the material universe (Comm. in Jh., I,17 22,16ff.). Origen equates it with "non-being" (Orat.,27,8. 367ff.). God takes the "material substrate" (hypokeimenon: C. Cels. IV.60.332,9f.) and it is "informed with qualities" (De Princ., IV,4,6. 357,10f.). It is something that can only be grasped "by an artificial mode of thought" stripped of all qualities (simulata quiodammodo cogitatione: De Princ., IV,4,7 358,24).

Origen's doctrine of matter is different from those of earlier Middle Platonists such as Clement (Strom., v.89.6), Moderatus (Simpl., In Phys., 231,4-5), and Numenius (Proclus, In Tim., 299c). His doctrine of matter is discontinuous with the Middle Platonic doctrines of an eternal matter held by Plutarch, Apuleius, and Albinus (cf., as Lilla, C., 193-196). Origen does not identify matter as eternal as did several Middle Platonists (cf. Plutarch, De An Procr. in Tim., 1014b, f.; Apuleius, De Plat., i, 191, Albinus, Did., 162,25ff.; 163,3-7). However, his view that being contains form, and that which is devoid of form is not being, does go back to the Aristotelian doctrine of matter without form as 'non-being' (cf., Arist. Phys., 1. 191a 8-12). This Aristotelian maxim underlies Origen's definition of matter, and frames the ontological status it has in Origen's metaphysic. Since the material substrate is formless and without quality it is not being. Once it has been formed and given quality it gains the status of being.

Origen's refusal to equate the Logos or Holy Spirit with the world-soul is clear from his doctrine of matter. Matter (hypokeimenon) is a kind of "non-being." (ex ouk ontôn: Comm. in Jh. I.17 22.16f. cf. De Princ., II,1,5 111,17). Once formed material things become "accidental" being (kata symbebêkos: e.g., Comm. in Jh., II,18 75,8) they exist as a type of Being once created (or formed), but they do so only to serve God's "will and thought" (boulêsis, noêsis: De Princ., II,9,1 164,1ff.). Such a conception excludes any consideration of identifying the Logos or the Holy Spirit with the soul of the world and with matter.

Given the fact that: 1) the substrate of all material things is not being; and 2) that once formed all created material things are "accidental," it follows that it would not be possible for Origen to equate any of the lower hypostases, viz., the Logos or Holy Spirit, with the soul of the world. Soul is a created composite of hylê and eidos, and hence a kind of "accidental" being. The Logos and the Holy Spirit are generated (created) but they are not a composite of matter and form. They are non-corporeal and, a kind of "essential" being (De Princ., I,2,2, 28,17ff.; I,3,4 54,7ff.). They participate in the Being of the Father (Comm. in Jh., II, 10. IV 64-65; cf. Comm. in Jh., fr. 1. iv. 483-85), and are not equated with a soul of any type, nor defined as such in any context.

Origen, thus, does not postulate a Third One immanent in the created universe that participates in the First and Second "Ones" like Moderatus, Nichomachus, Numenius, or Albinus. Like Nichomachus, Numenius, and Albinus, however, his second intellect is the formative agent of creation and orders matter into bodies. Hence, Origen's first principles parallel antecedent Middle Platonic proposals in both its doctrines of the first two hypostases, and its doctrine of matter. It differs in its absence of a third hypostasis defined as a world-soul, and in a theory of creation based on the cosmology of the divine ideas. Still less does Origen's theoretic compare with those proposed by Philo and Clement. It is as if Origen has set out on a new path metaphysically. In our next sections we shall attempt to reconstruct this fresh approach to Middle Platonic metaphysics.

The material realm consists of all entities made from form and matter. This includes all created entities such as rational creatures.[136] These include angels, rational spirits, and human souls. Since they are created these rational creatures are not good essentially. They do, however, possess free-will to choose the good and the moral responsibility to do so. This assumption made it necessary for Origen to postulate the fall of rational creatures away from God, and this fall accounted for the creation of the material world. Those that fell least were the angels, and those that fell the farthest were the powers of wickedness.

Although these considerations take us out of the realm of philosophy they do inform us of the religious side of Origen's theoretical formulations. The fall and rise of rational creatures from and to God reflects the dynamic nature of Origen's universe, and the degrees of reality it constitutes. The angels are the least corporeal of the rational creatures, and the human being is at the bottom of the psychic scale. Origen's belief that rational spirits animate the heavenly bodies reflects the scientific assumptions of his time. The stars are animate creatures, who will be released from their bondage to material bodies when in the consummation God is all in all.

4. Doctrine of Being

4.1   In our description of Origen's first principles we neglected to investigate in detail his answer to the three problematics which confronted Middle Platonism: 1) what is the relation of the sensibles to the intelligibles; 2) what is the relation of the intelligibles to each other; and 3) how is God the first principle of all things? In the following sections we shall offer a thesis that illustrates how Origen proposed to answer them. From the preceding analysis we have hints which point toward his solution to these problems. It is now our task to unpack them.

Origen proposed a series of new answers to the perennial problematics of Middle Platonic metaphysics. Much of the material he introduces is new to the Platonic milieu. Hence, there results a formulation of new norms for the Platonic philosophy. These norms arise from Origen's imaginative use of Peripatetic theories within a Platonic context.

At the core of Origen's theoretic lies the theory of necessary and contingent Being, and the correlate theory of essential and accidental existence. The theory begins with a distinction in the being and existence of the hypostases, and it ends with a new norm proposed for the definition of the being and existence of the created intelligibles and sensibles. The theory states, roughly, that God the Father is the only necessary Being, and hence the only Being who has an essential existence. In God essence and existence are one. The Logos-Son is a necessary Being, but it has an existence which is superadded to its essence. It has a kind of accidental existence. The Holy Spirit is a necessary Being as well, but its existence is also accidental.[137] Its existence is even less than that of the Logos-Son and the Father. All the rational and non-rational things are fully contingent Beings, and the existence superadded to their essence is wholly accidental.

Our entrance into Origen's proposal is from the pericope which opened our examination of Origen's first principles, viz., De. Princ., I, 3, 5, 55, 4-56, 8). Origen lays out a triadic hierarchy of hypostases in which each is related to one another in terms of an economy of energy and power. God extends to all things, the Son to rational and non-rational things, and the Holy Spirit to the "saints" alone. God the Father, the hyperousion hen, stands at the apex of the hierarchy. The Son, the ousion hen, is "less" (in degree) than the Father according to Justinian (Ep ad Men.=Mensi IX 524), and "inferior" according to Jerome (Ep. ad Av. 2=Mensi XXII 1066). Dillon raises the important point of whether this formula suggests an essential subordinationism among Origen's hypostases (NPT., 20). It appears that he is correct that it does not. Origen is careful to argue that all the hypostases are equal essentially (e.g., De Princ., I, 3, 54, 12). However, the question remains does Origen propose an existential subordinationism among the hypostases?

In all the variants, the hierarchy proposed is one of energy, power, and degree to which each hypostasis reaches into the universe. The Father is "more" than the Logos and Holy Ghost because God's energy and power extends farther, and encompasses more entities than the energy and power of the Son or Holy Spirit.

Examining the Neo Platonic sources Dillon finds convincing parallels between Origen's formulation and propositions (7) and (57) of Proclus' Elements of Theology (CNPT., 21):

7)   every productive cause is superior to that which it produces all that is produced by secondary beings is in a greater

57)   measure produced from those prior and more determinative principles from which the secondary ones were derived.

According to Proclus' model the supreme principle (the Good) extends its _enargeia_ to the lowest levels of creation, even to what is unformed. The second principle, (Nous), extends its _enargeia_ to rational and non-rational beings. The third principle, (Soul), extends least for taking in only what has life.

Dillon is correct to be cautious in identifying Origen's formula with Proclus' (CNPT., 22). First, this model can only be traced as far back as Syrianus. Second, Proclus' formulation is structurally distinct in several of its features from Origen's proposal. Thus, for the moment, let us bracket the Origen-Proclus hypothesis.

The Middle Platonic and Neo Pythagorean parallels offer another road to us. Dillon notes (CNPT., 23) striking similarities between Origen's formulation and those of Moderatus, Nichomachus, Numenius and Albinus.[138] However, the deficiencies here are equally obvious. Although these Middle Platonists present God, Nous, and Soul in a hierarchy with concentric spheres of influence, there is either no specific definition of the nature of the relation between the hypostases, viz., the Pythagoreans, or if one is postulated the three entities are equivocal in essence and existence, viz., Albinus. How the divisions of Being are proposed, and how the structures of Being are defined by these thinkers does not parallel Origen's _enargeia-dynamis_ model sufficiently to assert that they are the sources for Origen's model. Hence, the Middle Platonic-Pythagorean hypothesis must be bracketed as well. We must look elsewhere for Origen's paradigm.

A third option would be to examine the Peripatetic sources.[139] We shall now do this in detail. Special care will be taken to examine the writings of Alexander Aprodisias, Origen's elder contemporary at Alexandria. The entrance into the Aristotelian proposal will be through a concept known to Alexander and ascribed to Plato by Aristotle — the tripartite division of Being.

4.2   The background to the notion that Being is tripartite can be traced back to the testimonies of Aristotle concerning Plato's definition and division of Being (Met. III.2, 1004a2; Phys. II.7, 198a29-31). Aristotle reports that Plato divided _ousia_ into the ideas (intelligibles), mathematicals, and sensibles. Merlan is correct (PNP; 58) that whether or not Plato actually divided being in this manner is not an important question. Nor is it an important issue whether Aristotle actually held this division. (Zeller is correct that it fits the preserved writings of Aristotle very badly (Phil. d. Gr. II/2[4] (1921), p. 179-181).) The important question is whether or not the mathematicals are _subsistentia_? This problem was debated by both Platonists and Peripatetics from the Old Academy through the Neo Platonic schools. The debate circled around the question of "multiple" realism, i.e. a realism asserting the subsistence of more than one type of non-sensibles and universals.[140]

In an answer to this question, Origen postulates three divine hypostases in descending order of energy, power, and value. They are the Father, Son, and Holy Spirit. All three hypostases are fully subsistent beings, but they exist in different ways (De Princ., I,3,5 55,4ff.). The Father is the only hypostasis which is a necessary existant (I. Sam., I,11 20,16ff.). The Logos and Spirit exist contingently. Hence, if the Son and Holy Spirit are hypostases which exist differently than the Father, is it possible that the power they exercise in the world is defined in terms of how they exist differently from the Father?

To answer this question adequately, but not completely, we have to turn to Speusippus and his doctrine of mathematicals. It is generally assumed that Speusippus' doctrine survives for the philosophy of late antiquity in the Neo Pythagorean schools. This is clearly accurate, but we must not ignore a second philosophical tradition it probably survived in, the Peripatetic. Aristotle's works were studied and commented upon extensively in this school tradition.[141] Speusippus was one of his major adversaries in his writings. This could not have gone unnoticed by Aristotle's pupils in the Old Lyceum as well as the New. If so, then we have a probable source for Origen's doctrine of the distinction he makes between necessary and contingent being. Let us turn now to a brief sketch of the doctrine of Speusippus on the mathematicals.

Speusippus substituted numbers for the ideas. Like Plato, Speusippus thought that without some kind of direct knowledge all knowledge and thought are impossible. He postulated direct knowledge of numbers because of the ontological priority of the ideal numbers to other kinds of entities. This is an important fact for at least two reasons. For Speusippus numbers are the first entities. The point is like the One, and the second principle of magnitude is like multiplicity, which is the second principle of number, but not identical with it (Arist., Metaphys., 1085a 32-34; Top., 108b 26-31). He speaks of the priority and self-subsistence of the decad, using wording based upon the Timaeus, which Plato used to describe the ideas (cf. Iamblichus, Theol. Arith., 82, 10-85, 23). According to Speusippus, magnitudes imitate or are similar to the numbers. The point is associated with one, the one with two, the triangle with three, and the pyramid with four. In magnitudes Speusippus sees the presence of the decad (1+2+3+4=10). Magnitudes presuppose numbers. Thus all entities, save numbers and the soul, are like a point. Each thing is the focus of all relations that make it different from everything else (Arist., Metaphys., 1044a 7).

Given his assumptions that there must be a direct knowledge, and his rejection of the ideas as the hypostatization of all universal concepts, Speusippus was led by epistemological and ontological considerations to postulate the mind's direct knowledge of the separately existing mathematical numbers.

Speusippus' numbers are not mere abstractions or concepts, but individual entities that exist outside of time and place, like Plato's ideas. Although there is some difficulty in deciphering exactly what Speusippus meant, it appears that he maintained that each number is a congeries of homogeneous and undifferentiated monads which equal a mathematical number. If he maintained this, then he postulated the existence of separately existing mathematical numbers. He proposed that if numbers have separate existence there is a first One, a first Two, and first Three and so on. However, these numbers are not Plato's ideal numbers, which are congeries of units, but separately existing numbers. In short, Speusippus postulated what Aristotle criticized him for postulating, namely, the existence of separately existing mathematical numbers, and incomparable numbers (Arist., Metaphys., 1083a20-b1).

The significance of Speusippus' formulation is its impact on subsequent Platonic thought. His One becomes a metaphysical principle equated with Aristotle's own unmoved mover (Arist., Metaphys., 1075a31-b1). For Speusippus mathematical numbers are the cause and substance of things (Arist., Metaphys., 1090a10-13;p 1075b27-28; b37-1076a4). It appears that Speusippus did not single out a single, separate, final cause of the universe (Arist., Metaphys., 1075b37-1076a4). He maintained different kinds of substances with their own particular principles with the connection between substances and principles as similarity (Iamblichus, Theol. Arith., 82, 10-85, 23 de Falco).

Speusippus, at least according to Aristotle, posited a One (to hen, monas) and a multiplicity (to plêthos, polla) as the principles (archai) of mathematical numbers. He also maintained that the point (stigma) was similar to the One and multiplicity and was the principle of mathematical magnitudes (Arist., Metaphys., 1083a20-b1; 1092a35-b3; 1087b4-9, 26-33; 1085b4-27; 1091b22-26, 30-35; 1075a31-b1; 1085a31-b4, b27-34; Top., 108b23-31).

It is unclear if the One is beyond being, or if it is non-existent (Arist., Metaphys., 1092a11-17). We only know that the One is identical with the number one, and is the principle or beginning of number. Furthermore, as a number the One has a separate existence as all the other numbers have. Thus, the numbers are first entities, and the One is the principle of number as a numerical monad (Arist., Metaphys., 1083a20-b1; 1085b4-27). The unity of any entity is due to its relation in similarity to this One or Monad.

Speusippus, according to Aristotle's testimony, posited multiplicity as the material element of number and as a contrary to the One (Arist., Metaphys., 1087b4-9, 26-33). It may be that multiplicity is the second principle of number, and not an element of number, or the material cause of number, or contrary to the One (cf. Taran, S., 39-41). However, the evidence is too incomplete to make a firm decision on this question even if the inner consistency of Speusippus' first principles points to the latter interpretation. In any case he posited two first principles, or at least one, and identified them with number. This theory would have important impacts upon later Platonic interpretations.

Upon these postulates Speusippus maintains that there is a first One, or incomparable number. This is the first principle of all mathematical numbers since it is the first mathematical number (Aelian, Varia Historia, 3, 19; cf. Arist., Metaphys., 1028b21-24). In positing the One as the first ousia he sows the seeds of the Neo Pythagorean theology which becomes so influential in later Platonic thought. Proclus says as much in his (In Parm., 38, 32-40, 7). Although his testimony is of little value for the reconstruction of Speusippus' first principles it does point out that he was considered as a source for this doctrine.

In summary, Speusippus' doctrine of mathematicals arises out of a criticism of Plato's doctrine of ideas. Replacing the ideas with the mathematicals as the eternally subsisting ground of being, Speusippus postulated that there existed a distinction between the number One, the number Two and so on. These mathematicals became first principles in themselves.

The interpretation and transmission of this doctrine is almost impossible to trace and explain in Aristotle's writings let alone in the writings of Alexander who comes to this doctrine, probably through the Peripatetic literature, almost five centuries later. To reconstruct the doctrine we must view it as these Peripatetics viewed it. Since Speusippus was a member of the Old Academy it is likely that he represents the "platonists" Aristotle refers to in his discussion. This is conjecture. It cannot be demonstrated conclusively.

The doctrine of the tripartition of being was known to Alexander of Aphrodisias. He responds to Aristotle's discussion of the threefold division of being (Metaphys., III.2, 1004a 2) in his commentary (In Metaphys., 250f. Hayduck). Another Peripatetic, the so-called pseudo-Alexander, also comments upon this doctrine (In Metaphys., 446,35-447,3).

Alexander amends Aristotle's division of being (ousia). The theologicals, astronomicals, and physicals, rather than theologicals, mathematicals, and physicals, constitute the three types of being. The theologicals are immaterial and unmoved; the astronomicals are imperishable but moveable, and the physicals are perishable and movable. The motives of Alexander's reformulation lie within the context of a Peripatetic problematic, and are not of importance for this study (cf. In Metaphys., 251,34-38). What is important is that he is the first source from the philosophical literature of the second century who accepts the postulate of three different spheres of being.

The pseudo-Alexander also accepts this tripartite division (In Metaphys., 446,35-447,3). However, he keeps the Aristotelian division of being into theologicals, mathematicals, and physicals. This triadic division is then placed within an ontological scheme wherein the theologicals and mathematicals are described as non-moved and immaterial (akinêta, chôrista), and the physicals described as moved and material (kinêta, achôrista). This amounts to a division between those things which are unmoved and immaterial, and those which are moved and material. The only distinction made between the theologicals and mathematicals is that the latter may be abstracted by thinking. Apparently the theologicals cannot be abstracted by thinking.

The Peripatetic doctrine of the tripartition of being is important because it suggests a theory which could be easily adapted to a Platonic metaphysics. There are three divisions of being with the mathematicals (astronomicals) constituting a tertium quid between the theologicals and physicals. The evidence suggests that it was introduced into Platonism proper by Ammonius Saccas (cf. Porphyry, Isag., 11,30-12,8 Busse). It is from this source that Origen probably culled the doctrine.

4.3   Origen's theoretic adapts two important aspects of this doctrine. First, there is the postulate of a triadic division of Being. Second, there is the identification of the lower theologicals with the mathematicals. The importance of this threefold division is that it permits Origen to postulate spheres of influence for each theological (De Princ., I,3,5 55,6ff.) and to propose that the theologicals exist differently from one another (e.g., In Lib. I Sam. Hom., I,11 20,16ff.).

From our sketch of Origen's theoretic it is clear that he called the Father a monas and hen and the Logos-Son a monada and henada. It was on the basis of Origen's terminology that Justinian accused him of proposing a Pythagorean first principles (Just., Ep. ad Men.=Mansi IX 536d). Terminologically Justinian was correct. Conceptually he may not have been. The inner logic of Origen's proposal suggests a Peripatetic pedigree to his doctrine.

Origen proposed a theoretic which combined the first two hypotheses in Plato's Parmenides and the Peripatetic doctrine of the tripartite division of being originally proposed by Aristotle in his Metaphysics. Let me explain.

Origen's hypostases are immaterial and without movement (chôrista, akinêta). They are defined in terms of the first two hypotheses of the Parmenides. They are hen and henada respectively.

Origen's first One is absolutely transcendent and is not a countable unit. He is the absolutely simple One of the first hypothesis of Plato's Parmenides. Origen's second One is both transcendent and a countable unity. He is the pregnant One of the second hypothesis of Plato's Parmenides. God the Father is God par excellence for Origen and is not identified with any mathematical number. The Son (and Holy Spirit) are God only by attribution. The Logos is not the henad which is utter unity and simplicity, rather he is the henad which is unity in plurality, demiurge, prefiguration of the world.

The Logos-Son thus stands as something distinct and derivative in relation to God, but as something which mediates between God and the World. In short, the Logos is that tertium quid between God and the universe distinct from both, and yet mediating between both.

In the Platonic and Peripatetic sources we have examined in this study we have seen that the ideas mediate ontologically and epistemologically between God and the world. The Logos is the primary intelligible of Origen's theoretic. As the primary intelligible called Unity and One is it possible that Origen identified the Logos with the mathematical One of the long lost Speusippan theoretic? This we cannot know, but we do know that Speusippus' doctrines lived in the Lyceum and the Academy. Could it be that Origen tapped into this dormant doctrine to offer a new doctrine of his own? If he did this is what it would look like.

God the Father is the absolutely transcendent One above the Logos and the world. The Logos-Son is transcendent but a Unity, an idea of ideas, a form of forms. He is eternally generated by his Father, thus he is of the same substance. Since he is generated he exists differently than the Father who created him. In Origen's proposal God is the first theological and the Logos is the second. Furthermore, God is not a countable unit and the Logos is. Hence, the Logos is a mathematical as well as a theological.

The Spirit is difficult to define within this framework. Since he is generated by the Logos and distinct in his own right from the other created creatures he is like the Logos and unlike God and the world, at least existentially. In this sense the Spirit too is a tertium quid between the Father and the universe.

In summary, it appears that Origen makes a distinction between theologicals, mathematicals, and physicals. He identified God with the first, the Logos and the Spirit with the second, and the created world with the third. The background to his theory is difficult to trace but it has its origins in Peripatetic sources that contain and sustained debates about Speusippus' mathematicals. The importance of Origen's adoption of this doctrine is that it aids him in making the distinction between necessary and contingent existence, God par excellence and God by attribution.

In Origen's division of types of being, the second and third theologicals (the Son and Holy Spirit) play an important role. They mediate between the first theological (the Father, and the realm of the eternally unchanging and "really" real), and the created physicals (the realm of the permanently changing and "relatively" real).

4.4 Origen's theory of being and existence is also based upon the distinction between "essential" and "accidental" being and existence. This theory, in turn, is based upon the notion that there are three ways in which the entities of the universe exist. There is God the Father who exists as a necessary being, the Logos and the Spirit who exist as contingent beings, and the physicals who exist as contingent beings. Finally, since God is the necessary existent his power stretches to all levels of the universe. The Logos, as the first in rank among contingent beings, has his power extent only to the rational creatures. The Spirit, as the second in rank among contingent beings, has his power extent only to the select among the rational creatures who are called the "saints." The key to Origen's formulation is the postulate that all three types of being exist differently. Upon this axiom he proceeds to structure being making the distinction between essential and accidental being and necessary existence and contingent existence. On the basis of this postulate, Origen can claim that all things save God exist accidentally, until God is all in all. The Logos, Spirit, and the other created entities are not accidental because they are a different substance from the Father. They are accidental because they exist differently than the Father. Only the Father exists necessarily. All else exists contingently.

Origen's doctrine does not exhibit the tight technical terminology of the Peripatetic doctrine. Origen never uses the terms symbebêkota-per accidens to define the second and third theologicals, only to define the rational-created entities (logikai ousiai, psychai). Nonetheless, how he goes about defining the existence of these entities points to the paradoxical datum that per definitionem they are 'accidental.'

How this can be so, and how Origen unfolds this theory, will be unpacked below. The first question to be asked is what is the nature of the relation between the subsistents? The relation is hierarchical, as Origen's language clearly shows, but how is it possible for Origen to postulate three hypostases which are different and also the same (De Princ. I,2,6 p. 34,22f.; 36,7ff.)?

5. Being and Existence

5.1 Origen isolates one hypostasis and calls it the ground of Being-itself (In Lib. I Sam. Hom., I, II (20, 19ff.).[142] Universality and necessity are the characteristics of God the Father, and they belong to him alone. Only he, as first God and first intellect, is the first principle and cause of all things. However, God's universality and necessity manifests itself in different ways throughout the different levels of Being.

God pertains to one nature, per se viz., himself, (In Lib. I Sam. Hom., I. II 20, 19ff.). He also pertains per se to the Son and Holy Spirit and the rational beings (Comm. in Jh., II, 10 64-65; fr. 1. 483-85). He pertains per accidens to the non-rational things (Comm. in Jh., II 18, 75, 8). The reason for this is implied in the notion of "first" or "highest." If the first cause did not pertain to God alone necessarily and universally, he could not be a first cause of all things (e.g., De Princ., I, 1, 6 22, 1, 25; C. Cels., I, 21 72, 14). If this were not the case, cause would pertain to God's nature by reason of prior cause or causes, and he would be neither universal or necessary. Yet, he is the first cause of Being (e.g., Comm. in Jh., II, 10 64, 5 ff.), and pertains to all the other types of being (In Lib. I Sam. Hom., I.II 20,19ff.). Let us examine this briefly.

Origen understands the cause of the universe as the result of a first cause. God is the cause of Being in all of its different types, in all the levels of generated and created Being. This is clear when Origen lists the four causes, e.g. final, efficient, instrumental, and material, and reduces them to a unity of causes subsisting in the realm of the two "Ones" (Comm. in Jh., II.10 iv 64-65).

This is the premise upon which Origen postulates that God is the first principle of all things. This is the conclusion which must be drawn from (In Lib. I Sam. Hom., I, 11 20, 19ff) and (De Princ., I, 1, 6 22, 1, 25). The claim is that God the Father is the cause of Being per se, and the Logos-Son the cause of Being per accidens, but since the second presupposes the first, it follows that God's energy and power extends through the entire universe. It is on this basis that Origen asserts that God the Father holds together all things, and extends his power to every level of Being (e.g., De Princ., I,3,5 55,6ff.). The Father has power over all of creation (De Princ., I, 3, 5 55, 6ff.), and he made the world through the agency of his Son (Comm. in Jh., II.10 iv, 64-65). However, Origen does not hold that all types of Being exist in the same way. The Father exists differently than any other entity (In Lib. I Sam. Hom., I,11 20-21), and the Son and Holy Spirit exist differently than the Father, and the created entities (Comm. in Jh., fr. 1 483, 20ff.).

5.2   In a number of passages scattered throughout Origen's works a distinction is made between the essence and existence of the Father, and the essence and existence of the generated and created entities (e.g. De Princ. I,2,6 p. 34,18ff.; In Lib. I Sam. I,11 p. 20,19ff.; cf. De Princ. I,2,6 p. 36,4ff.; I,3,3 p. 50,4ff.; IV,4,1 p. 348,5-351,6.; P 4 p. 9,12f.; Comm. in Jh. II,4 p. 58,4f.; II,10 p. 65,22f.; C. Cels. VIII 13 p. 231,3ff. cf. Jerome, Ep. ad Av. 2 = Migne SL XXII 1061). It appears that Origen holds a theory of 'essential' and 'accidental' existence which can be formulated: "The Father is a being whose existence and essence are identical. In the case of all other beings existence is something superadded to their essence."[143] First the evidence will be introduced which supports this interpretation, and then the analysis of the evidence will follow.

In his (In Lib. I Sam. I,11 p. 20, 16ff.) Origen interprets the phrase:

...non est praeter te...

to mean:

...nihil eorum, quae sunt, hoc ipsum, quod sunt, naturaliter habent...

Nothing save the Father is (or exists) by virtue of its own nature.

In his (De Princ. I,2,9 p. 40,12-41,9. cf. I,2,9 p. 39,12-40,11) he interprets the phrase:

...vapor est quidam virtutis dei et aporroia (id est manatio) omnipotentis gloriae purissima et speldor lucis aeternae et speculum inmaculatum inoperationis sive virtutis dei et imago bonitatis eius.

to mean:

Quinque igitur haec de deo definiens ex singulis quibusque certa quaedam inesse sapientiae dei designat; "virtutem," namque "dei" nominat et "gloriam" et "lucem aeternam" et "inoperationem" et "bonitatem." Ait autem sapientiam "vaporem" esse non gloriae omnipotentis ... neque enim conveniens erat alicui horum adscribi vaporem; sed cum omni proprietate ait "virtutis dei vaporem" esse sapientiam. Intellegenda est ergo "virtus dei," qua viget, qua omnia visibilia et invisibilia vel instituit vel continet vel gubernat, quod ad omnia sufficiens est, quorum providentiam gerit, quibus velut unita omnibus adest.

After saying this he asserts that:

Huius ergo totius "virtutis" tantae et tam immensae "vapor" et, ut ita dixerim, vigor ipse in propria subsistentia effectus quamvis ex ipsa virtute velut voluntas dei nihilominus dei virtus efficitur. Efficitur ergo virtus altera in sua proprietate subsistens, ut ait sermo scripturae, "vapor quidam" primae et ingenitae "virtutis dei," hoc quidem quod est inde trahens; non est autem quando non fuerit.

This he takes to mean:

Ex quo ostenditur semper fuisse vaporem istum virtutis dei, nullum habentem initium nisis ipsum deum. Neque enim decebat aliud esse initium nisi ipsum, unde et est et nascitur, deum.

We take this to mean that only the Father's existence (esse) is 'subsistent' and not 'inherent.' The existence which characterizes all generated and created beings is not 'subsistent,' but 'inherent.' Thus, the Father is the only non-generated, non-created existant (De Princ. I,2,6 35,8ff.; Comm. in Jh. II,10 65,17f.; Jerome, Ep. ad Av. 2 Migne SL XXII 1061). He is the only entity whose essence and existence are perfectly identical (In Lib. Sam. Hom. 1.11 20-21). This is implied at (De Princ. I,3,3 50,14-51,9), and worked out at (De Princ., I,3,5 55,6ff.).

Reconstructing Origen's thesis from these pericopae, the following proposal is offered: Origen holds that nothing existed before God or was co-eternal with him, and that God the Father is a kind of necessary existence. Thus, God alone always had existence and never received any beginning of being (In Lib. I Sam. I,11 p. 20,25-26).

The essence of the Father exists by itself as a concrete thing. It is a singular essence which has unity in a higher degree than any other concrete thing. As an hypostasis it is substance in the truest sense, and existence belongs to it absolutely and primarily. Its existence is not the result of a particular substance achieving form, or of a specific set of causes.

This is not the case with the Son (Wisdom-Logos) whose substance is the impress of the Father's (e.g. De Princ. I,2,5 p. 33,4ff.; I,2,6 p. 35,1ff. I,2,8 p. 38,1-39,11; cf. IV,4,1 p. 349,10ff.). Nor is it the case with the Holy Spirit (e.g. De Princ. P 4 p. 11,3ff.; I,3,5 p. 54,20ff.; cf. Just. Ep. ad Men. = fr. 9 Koe.). The Holy Spirit is the first generated entity who participates in the existence of the Father through the agency of the Son (e.g. Comm. in Jh. fr. 1 p. 483 Koe).

This is not the case with the created intelligibles and sensibles. They are particular substances that receive their form from the Father through the agency of the Logos (e.g. De Princ. IV,4,5 p. 356,6ff. cf. Anath. VII Con. Syn. = Mansi IX 506d.; IV,4,6-7 p. 356,21-358,10).

5.3   If we reconstruct Origen's thesis further, it appears that although the Father, Son, and Holy Spirit make up an "essential unity," and constitute "essential being" insofar as they are of one nature and substance (e.g. De Princ. I,2,6 p. 34,23-35.; I,3,8 p. 60,22), the Son and Holy Spirit exist in a different manner than the Father. The Son and Holy Spirit are ktisma-gennêma and exist by the will of the Father (De Princ. IV,4,1 p. 349,11-15.; P 4 p. 11,3-5.; Comm. in Jh. II,10 p. 65,15). They receive their existence from the Father (In Lib. I Sam. I,11 p. 20,21-22,7.).

...nihil eorum, quae sunt, hoc ipsum, quod sunt, naturaliter habent...

The Father:

...solus est....

(In Lib. I Sam. I,11 p. 20, 19-20)

If our reconstruction is correct, then the type of existence which characterizes the Son and Holy Spirit is contingent because their existence is dependent upon factors outside their essence. Is this not what Origen means when he asserts:

...(hoti) ho men theos kai patêr synechôn ta panta phythanei eis hekaston tôn ontôn metadidous hekastô apo tou idiou to enai, hoper estin...

(De Princ. I,3,5 p. 55,4-56,2)

That is, only the Father exists "essentially" because his existence is not due to any factor outside his essence. The Son and Holy Spirit exist "accidentally" because their existence is due to factors outside their essence.

Analysis exhibits two distinct understandings of existence (e.g., Comm. in Jh. fr. 1 Koe. p. 485). 1) Existence represents what generated things are in the timelessness and constancy of being; and 2) Existence represents essence thrown into combination with matter, or intelligible form, or divine impress. In this second sense existence is always accidental to essence. All generated existence is contingent existence because it does not exist by virtue of its own nature.

A good example of this is Origen's definition of the Son's existence. Origen says:

> Imago ergo est invisibilis dei patris salvator noster, quantum ad ipsum quidem patrem veritas, quantum autem ad nos, quibus revelat patrem, imago est...genomenoi toinun hêmeis kat'eikona, ton hyion prôtotoupon hos alêtheian echomen ton en hêmin kalôn tupôn. autos de ho hyios hoper hêmeis esmen pros auton, toioutos esti pros ton patera alêtheian tugchanonta.
>
> (De Princ. I,2,6 p. 36,7ff.)

To Origen's critics this meant that the Son, who was the image of the invisible Father, is not the truth when compared with the Father, but a shadow and semblance of the truth (Jerome, Ep. ad Av. 2 Migne SL XXII 1060; Photius Cod. 117 p. 92a 33b; Theophil. Ep. Syn. 2 = Hieron. Ep. 92 Migne SL XXII 762). However, Origen did not mean this at all. The distinction between the Father and the Son was a distinction based on Peripatetic not Platonic grounds, i.e. analogice as distinct from aequvoce and univoce in the Peripatetic sense, not analogice as non esse veritatem...non possumus recipere veritatem.

This view goes back to Aristotle, who, when speaking of the senses of being as related to the categories, made it clear that that which is primarily and absolutely is substance, and that the being of the other categories, while still essential, is not primary. It was permissible to use the term being in this variety of senses because it may be used neither equivocally nor in the same sense, but in relation to one and the same thing. In this sense then, the type of existence which characterizes the Son and Holy Spirit is not 'subsistent,' or as Origen would say 'by virtue of their own nature,' but rather 'inherent,' or as Origen says their being is "made according to the image" or "imparted to them from the Father" (In Lib. I Sam. I,11 p. 20,19f.; De Princ. I,3,5 p. 55, 4-55,2).

Although the Father is beyond the type of qualified essence that characterizes other entities, does this mean nonetheless that he is an essence? Origen answers in the affirmative. God the Father is an essence and an intellect (De Princ. I,2,5 p. 33,8.; p. 34,23ff.; I,2,8 p. 39,4-11; I,3,6 p. 57,2). Indeed, the Father is a supreme intellect, and an essence that is the ground of all being. He is the entity that gives being and existence to all things (De Princ., I, 35 55, 4ff.). However, God is an absolutely simple essence and intellect. That is, he is eternal and ungenerated. Simply stated God's essence and intellect is in <u>toto caelo</u> different from the essence and intellect which characterizes all other beings.

Just as Origen uses the term "essence" in a special sense with the Father. He also employs the term "existence" in a special sense. This is reflected in (<u>I Lib. I Sam.</u>, I,11 p. 20,16-21,7) where Origen states that the existence of the Father is "by virtue of its own nature." When he speaks of the Son, Holy Spirit, and the other created entities it is clear that their existence is dependent upon something prior to themselves, i.e., the Father (e.g., <u>De Princ.</u> I,3,1 48,17ff.; <u>Comm. in Jh.</u>, II,10 64-65; <u>Comm. in Jh.</u>, fr. 1 Koe iv. 483-485). The crucial distinction between the type of existence which characterizes the Father and that which characterizes the other entities is that the Father's existence is not a generated or created type of existence. It is a bare existence which never received any beginning of being (<u>I Lib. I Sam.</u> I,11 20,16ff.). This is the meaning, according to Origen, of the statement "there is none besides thee."

From his statement that the Father is the only entity to whom existence is given by none, and never received any beginning of being (<u>I Lib. I Sam.</u> I,11 20,16ff.), it is proposed that for God the Father, existence and essence are identical. The Father exists by virtue of his own nature. He is a necessary existant. Furthermore, not only does he exist in himself he is also the <u>fons-archê</u> of all existence and being. He is the source of the intelligible entities within the universe (<u>De Princ.</u> I,1,6 21,13), if not all the creatures within the universe (<u>De Princ.</u> I,3,3 50,14ff, I, 3, 5 54,8ff.). Hence, as the source of all being, Origen defines the Father as a necessary being and a necessary existant (<u>De Princ.</u> I,3,6 p. 57,2ff.). God's being and his existence were given to him by none. This is what Origen means in his use of the statement "I am that I am" (e.g. <u>De Princ.</u> I,3,6 p. 57,2ff.).

In summary: The essence and the kinds of essence and intellect of the Father are distinct from all other entities. The existence of the Father is also different from the type which characterizes all generated and created entities. Hence, the type of being and existence which belongs to this first intellect is necessary. Since the Father is necessary being and existence, Origen calls him a type of being and existence that is "<u>epekeina</u>" and "<u>naturaliter.</u>"

Now the question must be asked: "how can a substance be 'accidental'?" Is not substance by definition 'essential'? That is, if substance is called 'accidental' are we not involved in a contradiction?

<u>5.5</u>   In order to understand what is meant by 'accidental being' it is necessary to define this idea within the context of the correlative notions of 'accidental unity,' 'essential being,' and 'essential unity.' These concepts are discussed in the writings of Aristotle, and were known to his commentator Alexander of Aphrodisias. It is proposed that Origen knew of these notions from his own studies in the school of Ammonius Saccas.[144] Although Origen's use of these concepts differs from Alexander's we may use these Peripatetic <u>loci paralleli</u> as a means of interpreting Origen's own doctrine. No claim is made that Alexander's writings serve as direct <u>fontes</u> for Origen. Aristotle presents these ideas in his (<u>Met.</u> IV, 7, 1017a7-22; VI,6 1015b-17-34; V,4 1027b33-1028a4) and (<u>Met.</u> IV,7, 1017a22-30; I,2, 1054a13-18; <u>Eth. Nic.</u> 14, 1096a20-22; <u>Anal. Post.</u> 63b3-5;

De Interp., 16b22-25). Alexander comments upon them in his (In Met. p. 370,9ff.; 371,18-36; 614,25-26).

In the seventh chapter of Metaphysics IV Aristotle begins his discussion of the use of the terms to einai and to on with the concept of to kata symbebêkos on.[145] Aristotle understood 'accidental being' as the being which is implied in the proposition 'the man is musical.' The being which is "accidental," at least in this example, is merely the temporary connection between subject and attribute (predicate). As such the term to kata symbebêkos refers to the accidental relation consisting between the subjects (S) and the predicate (P) of a proposition. This propositional or logical character seems to be an essential mark of accidental being. Indeed, all the instances given by Aristotle bear the form of the proposition (Met. IV,7 1017a7-22). Aristotle does not speak of ta onta in the sense of things existing independently from thought. He means by to on and to einai copulative esse or being. It primarily indicates the logical connection between S and P but even copulative being is based on reality.[146]

The counterpart of 'accidental' being is 'accidental unity (cf. Met. IV,6 1015b17-34). It also has a logical character. Indeed Alexander associates to on kata symbebêkos with to hen kata symbebêkos (In Met. 362,13). In his Met. IV,6 Aristotle lists the various kinds of accidental unity (to hen kata symbebêkos). By accidental unity Aristotle means a unity grounded on a de facto conjunction, not a unity grounded on the essential nature of that which forms a unity. For the purposes of our study it is best if we turn to Alexander's interpretation of Aristotle.

Alexander knew of Aristotle's examples, and listed the three cases of accidental unity as: (In Met. 362,13).[147]

1)   the unity of substance and accident (b17-18; cf. b22-23).

2)   the unity of accident and co-accident (b19-20; cf. b21-22).

3)   the unity of substance+accident and the same substance+another accident (b20; cf. b26-27).

In addition Aristotle adds an analogue to (1) and (3):

1a)   the unity of substance+accident and substance (b23-26).

3a)   the unity of genus+accident and genus (b28-36).

According to Alexander the division of accidental being in IV,7 runs parallel to that of accidental unity in IV,6. (1) answers the first kind of accidental being (1017a8-10): P is an accident of S. (2) answers the third kind of accidental being (1017a20-22): P and Q are accidents of S. (3) answers to the same kind of accidental being as (2). (1a) and (3a) are of the type of accidental being as (1) and (3). (There is no correspondence of a (2a) with

(2) because it does not matter whether accidental unity is of SP or PS.) The point Aristotle makes, and Alexander concurs with, is that there is no difference between the mark of "accidental being" and "accidental unity." Both have a logical character and are closely related to the proposition (In Met. p. 370,9ff.; 371,8-13).

According to Aristotle and Alexander that which is "accidental," including accidental being, does not have any "real" character of its own. Both consider "accidental being" as something logical and in contrast to "essential being" (Met. V,4,1027b33-1028a4.; V,2 1026b13). This means that the term "accidental being" is closely related to the proposition and predicating, and denotes the temporary connection between subject and predicate.[148]

If Aristotle means by "accidental being" the being which is a temporary connection between S and P, it follows that "essential being" is an essential and necessary connection between S and P[149] (Met. IV,7, 1017a22-30). In order to grasp what Aristotle means by "essential being" it is necessary to draw a parallel with his understanding of "essential unity."

Aristotle lists the various types of essential unity at (Met. IV,6 1015b36-1017a3). None of the instances given by Aristotle has the form of a proposition. Only entities are always given as examples. This means that by "essential being" Aristotle means the "essential unity" of predicate and copula (esti). This follows from Aristotle's views about the copula. The copula by itself is meaningless, and takes its meaning only by its connection with the predicate (cf. De. Inter. 16b22-25.; Met. I,2 1054a13-18).

Alexander (In Met. p. 614,25-26.), commenting upon Aristotle's proposal, broadens it by asserting that the copula forms in connection with the predicate an "essential unity," which is comparable to the substantial unity formed by the indefinite prime matter (protê hylê) and the defining form (eidos). According to Alexander, the copula cannot exist apart from its predicate any more than matter can exist apart from form. Essence must always be the essence of "something" (In Met. p. 371,18-36). The copula and predicate together indicate a certain form of being. This is an important addition to Aristotle's original definition of "essential unity." The shift in emphasis is away from the logical and towards the ontological. Alexander's reformulation must have had a profound impact in Middle Platonic circles.

In order to complete what Aristotle means by essential and accidental being we shall conclude with a discussion of the essential attribute, and its opposite the accidental attribute. In the (Anal. Post., I,4, 73a34-b3, esp. 73a34-b5) Aristotle asserts that "essential" attributes are those which belong to their subjects as elements in their essential nature, and are those which while belonging to certain subjects cannot be defined without mentioning these subjects. In the (Anal. Post., 73b3-5) he separates them from "accidental" attributes, i.e. that which is "musical" or "white" is an accident of "animal."

5.6 Now that we have examined the Peripatetic evidence, let us turn to Origen's use of these theories. The character of the relationship between the Father, Son, and Holy Spirit is primarily logical. The Father thinks or wills them, and they are generated as a product of his thought inasmuch as he is the mind from which originates all intellectual existence (e.g. De Princ. I,1,6 p. 21,13.; cf. Comm. in Jh. II,10 iv. p. 64-65). Now it is proposed that the type of unity which characterizes the Father, Son, and Holy Spirit is the logical unity of substance+accident or substance+accident and substance (cf. Arist. Met. IV,6 1015b17-18; b22-23; b23-26; Alex. In Met. p. 362,13). The unity has a logical character, and is closely related by Origen to the proposition from Jn. 1:3 "all things were made through him" (e.g. Comm. in Jh. II,10 iv. p. 64-65). In this 'metaphysics of prepositions' the Father is the Intellect through which the Son, Holy Spirit, and created things are made, and the principle in which they reside.

As we have noted anything which is accidental does not have any real character of its own. In the sense that all existence comes from the Father (e.g. In Lib. I Sam. I,11 p. 20,16ff.; De Princ. I,1,6 p. 21,13,13ff.; I,3,3 p. 52,1f.) generated existence does not possess a real character of its own. Generated existence does not exist by virtue of its own nature as does the Father, and is something accidental. That is, the Son and Holy Spirit, logically at least, are accidents of the Father (De Princ. I,2,5 p. 35,4).

Categorically, the relationship would be that between substance (ousia) and accident (pros), or substance (ousia), and accident (pros) and substance (ousia). There is both an Academic and a Peripatetic aspect to how this categorical model is presented. We shall examine first the Academic moment, and then the Peripatetic.

We know that the Father is a substance and that the Son is the image of the Father's substance (e.g. De Princ. I,2,5 p. 33,8). In turn we know that the Holy Spirit participates in the Father through the agency of the Logos-Son (Comm. in Jh. II, 10 p. 65,26). We know that the substance of the Father is the only ungenerated substance and that the substance of the Son and the Holy Spirit is generated (e.g. De Princ. IV4,1 p. 349,11ff. cf. Just. Ep ad Men. = Mansi IX 525,489b; In Jh. II,10, p. 65,15ff. cf. De Princ., P 4 p. 11,3ff.). We know that the Son:

> ...imago patris deformatur in filio, qui utique natus ex eo est velut quaedam
> voluntas eius ex mente procedens.
>
> (De Princ. I,2,5 p. 35,3f.)

We know that the Holy Spirit is:

> ...prosiemetha to pantôn dia tou logou genomenôn to hagion pneuma pantôn
> einai timiôteron...
>
> (Comm. in Jh. II,10 p. 65,18ff.)

Since the Son proceeds from the mind of the Father, and the Holy Spirit was made by the Father through Christ the categorical relation is between the Father's substance and that which is produced from this substance, which is in relation to it (De Princ. I,2,6 p. 36,7ff. cf. Jerome, Ep. ad Av. 2 = Migne SL XXII 1060.; Photius, Codex 117 p. 92a,33b). The nature of this relation is expressed by Origen in the following manner:

epeiper ho ton logon tetheôrêkôs tou theou theôrei ton theon, anabainôn apo tou logou pros ton theon.

(Comm. in Jh. XIX,6 p. 305,7f.)

Now given the statement that the Son is,

...splendor gloria et figura expressa substantiae eius (the Father's)...

(De Princ. I,2,5 p. 33,7f.)

the relation between the Father and the Son is that of substance (the Father's) to that of accident (the Son proceeds from the mind of the Father) as well as that of substance (the Father's) to that of accident (relation or image) and substance (generated substance). The relation of the Father to the Holy Spirit is similar, but one step removed since the Logos-Son is the intermediary between the Father and the Holy Spirit.

The Son and Holy Spirit are a kind of logical accident. The question arises are they also characterized as ontological accident?[150] Are they entities which cannot exist in themselves, but their existence depends on a prior entity in which they inhere? Let us examine the notion of ontological accident, and see if the Logos-Son and Holy Spirit are accidental beings in the sense of being ontological accidents.

5.6   Origen mentions the Father and the Son in ontological relation to one another at (e.g. De Princ. I,2,6 p. 36,4ff.; cf. Jerome, Ep. ad Av. 2 = Migne XXII 1060.; Just. Ep. ad Men. = fr. 4 Koe. = Mansi IX 515, 489d.).[151]

We know from Aristotle that the category of relation (pros) is mentioned as one of the symbebêkota (Eth. Nic. 14, 1096a20-22). Here we see ousia (qua subsistent being) defined in opposition to accident, i.e. relation (qua inherent being).

The commentator Eustratius comments on this passage as follows:

oudemia de tôn allôn kategoriôn echei to hyphestêkani kath'auto (i.e. being subsistent) kai mê en hypokeimenô einai ê mona he ousia.

(In Arist. Eth. Nic. Comm. 43, 9-11)

Hippolytus, in turn, calls the secondary categories, in opposition to ousia:

ta symbebêkota: Aristotelês toutou (i.e. Platônos) genomenos akroatês eis technên tên philosophian êgagen kai logikôteros egeneto, ta men stoicheia tôn pantôn hypothemenos ousian kai symbebêkos. tên men ousian main tên pasin hypokeimenên, ta de symbebêkota ennea. poson poion pros ti pou pote exhein keisthai poiein paschein.

(Ref. omn. haer. I,20 DG 570ff.)

The point is that the concept of ontological accident is a transcendental one which can be said, analogically, of all praedicamenta, except ousia.[152] Origen appears to hold the same position on this issue.

Origen appears to know the concept of ontological accident yet he does not distinguish it from that of logical accident. In his scheme only the Father is ontological necessity. Hence, the notion of ontological accident can be said of all entities, ontologically, save the Father. We can say this because the character of ontological accident is that it indicates something that is not "by virtue of its own nature" (In Lib I. Sam. Hom. I,11 p. 20,16ff.), or to use Aristotle's language that which is not subsistent, but inherent. The Father alone exists "by virtue of its own nature." The Son and Holy Spirit exist by virtue of the Father's nature.[153]

To summarize: That which is not per se logically is a logical accident, and that which is not per se ontologically is an ontological accident. In Origen, the distinction between logical and ontological accident is not as sharp as it is with later thinkers. Thus, ontological accident has a logical aspect to it. Origen defines accident by way of the proposition, i.e. via predicating. For example, in his (Comm. in Jh. II,10 p. 65) he defines the Holy Spirit as the most honorable of all the things that was made through the Logos, and first in rank of all that has been made by the Father. The act of making the Logos and Holy Spirit is clearly logical. Yet at the end of the pericope Origen distinguishes between the predicates that indicate the essence (being) of this divine species (we know that they are of the same species as the Father, e.g. De Princ. I,2,6 p. 34,19ff.), and those that indicate the quality and relation of the Logos and Holy Spirit to the Father. Both aspects of the concept accident merge into one another. The two divine entities, who are generated, are characterized by logical as well as ontological accident. The same conclusion holds for the created things.

5.7   The problem which confronts us is that although Origen views the created things as 'accidental' (e.g. De Princ. I,2,13 p. 48,5ff.; Comm. in Jh. II,18 p. 75,8) nowhere does he explicitly employ the term symbebêkos-accidens to define the Son and Holy Spirit. The definition symbebêkos-accidens is used only to define the physicals. To state it in another way, if the term 'accidental' is only used to define the sensibles how can it be asserted that second and third theologicals are 'accidental'? To answer this question we must call to mind the propositional character of logical accident, and the ontological character of ontological accident. Both of these understandings of accident are utilized by Origen when he explains the creation of the Son and Holy Spirit.

Origen asserts that the Son and Holy Spirit are created. The testimonies of Jerome and Justinian, the redactions of Rufinus, and the writings from Origen's own hand concur on this point (e.g. De Princ. IV,4,1 349,11ff.; In Lib. I Sam. Hom. I,11 20,16ff. cf. Jerome, Ep. ad Av. 2 = Migne SL XXII 1060.; Just. Ep ad Men. = Mansi IX 525. cf. Comm. in Jh. II,10 65,17ff.).

Origen presents the concept of creation first propositionally, and then cosmo-logically. Working off the Bible as a proof-text Origen postulates the eternal generation of the Son, and that the Spirit was the first of the generated beings (e.g. In Jerem. Hom. IX, 4 iii. p. 70.; Comm. in Jh. II,10 p. 65,17ff.). Laying stress on the identity between ên and egenêto in Jn. 1:1, Jn. 1:3 and Gen. 1:1 (Comm. in Jh. fr. 1 Koe. p. 483-485) he asserts that the meaning of the verse "in the beginning was the Logos" is "in the beginning of the creation of the world the Logos came into being." Although in classical Greek ên means "was" and not "came into being," which in Greek is egenêto, Origen justifies this interpretation of ên as meaning egenêto on the ground that the Greek translation of the Hebrew scripture in the LXX renders hayah as both "was" and "came to be." He then takes the verb "was" (ên) to mean "is" (esti) on the ground that in respect to the Logos time has no bearing, and upon this postulate asserts the eternal generation of the Son and the first generation of the Holy Spirit. Thus, although the Son and Holy Spirit were created (gennêma) they represent a different type of created entity than those created by the Father through the Logos. The distinction is between that created logically (e.g. De Princ. I,2,5 p. 35,3ff.; IV,4,1 p. 349,11ff.), and that created temporally (e.g. Comm. in Jh. fr. 1 Koe. p. 483-485).

Next, Origen presents the Father as the begettor of things after the analogy of natural procreation. He defines the existence of the Son and Holy Spirit as the result of the Father's act of begetting or generating. As in any act of natural generation, that which is generated is like that which generated it. Hence, the Son and the Holy Spirit are like the Father. Subsequently the term God is extended to each of the lower hypostases, and each entity of the Trinity is called divine. It is within the context of this model that we must understand that the Son and Holy Spirit are logically and ontologically 'accidental.'

In summary: The Son and Holy Spirit are logically generated. Hence, they are 'accidental' (even though Origen does not use this term in respect to the hypostasis). Origen does not use the term symbebêkos-accidens to define these theologicals because the nature of their generation is different from the other created intelligibles and sensibles. They are created logically, and not temporally, from the mind of the Father. This constitutes their 'accidental' character.

5.8   The counterpart of the term symbebêkos are the terms ousia and ti esti. Just as the former term has its logical and ontological aspects, so too do the latter terms. These terms denote essence or substance.[154] They refer to a concrete individual substance, and to a general sense of essence. That is, they are said either of a substance or an accident. Origen uses the term ousia (ti esti) in both senses, and defines the non-substantial and substantial things as essence (substance). Origen holds no sharp distinction between the Aristotelian and Platonic meanings and uses of the term essence (substance). The term is employed by Origen to indicate the highest essences, or principle forms of being, and secondary forms of being, the noêrai ousiai and psychai (Just. Ep ad Men. = Mansi IX 489).

Origen does not assert that all beings are identical with their essence. This only holds for those beings which are a self-subsistent unity, either in the category of substance or in one of the secondary categories. The only entity which is characterized by this 'essential being' is the Father, and those who are of the same species as the Father, i.e. the Son and Holy Spirit (e.g. De Princ. I,2,6 34,19f.; Comm. in Jh. II,10 65). Origen states that the Son and Holy Spirit are of the same species of the Father because their substance is the express image of the Father's or participates with the Father's (e.g.

De Princ. I,2,5 33,7; e.g. Comm. in Jh. II,10 65,17f.). He explains what he means by the Peripatetic analogy of the statue composed of form and matter (De Princ. I,2,8 38,13ff. cf. Ep ad Av. 2 = Migne XXII 1060).

Origen holds that the Father is an 'essential being' in an 'essential unity' with the Son, and the Holy Spirit (e.g. Comm. in Jh. II,10 p. 65). To use Origen's language the 'essential unity' between these entities is comparable to the unity formed by the substance of the Son and Holy Spirit and the form of the Father. Essence must always be the essence of something. Hence, the Son and Holy Spirit are of the same essence as the Father's essence. This is not the case, however, with the created essences.

Indeed, Origen affirms an essential unity of the Father, Son, and Holy Spirit. However, he does not assert that the essence (substance) of the three are identical (e.g. De Princ. I,2,6 p. 36,7ff. P 4 p. 10-11). The Son and Holy Spirit are generated essences that do not exist "by virtue of their own nature" as the Father does (In Lib. I sam. Hom., I,11 20,16ff.). For Origen the Father is the only essential being and necessary existant, while the Son and Holy Spirit are essential beings that exist accidentally. They are the only generated entities that are characterized as 'essential' because they are the only beings that are in an 'essential' unity with the Father.

Origen also asserts the essential unity of the three hypostases (e.g. De Princ. I,2,6 p. 34,19-35,7.; I,3,5 p. 54,20ff.; Comm. in Jh. II,10 p. 65). As such, the Father, Son and Holy Spirit are the protai ousiai or the non-material primary forms of the universe. The Father is the ground of the whole world (De Princ. I,3,5 55,6ff.; De Princ., I,3,5 55,6ff., I,1,6 p. 21,13), the Son the ground of the intelligible and sensible worlds (Comm. in Jh. fr. 1 Koe. iv. p. 483ff.), and the Holy Spirit the condition for the possibility of the saints to share in the Son and the Father (De Princ. I,3,5 55,6ff. II,7,2 p. 149,1ff.; Comm. in Jh. II,10 p. 65.). Hence, Origen proposes a realism which asserts the subsistence of more than one type of non-material universal. They are the protai ousiai of the universe and the archai of all things in the universe.

If we understand Origen's scheme correctly only God the Father is pros auto (kath auto). The Son, Holy Spirit, the intelligible cosmos, and the sensible cosmos are pros ti (In Lib. I Sam., II 20,16ff.; Just. Ep. ad Men. = Mansi IX 525.; cf. Comm. in Jh. XIX 6 iv. 305,7). To this Origen adds that God the Father is the only entity who is unbegotten (De Princ. I,2,6 35,8ff.; Jerome, Ep. ad Av. 2; Comm. in Jh. II,10 65,17f.). The Son is the image of the Father and is eternally begotten (De Princ. I,2,6 34,20ff.; Comm. in Jh. XIII 36 260f).

It is significant that Origen speaks of the second principle as not only being an image of the Father but in relation to him as well as to us. (In this sense the Son functions in a manner akin to the Idea in Albinus' theoretic, Did., 163, 12ff.) Origen states that the Son:

Imago ergo est "invisibilis dei" patris salvator noster, quantum ad ipsum quidem patrem "veritas," quantum autem ad nos, quibus revelat patrem "imago" est...

(De Princ. I,2,6 p. 36,7ff.)

This statement, when coupled with the testimonies of Jerome (Ep. ad Av. 2 = Migne 52 XXII 1060) and Photius (Bibl. Cod. 117 p. 92a, 33b), suggest that Origen viewed the substantia-subsistentia of the Father as distinct from the Son's, and all the other generated and created substances (De Princ. I,2,8 p. 38,1-5; 18-25f.; I,3,3 p. 52,1f.; Just. Ep. ad Men. = fr. 7 Koe.). The Father is distinct from the generated Son and Holy Spirit, and from the created non-corporeal and corporeal entities. Yet they are in relation (pros) to him. Thus, the term pros suggests: 1) the relation of copy to model; and 2) the relation of substance in itself to substance in relation to something else, viz. the Father.

Origen divides Being into two categories -- the Absolute, to which only the Father belongs per se, and the Relative, to which the Son, Holy Spirit, and the other created entities belong per accidens.[155] This does not mean that the Son and Holy Spirit are not 'real,' viz., that they have no Being. It means they are Being insofar as they are related to the Father (In Lib. I Sam. I, 11 20, 16ff.; De Princ. I,3,5 p. 55,4ff.; Just. Ep. ad Men. = fr. 9 Koe.). However, they cannot be or exist without the Father. God the Father is the necessary being and existence who imparts (phthanei) to each one from his own existence (apo tou idiou to einai) what each one is (De Princ. I,3,5 p. 56,1ff.). The Son is the first and only eternally generated essence (substance), and the Holy Spirit is the first generated essence (substance) (De Princ. I,3,5 p. 56,1ff.; Comm. in Jh. II,10 64-65; cf. Jerome, Ep. ad Av. 2 = fr. 9 Koe.).

The Father exists in a toto caelo different manner than all other Beings. Origen's own remarks seem to support this claim (e.g., In Lib I Sam II, 11 20, 16ff.). Hence, God the Father, the hyperousin hen "exists" differently from the Son, the ousion hen, the Holy Spirit, and all the created entities.

To summarize: In his division of Being (ousia) into the Absolute and the Relative, Origen reduces necessary existence to God the Father. The Logos-Son-Christ and the Holy Spirit are distinct from the Father. They are characterized as eternally generated and generated existences respectively (cf. De Princ. I,3,3 p. 52,1f. cf. Just. Ep. ad Men. = fr. 7 Koe = Mansi IX 528). They are the first in rank among the generated entities, but they do not exist per se (Just. Ep. ad Men. = fr. 9 Koe. p. 55,4ff.; De Princ. I,2,6 p. 34,20ff.; I,2,8 p. 38,1-5, 18-25ff (Ep. ad Men. p. 161 Koe. Ep. ad Men. p. cviii, 1ff. Koe.). This clear separation of the second and third theologicals and the intelligibles from God the Father distinguishes Origen from antecedent Middle Platonists, who place the theologicals and intelligibles (ideas) within the realm of the 'really' real. Nonetheless, Origen's formulation is based on sound philosophical principles.

5.9   Origen solves the first two problematics of Middle Platonic metaphysics in a novel way. First, he postulates a tri-fold division of Being. Second, he distinguishes the type of existence which characterizes each level of Being. These theories he culls from the Peripatetic speculation upon the writings of Aristotle.

Origen also defines the Being and Existence which characterize the entities of each realm of reality by means of the Peripatetic categories. The categories are about things or beings, and show the referential efficacy of each thing (being) to its first cause and ground. The categories exhibit the characteristics shared by the three groups of Being in the two major divisions of reality Origen postulates. They permit Origen to offer loose classifications of Being, and to show the unifying energy and power the three hypostases have over creation. These theories Origen again draws from Peripatetic speculation upon Aristotle's corpus.

We have spent so much time on Origen's doctrine of being and existence because it illustrates how different Origen's theoretic is from those of Philo and Clement. Philo and Clement diligently worked to overcome the ontological fault-line between Being and Becoming proclaimed in the Neo Pythagorean theoretics. For them Being per se extended beyond God alone to the whole intelligible world. Only the sensible world is being per accidens. With Origen we appear to return to the radical ontological dualism of these Neo Pythagoreans. God is being per se and existence necessitaliter, all else is characterized by being per accidens and existence accidentaliter. The Son and Holy Spirit appear to stand between God and the Universe as entities who are like the Father, but who exist differently from the Father. However this tertium quid is and exists differently than the rational creatures of the universe.

However, to characterize Origen's theoretic as a return to a Neo Pythagoreanism is a misinterpretation. Origen couples his division of reality to a Peripatetic understanding of the nature of reality. God, the Logos, and the Spirit form a hypostatic triad that is one in substance. Substance extends to creation, and each of the divine hypostases has power over the universe. God's power extends to all of creation, the Logos' power to the rational creatures, and the Spirit's to the "saints" of the church.[156] In substance all three form an essential unity. When God is all in all, the world will also become one in this essential unity. Before this end time, however, God is the only being who exists as a necessary being. All others exist in varying degrees of contingency.

There is a dynamic element to Origen's theoretic which makes it quintessentially anti-Pythagorean. The ontological distinctions between God and all of creation from the Logos to material things are not permanent, but transitory, not predetermined onto-logically, but determined willfully. The world is good but not ultimately good, the world is not evil in-itself but was created because of a failure of rational will. Origen's belief in these principles serves to frame his theoretical postulates. Distinctions between essential and accidental being, necessary and contingent existence are not determined for eternity. When God is all, and all accidental and contingent distinctions pass away, all things become essential and necessary like the Father.

God's providence and the free will of rational creatures shapes his understanding of the world.[157] God leaves souls free, but in the creation of the world sets the conditions for their return to God willingly. Existence is a preparatio dei, a road on the way back to God. The ultimate telos of all created existence, corporeal and incorporeal, is in union with God. This union is preordained. Origen is confident of the providence of God and of the union of not only divine noêsis, but also boulêsis.

We began our analysis with an analysis of the doctrine of the powers of God, the Logos, and the Spirit in the created world (De Princ., I,3,5 55,4-56,8). We asked the questions of Origen that Jerome, Rufinus, and Justinian did. Does Origen propose a subordinationist doctrine? If so how does it present itself? Indeed, Origen does offer a subordinationist doctrine, but the subordination of the Son and Holy Spirit to the Father is not an essential one, it is an existential one. The fact that the hypostatic triad constitutes an essential unity and an existential disunity frames not only the relation between God, the Logos, and the Holy Spirit, but also the relation between God and the universe. It points backward to an original unity of the Logos and Holy Spirit with God, it expresses a present distinction between the Logos and Holy Spirit, and God, and it points forward to the final unity between the Logos, the Holy Spirit, and God.

Although the materials left to us are ambiguous about the nature of the final restoration of all things in God, whether it includes the non-rational as well as rational things, it appears that materiality will cease altogether and that all things will return to the divine unity from which they fell.[158] The fact that even materiality will cease to exist attests to the unity Origen maintained existed between God and the universe. The achievement of unity with God is the ultimate expectation, not just for the few trained in philosophy, but the entire universe. This could not be asserted if Origen did not see the possibility for the elimination of accidentality and contingency as the destiny of all things.

We shall now turn to the philosophical basis which supports Origen's optimism about both the nature and the destiny of the world. We shall examine his doctrine of how God is the first principle of all things. It is only because God is the ground of the universe that the universe ultimately returns to God.

6. God the Father: The First Principle of Being

6.1   The leitmotif of Origen's doctrine of Being does not commence by taking a one and asking how it can be many. He begins from the many, Being _in toto_, and asks how can it arise from the one? Hence, Being for Origen is _pros hen_ unity. Origen postulated that the first and second "Ones" were related to one another as a _pros hen_ unity. Since the noetic and psychic entities were within the second "One" and willed by the first "One," it followed that Origen proposed that the created things were related to the hypostases in a _pros hen_ manner as well.[159]

It is upon the doctrine of equivocals that Origen constructs his thesis that God the Father is the first principle of the universe.[160] Central to this thesis is his use of the Peripatetic doctrine of the categories, and the cognate doctrines of essential and accidental being and existence. These doctrines are coupled to his theory of causation.

In order to grasp Origen's postulate that God the Father is the first principle of all things, it is necessary to keep these other doctrines in mind. Without them Origen's proposal cannot be understood. No claim is made that Origen's conflation of doctrines works, or that he adequately solves the tensions involved in proposing his postulate. At this stage in the study of Origen's metaphysics we must be content to accurately describe his theoretic, and to also recognize the possibility that even this modest goal may not be met.

When Origen defines God as "first principle" (_prôton aition_: _C. Cels._, I, 24 75, 16) no distinction is made between 'principle' and 'cause,' the two always accompany each other whether or not they are explained by the same notion. This can be inferred when he speaks of the Son as instrumental cause pointing toward a cause prior to the Son. This cause is the Father, who presumably is the final-efficient cause of creation (Comm. in Jh. II.10 64, 12.) The echei to di ou or instrumental cause of creation is the Logos-Son. The point to be noted is that Origen's tendency is to reduce all the causes to a final or formal cause, and locate it in God the Father.

The instances of Origen identifying principle and cause are listed at (De Princ., I,1,6 22,1,5; C. Cels., I.21 i 72,14; VI.71 141,16). Origen attacks the Stoics and Epicureans on how they define the first 'principle' as 'cause' not that the two terms mean the same thing. The conflation of both terms offers no difficulty for Origen. Both refer to a beginning of some kind. If our reconstruction is correct then we have a major clue which points toward the presuppositions behind Origen's theory. Let us pursue this modest lead.

If Koch is right that Origen's understanding of archê is:

...in ingendeiner Weise von der Metaphysik Aristoteles' IV 1 (1012) abhängig...

(PP., 252)

then we must examine Aristotle's theory of archê. According to Aristotle aitia and archê are the same (Arist., Metaphys., V, 1 1013a16-17). They always accompany each other, whether or not they are explained by the same notion (Arist., Metaphs., IV, 2, 1003b 24ff.). Aristotle lists the instances at (Arist., Metaphys., V, 1, 1012b34-1013a23), and gives its definition at (Arist. Metaphys., V, 1, 1013a 17-19).

If Origen's understanding of 'principle' and 'cause' is Peripatetic, then we have the clues needed to reconstruct how he viewed God the Father as the first principle of all things.

Origen's effort throughout his works is to define the causes of the universe as the result of a first cause. God is the cause of the manifestation of Being in all of its different types, and in all the levels of generated and created Being. The four causes, e.g. final, efficient, instrumental, and material, are understood as a unity of causation subsisting in the Father and Son. This is the premise from which the notion of God as the first principle of all things is drawn. This conclusion is drawn from (In Lib. I Sam. Hom., I,11 20,19ff.) and (De Princ., I,1,6 22,1,25). As the cause of Being, God is the cause of Being per se, and through the Son he is also the cause of Being per accidens. The latter presupposes the former. Being per accidens is the temporal and spatial kind of Being that presupposes Being per se, the eternal type of Being.

Origen makes no attempt to solve the contradictions in his model. He is not interested in working out a defense of his thesis. He merely postulates it. The first cause pertains to all Being, and all the effects refer back to God the Father. Hence, all effects of first cause involve, either immediately or mediately, Primary Being itself. In this way God, as first cause, is the universal and necessary first principle of all things. It is by means of this postulate then, that Origen asserts that God holds together all things and extends his power to every level of Being (e.g., De Princ., I,3,5 55,6ff.).

6.2   Origen's doctrine of Being may be summed up in a few words. Absolute Being is a triadic group of pros hen equivocals, of which the primary entity is form in the sense of act. This first One is an entity unlike any other. It requires no other principle to account for its specific difference. It is characterized by essential being and necessary existence. The second One is an "image" of the first "One" and requires it to account for its specific difference. It is characterized by essential being and a specific kind of contingent existence. Both act to create the universe. The Father acts (creates wills) the realm of Being and the Son acts (noetically wills) the realm of Becoming. Since the Father is the primary act or cause he has energy and power over all creation. Since the Son is the secondary act he has energy and power over only rational beings. God as the energy extends to all things. He is their Beingness. The Logos-Son as energy extends to rational things. As the agent of God he is the medium for the Beingness of at least the intelligible things (e.g., De Princ., I,3,5 55,6ff.)

Being is expressed in two ways, viz., as primary and as secondary. Being in its primary instance is essential and in its secondary instance it is accidental. Primary Being is expressed by Origen in his hierarchy of hypostases. Being in its most universal sense as God the Father is not a genus, and so God the Father is above the type of being and intellect that characterizes genus, species, and differentia. Being in its most generic sense is expressed in the Logos-Son, who as primary intelligible and the sum-total of the secondary intelligibles, is the ground of all secondary Being.

In the philosophical theologies of Nichomachus, Moderatus, Philo, and Clement a hierarchy of first principles is postulated, but the relation between them is not one of an energetic cause and effect (correlation) so much as one of paradigmatic cause and effect (imitation). For Origen, as it was for Albinus, God is Mind that is the active first "principle" or "cause" of the lower hypostases, and through the second intellect he is the cause of all creation. Correlation and not imitation is how Origen defines the relation of the hypostases to one another, and the sensibles to the intelligibles.

Now Origen identifies universality with this first cause. Since he was seeking a single principle to explain the origin of all things, this principle had to be the most universal cause. Origen also identifies universality with the first cause of physical creation, the Logos-Son. Together they are the ground of all Being without exception. Thus, the first two hypostases are the universal first principles that extend Beingness to all creation. Origen defines Being so that there is no ontological gap between divinity and creation. Origen's adoption of a Peripatetic philosophical theology and ontology guarantees that the metaphysical lacunae that plagued the earlier theologies and ontologies of Middle Platonism do not affect his own.

6.3   The principle problem Origen faced was that if God the Father was not a genus, how could he extend his energy and power to all things and be the first principle of Being? What is this Being, which is universal, necessary, and yet is non-generic?

This problem also faced Albinus and it is perhaps his Middle Platonic metaphysical option that Origen is most indebted to in the formulation of his own solution. Origen fills out Albinus' theoretic by integrating the Peripatetic formulations of Alexander of

Aphrodisias into it, and thereby constructing his own proposal. Hence, in order to reconstruct Origen's doctrine of first principles we must turn to Alexander's De Anima. [161] Alexander asserts that:

(1)   God is the supreme good, and first cause (De Anima, I, 89, 2-3; 9-10; 17-18)

and that:

(2)   God is a transcendent intellect in act (De Anima, I, 89, 11-16).

Alexander calls the productive intellect to "cause the being of all the intelligibles" (Alex., De Anima I, 89, 4-11). The first intellect is an act by its own nature, giving intelligible things their intelligibility. Furthermore, this intellect is called the "supreme good" (prôton agathon), "the first cause" (prôton aition), that is called God (Alex., De Anima I, 89, 2-3; I, 89, 9-10; 17-18). Alexander's identification of the productive intellect with the supreme good harmonizes the Aristotelian notion of first cause, and the Platonic notion of supreme good. The supreme intellect is a productive intellect, and as the supreme good, this intellect is not only intelligible by its own nature, but is the cause of the being of all things (Alex., De Anima., I, 89, 10-11). Indeed, the productive intellect is the cause of all other existants (De Alex., De Anima., I, 89, 9-111).

In summary: Alexander identifies the productive intellect with the divine intellect, and calls it first cause (Alex., De Anima., II, 112, 19-20; I, 89, 9-10; 17-18). This first God is the source and cause for the being of all things as the supreme intellect of all things. Finally, God has properties of impassibility, incorruptibility, separability, and actuality (Alex., De Anima., I, 89, 11-16). Since every productive cause is superior to that which produced it, the supreme principle extends its "energy" (enargeia) from the highest to the lowest reaches of creation. The lower intellects possess the same characteristics as the first intellect, while the created things possess none of the characteristics of the divine intellects.

Origen defines God as the Good (De Princ., I,2,13 46f.), and as the first cause of all things (C. Cels., I,24 75,16). He also defines God as an intellect (De Princ., I,1,6 21,13; Cat. in Jh, 495,24) and the ground of the whole world (De Princ., I,1,6 21,13f.; In Lib. I Sam. Hom., I,11 20,16ff.). God is said to extend his energy and power to the whole of creation (De Princ., I,35 55,6ff.). Hence, the evidence suggests that Origen defined God in the same manner as Alexander.

The characteristics of the Father are possessed by the Son, although in a lesser degree (De Princ., I,2,13 47,4ff.; Comm. in Jh., II,10 64-65; cf. fr. 1 483-485; C. Cels., VII,38 ii,43). Hence, the Father and Son are equivocal Beings, analogice, and together constitute the first causes, intellects, and principles of the universe, who extend their energy and power throughout the cosmos (De Princ., I,3,5 55,6ff.).

Origen employs the terms "One" and "Unity" to define the Father and the Son (e.g., De Princ., I,1,6 21,10; IV,4,1 (28); fr. 31 K. 348,7; Just. Anath., VI cxxiii; VIII 142; II cxxii,29). Given the relationship between these hypostases it appears that they are pros hen equivocals. That is, they are equivocal by reference and analogy.[162] Their referential efficacy is defined both as paradigm and copy (e.g., De Princ., I,2,13 47,4ff.) and as reference to one form (De Princ., I,2,5 33,4ff.; I,2,6 35,1ff.; I,2,8 38,1-39,11). This means that the Son is a "One" and "Unity" expressed according to the Father's "One" and "Unity." The son is denominated from the source whence it came or proceeded from, the Father, and according to the form it has reference to.

This formulation has a Peripatetic pedigree (cf. Arist. Meta., III,2,1003b 14-15; Top., I,15,106b 13-20; V,2,129b 33-34), but it is no longer possible to suggest Origen's source for this doctrine unless we turn to Clement of Alexandria and Alexander. Following the assumption that Origen defines the Father and Son as pros hen equivocals, let us proceed with our inquiry.

6.4   Origen was seeking a principle that would explain all things, and that would be necessary in scope. It had to be not only the cause of a particular type of Being but of all Being without exception. Yet again the Being of God is not a genus. How then, does it extend to everything? What is this nature of Being, which is universal and necessary to all things, and yet is not generic?

As stated, Origen defines the Being of God as a pros hen equivocal. Thus, universal and necessary Being is located only in God the Father. The nature of God, designated by the word Being, is found in God alone. Being may be expressed in many ways, but it is always in reference to this one primary hypostasis. The Son and Holy Spirit are Beings because they are generated by the Father (De Princ. I, 2, 4 32, 15ff., Comm. in Jh., II, 10 64, 32ff.). The rational and non-rational creatures are Being because they have a way toward the Father (Comm. in Jh., XX, 7, 534), or they are the products of the creation initiated by the Father, and hence have privations, or physical qualities by reference to the Father (De Princ., IV, 5, 6 357, 10ff.; C. Cels., IV, 57 330, 7f.).

A review of Origen's writings will show the obvious ways in which Being extends "by reference" to its various instances. The first instance of the extension of being is in the Logos-Son; the second is in the Holy Spirit; and then through the Logos-Son being is extended to the created things. In this way Being qua Being is located in the Father alone, and extended "by reference" to all other things. Being in all its manifestations is defined by reference to the Father. Primary Being, or the Being of the Father, Son, and Holy Spirit, is presented as the extension of God's energy and power throughout the universe (De Princ., I, 3, 5 55, 6ff.). It is also presented in terms of first cause (generator) and its subsequent effects (the generated) (De Princ., IV, 4, 1 348, 5ff.). Origen is making one point. He wishes to show that the Being of the Father, without appearing as a genus, extends to all things universally.

However, does not Origen's locating of Being qua Being in an extra-generic hypostasis destroy the universal scope of Being, and make it impossible to postulate that the Father is the first principle of all things? It is precisely on this question that much confusion has arisen. How can Being qua Being be universal, if it is restricted to one type of Being?

The answer is stated in the pros hen way in which Being extends to its various hypostatic instances, and through the hypostases to the material realm. It is here that Origen's answer parallels Alexander's. Created, or Relative Being, is called Being because it is the effect of a first cause that extends its energy and power throughout the whole of creation (e.g., De Princ., I,3,5 55,6ff.). The only requirement of Being is reference, either immediate or mediate, to God the Father. Since Origen says all creatures had received existence from the Father:

quod ea esse volunt ille, qui fecit...

(In Lib. I Sam. Hom. I, 11 21, 6)

even though:

... ad naturam Dei pertinet, non sunt...

(In Lib. I Sam. Hom., I, 11 21, 5)

We can assume all Being has reference to (ad) God's Being. This follows consistently from Origen's definition of the referential nature of Being.

In summary: This conclusion brings us back to Origen's whole treatment of causes and powers. The first task was to define God as first cause. The second task was to show that all the causes after the first cause pertain to God the Father. We have shown that the first cause belongs to Being qua Being and pertains to God alone, but, from the Father it extends to the Logos-Son. The efficient and instrumental cause of creation he extends Being to the created things. Being, thus, extends its way to everything, and has its source, ultimately, in God the Father.

The lower theologicals, the intelligibles and all of the sensibles depend upon this unmoved-mover, and "inhere" in him. God extends by reference then to all types of Beings, and embraces in one way or another, all beings. Being, thus, taken in toto, constitutes groups of referential equivocals. Being is in reference to the Father either immediately, as in the case with the second and third hypostases, or mediately, as is the case with the created things. For both cases God the Father is the ultimate Being, and the foundation of all Being.

6.5   Origen's distinction between essential and accidental being, necessary and contingent existence constitutes the foundations of his late Middle Platonic theoretic. If we add to these his notions of potentiality and actuality we begin to see how he wove the diverse strands of Neo Pythagorean, Middle Academic, and Peripatetic metaphysical thinking into a diverse whole.

In the early Neo Pythagorean writings of Eudorus and Archytas, in the context of the Middle Academy of the first century B.C., we encountered a view of reality that was radically dualistic. Being per se was limited to the First One alone, and being per accidens characterized the Monad and Dyad, and hence the intelligible and sensible worlds respectively.

Philo's theoretic, which was strongly influenced by the early Neo Pythagorean philosophial theology, represented a modification of the radical ontological postulate of Eudorus. His modification was motivated principally to overcome the chôrismos between God and the universe. Philo accomplished his goal by postulating a categorical theory that linked God to the world through his Logos. The results were that the demarcation line between being per se and per accidens was redefined. Being per se was broadened to include God, the Logos, and the whole of the intelligible world, and being per accidens characterized the sensible world alone.

Clement adopted Philo's scheme, but went so far as to reinforce it. He postulated a new categorical theory which claimed that the same categories had referential efficacy to the intelligible and sensible realms. This meant that the basic principles of the Neo Pythagorean philosophical theology maintained by Philo were also modified. God remained transcendent, but was linked through the doctrine of equivocity to the Logos and through the mediation of the Logos to the sensible world. Although being per se referred to the intelligible world and being per accidens to the sensible world, as it did for Philo, the referential efficacy of a single set of categories to both made Clement's universe more closely linked to the God who created and sustains it through his Logos.

Second century Middle Platonism, as represented in Albinus, offered a new element to this picture. Albinus accepted the philosophical theologies of early Middle Platonism as his own. His categorical theory had close affinities to that of Clement. However, he introduced the notions of potentiality and actuality to the Academic cauldron. He argued that all being save God was in potentia. God was the only entity which was eternally active, or in actu. The intelligible world, which was made up of the Nous and the World Soul, was actualized by God out of potentiality. Once actualized the Nous and Soul actualized matter thereby creating the sensible world. Thus, added to the Middle Academic division of reality into being per se and per accidens is the Peripatetic notion of a universe becoming actualized. The Nous and Soul are actualized by apprehending God and his Idea. Matter is actualized by being formed in the image of the transcendent ideas by the demiurgic Nous, and sustained by being formed according to the immanent ideas by the World Soul.

The significance of Albinus' contribution was immense. Not only was God linked to the world paradigmatically and categorically, but we see the universe having God as its telos, and moving from potentiality to actuality. The static nature of the early Middle Platonic views of reality was replaced by a dynamic view of reality based upon a series of Peripatetic norms. The result of this transition in Middle Platonic metaphysical thinking is a lessening in the gap between God and the universe.

By the early third century we encounter a thinker, Origen, who combines these diverse elements into a coherent whole. First, he reasserts the Neo Pythagorean postulate of a radically transcendent God by arguing as Albinus did that God is the only entity that is actual. All other things are potential. He presented this notion a bit differently than Albinus. He framed his definition in terms of the distinction between necessary and contingent existence. God exists necessarily, all else exists contingently. Second, he reaffirmed the ontological postulate of his authorities Philo and Clement. Namely, that the noetic realm constituted being per se, and the material realm being per accidens. He folded the notions of actuality and potentiality into this division of being. Once essential, existentially, the Logos and Spirit became like their Father, and full members of an essential world. Matter, once accidental, became a cosmos made by the demiurgic Logos, and sustained by the power of God and the Logos.

Both doctrines allowed Origen to assert the distinctiveness of God, and the fundamental relationship God has with the universe. Existing, first alone, God creates the Logos, the Spirit, and through the Logos a sensible world out of matter. The intelligible and sensible worlds have God as their telos, and realize their actual states in conforming rationally and naturally to the intellect and will of God. This actualization of a world stretches from the two lower members of the divine triad, through the rational creatures, to matter. God's providence guarantees God, eventually, will be all in all, and one with the creatures who decide to conform to his will and message proclaimed in Christian scripture. It may be that even the non-rational creatures return to God because material bodily existence will cease when there is the final union of the cosmos with God.

The philosophical aspects of this final doctrine are what are important to consider, at least within the context of this study. Origen could not have proposed such a doctrine without creatively combining the variety of doctrines we have just reviewed. The Neo Pythagorean and Middle Academic distinctions between a radically transcendent God and the universe, and between Absolute and Relative being allow Origen to maintain the radical transcendence of God, and the distinction between orders of being. The Peripatetic notions of necessary and contingent existence permits Origen to underscore these differences. The Academic assertion of a link, paradigmatically and categorically between God and the world, and the Peripatetic doctrines of equivocity and natural teleology allow Origen to proclaim the eventual union of the all in all.

In summary, the theoretic proposed by Origen of Alexandria represents the consummation of a variety of Middle Platonic theoretics. In it we encounter the fruitful conflation of the principle postulates of Jewish, Christian, and Hellenic metaphysics.

As with any systematic interpretation of a philosopher, our interpretation of Origen may require some adjustments and qualifications. The core of Origen's philosophy is his theory of being and existence, and this is why we have spent a great deal of time upon it. Accordingly, the bulk of modern scholarship has focused upon his understanding of the hypostases, their relation to one another, and to the universe. Most textual and philosophical issues have been directed to questions of Origen's theology and not to his theoretic. However, we believe we cannot adequately answer these questions until we adequately describe some prior ones.

Within the limited parameters of this work we have completed the task set before us. We must now turn to Middle Platonic theories of knowledge. As a prefatory statement it can be said that knowledge and being are complementary areas of research for the Middle Platonists under examination in this study. Problems of knowledge and being are not mutually exclusive in Platonic metaphysics. Hence, the problematics addressed in this section reappear in the next. Indeed, without a firm grasp of the theoretics held by our thinkers we would not be able to begin with a study of their epistemologies.

PART TWO: EPISTEMOLOGY AND DIALECTIC

VI. EPISTEMOLOGY

Introduction

In this chapter we shall describe and analyze the structure and function of knowledge according to the Middle Platonists under examination. Just as transition characterized their doctrines of Being so does it characterize their theories of knowledge. It is clear that their epistemologies are intentional. Knowledge reflects the structure of Being each postulated. It is characteristic of Middle Platonic thought that the problems of Being and Knowledge are connected with one another. Thought cannot turn to the world of external objects without at the same time reverting to itself. In the same act it attempts to ascertain the truth of Being and its own truth.

Knowledge is not merely applied as an instrument and employed unreservedly. The justification of the use of knowledge and the quality of the instrument itself must be brought into question. The tendency manifests itself so that we must not grasp at any objects whatever and seek to investigate their nature on the basis of our knowledge. Instead the first question asked is what kind of object is commensurate with, and determinable by, knowledge. This question leads into the specific character of the human understanding and the asking of the question, "What is its realm?" and "How does it develop from its first elements to its highest forms?"

The critical problem of knowledge has its roots in a metaphysical problem. A really adequate explanation of the human mind is only to be found in a definition of its capacities and functions. Hence, ontology is designated as the foundation of epistemology. What the human mind knows and the veracity of the knowledge it procures is largely determined by the nature of the object is focuses upon and its place in the hierarchy of being. The problem of the truth of human knowledge is resolved into the question of the agreement between perceptions, conceptions, and objects.

Although our Middle Platonists differ over the extent of the relation between these distinct faculties of knowledge and their objects, they generally agree that there are degrees of knowledge commensurate with the objects under examination, and that sensibles and intelligibles yield different types of knowledge. The question about the connection of the ideas of the human mind with reality, or concerning the possibility of their application in cognition, is generally answered by postulating that there is no opposition between the structure of knowledge and the structure of things known. In addition, there is no opposition between how reason, as the system of clear and distinct ideas, and the world, as the totality of created beings harmonize. Their answers are that knowledge and Being represent different aspects of the same essence. The "archetypal intellect" of God is the ground of the bond between thinking and being, truth and reality. The connection between the ideas and reality, between concept and object is guaranteed and produced by the mind of God. It is through this agency that the human mind recognizes and acts upon external objects.

For Antiochus there is no true knowledge of things except insofar as the mind relates sense perceptions to the ideas of reason. Dillon is correct (MP., 91-96) that it is only through this relation that ideas gain objective meaning. Only then do ideas cease to be mere modifications of ego, and represent objective reality and order. Sense qualities in themselves contain no trace of any knowledge of being apart from being within the manifold world of sensation. The immediacy with which the mind fixes upon them and the mode in which they change from moment to moment provides no solid ground for a knowledge of Absolute Being. Scientific method alone can perceive in these states of mind and moments of sensation, the objectively subsisting and objectively valid order of nature. But such a knowledge is possible only by the procedure of relating the accidental to the necessary, the merely factual to something rational, the temporal to the eternal.

Antiochus argues that the human mind can only know nature and physical reality by relating it to God as the place of the ideas (Cicero, Or., 8ff). In this sense every act of cognition, every act of reason, brings about an immediate union between God and the human mind. The validity, the value, and the certainty of the fundamental concepts of our knowledge are only placed beyond uncertainty by the fact that in and through intellection (noêsis) we participate in the ideas. All logical truth and certainty are based on this metaphysical participation, which they require for their complete truth. True knowledge radiates from the realm of ideas and the eternal truth which produces them, not from the things of sense.

As we consider the transitions in Jewish and Christian Middle Platonic epistemology we can see most directly the point at which the epistemology of Antiochus was adopted. In the problem of knowledge the Middle Platonists found the approach and solution to the problem of knowledge as a modification of the solution offered by Plato. Nature and knowledge are placed on their foundations, the divine ideas, and explained in terms of their own conditions. The ideas of God mediate between subject and object. The problem of knowledge was solved on the ground of the apriorism of the ideas, and the divine intellect which produced them.

The logical and epistemological problem of the relation of knowledge to object is solved by the introduction of metaphysical considerations. Philo postulates that divine being is the source of the principles and concepts of the understanding. The problem of knowledge is solved through the postulate of a transcendent world created by God, which contains the basis for the order, structure, and value of knowledge. This postulate of the heteronomy of knowledge and the rejection of the autonomy of knowledge was expanded upon by Albinus and Clement following Philo.

With Clement, and later Origen, we encounter a conflation of Antiochus' and Philo's theories of knowledge, and a significant contribution to Middle Platonic epistemology. The postulate is offered that one ought not to merely observe the faculty of understanding as it synthesizes sense perceptions and produces its first sense ideas from perceptions or how it combines the primary intelligibles and produces the intelligible ideas. In addition one should examine the ultimate criterion of sensible and intelligible knowledge itself, the logoi-ideai of God proclaimed in scripture. When the demand is made for a precise characterization of the reasoned revelation of scripture the motive is not simply from pious introspection; on the contrary, they are led to this conclusion by a belief that the "words" of scripture represent highest knowledge in-themselves, and constitute the verification of the veracity of all knowledge. The logoi represent a different, a profound, a divine knowledge of reality. They represent a divine knowledge (gnôsis) upon which all epistêmê and doxa rest, and are judged.

Clement, for example, proposes a scheme wherein the 'knower' moves upward to divine knowledge. He begins from sensible knowledge and works up to intelligible knowledge. Knowledge of the sensible and intelligible worlds then brings him to the threshold of divine knowledge. Divine knowledge provides the criterion whereby the mind judges the validity of the content of perception and cognition.

In order to clearly distinguish between the object of gnôsis, and of pistis, Clement finds it necessary to recognize a special class of ideas. The logoi are neither a product of human cognition or perception. They would slip through our fingers if we regarded them as objects of human knowledge, to be approached and grasped by means of analysis and definition. They would also be lost if we treated them as objects of sensation because if we approach them from the sensible standpoint we forever lose the true meaning they hold.

Albinus postulates that the whole structure of knowledge was to stand on the ideas: knowledge of the physical world upon the ideas within matter, and knowledge of the intelligible world for the primary intelligibles or the transcendent ideas. All knowledge is ground upon the being and nature of God. With Albinus the system of the divine ideas is reinforced. They are traced back to God's creative force within nature, and to the eternal paradigms of the intelligible world which are the models for nature. The divine mind becomes the mirror of reality in its manifold forms. In this sense the understanding is active. Its function is to arrange its objects so that they correspond to the reality of the ideas which they mirror.

The division of the mind into its individual faculties represents an attempt by Albinus to segregate the different types of knowledge, and to arrive at a precise definition of the different realities the ideas reflect. Albinus asserts that rational and sense knowledge have specific meanings which cannot be confused. When he gives a precise characterization of intelligible intellection and distinguishes it sharply from sense perception he affirms that there are two entirely different modes of objective relations involved in these two types of intellection. The one yields epistêmê, the other doxa. The one presents to the mind the eternal ideas themselves, the other the mere quality of sensible objects.

On the basis of Philo's and Clement's considerations, and rejecting Albinus', Origen postulates an independent faculty of the mind. He calls it "divine perception" (theia aisthêsis). Only this agent intellect is capable of energizing the human intellect so that it can know reality and decipher the "inner meaning" Scripture holds. The divine, and agent intellect, leads the soul upwards to final felicity, conjunction with God.

From the seminal reflections of Philo, Clement, and Origen we enter into the realm of Jewish and Christian Middle Platonic epistemology. In conquering a place for divine perception, and in endeavoring to show that the divine mind is the most profound of mental faculties, these Christian Platonists bring about a change in the conception of the meaning and origin of knowledge. Knowledge is not merely the aggregate of innate ideas whose truth is determined by the inherent trustworthiness of reason itself. Nor is knowledge an accumulated mass of perceptual ideas and cognitive ideas whose truth is determined by an appeal to general principles and their apriori evidence. Philo, Clement and Origen argue that there is a relativity which extends to human knowledge from sense-perception to intellection. The question they ask is: is there a criterion of knowledge which is free from the bondage of human understanding? Are there invariable truths which transcend the relativity of the ideas themselves? Indeed there is. For the Jewish and Christian Platonists, scripture and the knowledge proclaimed therein, lead the philosopher to union with God.

These Platonists accept and adapt the postulate that human knowledge has a specific function, and certain limits. To this they add a new postulate that the validity of all human knowledge and the ideas they rest upon is ultimately determined by the revelation of scripture and the logoi proclaimed in Scripture. Divine knowledge becomes the agent and guarantor of the truth of human knowledge, and the criterion of the veracity of all human perceptions and conceptions.

These transitions in Middle Platonic epistemological theory shall be examined in this section. The attempt will be made to describe and analyze the presuppositions of the doctrines of knowledge proposed by Philo, Clement, Albinus, and Origen. We shall do this with an eye on the epistemological problematics which confront these representatives of the Middle Academy.

1. Philo of Alexandria

Philo does not present a succinct epistemology, nor does he present his theory of knowledge in systematic faction.[1] Nonetheless, it is possible to reconstruct its basis and premises.

In this section our goal is a modest one. We wish to describe Philo's theory of the human understanding, trace its origins, and note its limitations. The value of such an undertaking is that we are permitted to view the severe limitations Philo places upon human knowledge, and why he proposes that the human mind should turn to divine knowledge for the truths about reality it seeks to know.

It is characteristic of the Middle Platonic philosophy that the problem of being and the problem of knowledge are very closely connected with, indeed inseparably linked to, one another. Human thought cannot turn to the world of external objects without at the same time referring to itself. In this act it attempts to ascertain the truth of reality and its own truth. Knowledge is not merely applied as an instrument and employed unreservedly as such, but time and time again with growing insistence the question of the justification of this use of knowledge and of the quality of the instrument arises.

Philo was not the first to raise this question. He merely gave it a new formulation, a deeper meaning, and a new solution. The general task of defining the function of human knowing had already been clearly grasped by Plato. Philo places the same question at the foundation of his whole epistemology. The point of both is that we must not grasp at any objects whatever and seek to investigate their nature on the basis of human knowledge alone. The first question is what kinds of objects are commensurate with, and deter-minable by, human knowledge? The solution of this question requires exact insight into the specific character of human understanding. This can only be done by tracing the whole course of its development from its first elements to its highest forms.[2]

The fundamental problem of the truth of knowledge, and the agreement between perceptions, conceptions, and objects, is solved by Philo most pessimistically. He reduces the realm of perceptions and conceptions to the natural or physical realm of being, and asserts that a higher realm of being contains objects of knowledge that can only be found in prophecy and divine revelation.[3] To grasp these objects it is necessary to be trained not only in philosophy, but in the truths of biblical scripture, or divine prophecy.

Philo, thus, radically separates human understanding and its capacities from divine understanding, and asserts that the veracity of all human understanding has as its final criterion the wisdom proclaimed by God in his prophecy (Mut., 22, 122). Indeed, the prophecy of the divine intellect become the bond between thinking and being, between truth and reality in the philosophy of Philo. This basic claim of Philo's thought is even more apparent in his heirs Clement and Origen.

1.1   For Philo the nature of human knowledge can only be explained in terms of the ideas the mind finds within itself. These ideas are the objects the mind pursues, assuring it once and for all of its origin and destiny. According to Philo all philosophy begins with a consideration of the objects of perception. Corporeal objects are the initial objects of human knowledge. The mind grasps these material perceptions, orders them, and come to know the world.

Philo calls knowledge (epistême) perception (katalêpsis), and asserts that the criterion of human knowledge, at least as it comes to know the world initially, is the kataleptikê phantasia (Congr.,141). There is no need to ask further the provenance of his theory. As Dillon (MP., 141) notes this is the Stoic definition (SVF.,i,68), and presupposes the whole Stoic theory of knowledge. Philo as much as reproduces this theory in (Immut.,41-44) and (QG.,iii,3).

Philo's theory of knowledge maintains the Stoic notion, probably mediated through Antiochus (cf. Boyance, REG 72 (1959),367-379; Theiler, Parousia, 204-215), that all knowledge must be tested by a standard.[4] What is true in human notions may be distinguished from what is false. Since every kind of knowledge, no matter what its object, must be tested by this standard, it follows that the standard of human knowledge cannot be found in the subject-matter of human perceptions, but rather in something else. This something else is the wisdom of God proclaimed in scripture. This wisdom is the universally valid standard by which the truth of human notions are ultimately tested (QG.,iv.,140; ef.Post.,43,143; Fuga.,13,66; 18,aa; VM.,ii,8,48).

Philo's important statement in (Congr.,141), associating knowledge (epistémê) with conception (katalêpsis), tells us that he regarded sensation as the source of all perceptions and hence of all human knowledge.[5] The formation of perceptions gives rise to knowledge, and knowledge is a fixed and immoveable conception or system of conceptions. Hence, Philo's preoccupation with the Stoic theory of the proposition (lekta: AGR.,141), and etymology (e.g., Leg. Alleg.,ii.14-15).

However, it is the first claim that is significant, at least epistemologically. Philo always associates sensation and mind (Leg. Alleg.,i.11,29), sensation and thought (Conf.,26,133; Leg. Alleg.,ii.7,23;ii.8,24), and sensation and reason (Praem.,v.28). This tells us that perceptions and the conclusions based upon them are related to one another, and that human knowledge is a combination of sensations, and the faculty of understanding allied to sensation.

The standard of truth (to krinon) is the katalêptikê phantasia. This is the Stoic definition (SVF,i.68).[5] Assent, therefore, rests with the human mind. The human mind has the power of decision concerning the truth or falsehood of a conception. Hence, human perceptions are of such a kind that they bestow their own assent compelling us to regard them, at least initially, as true. They are valid if they correspond with the actual nature of things. Conformity to nature is the standard for the truth of human perceptions. Such a test of irresistibility (katalêptikai) applies to sensations, and sensations supply the material for human knowledge. However, sensation is not the only standard for truth. Sensation coupled with mind, thought, or reason is the complete standard of truth for human knowledge.

Philo maintains that the visible world is the starting point to higher knowledge (Somn.,i.32,187,188), but qualifies this assertion by claiming that God directs the activities of the human mind (Leg. Alleg.,ii.13,44-46; i.13,40; 11,29). This higher knowledge comes from God, and provides the human mind with a knowledge of the things incorporeal (Virt.,iii,12). The combination of sensible and divine knowledge yields knowledge of nature and of God (Leg. Alleg.,iii,33,100). This combination consists of scientific knowledge (epistêmai) and propositions (theorêmasi: Mut.,i.4-5). This is the content of reason (logismos) and sensation (aisthêsis). The former deals with intelligible things, and the latter with visible things. The first yields truth and the second opinion (Praem.,v.28).

In summary, knowledge, at least of the human variety, consists of sensation and reason, which yield both opinion and truth. There is no hint in Philo that sensation and reason are separate faculties of the mind, or that they present different types of knowledge. Rather knowledge has its origins in the sense-perceptions, which the mind organizes, and its end in the arrangement of these sense perceptions according to the intelligible ideas given to the human mind by God (Virt.,iii,12). In defining human knowledge, its activity, and its products Philo's epistemology reflects the theory of knowledge in the school tradition associated with Antiochus of Ascalon. Certain traditional elements of the Platonic epsitemology are wanting. There is no distinction between faculties of knowledge, the types of knowledge associated with each faculty, nor is there a theory of recollection proposed which accounts for how the human mind comes to know the higher things. Rather the universal is summed up from the particular by the human mind, and the validity of the particular as well as the universal is tested by the knowledge God implanted in man at the time of creation which man later discovers just as Moses did (VM.,i.5,21). Philo's theory of knowledge is a monotonic theory of knowledge, and it becomes paradigmatic for the epistemologies of Clement and Origen. Its counterpoint is the theory of knowledge called dichotomic exemplified in Albinus. The distinction between the two is what distinguishes later Hellenic and Christian Academic theories of knowledge.[6]

Human knowledge is applicable to sensible reality because it arises from the same source as its objects. Given this there is no fundamental dissonance between the structure of knowledge and the structure of things. Reason harmonizes sense impressions and yields a system of clear and distinct ideas. Philo does not propose two faculties of knowing, one directed toward sensible objects, and the other toward intelligible objects. Rather, as Drummond suggests, (PJ.,i.356) the activity of knowing is the movement from perception to conception. Perception (aisthêsis) is one of the activities of knowing that leads to thought (dianoia) and reason (logismos). All three activities are phases in human knowledge, and represent the degrees the mind (nous) goes through in its processes of knowing (Leg. Alleg.,i.11,29; Conf.,26,133; Praem.,v.28; cf. Leg. Alleg.,ii.7,23; ii.8,24).

1.2   As we consider the basic principles of Philo's theory of knowledge we can see most distinctly the point at which nature and knowledge are placed on their own foundations and explained in terms of their own conditions. Out of cognitive impressions (kataleptikê phantasia) a world comes to be known. Knowledge is the product of the combined activity of sensations and the mind working upon these sensations. Philo does not deprecate human knowledge. He merely recognizes its limitations. The human mind knows only sensations. It possesses no ability whatsoever to gain knowledge of being or of the world. It offers only states of mind which change from moment to moment. All logical truth and certainty are based ultimately upon metaphysical participation with the Logos. God's Logos is the source of principles and pure concepts of the understanding (QG.,iii.9; Virt.,39.21).[7] Philo calls the knowledge of the Logos prophetic knowledge, or unmixed knowledge (Fuga, v.22). Prophecy presents a divine knowledge independent of sensation placed in the soul of man. Divine knowledge complements human knowledge formed by the mind out of sensation (Spec. Leg.,iv.8,49: Virt.,39,217; Heres,53,265).

1.3   Philo solves the problem of the transitory nature of human knowledge by postulating a transcendent knowledge. Transcendence is the bridge between the ego and the external world, between subject and object. There is not true knowledge of things except insofar as the human mind relates its sense perceptions to the divine knowledge. It is only through this relation that human notions gain objective meaning, and thus cease to be mere modifications of the ego and come to represent objective reality and order. (Fuga, 137; Plant.,121)

Scientific reasoning alone perceives in these states of mind the objectively subsisting and objectively valid order of nature. But such perception is possible only through the procedure of relating the accidental to the necessary, the merely factual to something rational, the temporal to the eternal. Indeed, the human mind can only know nature and physical reality through the concept of intelligible extension, but the mind can only grasp this concept by relating it to God as the source of the ideas (Leg. Alleg., iii.33,100: cf.ABR.,24,122). The validity, the value, the certainty of the fundamental concepts of human understanding are placed beyond doubt by virtue of the fact that in and through them we participate in divine being (QG.,iv.140). All logical truth and certainty are ultimately based upon such metaphysical participation, which they require for their complete proof. The light that illuminates the path of knowledge shines not from within, but from without. It radiates from God, his divine truths, and divine prophecies (Abr.,102; Fuga, 108; Somn.,i.215).

The pandora's box has opened. The divine and prophetic spirit is the source of all true knowledge, and the final criterion of all transitory knowledge. this spirit of divine wisdom is breathed into man's incorporeal and rational soul as the breath of God was breathed into Adam (Fuga, 33,186: VM.,i.50,277). The apriorism of divine rationalism now enters into the lexica of Middle Platonism in the Judaic Platonism of Philo. A deus ex machina becomes the determination of the origin of true knowledge, and the validity of all knowledge. We encounter the first metaphysics of the soul based upon the prophecy of biblical scripture, and the Logos (Somn.,i.191).

As Wolfson and Drummond note (P.,ii,31-33; PJ.,ii.216) Philo associates the divine spirit with the Logos. This divine spirit is also given to a few men to understand since it is associated with scriptural wisdom, and the prophet who deciphers the wisdom proclaimed in scripture (Gig.,v.22; Immut.,i.33,190; Mut.,31,169: Somn.,i.33,190). The significance of Philo's suggestions cannot be underestimated. They form the foundations of a doctrine of divine knowledge and its demonstration in the later Christian Platonisms of Clement and Origen. Implicit in his brief comments is the notion that biblical scripture is a divine source of philosophical knowledge. This knowledge is identical with the Logos and the thoughts he contains within himself. The Logos contains this knowledge and imparts it to human understanding. Indeed, not only is the Logos the place and transmitter of this knowledge, he also provides to the human mind the rules and principles to decipher the meaning of this divine knowledge by scientifically relating the perceptions of the human imagination to the ideas situated in the divine mind.

Philo is not content to merely present the growth of the human mind, he wants to penetrate into its real moving forces. A survey of Philo's epistemology shows that its central problem is grouped around a common center. The investigation of the activity of human knowledge comes back again to the theoretical problem in which all the threads of this study unite. Is the experience derived from the world a sufficient basis to construct a true view of reality? If not, is there an inner connection which permits us to make a transition from the world of Becoming to the world of Being, and hence to God?

No uniform solution of this problem is found in Middle Platonic thought all at once. But now that the problem has been formulated, and in a sense answered by Philo through his doctrine of divine wisdom and prophecy, does Philo plant those germinating cells from which a whole epistemology of divine wisdom is built? The general question is, is there a body of knowledge upon which we can ground human knowledge and make metaphysical sense out of the physical and the noetic world in which we find consciousness? Does the human mind cooperate in this process of gaining true knowledge? If so, how is this determined?

Philo's epistemology proceeds from the anomaly that the only material available for the erection of the structure of our perceptual world consists in simple sense perceptions, but that these perceptions do not contain the slightest indication of those forms in which perceptual reality is given. Yet we believe that we see this reality before us as a solid structure in which every individual thing has its assigned place, and its relation to all other parts is exactly determined. Indeed, the fundamental character of all reality lies in this definite relationship. Without the presence of order in the co-existence and sequence of our individual perceptions, without a definite spatial and temporal relationship, there can be no objective world, no nature of things.

The material world shows us the world of products not of process. It confronts us with objects bearing definite shapes without telling us how they acquired these shapes. Yet we ascribe to ever individual object a certain magnitude, a certain position, and a certain distance from other objects. But if we try to establish the foundations of all these assertions, we find that it is not to be discovered among the data given to us by the senses. A gap exists between being perceived and being.

This attitude forces Philo to postulate an inviolable order among phenomena and explain it in the paradigmatism of his physics (e.g. Opf.,102;Heres,156; cf.Opf.,16) and in the categorical ontology of his theoretic (Dec.,30ff). If he does not, this phenomenal world will dissolve into mere illusion, and the attitude towards the world will become the attitude of the Sceptic. It is clear that Philo does not take the Sceptic's course. His ten points against dogmatism shows this (Ebr.,162-205). Thus, the cardinal question of Philo's theory of knowledge is that of the meaning of this order and its derivation. For Philo the origin of human knowledge is certainly sense perceptions, but we cannot expect reliable guidance in following perceptions. Without God's grace we cannot comprehend truth. Hence, Philo postulates that the end of human knowledge is the apprehension of divine knowledge, and the meaning of divine knowledge is found in biblical scripture and the Logos.

1.4   Philo overcomes this dilemma by giving a broader meaning to his basic concept of perception, by including in its definition not only simple perception but also prophetic perception (Leg. Alleg.,iv.8,49; Virt.,39,217; Heres,53,265).[8] This prophetic perception is associated with a kind of ecstasy (QG.,iii.9). Ecstatic knowledge transfers the human mind into another realm (QG.,iv.90). Every sense impression possesses such a power of representation if seen in the context of prophetic perception. It not only presents itself with its specific context to consciousness, but it causes all other content with which it is joined to be visible and present in consciousness. This reciprocal play of impressions, this regularity with which sense impressions are linked to prophetic impressions, is the ultimate ground of human knowledge and knowledge of the world.

Philo argues that this transition is a rational transition. It is of a logical and mathematical kind. Epistemological analysis reveals these intermediary steps and teaches us how indispensable they are. It shows us that a connection exists between different fields of sensory experience just as it does between the symbols of language and their meaning (Dec.30ff.). Just as the speech symbol is in no sense similar to the content in which it refers at first glance, at deeper glance we see that relations hold for the connection among disparate impressions. Out of these impressions we see not only the true meaning of the symbols of speech, but their objective ontological relations expressed categorically.

The pedigree of Philo's analysis in (Dec.,30) has philosophical antecedents which are probably Stoic (cf. Dillon, MP.,178-179). Philo is quick to assert that the universality and regularity of these arrangements, which distinguish the symbols of sense impressions from those of speech, has its origins in a power of divine reason arising in a realm beyond human knowledge. The logic and metaphysics of sense impressions and language comes from the sphere emancipated from the bondage of the sense organs. The validity and objectivity of such knowledge could not be found in the activity of human reason alone. The human mind is but a mirror of reality. It is and remains a mirror of the universe which is the product of God.

Here we have reached the point where the inner unity of the relation between human and divine knowledge arises. Human knowledge may begin from perceptions but is based upon the thought of a divine mind. The goal of the philosopher is to correlate his impressions with God's conceptions. He can do this if he recognizes the origin of all human knowledge in the world is limited, but that all human knowledge of the world is divinely grounded. The locus of this latter knowledge is in biblical scripture, and proclaimed in prophetic perception.

Now that we have outlined Philo's programmatic statement, let us turn to its expression in the writings of Clement. If Philo's epistemology is characterized by a want of explicit expression, Clement's is characterized by an abundance of expression.

2. Clement of Alexandria

2.1   We can situate Clement's epistemological doctrines within the trajectory of Middle Academic theories of knowledge extant in Antiochus and Philo.[9] The evidence for this is that he views knowledge as the product of the combined activities of sensation and mind. Following Antiochus he identifies pistis as a type of metaphysical knowledge, by calling pistis sygkatathesis and prolepsis, and asserts that evangelical pistis is on the same level, at least epistemologically, as metaphysical pistis. For Clement both pistis refer to immediate knowledge, and the raw material for the faculties of the mind to construct the concepts of scientific knowledge.[10] Clement's proposal that evangelical faith is a type of epistemological knowledge is his original contribution to the history of Middle Platonic epistemology.

Clement made the most strenuous efforts to gain an epistemological foot-hold for biblical faith. The whole material of knowledge was held to grow out of sensuous presentations, but the truth or falsity of this knowledge is in its assent (sugkatathesis) to both the mind and the content of divine knowledge (Strom.,ii.8.4: (ii.117.8-9). Although the content of all knowledge arises solely from perception and results in mental presentations (prolêpseis), it is trustworthy because its demonstrations are based on the principles of all things which are undemonstrated (Strom.,viii.6.7-7.2: (iii.83.16-24; ii.13.4-14: (ii.119-26-32).

Unlike the earlier Peripatetics (Arist, EN.,vi.1140b31-1141a3) or those contemporary with himself (Galen, In Log.,i.5;xvii.1;xvii.2; De meth. Med., x.p.33.15-18; cf. Alexander Aph., In Top.,ii.2.p.18.16, p.16.4-8), Clement identified the undemonstrable first principles (anupothetoi archai) of knowledge with the statements (lêmmata) and axioms (axiômata) of biblical scripture. He considered them as principles of demonstration not only for the universal and trustworthy principles of scientific knowledge, but also for what appears evident to both sensation and to mind (Strom.,viii.7.3:(iii.83.24-29); v.35.5: (ii.349.18-350.2). It is also the case that these first principles are found in the Logos who is wisdom, science and truth (Strom.,iv.156.1: (ii.317.21-23; cf. vi.2.2 (iii.6ff.); vii.13.2: (iii.10.7-8).

The mind's activity according to Clement is akin to what we encountered in Philo.[11] It is characterized by energy and actively synthesizes the sense-perceptions into conceptions (prolêpseis: Strom., viii.14.3: (iii.88.20-21); ii.9.5: (ii.118.2-4): ii.16.3: (ii.121.8-12); ii.28.1 (ii.128.1-2). The origins of his doctrine of knowledge can be traced back to Antiochus (Cicero, Ac.Pr.,ii.30-31).[12]

Belief or faith (pistis) for Clement is termed as assent (sygkatathesis Strom.,ii.8.4: (ii.117.8-9); ii.54.5-55.1). This positive assent of the mind to sense-perceptions is theory which has its origin in the tradition of Academic epistemology associated with Antiochus (Cicero, Ac.Post.,i.40.1). The association of assent and faith is made by Varro speaking from the standpoint of Antiochus (Cicero, Ac.Pr.,ii.37;ii.38;ii.39; Fin.,iv.9). The principal difference between the theory as expressed by Clement and that of Antiochus is the grounds for assent. For Clement assent is based upon the assumption that divine knowledge is the guarantor of human knowledge. For Antiochus there is assent based upon a firm conviction that the human mind itself has the ability to test the veracity of its own perceptions and conceptions.

Clement, thus, holds faith (pistis) to be the acceptance of the first undemonstrated principles of demonstration, the acceptance of what is evident to sensation and to mind, and any kind of immediate knowledge associated with the sense-perceptions. As Lilla has noted (C.,118-131) there is little in Clement's epistemological doctrine, at least up to this point which we have not seen in Antiochus and Philo. The activity of human knowledge is the combined activity of sensations and mind.

2.2 Faith can also be produced by demonstration (Strom.,viii.5.1: iii.82.12-14); viii.5.3: (iii.82.16-17); viii.7.6 (iii.83.31-33). This is not a new notion in hellenistic philosophy. It can be traced back to Aristotle (Top.,103b7,131a23; An.Pr.,68b12,68b13-14; An.Post., 72a25-26,72a30-31,72a35-36; EN.,1139b33-34; AR.,1355a5-6,1377b23), and Alexander (In An.Pr.,ii.p.4.23-25;ii.43.6-9,10-12;44.6-8;68.20-21; In Top.,ii.62.6-7 Wallies; cf, Cicero, Ac.Post.,i.32).

For Clement there are two types of faith and demonstration. One is scientific and the other is doxatic (Strom.,ii.48.1 (ii.138.20-24);viii.5.2-3 (iii.82.14-18). If premises are true and conclusions deduced from the scientific syllogism, then the mind is presented with scientific faith (epistêmonikê pistis). If the premises are probable and the conclusions deduced from the dialectical or rhetorical syllogism, then the mind is presented with opinion (doxastikê pistis: Strom.,viii.7.8: (iii.84.4-7); viii.6.2: (iii.83.1-3).[13] Thus, Clement argues that faith (pistis) is the direct product of demonstration which yields knowledge and opinion.[14] Scientific knowledge is associated with gnôsis (Strom.,ii.49.3): ii.139.5-8). Since the anapodeiktoi archai of scientific knowledge are found in the Logos and based upon biblical scripture (Strom., iv.156.1: (ii.317.21-23);vi.2.2 (iii.6ff.); vii.13.2: (iii.10.7-8), Clement claims that faith (pistis) is a higher type of knowledge than knowledge (epistêmê: Strom.,ii.15.5: (ii.120.26-27).

Clement distinguishes between a common faith (koinê-philê pistis) and a scientific faith (exairêtos pistis). The first type is a lower type of knowledge than the second (Strom.,v.5.2 (ii.328-27-29); vii.95.9 (iii.68.2-4);i.43.1: (ii.28.30); iv.100.6: (ii.293.2); v.9.2 (ii.331.19); v.11.1 (ii.332.27);v.26.1 (ii.342.2);v.53.3 (ii.362.27). He associates scientific faith with the scientific epistemological faith mentioned above.

After having associated faith with knowledge Clement associates two types of faith with corresponding types of demonstration. Arguing that scientific demonstration from true premises yields scientific faith Clement proceeds to claim that faith is a higher form of knowledge than scientific knowledge. He calls this knowledge gnôsis. By means of these procedures he succeeds in raising faith to a type of knowledge, and turning faith into the highest kind of knowledge. This schemata is important to grasp because it forms the basis of his theory of religious and epistemological pistis.

2.3   The words of scripture are considered by Clement as the ground (archê) of demonstration. The study and interpretation of scripture practiced scientifically, and demonstrated scientifically, yields trustworthy and true metaphysical knowledge. The problem Clement faces is not is scripture true, but how is it true? If it is interpreted so that it yields its inner meaning, then it offers to the human mind the higher faith Clement associates with gnôsis.

Lilla compares (Strom.,vii.96.1) and (Strom.,vii.96.5) and illustrates how Clement regarded scripture as both the principle and object of demonstration.[15] The significance of Clement's proposal is that the scientific study of scripture discloses scripture's inner meaning, and yields scientific knowledge to the human mind (Strom.,ii.49.3: (ii.139.5-8); v.18.3: (ii.337.25-27); vii.57.3 (iii.42.4-7). Religious faith is accepted as the principle of demonstration and demonstration yields the interpretation of scripture. Hence, faith becomes the basis of gnôsis (Strom.,v.1.3:(ii.326.9), and gnôsis reveals the truth of knowledge and being.

Clement asserts that the acceptance of the truth of scripture is the preliminary condition for religious as well as epistemological faith. Furthermore, it is the basis for all metaphysical knowledge as well. The acceptance of scripture begins as a common faith and ends as a scientific faith. This movement of the mind from primitive to philosophical knowledge has two dimensions. One is epistemological, and the other is religious. Clement does not separate the two. He combines them. In so doing he coherently presents a doctrine of pistis as knowledge which leads to gnôsis. This activity of the mind in gaining knowledge of the world and the principles of the universe constitutes the leit-motif of his philosophy.

2.4 Clement has asked the question what kind of objects are commensurate with, and determinable by, human and divine knowledge? He answers this question by examining the whole extent of the realm of human knowledge, and by tracing the whole course of its development from its first elements to its highest forms. This critical problem has its roots in a genetic problem, and the adequate explanation of knowledge is found in its arehê and telos. Hence, ontology is the foundation of epistemology (Strom.,i.176.3: (ii.108.30-109.1); i.177.1: (ii.109.6-9); vi.8.40: (ii.471.30-472.1). It is through the encyclical disciplines that the human mind strives toward an understanding of reality, and the contemplation of divinely created being (Strom.,i.93.5: (ii.60.10-11); i.30.1: (ii.19.22); vi.91.1 (ii.477.20).

The objective validity of the perceptions and conceptions of human knowledge is determined and judged both by its origin in experience and its end in divine revelation. Divine wisdom thus becomes an epistemological criterion. In view of this knowledge (pistis) belongs to the metaphysical and divine sciences. Its function is to know the cosmos. The fundamental question of the truth of human knowledge, of the agreement between concepts and objects has been solved by reducing the realm of concepts and objects to a single stratum of being. In this divine stratum concepts and objects meet, and from this conjunction is derived all true correspondence. The nature of human knowledge can only be explained in terms of the perceptions the mind finds in the world, in God's Logos, and in biblical scripture. The goal of human knowledge is homoiôsis theô (Strom., vi.113.3: (ii.488.27).

According to Clement, all knowledge begins with a consideration of experience. Among these notions are the concepts of extension, form, motion, place and so on in the physical world, and numbers, the ideas, being and so in the noetic world. These models point backward to their origin, and forward to their end. Both are the trademark that the divine workman has placed before the human mind. As such there is no need to ask further concerning the connection of human knowledge with reality or concerning the possibility of its application to reality. It is applicable to reality because it springs from a divine source and because, accordingly, there is no opposition between the structure of knowledge and the structure of things. Reason, as the system of clear and distinct perceptions and ideas, and the world as the totality of created and eternal being, can fail to harmonize nowhere. They merely represent different expressions of the same essence. The archetypal intellect, the Logos, becomes the bond between human thinking and being, between the truth of human knowledge, and reality. There is no union between soul and body, between our perceptions, conceptions, and ideas, except that which is given or produced by the being of God. The way from pistis to gnôsis leads from one level of reality to another, but it always moves through the center of divine being and activity. It is only through this medium that the human mind recognizes and acts upon external objects. We see all things in God, and in the sacred scriptures which contain his wisdom. It is only through this relation that human knowledge gains objective meaning, only thus that its products cease to be mere modifications of ego, and come to express objective reality and God's order.

First sense qualities contain no trace whatsoever of any knowledge of being or of the world (Strom.,i.71.1: (ii.45.17-18); v.6.1(ii.336.1); v.67.2: (ii.370.29-371.2); v.67.2: (ii.370.29-371.2); v.67.3 (ii.371.4-5); v.73.1 (ii.375.14-15). Through the immediacy with which we experience them they represent mere states of mind which change from moment to moment. Scientific method alone can perceive in these states of mind the objectively subsisting and objectively valid order of nature. This perception is possible by relating the accidental to the necessary, the merely factual to something rational, the temporal to the eternal. We attain knowledge of the world by reducing it to the laws of divine reason rather than by merely attributing to it the qualities perceptible to sense. Scientific knowledge is contemplation by the mind (nous) of the intelligible world (Strom., i.15.2: (ii.11.13-4); i.166-2 (ii.104.1-2); ii.46.1: (ii.137.14-15); ii.47.4: (ii.138.11-13); ii.77.4: (ii.153.19); iv.40.1: (ii.266.5-9); iv.136.2: (ii.308.22-23); iv.136.4:(ii.308.26-27); iv.152.3: (ii.315.31-316.2).[16] This reduction is followed by a further reduction which penetrates more deeply. In order to grasp the true meaning of the world the mind must be purged of all sensible content, and proceed from a merely imaginative to an intelligible content. The human mind can know nature and physical reality only through the ideas of God, and it can only grasp this concept by relating these ideas to the Logos as the place of the ideas, and to biblical scripture as the place these ideas reside awaiting proper discernment. The validity, the value, the certainty of the fundamental concepts of human knowledge are placed beyond doubt by the active participation of God in the world, and the fact that in and through the divine ideas and divine revelation we participate in divine being, and the objects of the divine intellect. All logical truth and certainty is based ultimately on such metaphysical participation, which it also requires for its complete truth. The light that illuminates the path of knowledge shines from without, not from within. It radiates from the realm of ideas and eternal truths, not from the things of sense. This light of the human understanding points toward another and higher light, which is the light of the divine intellect (Strom.,i.97-2: (ii.62.17); ii.45.7): (ii.137.11-12); v.12.3: (ii.334.8); vii.2.2: (iii.68&); vii.13.2: (iii.10.7-8); vii.16.6: (iii.12.20-22).

In summary, the logical and epistemological problem of the relation of knowledge to its objects is solved by metaphysical considerations. God is the source of principles and concepts of the understanding. The problem of knowledge is solved by means of a transcendent world and the God who sustains and creates it. The relation between ego and the external world, between subject and object is the bridge of transcendence. This alone, at least according to Clement, overcomes the gap, between the human mind's idea and its object. As with Philo, in Clement, we encounter another metaphysics of the soul.

2.5   Clement's epistemological doctrine has a number of characteristics which suggest a Platonic theory of knowledge. However, one element is strikingly absent. This is a theory of recollection (anamnêsis). Knowledge according to Clement is not a recollection of things implanted in the should before its earthly life. Rather, knowledge begins from sense experience, and develops an understanding of the universal, inductively, out of the opinions and perceptions of sensible knowing. The comprehension of the sensible world leads to an understanding of the intelligible world, and finally to a gnôsis of God.

The basis for Clement's rejection of the doctrine of recollection, at least epistemologically, rests upon the view he holds concerning the structure and activity of human understanding. Following the trajectory of epistemological speculation as represented in Antiochus and Philo, Clement maintains a canonic theory of knowledge. Knowledge of the intelligible world begins with knowledge of the sensible world. There is no chôrismos either between knowing faculties in man, or the objects that the knowing faculty directs its attention towards. Both sensible and intelligible knowledge possess the validity which Clement terms belief or faith (pistis). The content for conceptions is given to the human mind by God as perception.

The division of the ideas into class-concepts or logical genera with species is held by Clement. The union of sensible perceptions with their transcendent ideas is brought about by the apprehension of these universals from the particulars of sense-perception itself. The individual sensible things partake of the universe essence by imitating them. In this sense the intelligible world of the ta noêta is of higher epistemic value than the sensible world of the ta aisthêta; but a knowledge of the latter does not preclude a knowledge of the former.

The essence of the ideas applies to all class concepts and the immaterial world is made up of the archetypes of the material world. It is the function of human knowledge to gain a comprehension of the connections between the two. This it does inductively out of the perceptions and opinions initially presented to the human mind by sense experience. Knowledge of the ideas comes from conceptions found in the content of perception. They present suggestions to the mind of things immaterial which are then perceived by the mind as it sheds itself of its corporeal way of assessing things.

The probable grounds for the rejection of the doctrine of recollection apart from those mentioned above is that Clement, like Philo, possessed knowledge of the intelligible world and of the Logos in the revealed wisdom of biblical scripture. With this higher knowledge at hand there was no need to propose an explanation of how the human mind remembers this higher knowledge. It is available if the knower deciphers the inner meaning of scripture.

3. Albinus

3.1   We shall now turn to Albinus' theory of knowledge.[17] As we consider this example of Middle Platonic rationalism, we can see most distinctly the point at which it agrees with the epistemologies of Philo and Clement. There is no true knowledge of the corporeal world and its changing states, but only perceptions and opinions. The point at which there is disagreement is that the incorporeal world forms the object of science, and this world exists side by side with the corporeal world as independently as knowledge (epistêmê) does with opinion (doxa). Here we have for the first time, in the Middle Platonic tradition at least, the claim of an immaterial reality and a faculty of knowledge that has this reality alone as its object brought forward expressly, and with full consciousness. This springs from the need for a knowledge that is raised above all ideas gained by sense-perception.

With Albinus we encounter a system of knowledge which explicitly rejects the monotonic approach to knowledge and its objects proposed in early Jewish and Christian Middle Platonic circles. Albinus builds upon an older dichotomic tradition of Platonic epistemological speculation, which grounds true knowledge and being in the intelligible world alone, and does not trouble itself about the world of generation and occurrence, of opinion and becoming, which is left to perception.[18] There are two faculties of knowledge directed to two distinct objects of knowledge, the immanent forms and the transcendent ideas. Human knowledge does not begin in perceptions and end in conceptions. One aspect of human knowledge knows the sensibles and another the intelligibles.

For Albinus, the transcendent ideas are that incorporeal being which is known through conceptions. This immaterial reality is related to the material, as being to becoming, as the simple to the manifold. If the ideas are something other than the perceptible world, knowledge of them through conceptions cannot be found in the content of perception.[19] With this turn of thought, which emphasizes more sharply the separation of the two worlds than do the doctrines of Philo and Clement, Albinus' doctrine of knowledge becomes more rationalistic than that of others we have examined. It also goes decidedly beyond that of Antiochus of Ascalon. These thinkers had developed the universal partially out of the opinions and perceptions of the particular. The universal was the common content of perceptions and opinions, however fragmentary and incomplete both were. Albinus sees in perceptions only the suggestions of the nature of physical reality, not a first step on the way to the conception of noetic reality.

Albinus divides human knowledge into two faculties with two distinct objects for the human mind to apprehend. Perception (aisthêsis) attends to knowledge of the sensibles (ta aisthêta), and intellection (noêsis) to the intelligibles (ta noêta). His theory of sensible knowing reflects the teachings of Antiochus, Philo, and Clement (cf. Witt, A., 47-49). Sensible knowledge is not denied its place, nor is its data deprecated. The natural mind (logos physikos) engages in receiving impressions from the outside world (Did., 154, 15.). Sense perception, which is an affection (pathos) of the soul, presents two types of object (Did., 154, 29ff.). One corresponds to qualities (poiotetês) and the other to embodied qualities (poia) from which composite bodies (athrosima) find their form. Dillon refers to these two types as primary and secondary perceptibles (MP., 274).

Nonetheless, the mechanics of sensible knowing are explained in Antiochean fashion. Albinus makes the distinction between three elements of perception (aisthêsis).

These are the faculty making the judgement, the object of judgement, and the judgement or criterion itself (Did., 154, 8ff.). Dillon notes that the first distinction, the to krinon, krisis, is analogous to a cognitive impression (kataleptikê phantasia: MP., 273). This distinction between agent and instrument of judgement, expressed using prepositional phrases, goes back to Antiochus as well (Seneca, Ep., 65, 8; cf. Theiler, VN., 18). In another parallel with Antiochus, Albinus maintains that the natural mind (logos physikos) corresponds to the force of mind (dynamis physikê) extant in Antiochus' theory (Cicero, Ac. Pr., 30). The instruments of judgement for this mental faculty are the sense impressions. Albinus calls the type of logos which apprehends the sensibles the doxastikos logos. Its product is opinion (doxa).

We have in sense perceptions a distinction made between qualities such as color or whiteness, and accidents (ta kata symbebêkota) or embodied qualities. The objects of the human knowing faculty directed toward sensibles are these composite bodies, which are the aggregate of sense-data. Apprehension of the sensibles yields the impressions of immediate thought. The doxastikos logos focuses upon unanalyzed primary impressions and forms mental constructions out of them. These constructions in turn conform to innate concepts (physikê ennoia), which are the metra of all right reason (orthos logos: Did., 156, 13ff.), and constitute the forms-in-matter (eidê). Dillon calls these the 'secondary' objects of intellection (MP., 274).

The second faculty of knowing Albinus calls the epistêmonikê logos. It apprehends the intelligibles (ta noêta), and its product is scientific knowledge (epistêmê). This category of knowledge is completely independent of sense-perception. It is the activity of mind (noêsis) which apprehends the primary intelligibles (ta prota noêta), or the transcendent ideas (ideai: Did., 157, 15f.). Again the logos is brought to bear on its respective object and receiving unanalyzed primary conceptions proceeds to construct them into mental constructs. These constructs are not the qualities in bodies of sensible perception, but the laws of mathematics, ethics, and so on. The activity of intellection (noêsis) has knowledge of the intelligible world as its goal.

For Albinus the doxastikos and epistêmonikos logos have as their objects the sensibles (ta aisthêta) and intelligibles (ta noêta) respectively. Albinus does not agree with Antiochus, Philo or Clement that sensible knowing (aisthêsis) is the source of any scientific knowledge (epistêmê). It yields only opinion (doxa: Did., 154, 23ff.). Hence the distinction between these two trajectories of Middle Platonic epistemology is that the former tradition maintains a canonic theory of human knowledge, and the latter a dichotomic one.

3.2   Both the doxastikos and epistêmonikos logos are agents of the human mind (nous). One uses the senses to interpret the sense world as well as the mind to interpret the intelligible world. It is as if the mind works with two halfs, one directed to the sensibles and the other to the intelligibles, but they function distinctly and do not combine their data to form mental constructs.

We have encountered Albinus' theory of the activity of sensible human perception previously. Activity characterizes simple sensation, and the activity of representation.

There is an activity which the sensible faculty possesses which reflects the dynamic nature of the world and the objects it focuses upon. Albinus' theory of intelligible human conception is also characterized by this activity of representation. The intelligible world is activity synthesized and the faculty which apprehends its objects reflects this active process.

The problem such an epistemology presents is self-evident. How does a mind initially engaged in sensible sensation come to know of the world above the material world? How does he come to use his faculty of intelligible intellection to understand this world?

For Albinus the human mind cannot move from an apprehension of sensibles to a conception of intelligibles. Neither the faculties of human understanding nor the objects each apprehend, share a common ground or starting point. Thus, how does the human mind ascend from sensible becoming to intelligible being if these two realms and the faculties of knowledge associated with each are toto caelo different? To answer this we must examine another aspect of Albinus' epistemology -- his doctrine of recollection.[20]

A monotonic theory of knowledge asserts that the human mind inductively develops an understanding of the universal out of the opinions and perceptions, and finds the common content in these perceptions and opinions. A dichotomic theory of knowledge does not conceive of the process of induction in this analytical manner, but rather sees in perceptions the suggestings or promptings with which the soul remembers conceptions and knowledge of the ideas.

Albinus expressed this rationalistic principle in the form that scientific knowledge (epistêmê) is a recollection (anamnêesis). In a series of implied propositions Albinus shows that mathematical and theoretical knowledge is not extracted from sense-perception, but that sense-perception offers only the opportunity for the soul to recollect the knowledge already present in her, the knowledge which has pure rational validity. He points out that mathematical relations are not present in corporeal reality, and he extended this observation to the sum-total of scientific knowledge (Did., 177, 35ff.).

This position, which reflects on that which is rationally necessary, recognizes the creative activity of the consciousness. The mind orders, or arranges, its sensible content. The content of knowledge is ordered according to the natural or 'innate concepts' (koinai ennoia: Did., 156, 13ff.; 178, 7) and the ideas (Did., 157, 17f.).

For the act of intelligible reception and the ordering of intelligible knowledge, Albinus follows the mythical representation extant in Plato (cf. Phaed., 246ff.). Before the earthly life the souls behold the pure forms of reality in the incorporeal world. The perception of similar corporeal things calls back the remembrance of forms forgotten in the corporeal life. From this awakens the philosophical impulse, or the love of the ideas. It is in this manner that the soul is raised again to the knowledge of true reality.

The argument is made that each faculty does this independently of the other. The canonic doctrine that one can form general concepts from sense data is argued against. Hence, in presenting his thesis Albinus stands in opposition to the tradition of Middle Platonic epistemological speculation beginning with Antiochus.

What Antiochus, Philo, and Clement, in their doctrines of knowledge, had designated as inductive knowledge becomes transformed in Albinus into an intuition that proceeds by recollecting a higher and purer perception. This perception yields a plurality of ideas which corresponds to the multiplicity of objects which occasion such perceptions. From this arises the task of scientific knowledge, which is the definition of the relations of the ideas to one another. This ascertainment of the logical relations between conceptions is presented as the division of the class-concepts or logical genera into their species. These logical operations, taken as a whole, Albinus calls dialectic (Did., 156, 21ff.).[21] We shall have the opportunity to discuss this concept of Albinus' thought later.

The doctrine of knowledge as recollection stands in close relation with Albinus' relation of ideas to the sensible world. Between the higher world of ousia and the lower world of genesis, between what is, and what is becoming, Albinus found that a relation of similarity exists. The relation is between archetypes (paradeigmata) and their copies or images (eidôla). Individual things correspond to their class concepts. This notion is expressed through the doctrine of imitation (mimêsis).

The class-concept or species is present in the sensible insofar as it possesses the qualities which dwell in the immanent idea. The precise designation of this relation, defined through dialectic, underscored the dependence of the sensibles upon their intelligible archetypes. The mind grasps what truly and really is by means of conceptions.

There is a logico-metaphysical aspect which cannot be separated from Albinus' theory of knowledge. The ideas apply to all class-concepts, and the immaterial world is the archetype of the entire sensible world. Albinus expresses this notion in his definition of the paradigmatic idea (Did., 163, 10ff.). The Idea is the paradigm of all things natural (Did., 163, 21). This purely formal understanding of the Idea as a class-concept permits him to assert that every class-concept belongs to the higher world of the forms.

In terms of epistemology the whole conception outlined above is explained by the process of recollection. Knowledge begins with sense experience which is suggestive of and pregnant with truths of an intelligible order. Sensible knowledge itself does not adequately establish this higher intelligible knowledge. It merely awakens in the human mind associations which point toward the knowledge of the higher world of the forms. The forms themselves are contained in the sensible world through the natural or innate concepts, what Albinus calls the physikê ennoia (Did., 156, 13ff.). These innate concepts may fall short of a complete realization of the transcendent ideas they are patterned on, but at least they lead to a recognition of a world of ideas which the human mind must know to fully understand the true nature of reality and knowledge. This is the teleological aspect of Albinus' theory of knowledge.

In summary, Albinus postulates two faculties of human knowledge directed toward sensible and intelligible objects respectively. The knowledge each faculty yields is radically distinct, and there is no connection between them.[22] It is not possible to rise from perception (aisthêsis) to conception or intellection (noêsis). This dichotomic theory of knowledge poses a problem which can only be solved through the theory of recollection (anamnêsis). Sensible knowledge is suggestive of a higher knowledge of the forms, or scientific knowledge. Individual sense-data recollecting and the formation of concepts from them is based upon a knowledge the soul possessed in a previous existence which the soul forgot when she entered the body. The associations raised of sensible perception awaken the philosophical impulse in the human mind, and the love of the ideas results in the acquisition of knowledge of the ideas. This theory of recollection provides Albinus with the quantum leap over the obstacles presented by his dichotomic theory of knowledge. He buttresses his anamnêsis postulate by demonstrating the proofs for the soul's immortality (Did., 177, 15ff.).

3.3   Albinus' theory of knowledge is significant for our study not because it becomes a norm for the Christian Middle Platonism of the early third century, but precisely because it does not. Albinus' epistemological norms are explicitly rejected by Origen. He argues that one can form general concepts from an accumulation of sense-data, and move from sense-perception to intelligible intellection. This rejection of the dichotomic theory of knowledge leads him to also reject the theory of recollection, and offer in its place a theory of the agent intellect. The fundamental question of the truth of human knowledge, of the agreement between concepts and objects, is to reduce both the realm of concepts and objects to the same stratum of being. Origen, like Philo and Clement, employs many pericopae from biblical scripture to argue this postulate. The nature of human knowledge can only be explained in terms of the ideas which the human mind finds in itself, the Logos, and biblical scripture.

According to Origen, philosophy begins with a consideration of divine knowledge expressed metaphysically through the Logos and in scripture. There is no union between human perceptions and reality except that which is given or proclaimed by God and the Logos. The way to knowledge never leads from one pole of being indirectly to another, but always through the center of divine being and its revelation in the metaphysical wisdom of the Bible. Origen's assertion is that we see all things in God. There is no true knowledge of things except when we relate our perceptions and conceptions to divine perceptions. It is only through this association that human knowledge gains objective meaning, and ceases to be mere modifications of the ego. Scientific method perceives the objectively subsisting and valid order of being. This is done by relating the accidental to the necessary, the factual to the rational, the temporal to the eternal. The human mind can only grasp these concepts by relating them to God. In this sense every act of cognition, every act of reason, brings about a union with the agent intellect which ends in union between God and the human soul. The validity, the value, the certainty of human knowledge is placed beyond doubt by the fact that in and through our perceptions and conceptions we participate with the divine agent intellect and divine being. All truth and certainty is based ultimately on this metaphysical participation.

Origen's theory of knowledge radically differs from Albinus'. Perhaps it is a reaction against the doctrine of knowledge proposed by the theory of knowledge emerging in the Hellenic Middle Platonism of the late second and early third centuries. In any case let us turn to Origen and describe the direction Christian Middle Platonic epistemology takes away from the example proposed by Albinus.

4. Origen: Knowledge

4.1   To initiate reflection on these broad concerns, this section considers only one context against which Origen's theory is considered. This is the intellectual or cognitive world that any philosophical document might be said to inhabit. The reconstruction of Origen's theory of knowledge to follow is neither strictly interpretive nor programmatic. It is merely offered as one context within which an understanding of Origen epistemology may be analyzed. It limits its focus of enquiry to the Middle-platonic context of Origen's thought, and examines the continuities and discontinuities Origen's option has with other 'contemporary' theories of knowledge such as the Peripatetic and Stoic.

Given the text-critical problems we face n Origen's writing, certain caution is assumed. Whenever possible the attempt is made to explain what Origen's theory of knowledge contains. At times, however, when we have to pass over the threshold of description to interpretation, certain cognitive contexts are proposed as analytical hypotheses. This attempt reflects the motive of the student to participate in the thought processes of the author himself, and to propose solutions to problems which Origen's theory of knowledge raises.

The term epistêmê and its cognates, e.g., pistis, logos, epistêmonikê pistis, logikê pistis; sophia, sophia pisteôs, are perhaps the most difficult terms in Hellenistic philosophy to define. Hellenic, Jewish, and Christian Platonists of the first centuries, A.D., employed these terms to designate "knowledge," and set them above what was held to be mere "opinion" or doxa. Although the general distinction between "knowledge" and "opinion" in Greek theories of knowledge received their first systematic expression in the writings of Plato, there is no direct link between Plato's theory of knowledge and the theory we encounter in the writings of Origen. Origen draws from more recent tradition(s) of reflection upon the nature of knowledge.[23] In addition, he complements the traditional Hellenic theories with a singular Jewish and Christian theory -- that the content of scripture presents a 'divine knowledge' in-itself, and that the "words" of scripture are the criterion of all human knowledge. Indeed, in pushing this postulate to its fullest conclusion, the claim is made that only scripture constitutes epistêmê, and the activity of human reason presents doxa in varying degrees.

In this examination of Origen's theory of knowledge we shall first examine the general principles and architechtonic of his epistemology. Next we shall unfold the relation he saw between the sêmeia-dicta of scripture and knowledge, and how the logoi of scripture are demonstrated as divine knowledge. Finally, we shall examine Origen's concept of ultimate felicity, the apprehension of the divine intelligible, through the doctrine of conjunction with the agent intellect.

4.2   It is characteristic of Middle Platonic thought that the problem of nature and the problem of knowledge are very closely connected with one another. In the epistemologies of Philo, Clement, and Albinus we have seen this relation between knowledge and reality touched on again and again. Thought cannot turn to the world of external objects without turning toward itself and to God in an attempt to ascertain the truth of itself and of the world.

Knowledge is not merely applied as an instrument and employed unreservedly as such. Time and time again with growing insistence the question of the justification of the use of human knowledge, and the quality of the instrument arises. This is clear in the debates the Jewish and the Christian Platonists have with the so-called literalists in their midsts. Philo was no means the first to raise this question and answer it. He merely gave it a new formulation that became paradigmatic for his heir Clement, and as we shall see for Origen.

The general task of defining the limits of the man mind begun by Plato had been picked up with new vigor in the New Academy with Carneades and Anesidemus. The sceptical attitude concerning the capacities of human knowledge were in a curious way upheld by the Jewish and Christian Middle Platonists, but with one major qualification. The human intellect cannot apprehend truth on its own merits unaided by God's grace. Hence, they accept the sceptics' arguments concerning the limits of human knowledge so they can offer divine knowledge as proclaimed by God's Logos and scripture as the way to the knowledge of higher things, both intelligible and divine.

Origen takes up the tradition of Middle Academic discourse on knowledge. He repeats much that we have encountered earlier, and adds something quite new within the context of our study.

Origen offers an epistemoloy strikingly familiar to those of Antiochus, Philo, and Clement, and unlike Albinus',[24] Perception (aisthêsis) and mind (nous) are linked, and human knowledge begins with apprehension of the sensibles (ta aisthêta) and ends with apprehension of the intelligibles (ta noêta: De Princ., IV,1,1, 292,9ff.). Even divine knowledge (theia aisthêsis) presents itself in the language of perceptions (Com. in Jh., XX,43,386). The human mind has levels of reality and objects to know, but the ground of all knowledge, be it sensible, intelligible, or divine has its ground in sensible perception (De Princ.,I,1,7,24; I,1,9,27,9f.), and its criterion of validity in scripture.

Opinion yields (doxa), scientific knowledge (epistêmê), and now prepare the way to divine knowledge (gnôsis). Knowledge begins as pistis eytychês becomes pistis exetasmênê, and ends as gnôsis (C. Cels.,I,9-11; cf. III,38,234ff.). Following Clement, Origen associates epistemological faith with religious faith (pistis), and asserts that both lead to a knowledge of the world, and to a knowledge of God. Although the human mind knows corporeal substances, and they are its objects (De Princ.,I,1,7,24,4) it is not characterized by physical space, sensible magnitude, bodily shape or color. Indeed, the human mind is incorporeal. It is not a corporeal entity.[25]

Sense-perception is imperfect and yields opinion, but it is the foundation for all subsequent knowledge. Human knowledge is the product of sense-perceptions and the activity of mind working from apprehension of the sensibles to intellection of the intelligibles (De Princ.,IV,1,1,292,9). Origen calls sense-perception enargeis, and all that possesses enargeia is accepted as valid on faith. Faith is a belief in the first principles of knowledge and demonstration supplied to the mind by the Logos and biblical scripture.[26] This is evident in his use of the term katalêptikê phantasia (C.Cels., I,4,92,6f.; VII,37,187,25f.). The koinai ennoiai of the human mind are trustworthy because they correspond to the _physikê ennoiai_ of God (C. Cels.,IV,14,284,26; IV,32,302,17).[27] The background of Origen's theory can be traced back to the epistemological theories of Antiochus (Cicero, Ac.Pr.,ii.37;38;39), and Clement (Strom.,viii.7.3-4: (iii.83.24-29); ii.8.4: (ii.117.8-9); v.86.1: (ii.383.1). Faith (_pistis_) is assent (_sygkatathesis_) to the veracity of sense-perceptions.[28] Origen virtually reproduces this doctrine in (De Princ., III,1,1,195,7;IV,3,1,325,3). For Origen sense-perception yields trustworthy knowledge albeit incomplete knowledge (C.Cels.,VIII,46,198,1).

The fundamental question of the truth of human knowledge, of the agreement between concepts and objects, has been solved by reducing the realm of concepts and objects to a common stratum of being. In this stratum, concepts and objects meet and from this original mingling all their later correspondence is derived. The nature of human knowledge is explained in terms of the common notions it has within itself, and their correlation with the common notions of God. These innate concepts (_koinai ennoiai_) are the seal that is from the first stamped on the human mind by its divine maker.[29] This assures it once and for all its origin and destiny.

4.3   Origen makes no mention of the doctrine of recollection, and comments upon the doctrine of ideas only to repudiate it (De Princ.,II,3,6,122,4). Knowledge is not grounded upon the _phantasia mentis,_ nor are such ideas to be recollected once sense-perception suggests the higher world they constitute. If the ideas are mere mental images, and the soul does not recollect and rediscover them through the process of recollection, how does the human mind know the truth of reality, and the God who created and sustained it?

As noted Origen rejected the Antiochean postulate that the criterion of knowledge is the uniformity of the human reason itself. He also rejected Albinus' theory that the ground and criterion of knowledge are the ideas. In its place he offered theories proposed by Philo and Clement to explain the criterion of human knowledge. These are that all perceptions and conceptions held by the human mind are to be tested by the _metra_ of scripture, and that the human mind working from these divine truths adjudicates the content of the mind's perceptions and conceptions.

Origen's theory of knowledge rests on the postulate that scripture, and the divine words contained therein, constitute the final arbiter of the veracity of all human knowledge (Com. in Math.,ii. Lomm.,iii,3-6;xxv.49-50). Once tested human knowledge may be accepted as _pistis._ The conditions for the possibility of divine knowledge, however, rest on an act of will (e.g., Comm in Ep. ad Rom. I,17 p. 53).[30] We shall examine the stages on the way of knowledge.

The _koinai ennoiai_ present man with a knowledge of God, but this knowledge is not derived from the study of the universe alone. The universal notions given to man by God are a _lex naturalis_ whereby man makes theoretical and moral judgments. Apprehension of the common notions yields an awareness of the universe, and the difference between good and evil (Comm. Ep. ad Rom. III,7 p. 201f. cf. Comm. in Cant. Cant. II p. 160,1). However, this is a knowledge which is not complete (Comm. in Ep. ad Rom. V,i p. 332ff. cf. Comm. in Jh. I,37 p. 48, 18ff). Indeed the _communes rationes-koinai ennoiai_ do not always present correct theoretical and moral ideas (cf. C.Cels. I,4 p. 58,9; Hom. in Luc. XXXV,lp. 205, 21ff. C.Cels. VIII,52, p. 267-15). Therefore, the universal notions must be tested by testimonies drawn from the scriptures (e.g., DePrinc. IV,1,1 p. 292,9ff).

Central to Origen's theory of knowledge is that every act of knowledge assumes an act of will, and every act of will is an act of faith (pistis). Rational power and free-will involve one another, and each belongs to the activity of cognition. Knowledge is a prolêpsis hekousios, a psychês autoexousiou ogikê sugkatathesis.[31] Knowledge begins from the perceptions of sense, and with the aid of the divine sense the mind moves to a knowledge of the intelligible things. Origen calls the movement from sensible to intelligible knowledge an: "...anabênai men apo tês philês pisteôs"....(C.Cels. III, 33 p. 229,30; cf. Comm. in Jh. XIX,3 p. 301,15; Cat. in Jh. p. 556; Comm. in Mt. XII, 15 p. 157; XVI,9 p. 31). Thus, the study of scripture yields the initial data whereby one begins his ascent to a knowledge of God, having left behind his philê pistis. It is through the study of scripture that one exercise his rational powers fully and becomes knowledgable of the sensible and intelligible things.[32]

The way to higher knowledge is the study of scripture, complemented by the decision to accept it as the foundation of all higher knowledge.[33] This study of scripture involves a movement from pistis eytychês to pistis exêtasmenê (e.g., C.Cels. I,9-11 p. 61ff).[34] The final goal of pistis is the knowledge of divine things, or gnôsis (DePrinc. II,11,6 p. 190,3ff). This growth in knowledge is an ascent that culminates in gazing 'face to face' with the divine itself (DePrinc. II,ii,7 p. 191,20ff). This is a theoreia et intelletus Dei.

4.4   The human mind for Origen is characterized by perpetual activity and volition. Its telos is union with God, and this union itself is prepared by a dialectical journey of the soul through acquired stages -- from knowledge of the sensible world, to knowledge of the intelligible world, to knowledge of the Intelligible itself, God.

This ascent of the intellect to final union with God begins with a clearing of the mind. Platonic dialectic, and the use of certain intellectual forms supplied by logic, are employed to move from sensible knowledge to intelligible knowledge. This process is complemented by a systematic reading and study of the scriptures whose data tests the conclusions arrived at by scientific reflection. This ascent is Platonic in its hue, but there are certain Peripatetic elements as well. The most important Peripatetic concept is the notion that ultimate felicity is the apprehension of the separate intellects. Central to this notion is the concept of the conjunction of the separate intellects.

Origen claims that man's ultimate felicity and perfection is gazing upon God 'face to face' (DePrinc. II,11,7 p. 191, 20ff). The ultimate felicity of man is his apprehension of the divine intellect(s).

Origen's concept of felicity and perfection comes from the Platonic tradition where utmost happiness is contemplation of the supernal world of forms. Origen modifies the notion, slightly, by postulating that utmost happiness consists in contemplation of the divine hypostases or intellects themselves. The object of desired vision are not the Platonic forms since Origen denies the existence of self-subsistent forms (e.g., DePrinc.

II, 3, 6 p. 122, 2). Rather it is knowledge of the separate intellects which constitutes ultimate felicity and knowledge. The problem we face in our analysis is how did Origen conceive of knowledge of the divine substances? Our thesis is that he conceived of it as the 'conjunction' of separate intellects, the human and divine, and that his theory of conjunction was grounded upon the theory of the agent intellect proposed in the Old and New Lyceum.

4.5 This section explores Origen's theory of the conjunction of the separate intellects. We shall begin with a brief discussion of this theory in the De Anima of Aristotle. Next we shall examine the presentation of this doctrine in the De Anima and De Intellectu of Alexander of Aphrodisias.[35] Finally we shall explore Origen's adoption of this theory in the Periarchôn (De Principiis). The goal of this study is to describe and analyze a late Middle Platonic adoption of a Peripatetic theory, and its place in Origen's epistemology.

In De Anima 3.5. Aristotle distinguished two aspects in the activity of intellection: one active, the other passive. The Stagarite's remarks are obscure, and have resulted in an enormous exegetical literature beginning with Alexander. In any case, Aristotle's remarks are important because they set the foundation of an epistemological ediface that was central in Peripatetic and Platonic thought for two millenia. The central idea was that human perfection consisted in union or conjunction with the active power in intellection. The active power unites or conjoins itself with the human intellect (or at least a part of the human intellect). Let us examine the psychological presuppositions of the theory.

In De Anima 3.5 Aristotle proposed a specific model of cognition according to which knowledge is essentially a passive function in which the human mind receives its contents from external sources. Aristotle's analogy is seeing. The eye receives its visual images from external objects through the medium of light, which illuminates both the objects and the eye. Aristotle builds from this model analogically to assert that the mind receives its contents through a power that stimulates the act of cognition by doing something to the mind and the objects from which the mind receives its data. This last notion is vague because Aristotle does not clarify what the active power in intellection is, and how it performs its operations.

In the doctrine of intellection proposed by Aristotle, the notion of 'conjunction' does not appear. By the time of Alexander, the matter-form relationship is no longer understood on the analogy of the passive and active aspects of intellection in the organism man. It is at this point in the interpretation of Aristotle's epistemology that the notion of 'conjunction' appears in the long tradition of Peripatetic exegesis. We shall examine the introduction of this idea by Alexander in his De Anima and De Intellectu.

Commentating upon Aristotle's obscure remarks, Alexander noted that in the Stagarite the active function in intellection is anonymous, while the passive aspect or the "passive intellect" (ho pathêtikos nous) is given a name (Arist. DeAnima, III, 5, 430a 24-25). Building from this, Alexander gave the active power a name -- "the agent or active intellect" (ho poiêtikos nous) (Alex. DeAnima, 88-89), and renamed the "passive intellect," or potential aspect of intellection -- "the material intellect" (ho hylikos nous) (Arist. DeAnima), 81).

This terminological reformulation has its analytical correlate. Alexander analyzed both the material and agent intellects. In Alexander's exegesis of Aristotle the material intellect is interpreted as a potential intellect, or disposition (epitêdeiotês)for knowledge (Arist. DeAnima, 85). Hence the material intellect is not hypostasized. It is not viewed as a substance, which would imply (as it did for Aristotle) that it is a separately existing thing, or a substance capable of separate existence. It is rather a natural capacity of the organism, through which it can engage in a specific type of noetic activity.

The agent or active intellect, however, is understood by Alexander, as a separately existing substance, radically different from the organism man, and from any human capacity. Alexander also viewed the Agent Intellect as coming into contact with the human material intellect, and helping it to energize its intellectual powers. In addition, in Alexander's interpretation of DeAnima 3.5, the Agent Intellect is identified with the Primal Nous or God (Arist. DeAnima, 112). Thus, with Alexander we encounter two distinct entities: the human and divine Agent Intellect. The former possesses the potentiality to know, and the latter is actively knowing. This represents a distinct reformulation of the Aristotelian theory that the intellect "becomes" the intelligible, viz., that the intellect itself makes a transition from potentiality to actuality -- from matter to form insofar as the active stage of intellection is the "form" of the potential intellect.

In the De Intellectu Alexander introduced the term "material intellect" once again to define the "potential intellect." In addition, in his De Anima, he described the ultimate stage of intellection for the human mind as the stage in which it becomes active, represented by the Divine Intellect from without. If we view these two statements in light of a third in the De Intellectu we encounter Alexander's theory of cooperation (synergos).

Alexander defined the cooperation between the material intellect and the Agent Intellect (or the intellect from without) as the synergos of two kindred intellects. Alexander gives us two answers on the question of whether or not the Agent Intellect is active and present in the material intellect from the beginning of the intellection. In the De Anima he stated that the Agent Intellect "comes to be" only at the final stage of intellection (Arist. DeAnima, 89, 21-22; 90, 19-20), while in the De Intellectu he asserted that the Agent Intellect is active in human intellection at all of its activity (Arist. DeIntellectu, 112,2-4). In both interpretations, however, Alexander distinguished between a passive (material) and active (Agent Intellect); asserted that the material intellect has a potential for knowing at a variety of stages; and that the Agent Intellect comes into contact with the human intellect and helps it energize its intellectual powers. The unresolved question is whether or not the Agent Intellect is wholly a transcendent entity which the human mind cooperates with at the final stage of intellection, or whether it assists the human intellect in all of its stages of intellection? To solve this question we shall examine how Alexander described the career of the human intellect.

When the human intellect is put into action by the joint effort of the objects of knowledge which are non-material, viz., the noêta, and the Agent Intellect, it becomes an intellect in actu (ho nous kat' energeian) (Arist. DeAnima, 112). When the human mind is not engaged in the activity of knowing the enoêta, the human intellect is an intellect in habitu (ho nous kath' hexin) (Arist. DeAnima, 86). It appears that it is only when the human mind is actively engaged that it cooperates with the Agent Intellect.

It is the case that the human mind is not always an intellect in act, whereas the Agent Intellect always is. Nonetheless, it is not the case that the human mind loses its already actualized capacity to know when it is not an intellect in actu. If intellection constitutes a habit that has been established in the organism which is sometimes active and at other times passive then the two apparently divergent remarks in the De Anima and De Intellectu are in fact complementary. When Alexander spoke in the De Intellectu of the Agent Intellect, as being active in human intellection in all its aspects, he meant there is a cooperation between the human and Agent Intellects even when the (human intellect) is in habitu. When he spoke in the De Anima of the Agent Intellect as being active in human intellection only in the final stage of intellection he meant there is a cooperation between the human and Agent Intellects when the human intellect is in actu.

In summary, the human mind has two momenta. It has an actualized, but not always exhibited power to know -- the intellect in actu and in habitu. It also has a set of accumulated cognitions, or pieces of knowledge, which operate whenever the mind is in actu, but not when it is in habitu. It is when the human mind is actively working upon the pieces of knowledge that it has acquired that it actively cooperates with the Agent Intellect. Alexander of Aphrodisias also states that in every act of intellection, even in the intellection of material forms, the intellect is but the intelligible form (Bruns, p. 86, 14ff.) Alexander also differentiates between the partial identity in the case of the intellection of material forms, and the total identity in the case of intellection of non-material forms. Only in this last case does the whole object of intellection enter into identity with the intellect (Bruns, p. 87, 24ff.). Hence, Alexander postulates a theory of potential and actual conjunction. The first type occurs ab initio in human intellection, and the second type is the consummation of human intellection.

In the Aristotelian doctrine of the intellect the concept of 'conjunction' does not appear. The intellect "becomes" the intelligible, and since all becoming is a transition from potentiality to actuality, i.e., from matter to form, the intelligibles are, in a sense, the "form" of the potential intellect. By the time of Alexander, however, a subtle change has occurred. In the case of intellect the relationship of matter-form is no longer understood on the analogy of things composed of matter and form. The term 'material intellect' is introduced as an alternative term for 'potential intellect (cf. DeIntel. ed. Bruns, p. 106, 20-23). The ultimate state of intellection is one in which we "become" the pure intelligible represented by the Divine Intellect from without. We "become" the pure intelligible when this intellect comes to be in us (cf. DeAnima Liber ed. Bruns, 89, 21-22; 90, 19-20.)

In the DeIntellectu Alexander speaks of a cooperation between the material intellect and the intellect from without, i.e., the Agent Intellect (Bruns, p. 111, 27). The intellect which is such-like in nature, and is from without, cooperates (synergos) with the one in us. As to the question of whether or not the Agent Intellect is active and present in all our thinking, or only at the final state, Alexander's answer is complementary. In the DeAmina the Agent Intellect "comes to be" only at the final stage, and in the DeIntellectu he speaks of it as being active in all our thinking, including the thinking of the material intelligibles (Bruns, p. 89, 21-22; 90, 19-20; 112, 3-4; 112, 2-3).

4.6   Origen was introduced to the writings of Aristotle while a student in the circle of Ammonius Saccas. Ammonius represented a school of Platonism which was not hostile to the Peripatetic philosophy.[36] He viewed Aristotelianism an an authentic interpretation of Plato's own teachings, and attempted to harmonize the philosophies of the Academy and the Peripatos. In this respect, Origen was a faithful follower of his teacher, Ammonius.

Alexander was known and widely read at Alexandria in Origen's time. Although Alexander's interpretation and development of Aristotle shaped subsequent Platonic interpretations of Aristotle as well, his reading of De Anima 3.5 was not universally followed. In the case of the Middle Platonist Origen there was divergence on two points. First, Origen rejected the Peripatetic's dispositional and naturalistic analysis of the material intellect. He claimed that the latter is an incorporeal substance with a separate and independent existence from matter. Second, Origen also viewed the Agent Intellect as an immanent and inherent power of the human mind as well as an external supervenient factor in human cognition.

Thus, Origen presents different epistemological theses than Alexander, but in the Periarchôn (De Principiis) he offers a Platonic interpretation of the Peripatetic doctrine of conjunction with the Agent Intellect. Hence, it is this work that we shall primarily focus upon.

Origen's theory does not represent a radically different psychology from Alexander's. It is based on Alexandrian assumptions. For purposes of our discussion, it will be helpful to represent the different interpretations of Aristotle's De Anima 3.5 in terms of a tree (Aristotle) with two branches (Alexander and Origen).

Before we sketch our thesis, a number of points need to be made in respect to Origen's utilization of this Peripatetic theory. First, Origen's technical terminology differs from that of the Aristotelians. Specifically, Origen's calls the Agent Intellect (poiêtikos nous) Divine Perception (theia aisthêsis). This term is individually Platonic and Christian. Nonetheless, the Divine Intellect functions like Alexander's Agent Intellect. Second, Origen folds this theory into his Platonic epistemological model. This means implicit in his presentation is the Platonic notion of the ascent of the soul through various stages of reality, viz., the sensible, the intelligible, and the divine. Third, although we shall focus only upon the possibility of conjunction of the human intellect with the Agent Intellect, Origen also holds the possibility of a union of the Agent Intellect with other intellects that populate the created universe. We will not examine this aspect of his theory.

Origen employed this epistemological construct in a radically different terminological and metaphysical paradigm than it was originally proposed by the Peripatetics. Origen's model represents a harmonization of Platonic and Peripatetic epistemological theories. This is consistent with the philosophical activity that characterized the philosophical school traditions of the late second and early third centuries. Let us now sketch another.[37]

Aristotle

De Anima 3.5:   "...in the intellect there are differences."
1.   The intellect that becomes all things, the passive intellect.
2.   The intellect that makes all things.

Alexander

De Anima/De Intellectu:

1.   The passive, potential, or material intellect (1) is not identical with the Agent Intellect (2).

2.   The material intellect (1) is:
      a.   a disposition of the organism.
      b.   corporeal.
      c.   corruptible.
      d.   many.

3.   The Agent Intellect (2) is:
      a.   a transcendent substance which energizes the material intellect in cognition.
      b.   incorporeal.
      c.   eternal (divine).
      d.   one.

4.   The material intellect (1) attains immortality only if it has reached the degree of perfection capable to it -- apprehension of the incorporeal forms.
      a.   at this level it is called the 'acquired intellect.'
      b.   it becomes identical or like the Agent Intellect
      c.   the material intellect apprehends the Agent Intellect which knows the immaterial forms.
      d.   through this apprehension the material intellect is assimilated to the Agent Intellect.

Origen

1. The (human) potential intellect (<u>mens-nous</u>) (1) is not identical with the Agent Intellect (2). It is:
   a. a substance.
   b. separable from the body.

2. The Agent Intellect (<u>theia aisthêsis</u>) (2) is:
   a. immanent in the human intellect.
   b. a transcendent intellect.
   c. a substance.

3. The Agent Intellect (2) constitutes the energizing aspect of the human intellect (1):
   a. it energizes the human intellect in cognition.
   b. it is incorporeal.
   c. it is eternal (divine).
   d. it is one and many.

4. Union or conjunction of the human intellect with the Agent Intellect means that:
   a. it becomes like the Agent Intellect.
   b. it apprehends the Agent Intellect which knows the Primal Intellect (God the Father).
   c. it is assimilated to the Agent Intellect and comes 'face to face' with the Primal Intellect (God the Father).

5. Immortality is possible through union with the Agent Intellect. Immortality is:
   a. incorporeal.
   b. eternal.
   c. individual.

<u>4.7</u>   In the third century the Aristotelian theory of the intellect, as developed by Alexander, already had recognizable Platonic elements. For example, Alexander explains the productive intellect as a transcendent intellect that acts by its own nature. This interpretation makes the intellect resemble the Platonic supreme good (<u>prôtê archê</u>). This interpretation of the productive intellect as the supreme active intelligible influenced Origen's notion of the two "Ones", the Father, and the Logos. Following the concept of the productive intellect as divine and intelligible Origen proposed the notion of the first one, or God the Father, as the supreme intelligible, and the second One or the Logos as its first product. This divine intelligible second One corresponds to the Aristotelian intellect which is the cause and agent of all human intellection.

   Alexander played an important role in Origen's identification of the intellect (<u>nous-mens</u>), and the intelligible (<u>noêton</u>) in the divine intellect whereby the intellect is identified with its object. This notion and the proposal that God is not above thought and being, but is himself the ground of thought and being, set up the conditions for the possibility of Origen's own proposal of the conjunction of the human and Agent Intellect, and their final union with the First Intellect, or God the Father. We shall reconstruct Origen's theory of conjunction, within the context of our generic tree.

Origen's theory of conjunction consists of the following theses:

1.   The human intellect is always in conjunction with the Agent Intellect (e.g. C.Cels., vii, 34 184). This correlation results from Origen's own Platonic-Christian theory that the material intellect is not merely a pure disposition, as Alexander maintained, but is itself a separate substance or a dimension of a separate substance, i.e., the Agent Intellect (e.g., DePrinc., I, 1, F 24.4).

   This formulation may stem from Origen's own reading of the DeAnima. For Origen, the Agent Intellect is constitutive of the human intellect. The Agent Intellect (theia aisthêsis) is immanent, in the human mind, as well as transcendent above the human mind (Comm. in Jh., XX, 43, 386). Hence, the nature and essence of man is constituted by the Agent Intellect.

   In its immanent aspect the Agent Intellect is the power (dynamis) of the one primary Agent Intellect, and is referred to as activity (enargeia) (Comm. in J., I, 26 39, 29ff). Insofar as all human intellects are constituted by the Agent Intellect, they are joined to the Agent Intellect. Hence, the Agent Intellect (theia aisthêsis) is the activity of the human intellect (C.Cels., VII, 34 184; DePrinc., I, 1, 9 27, 9ff).

2.   The Agent Intellect (theia aisthêsis) exists by itself, and it cooperates with individual human intellects (Comm. in Jh., vi, 30, 140, 20; Cant. in Jh., xvii, 297, 15f). When the Agent Intellect exists per se it is the Agent Intellect essentialiter. When it exists, embodied in man, it is the agent intellect accidentaliter. In its former state the Agent Intellect is engaged in knowledge of this intelligible and divine. In its latter state it knows sensible objects of knowledge, that are in and derived from bodies, and knows the sensible things. The human mind apprehends sensibles and intelligibles in the stages of its conjunction with the Agent Intellect (DePrinc., I, 1, 7, 24, 1ff; 23, 15ff; I, 1, 8 26, 2; IV, 4, 7 357, 29ff).

3.   The human intellect is a composite mind. It possesses self-perceptions in the activity of aisthêsis (DePrinc., IV, 4, 7 357, 29ff), and these sense-perceptions are stored in the mind as ta aisthêta (C.Cels., I,42,92, 6f, VII, 37,187, 25). The human intellect also possesses intelligibles in its activity of noêsis. These intelligibles are stored in the mind as ta noêta. Hence, every human mind is a composite containing sensibles, and intelligibles. The Agent Intellect energizes the human mind giving it the power to apprehend sensible and intelligible objects (C.Cels., I, 9-11,61ff.; III, 38,234f).

4. Each human mind shares one and the same Agent Intellect, but human
    minds differ insofar as each mind acquires different sense-images. The
    rational dimensions of the mind are common to all men, as are the
    intelligibles it apprehends. The off-shoot of this is that the rational
    dimension of the human mind is eternal and noncorruptible, while the
    products yielded by the human mind are transitory and corruptible. This
    reflects Origen's postulate that perception yields opinion, which is a
    transitory knowledge; and intellection yields scientific knowledge which
    is true knowledge. These four theses constitute the main elements of
    the doctrine of the intellect developed by Origen from Peripatetic
    themes.

Origen's thesis of conjunction represents only a small aspect of his doctrine of
knowledge. Nonetheless, it is an important one. It represents the theory which grounds
the condition for the possibility of a union of the human intellect and divine intellects.
For Origen, conjunction is not merely the return of the Agent Intellect to its primordial
and pristine state of separate existence divorced from its embodiment in individual and
corporeal knowers. Conjunction is the condition for the possibility of ultimate felicity, of
union of the human and divine intellects.

The claim is that the human intellect is <u>ab initio</u> in conjunction with the Agent
Intellect, and that we are the Agent Intellect. If this is so, then the importance of this
theory for Origen is self-evident (<u>Comm. in Jh.</u>, VI, 30 140, 20; X, 34, 209, 10; ef. <u>Cant. in
Jh.</u>, XVIII 297, 15f).

<u>4.7</u>   The Platonic elements in Origen's theory are the most evident. Union with
God involves liberation from matter. The imagery employed to describe the soul's ascent
is that of shadow and light, and the final unity is described in the language of the soul's
ascension and contemplation of God. However, we must not ignore some of the
Peripatetic aspects of Origen's theory. Final union is depicted as a unity of separate
substances and intellects. This union of separate intellects is presented through the
imagery of the conjunction of separate substances and intellects.

As stated, the origin of Origen's notion arises from Aristotle's unfulfilled promise to
investigate the possibility of knowing something of the 'abstract' things (<u>De Anima</u> III,7
431b16), taken up by Alexander in his <u>De Anima Liber</u> and <u>De Intellectu</u> as the 'conjunction' of separate intellects. Origen maintains that the human intellect is a substance
(<u>DePrinc.</u>, I, 1, 7 24, 4), and that the agent intellect is both transcendent and immanent
(<u>Comm. in Jh.</u>, XX, 43 386). He also holds that the human intellect is a substance which
has the capacity to know, and the Agent Intellect is a substance that always knows and is
identical with God (<u>DePrinc.</u>, I,I, 9,27, 10f).

Although Origen is not clear on this issue it appears that conjunction takes place on
two levels. First, an initial conjunction of the two intellects is the condition for the
possibility of human intellection at any level, viz., <u>aisthêsis</u> and <u>noêsis</u> (<u>C.Cels.</u>, Vii, 34
184; <u>Comm. in Jh.</u>, I 26 39, 29ff). Second, a final conjunction of the two intellects occurs
at the end of a specific kind of intellectual activity, viz., <u>gnôsis</u> (<u>DePrinc.</u>, II, 11 7 191,

20ff). In Origen, then, the function of the Agent Intellect is to bring about human thinking on all levels of its noês. It is the cause of knowledge because it possesses in actuality the knowledge it either stimulates in, or dispenses to the human intellect.

In Origen's version of final conjunction, man attains union with God (henosis) at the end of a long and arduous process of intellectual activity. When this state is attained the human intellect becomes the Agent Intellect. They achieve a kind of cognitive identity. This reflects the Aristotelian epistemological maxim: in the state of knowing, the knower and the object of knowledge are identical (Arist. Meta. XII, 9 1074b 39-1075 a 11; Alexander, In Meta., 90-91).

In Origen's scheme the human intellect comes to know the ta aisthêta, the ta noêta, and the divine ousiai. Because of the conjunction (sensible and intelligible) with this agent intellect, objects are perceived with the aid of the Agent Intellect, the human mind is, ab initio, in conjunction with the Agent Intellect (Comm. in Jh., VI, 30 140, 20; X, 34 209, 10; cf. Cont. in Jh., XVIII 297, 15). Since the divine substances are identical with the Agent Intellect the human mind becomes identical with the Agent Intellect when it comprehends them (DePrinc., II, 11, 7 191, 20ff).

In proposing this theory Origen maintains the individuality of the human intellect (cf. DePrinc., II, 11 7 20ff) throughout its ascent from the material to the divine realms. Conjunction is the condition for the possibility of final union with God, and even at this state the human and divine intellects remain distinct (DePrinc., II, 11 7 191, 24f). Ultimate felicity does not involve the elimination of individuality because conjunction does not eliminate at any level, the elements to be joined (DePrinc., III, 6, 5 257, 5ff), which are the separate intellects.

Origen's doctrine of conjunction with the Agent Intellect must be placed within the context of his theory that all intelligible creatures seek to return to their source and that God will be all in all (DePrinc., III, 6, 8 289, 23ff). This is why he formulates the telos of his doctrine as a kind of contact, or unification, with a divine transcendent being (DePrinc., III, 6, 9 290, 21ff). Man is to devote himself to the acquisition of that which is humanly attainable, pistis, which is the knowledge of the created world, and that which is humanly attainable, gnôsis, which is knowledge of God himself. Both are possible by virtue of, and in cooperation with the Agent Intellect (theia aisthêsis). In this final state there is an identity of both the human intellect and its agent. Beyond the Agent Intellect there is another intellect which is its source, and the source of truth and being. The Agent Intellect is subordinate to this first intellect, God the Father. No identification with the Father is possible for the human intellect. Human conjunction with the divine intellect is in the Logos.

For Origen, felicity consists in the pursuit of human knowledge and the attainment of divine knowledge (DePrinc., III, 6 9 290, 14ff). This is the leit-motif of Origen's philosophy. Expressed epistemologically it is the journey from faith (pistis) to knowledge (gnôsis). This process ends with the human intellect understanding the first principles and of all things and being 'face to face' with God. This recognition does not terminate in the obliteration of the self in a transcendent being. Origen proposes no unio mystica. To use Merlan's terminology (PS., 20ff) Origen offers a 'rationalistic mysticism.'

<u>4.8</u>   By his formulations concerning the function of scripture in the adjudication of human knowledge, and the conjuncton of the human and divine intellects, Origen proposes two theories which make the doctrines of the ideas and their recollection unnecessary for inclusion in an epistemological system.

All philosophy begins with a consideration of these primitive notions in our minds because they are the notions of the divine mind energized in our own. In the corporeal world they are the concepts of form, extension, motion, place, and the like. In the immaterial world they are the concepts of being, number, duration and the like. In these prototypes are included all reality, and all variety of objects. They point forward to reality, and backward to their origin in the Logos and God.[38]

For Origen there is no need to ask questions concerning the connection of perceptions and conceptions with reality, or concerning the possibility of their application to it. They are applicable to reality because they spring from and are analogous to divine knowledge. There is no opposition between the structure the human mind perceives in things, and the structure of things. Knowledge, as the system of clear and distinct ideas, and the world, as the totality of created being, cannot fail to harmonize. They merely represent, different versions or expressions of the same created essence. The archetypal agent intellect of God is the bond between thinking and being, between truth and reality in the philosophy of Origen. This union between soul and body, between ideas and reality is firm because it is produced by God.

In summary, according to Origen, human knowledge in all its varieties and forms gain objective meaning because it grasps the objective reality and order created by God. Human knowledge is not merely the expression of the human ego. Certainly sense qualities, sensations of color and tone, of smell and taste, contain no complete trace of the reality of the world. They reflect states of mind which change from moment to moment. But through scientific method the human mind perceives in these states of mind the objectively subsisting and objectively valid order of nature. How they reflect such states is determined by the now familiar procedure of relating the accidental to the necessary, the merely factual to something rational, the temporal to the eternal. Perception becomes true knowledge by relating it to the wisdom of God proclaimed in scripture, and contained in the Logos. In this sense every genuine human act of cognition is a divine act of cognition. The validity, the value, and the certainty of the fundamental perceptions and conceptions of human knowledge are placed beyond doubt, and in the realm of belief, by virtue of the fact that in and through faith we participate in divine being. Epistemological certainty is based on the metaphysical participation between human knowing and divine knowing.

The light that illuminates the path of knowledge shines from within as well as from without. It radiates from the realm of sensible as well as intelligible objects. Yet this inner light is not due to man's mind, but points back to another and higher mind and light. The logical and epistemological problem of the relation of knowledge to its object is solved by its reduction to metaphysical considerations. Divine being is the source of the principles and concepts of the understanding.

VII. DIALECTIC: LOGIC

Introduction

A discussion of dialectic is central to an explanation of the Middle Platonic philosophy. First, dialectic was a method whereby philosophers demonstrated the efficacy of their first principles. Second, dialectic concerned itself with the epistemological and ontological theories, as well as the purely logical ones. Propositions were viewed as combinations of conceptions that had epistemological and ontological significance. Third, Jewish, Christian, and Hellenic Middle Platonists identified the statement of both biblical and philosophical scripture as types of first propositions. From these propositions philosophical systems were deduced. Fourth, propositions were viewed as constituting a type of intelligible, if not divine, knowledge.

The Middle Platonists were heirs to a system of dialectic hammered out in the Stoa, Lyceum, and Academy. They offered little, theoretically, to the field of dialectic. They were involved principally in harmonizing the principles of class and propositional logic, and attributing them to the thought of Plato. As early as the New Academy, if not before, Platonists accepted the old Stoic definition of dialect as constituting both logic and rhetoric. Both were practiced in the Academy as the writings of Cicero and Philo show. Later Platonists, such as Clement, Albinus, and Origen, are fully versed in the principles of both, and utilize them in their own metaphysical endeavors.[39]

Few new dialectical norms were proposed by the Academy in the first three centuries of the common era. Only among Jewish and Christian Middle Platonists are new norms offered. These proposals were: (1) to include under the definition of a proposition (lekton) statements from biblical scripture; and (2) to call the words (lêmmata) of scripture axioms (axiômata) and to demonstrate from scripture philosophical propositions.

This constellation of dialectical norms were first introduced by Philo, and institutionalized by Clement and Origen. Modes of syllogistic differ in each of their works, depending upon their genre of composition, but both logical and rhetorical argumentation were used by Jewish and Christian Middle Platonists to demonstrate metaphysical propositions from biblical scripture. It was often the case that these thinkers correlated their biblical propositions with Platonic philosophical propositions thereby demonstrating a Jewish or Christian metaphysic.

In this section we shall also examine the system of biblical demonstration (apodeixis biblikê) hammered out by Philo, Clement, and Origen, and its basis in the principles of Hellenistic and Roman dialectic. First, we shall investigate the logical dimensions of the theory of biblical demonstration. Second, we shall define the rhetorical elements of this theory. Our study shall focus upon Philo, Clement, and Origen.

This area of Jewish and Christian Middle Platonic thought has been little investigated by modern scholarship.[40] Some work has been done on the logic of these

- 201 -

thinkers, but only recently has any work been done on their rhetoric. Rhetorical studies have been principally done upon Philo. Clement and Origen's rhetoric, especially their rhetorical logic, have not been investigated at all.

This massive lacuna cannot be filled by this study.[41] The most that can be done is to offer a prolegommenon for future studies. Within the context of this work our brief examination of Jewish and Christian dialects serves a limited end. We shall take one work of Origen's as an example of how this system of biblical demonstration (apodeixis biblikê) works as evangelical demonstration (apodeixis euaggelikê). Our goal is to show how one Christian Middle Platonist demonstrated the truth of his metaphysical and epistemological theories from the premises of his sacred scripture.

First we shall sketch the dialectical assumptions which underly scriptural demonstration. This entails examining the logical and rhetorical theories of Philo, Clement, and Origen.[42] Second, we shall define Origen's use of the principles of one branch of dialectic, rhetoric, to demonstrate a Christian Platonism in the Periarchôn (DePrincipiis). Our examination of Philo and Clement is brief and serves as a proem to our exegesis of Origen's (apodeixis euaggelikê) in Part Three.

1. Philo of Alexandria

No systematic study has been undertaken to examine Philo's theory of logic. Wolfson and Drummond devote only a few pages to this topic, and the studies of Dillon, Conly, and Leopold focus principally upon Philo's theory of rhetoric. In this section we shall sketch the principles of Philo's system of dialectic, and attempt to describe its major tenents. This study is limited and incomplete. Our goal is a modest one. We merely want to identify Philo's logical assumptions in order to trace their subsequent developments by Clement and Origen.

1.1   Philo's acquaintance with logical theory arose out of his Hellenic philosophical education. Dillon has correctly noted (MP., 178-182) the use Philo makes of standard early Middle Platonic logical doctrine. His own comments leave little doubt of his awareness of the basics of theories of dialectic. Heinemann (PGB., 436; 549) has amply noted Philo's use of logic in his writings, and Leopold and Conly (TTP., 129-135; CCHS., 15 [1975] point out Philo's knowledge of rhetoric.[43] There can be little doubt that Philo was conversant with both logic and rhetoric, and that he used both in the presentation of his philosophical ideas.

Philo's dialectic is closely linked to his epistemology. At (Mut., i, 4-5) he couples sensible and scientific knowledge with its objects. Among these objects are doctrines (dogmosi) and propositions (theôrêmasi). Wolfson correctly (P., ii, 7) identifies the doctrines and propositions referred to in this pericope with the knowledge of the ideas which do not rest on sensation at all. This is an important insight into Philo's theory of propositions.

Philo identifies this form of knowledge and its propositions with prophecy. He associates prophecy with the statements extant in biblical scripture, the divine command, and the divine Logos (QG., iv, 140). This is an important postulate. It represents in

Philo: (1) The association of biblical sayings with propositions; and (2) the claim that biblical propositions represent the highest type of knowledge, as prophecy. This Philonic doctrine becomes the cornerstone of all subsequent interpretations, at least by Christian authors, of biblical scripture. Furthermore, it sets the context for the theory of scriptural demonstration (apodeixis biblikê).

Wolfson (P., ii, 11-13) outlines the four functions of prophecy. They are to: (1) predict the future; (2) mollify deity; (3) receive divine communications, and (4) to know things which cannot be known by the senses. To this may be added, (5) scriptural prophecy functions as philosophical wisdom that can be deduced from scripture. The one who receives this prophetic wisdom receives the divine spirit (QG., III, 9). The divine spirit is received by the rational soul of man (Fug., 33, 186; VM., I, 50, 2ff).

Prophetic knowledge, also called scriptural knowledge by Philo, is entirely free from sensation. It is an unmixed knowledge (akrêtos epistêmê Gig., 5 22), imported from another region by the divine spirit, and instilled in the rational soul of man. Once apprehended by the human mind it takes on the character of a rational concept. Philo maintains that this divine wisdom carried to man by the divine spirit plays upon the vocal organism and dictates words which clearly express its prophetic message (Spec. Leg., iv, 8, 49). This is an important notion. Philo associates the logos prophôrikos with theôrêmosi, and the prophetic word with propositions. He does this because the term divine Logos (logos theios) is used as a description of the prophetic revelations contained in scripture (Met., 31, 169; Somn., i, 33, 190).

Philo fills out this notion by calling the prophetic revelations of scripture, the speech or voice of God (Dec., 9, 32). This voice is not physical speech heard by means of physical learning. It is an invisible incorporeal sound (echon aoraton) from an articulate voice (phônê enarthros) heard by the rational soul (psychê logikê: VM., II, 39, 213; Dec., 9, 33; cf. Dec., 11, 46).

1.2   One of the difficulties we have in reconstructing Philo's thought is that much of what Philo says is stated incompletely, or is scattered through out his writings. Hence, we have to work inductively to reconstruct his doctrines. This is especially the case with his theory of dialectic. Nonetheless, if we take Philo's statements that scriptural prophecy comes to man in speech and through a voice, and couple it to his definition of what a proposition is, a fascinating pattern emerges.

In (Agr., 141) Philo presents us with the Stoic theory of the proposition (lekton), and the theory of demonstration (apodeixis) that accompanies it. He maintains that thoughts and words are the same things regarded from different aspects. An idea which is a thought is a word, and then a proposition as soon as it is uttered. Hence, a proposition (lekton) is an entity indicated or revealed by the sound of the uttered word which the human mind apprehends as subsisting together in thought. A lekton may be translated literally as that which is meant. Our question is did Philo associate the speech of prophecy heard by the rational soul with the lekton? If so, can prophetic words be understood as propositions?

Sextus Empiricus tells us (Adv. Math., VIII, 245) that the Stoics defined the proposition (lekton) as incorporeal. Galen (In. Log., 7, 22-8, f., Kalbfleisch) concurs with this observation and informs us that notions that do not derive from sense-perceptions were called propositions (axiôma) by the Stoics [axiôma are a species of lekton].

Propositions were also called significates by the Stoics (Seneca, Ep., 89, 17; Diog. Laer., V., VII, 57). The significates (ta sêmainomena) were thought of as non-material. Furthermore, they were divided into two types, commemorative and indicative, and indicative signs were defined as antecedent propositions in certain types of true conditionals (Sextus Empiricus, Adv. Math., VIII, 245). This implies that indicative signs are propositions.[44]

This distinction of significates into commemorative and indicative has the corresponding distinction between common and special significate. The common significate reveals something evident, and the special significate something non-evident (Sextus Empiricus, Adv. Math., VIII, 143). From Sextus' testimony it appears that the Stoics defined indicative significates as lekta. It not clear of they defined commemorative significates as purely non-sensible. This contradiction is noted by Sextus (Adv. Math., VIII, 264). Nonetheless, indicative significates are wholly non-corporeal. This much can be affirmed.

The Stoic definition of lekton, as reported by Sextus and Diogenes, is that which exists in conformity with a rational presentation (Adv. Math., VIII, 70; V., VII, 63). Sextus tells us that his rational presentation is conveyed by discourse (logô). To say something is to utter a sound capable of signifying the object conceived (Adv. Math., VIII, 80).

We know that Philo knew of the Stoic theory of the lekton and demonstration (apodeixis) (Agr., 141). We also know that he referred to scripture as containing the voice (phonê) of God received by the rational soul (psychê logikê) (VM., II, 39, 213; Dec., 9, 33; 11, 46). The voice of the prophetic word (logos prophorikos) was called propositions (theôrêmasi) of the divine Logos (Logos theios) contained in scripture (Mut., 31, 169; Somn., I, 33, 190). Hence, it is likely that he understood the voice (phonê) of God as a sign (sêmainon) of the prophetic word (logos prophorikos) that presented itself as a significate (sêmainomenon) or proposition (lekton).

Any proposition, conveyed by divine discourse, is a mon-material, indicative proposition (axiôma). These propositions constitute types of true conditionals because they are the words of God proclaimed in scripture, viz., a knowledge inspired by God.

The importance of Philo's formulation is self-evident. He equates prophecy with wisdom, and assents that it constitutes propositions. Having defined prophecy as propositional knowledge he can: (1) postulate that biblical knowledge is the highest kind of philosophical knowledge; and (2) that it can be demonstrated in a logical manner. Let us turn to this aspect of this theory.

1.3   Dillon (MP., 145) is correct that Philo's definition of the criterion and content of knowledge is strongly Stoic in dimensions (cf. SVF., I, 68; e.g., Immunt., 41-44; QG., iii, 3).

Likewise in his theory of the lekton (Agr., 141) Philo shows a knowledge of the Stoic distinction between the physical object which the significate-proposition refers to, the sound, or significans, and the significate-proposition itself. These distinctions permit Philo to equate the lekton with the cognitive impressions of which it is the content. The proposition is that which exists in conformity with a rational presentation, or kataleptikê phantasia. Indeed, a rational presentation is one in which the phantasthen (that which is presented) can be conveyed by discourse (logô).

Next in (Agr., 141) Philo attacks the scholastic quibbling of arguing the opposite sides of the same question. He states that this is not the goal of those who aim for the truth. Nonetheless, he recognizes that dialectical arguments can be used to demonstrate the connectivity of things in nature. He maintains that propositions convey meanings which are useful for man's understanding of the cognitive impressions the mind synthesizes from sense-impressions. He affirms that there is a connection between the things which are signified by propositions, and the meanings conceptions convey. Philo maintains that this correlation of proposition, signification, and perception, may be demonstrated through the rules and theorems of syllogistic reasoning. If this is so for the connectivity of human knowledge with things natural, why cannot it also be so for things divine?

Philo offers no systematic presentation of the rules of syllogistic, but an examination of his works illustrate that he knew the formulae of the pure and mixed hypotheticals, if not the categorical syllogisms. There is no indication that he distinguished between a logic of terms and one of propositions, but it is clear that he utilized their forms for the demonstration of a wide range of concepts. No study has yet been undertaken to define Philo's theory of demonstration. However, it appears he utilizes the "undemonstrated arguments" (anapodeitikos syllogismos) of Stoic logic to demonstrate his philosophical theories.

This knowledge of Stoic argument forms is indirectly presented in his art of rhetorical logic. First, Philo's theory of argumentation is based on rhetorical principles. Conly has shown this in his work on "Philo's use of Topoi" (TTP., 171-180). Second, we know that topical argumentation has strong connections with Stoic propositional logic. Cicero links rhetorical enthymemes with the Stoic undemonstrables (Top., 54, 56, 57). Indeed, Mates (SL., 67-74) has shown that the forms of Stoic argumentation evidence apodectic, dialectical, and rhetorical argument structures in Philo's time. Third, Dillon has illustrated (TTP., 77-88) that Philo's texts to be commented upon are divided up into lêmmata.

We know that lêmmata are premises for arguments in Stoic logic (Sextus Empiricus, HYP., II, 135ff.; 172 ff.; Galen, In. Log., IV, 8; XX, 20, 5, 2). Diogenes Laertius tells us they were defined as the major premises of a two premised argument (V., VII, 76). Hence, it is possible that Philo understood scriptural lêmmata as premises of propositions (lekta, axiômata), that could be argued dialectically, viz., either logically or rhetorically.

Philo's use of these argument forms is generally within the context of the allegorical exegesis of biblical scripture. He takes a verse from the Pentateuch and argues for and against other allegorical and literal interpretations. He generally passes from a literal to an ethical interpretation of the verses under consideration (e.g., Leg. Alleg., 1, 16, VM., II, 96, cf. Dillon, TTP., 80; 83-84: e.g., Leg. Alleg., 1, 59; QG., I, 10). His goal, as Dillon correctly notes, is to refute specific literal and materialistic interpretations of scripture (TTP., 83). The irony is that Philo uses Stoic logical devices to refute a Stoicized Judaica. Finally, Philo forms his arguments rhetorically. This is his strategy of argumentation. How he does this is nicely sketched by Conly (TTP., 171-180), and Leopold (TTP., 155-170).

In summary, Philo uses the lêmmata of the Pentateuch as premises for propositions (lekta). These propositions are called (theôrês masi). These divine sayings constitute the premises from which allegorical interpretations of the Bible are argued and first principles deduced. His interpretations are argued rhetorically, and are based upon the argument forms of Stoic logic.

Philo's theory of argumentation when coupled to his theory of prophecy and proposition constitute his doctrine of scriptural demonstration (apodeixis biblikê). His importance for the subsequent Christian Middle Platonic doctrine of evangelical demonstration (apodeixis euaggelikê) is immense. First, his definition of biblical scripture as divine philosophical wisdom is accepted in toto by Clement and Origen. Second, Philo's definition of scriptural sayings as propositions, from which philosophical interpretations are deduced, is also a corner-stone of later Christian theories of demonstration. Clement, and later Origen, build upon Philo's dialectical norms, and offer, upon them, the first systematic demonstration of a Christian Platonism.

2. Clement of Alexandria

2.1   No study of Clement's logic has been undertaken since Witt's monogaph on Albinus (A., 31-41). Witt is primarily concerned with the fontes of Albinus' theory of logic, and Clement is analyzed for these purposes. Lilla briefly touches upon this topic, but his work is chiefly concerned with Clement's epistemology and theoretic (C., 132-136; 163-173). Clement's rhetoric has not been examined at all. Nonetheless, these two studies provide an introduction into Clement's understanding of the content and function of dialectic. Hence, it is upon their works that our brief analysis depends.

Witt is correct (A., 31) that book eight of the Stomateis contains the theoretical heart of Clement's theory of logic. Witt argues that the origin of Clement's doctrine arises from the reflections of Antiochus. This is largely correct, and Clement's theories point back to a doxological source from the school activity around Antiochus. The Antiochean character of Clement's presentation is illustrated by the conflation of Stoic and Peripatetic logical principles (Strom., VIII, 14, 1). Similar passages can be found in the Ciceronian treatises connected with Antiochus (Fin., II, 3; De Off., I, 7; Part. Or., 126).

Clement's addition to this scheme is to maintain that the inquirer must keep to both common notions (koinai ennoiai), and to biblical scripture to advance by means of scientific demonstation to knowledge (Strom., viii, 2, 5). While the first proposal is typically Platonic (Cic., Luc., 26; 30), the second illustrates a Philonic norm. Clement maintains that the sayings of scripture have epistemological validity, and are to be utilized by the philosopher in his demonstration of philosophical principles. From these postulates, Clement introduces to Christian Middle Platonism the theory of evangelical demonstration (apodeixis euaggelikê).

In an important transitional step in Middle Platonic logic, Clement associates the undemonstrated principles of knowledge with the pistis of scripture (Strom., viii, 7, 2). This association, hinted at by Philo, is explicitly affirmed by Clement. Clement is influenced by the Antiochean doctrine, that pistis is the attitude of mind which is produced by the katalêptikê phentasia possessing enargeia (Cic. An. Post., 41). Working from this, and the assertions of Philo (Opf., 8 & 2; Cong., 178; VM., II, 12; Flac., 35), Clement asserts the identity of scriptural pistis and epistemological pistis. The result is a new norm for Christian Middle Platonic epistemology (Strom., viii, 11, 13).

Clement maintains that the philosopher who practices demonstration (apodeixis) must make sure that the premises he assumes are proven true. Since biblical premises are by definition true. He calls these biblical premises protaseis (with the Peripatetics), and axiômata and lêmmata (with the Stoics). It is a brief step to associate the sayings (lêmmata) of scripture with the propositions (axiômata, protaseis) of demonstration.[45] This association constitutes one of the pillars of his theory of evangelical or scriptural demonstration (apodeixis euaggelikê).

2.2 Clement holds that the categorical and hypothetical syllogism are modes of demonstration (apodeixis). All types of syllogism are useful in philosophical discourse. Lilla is right (C., 134) that Clement makes a distinction between scientific syllogistic that draws a conclusion which is true, and dialectical and rhetorical syllogistic that draws a probable conclusion. This means that in categorical syllogisms the premises are proven, the conclusions true, and in a hypothetical syllogism the premises are assumed, and the conclusions not necessarily true. However, scriptural premises are always true and need not be demonstrated. This point is important because it suggests that scriptural premises may underly a categorical syllogism as well as a hypothetical one, and that the conclusions deduced from a hypothetical syllogism are as valid as those demonstrated from a categorical syllogism. This is noteworthy because premises of scripture may serve both types of argument, and the conclusions deduced-demonstrated from both would be accepted as true. cf. epi tên anapodeikton pistin he passa apodeixis anagêtai (Strom., viii, 4.7.2 (iii. 83. 23f).

Clement expands upon this suggestion in a manner most Stoic. He states that basic to argumentation as a whole are certain "undemonstrables" assumed as true premises. That they are true is accepted on faith (pistis). Indeed, this type of premise is believed without demonstration, and it serves as the starting point for apodeixis (Strom., viii. 3.8, 1-6) (iii. 84.9-33). This presentation of a logical definition of the undemonstrables (ta anapodeikta) is of capital significance. It suggests that underlying types of categorical and hypothetical arguments are premises which need not be formally proven because it is immediately clear that they are valid. This presupposition is one of the presuppositions of

Stoic propositional logic (e.g., Sextus Empiricus, Adv. Math., VIII, 223), and it is adopted by Clement.

If we couple these statements to those which call the knowledge of scripture gnôsis kataleptikê a fascinating pattern emerges (Strom., viii, 1.2, 1F. (iii. 80.13-17). These "gnostic perceptions" are comprehended dia tês logikês. This means that demonstration (apodeixis) has the task of decoding the utterances and propositions of human speech, and biblical scripture.

The goal of demonstration is to determine whether or not propositions (pro-taseis-axiomata) have signification (sêmainêsthai) or not. Although Clement's logical nomenclature is mixed (he employs the Peripatetic term protaseis and the Stoic axiômata and lêmmata), his point is clear. The content of human as well as divine knowledge serves as the premises for metaphysical demonstration. The goal of demonstration is clear definition. We shall now discuss how definition and demonstration are coupled to yield: ho logos ex heteron heterôn ti pisttoumenos.

<u>2.3</u>   Definition begins with division. Clement tells us that division is a means by which the universal is summed up by sensation from the particular (Strom. viii. 6.17, 6 (iii. 90. 24ff), as well as a proseche eide whereby one divides a genus into its species, a whole into its parts, and a subject into its accidents (Strom. viii. 6.18, 2 and 7 (iii. 91.55ff). Of the three types of diairesis Clement holds the division of genus into species as most valuable. This is important because it means that through this type of logical analysis the essential attributes of things are reached by the exclusion, at every stage, of members of coordinate yet distinct species.

Witt is correct (A., 32ff) that Clement's understanding of definition is similar to Albinus'. Like Albinus, Clement links Platonic diairesis with the Peripatetic theory of definition by the aid of demonstration. Although Clement's technical terminology is Stoic in hue, with division called proseche eide (Strom. viii. 18.2 (iii. 91.4-7), there is no indication that Clement utilized Stoic methods of division.

The division of a thing into genus and species is done within the context of Academic and Peripatetic categorical division. Clement divides things initially into that which is Absolute and Relative, and then proceeds to employ the ten Peripatetic categories for a precise definition of the properties of a thing (Strom. viii. 23, 1ff. (iii. 94. 5ff); viii. 24, 1ff. (iii. 95.4ff). In this respect Clement's methods of division and demonstration are linked to the analysis of things by means of the categories. In fundamental respects Clement's approach is akin to the approach we witnessed with Albinus.

There is an aspect of Clement's theory, however, which differs from Albinus'. It appears that he holds that it is possible to analyze the elements of speech by means of these procedures. He gives no examples as what he understands by the analysis of the elements of speech. He merely asserts that the elements of words must be determined, and that their properties rest on definable principles (Strom. viii. 23.2ff. (iii. 94. 12-19).

Although chapter eight is rather confused given to its doxographical character, it presents a Stoic theory of grammatical analysis reminiscent of that encountered with Philo. Clement's point is that it is possible to analyze language and say something about being in its absolute and relative dimensions. Since language consists of univocal terms, heteronyms, polynyms, and paronyms, he suggests that some sort of classification of reality can be done linguistically. Apparently this would be accomplished by noting how things are stated and pointing out the essence, quality, quantity, relation, where, when, position, possession, action, and passion exhibited by a thing.

To summarize: We know from Strom. viii. 6, 7 and 8 that Clement thinks it possible to divide all things into the categories of the Absolute and the Relative, and that the specific determinations of what things are can be determined by means of predicative analysis. In addition, he holds that names and symbols are expressions of what things are, and that it is possible to define things as they present themselves in language. Definition, thus, is accomplished by division and classification. Its objects are the things sensible and intelligible and their expressions in language. Clement's doctrine of logical diairesis is significant because once metaphysical doctrines are deduced from Scripture dialectically, Clement utilizes logical analysis to defined the precise nature of the sensibles and intelligibles that populate reality.

Division yields definition, which then can be demonstrated from biblical as well as philosophical premises. The results of these processes are the content of what he calls epistêmonikê pistis, and gnôsis kataleptikê, viz., philosophical and divine wisdom.

Clement continues in the trajectory of scriptural interpretation, and dialectical theory proposed by Antiochus and Philo. He accepts their assumptions, and gives an evangelical emphasis to them. Using the New and Old Testaments he offers a demonstration of first principles from biblical scripture. This apodeixis euaggelikê, based upon the theories of Antiochus and Philo, is utilized, next, by Origen.

3. Origen of Alexandria

3.1 Modern scholarship has shown little interest in examining the logical apparatus employed by Origen. Although there has been a recognition that Origen utilized a system of logic, no attempt has been undertaken to define its theoretical bases or what its content looked like.

Hal Koch states:

...dass die greschische wissenschaftliche Methode ihm (Origenes) in vielen Punkten von Nutzen gewesen ist, sucht der Verfasser des Contra Celsum garnicht zu verbergen... Wenn man in der Wahrheit der göttlichen Schriften nicht irren will, muss man die Logik und die Begriffsbestimmung kennen. Und selbst wenn Origenes den Einfluss der wissenschaftlichen Methode leugnen wollte, brauchen wir nicht im Zweifel zu sein. Sein ganzer Systemaufbau und seine Beweisfuehrung waeren ohne die griechische Wissenschaft undenkbar.[46]

René Cadiou proclaims that:

Il l'appele aussi la couronne qui honore et eleve la raison.[47]

Eugene de Faye asserts that Origen's reasoning is carried on according to the strictest rules of Aristotelian dialectic.[48] Yet none of these authors explained what the parameters of Origen's system of logic was, or its relation to his understanding of the art of rhetoric. Robert Walzer refers to the development in Clement and Origen of a theory of apodeixis euaggelikē based on the critical apparatus of Galen and Celsus, but he does not explain its content.[49]

In several cases Origen's theory of dialectic is not mentioned at all. Neither René Cadiou nor Jean Danièlou discuss this aspect of Origen's thought at all. Henri de Lubac, in a solid presentation of Origen's "le sens litteral-spirituel," does not think logic has an important function at all in Origen's theory of scriptural exegesis.[50]

Thus, apart from brief statements that Origen utilized a system of logic to present his ideas, no study has been undertaken to examine the logical principles utilized by Origen, why they were used, or the philosophical implications of their use. Koch's statements suggest the importance of such an inquiry, and Walzer's association of Galen and Origen make such an undertaking an important one. Such a study could tell us a great deal about the type of Christian Platonism Origen proposed in the early third century, and the role logic served in the presentation of a Christian philosophy.

3.2   Origen presents us with no systematic theory of dialectic. However, analysis of his thought points toward a theoretical basis in common with Philo and Clement. Indeed an examination of his works suggests that he held no specific theory as such, but that he understood the application of dialectic as the art of rhetorical logic.

It is this aspect of Origen's philosophy which has been least studied, and in its presentation there are lamentable lacunae. Two errors in particular have prevented a proper appreciation of Origen's understanding of dialectic. The first was the tendency to separate rhetoric from dialectic. The second was the belief that Origen being a Christian was hostile to dialectic, i.e., logic and rhetoric. In summary, it was assumed that as a Christian, and thus one hostile to the use of dialectic and rhetoric, Origen did not employ its rules and theorems in the presentation of a Christian philosophy. However, in the Contra Celsum (e.g., VI, 7 p. 76, 25ff.) Origen explicitly states the value dialectic has to the Christian philosopher, and how it may be employed for the definition of philosophical wisdom revealed in scripture (Comm. in Gen. 9, p. 47; Comm. in Jh. XIII, 13 p. 237ff; Hom. in Gen. XI, 2 p. 103). Hence, there is no validity to the assumption that Origen avoided the use of logical and rhetorical modes of argumentation to present his apodeixis euaggelikē. His dependency upon this aspect of Hellenistic science is without question from Origen's own statements (C. Cels. VII, 46 p. 197, 14).

Origen employs a number of technical terms common to the traditions of Hellenistic logic when he defines scripture. Among the more important is his use of the word sēmeion in connection with the statements of scripture.

As we have suggested it is probable that the rules and theorems of rhetoric underly Origen's theory of demonstration. Through them he attempts to deduce his metaphysical postulates. The term sēmeion is important in this context because Origen accepts the notion that the premises (lekta-axiomata-lēmmata) of scripture present signs (sēmeia) which disclose the nature of reality. Indeed, he asserts that the premises of scripture yield definitions which 'signify' metaphysical truths.

It is proposed that the basis of Origen's concept of the sêmeion has its ground in the Stoic theory of logic. We shall first give a general explanation of their role in Origen's dialectic. Next we shall explain how commemorative and indicative sêmeia are defined by the Stoics. Finally we shall present an example from Origen's own writings which illustrate Origen's adoption of this doctrine.

The signs of scripture present themselves to the human mind initially on the level of the 'common notions' (koinai ennoiai) (e.g., Comm. in Jh. XX, 43 p. 386. cf. C. Cels. VII, 34 p. 184). This is clear, Origen argues, because God communicates to man, as reported in scripture, through the senses and the faculty of sensible knowing (e.g., De Princ. IV, 1, 1 p. 292, 9ff.). On this level of knowledge the signs function as commemorative signs. That is, they reveal that which is observed in conjunction with it. The signs of Scripture also present themselves to the mind indicatively. The indicative signal can never be observed in connection with the object signified, since what is not observable is a fortiori not observable in connection with something else.

The commemorative sign is the sign in its common sense, while the indicative sign is the sign in its special sense. In its common usage the word refers to anything which serves to reveal that which has been observed in conjunction with it. In the special sense it means that which is indicative of something non-evident. It appears that Origen understands sêmeion in the indicative sense when he refers to the literal interpretation of scripture, and in the commemorative sense when he refers to the inner meaning of scripture. There are a variety of ways of understanding the 'signs' of Scripture. One can understand them as the faculty of sensible knowing interprets them, or one can understand them as the faculty of intelligible knowing interprets them. Hence, Origen's theory of sêmeion complements his theories of the literal and allegorical interpretation of scripture.

An example from the Periarchôn illustrates Origen's meaning (De Princ. III, 1, 8 p. 207, 11-30). The discussion centers upon statements made to Pharaoh, who is said to have been hardened by God in order that he might let the people go. Along with this is discussed Paul's saying he has mercy on some and others he hardens. These statements from the Old and New Testaments are then harmonized to refute a definition offered by the opponents of Origen. What is significant in this pericope is that Origen terms these statements signs (sêmeia) and suggests that they function to reveal the proposition that God, in order to display his mighty works for the salvation of the many, needs Pharaoh to proceed to a further degree of disobedience and hardens his heart on this account.

Origen distinguishes between the common and special sense of the sêmeia presented in Ex. 4:21, 7:3, and Rom. 9:18. His assertion is that there is a non-evident meaning, which this sign reveals. The signal is not commemorative, but indicative. Nonetheless, the commemorative signal leads us to an understanding of its indicative signal. That is, the commemorative sign, when observed together with the object signified, makes us remember that which was observed along with it, when the object signified is not evident. Thus, if one reads the sign in merely a commemorative sense, at the level of the commemorative sign, then one will not be able to comprehend the real or indicative meaning of the sign. However, at the indicative level, when the sêmeion is understood as a lekton-dicta (p. 207, 16, 34) the true, and deeper meaning, of the sêmeia is revealed.[51] Not only do the sciences, in the stricter sense of the term, receive a new direction and definition through this understanding, but the content of scripture is also to be measured and the knowledge derived from it tested, by the rules of reason. For Origen, only scientific examination shows that scripture contains knowledge which is everlasting, genuine, and essential.

The divine wisdom of scripture contains knowledge as a whole and in all its particular forms. He arrives at this notion of scripture as the reservoir of the entirety of knowledge by reducing its content to a single principle, i.e., that it is the reasoned revelation of God. Thus, all its sêmeia may be explained and demonstrated through the principles of reason, and it is the highest task of knowledge to formulate these principles in such a manner that they may be employed in the philosophical exegesis and defense of what is stated in scripture.

3.3   The determination of the meaning of philosophy rests upon two principles: the doctrines and teachings of the church, and the examination of the sacred writings through the scientific principles of demonstration (apodeixis). Whenever possible the results of the former must conform to the teachings of the latter. We shall focus upon what Origen meant by apodeixis, and how this 'way' leads to knowledge.

Origen equates apodeixis with the horos apodeiktis. The exact meaning of these terms is difficult to ascertain in Origen but it appears that a fundamental assumption of the notion is the assertion that the sayings of scripture function as both the principle of demonstration and the object of demonstration.

The 'demonstrative way' is an approach to scripture whereby the exegete aims at deciphering its 'inner' meaning.

> ...all' hekastô kata to prepon autou tô êthai kai tê katastasei prosagomen ton logon, mathontes "eidenai pôs dei hêmas heni hekastô apokrivasthai." kai eisin ois pleion mê dynamenois tou protrapênai eis to pisteuein touto khêruttomen, allois de hosê dynamis apodeiktikôs di' erôteseôn kai apokriseôn proserchometha.

(C. Cels. VI, 10 p. 80, 21-26)

The demonstrative analysis of scripture yields a certain 'divine scientific wisdom' (C. Cels. III, 72 p. 264, 1ff.), which is the condition for the possibility of gnôsis (C. Cels. VII, 33 p. 183, 24ff.).

Origen employs the term pistis to denote an attitude of belief on the part of Christians of the truth of their sacred scripture. This pistis is called philê pistis by Origen. It is not the fullest expression of faith for:

> eti de hoti kai kata to tô logô areskon pollô diapherei meta logou kai sophias sugkatatithesthai tois dogmasin êper meta philês tes pisteôs, kai hoti kata

peristasin kai tout' eboulêthê ho logoshina mê pantê anôpheleis easê tous
anthropous dêloi ho tou Iêsou gênsios mathêtês Paulos eipôn...

(C. Cels. I, 13 p. 66, 8-12)

This is why Origen is careful to distinguish between this type of knowledge which is alogon
(C. Cels. I, 41 p. 93, 2-8), and that which is "peri tês pisteôs apodeixesin" (C. Cels. VII, 4
p. 156, 16-21). He exhorts Christians to go beyond this notion of pistis philê to search out
the

...ton en tais Theiais graphais noun...

(C. Cels. III, 33 p. 229, 30f.)

which is called gnôsis.

What Origen means is clear when he argues that the full meaning of Christian
teaching cannot be fully comprehended by means of a simple and literal reading of
scripture. Scripture requires study and analysis in order to understand its hidden
meanings, its spiritual meanings. This is why:

...protrepei kai ho Theois logos hemas epi dialektikên...

and the basis for asserting that:

...eumêneis oun elegchoi par' hêmin eisi mallon...

Thus,

ei de rathumousi tines, ouk askountes proseichein tais Theiais anagnôsesi kai
ereunan "tas graphas" kai kata tên entolên tou Iêsou zêtein tên dianoian tôn
graphôn kai aitein peri autôn apo tou Theou kai krouein autôn ta kekleismena,
ou para touto ho logos kenos esti sophias.

(C. Cels. VI, 7 p. 77, 16-20)

The important point to note is that the zêtesis of which Origen speaks is the attempt to
disclose the hidden and higher meaning of scripture. This term is linked to dianoian,
which in the language of the Hellenistic philosophies of the period denoted discursive
reasoning. The seekers, thus, employ discursive reasoning to unlock the truths contained
in scripture.

The common point which unites all Christians is a faith (pistis) that what is said by
scripture is true. All Christians partake of and share in this common faith. The major

problem is to determine in what sense scripture is true, and what meanings, definitions, and doctrines are in accordance with the meanings of scripture.

The scientific evaluation of the content of revelation yields a type of knowledge which is akin to scientific knowledge. The scientific apprehension of revelation results in a knowledge which Origen calls pistis tês apodeixeôs. One attains wisdom by critically interpreting the sayings of scripture. This interpretative process leads the philosopher to the threshold of gnôsis and absolute truth.

Starting from II Cor. 4:18 in the (C. Cels. VII, 46 p. 198, 9f.) Origen describes how one moves from an understanding of the sensible world to a comprehension of the intelligible world, and finally to an apprehension of divinity. The epistemic dimensions of this are detailed by Origen in the (De Princ. IV, 1 p. 292, 9ff.):

Epei de peri têlikoutôn exetazontas pragmatôn, ouk arkoumenoi tais koinais ennoiais kai tê enargeia tôn blepomenôn, prosparalambanomen eis tên phainomenên hêmin apodeixin tôn legomenôn martupia ta ek tôn pepisteu-menôn hêmin einai Theiôn graphôn, tês te legomenês palaias diathêkês kai tês kaloumenês, kainês logô te peirômetha kratunein hêmôn tên pistin, kai oudepô peri tôn graphôn hôs Theiôn dielexthêmen.

Verum quoniam de tantis et talibus rebus disserentibus non sufficit humanis sensibus et communi intellectui summam rei committere et, ut ita dixerim, visibiliter de invisibilius pronuntiare, assumenda sunt nobis ad probationem horun, quae testimonia ut certam et indubitatam habeant fidem sive in his, quae dicenda a nobis, sive quae iam dicta sunt, necessarium prius videtur ostendere quod ipsae scripturae divinae sint, id est dei spiritu inspiratae.

In summary, Origen's use of terms such as koinai ennoiai, enargeia, apodeixis, and pisteuô (sens, communus, intellectus, probatio, fides in Rufinus' version) and the claim that knowledge of the sensibles and the intelligibles must be tested by the criteria of scripture, represent an attempt on his part to ground knowledge on the testimonies of divine revelation. Origen's claim is that the validity of all knowledge must be tested from scripture, and that the deeper meaning of scripture can be revealed through the scientific study of its contents (C. Cels. VI, 7 p. 76, 25ff.).

In summary, what we encounter with Origen is the hammering-out of a Christian epistemology. It is fundamentally Christian because the criterion of knowledge rests upon the sayings of scripture. It represents an epistemology because Origen accepts from the philosophical tradition of his day the standard 'Platonic' understandings of the processes of knowing and demonstration. The immediate belief the Christian has for his scriptures and its contents is akin to the immediate belief one has when one assents (sugkatathesis) to any common perception. The task before the Christian is to study scripture and explain the rational thoughts they contain. The knowledge scripture yields is a scientific knowledge because the contents of the sacred writings are studied through the rules and theorems of dialectic.

VIII. DIALECTIC: RHETORIC

1. Rhetoric in the Middle Academy

1.1   The Platonic schools of first, second and third century Alexandria did not consist solely of scholarly commentators, nor did the philosopher confine his work to philosophical issues alone. The philosopher moved in those circles with the intellectual currents of the age -- philosophy, rhetoric, sophistry, and medicine blended. In these circles philosophical issues were debated publicly, and the method of debate was rhetorical.[52]

Philosophy and rhetoric characterize from diverse angles the fundamental intellectual energy which permeated the era to which it owes its trends of thought. The union of philosophy and rhetoric is evident in all the eminent minds of this period. This is in no case an accident. It is based on a deep and necessary union of these two fields of thought.[53]

There is a close relationship between the questions of logic and rhetoric in the writings of Plato, Aristotle, and the early Stoa.[54] In the renewal of the philosophic spirit in the Middle Academy, and the art of rhetoric in the renaissance of the Second Sophistic, there developed a direct and vital reciprocity between these disciplines. This correlation was an original and substantial one.[55] Logic and rhetoric were understood as branches of dialectic. A formal unity between these modes of argument, and the rhetorical logic employed by these thinkers in debate, sprang from the conception of the interdependence and unity of logic and rhetoric.

The various threads which had been spun in previous centuries by rhetoricians and philosophers were woven together into one fabric in this period. The materials offered in such abundance in the handbooks and doxographies of the Hellenistic-Roman periods were ordered and arranged from unified points of view. This demand for clarification and order between the two disciplines was characteristic of the age. From the recognition of this nexus between rhetoric and logic there followed a conflation of the functions of these two arts. This union was hammered out on grounds originally proposed by Aristotle in his Ars Rhetorica and Topica and Chrysippus in his numerous writings. Thinkers in the New and Middle Academies such as Cicero, Seneca, Philo, Clement, and Origen argued ideas rhetorically. This activity was central to all efforts to debate philosophical issues in this period.

The parallelism between logic and rhetoric had its origins in Aristotle and the Stoa. The latter, expanding upon Aristotle's suggestion, asserted that dialectic and rhetoric were parts of logic along with canonics. This was picked up by Cicero who viewed the syllogisms of rhetoric and logic as related hypothetical types of argument which could be reduced to one or more of the five undemonstrated arguments.[56] This tendency in the philosophical schools to develop a type of rhetorical logic was assented by the doxographer Quintilian, to have begun in the Peripatetic and Stoic schools of the early Hellenistic age.[57]

Little is known of the Stoic treatment of rhetoric or how, if at all, rhetoric was practiced in the Peripatetic schools prior to the first century B.C. The most which can be said about the place of rhetoric, within the context of dialectic or apodictic, was that it was treated as a type of logic by the Stoics, but not by the Peripatetics. However, the Stoic affirmation of the logical dimensions of rhetorical argumentation was accepted by the time of Cicero.[58] Hence, in the New and Middle Academies it was assumed that the rules and theorems of rhetoric correlated with those of logic. Rhetoric was thought to have a logical complexion much deeper than mere stylistic potentialities. We shall now examine the major theoretical tenets of the rhetorical logic of this age.

1.2   At the dawn of our era philosophers fully accepted the postulate of a union between rhetoric and logic. This is attested by Philo who uses its rules and theorems in his own works. We shall now sketch the elements of Middle Academic rhetorical logic.

The epicheirêma was understood as a rhetorical argument whose parts are fully expressed and which is based on probability. This understanding of the rhetorical syllogism was introduced by Hellenistic rhetoricians because they understood Aristotle to say that an enthymêma was a rhetorical syllogism with one of its part suppressed. In the Hellenistic and Roman period this type of argument was thought to have five parts. It contained the basic syllogism plus reasons to support each of the premises. The following illustrations clarify the difference between an enthymêna and epicheirêma.

Enthymêma:

It is unthinkable, that Socrates, who is a good man, would commit murder.

The enthymêma is an argument from probability. It is non-syllogistic in form and has an unstated premise.

Epicheirêma:

(1) Socrates is a good man. (2) As is proven by his life and writings. (3) As we know a good man would not commit murder (4) because murder is an injustice. (5) Therefore Socrates could not have committed murder.

The epicheirêma has five parts although sometimes it has three. It has two premises with reasons and a conclusion. It is considered to be an argument from probability.[59]

The rhetorical arguments were understood to be based on evidence which was either eikota (probabilis) or tekmêria (necessaria) and sêmeia (signa).[60] Probable arguments (and according to some such as Cicero and Galen necessary arguments)[61] constituted the material for the "artistic" proof.[62] Probable arguments were viewed as types of rationes essendi, and the arguments from signs were viewed as types of rationes cognoscendi. The former is an argument which attempts to account for the fact or principle maintained by postulating that its truth must be granted. It then assigns a cause or reason for the being of this fact. The latter is an argument which attempts to supply a reason which will establish the existence of a fact without any effort to explain what has caused it. Evidence garnered from these served as the premises for the enthymêma-epicheirêma.[63]

Central to the rhetorical syllogism were the topoi (loci). They were employed as the "commonplaces" wherein arguments were formulated. As aphormê pisteôs (sedes argumentorum) they operated analytically, i.e. within a highly formalized or structured logical argument.[64] These dialectical topics were at the center of the rhetorical logic practiced in the philosophical schools, and formed the core of the art of rhetorical invention. They go back to the lists of topics collected by Aristotle, i.e. the twenty-eight topics and nine paralogisms of the Ars Rhetorics and the Topica. Also in evidence were the so-called stasiastic topics (status causae).[65] For example, an argument could be constructed from the antikeimena topoi by arguing ex causa, ex persona, or ex facto. The function of the topics and proofs was the demonstration of theseis.

The demonstration of theses was presented through one or more of the genê (tria genera causarum).[66] In the type of debate encountered in the philosophical schools the genus most commonly employed was the iuridicale. The goal of such debate within this genus was to demonstrate the validity of one's own thesis and the non-validity of an opponent's. The theses themselves were placed under specific moria logou (partes orationes). In the period under consideration a quinquepartite scheme was generally followed, but this was by no means dogma among rhetoricians. The art of rhetorical invention was a fluid one, and no one set of theoretical principles governed any rhetorical composition.

These elements formed the core of the rhetorical logic practiced in the Middle Academy. It is unlikely that the art of rhetorical logic was practiced by Philo, Clement, and Origen to argue for, and deduce, metaphysical principles from biblical scripture. For the next section we shall turn to Origen's practice of this art (technê) as an example of Christian Middle Platonic dialectic. We may assume that what we say of Origen is applicable to Philo and Clement as well. We analyze Origen's theory of biblical demonstration as an initial step in the eventual analysis of the theories of Philo and Clement.

2. Origen's Knowledge of Rhetorical Theory

2.1 Modern scholarship has shown limited interest in Origen's art of rhetoric. In addition there is little consensus on what the art of rhetoric means. In this section we shall examine the variety of approaches to the study of Origen's rhetoric, and suggest an approach which may clear up these ambiguities.

Few authors address the rhetorical aspect of Origen's compositions except in general terms. C.A.T. Keil states:

Im 3. Jahrhundert setzen Philosophen mit rhetorsichen Lehrbuechern und Commentaren ein... man nahm die Rhetorik ex officio wieder in den

philosophischen Lehrgang auf. Und keiner Schule ward das leichter als dem
Neu-Platonismus... Und von Seiten des Platonismus stand das einseitig ethisch
fundierte Anathem des Begründers der Schule nicht mehr in Weg, seit dem
Arkesilaos der praktischen Beredsamkeit durch die Einführung des pithanon die
Tore der Akademie weit göffnet hatte.[67]

The first work which directed full attention to Origen's art of rhetoric was Joseph
Borst's Beitraege zur sprachliche-stilistischen und rhetorischen Würdigung des
Origenes.[68] This monograph is important because Borst's approach to and definition of
rhetoric influenced later studies in this field, and convinced scholars who worked on
Origen's philosophy and theology that rhetoric stood apart from, and had little influence
upon, Origen's conceptual universe. Borst's study was limited to Origen's homiletical
literature. His definition of rhetoric as referring only to vocabulary, grammar, and syntax
convinced scholars that Origen's art of rhetoric was important only in regard to his
non-philosophical and non-theological writings, and that rhetoric was primarily an issue
which addressed questions of "style."

Borst's influence is evident upon René Cadiou. Cadiou limits his brief overview of
Origen's technê to the commentaries. Although his work represents an advance upon
Borst's, he sees the connection between rhetoric and logic but he does not follow up on his
insight that:

conaissait aussi un lexique d'Aristote, un dictionnaire du rhetorique qui
distinguait le sens des termes voisins ou synonymes, e un repertoire ou les
mots etaient classes selon la derivation, a patir des noms, ue l'on considerait
comme l'element primitif de la semantique.[69]

He merely states in his comment upon Origen's (Com. in Ps. IV, 7 [PG XII, 1164-65]), that:

Le mot logikon doit s'entendre de la science du discours.[70]

Cadiou does not examine the relationship of rhetoric to logic in Origen's works, nor does
he discuss the function of rhetoric in Origen's philosophical writings.

It is not until Robert Smith's work, The Art of Rhetoric in Alexandria, that Origin's
art of rhetoric is examined.[71] This monograph is in the tradition of scholarship initiated
by Borst. The study is limited to Origen's homiletical literature, and ignores Cadiou's
insight that there was a relation between rhetoric and logic in antiquity. Smith's focus is
upon the stylistic dimensions of rhetoric, and how Origen employed the conventions of
style common in the Second Sophistic to preach the gospel.

In summary: there is no critical study of Origen's rhetoric. In the following pages
we shall attempt to reconstruct Origen's rhetorical theory.

2.2 Origen's acquaintance with rhetorical theory arises from his Hellenic
education, dominated in his time by grammar, rhetoric, and logic. It can also be inferred
from his use of rhetorical devices in his own writings, and his knowledge of dialectic.

His own mode of demonstration, i.e. the horos apodeiktos, leaves the reader in little doubt of his awareness not only of the basics of rhetorical and logical theory, but also the use of rhetorical logic in philosophical debate. In various pericopae scattered throughout his writings we encounter a knowledge of the parts and types of speech, of topics and proofs, and of his knowledge of the rules and theorems of logical argumentation.

Origen came into contact with the art of rhetorical logic through the Academic and Peripatetic practice of debating philosophical theses through the topics of rhetorical invention. They were known in the New Academy and in Middle Platonism, as a study of Cicero's and Philo's rhetoric illustrates.

In the area of rhetorical invention Origen was aware of the reliance of the dialectic of his time on probable rather than necessary premises in arguments aimed at a popular audience. He does not seem to be uncomfortable with this methodological datum. Since the premises he argues from are the revelation of scripture, he takes them to be necessary premises. This reductionist theory in the art of demonstration is echoed in other Hellenistic thinkers such as Galen. By means of this reduction they overcome the problem of demonstrating valid arguments from probable premises, which was the goal of rhetorical and logical argumentation in the second and third centuries.

Given the educational milieu in Alexandria it is not a surprise to find topics and proofs in his compositions, their division into parts of speech, and their compositions written according to specific rhetorical genres. The fact that these elements are found in the Periarchôn (De Principiis) attests to the rhetorical nature of Origen's philosophical writing, and the central role rhetoric played in Christian philosophical debate of the early third century.

Topoi-Loci

Origen employs the topics in both of the senses in which it was defined in late antiquity. They are employed as aphorme pisteôs or sedes argumentorum with epicheirêma-enthymêma or argumenta. They also function as the topoi-loci (commonplaces) or argumentation. In the first case the topics operate analytically, i.e. within a highly formalized, structured rhetorical logic.[72] In the second case the topics are places in which specific themes are amplified. The first use of the topics reveals a knowledge of the subtle workings of rhetorical theory garnered from the handbooks and doxographies on rhetorical invention. The second use illustrates Origen's knowledge and use of the lines of argumentation he perceived to exist in the speeches of the Attic Ten.[73]

A close examination of the Praefatio (1-4) and the De Deo (I, 1, 1-9) shows that Origen used the so-called dialectical topics for the important task of "demonstrating" Platonic metaphysical postulates from Christian scripture. These in turn have both their theoretical and practical application, i.e. the demonstration of theseis.[73] Here the topics stand at the heart of his art of rhetorical invention. The so-called stasiastic topics are also in evidence.[74] Origen argues ex causa, e.g. if God is incorporeal, then knowledge of him cannot be a sensible type of knowledge; ex persona, e.g. from the statements of Paul, John, or other figures in the Old and New Testaments; ex facto, e.g. God is incorporeal and a unity, therefore he cannot be divided into parts as physical things are. It is, thus, within the status causae of conjectural issues that the topics serve to shape the case brought before the audience.

The speeches of the Attic Ten provide Origen with the many exempla from which he can structure his argument along the lines of authoritative cliches. The commonplaces extant in the writings of Plato and the Bible, such as the divided line, the sun simile and its light imagery, God is light or God is spirit, the letter kills but the spirit gives life, the heavenly and material Jerusalem, and seeing with the heart, are also used by Origen in the development of his argument.

The standard or commonplace topics go back to his training in Hellenic education in the speeches of the Attic Ten, Homer, and his Christian education in the stock phrases of the Bible.[75] He generally employs these topics as a complement to the dialectical topics, for they give a certain authority and status to his analytical lines of argu- mentation. His primary goal is to persuade his audience of the validity of his inter- pretation of scripture and church teaching. If he forms his argument in a manner akin to a Demosthenes and asserts that the theses proposed are based upon the sayings of Paul or John, then he is well down the road towards convincing his audience of the efficacy of his apodeixis euggelikê.

The analytical topics go back to the lists of topoi collected by Aristotle in his Ars Rhetorica and Topics and later catalogued in the Hellenistic-Roman handbooks.[76] Origen's favorite topics of this sort are the antikeimena topoi and the argument ek kriseôs and its cognates. Thus, in the area of rhetorical invention Origen displays a knowledge of rhetorical theory which has a Peripatetic pedigree, although by his time this technê was not limited to any one rhetorical or philosophical school. He knows of and utilizes the enthymêma-epicheirêma-paradeigma, and the basics of tekmêria and the eikota. He learned to use these devices through the Academic practice of debating these through topical reasoning.

Enthymêma-Epicheirêma

Origen employs both types of rhetorical syllogism in the Periarchôn (De Principiis). The technical distinction between the two is difficult to discern in Origen's composition. His inventio, at least in the Periarchôn (De Principiis), shows evidence of syllogisms consisting of anywhere from five to two parts. His use of them reflects the confusion which surrounds the enthymêma-epicheirêma concerning its proper form, i.e. whether or not it has a five, four, three, or two part ratiocination.[77]

It is clear that Origen assumes that the rhetorical syllogism is a type of logical syllogism. Although he never explicitly states this as such it appears that he knows that the investigation of causes is understood as both ratio essendi, i.e. the reasons for the being of a fact, and as ratio cognoscendi, i.e. reasons for acknowledging its being.[78] In addition his rhetorical syllogisms take the form of argument from probability. He attacks and defends given theses from such principles, i.e. from the metaphysical postulates of the Middle Platonism he held.[79] However, at the same time, he attempts to overcome the probable aspect of conventional rhetorical argumentation by arguing from the premises of scripture. This has the effect of converting a probable argument into a necessary one.[80]

It appears that his metaphysical arguments are what the handbooks call "artistic" proofs, i.e. they are means of persuasion based on sound philosophical reasoning. His use of scriptural premises functions as types of "inartistic" proofs, i.e. they are the evidence or hard facts not supplied by human efforts but they constitute the reasoned revelation of God.[81] The materials of the first type of enthymêma-epicheirêma are probabilities (eikota), and the second are signs (sêmeia). Probable arguments are thus types of rationes essendi, and the arguments from signs are types of rationes cognoscendi. The former is an argument which attempts to account for the fact or principle maintained, supposing its truth granted: it assigns a cause or reason for the being of fact, i.e. God is immaterial, therefore knowledge of God cannot arise from sensible perception. The latter is an argument which attempts to supply a reason which will establish the existence of this fact without any effort to explain what has caused it. It is the reason for acknowledging the being of a fact, i.e. God is immaterial because God is spirit (Jn. 4:24), e.g. De Princ. (I, 1.1 p. 17, 1ff.). When Origen argues rhetorically he seems to have these distinctions in mind.

The enthymêma-epicheirêma are the syllogistic structures in which the topics are placed. The syllogism is the form the argument has and the topics provide the lines of argument or methods of persuasion to be employed. The materials for the formal construct are provided by Origen's metaphysical and scriptural postulates. Origen goes to the postulates of Platonic and Christian scripture for his premises, and to the enthymêma-epicheirêma-topoi for the form and the lines of argument he pursues. All these elements together constitute the content of his rhetorical syllogism. If it combines these elements in such a way as to constitute a ratio essendi, it is an eikos argument. If it combines them in such a way as to constitute a ratio cognoscendi it is an argument from a sêmeion. Origen generally employs both together, and forms them into a syllogism with two or more parts.[82]

Origen employs both the demonstrative and refutative syllogism in the Periarchôn (De Principiis). At the heart of his art of rhetorical invention are two methods of refutation. These are the "counter-syllogism," and refutation by bringing up an objection. Both are based upon scriptural premises (the two are mutually inter-changeable). The metaphysical arguments of his opponents are not refuted merely from the bases of Origen's own metaphysical arguments. One argument from probability cannot be refuted by another. They are refuted by illustrating that they are not cogent given what the "inner" meaning of scripture reveals. The reason for this is that one does not refute an enthymêma-epicheirêma, which reasons from a probable cause, by showing that its premises are merely probable. It is impossible to demonstrate any metaphysical premise as anything but probable. Probability is all that is claimed from the results of human reasoning. However, it is possible to show that a metaphysical argument is invalid by demonstrating that it does not agree with what is said in scripture. Scripture is the final arbitrator of the validity of all metaphysical knowledge. The point Origen makes is that no argument is false because it is formally deficient. It is false because its conclusions do not correlate with what scripture says.

We know from an examination of Origen's Praefatio (1-4) and De Deo (I, 1.1-9) that the enthymêma-epicheirêma often appears with one or more of its premises suppressed. This must be taken as a matter of fact because there is no evidence which suggests that Origen thought of the rhetorical syllogism as an elided syllogism, i.e. an incomplete logical syllogism. He also thinks it possible to make valid arguments from probable premises, as long as these premises are buttressed by statements from scripture. Many premises are suppressed because this is the nature of rhetorical argument building. In addition, it is often the case that Origen expects his audience to provide premises. The latter device is basic to the art of persuasion.[83]

Moria Logou-Partes Orationes

Origen organizes his argument under the heading of parts of speech. On the basis of our evidence we can assert that Origen employs these divisions. However, the large amount of redaction upon the Periarchôn (De Principiis) does not permit us to say whether or not he employs the quinquepartite scheme, proposed by Cicero and Quintilian, and codified by Martianus Capella and later Byzantine doxographers.[84] The most we can say is that the Praefatio and the De Deo exhibit what the ancient called the prooimion-prooemium (proem-exordium) and the eurêsis-inventio respectively. Within the inventio we have a partitio of the argument into refutatio and confirmatio. Origen's composition does not exhibit a division of the argument into specific sections, each dealing with one part of speech alone. We must add at once, however, that few rhetorical compositions present the parts of speech in the highly schematized form that the handbooks suggest. Compromises with theory are a regular and normal feature of rhetorical invention. The evidence suggests that Origen did not organize his rhetorical material under the headings of the moria logou-partes orationes alone. He organized it under the themes of the syggramma of each chapter.

Genê-Tria Genera Causarum

Of the three parts of speech of rhetoric, the one which dominates the Periarchôn (De Principiis) is the genus iuridiciale. This is clear from: 1) the polemical nature of the composition; 2) his use of forensic topics; 3) his emphasis upon the adikaion of his opponent's interpretation of scripture, and 4) the dikaion of his own. This almost exclusive concentration upon the forensic genus is typical of the Imperial Era.[85] Cicero and Quintilian at the dawn of this era, and Hermagoras after Origen, fit the system of the status wholly within the forensic branch of rhetoric. Hence, Origen's composition reflects the preferential treatment that the forensic branch received among rhetoricians. In addition the forensic genre complements the literary genre employed in the Periarchôn (De Principiis).

From our study of the art of rhetorical invention practiced by Origen the following conclusions can be made about Origen's knowledge of rhetorical theory: 1) the topics and the rhetorical syllogism(s) stand at the heart of Origen's technê, and his use of them suggests a sophisticated knowledge of their use; 2) the parts and genres of speech are known to Origen, but are of secondary importance in his rhetorical scheme; 3) the enthymêma-epicheirêma is the syllogism of Origen's rhetoric and it has the same function the syllogism has in logic. His syllogistic premises are probable causes and signs which are drawn from topics which vary in specificity and exactness; 4) Origen's premises are taken from his philosophical and religious literature. The former premises are validated by the latter; and 5) Origen views the art of rhetoric as reasoned discourse that is constructive and refutative. Its persuasive force is logical, and it draws its premises and lines of argument from topics which are combined to enunciate a ratio essendi and/or ratio cognoscendi. These tie the form of probable causes and their examples with a reason, usually a sign from scripture.

We shall now turn to an examination of how Origen practices his art of rhetorical logic through a rhetorical analysis of the Periarchôn (De Principiis). We shall limit our analysis to a form-critical exegesis of the Praefatio (1-4) and the De Deo (I,1,1-9). In these chapters he deduces his theoretical and epistemological postulates from the premises of scripture. This study permits us to view not only Origen's art of rhetorical logic, but also how a Christian Middle Platonist, in the trajectory of Middle Platonism examined in this study, argues against and defends metaphysical principles.

PART THREE:
THE DEMONSTRATION OF A MIDDLE PLATONIC
THEORETIC AND EPISTEMOLOGY:
THE EVIDENCE OF THE <u>PERIARCHON</u> (<u>DE PRINCIPIIS</u>)

IX. THE PERIARCHON (DE PRINCIPIIS):
PRAEFATIO (1-4); DE DEO (I, 1, 1-9)

1. Literary Structure

1.1   We turn to Origen's Periarchôn (De Principiis) as an example of Middle Platonic philosophical composition arising out of the trajectory of Christian Middle Platonism examined in this study. The purpose of our analysis is to show how a Christian Middle Platonist demonstrated theoretical and epistemological postulates from the premises of biblical scripture.

Origen composed the Periarchôn (De Principiis) around 229. The work represents Origen's mature philosophical vision, and contains the philosophical premises which underly his later works as well. Although we no longer have the original composition we do possess Rufinus' Latin translation of the entire treatise, and Greek fragments of the text preserved in testimonies by Pamphilius, Basil, Gregory of Nanzianzus, and Jerome. We must use Rufinus' redaction as well as the Greek fragments with caution. Rufinus consciously altered passages which he considered of doubtful orthodoxy for his audience in the Latin West, and the opponents and supporters of Origen in the Greek East changed Origen's composition as well.

Modern research has done much to clarify the literary structure of the Periarchôn (De Principiis). Koetschau was the first to offer a reconstruction of the work.[1] Working from the division of the text reported by Pamphilius, Basil, Gregory of Nanzianzus, Rufinus and Photius, Koetschau accepted the four part division of the document extant from these later testimonies.

Thirty years after Koetschau's critical edition scholars began to ask questions concerning the nature and purpose of the work. One of the first questions asked was the genre question. Kübel was the first to suggest that the Periarchôn was a philosophical treatise with genre-parallels to writings in the philosophical literature of the same period.[2] He claimed that the work was not a summa on the scale with those of the mediaeval schoolmen, but something quite different. Working with the same problematic, Steidle suggested that Origen's work had genre affinity to Plotinus' Enneads.[3] Later genre-critics, notably Harl, pushed research on this question to a fruitful conclusion.[4] Works by the pseudo-Aristotle and Sallustius were shown to be kindred works to Origen's Periarchôn.[5] Indeed, Origen's work belongs to a recognized genre of philosophical literature dealing with questions of physics; hence, its title "On First Principles".[6]

Most recently Crouzel and Simonetti have published a new edition of Rufinus' redaction of the Periarchôn, the De Principiis.[7] Utilizing the results of scholarship from Koetschau to Harl they offer a reconstruction of the original literary structure of the Periarchôn. They show that Origen divided the treatise into four books with fourteen divisions. The four books were prefaced by an Introduction (eisagôgê), and were divided into separate Treatises (syggrammata) dealing with specific philosophical questions.[8]

1.2   The importance of the results offered by literary-criticism on the Periarchôn (De Principiis) cannot be underestimated. First, they show that the original intention of the composition differs from the redacted intention attributed to it by fourth and fifth century editors. Second, the data suggest that the issues and concepts attributed to Origen by Patristic and Neopatristic commentators better represent the concerns of the commentators than Origen's own. Third, given the probable literary structure and conceptual context of the Periarchôn it is best to look to literary and conceptual parallels from the first to the third centuries rather than from the fifth to the thirteenth centuries if we are to historically reconstruct the nature and purpose of Origen's treatise.

It is on the basis of these conclusions that the final section of our study commences. Our goal is to place the Periarchôn (De Principiis) within its proper literary context, and to show how Origen rhetorically argued for a system of first principles based upon biblical premises and philosophical postulates. In an attempt to define more precisely the literary situation of the treatise we draw attention to its parallels with a series of monographs on philosophical topics written by Alexander of Aphrodisias. In an attempt to define the text's rhetorical strategy we examine Origen's art of rhetorical argumentation and its parallels to the rhetorical handbooks of the early Graeco-Roman period and their advice on how to construct arguments on exempla offered in the speeches of the Attic Ten.

Working from the conclusions of the genre-critics, we can determine the literary function of the Periarchôn (De Principiis). The Periarchôn (De Principiis) is a monograph (syggramma) composed to treat the problematic issue of first principles within a Christian context, and to respond to a variety of opposing Christian views on this subject. This genre of composition was widely employed in philosophical circles in late antiquity and seemed to have developed among the Alexandrian commentators on Homer, and then was adopted later for purposes of philosophical discourse.[9] A syggramma is a polished work which addresses a specific problem.

Alexander composed several monographs. The most important was his long essay, the de anima, an interpretive paraphrase of the Aristotelian work of the same title. In this work Alexander presented views on the formation of the soul and the nature of the intellect. It was written for a wider public than would have had access to the commentaries (hypomnêmata).[10] This monograph has a literary parallel with Origen's Periarchôn.

Two other essays by Alexander were also composed as monographs. These were the de fato and the lost treatise, the de providentia. The de fato was a long treatise which critiqued the Stoic doctrine of fate and the establishment of a parallel Peripatetic theory. The de providentia, as far as can be determined from the fragments, was a treatise which integrated a theory of providence with an Aristotelian cosmology. Both contributed to a long standing philosophical debate on philosophical questions. They also are kindred to the literary genre of the Periarchôn.

There is a strong polemical element in the monograph (syggrammata).[11] In the Periarchôn (De Principiis) Origen's main opponents are adherents of a Stoa Christiana and

Gnosis. In his anti-Stoic and Gnostic positions we observe his affinities with the Platonic and Peripatetic philosophical culture of Alexandria. He attacks Stoic and Gnostic positions in the same manner as his contemporaries Clement (Strom. I. 83.5) and Alexander (de fato 196. 25-26; 197. 1-2 206, 1; 206, 28-30; 209, 20-210, 3) did. Hence, Origen shared in an anti-Stoic and anti-Gnostic fons communis with other Platonic and Peripatetic philosophers, Christian and Pagan.[12]

In summary, Origen's Periarchôn (De Principiis) is a collection of syggramma and exhibits literary parallels with those composed by Alexander. The Periarchôn (De Principiis) is a Christian Middle Platonic attack on a rival Stoic Christian theory of first principles just as Alexander's writings are directed against Stoic opponents. The work afforded Origen the opportunity for a defense of his Christian Platonic doctrines of divinity, creation, providence, the soul, and so on. It also afforded Origen the opportunity for a continuous critique of opposing Christian doctrines on these topics.

2. Rhetorical Structure

2.1 A rhetorical analysis of the Praefatio 1-4 and the De Deo I, 1.1-9 is extremely difficult because the major bulk of the work is extant only in the redaction of Rufinus. Thus, the analysis offered is provisional, and only suggests what Origen's art of rhetoric and his apodeixis euaggelikê may have looked like. Nonetheless, it appears that the De Principiis contains the rhetorical formulae utilized by Origen when he composed the Periarchôn. It is likely that the rhetorical structure of argumentation is altered by Rufinus only when he changed Origen's theological formulations. Thus, Rufinus left major portions of the composition in its original rhetorical form.

Origen's Periarchôn was composed according to the rules and theorems of rhetoric. In order to facilitate our rhetorical analysis of the Periarchôn (De Principiis), we use the division of the work proposed by Crouzel and Simonetti.[13]

The literary and rhetorical structure of the Periarchôn complement one another. The literary (and rhetorical) structure of the Periarchôn has the following outline. The Eisagôgê constitutes ten sections. Of these we shall examine the first four (Praef. 1-4). The De Deo has nine chapters. Of these we shall examine the first syggramma, which is the refutatio and the confirmatio: I,1,1-5 and I,1,6-9.

2.2 The goal of rhetorical exegesis is to identify the formal dimensions of rhetorical composition utilized by a writer. These formal units comprise the building blocks of argumentation. The description and analysis of the forms and formulae of rhetorical argumentation permit us to reconstruct the strategy of philosophical debate a text reflects, and to precisely define the situation of the philosophical debate in which the author is engaged. Our purpose is to reconstruct the rhetorical context of Origen's metaphysical world. Many of the central philosophical postulates outlined in sections one and two of this study surface in these sections.

The literary and rhetorical nature and purpose of the Periarchôn (De Principiis) are complementary. Origen employs the art of rhetorical logic to argue for and demonstrate the efficacy of a series of Christian Middle Platonic postulates.

There is little recent research which examines the art of rhetorical logic employed by Origen. However, we know that Origen's education was centered on the study of Greek literary and rhetorical treatises. These included the study of Homer, Hesiod, Aeschyles, Sophocles, and Euripides in the literary canon, and the Attic Ten in the rhetorical canon. It is probable that his art of rhetorical logic belongs to a long tradition of philosophical argumentation in the Middle Academy dealing with questions of physics. Since rhetorical the demonstration of such issues was known since the time of Philo and Cicero. We may assume that Origen utilized the art of rhetorical logic to argue his first principles as well.

Origen composed the four books and fourteen sections of the Periarchôn (De Principiis) rhetorically by utilizing the common places, proofs, types, and genres of speech common to ancient rhetoric. Each book is composed in a primary rhetorical genre, usually forensic, and each section argues for and against a philosophical topic through proofs and common places arranged so as to persuade an audience of the efficacy of the position the author champions.

Since the Periarchôn comes down to us in fragments and in redacted form, we do not claim that we cannot claim a generic connection between the argument forms of the Periarchôn (De Principiis) and those cited in the rhetorical handbooks. All reference to, and discussion of, the twenty-eight types of argument from Aristotle's Ars Rhetorica, and the works of Cicero and Quintilian, are analogical in character. Our goal is to uncover the formal similarity between Origen's art of rhetoric and compare it with the art of rhetoric proposed in the rhetorical handbooks. Although this type of formal analysis is tenuous it is helpful in our attempt to reconstruct the situation and strategy of Origen's composition.

In summary, in the exegetical sections we have tried to set the pericopae in the perspective of Origen's art of rhetoric. Focus is primarily upon the argument structure employed by Origen, and how he employs the technê to argue for and demonstrate that his interpretation of scripture is the 'true' one. The definition of God the Father associated with his interpretation of scripture is the point of rhetorical debate. Within the context of the Periarchôn (De Principiis) it appears that if Origen can persuade his audience of the validity of his scriptural exegesis then his apodeixis euaggelikê has succeeded. The reader should concentrate on how the argument unfolds rhetorically. The conceptual assumptions Origen holds have been presented in the previous sections. If clarification is necessary as to what Origen means by substance or knowledge, for example, the reader should refer to preceding sections.

Although we mentioned that little work has been done on Origen's logic and rhetoric, we are fortunate to have at our disposal much research on the art of ancient rhetoric. Spengel, Walz, and Gebauer have collected the writings of the ancient rhetors, and Spengel, Cope, Solmsen, and Palmer have presented historical reconstructions of the art of rhetoric as it was practiced in late antiquity.[14] It is from their research that we begin our own attempt to extend the reach of rhetorical analysis into uncharted waters toward a reconstruction of the rhetorical structure of the Periarchôn (De Principiis).

To facilitate our rhetorical analysis we shall present an analytical outline of the sections of the treatise to be studied.

3. Analytical Outline

The analytical outline preceding the exegesis is presented to help the reader follow the general argument of the sections of the treatise under examination.

3.1 Praefatio (1-4)

P1.   A presentation of a Christian first principles rests upon the postulate that all knowledge is based on the belief that Christ is the truth, and that the word of God proclaimed in the scriptures constitutes the basis for the interpretation of this truth. Origen holds that the premises for the definition of first principles reside in the words and teaching of Christ as proclaimed in scripture. The basis of a valid first principles is the correct interpretation of scripture and church doctrine.

Origen outlines the goal of his work in this pericope. He outlines the conflicting opinions on the nature of God, Jesus Christ, the Holy Spirit, and the created beings. His aim is to define the correct doctrines on these issues. The truth proclaimed in scripture and the teachings of the church are the basis for correct interpretation of philosophical issues. It is clear that his audience is Christian. He postulates that truth resides in Christ. What the audience must decide is which interpretation of first principles under debate corresponds to the teachings of Christ and the doctrines of the church.

P2.   Origen presents his theory of the threefold sense of scripture, and the three types of knowledge man possesses. The necessary doctrines proclaimed in scripture are those understood by all believers. These are grasped by the mind as objects of perception and yield a somatic understanding of scripture. There are other meanings of scripture that are grasped by the faculties of intelligible and divine intellection.

P3.   The first type of knowledge is full of illusion, yet it is partially true. The higher types of knowledge are not opinions but constitute knowledge and wisdom. They represent a deeper understanding of the truth proclaimed in scripture. To understand the inner meaning of scripture and grasp its higher knowledge it is necessary to investigate its doctrines through a systematic study of them by means of these higher faculties of knowledge.

P4.   Origen lists the doctrines to be investigated, which form the basis for a study of first principles. The topics are God the Father, Jesus Christ, and the Holy Spirit. The definitions offered of these doctrines are postulated in accordance with Apostolic doctrine.

3.2 De Deo (I, 1.1-9)

1.1   In this opening section Origen argues for the __asomatic__ interpretation of scripture. Origen defines the nature of God as incorporeal, i.e. as spiritual. Here we encounter Origen's correlation of the three-fold meaning of scripture, and the tri-partite division of the faculties of knowledge, cf. P 3. The distinction is made between corporeal light and spiritual light. Only Spiritual light is associated with the Father and the Son.

1.2   Working from the postulate that God is non-corporeal Origen attempts to refute the corporealists' interpretation of divine light, and their thesis that God is material. He builds a series of arguments that point out the implausibility of such an interpretation. The epistemic basis he works from is the distinction between sensible and intelligible knowledge. He correlates this distinction with the somatic and asomatic interpretations of scripture.

1.3   This pericope continues the argument of the first two. Origen couples his postulates concerning the nature of knowledge and the meaning of scripture, with an ontological postulate. The Holy Spirit, the focus of this section, is an intellectual existence with a subsistence and being of its own. The nature of the Holy Spirit precludes the possibility that it can be known through the faculty of sensible intellection. Since it has intellectual existence its nature is known only through the faculties of higher knowledge, i.e. either intelligible or divine intellection (Origen does not specify which one; we assume that he holds the Holy Spirit is known through the faculty of intelligible and divine intellection, cf. I, 1.8-9). Origen attempts to argue that the position of the corporealists is untenable by showing the contradictions inherent in their interpretation.

Origen postulates an asomatic reading of the dictum "deus spiritus est." His example is based upon the distinction between the literal and spiritual interpretation of scripture. His example is the women of Samaria who receive the exhortation to believe, but are incapable of understanding the inner meaning of belief. Origen's point is that the somatic sense of scripture has to do with language and mere words, with things which are the object of perception. Hence, the understanding of Jerusalem as a material place, rather than as the abode of spirit and truth. Origen's argument is that since God is spirit and truth (cf. I,1,1), he cannot be understood as something corporeal. He must not be worshipped as a shadow or image of what he really is.

1.4   With this chapter begins Origen's defense of his interpretation of God the Father. God has no material characteristics. He can only be known through the faculty of intelligible intellection, but even this knowledge of God is not a full one. Origen postulates that God is above materiality. He asserts that God is only known by the faculty of intelligible knowledge, which is above sensible knowing. These Platonic postulates are unpacked through the use of the analogy of the sun. This draws the audience's attention to the analogy of the sun and the Platonic interpretation of knowledge and its objects. God is incomprehensible and immeasurable, but just as the sun, is supremely visible. He renders other things visible to the eye. Thus, God, the supreme intelligible, renders his nature, indirectly, to the higher faculties of knowledge.

1.5   This pericope continues the analogy of the sun. Origen stresses the dependence of the universe on divine providence, and postulates that he cannot be thought of as any kind of body. God is an intellectual existence devoid of all physical attributes. Origen argues that deity exists apart from all material intermixture. He is a noetic first principle, a "One" and a "Unity" that cannot be perceived by sensible intellection. Against the Stoics, Origen argues that God is not material, and he does not pervade matter.

1.6   Next, Origen moves into a definition of the higher faculties of the human mind. The "mens intellectus" is characterized by the same want of material attributes as the divine mind. It exists in the body but is not co-mingled with it. The mind is non-corporeal. Origen attacks the Stoic doctrine of mixture, in which mind and body are postulated as one. Origen argues that this definition cannot be applied to the mind and body. He then shows that this doctrine does not hold to God either. God is a unitary intellect and being.

1.7   Origen continues the arguments and conclusions of (I, 1.5-6) in this pericope. The focus now is upon the nature of knowledge. If the soul is a body, how could it apprehend the intelligibles or the theologicals? Furthermore, how could the mind discern the divine doctrines of scripture which are also incorporeal? He repeats the doctrine of the three-fold sense of knowledge: the aesthetic, the intelligible, and the divine. He concludes that Mind, in toto, has different objects to act upon. Sensible knowing does not have a substance connected with it, and does not have anything substantial as its object of knowledge. This proves Origen's postulate that God is incorporeal.

1.8   The first part of this chapter is a continuation of the argument in (I, 1.5-7). The goal of the argument is to refute those who assert that although God's nature surpasses the nature of bodies, it is visible to some and not to others. This is an attack on those who claim that knowledge is not available to all men, but only to the Pneumatici chosen by God. Origen argues that spiritual knowledge is available to all men. Pistis is available to all, and epistêmê and gnôsis is not limited to a privileged few.

In this section Origen also expands his definition of God the Father, and further unpacks his epistemological presuppositions. A distinction is made between seeing and knowing, and upon this distinction Origen explains why God's nature is invisible, and why it is invisible even to him. To see and be seen is a property of bodies, while to know and to be known is the property of intellectual existence. Since the Father and the Son are intelligible existences they know each other, and man knows them through his faculty of intelligible knowing.

1.9   In this pericope Origen addresses some final objections to his opponents. They focus on his opponents' metaphysical presuppositions and their interpretations of scripture. Again epistemic assumptions postulated earlier are utilized to show that there are different faculties of knowing, and that scripture is interpreted differently by each of these faculties. There are degrees of knowing and Origen lists them, from lowest to highest, i.e. perception, intellection, and divine perception.

4. Text and Translation

The rhetorical structure of the Praefatio (1-4) and the De Deo (I,1,1-9) will be examined in the commentary. The analytical outline is based upon the following pericopae from the Periarchôn (De Principiis).

We provide Rufinus' redaction of Origen's work, and Butterworth's translation into English. For the complete text and the critical apparatus we refer the reader to Koetschau's edition of the Periarchôn (De Principiis), and Butterworth's translation of Koetschau's edition. We provide text and translation only to serve as a guide to the rhetorical commentary which follows in part five.

Praefatio

1. [Omnes qui credunt et certi sunt quod gratia et veritas per Iesum Christum facta sit, et Christum esse veritatem norunt, secundum quod ipse dixit: "Ego sum veritas",] scientiam quae provocat homines ad bene beateque vivendum non aliunde quam ab ipsis Christi verbis doctrinaque suscipiunt. Christi autem verbis dicimus non his solum, quae homo factus atque in carne positus dociut; et prius namque Christus dei verbum in Moyse atque in prophetis erat. Nam sine verbo dei quomodo poterant prophetare de Christo? Ad cuius rei probationem non esset difficile ex divinis scripturis ostendere, quomodo vel Moyses vel prophetae spiritu Christi repleti vel locuti sunt vel gesserunt omnia quae gesserunt, nisi studii nobis esset, praesens hoc opus omni qua possumus brevitate succingere. Unde sufficere aestimo uno hoc Pauli testimonio debere nos uti ex epistula, quam ad Hebraeos scribit, in qua ita ait: "Fide magnus factus Moyses negavit se dici filium filiae Pharaonis, magis elignes afflictari cum populo dei quam temporalem habere peccati iucunditatem, maiores divitias aestimans Aegyptiorum thesauris inproperium Christi". Sed et post adsumptionem eius in caelos quod in apostolis suis locutus sit, hoc modo indicat Paulus: "Aut numquid probamentum quaeritis eius, qui in me loquitur Christus?"

2. Quoniam ergo multi ex his, qui Christo se credere profitentur, non

1. All who believe and are convinced that grace and truth came by Jesus Christ, and who know Christ to be the truth (in accordance with his own saying, 'I am the truth'), derive the knowledge which calls men to lead a good and blessed life for no other source but the very words and teaching of Christ. By the words of Christ we do not mean only those which formed his teaching when he was made man and dwelt in the flesh, since even before that Christ the Word of God was in Moses and the prophets. For without the Word of God how could they have prophesied about Christ? In proof of which we should not find it difficult to show from the divine scriptures how that Moses or the prophets were filled with the spirit of Christ in all their words and deeds, were we not anxious to confine the present work within the briefest possible limits. I count it sufficient, therefore, to quote this one testimony of Paul, taken from the epistle which he writes to the Hebrews, where he speaks as follows: 'By faith Moses, when he was grown up, refused to be called the son of Pharaoh's daughter, choosing rather to suffer affliction with the people of God than to enjoy the pleasures of sin for a season, accounting the reproach of Christ greater than the treasures of Egypt. And as for the fact that Christ spoke in his apostles after his ascension into heaven, this is shown by Paul in the following passage: 'Or do ye seek a proof of him that speaketh in me, that is, Christ?

2. Many of those, however, who profess to believe in Christ, hold con-

solum in parvis et minimis discordant, verum etiam in magnis et maximis, id est vel de deo vel de ipso domino Iesu Christo vel de spiritu sancto, non solum autem de his, sed et de aliis creaturis, id est vel de dominationibus vel de virtutibus sanctis: propter hoc necessarium videtur prius de his singulis certam lineam manifestamque regulam ponere, tum deinde etiam de ceteris quaerere. Sicut enim, multis apud Graecos et barbaros pollicentibus veritatem, desivimus apud omnes eam quaerere, qui eam falsis opinionibus asserebant, posteaquam credidimus filium esse dei Christum et ab ipso nobis hanc discendam esse persuasimus: ita cum multi sint, qui se putant sentire quae Christi sunt, et nonnulli eorum diversa a prioribus sentiant, servetur vero ecclesiastica praedicatio per successionis ordinem ab apostolis tradita et usque ad praesens in ecclesiis permanens, illa sola credenda est veritas, quae in nullo ab ecclesiastica et apostolica traditione discordat.

3. Illud autem scire oportet, quoniam sancti apostoli fidem Christi praedicantes de quibusdam quidem, quaecumque necessaria crediderunt, omnibus credentibus, etiam his, qui pigriores erga inquisitionem divinae scientiae videbantur, manifestissime tradiderunt, rationem scilicet assertionis eorum relinquentes ab his inquirendam, qui spiritus dona excellentia mererentur

flicting opinions not only on small and trivial questions but also on some that are great and important; on the nature, for instance, of God or of the Lord Jesus Christ or of the Holy Spirit, and in addition on the natures of those created beings, the dominions and the holy powers. In view of this it seems necessary first to lay down a definite line and unmistakable rule in regard to each of these, and to postpone the inquiry into other matters until afterwards. For just as there are many among Greeks and barbarians alike who promise us the truth, and yet we gave up seeking for it from all who claimed it for false opinions after we had come to believe that Christ was the Son of God and had become convinced that we must learn the truth from him; in the same way when we find many who think they hold the doctrine of Christ, some of them differing in their beliefs from the Christians of earlier times, and yet the teaching of the church, handed down in unbroken succession from the apostles, is still preserved and continues to exist in the churches up to the present day, we maintain that that only is to be believed as the truth which in no way conflicts with the tradition of the church and apostles.

3. But the following fact should be understood. The holy apostles, when preaching the faith of Christ, took certain doctrines, those namely which they believed to be necessary ones, and delivered them in the plainest terms to all believers, even to such as appeared to be somewhat dull in the investigation of divine knowledge. The grounds of their statements they left to be investigated

et praecipue sermonis, sapientiae et scientiae gratiam per ipsum sanctum spiritum percepissent; de aliis vero dixerunt quidem quia sint, quomodo autem aut unde sint, siluerunt, profecto ut studiosiores quique ex posteris suis, qui amatores essent sapientiae, exercitium habere possent, in quo ingenii sui fructum ostenderent, hi videlicet, qui dignos se et capaces ad recipiendam sapientiam praepararent.

4. Species vero eorum, quae per praedicationem apostolicam manifeste traduntur, istae sunt. Primo, quod unus est deus, qui omnia creavit atque composuit, quique, cum nihil esset, esse fecit universa, deus a prima creatura et conditione numdi, omnium iustorum deus, Adam Abel Seth Enos Enoch Noë Sem Abraham Isaac Iacob duodecim partiarcharum Moysei et prophetarum; et quod hic deus in novissimis diebus, sicut per prophetas suos ante promiserat, misit dominum Iesum Christum, primo quidem vocaturum Israhel, secundo vero etiam gentes post perfidiam populi Israhel. Hic deus iustus et bonus, pater domini nostri Iesu Christi, legem et prophetas et evangelia ipse dedit, qui et apostolorum deus est et veteris ac novi testamenti.

Tum deinde quia Christus Iesus, ipse qui venit, ante omnem creaturam natus ex patre est. Qui cum in omnium conditione patri ministrasset, "per ipsum" namque "omnia facta sunt", novissimis temporibus se ipsum exin-

by such as should merit the higher gifts of the Spirit and in particular by such as should afterwards receive through the Holy Spirit himself the graces of language, wisdom and knowledge. There were other doctrines, however, about which the apostles simply said that things were so, keeping silence as to the how or why; their intention undoubtedly being to supply the more diligent of those who came after them, such as should prove to be lovers of wisdom, with an exercise on which to display the fruit of their ability. The men I refer to are those who train themselves to become worthy and capable of receiving wisdom.

4. The kind of doctrines which are believed in plain terms through the apostolic teaching are the following: --

First, that God is one, who created and set in order all things, and who, when nothing existed, caused the universe to be. He is God from the first creation and foundation of the world, and God of all righteous men, of Adam, Abel, Seth, Enos, Enoch, Noah, Shem, Abraham, Isaac, Jacob, of the twelve patriarchs, of Moses and the prophets. This God, in these last days, according to the previous announcements made through his prophets, sent the Lord Jesus Christ, first for the purpose of calling Israel, and secondly, after the unbelief of the people of Israel, of calling the Gentiles also. This just and good God, the Father of our Lord Jesus Christ, himself gave the law, the prophets and the gospels, and he is God both of the apostles and also of the Old and New Testaments.

Then again: Christ Jesus, he who came to earth, was begotten of the

aniens homo factus est, incarnatus est, cum deus esset, et homo factus mansit quod erat, deus. Corpus assumsit nostro corpori simile, eo solo differens, quod natum ex virgine et spiritu sancto est. Et quoniam hic Iesus Christus natus et passus est in veritate, et non per phantasiam, communem hanc mortem vere mortuus; vere enim et a mortuis resurrexit et post resurrectionem conversatus cum discipulis suis assumtus est.

Tum diende honore ac dignitate patri ac filio sociatum tradiderunt spiritum sanctum. In hoc non iam manifeste discernitur, utrum natus aut innatus, vel filius etiam ipse dei habendus sit, necne; sed inquirenda iam ista pro viribus sunt de sancta scriptura et sagaci perquisitione investiganda. Sane quod iste spiritus sanctus unumquemque sanctorum vel prophetarum vel apostolorum inspiraverit, et non alius spiritus in veteribus, alius vero in his, qui in adventu Christi inspirati sunt, fuerit, manifestissime in ecclesia praedictur.

Father before every created thing. And after he had ministered to the Father in the foundation of all things, for 'all things were made through him', in these last times he emptied himself and was made man, was made flesh, although he was God; and being made man, he still remained what he was, namely, God. He took to himself a body like our body, differing in this alone, that it was born of a virgin and of the Holy Spirit. And this Jesus Christ was born and suffered in truth and not merely in appearance, and truly died our common death. Moreover he truly rose from the dead, and after the resurrection companied with his disciples and was then taken up into heaven.

Then again, the apostles delivered this doctrine, that the Holy Spirit is united in honour and dignity with the Father and the Son. In regard to him it is not yet clearly known whether he is to be thought of as begotten or unbegotten, or as being himself also a Son of God or not; but these are matters which we must investigate to the best of our power from holy scripture, inquiring with wisdom and diligence. It is, however, certainly taught with the utmost clearness in the Church, that this Spirit inspired each one of the saints, both the prophets and the apostles, and that there was not one Spirit in the men of old and another in those who were inspired at the coming of Christ.

De Deo

1.   Scio   quoniam   conabuntur
quidam   etiam   secundum   scripturas
nostras dicere deum corpus esse quoniam
inveniunt scriptum esse apud Moysen
quidem: "Deus noster ignis consumens
est", in evangelio vero secundum Iohan-
nem: "Deus spiritus est, et eos qui
adorant eum, in spiritu et veritate
oportet adorare". Ignis vero et spiritus
non aliud apud eos quam corpus esse
putabitur. Quos interrogare volo, quid
dicant de eo quod scriptum est, quia
'deus lux est' sicut Iohannes in epistola
sua dicit; "Deus lux est, et tenebrae non
sunt in eo". Ista nempe 'lux est', 'quae
inluminat' omnem sensum eorum, qui
possunt capere veritatem, sicut in
tricesimo quinto psalmo dicitur: "In
lumine tuo videbimus lumen". Quid enim
aliud lumen dei dicendum est, in quo quis
videt lumen, nisi virtus dei, per quam
quis inluminatus vel veritatem rerum
omnium pervidet vel ipsum deum
cognoscit, qui veritas appellatur? Tale
est ergo quod dicitur: "In lumine tuo
videbimus lumen", hoc est, in verbo tuo
et sapientia tua, qui est filius tuus, in
ipso te videbimus patrem. Numquidnam
quia lumen nominatur, simile putabitur
solis huius lumine? Et quomodo vel levis
aliquis dabitur intellectus, ut ex isto quis
corporali lumini causam scientiae capiat
et veritatis inveniat intellectum?

2.   Si   ergo   adquiescunt   huic
assertioni   nostrae,   quam   de   natura
luminis ipsa ratio demonstravit, et
fatentur non posse corpus intellegi deum
secundum luminis intellectum, similis

1. I am aware that there are some
who will try to maintain that even
according to our scriptures God is a
body, since they find it written in the
books of Moses, 'Our God is a consuming
fire', and in the Gospel according to
John, "God is spirit, and they who
worship him must worship in spirit and in
truth'. Now these men will have it that
fire and spirit are body and nothing else.
But I would ask them what they have to
say about this passage of scripture, 'God
is light', as John says in his epistle, 'God
is light, and in him is no darkness'. He is
the light, surely, which lightens the
whole understanding of those who are
capable of receiving truth, as it is
written in the thirty-fifty psalm, 'In thy
light shall we see light'. For what other
light of God can we speak of, in which a
man sees light, except God's spiritual
power, which when it lightens a man
causes him either to see clearly the
truth of all things or to know God
himself who is called the truth? Such
then is the meaning of the saying, 'In thy
light shall we see light'; that is, in thy
word and they wisdom, which is thy Son,
in him shall we see thee, the Father.
For can we possibly think that, because
it is termed light, it is like the light of
our sun? And how can there be the
slightest reason for supposing that from
that material light the grounds of
knowledge could be derived and the
meaning of truth discovered?

2. If then they accept this argument of ours, proved by reason itself,
about the nature of light, and will admit
that the use of the word light cannot
possibly mean that God is to be thought

quoque ratio etiam de 'igni consumenti' dabitur. Quid enim consumit deus secundum hoc quod 'ignis' est? Numquidnam putabitur consumere materiam corporalem, ut est 'lignum vel faenum vel stipula'? Et quid in hoc dignum de dei laudibus dicitur, si deus ignis est huiuscemodi materias consumens? Sed [si] consideremus quia deus consumit quidem et exterminat, sed consumit malas mentium cogitationes, consumit gesta turpia, consumit desideria peccati, cum se credentium mentibus inserit et eas animas, quae verbi eius ac sapientiae efficiuntur capaces, una cum filio suo inhabitans secundum quod dictum est: "Ego et pater veniemus et mansionem apud eum faciemus", omnibus eorum vitiss passionibusque consumtis purum sibi eas seque dignum efficit templum.

Sed et his, qui per hoc quod dictum est quoniam "deus spiritus est" corpus esse arbitrantur deum, hoc modo repondendum est. Consuetudo est scripturae sanctae, cum aliquid contrarium corpori huic crassiori et solidiori designare vult, spiritum nominare, sicut dicit: "Littera occidit, spiritus autem vivificat". In quo sine dubio per litteram corporalia significat, per spiritum intellectualia, quae et spiritalia dicimus. Apostolus quoque ita dicit: "Usque in hodiernum autem, cum legitur Moyses, velamen est positum super cor eorum; cum autem conversus quis fuerit ad dominum, auferetur velamen; ubi autem domini spiritus, ibi libertas" Donec enim quis non se converterit ad intellegentiam spiritalem. 'velamen est positum super cor' eius, quo velamine, id est intellegentia crassiore, scriptura ipsa velari dicitur vel putatur; et hoc est quod ait superpositum esse velamen vultui Moysi,

of as being a body, they will allow a similar reasoning in regard to the phrase 'a consuming fire'. Are we to suppose that he consumes bodily matter, 'wood or hay or stubble'? What is there in this statement consistent with the praises due to God, if he is a fire that consumes material substances like these? Let us rather consider that God does indeed consume and destroy, but that what he consumes are evil thoughts of the mind, shameful deeds and longings after sin, when these implant themselves in the minds of believers; and that he takes those souls which render themselves capable of receiving his word and wisdom and dwells in them according to the saying, 'I and the Father will come and make our abode with him', having first consumed all their vices and passions and made them into a temple pure and worthy of himself.

To those, however, who think that God is a body in consequence of the saying, 'God is spirit', we must reply as follows. It is a custom of holy scripture, when it wishes to point to something of an opposite nature to this dense and solid body, to call it spirit, as in the saying, 'The letter killeth, but the spirit giveth life'. Here undoubtedly the letter means that which is bodily, and the spirit that which is intellectual, or as we also call it, spiritual. The apostle also says, 'Even until this day, whenever Moses is read, a veil lieth upon their hearths; but when a man shall turn to the Lord, the veil shall be taken away; and where the Spirit of the Lord is, there is liberty'. For so long as a man does not attend to the spiritual meaning 'a veil lies upon his hearth', in consequence of which veil, in other words his duller understanding, the

cum loqueretur ad populum, id est, cum lex vulgo recitatur. Si autem 'convertamus nos ad dominum', ubi est et verbum dei, et ubi spiritus sanctus revelat scientiam spiritalem, tunc' auferetur velamen', et tunc 'revelata facie' in scripturis sanctis 'gloriam domini speculamur'.

3. Sed et cum de spiritu sancto multi sancti participant, non utique corpus aliquod intellegi potest spiritus sanctus, quod divisum in partes corporales percipiat unusquisque sanctorum; sed virtus profecto sanctificans est, cuius participium habere dicuntur omnes, qui per eius gratiam sanctificari meruerint. Et ut facilius quod dicimus possit intellegi, ex rebus quamvis inparibus sumamus exemplum. Multi sunt qui disciplinae sive artis medicinae participant, et numquid putandum est omnes eos, qui medicinae participant, corporis alicuius, quod medicina dicitur, in medio posit sibi aufere particulas et ita eius participium sumere? an potius intellegendum est quod quicumque promptis paratisque mentibus intellectum artis ipsius disciplinaeque percipiunt, he medicinae participare dicantur? Sed haec non omnimodis similia exempla putanda sunt de medicina sancto spritui comparata; sed ad hoc tantummodo conprobandum, quia non continuo corpus putandum est id, cuius participatio habetur a plurimis. Spiritus enim sanctus longe differt a medicinae ratione vel disciplina, pro eo quod sanctus spiritus subsistentia est intellectualis et

scripture itself is said or thought to be veiled; and this is the explanation of the veil which is said to have covered the face of Moses when he was speaking to the people, that is, when the law is read in public. But if we turn to the Lord, where also the Word of God is, and where the Holy Spirit reveals spiritual knowledge, the veil will be taken away, and we shall then with unveiled face behold in the holy scriptures the glory of the Lord.

3. Further, although many saints partake of the Hold Spirit, he is not on that account to be regarded as a kind of body, which is divided into material parts and distributed to each of the saints; but rather as a sanctifying power, a share of which is said to be possessed by all who have shown themselves worthy of being sanctified through his grace. And to make this statement more easily understood let us take an illustration from things admittedly of lesser importance. There are many who share in the teaching and art of medicine; yet are we to suppose that all who share in medicine have some material substance called medicine placed before them from which they take away little particles and so obtain a share of it? Must we not rather understand that all who with ready and prepared minds gain a comprehension of the art and its teaching may be said to share in medicine? These illustrations from medicine must not be supposed to apply in every detail when compared with the Holy Spirit; they establish this point only, that a thing in which many have a share is not necessarily to be regarded as a body. The Holy Spirit is far different from the

proprie subsistit et extat; nihil autem tale est medicina.

4. Sed et ad ipsum iam sermonem evangelii transeundum est, ubi scriptum est quia "deus spiritus est", et ostendendum est quam consequenter his quae diximus intellegi debeat. Interrogemus namque quando ista dixerit salvator noster vel apud quem vel cum quid quaereretur. Invenimus sine dubio quod ad Samaritanam mulierem loquens ista protulerit, eam quae putabat quod in monte Garizin secundum Samaritanorum opinionem adorari oporteret deum, dicens quoniam "deus spiritus est". Quaerebat enim ab eo Samaritana mulier, putans eum unum esse ex Iudaeis, utrum 'in Hierosolymis' adorari oporteret deum, aut 'in hoc monte'; et ita dicebat: "Patres nostri onmes in hoc monte adoraverunt, et vos dicitis quia in Hierosolymis est locus, ubi oportet adorare". Ad haec ergo quae opinabatur Samaritana, putans quod ex locorum corporalium praerogativa minus recte vel recte adorabitur deus aut a Iudaeis in Hierogolymis aut a Samaritanis in monte Garizin, respondit salvator recedendum esse a praesumptione corporalium locorum huic qui vult deum sequi, et ita ait: "Venit hora ut veri adoratores neque in Heirosolymis neque in hoc monte adorent patrem. Deus spiritus est, et eos qui adorant eum, in spiritu et veritate oportet adorare". Et vide quam consequenter veritatem spiritui sociavit, ut ad distinctionem quidem corporum 'spiritum' nominaret, ad distinctionem vero umbrae vel imaginis 'veritatem'. Qui enim adorabant in Hierosolymis,

system or science of medicine, for the Holy Spirit is an intellectual existence, with a subsistence and being of its own, whereas medicine is nothing of the sort.

4. We must now turn to the Gospel passage itself, where it is written that 'God is spirit', and must show that this is to be understood in a sense agreeing with what we have just said. Let us ask when our Saviour spoke these words, and to whom, and in what connexion. We find undoubtedly that he uttered them when speaking to the woman of Samaria, who thought that men ought to worship God in Mount Gerizim according to the belief of the Samaritans. 'God,' he told her, 'is spirit'. The woman of Samaria, supposing him to be an ordinary Jew, was asking him whether men ought to worship God 'in Jerusalem' or 'in this mountain'. These were her words: 'All our fathers worshipped in this mountain, but ye say that in Jerusalem is the place where men ought to worship.' It was this belief of the woman, who thought that God would be worshipped rightly or wrongly by Jews in Jerusalem or by Samaritans in Mount Gerizim because of some special privilege attaching to the material places, that the Saviour contradicts by saying that the man who desires to seek for God must abandon all idea of material places. These are his words: 'The hour cometh, when the true worshippers shall worship the Father neither in Jerusalem nor in this mountain. God is spirit, and they that worship him must worship in spirit and in truth.' See, too, how appropriately he associated truth with spirit, calling God spirit to distinguish him from bodies, and truth to distinguish him from a shadow

'umbrae et imagini caelestium deservientes' non veritati neque spiritui adorabant deum; similiter autem et hi, qui adorabant in monte Garizin.

5. Omni igitur sensu, qui corporeum aliquid de deo intellegi suggerit, prout potuimus, confutato, dicimus secundum veritatem quidem deum inconprehensibilem esse atque inaestimabilem. Si quid enim illud est, quod sentire vel intellegere de deo potuerimus, multis longe modis eum meliorem esse ab eo quod sensimus necesse est credi. Sicut enim si videamus aliquem vix posse scintillam luminis aut brevissimae lucernae lumen aspicere et eum, cuius acies oculorum plus luminis capere quam supra diximus non valet, si velimus de claritate ac splendore solis edocere, nonne oportebit nos ei dicere quia omni hoc lumine quod vides ineffabiliter et inaestimabiliter melior ac praestantior solis est splendor? -- ita mens nostra cum intra carnis et sanguinis claustra concluditur et pro talis materiae participatione hebetior atque obtusior redditur, licet ad comparationem naturae corporeae longe praecellens habeatur, tamen cum ad incorporea nititur atque eorum rimatur intuitum, tunc scintillae alicuius aut lucernae vix obtinet locum. Quid autem in omnibus intellectualibus, id est incorporeis, tam praestans omnibus, tam ineffabiliter atque inaestimabiliter praecellens quam deus? cuis utique natura acie humanae mentis intendi atque intueri, quamvis ea sit purissima mens ac limpidissima, non potest.

or an image. For those who worshipped in Jerusalem, 'serving a shadow and image of heavenly things', worshipped neither in truth nor in spirit, and the same is true of those who worshipped in Mount Gerizim.

5. Having then refuted, to the best of our ability, every interpretation which suggests that we should attribute to God any material characteristics, we assert that in truth he is incomprehensible and immeasurable. For whatever may be the knowledge which we have been able to obtain about God, whether by perception or by reflection, we must of necessity believe that he is far and away better than our thoughts about him. For if we see a man who can scarcely look at a glimmer or the light of the smallest lamp, and if we wish to teach such a one, whose eyesight is not strong enough to receive more light than we have said, about the brightness and splendour of the sun, shall we not have to tell him that the splendour of the sun is unspeakable and immeasurably better and more glorious than all this light he can see? In the same way our mind is shut up within bars of flesh and blood and rendered duller and feebler by reason of its association with such material substances; and although it is regarded as far more excellent when compared with the natural body, yet when it strains after incorporeal things and seeks to gain a sight of them it has scarcely the power of a glimmer of light or a tiny lamp. And among all intellectual, that is, incorporeal things, what is there so universally surpassing, so unspeakable and immeasurably excelling, as God, whose nature certainly the vision of the

6. Verum non videtur absurdum, si ad evidentiorem rei manifestationem etiam alia utamur similitudine. Inderdum oculi nostri ipsam naturam lucis, id est substantiam solic, intueri non possunt; splendorem vero eius vel radios fenestris forte vel quibuslibet luminum brevibus receptaculis infusos intuentes, considerare ex his possums, fomes ipse ac fons quantus sit corporei luminis. Ita ergo quasi radii quidam sunt dei naturae opera divinae providentiae et ars universitatis huius ad comparationem ipsius substantiae ieus ac naturae. Quia ergo mens nostra ipsum per se ipsam deum sicut est non potest intueri, ex pulchritudine operum et decore creaturarum parentem universitatis intellegit.

Non ergo corpus aliquod aut in corpore esse putandus est deus, sed intellectualis natura simplex, nihil omnino in se adiunctionis admittens; uti ne maius aliquid et inferius in se habere credatur, sed ut sit ex omni parte monas, et ut ita dicam henas, et mens ac fons, ex quo initium totius intellectualis naturae vel mentis est. Mens vero ut moveatur vel operetur, non indiget loco corporeo neque sensibili magnitudine vel corporali habitu aut colore, neque alio ullo prorsus indiget horum, quae corporis vel materiae propria sunt. Propter quod natura illa simplex et tota mens ut moveatur vel operetur aliquid, nihil dilationis aut cunctationis habere potest, ne per huiusmodi adiunctionem circumscribi vel inhiberi aliquatenus videatur divinae naturae simplicitas, uti

human mind, however pure or clear to the very utmost that mind may be, cannot gaze at or behold?

6. But it will not appear out of place if to make the matter clearer still we use yet another illustration. Sometimes our eyes cannot look upon the light itself, that is, the actual sun, but when we see the brightness and rays of the sun as they pour into our windows, it may be, or into any small openings for light, we are able to infer from these how great is the source and fountain of physical light. So, too, the works of divine providence and the plan of this universe are as it were rays of God's nature in contrast to his real substance and being, and because our mind is of itself unable to behold God as he is, it understands the parent of the universe from the beauty of his works and the comeliness of his creatures.

God therefore must not be thought to be any kind of body, not to exist in a body, but to be a simple intellectual existence, admitting in himself of no addition whatever, so that he cannot be believed to have in himself a more or a less, but is Unity, or if I may so say, Oneness throughout, and the mind and fount from which originates all intellectual existence or mind. Now mind does not need physical space in which to move and operate, nor does it need a magnitude discernible by the senses, nor bodily shape or colour, nor anything else whatever like these, which are suitable to bodies and matter. Accordingly that simple and wholly mental existence can admit no delay or hesitation in any of its movements or operations; for if it did so, the simplicity of its divine nature would

ne quod est principium omnium, compositum inveniatur et diversum et sit multa, non unum, quod oportet totius corporeae admixtionis alienum una sola, ut ita dixerim, deitatis specie constare.

Quia autem mens non indigeat loco, ut secundum naturam suam moveatur, certum est etiam ex nostrae mentis contemplatione. Haec enim si in sua mensura consistat, nec ex qualibet causa aliquid ei obtusionis eveniat, nihil umquam ex locorum diversitate tardabitur, quominum suis motibus agat; neque rursum ex locorum qualitate augmentum aliquod vel incrementum mobilitatis adquiret. Quodsi obtendat aliquis, verbi gratia, quia navigantibus et fluctibus maris iactatis minus aliquanto mens vigeat quam vigere in terris solet, non eos ex loci diversitate id pati, sed ex corporis commotione vel conturbatione credendum est, cui mens adiuncta est vel inserta. Videtur enim velut contra naturam in mari degere corpus humanum, et propter hoc velut quadam sui inaequalitate motus mentis inconposite inordinateque suscipere et acuminis eius ictus obtunsiore ministerio dispensare, non minus quam si qui etiam in terra positi febribus urgeantur; quorum certum est quod, si minus aliquid per vim febrium mens suum servet officium, non loci culpam, sed morbum corporis esse causandum, per quem perturbatum corpus atque confusum nequaquam notis ac naturalibus lineis solita menti dependit officia, quoniam quidem nos homines animal sumus compositum ex corporis animaeque concursu; hoc enim modo habitare nos super terras possibile fuit. Deum vero, qui omnium initium est, compositum esse non est putandum;

appear to be in some degree limited and impeded by such an addition, and that which is the first principle of all things would be found to be composite and diverse, and would be many and not one; since only the species of deity, if I may so call it, has the privilege of existing apart from all material intermixture.

That mind needs no space in which to move according to its own nature is certain even from the evidence of our own mind. For if this abides in its own proper sphere and nothing occurs from any cause to enfeeble it, it will never be at all retarded by reason of differences of place from acting in conformity with its own movements; nor on the other hand will it gain any increase or accession of speed from the peculiar nature of any place. And if it be objected, for example, that when men are travelling by sea and tossed by the waves, their mind is somewhat less vigorous than it is wont to be on land, we must believe this experience to be due not to the difference of place but to the movement and disturbance of the body with which the mind is joined or intermingled. For it seems almost against nature for the human body to live on the sea, and on this account the body, as if unequal to its task, appears to sustain the mind's movements in irregular and disordered manner, giving feebler assistance to its keen flashes, precisely as happens even with men on land when they are in the grip of a fever; in whose case it is certain that , if the mind fulfils its functions less effectively through the strength of the fever, the cause is to be found not in any defect of locality but in the disease of the

ne forte priora piso principio esse inveniantur elementa, ex quibus compositum est omne quicquid illud est quod compositum dicitur.

Sed nec magnitudine corporali mens indiget, ut agat aliquid vel moveatur, sicut oculus, cum in maiora quidem corpora intuendo diffunditur, ad parva vero et exigua coartatur et adstringitur ad videndum. Indiget sane mens magnitudine intellegibili, quia non corporaliter, sed intellegibiliter crescit. Non enim corporalibus incrementis simul cum corpore mens usque ad vicesimum vel tricesimum annum aetatis augetur, sed eruditionibus atque exercitiis adhibits acumen quidem elimatur ingenii, quaeque sunt ei insita ad intellegentiam provacantur, et capax maioris efficitur intellectus non corporalibus incrementis aucta, sed eruditionis exercitiis elimata. Quae idcirco non statim a puero vel a nativitate rrecipere potest, quia invalida adhuc et inbecilla membrorum conpago, quibus velut organis ad exercitium sui mens utitur, neque operandi vim sustentare valet neque percipiendae disciplinae exhibere sufficit facultatem.

body, which renders it disturbed and confused and altogether unable to bestow its customary services on the mind under the well-known and natural conditions. For we men are animals, formed by a union of body and soul, and thus alone did it become possible for us to live on the earth. But God, who is the beginning of all things, must not be regarded as a composite being, lest perchance we find that the elements, out of which everything that is called composite has been composed, are prior to the first principle himself.

Nor does the mind need physical magnitude in order to perform any act or movement, as an eye does when in looking at large bodies it expands and at small ones narrows and contracts for the purpose of seeing. Mind certainly needs intellectual magnitude, because it grows in an intellectual and not in a physical sense. For mind does not increase by physical additions at the same time as the body does until the twentieth or thirtieth year of its age, but by the employment of instructions and exercises a sharpening of the natural faculties is effected and the powers implanted within are roused to intelligence. Thus the capacity of the intellect is enlarged not by being increased with physical additions, but by being cultivated through exercises in learning. These it cannot receive immediately from birth or boyhood because the structure of the bodily parts which the mind uses as instruments for its own exercise is as yet weak and feeble, being neither able to endure the force of the mind's working nor sufficiently developed to display a capacity for receiving instruction.

7. Si qui autem sunt qui mentem ipsam animamque corpus esse arbitrentur, velim mihi responderent, quomodo tantarum rerum, tam difficilium tamque subtilium, rationes assertionesque recipiat. Unde ei virtus memoriae, unde rerum invisibilium contemplatio, unde certe incorporalium intellectus corpori inest? Quomodo natura corporea disciplinas artium, rerum contemplationes rationesque rimatur? Unde etiam divina dogmata, quae manifeste incorporea sunt, sentire atque intellegere potest? Nisi si forte aliquis putet quod, sicut forma ista corporea et habitus ipse aurium vel oculorum confert aliquid ad audiendum et ad videndum, et ut singula membra, quae a deo formata sunt, habent aliquid oportunitatis etiam ex ipsa formae qualitate ad hoc, quod agere naturaliter instituta sunt: ita itiam habitum animae vel mentis intellegi debere arbitretur quasi apte accommodeque formatum ad hoc, ut de singulis sentiat vel intellegat atque ut vitalibus motibus moveatur. Verum qualem colorem mentis secundum hoc, quod meus est et intellegibiliter movetur, describere quis posset aut dicere, non adverto.

Adhuc ad confirmationem atque explanationem eorum, quae de mente vel anima diximus, eo quod praestantior sit totius naturae corporeae, etiam haec addi possunt. Unicuique corporeo sensui substantia quaedam sensibilis subiacet proprie, in quam ipse sensus corporalis intenditur. Verbi gratia visui subiacent colores habitus magnitudo, auditui voces et sonus, odoratui nidores boni vel mali, austui sapores, tactui calida vel frigida, dura vel mollia, aspera vel levia. Horum

7. But if there are any who consider the mind itself and the soul to be a body, I should like them to tell me how it can take in reasons and arguments relating to questions of great importance, full of difficulty and subtlety. Whence comes it that the power of memory, the contemplation of invisible things, yes, and the perception of incorporeal things reside in a body? How does a bodily nature investigate the teachings of the arts and the meanings and reasons of things? And divine doctrines, which are obviously incorporeal, how can it discern and understand them? One might perhaps think that, just as the bodily form and shape of the ears or eyes contributes something to hearing or to seeing, and as the various parts of our body, which have been formed by God, each possess some special capacity, due to their particular form, for doing the work for which they were by nature designed, so too, the soul or mind must be supposed to have an outward shape fitly and suitably formed, as it were, for the purpose of perceiving and understanding individual things and of being set in motion by vital movements. But what sort of appearance the mind could have, seeing that it is a mind and moves in an intellectual way, I do not know who could describe or tell us.

In further confirmation and explanation of what we have said about the mind or soul, as being superior to all bodily nature, the following remarks may be added. Each of the bodily senses is appropriately connected with a material substance towards which the particular sense is directed. For instance, sight is connected with colour, shape and size;

autem sensuum, de quibus supra diximus, quia multo melior sensus sit mentis, omnibus clarum est. Quomodo ergo non videtur absurdum, his quidem, quae inferiora sunt, substantias esse subiectas ad intendendum, huic autem virtuti, quae melior est, id est mentis sensui, nihil omnino subici substantiale, sed esse intellectualis naturae virtutem corporibus accidentem vel consequentem? Quod qui dicunt, sine dubio in contumeliam eius substantiae, quae in ipsis melior est, haec proferunt; immo vero ex hoc etiam ad ipsum deum refertur iniuria, cum putant eum per naturam corpoream posse intellegi, quo scilicet secundum ipsos corpus sit et illud, quod per corpus potest intellegi vel sentiri; et nolunt hoc intellegi quod propinquitas quaedam sit menti ad deum, cuius ipsa mens intellectualis imago sit, et per hoc possit aliquid de deitatis sentire natura, maxime si expurgatior ac segregatior sit a materia corporali.

8. Verum istae assertiones minus fortasse auctoritatis habere videantur apud eos, qui ex sanctis scripturis de rebus divinis institui volunt et inde sibi approbari quaerunt, quomodo natura dei supereminet corporum naturam. Vide ergo si non etiam apostolus hoc idem ait, cum de Christo loquitur dicens: "Qui est imago invisibilis dei, primogenitus omnis

hearing with the voice and sound; smelling with vapours pleasant and unpleasant; taste with flavours; touch with things hot or cold, hard or soft, rough or smooth. But it is clear to all that the sense of mind is far superior to the senses above mentioned. Does it not then appear absurd that these inferior senses should have substances connected with them, as object towards which their activities are directed, whereas this faculty, the sense of mind, which is superior to them, should have no substance whatever connected with it, and that this faculty of an intellectual nature should be a mere accident arising out of bodies? Those who assert this are undoubtedly speaking in disparaging terms of that substance which is the better part of their own nature; nay more, they do wrong even to God himself in supposing that he can be understood through a bodily nature, since according to them that which can be understood or perceived through a body is itself a body; and they are unwilling to have it understood that there is a certain affinity between the mind and God, of whom the mind is an intellectual image, and that by reason of this fact the mind, especially if it is purified and separated from bodily matter, is able to have some perception of the divine nature.

8. But these assertions may perhaps seem to be less authoritative to those who desire to be instructed in divine things from the holy scriptures and who seek to have it proved to them from that source how God's nature surpasses the nature of bodies. See then, whether the apostle, too, does not say the same thing when he speaks as follows

creaturae". Non enim, ut quidam putant, natura dei alicui visibilis est et aliis invisibilis; non enim dixit apostolus 'imago invisibilis dei' hominibus aut 'invisibilis' peccatoribus, sed valde constanter pronuntiat de ipsa natura dei dicens "imago invisibilis dei". Sed iet Iohannes in evangelio dicens: "Deum nemo vidit umquam" manifeste declarat omnibus, qui intellegere possunt, quia nulla natura est, cui visibilis sit deus; non quasi qui visibilis quidem sit per naturam et velut fragilioris creaturae evadat atque excedat aspectum, sed quoniam naturaliter videri impossibilis est.

Quodsi requiras a me, quid etiam de ipso unigenito sentiam, si ne ipsi quidem visibilem dicam naturam dei, quae naturaliter 'invisibilis' est: non tibi statim vel impium videatur esse vel absurdum; rationem quippe dabimus consequenter. (Sicut enim incongruum est dicere quod possit filius videre patrem, ita inconveniens est opinari quod spiritus sanctus possit videre filium.) Aliud est videre, aliud cognoscere: videri et videre corporum res est, cognosci et cognoscere intellectualis naturae est. Quicquid ergo proprium corporum est, hoc nec de patre nec de filio sentiendum est; quod vero ad naturam pertinet deitatis, hoc inter patrem et filium constat. Denique etiam ipse in evangelio non dixit quia 'nemo vidit patrem nisi filius neque filium nisi pater', sed ait: "Nemo novit filium nisi pater, neque patrem quis novit nisi filius". Ex quo manifeste indicatur quod quicquid inter corporeas naturas videre et videri dicitur, hoc inter patrem et filium congnoscere dicitur et cognosci,

about Christ: 'Who is the image of the invisible God, the firstborn of all creation'. It is not, as some suppose, that God's nature is visible to one and invisible to others; for the apostle did not say 'the image of God who is invisible' to men or 'invisible' to sinners, but he makes an absolutely unvarying declaration about God's very nature in these words, 'image of the invisible God'. And John, too, when he says in the gospel, 'No one hath seen God at any time', plainly declares to all who are capable of understanding, that there is no existence to which God is visible; not as if he were one who is visible by nature and yet eludes and escapes the gaze of his creatures because of their frailty, but there he is in his nature impossible to be seen.

And if you should ask me what is my belief about the Only-begotten himself, whether I would say that God's nature, which is naturally invisible, is not even visible to him, do not immediately think this question to be impious or absurd, because we shall give it a logical answer. (For as it is incongruous to say that the Son can see the Father, so it is unbefitting to believe that the Holy Spirit can see the Son). It is one thing to see, another to know. To see and to be seen is a property of bodies; to know and to be known is an attribute of intellectual existence. Whatever therefore is proper to bodies must not be believed either of the Father or of the Son, the relations between whom are such as pertain to the nature of deity. And finally, Christ in the gospel did not say, 'No one seeth the Father except the Son, nor the Son except the Father' but

per virtutem scientiae, non per visibilitatis fragilitatem. Quia ergo de incorporea natura et invisibili nec videre proprie dicitur nec videri, idcirco neque pater a filio neque filius a patre videri in evangelio dicitur, sed agnosci.

'no one knoweth the Son except the Father, nor doth anyone know the Father except the Son' This clearly shows that what is called 'seeing' and 'being seen' in the case of bodily existences is with the Father and the Son called 'knowing' and 'being known', through the faculty of knowledge and not through our frail sense of sight. It is, therefore, because the expressions 'to see' and 'to be seen' cannot suitably be applied to incorporeal and invisible existence that in the gospel the Father is not said to be seen by the Son nor the Son by the Father, but to be known.

9. Quodsi proponat nobis aliquis, quare dictum est: "Beati mundo corde, quoniam ipsi deum videbunt", multo magis etiam ex hoc, ut ego arbitror, assertio nostra firmabitur; nam quid aliud est 'corde deum videre', nisi secundum id, quod supra exposuimus, mente eum intellegere atque cognoscere? Frequenter namque sensibilium membrorum nomina ad animam referuntur ita, ut 'oculis cordis' videre dicatur, id est virtute intellegentiae aliquid intellectuale conicere. Sic et audire auribus dicitur, cum sensum intellegentiae profundioris advertit. Sic et uti eam posse dentibus dicimus, cum mandit et comedit panem vitae, qui de caelo descendit. Similiter et ceteris uti membrorum officiis dicitur, quae ex corporali appellatione translata virtutibus animae coaptantur, sicut et Salomon dicit: "Sensum divinum invenies". Sciebat namque duo genera esse sensuum in nobis, unum genus sensuum mortale, corruptible, humanum, aliud genus immortale et intellectuale, quod nunc 'divinum' nominavit. Hoc ergo

9. But if the question is put to us why it was said, 'Blessed are the pure in heart, for they shall see God', I answer that in my opinion our argument will be much more firmly established by this passage. For what else is 'to see God in the heart' but to understand and know him with the mind, just as we have explained above? For the names of the organs of sense are often applied to the soul, so that we speak of seeing with the eyes of the heart, that is, of drawing some intellectual conclusion by means of the faculty of intelligence. So too we speak of hearing with the ears when we discern the deeper meaning of some statement. So too we speak of the soul as being able to use teeth, when it eats and consumes the bread of life who comes down from heaven. In a similar way we speak of it as using all the other bodily organs, which are transferred from their corporeal significance and applied to the faculties of the soul; as Solomon says, 'You will find a divine sense'. For he knew that there were in us two kinds of senses, the one being

sensu divino non oculorum, sed 'cordis mundi,' quae est mens, deus videri ab his, qui digni sunt, potest. Cor sane pro mente, id est pro intellectuali virtute nominari in omnibus scripturis novis ac veteribus abundanter invenies.

Hoc igitur modo quamvis longe inferius quam dignum est, utpote pro infirmitate humanae intellegentiae naturam dei intellegentes, nunc quid sibi nomen Christi velit videamus.

mortal, corruptible and human, and the other immortal and intellectual, which here he calls 'divine'. By this divine sense, therefore, not of the eyes but of a pure heart, that is, the mind, God can be seen by those who are worthy. That heart is used for mind, that is for the intellectual faculty, you will certainly find over and over again in all the scriptures, both the New and the Old.

Having thus investigated the nature of God, though in a manner farrom worthy by reason of the weakness of our human understanding, let us now see what meaning is to be given to the name Christ.

(Tr. Butterworth)

X. THE PERIARCHON (DE PRINCIPIIS): COMMENTARY

In preparing this part of the work we have been greatly assisted by Crouzel and Simonetti's critical edition of Rufinus' redaction of Origen's Periarchôn (Traité des Principes, I, p. 76-80; 90-110),[13] and the Görgemann-Karpp commentary of the Periarchôn (Origenes Vier Bücher von den Prinzipien, p. 82-90; 99-122). Since Koetschau's critical edition of the Periarchôn (De Principiis) constitutes the basis for the two commentaries mentioned above, his work [(Origenes. Werke Fünfter Band. De Principiis (PERIARCHON), Leipzig: 1913 = GCS 22)] is utilized as the basis for our commentary.

The goal of our rhetorical exegesis of the Praefatio (De Principiis) is limited. We want to show how Origen formally argued his first principles, and demonstrated a Middle Platonic theoretic and epistemology from the premises of his sacred scripture. The purpose of such a study is to illustrate the strategy of philosophical debate in the Middle Academy, and to gain an insight into the situation out of which philosophical postulates were formed. This permits us to more accurately reconstruct the intellectual world of Middle Platonism.

There are a number of risks involved in this undertaking. First, we work from the postulate that the underlying rhetorical structure of the Periarchôn is extant in the De Principiis. This is at best a tenuous assumption. It may well be that our rhetorical exegesis of Origen's Periarchôn is really a rhetorical exegesis of Rufinus' De Principiis. Second, we work from the assumption that Origen composed his work fully versed in rhetorical theory, and with the speeches of the Attic Ten at his finger-tips. It could be that he was versed fully in neither. Third, we make the assumption that the Periarchôn (De Principiis) represents an example of Christian Middle Platonic philosophical writing which may be utilized to inform us about the philosophical compositions of Philo and Clement. If Rufinus' redaction represents his rhetorical composition and not Origen's, and if Origen was not educated in the art of rhetorical logic practiced in the Middle Academy, then this thesis also would fail.

We mention these problems so the reader is fully aware of the provisional nature of the commentary which follows. It is an experiment, and no more. Nonetheless, we think that internal as well as external evidence supports the claims we make about the Periarchôn (De Principiis). The literary critics have uncovered the original genre and structure of the Periarchôn from the De Principiis. We believe we can uncover the rhetorical structure of its composition as well. Studies on Origen's other works illustrate that he was fully versed in the art of rhetoric, and that the Attic Ten were the bed-rock of elementary education at Alexandria in Origen's time. We maintain that knowledge of both is evident even through the remnants of the Periarchôn (De Principiis). Finally, the literary and rhetorical studies undertaken in the last decade on Philo's writings show that Philo utilized the same literary genres of composition and modes of rhetorical argumentation that we claim Origen did. Indeed, the parallels between the art of rhetorical logic utilized by both is striking. Hence, we maintain that Origen's composition literarily and rhetorically reflects the philosophical writings of the Middle Academy.

With debits and assets in hand we commence on uncovering the rhetorical skeleton of the Periarchôn (De Principiis). In so doing we enter upon uncharted waters.

Each section analyzed has two to three parts. In part one the commonplaces (topoi), part of speech (pars orationes), and the genre of speech (genus causarum) are listed. Here we unpack Origen's mode of rhetorical argumentation by examining its parallels with forms of rhetorical argumentation extant in the doxographical literaure of the period, and in the speeches of the Attic Ten which were the exempla for rhetorical argumentation at Alexandria. In part two the structure of the syllogistic argument (enthymêmata-epicheirêmata) is unpacked. Here the attempt is made to uncover the strategy of rhetorical composition. Parallels again are made with suggestions extant in the rhetorical handbooks on the art of argument building. Formal parallels are drawn with speeches from the Attic orators. In part three the situation of the argument is disclosed. Here the goal is to enter into the debate proper, and grasp the generative problematic which motivates it. In some chapters such as De Deo (I,1,6) and (I,1,7) we preface rhetorical exegesis with a statement which explains the theses Origen is arguing against. In (I,1,6) we briefly sketch the central premises of the Stoic theology Origen opposes, and in (I,1,7) we outline the assumptions of the Stoic epistemology he attempts to refute. This aids us in our attempt to comprehend both the situation and strategy of composition.[14]

The conceptual assumptions Origen argues from have been presented in Parts One and Two. Our focus in this section is limited. We intend to reconstruct Origen's art of rhetorical logic and no more. We wish to complement the literary-critical studies on the Periarchôn (De Principiis) by offering a rhetorical-critical exegesis of the text. If our endeavors prove successful and helpful in understanding the strategy and situation of this Middle Platonic composition, then a continuation of this type of exegesis can be undertaken.

1. Praefatio 1-4

P 1 p. 7,6-8.13

1.   The opening of the treatise is missing. It is preserved in Eusebius' Contra Marcellum 1,4 (= fr. 1. Koe.). Origen announces the progammatic basis upon which his definition of Christian first principles rests. The topos of (P 1 p. 7,6-11) is ek kriseôs.[15] This is one of the most popular of the rhetorical common places. It functions to establish Origen's postulate as legitimate by appealing to authority. It is an appeal from what the rhetors called the palaioi martures.[16] The use of the topic sets up the unshakeable ground upon which Origen's arguments unfold.

From the datum that Christ is the truth, Origen persuades his audience that the knowledge which calls men to lead a good and blessed life comes from no other source than the words and teachings of Christ. Although this is assumed by his audience, his motive is to persuade his listeners-readers that the knowledge he will present them is in agreement with the words and teachings of the Christ (P 1 p. 7,6-13), and with the word of God proclaimed in both Testaments (P 1 p. 7,13-8,13). Origen presents a scientia that is in full accord with the teachings extant in scripture. This also suggests an attempt to convince a Christian audience that the words of scripture constitute a scientia. Scripture yields a type of knowledge that is not mere opinion. It is knowledge defined as reason. The logoi of scripture are the objects of intelligible and divine intellection.[17] They are not grasped merely by the faculty of sensible intellection.

2. Origen sets his topic up in a standard rhetorical enthymêma.[18] The premise is: (Rufinus' redaction will be used since it presents the argument in its totality).

> Omnes qui credunt et certi sunt quod gratia et veritas per Iesum Christum facta sit, et Christum esse veritatem norunt, secundum quod ipse dixit: "Ego sum veritas."

The conclusion runs:

> ...scientiam quae provocat homines ad bene beateque vivendum non aliunde quam ab ipsis Christi verbis doctrinaque suscipiunt.
>
> (P 1 p. 7,9-12)

From this proof Origen constructs an auxêsis (P 1 p. 7,13-8,2). This amplification informs us of the forensic character of the pericope. Origen's use of the topos ek kriseôs hinted at this, but now he informs his audience of the polemical function that the opening proof has. We do not know who Origen is directing this auxêsis against, but it is against those who assert that the word of God was not in Moses and the Prophets. This suggests that it is directed against those who would claim that the Old Testament is not to be taken as sacred scripture. Origen refutes this postulate by presenting two passages from the New Testament which verify that the word of God filled Moses, and that Christ spoke to his apostles after his ascension into heaven (P 1 p. 8,6-13). The function of presenting apostolic doctrine and the knowledge which can be deduced from it, is to set up the agatha from which Origen deduces his system of first principles.[19] It also permits him to refute the assumptions of his opponents.

In summary, Origen argues that the criteria of all knowledge is scripture, and the object of knowledge is the "Christus verbis" extant in Moses, the Prophets, and the Apostles. Grace, truth, and knowledge came by Jesus Christ, and are present in his word. Origen's meanings for grace, knowledge, and truth will be unfolded in (I,1,1-9). At this stage he merely sets up his first postulate, and by means of it refutes two incorrect assumptions held by his opponents.

Rhetorically the argument functions to win the audience over to a basic postulate (P 1 p. 7,6-13), even though Origen knows it is not in dispute. The reason for doing this becomes clear in (P 1 p. 7,13-8,14). Origen hopes that the force (ek kriseôs) of the scriptural argument will persuade his audience of the veracity of his argument.[20]

P 2 p. 8,14-9,11

1.   Origen asserts a contradiction in the opinions some Christians and barbarians propose as the truth. We must remember that the audience has just been introduced to the postulate and arguments of (P 1). They know the criterion of truth and the true objects of knowledge.

The rhetorical thrust of the argument in (P 2) is well conceived. First Origen tells them of the confusion which reigns among some Christians who profess to hold truths (P 2 p. 8,14ff.) which are really opinions, and non-Christians who promise the truth (P 2 p. 8,20ff.). Second, he proceeds to remind them of the criterion of truth, which are teachings of the Son of God, and the doctrines of the church handed down by the apostles (P 2 p. 8,22-27).

His conclusion is directed at his opponents:

...servetur vero ecclesiastica praedicatio per successionis ordinem ab apostolis tradita et usque ad praesens in ecclesiis permanens, illa sola credenda est veritas, quae in nullo ab ecclesiastica et apostolica traditione discordat.

(P 2 p. 8, 25-27)

The inference is that he is among those who maintain the truth, while his opponents are not.

2.   We shall now examine the rhetorical structure of this pericope, and how it guarantees the end Origen seeks.

The rhetorical structure of the pericope is formally parallel to (P 1). (P2 p. 8. 14-28) is an auxêsis[21] of (P1 p. 7.6-8-13). The topics utilized are: ek tôn enantiôn[22] and ek tôn pros allêla.[23] They are linked to the topic ek kriseôs.[24] The argument is an enthymêma. The genus causarum is forensic and the partes orationis is the proem.

The use of auxêsis with an argument originally formed ek kriseôs is a favorite device of Origen's. It had wide usage. It was employed by the Attic Ten[25] and the Hellenistic[26] and Roman[27] orators who copied them. Its function was to support a course of conduct and to establish a fact. The topical schema employed by Origen was thought to have been known to the Attic rhetors,[28] and has many loci paralleli in the Hellenistic and Roman handbooks. It is called ek tou enantiou by Maximum Planoudes[29] and ex contrariis by Quintilian.[30]

Once the criteria of demonstration are established (P1 p. 7.6-8.13) it is necessary to refute the inferences and arguments of one's opponents. This is undertaken in (P2 p. 8.14-28). The false opinions of Origen's opponents are underscored through the use of the topos ek tôn pros allêla. Origen equates the opinions of some Christians with those of the Greeks and barbarians. Origen's true beliefs are associated with the doctrines handed down by Christ to the Apostles and the Church Fathers.

The relation between this topic and the two previously outlined is clear. The demonstrative argument from authority and the refutative argument from opposites are united in the use of the demonstrative-refutative argument from the identity of the attributes (ek tôn pros allêla). This topic functions to establish: 1) an identity between the opinions of some Christians, Greeks, and barbarians, and the identity between the beliefs of Origen, and the doctrines established by Christ received by the Apostles and Church Fathers. The argument is carefully formed to enhance the ethos of Origen and to discredit the ethos of Origen's Christian opponents.[31] The intent is to arouse the pathos of the audience to side with him and to oppose his adversaries.[32]

The argument is formed rhetorically to associate Origen with apostolic tradition and accepted Church dogma, and to associate his opponents with pagan tradition, Greek and barbarian. This is a very effective rhetorical construct and is one whose form was known to and favored by the Attic orators at Alexandria. It was utilized by Maximum Planoudes,[33] Minucianus[34] and Dionysius of Halicarnassus,[35] among the Hellenistic rhetors; and Cicero[36] and Quintilian,[37] among the Latin orators.[38] These loci paralleli reflect a utilization of this topic which is formally akin to the use of it in (P2 p. 8.14-28).

Origen wants to persuade his audience that much opinion circulates as truth, and that the doctrine he proposes is truth because it is in agreement with scripture and Apostolic teaching. The persuasive force of Origen's argument is constructed to convince the audience that there needs to be a definite line and unmistakable rule in regard to the interpretation of scripture and church doctrine (P 2 p. 8,18-20), and that he is in accord with this line and rule. If he succeeds he can discredit his opponents, and set up the audience so that they will accept his interpretation of scripture and church dogma as authoritative.

To summarize: The goal of this pericope is to set in the mind of the audience the distinction between what the theoreticians called a necessaria and probabilis argumenta-tio and to associate the former with those proposed by Origen.[39] Rhetorically, at least, Origen has set this up through his use of the commonplaces of authority, relation, and opposites. The argument is formulated carefully so that his own position is allied with the authority of scripture and the church, and his opponents' position is not. If he succeeds in his goal Origen not only postulates what apostolic doctrine is, he also convinces the audience that apostolic and Origenist doctrine are correlative because both are true.[40]

P 3 p. 9,1-11 Koe

1.   The postulate presented in this pericope is an important element of Origen's rhetorical polemic. He reaffirms the postulate that scripture is the criterion of knowledge (fides), and that scripture contains the doctrines of metaphysical knowledge. Knowledge is investigated by those who possess the higher graces of the Spirit, i.e. language, wisdom, and knowledge. The lovers of wisdom have the divine task of interpreting the inner meaning of scripture. If Origen persuades his audience that there are different levels of meaning in scripture, and that a certain group has the ability to decipher what scripture means, then he accomplishes a major breakthrough.

In P 1 Origen sets up the standards of what true knowledge constitutes. In P 2 he establishes the line and rule of this criterion. In P 3 he proposes that although the criterion of knowledge is scripture, and the line and rule of determining which interpretations of it are true are based on apostolic and church teaching, the criterion itself has manifold meanings.

He postulates that the trifold meaning of scripture corresponds to the three faculties of knowing. Thus when the mind focuses upon its object, scripture, it understands it somatically, asomatically, and as wisdom.

Origen proposes that he is one of those:

... qui dignos se et capaces ad recipiendam sapientiam praepararent.

(P 3 p. 9, 10f.)

Hence, our question is how does Origen persuade his audience of this postulate and how does he convince them that he is one of the lovers of wisdom? We shall answer these questions below.

2.   This pericope is linked rhetorically to the two which preceded it. Rhetorically (P3 p. 9, 1-11) is an auxêsis of the arguments and postulates demonstrated at (P1 p. 7, 6-8.13) and at (P2 p. 8,14-28). The topical arguments of the chapter are ek kriseôs, and the related topic ta protreponta.[41] The genus causarum is forensic. The pars orationis is the proem.

The rhetorical dimensions of the proof are clear to see. The premises of the argument imply the previous demonstrations "Illud autem scire oportet". The conclusions deduced follow in the remainder of the pericope (P3 p. 9, 1ff.). The argument is presented as an implied argument. Not all the premises are listed.[42] The topical arrangement informs us how Origen succeeds at the dual purposes he has set himself. In P 1 and P 2 he argues from authority, and from relation of attributes, and opposites. In this chapter he invokes and argues from authority once again, and this time couples it to an argument from advantages.[43] What are the advantages to be gained? They are divine wisdom, and the establishment of a true interpretation of those doctrines the apostles left unclear. Two agatha, wisdom and truth, are the benefits to be gained from the acceptance of Origen's argument.[44]

This mode of persuasion was popular among rhetors in antiquity, which attests to its widespread use. The virtues to be gained are scientia and sapientia (P 3 p. 9,6). Knowledge and wisdom are intelligible and gnostic (or divine) perception.

To summarize: Rhetorically, the audience has been molded to accept Origen's thesis. Origen's position is perceived to be in accordance with what the audience holds as authoritative, i.e. scripture and church teaching. Hence there are benefits to be gained from accepting this postulate. One hears the words of a most popular rhetor at Alexandria, Demosthenes, through Origen:

One must always bear in mind and do what is just, but take care at the same time that it may likewise be beneficial.[45]

Origen's argument reflects this sentiment entirely. Origen merely substitutes truth for justice.

P 4 p. 9,12-11, 11 Koe

1.   Origen reduces the doctrines of apostolic teaching to a series of compact definitions. His definitions were no doubt controversial. We can conclude this from the rhetorical strategy he employs. From (P 4 p. 9,12-11,2) Origen postulates a series of doctrines whose acceptance is crucial for the building of his first principles. Within the context of his rhetorical scheme he attempts to persuade the audience of the validity of their content by asserting that it is apostolic doctrine, not his own (P 4 p. 9,12f.). This is accomplished through the common place argument from relation (ek tôn pros allêla). Origen ascribes these doctrines to the Apostles. Since such a source is authoritative, and the criteria of any dogmatic postulate must meet the line and rule of these criteria, Origen persuades his audience to accept them as true.

2.   Origen unfolds his definition of the Father, Son, and Holy Spirit through the topic ek kiriseôs[46] and ek tôn pros allêla.[47] The postulate is argued through the genus causarum of forensic oratory. The pars orationis is the proem.

The topics function to convince the audience of the legitimacy of Origen's definition and to persuade the audience of the relation between Origen's definition and the teachings of the church.[48]   Origen structures his composition so that his definition appears authoritative, ek tôn pros allêla, with the teachings of the church, which arise ek kriseôs.[49]   The goal of Origen is to show that his definition is valid, because it is in accord with the dogmas of scripture and apostolic teaching.[50]

The premises upon which Origen rests his definitions are posited at (P 4 p. 9,12-13), and the deductions follow in (P 4 p. 9,13-11,2). (P 4 11,3-10) is an auxêsis in which Origen attempts to explain that, although the definition proposed is problematic, it is likely valid because of the manner of inquiry undertaken:

> ...sed inquirenda iam ista pro viribus sunt de sancta scriptura et sagaci perquisitione investiganda.
>
> (P 4 p. 11,5-7)

The definition of Divinity presented in (P4 p. 9,13-11.2) is an argument from the whole:

> Primo, quod unus est deus, qui omnia creavit atque composuit, quique cum nihil esset, esse facit universa, deus a prima creatura et conditione mundi...
>
> (P4 p. 9,13-15)

to its parts:

> Tum deinde quia Christus Iesus, ipse qui venit, ante omnem creaturam natus ex patre est. Qui cum in omnium conditione patri ministrasset "per ipsum" namque "omnia facta sunt", novissimis temporibus se ipsum exinaniens homo factus est, incarnatus est, cum deus esset, et homo factus mansit quod erat, deus.
>
> (P4 p. 10,5-9)[51]

The argument presented in this pericope offers a variety of insights into how Origen conceived and constructed his apodeixis euaggelikê. By means of the devices of rhetorical argumentation Origen attempts to persuade his audience of the validity and truth of his own definitions of first principles. These rhetorically argued definitions are employed against other definitions of divinity proposed by other Christians. Origen's suggestion is that his opponents hold a number of untenable definitions based on an unreasoned faith. Origen rhetorically implies this when he asserts that he:

> ...et sagace perquistione investigenda...
>
> (P 4 p. 11,6-7)

Origen's goal is to convince the audience that the same inquiring wisdom and diligence which motivated the Prophets and Apostles also motivate him. Indeed, by means of the Holy Spirit he argues that he is imbued with the same attributes of wisdom and diligence as the great teachers of the church. Origen is aware that many problems concerning the nature of divinity have not been solved, e.g. whether or not the Son is "natus aut innatus," but he is confident that a careful examination of scripture and church teachings will yield results to these problems. Indeed, he lets it be known that his Periarchôn is an attempt to correctly solve some of these problems. Let us now examine now he defined the postulates in P 4 which relate to God the Father in the Deo Deo I, 1,1-9.

3.   Within the context of Origen's scheme of apodeixis his purpose is to set up a series of postulates from which he will argue his first principles in the main body of the text. No attempt is made in this pericope to define the philosophical and dogmatic assumptions which underly these definitions. This chapter is an eisagogê to the syggrammata which deal with these issues in the main body of the text. Within this exordium proofs are offered to validate the definitions he proposes. His goal is to have his audience accept his postulates as valid. He assumes if the audience accepts these postulates as apostolic and in accord with the teachings of scripture, his task in this section is accomplished.

Within the limited parameters of Origen's rhetorical scheme we can discern a series of important insights which transcend the motives of argument building. The primary genus causarum of these first four pericopae is forensic. It is likely that each doctrine presented by Origen is problematic, and the basis of intense debate within the Christian community at Alexandria in the early third century. The mere assertion that:

> ...quod unus est deus, qui omnia creavit atque composuit, quique, cum nihil
> esset, esse fucit universa, deus a prima creatura et conditione mundi...
>
> (P 4 p. 9,13-15)

is a statement of immense controversy, and a doctrine not held by Gnostic Christians at Alexandria. The assertion that the figures of the Old Testament, as well as the New

Testament, were messengers of God was not universally accepted by the Christian community at Alexandria in the early third century (P 4 p. 9, 15-10,4). Origen's christological formulation came under intense criticism in the centuries which followed. It is likely that they were problematic at the time he formulated them given his reservations about the absolute validity of what he proposed (P 4 p. 11,3-10).

In summary, it is clear that what Origen proposed as apostolic doctrine was not universally accepted as such. This is where his rhetorical apodeixis euaggelikê takes on such magnitude. Initially, in the proem at least, his only recourse is to persuade the audience of the validity of a series of definitions and by means of rhetorical argumentation he attempts to persuade his audience of the validity and truth of his propositions. The precariousness of his position is that in order for the audience to accept these postulates as valid and true they must first accept that they are something more than Origen's own. They are part of the teachings and traditional doctrines of the church.

If he succeeds in persuading his audience of the truth of his definitions then Origen has accomplished a great deal. From postulates demonstrated from scripture and church dogma Origen uses the resources at his disposal to hammer out a scientific system of first principles.

2. De Deo I, 1.1-9

De Deo, I, 1.1-9 p. 16,19-27,17 Koe

We know from our analysis of Origen's philosophical theology why he defines God as a non-corporeal ousia. We know from the analytical outline of the De Deo (I, 1,1) what the purpose of the argument in this pericope serves. We know from the outline of the literary and rhetorical structure of the Periarchôn (De Principiis) that this section fits into an overall literary and rhetorical scheme. However, we do not yet know how Origen demonstrates his definition of God the Father. In this section, and those which follow, we shall attempt to reconstruct his rhetorical strategy, and chart the architechtonic of his apodeixis euaggelikê.

These syggrammata are framed within a refutatio and a confirmatio argued through rhetorical proofs, and placed within a set of common places. Thus, the weapons Origen employs are the persuasive devices of rhetoric. However, unlike the Praefatio, where the rhetorical pace is dictated by short and non-explicatory arguments and definitions, which is the rhetorical style common to an eisagôgê, the De Deo has a more complex rhetorical structure of argumentation. Definitions are carefully spelled out, which is rhetorically expected from a syggramma.

The problem to be solved in book one is twofold: First, Origen wants to refute the somatic interpretation of scripture held by adherents of the Stoa Christiana. Second, he wants to defend an asomatic interpretation of scripture and the Platonic definition of God the Father proposed by his pattern of Plato Christianus. In order to accomplish this goal Origen must demolish the conceptual and scriptural assumptions of the corporealists. This he does in (I, 1,1-4). Next, he must defend his own conceptual and scriptural assumptions. This he does in (I, 1,5-9).

I, 1.1 p. 16,19-27,17 Koe

1.   It is clear from the topics utilized and the manner in which the proofs are formulated that the genus iuridicale dominated this pericope. This suggests that the definition Origen presents is controversial. Furthermore, he is aware that conflicting conclusions are possible if one argues solely ek kriseôs. Thus, he does not merely argue from the authority of scripture. He couples arguments from scripture with arguments from philosophical reason. He formulates his argument so that it is philosophically cogent, and the only possible definition that correlates with the wisdom of scripture. Scriptural statements are always taken as true. However, it is not the case that all definitions deduced from them are necessarily true. Definitions are deemed true if they can be demonstrated scientifically and dogmatically valid. If definitions meet apostolic and metaphysical criteria then they are held to be true, and are correlated with the scientia and sapientia of scripture. Origen's goal is the refutation of a materialist ontology and epistemology deduced from Christian Scripture.

2.   The rhetorical structure of (1.1.1) contains the following elements. The argument is formed through the topics ek tôn enantiôn and ek kriseôs, the proof utilized is the deductive enthymêma, the pars orationis the refutatio, and the genus causarum is the iu ridicale or forensic oratory.

The topics employed in this pericope are the two most popular in Hellenistic oratory. The ek tôn enantiôn is the primary topic of the pericope, and the ek kriseôs is utilized to support the argument from opposites.

For purposes of illustration Aristotle offers an excellent description of the function of this topic.

> One line of positive proof is based on consideration of the opposite of the thing in question (ek tôn enantiôn). Observe whether the opposite has the opposite quality. If it has not you refute the original proposition; if it has, you establish it.[52]

The argument enantiôtes or contrarium was commonly utilized by orators in the Imperial period.[53] The line of argument is if A has a relation to B, X the opposite of A is similarly related to Y the opposite of B, with the truth or falsehood of either statement determined by reference to the other. There are four antikeimena topics possible, and our author employs contradiction.

There is a close connection between the rhetorical and logical dimensions of the topic ek tôn enantiôn. As early as Aristotle's Topics[54] a correlation between the rhetorical and logical aspects of the argument from opposites is mentioned. Cope explains how this rhetorical topic functions logically, at least according to Aristotle:

> Then look also at the case of the contraries S and P in the thesis (epi tôn enantiôn), and see if the contrary of the one follows upon the contrary of the other, either directly or conversely, both when you are demolishing and defending a view.[55]

This coupling of the argument from opposites within a rhetorical syllogism was done at an early period by the Attic orator Lysias. His example is based on a tekmêrion and argued syllogistically in the form of the syllogism of Festino.[56] Hellenistic orators are also aware of this mode of persuasion. Apsines, Minucianus and Maximus Planoudes all argue in this fashion.[57]

3. For Origen this topic functions to demonstrate that the postulate "deus spiritus est" arises, not only from a dogmatically valid exegesis of scripture, but that it is a logically cogent interpretation given the nature of divinity and our knowledge of him. On the basis of these criteria Origen presents his opponents' arguments as incoherent and invalid.[58] To underscore the falsity of their arguments Origen adds:

Et quomodo vel lecis aliquis dabitur intellectus, ut ex isto quis corporali lumine causam scientiae capiat et veritatis inveniat intellectum?

(1.1.1 p. 17.15-17)

Origen presented his opponents' arguments as eikota arguments, and his own arguments as tekmêria.[59] This is good rhetoric because that which is probable is not absolutely true. It can be refuted. However, that which is necessary requires no qualification and cannot be refuted. This can be illustrated by the following example.

Origen opens the argument with two scriptural statements, and the conflicting interpretations of the nature of God deduced from them. First he presents his opponent's position:

Scio quoniam conabunter quidam etiam secundum scripturas nostras dicere deum corpus esse, quoniam inveniunt scriptum esse apud Moysen quidem: "Deus noster ignis consumens est," in evangelio vero secundum Iohannen: "Deus spiritus est, et eos qui adorant eum, in spiritu et veritate oportet adorare." Ignis vero et spiritus non aliud apud eos quam corpus esse putabitur.

(I,1,1 p. 16,19-17,4)

The conceptual assumptions which form the basis of their interpretation of scripture are invalid, Origen argues, because they understand fire and spirit in a corporeal sense, and interpret scripture only in the somatic sense.

The rhetorical agendum is clear. Origen must persuade his audience that his opponents interpretations of scripture are false. He does this by refuting the notion that fire and spirit always refer to something material, and that scripture only has one sense, the somatic. In his arsenal of demolition are the postulates that God is incorporeal, that the statements of scripture which refer to an intellectual entity such as deity must be interpreted through the faculty of knowing which corresponds to the object it perceives, and that any statements of scripture which refer to God must be understood asomatically.

The auxêsis, which begins at (I,1,1 p. 17, 14-17), is illustrative of an attempt by Origen to refute his opponents on the basis of a rhetorical argument. Origen employs an epicheirêma with three parts, which is argued through the topics of opposition and authority. The argument begins at (I,1,1 p. 17, 45):

(1)   Quos interrogare volo, quid dicant de eo quod scriptum est, quia "deus lux est," sicut Iohannes in epistola sua dicit: "Deus lux est, et tenebrae non sunt in eo."

continues at (I,1,1 p. 17,6ff.).

(2)   Ista nempe "lux est," "quae inluminat" omnem sensum eorum, qui possunt capere veritatem, sicut in tricesimo quinto psalmo dicitur: "In lumine tuo videbimus lumen." Quid enim aliud lumen dei dicendum est, in quo quis videt lumen, nisi virtus dei, perquam quis inluminatus vel veritatem rerum omnium pervidet vel ipsum deum cognoscit, qui veritas appellatur?

The conclusion is keyed by the word "ergo" (I,1,1 p. 17,12ff.).

(3)   Tale est ergo quod dicitur: "In lumine tuo videbimus lumen," hoc est in verbo tuo et sapienta tua, qui est filius tuus, in ipse te videbimus patrem. Numquidnam quia lumen nominatur, simile putabitur solis huius lumini? Et quomodo vel levis aliquis dabitur intellectur, et ex isto quis corporali lumine causam scientiae capiat et veritatis inveniat intellectum?

Origen's interpretation of scripture holds the true definition of the nature of deity because it is in accord with the criteria of coherence he has set up. He skillfully presents this through the philosophical distinction between corpus and spiritus. Body connotates becoming, and mutability, while spirit connotates being, and eternity. The question he asks is which attributes are deity's and which are not? Corpus is proper to the physical world, and spiritus to the intelligible world. Is God a body or is he spirit? Rhetorically, this is the agendum Origen will answer in the following chapters.

To summarize: it is within the context of the rhetorical syllogism that Origen attempts to convince his audience of the validity of his interpretation of the scriptural passage "deus spiritus est." His opponent's definition is formulated in such a manner that the audience would be disposed to reject it on scriptural-apostolic, and philosophical grounds. We can begin to discern how deftly Origen weaves his dogmatic and conceptual assumptions together, attempting to convince an audience of their validity. Not only is Origen's thesis in agreement with scriptural postulates, it is conceptually cogent as well.

I, 1,2 p. 17,18-18,19 Koe

1.   In this chapter Origen continues the attack against his Stoic opponents begun in (I,1,1). Focus is upon the inconsistencies in the corporealist's understanding of the

nature of knowledge. The topics through which the argument is presented are: ek kriseôs,[60] ek tôn enantiôn,[61] and to ta anomologoumena skopein.[62] The proof utilized is the deductive epicheirêma. The genus causarum is forensic, and the pars orationis is the refutatio.

Origen is careful to refute his opposition by demonstrating the inconsistencies of their argument. The inconsistencies arise from an incorrect definition that God is material. This not only contradicts a correct reading of scripture, but it also contradicts reasoned thinking. Hence their contradictions not only invalidate their thesis, but they also demonstrate the validity of Origen's own definition that God is spirit, and non-corporeal.[63]

The topoi employed by Origen in this chapter were employed by the Attic Ten. Isocrates and Lysias[64] offer fine examples of the use of these topics. They were also known and explained by the Hellenistic rhetors Apsines and Minucianus.[65] Both Cicero and Quintilian tell the orator how to construct arguments with this topic, and Cicero is careful to emphasize the close relation between the rhetorical and logical aspects of the topics echoing a notion already introduced by Aristotle.[66]

The close formal relationship between (1.1.1) and (1.1.2) is evident from the topics utilized in both pericopae. (1.1.2) is an auxêsis of (1.1.1). In both chapters Origen couples the topoi ek tôn enantiôn and ek kriseôs together in the attempt to persuade his audience that God is spirit.

In (I,1,2) he continues this line of argument. He employs a topic that is a cognate of ek tôn enantiôn, the topic to ta anomologoumena skopein.[67] Origen juxtaposes the inconsistencies of his opponent's position to bring them into further disrepute. The function of this topic is to discredit the ethos of the opposition. Origen accomplishes this by underscoring the eikota character of the argument presented by the corporealists.[68]

In his division of proofs we can discern how Origen structures his argument. Origen follows the formal rules of rhetorical argumentation common to Attic oratory. Parallel examples are extant in Isocrates.[69] Origen follows the rules of the rhetorical canon closely. Anaximenes[70] and Aristotle[71] suggest the use of this topic with tekmêria and enthymêmata. Cicero,[72] Quintilian,[73] Apsines[74] and Minucianus[75] suggest the same.

We are told that this topic is almost exclusively employed in forensic oratory[76] and thus this is our ground for asserting that this is the primary genus of the pericope. Origen's goal is to point out all contradictions in his opponents' theses to discredit them. First, Origen presents his thesis (1.1.2 p. 17.18-24), and its auxêsis (1.1.2 p. 17.24-18.2). Next, the opponents' argument is presented (1.1.2 p. 18.3-4). There follows a lengthy rebuttal (1.1.2 p. 18.4-18.19).

2.   The premise of Origen's argument is revealed in his first enthymêmê:

Si ergo adquiescunt huic assertioni nostrae, quam de natura luminis ipsa ratio demonstravit, et fatetnur non posse corpus intellegi deum secundum liminis intellectum, similis quoque ratio etiam de "igni consument" dabitur.

It is clear that this premise arises from the conclusion demonstrated in (1.1.1). We know this from the key word "ergo." The conclusion which follows from this premise is:

> Quid enim consumit deus secondum hoc quid "ignis" est?... Et quid in hoc dignum de dei laudibus dicitur, si deus ignis est huiuscemodi materias consumens?
>
> (1.1.2 p. 17.18-24)

It is important to note that in the opening paragraph of the pericope the author is careful to form his proof within the arguments from opposites and inconsistency. Next, to underscore the validity of his own proposition he links it to a scriptural passage using the argument from authority (1.1.2 p. 17.29-18.2). The argument functions to link Origen's thesis with scripture and rational consistency, and his opponents' thesis in opposition with scripture, and rational inconsistency. Origen hopes to persuade the audience that of the two arguments from opposites only one is consistent with scripture and reason -- his own.

The second proof is structured as a refutation of the argument:

> ...qui per hoc quod dictum est quoniam "deus spiritus est" corpus esse arbitrantur deum...
>
> (1.1.2 p. 18.3-4)

is again formed by means of the topics ek tôn enantiôn, to ta anomologoumena, and ek kriseôs. Indeed in the clause:

> Conseutudo est scripturae sanctae, cum aliquid contrarium corpori huic crassiori et solidiori designari vult, spiritum nominare, sicut dicit: "Littera occidit, spiritus autem vivificat." In quo sine dubio per litteram corporalia significat, per spiritum intellectualia, quae et spiritalia dicimus.
>
> (1.1.2 p. 18.4-9)

all three topics are evident. First is posited the argument from authority. This is followed by the argument from opposites. The formulation shows that the proposition that God a body is inconsistent. This is stated in the conclusion, when Origen asserts in fine rhetorical fashion "in quo sine dubio..."

The auxêsis which follows from the argument (1.1.2 p. 18.9-19) again is formed ek kriseôs. Origen's appeal is from the New and Old Testaments, Paul and Exodus respectively. Underlying this appeal from reason and authority is the argument from contraries. Origen's goal is to argue from all the contraries detrimental to his opponents' thesis in order to refute it.

Origen argues in a manner parallel to Cicero's and Quintilian's locus ex repugnantibus.[77] Cicero's example is informative. It offers an excellent illustration of the force this type of argument has rhetorically and logically. The example concludes:

...repugnant enim recte accipere et invitum reddere.

The thrust of this construct presents, in the words of Quintilian:

...ex repugnantibus, qui est sapiens stultus non est.

This is an important statement because Origen began (1.1.2) by affirming that his proof in (1.1.1) was:

...ipsa ratio demonstravit.

(1.1.2 p. 17.19)

The logical force of a persuasive argument must not be underestimated. The ancients understood this, and the manner in which Origen rhetorically formulates his arguments underscores this. One of the best rhetorical parallels is offered again by Cicero in the Topics. He states:

Ex hoc illa rhetorum ex contrariis, quae ipsi enthymêmata appellant; non quod omnis sententia proprio nomine enthymêma non dicatur, sed ut Homerus propter excellentiam commune poetarum nomen efficit apud Graecos suum, sic, cum omnis sententia enthymêma dicatur, quia videtur ea quae ex contrariis conficitur acutissima, sola proprie nomen commune possedit. Eius generis haec sunt:

hoc metuere, alterum in metu non ponere!
eam quam nihil accusas damnas, bene quam
    eritam esse autumas
    dicis male merere?
    id quod scis prodest nihil; id quod
    nescic obest?

Hoc disserendi genus attingit omnino vestras quoque in respondendo disputationis, sed philosophorum magis, quibus est cum oratoribus illa ex repugnantibus sententiis communis conclusio quae a dialecticis tertius modus, a rhetoribus enthymêma dicitur. Quae conclusiones id circo ratae sunt quod in disiunctione plus uno verum esse non potest. Atque ex eis conclusionibus quas supra scripsi-prior quartus posterior quintus a dialecticis modus appellatur. Deinde addunt coniunctionum negatiam sic: Non et hoc et illus; hoc autem; non igitur illud. His modus est sextus. Septimus autem: Non et hoc et illud; non autem hoc; illud igitur. Ex eis modis conclusiones innumerabiles nascuntur, in quo est tota fere dialektikê. Sed ne hae quidem quas exposui ad hanc institutionem necessariae.[78]

Although Cicero ends his description with a disclaimer it is still clear that the rhetorical and logical dimensions of argumentation were well established in late antiquity. What is important for our study is that Cicero does not hesitate to present both together. Origen, like Cicero, employs topics and proofs together to argue for and against philosophical postulates.

3. The rhetorical element of Origen's composition rises to the surface most eloquently in the opening line of this chapter:

Si ergo adquiescunt huic assertioni nostrae, quam de natura luminis ipsa ratio demonstravit, et fatentur non posse corpus intelligi deum secundum luminis intellectum, similis quoque ratio etiam de "igni consumenti" dabitur.

(I,1,2 p. 17,18-21)

There are a series of epistemological and ontological assumptions underlying Origen's formulation. When he states:

Et quomodo vel levis aliquis dabitur intellectus, ut ex isto quis corporali lumine causam scientiae capiat et veritatis, inveniat intellectum?...

(I,1,1 p. 17,15-17)

he infers the Platonic analogy of the sun with regard to sight and its objects, and the role of God (this is the later Platonic variation) with regard to knowledge and its objects. Although the light of the corporeal sun renders things visible to the eye, only the spiritual God, supremely intelligible in himself, renders knowledge intelligible to the mind. Origen stresses the dependence of scientia on the spiritual light provided by the Son, and the dependence of all knowledge upon his knowledge and wisdom. Human knowledge is based upon an order of knowledge grounded in an order of being.

Origen begins (1.1.2) affirming that his proof in (1.1.) is "ipsa ratio demonstravit" (1.1.2 p. 17.19). Next, he recapitulates the proposition which he proved in the opening section of the pericope (1.1.2 p. 17.17-18.2). To underscore this assertion, the first inconsistency is introduced that follows if the audience accepts the validity of the corporealist's argument (1.1.2 p. 17.21-24). Topically, ek tôn enantiôn and ek kriseôs, the corporealist postulate is inconsistent with the inner meaning of Scripture. If God consumes and destroys, Origen argues, it is only evil thoughts, shameful deeds, and longings after sin that are destroyed. He does not consume bodily matter.

(1.1.2 p. 18.3-16) continues this line of argumentation. Origen argues for interpreting Scripture in a spiritual sense, and not in a literal sense (1.1.2 p. 18.9-19). Origen illustrates through rhetorical argumentation how conceptual consistency and allegorical exegesis must complement one another if one is to present a cogent series of metaphysical definitions deduced from scripture. These activities yield a correct interpretation and exegesis of Scripture. Origen calls the results a scientiam spiritalem (1.1.2 p. 18.18).

The final section (1.1.2 p. 18.13-19) is formulated to give added credibility to Origen's argument. He argues ho tan ti enantion mellê prattesthai tois pepragmenois to refute the literal exegesis of scripture. Origen forces his audience to examine two definitions based upon these different exegeses of scripture so that they may compare them. The rhetorical function of this construct is to illustrate the conceptual contradiction and dogmatic inconsistency of his opponents. The force of the argument compels the audience to accept Origen's argument as the only cogent option among the two.

I. 1.3 p. 16. 20-19.10 Koe

1.   In the first two chapters (I,1.1-2) Origen's goal is to persuade his audience of the conceptual non-validity of the corporealist definition of God. The use of Middle Platonic conceptual assumptions is central to this argument process. The basis for refutation is the comparison of his opponents' materialist assumptions with his own non-materialist assumptions about the nature of God. In (I, 1.3) Origen continues this line of argumentation, but turns to his opponents' definition of the Holy Spirit.

(I.1.3) is an auxêsis of the arguments of (I.1.1-2). Origen employs the same method of combining the postulates of the Praefatio with his metaphysical assumptions. His goal is to convince his audience of the falsity of his opponents' interpretation of scripture and the definition of the Holy Spirit deduced from scripture. Origen has carefully built up his case. The conclusions presented in the antecedent chapters are assumed as premises for this chapter.

Origen places his argument in the common places ek kriseôs, ek tôn enantiôn, and to ta anamologoumena skopein. Again his pattern is to argue from authority, to illustrate that his opponents' thesis is in opposition to what constitutes correct philosophical and structural dogma. The topic of examining inconsistencies is utilized to effectively underscore the logical thrust of his argument. In this scheme of persuasion Origen uses a fourth commonplace, the argument ek tou mallon kai êtton. Origen attempts to compel his audience to choose which position is better and which is lesser.[79]

Origen uses the topics ek kriseôs, ek tôn enantiôn, and to ta anomologoumena skopein, and the inductive paradeigma in this pericope. These are placed within the refutatio and are argued by means of the forensic genus. Since the paradeigma is a syllogism adapted to common discourse Origen did not find it necessary to give all the premises of his argument. Some parts were left out. This is also the case when he presents his opponent's position.

2.   The chapter begins with the argument of his opponents and his response to the argument:

...non utique corpus aliquod intellegi potest spiritus sanctus, quod divisum in partes corporales percipiat ununquisque sanctorum; sed virtus profecto santificans est, cuius participium habere dicuntur omnes, qui per eius gratiam sanctificari meruerint.

(1.1.3 p. 18.20-24)

Origen argues from the topic ek tôn enantiôn in order to force the audience to decide which of the propositions is the better -- ek tou mallon kai êtton.[80] His own argument, which is stated in clause "sed virtus... sanctificare meruerint," is explained in the auxêsis at (1.1.3 p. 18.-19.4). The conclusion deduced from the premise (1.1.3 p. 18.22-24) is presented with the words:

> Sed haec non omnimodis similia exempla putanda sunt de medecina sancto spiritui comparata; sed ad hoc tantummodo conprobandum, quia non continuo corpus putandum est id, cuius participatio habetur a plurimis.
>
> (1.1.3 p. 19.4-7)

Origen structures his argument rhetorically in such a manner that he molds his audience to the conclusion that his definition of the nature of the Holy Spirit is in accord with the dogmas of scripture and the church. Furthermore, he wants the audience to accept that the wisdom of scripture and apostolic teaching is a "Platonically" grounded wisdom. His audience chooses ek tou mallon kai êtton, and Origen hopes that his interpretation is chosen as the better or true one. His utilization of the topic to ta anomologoumena skopein permits him to structure the argument in such a manner that the conclusion he wants his audience to accept must be his own. This is the function of the rhetorical argument. It forces his listeners-readers to examine the assumptions of his opponents, and by the argument's very presentation it is likely they will conclude that they are untenable. This is assumed by Origen because the audience, theoretically at least, has accepted the postulates of the Praefatio and the arguments of the De Deo (I,1,1-2). It will reason, ek kriseôs, that Origen's criticism will be accepted, and this acquiesence sets up Origen's formulations which follow in (I,1,5-9).[81] The rhetorical structure of the pericope, particularly the use of topics, illustrates that Origen argues in a way that the Alexandrian rhetors thought a Demosthenes or an Isocrates would argue. He read his handbooks carefully and crafted his argument accordingly.

Origen's coupling of the argument from the more and the less with an appeal to authority was a common device in ancient oratory. Demosthenes, whose speeches were among the most copied at Alexandria in the Imperial period, was thought to have used it.[82] The connection of this topic with the argument from opposites was also widely employed.[83] This was usually effected as a rhetorical question in the manner in which Origen formulates it. Over half of Demosthenes' arguments from the more and less are questions.[84] Of the three divisions, ek tou mallon, ek tou êtton, ei metê mallon metê êtton, the second form is the most common especially in the arguments from opposites.[85] It is to be noted that Origen follows the first and second forms of the construct in this pericope, and couples it with the arguments from opposites and authority. He employs these topics to bring out the non-validity of an eikos argument.[86] Again, this was a common device in ancient oratory.

The use of ek tou mallon kai êtton with ek kriseôs is formulated by Origen as an appeal to authority and to a previous judgment.[87] In Attic oratory, Isocrates makes appeals which are linked to decisions of ancestors, as does Dinarchus. This has a formal parallel to how Origen presents these topics, because his appeal is to Scripture and the Apostles. When these two topics are coupled with the argument from opposites we have a series of parallels with arguments presented by Aeschines, Lycurgus, and Demosthenes.[88] The fact that Origen presents the argument of his opponents in this pericope ek tou êtton and follows it with a question is also important. This type of formulation was a favorite of Demosthenes, who presented it in the opou oudê, medê, and pôs forms.[89] Finally both Demosthenes and Isocrates both appeal to aidôs in using these topoi.[90] Origen does the same throughout his appeal ek kriseôs.[91]

From this sketch of the topics and their use it is clear that Origen formulates his argument according to modes long established in Hellenistic oratory. It is also important that, in the Hellenistic period, these modes were perceived to have been utilized by the Attic Ten. It illustrates that Origen patterns his arguments on models considered rhetorically paradigmatic. He borrows freely from the rhetoric of late antiquity to argue his religious and philosophical ideas. Additionally he belongs to a tradition of Hellenistic and Roman rhetoric which viewed rhetorical invention as an aspect of dialectic. He is very careful to craft his arguments with certain logical considerations in mind.[92]

3.   Origen places his topics within a paradeigma which runs from (I,1,3 p. 18,20) to (I,1,3 p. 18,29). The exemplum which follows upon this (I,1,3 p. 18,24-19,10) underscores the non-validity of the assertion that the Holy Spirit is corporeal. The premise upon which his argument rests is the assertion that:

> pro eo quod sanctus spiritus subsistentia est intellectus et proprie subsistit et
> extat...
>
> (I,1,3 p. 19, 8ff.)

His point is:

> ...quia non continuo corpus putandum est id, cuius participatio habetur a
> plurimis.
>
> (I,1.3 p. 19,6ff.)

Unfortunately Rufinus does not provide us with a detailed explanation of what Origen means by subsistentia, intellectus, or participatio (Rufinus' translations are suspect in any case). However, we know from Origen's works that subsistentia translates as hypostasis, intellectus as nous, and participatio as methexis. The Holy Spirit is a noetic essence in a hypostatic relationship with the other noetic essences.

The basis for Origen's refutation that the Holy Spirit is a body is based on the assumptions of his Middle Platonic theoretic or first principles. The Holy Spirit, as one of the theologicals, is above materiality. He participates, or has a share in the same substance as the higher hypostases. The spiritus sanctus (=pneuma for Origen: In Jh. fr. 37 p. 513, 12 Koe.) does not participate with the other hypostases as material participation. Hence the Stoic doctrine of body going through body is rejected. Origen argues that the Stoic conception of sharing as mixture -- that the constituents are separable as self-subsistent bodies -- cannot be applied to relations between intellectual entities. This is unpacked more fully by Origen in (I,1,6-I,1,7).

I,1,4 p. 19,11-20,4 Koe

1.   (1.1.4) is rhetorically linked to the chapters which preceded it. The author explicitly states this when he asserts:

> Sed et ad ipsum iam sermonem evangelii transcendum est, ubi scriptum est qui "deus spiritus est," et ostendendum est quam consequenter his quae diximus intellegi debeat.

> (1.1.4 p. 19.11-13)

The key term is "consequenter" which means to follow as a logical consequence. This chapter constitutes the culmination of his first refutative argument. Origen ties together the various threads presented in (I,1,1-3) into a tapestry. He utilizes the notion of the asomatic reading of scripture to argue that "Deus spiritus est," and that by "spiritus" the scriptures mean that which is non-corporeal.

Origen must convince his audience that the corporealist is not in agreement with scripture. He attempts to do this through the topics ek kriseôs and hotan ti enantion mellê prattesthai tois pepragmenois.[93]   The use of the latter topic functions to refute the corporeal rendering of "deus spiritus est." Origen wants to show that it is inconsistent with the inner meaning of scripture. The aim is to change the mind of those in the audience that have accepted the corporealist's interpretation of scripture.

Origen attempts to convince his audience of the falsity of his opponents' definition by associating it, ek tôn pros allêla, with the position of the Samarian woman. The woman from Samaria incorrectly understood Jerusalem to be a material place, and attached a special privilege to its physical locus (I,1,4 p. 19,18-20). Origen uses scripture to refute this notion. He quotes Jesus who said:

> "Venit hora ut veri adoratores neque in Hierosolymis neque in hoc monte adorent patrem. Deus spiritus est, et eos qui adorant eum, in spiritu et veritate oportet adorare."

> (I,1,4 p. 19,26-29)

This rebuke of the Samarian by Jesus is turned upon the corporealists:

> "Et vide quam consequenter veritatem spiritui sociavit, ut ad distinctionem quidem corporum "spiritum" nominaret, ad distinctionem vero umbrae vel imaginis "veritatem."

> (I,1,4 p. 19,29-20,2)

Hebrews 8:5 is interpreted Platonically and within the context of Origen's argument scheme it works most effectively to refute the corporealist's definition that God is a body.

The scriptural argument is so strong in this pericope that no attempt is made by Origen to refute his opponents on philosophical grounds. It is apparent that he thinks scriptural refutation has priority over philosophical refutation. Let us now examine the rhetorical structure of his argument.

2.   Origen formulates his argument ex epagôgês. (I,1,4) is not a deductive proof, but an inductive proof.[94] He begins with his conclusion "Deus spiritus est" (I,1,4 p. 19,12), and an amplification is built upon this example (I,1,4 p. 19,13). Then he moves inductively to demonstrate his conclusion through the use of three passages from scripture (I,1,4 p. 19,12,17,18-20,25,26). The proof "Deus spiritus est," denotes non-corporeality is demonstrated by means of these proof-texts.

Origen's argument is effective because the argument ex epagôgôs is formulated in the commonplace hotan ti enantion melê prattesthai tous pepragmenous, hama skopein.[95] The use of ek kriseôs is again utilized but not only as an appeal to authority. There is also the appeal that the audience use its judgment. Origen wants them to agree that his is a reasonable argument in accord with scriptural authority. Since the topic is utilized in comparison it appears that Origen's use of it is close to Theon's apo sygkriseôs. He is asking his audience to decide ek tou mallon kai êtton which argument is the better and which is the worse.[96] The comparative topic asks the audience to look at what is about to be done as opposed to what has been done already. This decision could only be made in reference to which of the two has the better thesis. The ek kriseôs topic is used for rebuttal. As Aristotle states:

An argument can be refuted either by a counter syllogism (antisyllogisamenon) or by bringing an objection (enstasin).[97]

Since the counter-syllogisms to this proposition have already been presented in the previous chapters, Origen refutes his opposition by introducing an objection through the auxêsis of (1.1.4 p. 19.13-20.4). Parallels to the use of this topic in Greek, Hellenistic, and Roman oratory are too great to list in detail. The use of this topic was widespread in ancient oratory. There are a number of parallel examples in Isocrates, Demosthenes, and Lysias. Origen's use of the topic ek kriseôs has a number of parallels in Isocrates and Demosthenes.[98] The appeal is to an authority the audience will accept.[99] For the Attic orators, Solon is such a figure.[100] For the Christian orator, John or Hebrews is an authority.[101] For the Jewish orator such as Philo, the Pentateuch is an authority.[102] It suffices to say that an appeal to the gods is a common one in ancient persuasion and Origen's appeal is formally identical to the many which are extant in both Greek and Latin sources. Quintilian explains the use of this appeal to auctoritas as:

...neque enim durassent haec in aeternum, nisi vera omnibus viderentur. Ponitur a quibusdam et quidem in parte prima deorum auctoritas, quae est ex responsit, ut, <u>Socraten esse sapientissimum.</u> Id rarum est, non sine usu tamen.... Quae cum propria causae sunt, divina testimonia vocantur; cum aliunde arcessuntur, argumenta.[103]

This explains the function of Origen's counter syllogism quite nicely.

<u>I,1,5 p. 20,5-23 Koe</u>

1.   We shall begin our analysis of the chapter by tracing the rhetorical thrust of the argument. There then follows a rhetorical analysis of the argument. We shall conclude with a discussion of the epistemology Origen proposes, and the significance it has for the remainder of the argument in the <u>De Deo</u> (I,1,6-9).

This pericope is the first part of Origen's <u>confirmatio.</u> This is an important chapter because Origen presents an outline of his theory of knowledge, and an introduction to his understanding of first principles.

Origen formulates his argument through a series of <u>antikeimena</u> topics. These arguments from opposites are the bases upon which Origen hopes to persuade his audience of the efficacy of his conceptual assumptions concerning the nature of God the Father. The epistemic terms <u>sentire</u> (<u>aisthêsis</u>) and <u>intellegere</u> (<u>noêsis</u>) are contrasted, and the assertion is made that a noetic first principle can be known but not perceived (cf. <u>C. Cels.</u> VI,17). <u>Aisthêsis</u> is not the medium of divine apprehension, Noêsis is.

The epistemic distinction between the faculties of <u>sens,</u> and <u>mens intellectus,</u> is demonstrated by Origen without reference to scripture. The want of proof-texts from scripture can be explained. Origen carries over the conclusions derived from his first <u>apodeixis euaggelikê</u> from (I,1,1-4). His argument is formulated with these conclusions already assumed. Scripture is the final criterion of the truth of his assertions, but in this chapter Origen is content to work from within a philosophical matrix alone. In the chapters which follow he provides ample evidence from scripture and apostolic doctrine to support his position.

(1.1.5) is rhetorically linked to the chapters which preceded it. This is clear at the opening sentence when the author states:

Omni igitur sensu, qui corporeum aliquid de deo intellegi suggerit, prout potuimus, dicimus secundum veritatem quidem deum inconprehensibilem esse atque inaestimabilem.

(1.1.5 p. 20.5-7)

The key terms in the premise of the argument are <u>confirmatio</u> and <u>dico.</u> "Non ergo" links the conclusion of (1.1.1-1.1.4) with the premise of (1.1.5). Origen is satisfied that he has sufficiently demonstrated that the corporealist's definition of the nature of God is not in agreement with scripture, and that it is not philosophically cogent. The next step in his plan is to present the correct definition of God the Father, and how he is known.

In order to prove "deum inconprehensibilem esse atque inaestimabilem" Origen falls back on an epistemic presupposition of the Middle Platonic school tradition he draws from. He makes a distinction between sentire and intellegere, and asserts that neither is capable of presenting an adequate understanding of God (1.1.5 p. 20.7-9). The remainder of the pericope clarifies this assertion (1.1.5 p. 20.9-19), and leads into the conclusion presented at (1.1.5 p. 20.19-23).

The topical arrangement of (I,1,5) is complex. The antikeimena genus has four species of arguments. These are ek diareseôs, ek tou endexomenou kai epi merous, peri duoin antikeimenoin, and ek tou akolouthountos. At the outset Origen presents the argument within the ek tôn enantiôn commonplace that has the characteristics of a very sharp division, peri duoin antikeimenoin.[104] Maximum Planoudes called this conflation of topics the argument ek tou endexomenou kai epi merous.[105] The force of arguing through these topics is to force the audience to choose only one as valid, thus ek tou akolouthountos.[106] In review, the first topic sets up opposition, the second tells the audience how sharp the opposition is, and the third has the function of forcing the audience to choose only one of the two options offered.

Fundamental to the success of Origen's argument is the assumption his audience will carry over the postulates and conclusions from antecedent chapters of the Periarchôn (De Principiis). The argument is constructed so that the audience is predisposed to accept Origen's definition of God the Father. Rhetorically, the argument is set up as an antithetai ta'nantia with the choice between what is true and what is false.

Origen formulates his argument so that one line of positive proof is based upon consideration of the opposite proof. Next, the audience considers whether or not the corporealist definition of knowledge has the opposite conceptual assumptions as the spiritualist definition. Since it has, the corporealist definition is refuted, and Origen establishes the spiritualist definition as true. The structure of the argument is:

If A has a relation to B, X the opposite of A is similarly related to Y the opposite of B.

The truth or falsity of either proposition is determined by reference to the other.

Closely connected with this enantia construct is the argument ek diaireseôs.[107] The method of argument from division is to split your opponent's statement up according to the ways it may be true and then rebut the divisions. Origen follows this procedure insofar as he posits the proposition that:

...qui corporeum aliquid de deo intellegi suggerit, prout potimus...
(1.1.5 p. 20.5f.)

and then:

...confutato, dicimus secundum veritatem quidem deum inconprehensibilem esse atque inaestimabilem.

(1.1.5 p. 20.6f.)

The refutation is then spelled out specifically in the auxêsis which runs to (1.1.5 p. 20.7-19).

This topic complements the argument from opposites because it underscores the dichotomy between the two theories of knowledge proposed. The author employs ek tôn enantiôn and ek diaireseôs together to refute the assertion that God is known through sensible intellection. Hence, he undercuts the possibility of the validity of their assertion.

The rhetor Quintillian provides us with an explanation of what Origen is doing. He states:

Divisio et ad probandum simili via valet et ad refellendum.... Fit hoc et multiplex, idque est argumentorum genus ex remotione, quo modo efficitur totum falsum...

(In. Or. V.10.65-66)

Another illustration of the function of these antikeimena topoi is offered by Cicero. His explanation of them is also helpful in understanding the rhetorical dimensions of the topics utilized by Origen. Cicero speaks of the topic of consequence as:

...locus dialecticorum proprius ex consequentibus et antecedentibus et repugnantibus... Ea enim dico consequentia quae rem necessario consequintur; itemque et antecedentia et repugnantia. Quidquid enim sequitur quamque rem, id cohaeret cum re necessario; et quiquid repugnant, id eius modi est ut cohaerere nunquam possit.

(Top. XII. 52)

In the case of (1.1.5) Origen wishes to make it clear that what the audience is confronted with are two logically contradictory propositions concerning the definition of the attributes of God. If they accept the spiritualist definition as normative, then certain consequents follow from their choice.[108] If they assent to the proposition of the corporealists, then they cannot adhere to the consequences attached to the spiritualist proposition. Again Cicero explains the probable intention of Origen's argument:

Nam quid interest, cum hoc sumpseris, pecuniam numeratam mulieri deberi cui sit argentum: si pecunia signata argentum est, legata ets mulieri. Est autem pecunia signata argentum. Legata igitur est; an illo modo: Si numerata pecunia non est legata, non est numerata pecunia argentum. Est autem numerata pecunia argentum; legata igitur est; an illo modo: Non et legatum argentum est et non est legata numerata pecunia. Legatum autem argentum est; legata igitur numerata pecunia est? Appelant autem dialectici eam conclusionem argumenti, in qua, cum primum assumpseris, consequitur id quo annexum est conclusionis modum; cum id quod annexum est negaris, ut id quoque cui fuerit annexum negandum sit, secundus is appellatur concludendi modus; cum autem aliqua convincta negaris et ex eis unum aut plura sumpseris, ut quod relinquitur tollendum sit, is tertius appellatur conclusionis modus. Ex hoc illa rhetorum ex contrariis conclusa, quae ipsi enthymêmata appellant.

(Top. XIII. 54-55)

2.   Origen forms his argument in the form of an epicheirêma in five parts. The argument is presented as a demonstrative syllogism in which all the premises are not listed, but are assumed. That they are assumed is clear from Origen's statement:

...qui corporeum aliquid de deo intellegi suggerit, prout potuimus, confutato...

(I,1,5 p. 20,5ff.)

We shall now examine the structure of the argument.

The five-part epicheirêma runs as follows:

(1)   ...dicimus secundum veritatem quidem deum inconprehensibilem esse atque inaestimabiles. Si quid enim illud est, quod sentire vel intellegere de deo potuerimum, multis longe

(2)   modis eum meliorem esse ab eo quod sensimus necesse est credi.

(1.1.5 p. 20.6-9)

(3)   Sicut enim si videamus aliquem vix posse scintillam luminis aut brevissimae lucernae lumen aspicere et eum, cuius acies oculorum plus luminis capere quam supra diximus non valet, si velimus de claritate ac splendore solis edocere, nonne oportebit nos ei dicere quia omni hoc lumine quod vides ineffabiliter et inaestimabiliter meloir ac praestantior solis est splendor? -- ita mens nostra cum intra carnis et

(4)   sanguinis claustra concluditur et pro talis materiae participatione hebetior atque obtusior redditur, licit ad comparationem naturae corporeae longe praecellens habeatur, tamen cum ad incorporea nititur atque eorum rimatur intuitum, tunc scintillae alicuius aut lucernae vix optinet locum.

(1.1.5 p. 20.9-19)

Quid autem in omnibus intellectualibus, id est incorporeis, tam praestans omnibus,

(5)   tam ineffabiliter atque inaestimabiliter praecellens quam deus? Cuius
utique natura acie humanae mentis intendi atque intueri, quamvis ea sit
purissima mens ac limpidissima, non potest.

(1.1.5 p. 20.19-23)

3.   The importance of this argument for Origen's thesis is clear. Origen's theory
of knowledge holds that all objects of knowledge are not phenomena of sensible knowing.
Deity is an intelligible phenomenon and an object of intelligible knowing. To know God,
one must transcend the sense data, and exercise the higher faculties of knowledge
directed toward the intelligibles and the theologicals. Matter is the mirror of spirit, and
knowledge of material things presents only knowledge of sensible things. Hence, spiritual
things are unknown, and unknowable by, sensible intellection.

This epistemological postulate leads to the ontological postulate Origen will propose
in the next chapters. Just as there are degrees of knowing there are degrees of reality.
The source of reality and the principle of all intelligent nature and understanding is a
hypostasis of absolute simplicity. In order to establish this postulate on firm grounds
Origen had to remove a fundamental obstacle: that God is a body that can be known by
the mind as it sets it gaze upon the material elements which constitute its nature.

I,1,6 p. 20,24-23,14 Koe

1.   The major portion of this chapter is devoted to the ridicule and refutation of
the Stoic philosophical theology and epistemology. It is impossible to reconstruct these
theories from the statements of the Periarchôn (De Principiis) alone. Origen's composition is a syggramma not a hypomnêma, and thus he did not compose the work as a
detailed commentary on Stoic physical principles. Nonetheless it is important to
reconstruct from other sources the basic outlines of such first principles so that we may
better understand Origen's argument.

The theory of pneuma is the linchpin of the Stoic physical theory as it was
formulated by Chrysippus. It appears that Chrysippus' theory was still held by Stoics as
late as the second century A.D. Alexander's de mixtione 10 makes reference to it.[109]
Given this let us reconstruct the Stoic doctrine, which most likely underlies the position
of Origen's Stoic Christian opponents.[110]

The concept of pneuma was defined within the context of the Stoic theory of
archai.[111] They held to an active principle which totally pervaded a passive principle as
the passage of body through body (cf. SVF II,300; 299-328; Alex., de mixt. 224,34;
225,5-18). The passive principle could not interact with the active. It served as its
medium. This active principle was described as a substance (ousia). The passive principle
was defined as qualityless matter (hylê) from which bodies evolve (e.g., Diog. Laert.
V.,VII,134=SVF II 300). The result of this relation between principles was the formation of
a rational cosmos. The active reason or first principle of the cosmos was called Logos or
God.

The physical processes by which the active principle pervades and orders matter was explained in terms of the four elements. Hot and cold were the active qualities, wet and dry the passive qualities (SVF II 444; Alex., de mixt. 218,2-6). The active elements were thought to be fire and air, and the passive earth and water. The pneuma was held to be a compound formed of these two elements, which constituted a structured cosmos. The model provided an explanation in qualitative physical terms of the unity and continuity of the cosmos. The central feature of this theory of pneuma was the motion of body through a body. Galen tells us that the Stoics called pneuma a hylikê ousia and a sunêktikê aitia (SVF II 439, 440).

Against this theory Origen argues that God is not a body which expands and contracts (I,1,6 p. 21,10-22,4). He argues against the assertion that God needs magnitude; is known through the senses; is composite and diverse; is characterized by material intermixture; and needs space and place (I,1,6 p. 22,4-9). Origen's deity is wholly Platonic. He is immaterial, immovable, simple, unitary, and in no need of magnitude or place. Finally he is non-discernible to the senses. He is a non-material substance.

2.   The topical arrangement of (I,1,6) is complex. In addition to the standard arguments, ek kriseôs and ek tôn enantiôn, Origen employs ek diaireseôs and ek ton meron, as well as ex horismou.[112] The argument from authority and opposites is implied. The argument has two themes. What is the nature of knowledge and divinity? The argument has a four-part division: (I,1,6 p. 20,24-21,9; p. 21,10-22,3; p. 22,4-6; p. 23,1-14). No direct use of scripture is employed in this pericope. Rather Origen bases his argument on the authority of his Platonic philosophical assumptions.

A cognate topic to division is definition (ex horismou). As a dialectical topic it was most important. Definition of terms was considered the basis of all sound argument. It was utilized to eliminate ambiguity and consequent misunderstandings of definition. Division was a well known rhetorical topic, and was discussed in great length in the handbooks. It was known to Cicero and Maximus Planoudes.[113] Quintilian notes the logical and rhetorical, i.e. its dialectical use:

> Rhetorice est bene dicendi scientia; aut per partes, ut Rhetorice est inveniendi recte et disponendi et eloquendi cum firma memoria et cum dignitate actionis... Finitioni subiecta maxime videntur genus, species, differens, proprium; ex iis omnibus argumenta ducuntur. Genus ad probandum speciem minimum valet, plurimum ad refellendam... species firmam probationem habet generis, infirmam refutationem... His adiiciunt propria et differentia. Propriis confirmatur finition, differentibus solvitur...[114]

We must keep these words of Quintilian in mind as we analyze 1.1.6. The complement of definition is division, and the primary function of both topics is the elimination of opposing definitions. Hence, through these topics Origen asserts the validity of his own definition of God the Father, and rebukes his opponents.

3.   The argument begins with a three-part epicheirêma. The premise of the
argument is assumed in that it is carried over from the conclusion of the previous
argument. Origen states, that the premise of (1.1.6) is contained in (1.1.5):

(1)   Verum non videtur absurdum, si ad evidentiorum rei manifestationem
        etiam alia utamur similitudine...

                              (1.1.6 p. 20.24-21.1f.)

From this premise is deduced the first conclusion of (1.1.6):

(2)   Ita ergo quasi radii quidam sunt dei naturae opera divinae providentiae eius ac
        naturae. Quia ergo mens nostra ipsum per se

(3)   ipsam deum sicut est non potest intueri, ex pulchritudine operum et decore
        creaturarum parentum universitatis intellegit.

                              (1.1.6 p. 21.5-9)

A five-part epicheirêma follows (1.1.6 p. 21.10ff.). It forms the core of the ek ton
meron argument that continues to the end of the chapter. The major premise is:

(1)   Non ergo corpus aliquod aut in corpore esse putandus est deus, sed
        intellectualis natura simplex, nihil omnio in se adiunctionis admittens;
        uti ne maius aliquid et inferius in se habere credatur, sed ut sit ex omni
        parte monas, et ut ita dicam henas, et mens ac fons, ex quo initium
        totius intellectualis naturae vel mentis est.

                              (1.1.6 p. 21.10-14)

The minor premises are:

(2)   Mens vero ut moveatur vel operetur, non indigit loco corporeo neque
        sensibili magnitudine vel corporali habitu aut colore, neque alio ullo
        prorsus indiget horum, quae corporis vel materiae propria sunt. Propter
        quod natura illa simplex et tota mens ut moveatur vel operetur aliquid,
        nihil dialationis aut cunctationis habere potest, ne per huiusmodi
        adiunctionem circumscribi vel inhiberi aliquatenus videatur divinae
        naturae simplicitas, uti ne quod est principium omnium, compositiun
        inveniatur et diversum, et si multa, non unum, quod oportet totius
        corporae admixtionis alienum una sola, ut ita dixerim, deitatis specie
        constare.

                              (1.1.6 p. 21.14-22.4)

and:

(3)   Quia autem mens non indigeat loco, ut secundum naturam suam moveatur, certum est etiam ex nostrae mentis contemplatione. Haec enim si in sua mensura consistat nec ex qualibet causa aliquid ei obtunsionis eveniat, nihil umquam ex locorum diversitate tardabitur, quominus suis motibus agat: neque rursum ex locorum qualitate augmentum aliquod vel incrementum mobilitatis adquiret.

(1.1.6 p. 22.4-9)

An auxêsis follows at (1.1.6 p. 22.9-23). It functions to refine and amplify the conclusion (1.1.6 p. 22.4-9). This amplification results in another conclusion:

(4)   Deum vero, qui omnium initium est, compositum esse non est putandum; ne forte priora ipso principio esse inveniantur elementa, ex quibus compositum est omne quicquid illud est quod compositum dicitur.

(1.1.6 p. 22.23-26)

The argument of (1.1.6 p. 23.1ff.) adds the previous conclusions together to form a new premise. The deduction from this premise is:

(5)   Se ned magnitudine corporali mens indiget, ut agat aliquid vel moveatur... Indiget sane mens magnitudine intellegibili, quia non corporaliter, sed intellegibiliter crescit.

(1.1.6 p. 23.1-5)

(1.1.6 p. 23.5-14) is an auxêsis that clarifies the proposition that mind needs intellectual magnitude. It grows in an intellectual and not in a physical sense.

3.   It is clear that Origen did not choose to appreciate the complexity of the Stoic first principles, but his rhetorical plan was not to appreciate but to deprecate. He viewed the Stoic pneuma as an active material essence that went through and bound together passive matter. Hence, the Stoic categories of essence, place, quality, quantity have no referential efficacy to define God. The fact they are physical categories makes it impossible, to associate them with the non-material transcendent first principle of Origen's system.

In summary, Origen's argument is directed against a system of first principles and epistemology held by the adherents of a Stoa Christiana. The definition of divinity Origen proposes is a transcendent, non-material mind who is the first archê of all things. Since God is not characterized by physical qualities he is not knowable by the sensible faculty of knowledge whose objects are only the sensibles.

Once Origen has refuted the notion that God is a body (I,1,1-4), known through sensation (I,1,5), he can begin to systematically dismantle the elements of a Stoic first principles. (I,1,6) is the first constructive step toward this end. In this chapter Origen refutes the doctrines of the Stoic ontology and epistemology. The arguments presented in

(I,1,1-6) have set up the audience for a more detailed examination of knowledge and being. In the remaining chapters Origen focuses on these issues. In (I,1,7) he defines the different knowing faculties, and the knowledge they yield.

I,1.7 p. 23,15-24,21 Koe

1.   In this chapter Origen continues the epistemological debate of the preceding chapters. The argument focuses upon whether or not the soul is a body, and if it is, how is it possible for a corporeal mind to know the invisible things which are a part of the intelligible and divine spheres of reality.

In this pericope Origen assumes a series of premises concerning the soul and mind demonstrated in (I,1,5-6). Hence, his goal in (I,1,7) is to refute a series of Stoic epistemological assumptions, and complete the argument begun in (I,1,6).

Origen presents his opponents' conceptual assumptions incompletely, and offers them up to his audience as objects as ridicule. Although we cannot reconstruct the bases of the epistemic theory Origen is arguing against from this source, it would be helpful to sketch the outlines of this Stoic theory of knowledge so that we may better understand the situation of Origen's own argument.

We shall sketch the outlines of the epistemic theory Origen argues against from the Stoic fragments. The questions which need to be addressed are: 1) what is the nature of the soul, and 2) what is the criterion by which one judges that a thing or things really exist.[115]

One of the basic features of the Stoic epistemology is the rejection of the Platonic tripartite soul. The soul and body, both of which are corporeal, interpenetrate one another (SVF 471, 473, 634). Chalcidius preserves the doctrine Origen argues against, in most probability, and describes it in the following manner:[116]

> The whole soul extends its senses, which are functions of it, like branches, from that ruling part, as from a tree; and these senses are to be reporters of those things which they perceive (sentire) while the ruling part itself, like a king, passes judgement upon those things which are sensed, namely, bodies, are composites, and thus each sense perceives some one ingredient in the composition; this one color; another, sound; and while that one discerns the flavor of fluids; this one discerns the aromas of substances, and that one by touch distinguishes roughness and smoothness. And all this is concerned with what is present; however, no sense remembers what is past or apprehends what is future. Rather it is the peculiar function of inner deliberation and reflection to observe the affection of each sense and to infer what this object is from those data which the senses report, and to apprehend what is present, and moreover to remember what is no longer present, and to foresee what will happen.

(SVF II, 879)

The Stoic position is that the soul acquires knowledge of the external world from what the senses report from the qualities of the object which impinge upon it. From the data reported by the senses the soul reflects upon the object before it, and apprehends it. This soul, or its ruling faculty, also remembers objects no longer present, and infers from memory to a prognosis of things which will happen in the future.

From another fragment (SVF II, 866) we learn that according to the Stoics a pneumatic current extends from the ruling part of the soul through the eye and out beyond into the surrounding air. These pneumatic currents, which function as extensions of the soul, go out to each of the sense organs, and this is how one comes to know the world. Movements are transmitted through these currents, and they cause impressions in the soul. In short, the soul and the knowing faculty function as a single corporeal unit, and knowledge is the impression of the material objects upon the soul (SVF II, 56). The analogy employed is that of an impression upon a wax tablet (SVF II, 56).

From these testimonies it is clear that for the Stoics the criterion of knowledge are the "common notions" (koinai ennoiai). They are based upon a critical appraisal of "sensations" (aisthêta). The generation of these notions comes about when the soul deliberates upon the data before it, remembering past sensations/notions, and assents (sugkatathesis) to their veracity.[117] Hence, an existing object signals its existence and character by affecting the sense organs. Pneumatic currents transmit the movements in the sense organs to the ruling part of the soul. Here they change into images or common notions. The soul and the knowing faculty are wholly corporeal.

It is against this theory of knowledge that Origen argues in (I,1,7). Fundamental to his position is a theory that asserts a liability of perceptible things to change. This is an indication of the relative unreality of the data of sensible knowing. The assumption is that sensible perception and the data it presents to the mind is transitory. Its objects are within the realm of becoming, not being. The knowledge yielded from sensation is "unreal." Hence perception yields belief about sensible things, but it is not capable of giving knowledge about intelligible and divine things. This higher knowledge is the prerogative of the human understanding and divine wisdom.

Origen's polemical point is that knowledge is not merely about the changing mutable things we perceive. It is also about the intelligible world we scientifically know. The things perceived in the changing, transitory world of Becoming suggest a knowledge of the world of Being, but knowledge of Being, and of the divine hypostases is not possible from the data of sensible knowledge alone. Intelligible knowledge is something which the human soul acquires in its study of the intelligibles. This is what Origen means when he speaks of the affinity between the human and divine minds (I,1,7 p. 24,18ff.):

...quod propinquitas quaedam sit menti ad deum, cuius ipsa mens intellectualis imago sit, et per hoc possit aliquid de deitatis sentire natura, maxime si expurgatior ac segregatior sit a materia corporali.

Human knowledge begins, but does not end, in sense-perception. Origen's theory of knowledge is based on the Platonic-Peripatetic analogies of the sun and the divided line.

These different kinds or states of mind have corresponding classes of objects. The visible world is a kind of shadow of the intelligible world, and the intelligible world is a shadow of the divine world. This trifold image-original relation presents us with our three types of knowledge (pistis): opinion (doxa), knowledge (epistêmê), and divine knowledge (gnôsis).

Origen sees danger in the theory of knowledge proposed by the adherents of the Stoa Christiana. In his view it is an assault upon the dignity of God (I,1,7 p. 24,13ff.). It is this concern which is the thematic link between (I,1,7) and (I,1,1-6).

The arguments presented in this pericope are linked to the pericopae which preceded it. This chapter, along with (1.1.8-1.1.9), are the summation of the confirmatio of the first book of the Periarchôn.

(1.1.7) is an auxêsis of the arguments which preceded it (1.1.1-1.1.6). As such the topics utilized in the previous chapters present themselves in this one as well. They are: ek kriseôs, ek tôn enantiôn, ek diaireseôs-ek ton meron, and ex horismos. The arguments follow the familiar pattern of rhetorical demonstration, the primary genus causarum remains forensic, and the partes orationis are the refutatio-confirmatio.

(1.1.7) is an argument from division and definition. It presupposes the argument from opposites and seeks to legitimize its conclusions arguing from scriptural authority. The thesis to be refuted is:

...qui mentem ipsam animamque corpus esse...

(1.1.7 p. 23.15)

Origen assumes that it can be refuted because it cannot be demonstrated:

...rationes assertionesque recipiat...

(1.1.7 p. 23.17)

He assumes this because the premises which underlie the definition that the soul is a body are the same as those which underlie the refuted definition that the mind is a body. By coupling these assumptions together Origen makes it a simple task to demonstrate their non-cogency. The same principles which apply to the corporealist proposition concerning mind apply to the corporealist proposition concerning soul.

Rhetorically, this correlation is presented through the argument ek tôn pros allêla. This is the argument from mutual relation of terms or notions. It is another of the antikeimena topoi treated in the rhetorical canon under the head of oppositions or opposites.

This is one of the so-called dialectical topics utilized in rhetorical and logical argumentation.[118] It is a helpful device in argumentation. Inferences are drawn from knowing or knowledge, epistêmê, to the thing known, to epistêton, from the sight as a sensation, aisthêsis, to the thing seen as an object of sense to aisthêton.[119] Origen argues that one cannot gain knowledge of divinity through sensible perception. Hence the same line of reasoning which underlies the definition that the soul is material underlied the definition that the mind is material. The reasons which make the first definition false also make the second false. They are arguments from mutually related false presuppositions.

The form of Origen's argument was widely employed in Hellenistic and Roman oratory.[120] Quintilian and Cicero were aware of it, and explained it in a manner close to Aristotle's original definition in the Ars Rhetorica.[121] We have an excellent parallel from Dionysius of Halicarnassus in his Letter to Ammaeus which shows how a rhetor uses this topic.[122] This example illustrates Demosthenes' use of Aristotle's Ars Rhetorica. Although this example is more a product of the scholastic's pen than an historical datum we can see how the later Hellenistic writers integrated the Attic orators into their theoretical matrix. In this presentation Demosthenes is shown as arguing ek tôn pros allêla. The example is instructive because Origen read similar handbooks, and assumed that this model rhetor argued through this topic. He then formulated his own argument in accord with this paradigm.

There is an example from Demosthenes which is formally akin to the topical formulation of (1.1.7): What is right for one is right for another.[123] Other examples from Isocrates and Isaeus follow the same formal pattern.[124]

The function of the argument from the mutual relation of terms or notions is explained by Quintilian:

Illa quoque, quae ex rebus mutuam confirmationem praestantibus ducuntur (quae proprii generis videri quidam volunt et vocant ek tôn pros allela, Cicero ex rebus sub eandem rationem venientibus) fortiter consequentibus iun-xerium... Est invicem consequens et quod ex diversis idem ostendit; ut, qui numdum nasci dicit, per hoc ipsum et deficere significet, quia deficit omne quod nascitur.

(In. Or. V. 10.78-79)

The argument is, "If it may be said of one (of the two terms of the relation) then the same terms may be applied to the other." Let us now examine how Origen puts his argument together with these examples in mind.

Origen couples mens and anima to the proposition corpus esse at (1.1.7 p. 23.15). What is said of "mens corpus esse" applies also to "anima corpus esse." In the words of Demosthenes, "What is right for one is right for another." In the words of Isaeus, "If we would inherit our property we also should inherit his." Both examples are formally kindred to Origen's construct. This is outlined below.

This commonplace is, if one shares in misfortune then one should also share in benefits. The topic hinges upon the identity of attributes between the active and passive, or deed and doer. Origen uses this commonplace to infer that the proposition soul is body is as incorrect as the proposition mind is body. There is an identity between the conceptual assumptions of both postulates. Since the first is false the second is also false. Origen states it in this manner:

Unde ei virtus memoriae, under rerum invisibilium contemplatio, unde certe incorporalium intellectus corpori inest? Quomodo natura corporea disciplinas artium, rerum contemplationes rationesque rimatur? Unde etiam divina dogmata, quae manifeste incorporea sunt, sentire atque intellegere potest? Nisi si forte aliquis putet quod, sicut forma ista corporea et habitus ipse aurium vel oculorum confert aliquid ad audiendum et videndum, et ut singula membra, quae a deo formata sunt, habent aliquid oportunitatis etiam ex ipsa formae qualitate ad hoc, quod agere naturaliter instituta sunt: its etiam habitum animae vel mentis intellegi debere arbitretur quasi atque accommodeque formatum ad hoc, ut de singulis sentiat vel intellegat atque ut vitalibut notibus moveatur.

(1.1.7 p. 23.17-29)

Since this epistemological postulate was refuted by Origen at (1.1.5-1.1.6), he states:

Verum qualem colorem mentis secundum hoc, quod mens est et intellegibiliter movetur, describere quis posset aut dicere, non adverto.

(1.1.7 p. 23.29-31)

His conclusions are deduced ek tôn pros allêla. The objections or enstaseis brought against this thesis are unpacked in the pericope that follows at (1.1.7 p. 24.1-21).

Origen argues that the bodily senses are appropriately connected with the material substance toward which each sense is directed, i.e. sight with color, shape, and size, hearing with voice and sound, smelling with vapors, taste with flavors, and touch with things hot, cold, hard, soft, rough, or smooth. Hence:

Horum autem sensuum, de quibus supra diximus, quia multo, melior sensus sit mentis, omnibus clarum est. Quomodo ergo non videtur absurdum, his quidem, quae inferiora sunt, substantias esse subiectas ad intendendum, huic, autem virtuiti, quae melior est, id est mentis sensui, nihil omnino subici substantiale, sed esse intellectualis naturae vittutem corporibus accidentum vel consequentem?

(1.1.7 p. 24-7-13)

Through the argument from relation Origen demolishes this epistemological postulate. Origen moves in the final pericope from the topic ek tôn pros allêla to its cognate, ek tôn enantion. In (1.1.7 p. 24. 1ff.) Origen presents one line of positive proof based upon consideration of the opposite of the thing in question. The proposition that the mind is superior to the body with a superior reasoning faculty limited to itself, is demonstrated by a consideration of the opposite proposition that the mind is material with a reasoning faculty directed toward the particular senses as well as towards substance. The truth of Origen's proposition is demonstrated by referring it to the falsehood of his opponents proposition.

This enstatis results in the verdict presented at (1.1.7 p. 24.13ff.).[125] In this section Origen repeats the arguments ek ton meron and ex horismou presented in (1.1.5-1.1.6). The argument from division is the explanatio of the proof. The argument from definition is the confirmatio of the proof. Origen divides the senses into the material objects to which they are directed, and he divides the mind into the intellectual objects to which it is directed. The definition of their capacities and functions follows from this division. The senses perceive the accidents arising out of bodies and are incapable of knowing substance. The mind knows substance itself, and is thus capable of knowing God. Hence, the mind is the superior knowing faculty, and the senses are the inferior knowing faculty. The enstasis apo tou enantiou is employed to deduce the conclusion:

> Quod qui dicut, sine dubio in contumeliam eius substantiae, quae in ipsis melior est, haec proferunt; immo vero ex hoc etiam ad upsum deum refertur iniuria, cum putant eum per naturam corpoream posse intellegi, quo scilicet secundum ipsos corpus sit et illud, quod per corpus potest intellegi vel sentire; et nolunt hoc intellegi, quod propinquitas quaedam sit menti ad deum, cuia ipsa mens intellectualis imago sit, et per hoc possit aliquid de deitatis sentire natura, maxime si expurgatior ac segretatior sit a materia corporali.
>
> (1.1.7 p. 24.13-21)

According to Origen there is a faculty that makes judgments, but it has three divisions. One apprehends the sensibles, one apprehends the intelligibles, and one apprehends the theologicals. The objects of judgment for the mental faculty which apprehends material things are material things. The objects of judgment for the faculty of the mind which apprehends the intelligibles are the intelligibles. The objects of judgment for the faculty of the mind which apprehends the theologicals are the divine ousiai. Hence, there is knowledge derived from the senses, knowledge derived from the intelligibles, and knowledge derived from the theologicals. The last is a source of knowledge superior to the others because it is capable of an indirect apprehension of divine reality. In its pure form it is the mode of perception proper to God, but it is also possible for man. Hence, for a Middle Platonist such as Origen, the mens which apprehends the natura deitatis is called the mens intellectualis, and its product is sentire. The pistis-mens which apprehends the ta aisthêta-corporeo substantia is called the doxastikê pistis-mens sentire, and its product is doxa-sentire.[126]

2.   The proof utilized by Origen in this pericope is the epicheirêma. Not all the premises are listed or demonstrated in this chapter because the author carries a series of premises over from arguments in preceding pericopae. In (1.1.7 p. 23.15-24.7) the opponent's epicheirêma is presented, and in (1.1.7 p. 24.7-21) Origen's own proof is offered. The premise of the first argument runs:

> Si qui autem sunt qui mentem ipsam animamque corpus esse arbitrentur ...
>
> (1.1.7 p. 23.15f.)

The conclusions are:

> Nisi si forte aliquis putet quod, sicut forma ista corporea et habitus ipse
> aurium vel oculorum confert aliquid ad audiendum et ad videndum, et ut
> singula membra, quae a deo formata sunt, habent aliquid oportunitatis etiam
> ex ipsa formae qualitate ad hoc, quod naturaliter instituta sunt: ...
>
> (1.1.7 p. 23.22-26ff.)

The point is that judgment is the mind's assenting to an impression. The source of the impression are the things which are moved, i.e. sight, voice, smell, and touch. The mind in turn is directed to the things by which it is moved. This argument presents a picture of the mind working and receiving impressions from the physical world.

Origen does not argue that this model inadequately explains how the mind receives sense-impressions and constructs knowledge from them. He only argues against the proposition that a cognitive impression of this type yields apprehension of intelligible reality and a knowledge about God.

To counter this proposition he offers another argument at (1.1.7 p. 24.7-21). The premise is:

> Horum autem sensuum, de quibus supra diximus, quia multo melior sensus sit
> mentis, omnibus clarum est.
>
> (1.1.7 p. 24.7-9)

The conclusions are:

> Quomodo ergo non videtur absurdum, his quidem, quae inferiora sunt,
> substantias esse subiectas ad intendendum, huic autem virtuti, quae melior est,
> id est mentis sensui, nihil omnio subici substantiale, sed esse intellectualis
> naturae virtutem corporibus accidentem vel consequentem?
>
> (1.1.7 p. 24.9-13)

From these conclusions are deduced a series of others. Origen shifts his argument to focus upon the ta protreponta and the ta apotreponta involved if one assents to either proposal:

> Quod qui dicunt, sine dubio in contumelian eius substantiae, quae in ipsis
> melior est, haec proferunt; immo vero ex hoc etiam ad ipsum deum refertur
> iniuria, cum putant eum per naturam corpoream posse intellegi, quo scilicet
> secundum ipsos corpus sit et illud, quod per corpus potest intellegi vel sentiri;
> et nolunt hoc intellegi, quod propinquitas quaedam sit menti ad deum, cuius
> ipsa mens intellectualis imago sit, et per hoc possit aliquid de deitatis sentire
> natura, maxime si expurgatior ac segregatior sit a materia corporali.
>
> (1.1.7 p. 24.13-21)

Origen postulates an affinity between the knowing faculty directed toward the intelligibles and God. It is an image of God, and can perceive the divine nature. Arrayed against these ta protreponta are a series of ta apotreponta. If one accepted the postulate that knowing faculty directed to material things yielded a knowledge of God then they would not only disparage the better part of human nature, but would also insult God by implying that he is a body.

Origen's use of the argument from advantages and disadvantages is to persuade the audience of the correctness of his epistemological presuppositions. It is an attempt to force the audience to consider inducements and deterents. He wants them to refrain from assenting to his opponent's proposition because of the losses involved in agreeing to it. Likewise he wants them to assent to his proposition because it is useful to them. They are able to gain a correct insight into the true nature of Deity.

Origen wants his audience to know the criteria that determine his opponent's thesis as doubtful. His use of terms such as quomodo (1.1.7 p. 23.19; 24.11) and per quae facta sunt (1.1.7.23.26) calls to mind the explanation of the function of this topic by Quintilian:

In omnibus porro, quae fiunt quaeritur aut Quare. Aut Ubi? Aut Quando? Aut Per quae facta sunt? ...Nam fere versatur ratio faciendi circa bonorum adeptionem, incrementum, conservationem, usum, aut malorum evitationem, liberationem, tolerantiam; quae et in deliberando plurimum valent.

(In. Or. V. 10.32-33)

Origen's use of this topic is important because on the consideration of advantages and disadvantages he hopes to convince his audience of the cogency of his epistemological postulate. The use of this topic in rhetorical argumentation is as old as Aristotle and Anaximenes and appears in Cicero as well.[127] His comparationis locus compares the greater and lesser good. This is important because he links this argument with division and definition in a manner akin to the construct in (1.1.7):[128]

...in quibus spectantur haec: numerus, species, vis quaedam etiam ad res aliquas affectio.

(Top. XVIII.68)

This topic was also employed in Hellenistic circles. Syrianus and Sopater discuss this topic extensively in their commentaries on Hermogenes. This topic was thought to have been utilized in Attic oratory. The majority of examples are from Isocrates.[129] There are also examples from Lysias.[130] The Philip, which was a popular speech among the scholia exhumed at Alexandria and Oxyrhynchus, is the source of most of our examples for illustrations of the less evident goods in the Hellenistic-Roman Period. These parallels are important because these rhetors were among the models Origen copied for the construction of his own arguments. In addition they were known to his audience. Therefore, if he could formulate his argument along the lines of the masters he would have an additional basis from which to convince an audience of the validity of his proposition.

I,1,8 p. 24,22-26,14 Koe

1.   This chapter is divided into two sections (p. 24,22-25, 12; 25,13-26,14). In the first section he employs scripture as a proof-text for the arguments laid out in (I,1,6-7). In the second he provides an argument based upon the epistemological assumptions outlined in the antecedent pericopae.

For the first section Origen anticipates objections from the audience. It has been a while since scripture and apostolic teaching have been invoked to sustain his thesis. Thus, he brings forward a series of scriptural arguments to buttress his thesis. In the second section he returns to the line of argument laid out in (I,1,6-7). Once again the Platonic analogy of the line is utilized. The analogy offered here suggests that the upper division of the line, or knowledge of divine things, is known by the divine intellects. The Father knows the Son, and the Son the Father. His point is that since they are not sensible things they do not know one another through sense-perception. The argument again contrasts the opposites of _sentire_ and _cognoscere_ (I,1,8 p. 25,16-26,14). Let us turn to an analysis of how Origen's argument unfolds rhetorically.

The chapter also constitutes a defense of Origen's epistemology. Rufinus has preserved Origen's use of the terms _videre_, _corpus_, _cognoscere_, and _intellectus_. The distinction Origen focuses upon is between sensible and intelligible intellection. The thesis he argues is that "to see" is an activity of the lowest level of knowing, while "to know" is the activity of the second level of knowing. Hence it is incorrect to assert, as the corporealists do, that by means of sensible perception one knows Divine Being.

Rhetorically, Origen employs the topics of authority and opposition to argue his case. His appeal to authority is two-fold. On the one hand, he attempts to ground his epistemic presuppositions upon scriptural premises. On the other hand, he appeals to the authority of reason, and the cogent argument that follows from his epistemic presuppositions.

Origen's use of the topic _ek kriseôs_, thus, has parallels to Apsines' understanding of the topic as well as to Maximus Planoudes'.[131] This topic was among the _antikeimena topoi_, and generally utilized in rebuttal.[132] Hence the argument _ek kriseôs_ complements the argument _ek tôn enantiôn_. The criteria for determining the _agatha_ is from the evidence of the _palaioi martures_.[133] Origen utilizes the authority of scripture and reason to argue against the thesis that one knows God through the faculty of sensible intellection. These argumentative topics were commonly used in _auxêsis_.[134] Their function is to establish what Origen wants his audience to assume as a fact. This is the use of Platonic metaphysical assumptions with scripture to define the nature of God. The use of the argument from authority establishes the validity of his enterprise. His use of the argument from opposites forces his audience to consider the thesis proposed by his opponents, and reject it.

This chapter also represents a good example of what the rhetoricians called an *entasis apo tou enantiou.*[135] The use of these topics has had a long history in Greek, Hellenistic, and Roman rhetoric. Aristotle, in his <u>Topics</u>, speaks to the dialectical use of this topic.[136] Aristotle's definition is repeated by Anaximenes, Cicero, Quintilian, Apsines, Minucianus, and Maximus Planoudes.[137] These topical forms were employed extensively among the Attic Ten. The most copied orators at Alexandria in the Hellenistic period, Demosthenes, Isocrates, and Lysias, were thought to have utilized them.

It was common to make an appeal to the gods and the authority of wise men to argue <u>enantiou.</u>[138] Origen topically argues in the same manner, but substitutes the revelation of the Christian God and the teachings of scripture for those of Zeus and the Delphic oracle.

2.   Origen employs the <u>epicheirêma</u> to present his argument. He does not list all his premises. He carries them over from the arguments of preceding pericopae. The major premise of his proof is:

(1)   Vide ergo si non etiam apostulos hoc idem ait, cum de Christo loquitur dicens: "Qui est imago invisibilis dei, primogenitus omnis creaturae."

(1.1.8 p. 25,2-4)

The minor premises are:

(2)   Non enim, ut quidam putant, natura dei alicui visibilis est et aliis invisibilis; non enim dixit apostulus "imago invisibilis dei" hominibus aut "invisibilis" peccatoribus, sed valde constanter pronuntiat de ipsa natura dei dicens "imago invisibilis dei." Sed et Iohannes in evangelio dicens: "Deum nemo vidit umquam"

(3)   manifeste declarat omnibus, qui intellegere possunt, quia nulla natura est, cui invisibilis sit deus; non quasi qui visibilis quidem sit per naturam et velut fragilioris creaturae evadat atque excedat aspectum, / sed quoniam naturaliter videri impossibilis est.

(1.1.8 p. 25.4-12)

The conclusion presented in Jn. 1:18:

(4)   "Deum nemo visit umquam."

(1.1.8 p. 25,8)

also serves as the premise from which Origen deduces the conclusions of (1.1.8 p. 25, 13-26,14). Hence, from (I,1,8 p. 25,8) through (I,1,8 p. 26,14), we have a series of conclusions deduced from the major premise of (I,1,8 p. 25, 2-4), the minor premise of (I, 1,8 p. 25, 4-7), and the conclusion of (I,1,8 p. 28,8). This long construct constitutes the metrical syllogism of (I, 1,8).

Origen's epicheirêma is formulated as a refutation of the arguments:

Verum istae assertiones minus fortasse auctoritatis habere videantur apud eos, qui ex sanctis scripturis de rebus divinis institui volunt et inde sibi approbare quaerunt, quomodo natura dei supereminit corporum naturam.

(1.1.8 p. 24,22-25,2)

and

Quodsi requiras a me, quid etiam de ipso unigenito sentiam, se ne ipsi quidem bisibilem dicam naturam dei, quae naturaliter "invisibilis" est: non tibi statim vel impium videatur esse vel absurdum rationem quippe dabimus consequenter; (Sicut enim incongruum est dicere quod possit filius videre patrem, ita inconveniens est opinari quod spiritua sanctus possit videre filium.)

(1.1.8 p. 25.13-26.2)

3.   Origen's point is that God is "spiritual" and non-corporeal. He argues that his definition is in agreement with those of Paul and John. The claim that God's nature is invisible is demonstrable from the distinction between videre and cognoscere. This distinction, in turn, rests upon the epistemological and ontological presuppositions of Origen's Middle Platonic philosophy. From both assumptions Origen asserts that God is invisible, and not perceptible to the faculty of sensible intellection:

Ex quo manifeste indicatur quod quicquid inter corporeas naturas videre et videri dicitur, hoc inter patrem et filium cognoscere dicitur et cognosci, per virtutem scientiae, non per visibilitatis fragilitatem.

(I,1,8 p. 26,9-11)

I,1.9 p. 26,15-27,17 Koe

1.   This chapter is the final argument of the first syggramma (I,1,1-9). It is a continuation of the arguments of the antecedent pericopae, and addresses a question concerning the locus of mind in the human soul, and its origin. This argument is again directed against the Stoic definition of the human soul. Origen proposes the argument that although the mind is located in the heart it is not a corporeal entity (cf. SVF II, 56; II, 81). The higher energies of the soul, or better said its intelligible functions and activities are not corporeal, but non-corporeal.

Origen rests the validity of his interpretation upon an asomatic reading of Prov. 2:5. If read in this way, Prov. 2:5 (conveniently altered from standard LXX readings) means:

Sensum divinum invenies=aisthêsin theian aurêsis.[139]

(I,1,9 p. 27,8)

Rhetorically (1.1.9) is a continuation and culmination of the argument of (1.1.5-8). The topics utilized in this chapter are ek tou sumbainein ean ê tauton hoti kai ex sumbainei tauta, and apo tou onomatos.[140] The type of argument utilized is the epicheirêma. The genus causarum is forensic. The pars orationis is the confirmatio.

(1.1.9) constitutes a concluding argument to the thesis presented in (1.1.8). Again the focus is on the distinction between videre and intellegere-cognoscere (aisthêsis and noêsis). Although the topics utilized are that of concluding the identity of antecedents from the identity of results, and meanings derived from the meaning of a name, the topics of (1.1.8) are still operative here. These are the arguments from authority and opposites. The topical scheme which dominated the previous pericope dominates this one.

The pericope begins with the argument ek tou sumbainein... tauta. This argument is utilized to assert that the underlying principles of this argument are the same as the preceding ones in (1.1.8). Inference from results or consequents to antecedents means that the results of (1.1.9) are identical to those of (1.1.8). The two assertions are regarded as equivalent, or the same in their effect for purposes of argument. They both lead to the same result or consequent. Indeed, one can be put for the other if need be. This argument was known to Minucianus, who called it apo tou emperiechomenou.[141] Maximus Planoudes defines it as the argument ek metalepseôs.[142] In effect, the later Hellenistic rhetoricians characterize the topic as that of cause and effect. The argument was known among the Attic Ten and utilized by Demosthenes, Isocrates, and Lysias. Likewise Origen argues that, if one accepts the conclusions of (1.1.8), one is compelled to accept those of (1.1.9). Given the popularity of this argument among the Attic canon studied and copied at Alexandria, it is possible that Origen was aware of the many examples of the topic in the Timocrates and the Antidosis.[143]

The topos apo tou onomatos is also employed. It is simply a play on names. The intent is to draw an inference from the signification of a name. Aristotle defines it as a logical topic that is akin to the rhetorical. He tells us that the use of the topic is for the consideration of the derivation and significance of names.[144] Maximus Planoudes comments on the use of the topic as do Cicero and Quintilian.[145] In all these testimonies the suggestion is that arguments can be drawn from the meaning of names. Origen employs it to argue that his incorporeal designation is compatible with the deeper meaning of Scripture.

2.   Origen's argument is straightforward. From the major premise:

"Beati mundo corde, quoniam ipsi deum videbunt."

(1.1.9 p. 26.15-16)

Origen presents a series of minor premises which run through the remainder of the pericope (1.1.9 p. 26.16-27.14). His interpretation of (1.1.9 p. 26.15-16) is:

...nam quid aliud est "corde deum videre," nisi secundum id, quod supra exposuimus, mente eum intellegere atque cognoscere?

(1.1.9 p. 26.17-27.1)

This play on the names of the organs of sense and soul permits Origen to again offer his epistemological postulate as the correct one. The interpretation and play on names is predicated on the antecedent arguments of (1.1.8). It is his use of antecedent premises and conclusions that makes the argument of (1.1.9) rhetorically cogent and conceptually sound.

3.   By means of this topic he moves from the notion of the sensum divinum (theian aisthêsin) as encompassing all the faculties of intellection, sensible and intelligible, to the distinction between the genus of knowing which is:

...mortale, corruptible, humanum...

and the genus of knowing which is:

...immortale et intellectuale, quod nunc "divinum" nominavit.

(1.1.9 p. 27.8-11)

With this, he concludes:

Hoc ergo sensu divino non oculorum, sed "cordis mundi," quae est mens, deus videri ab his, qui digni sunt, potest. Cor sane pro mente, id est pro intellectuali virtute nominari in omnibus scripturis novis ac veteribus abudanter invenies.

(1.1.9 p. 27.11-14)

By means of this proof Origen utilizes his topics to further demonstrate the thesis offered in the previous pericope. In addition, he further repudiates the epistemological and ontological presuppositions of his opponents. With this final assault he concludes the first section of his inventio. He presents a defense of his theory of knowledge, and demonstrates that this tripartite theory of noês has its ground in scripture itself.

To summarize: this chapter functions as a conclusion to the arguments concerning the nature of God the Father and the nature and functions of knowledge. Within this short chapter we are given a brief review of the arguments which precede it. Origen presents his view of the asomatic nature of scripture (P 8), and his postulate that scripture is the final criterion of knowledge (P 1-4). He combines these with his Platonic epistemological and ontological premises to argue for the incorporeality of the human and divine intellect, and the types of knowledge it yields. This chapter recapitulates the arguments of the preceding pericope in solid rhetorical fashion.

5. Conclusion

Book One, Chapter One, concludes Origen's first series of arguments on God the Father. In these pericopae he attempts to refute a Stoic definition of God the Father, and the epistemology associated with it, and to defend a Platonic theology and epistemology.

The basis for refutation and defense is biblical scripture. The strategy Origen employs is scriptural demonstration (apodeixis euaggaelikê) based upon his theory of rhetorical logic.

Origen's knowledge and use of the persuasive art of rhetoric for the demonstration of a Christian first principles presents us with a picture of a Christian fully absorbed in the intellectual culture of his time. We have no vision of a figure outside of the Hellenistic world of intellectual discourse or a view of a Christianity situated on the frontiers of the cultural world of Alexandria. Indeed quite the opposite is the case. In Origen we meet a Christian philosopher and rhetor of first rank fully conversant in the subtleties of Academic nuance and Sophistic erudition. When we read his works we encounter a vibrant intellect actively translating the principles of Christianity in the language of Greek metaphysics, and through the languages of Graeco-Roman literature and rhetoric.

Origen's Periarchôn (De Principiis) represents not only an expression of late Christian Middle Platonism. It reflects much more. Through the fractured mirror of its redaction and fragments we see the consummation of a trajectory of Middle Academic thinking which began with Philo, and continued in Clement. In the mangled pages that are left to us we see an artful mode of composition wielded by Origen to proclaim the principles of a Christian Platonic philosophy, and disclaim those of a Christian Gnostic and Stoic philosophy.

Studies on the Philonic corpus show that Philo employed the same conceptual system, and modes of literary and rhetorical composition, to present the principles of Judaic Platonism in the first century as Origen did in the third century. Our brief examination of Origen's major philosophical work illustrates that from conceptual as well as literary and rhetorical vantage points a proponent of Christian Platonism continues and consumates this trajectory of thought begun by Philo. Hence, we offer the Periarchôn (De Principiis) as an example of how Origen, following in the footsteps of Philo and Clement, presents a demonstration of Platonic first principles from biblical scripture. Origen's apodeixis euaggelikê represents the completion of the first attempts at a apodeixis biblikê offered by Philo, and a apodeixis euaggelikê presented by Clement.

EPILOGUE

The time has now come to tie together, as best we can, the scattered threads of this book, and to face more directly than hitherto some of the fundamental changes of attitude, or shifts of emphasis, which met us in our study. These changes are hard to define and their connection can only be explained with difficulty. In the strict sense these changes defy definition, and the connection between them cannot be explained. It can only be exemplified indirectly through the philosophies of these thinkers. At the deepest levels of experience, in definitions of the nature of God and the economy of the universe, in new insights into the powers of God and their limitations, the changing scene of history has its focus and justification. We have seen in the preceding chapters many changes which seem to be primarily matters of philosophical speculation. We must now try to see them from within the context of the hellenistic philosophy of the early Empire. Necessarily we shall be concerned with generalizations. From these we draw the scattered experiences of an age, whose thoughts become the common property of later ages, and hence the property of our intellectual history.

We begin by reviewing very briefly the changes which stand out in the course we have pursued. We have seen the enlargement of the intellectual boundaries of Judaism and Christianity, and the realm of the thinkable for these religious traditions. At the beginning of the first century a deeply hellenized Judaism in Alexandria, Judaism represented in Philo, stands face to face with Hellenism and Hellenic Platonism and becomes an expression of both. Alexandrian Judaism and the philosophical activity of Philo prepared the way for Clement and Origen to express Alexandrian Christianity in the cultural system of Hellenism and the conceptual systems of Judaic and Hellenic Platonism.

These new views reflected the Platonization of first Judaism, and then Christianity, at Alexandria. Philo, Clement, and Origen looked at the universe and speculated about its origin, constitution, and destiny in light of the philosophical proclamation of scripture. They discussed, with all the confidence of a young philosophy, the relation of God to the universe, how God and his creation are known, and how God's revelation reveals a logically demonstrable metaphysical system. The visions which would later stir the imaginations of Gregory and Aquinas, Hallevy and Maimonides, were emerging into the light of day. The lessons of Philo, and his heirs Clement and Origen, would bear an abundant fruit.

These thinkers brought their religions to the frontiers of knowledge. They came to grips with the problematics of ancient metaphysics, knowledge, and dialectic, and hammered out what would become normative Judaic and Christian philosophy. Formative Jewish and Christian Platonism presented a picture of a created world in God's image, of God's limitedness, of the world's goodness, and of a final merging of the all in all in God.

The extension of the boundaries of knowledge was accompanied by the enlarging of the field of the knowable beyond the confines of nation and ethnos. The fruits of the intellectual changes of the first three centuries of the common era are to be seen in the cosmopolitanism of Jewish and Christian thought in the Middle Academy. The world of ideas reflected the world of the early Empire and the perpetual passing back and forth of litigants on the roads leading to Rome, to Edessa along the trade routes, or to Alexandria from distant ports. They were a part of a commonwealth of shared conceptual systems.

This was expressed in the study of God, of cosmos, and of thought with the linking of this effort to a metaphysical understanding of reality. We also noticed the fascination and authority with dialectic, which from the small beginnings of a school discipline attained the eminence as an instrument for the demonstration of truth. It is in the passion for persuasion and logic that we come nearest to finding a common factor in the manifold changes we have noticed. It expressed this striving toward universality. It knew nothing of time and place, and it absorbed all local peculiarities. It became what a later age would call the "universal ordinary", the bond between all subjects and the solvent of all metaphysical difficulties. The God who stands above space and time is amenable to the processes of dialectic.

The change in emphasis from the parochial to the universal, first in Jewish Platonism and then in Christian Platonism in the emergence of systematic thought, was paralleled by another. This is the change from the mere stating of Torah and Gospel to its philosophical explication and amplification. The contrast is not merely a literary one, though it is in literature it is most clearly seen. It is a reflection of a general change of attitude which found expression in many different ways. The study of scripture is now a seeking and a journeying to grasp philosophical revelation. Men begin to order their understandings of revelation in accordance with the conceptual system of Platonism and explain revelation in the language of the cultural system which underlies it. The spiritual ideal becomes movement to knowledge and the ascent of the soul to God. It meets us on all sides in the writings of these first Jewish and Christian Platonists. The imagery of movement towards that which itself remains unmoved, lays hold of the philosophical imagination. This was the beginning of a Pilgrim's Progress that passes well beyond the confines of our study.

This critical period of discovery was in the period from Philo to Origen. It occurred between the events of Actium and Dobruja. We must remember that these thinkers never met. Philo exercised no direct, and little indirect influence on Origen. Their points of likeness, which are striking, have nothing to do with personality. They are based upon the conceptual systems which both accepted as divinely sanctioned, and to which both gave luminous expression. They were followers of Plato, the student of Moses and the Christ, Plato. It was to this philosophical tradition that they turned in order to understand their experience and their world. With these thinkers we enter into an inner world of movement and a struggle to understand the wisdom of God. In their writings the static act of acceptance is replaced by a movement of the understanding, in which there is no resting place short of final illumination, or gnosis. An energy meets us in their attempts to gain union with God.

Revelation has a metaphysical order to it, and a dialectical mode of expression. This urge toward a greater measure of knowledge ran like fire through this emerging vision of Judaism and Christianity. Philo was the founder of this ardent and effusive disclosure, but for the men of what would become Christian antiquity, at least in the Greek East, the patrons were preeminently Origen and his teacher Clement. These thinkers would occupy the central position in the philosophical life of the fourth century and beyond through the Cappadocian Fathers. It was Christian Platonism above all which communicated to the ancient world the biblical vision begun by Philo.

We have said that the Jewish and Christian Middle Platonists of Alexandria were energetic thinkers. This might appear as a modern assessment, but it is meant quite in the ancient sense. [They transformed the religious world views of their respective traditions by expressing the central symbols of their faiths through a scientific conceptual system. The study of their scriptures was undertaken consciously and to a degree systematically, and their efforts would transform Judaism and Christianity in late antiquity. This "Platonic" program was a process in self-knowledge which culminated in divine knowledge. Its metaphor was the ascent of the soul to God. It is an ascent in which each step in knowledge proceeds by an intelligible development from the one which has gone before. It is a movement through self-knowledge to knowledge of the world to a knowledge of God. This began as a way of life for a few isolated men. It culminated as a way of life for many in antiquity.]

This power to think new thoughts is most impressive, and it was clearly more than the mere expression of the hellenization of Judaism and Christianity as many scholars have claimed. They arranged their thoughts in such a manner because they were certain that such an arrangement reflected the thinking of their God. This power of Philo, Clement, and Origen to give a metaphysically coherent expression to human experience and divine revelation was a turning point for the history of western thought.

This union of philosophical learning and religious expression is something that become universal everywhere in Judaism and Christianity in late antiquity. A world molded in the conceptual systems of Greek metaphysics emerged in the formative period of Judaism and Christianity. It would culminate in the Platonization of Christianity, in the Christianization of Rome, and in a new period in western philosophy and history.

NOTES

Preface:

[1]See J. Owens, The Doctrine of Being in the Aristotelian Metaphysics, Toronto: 1951, ix-x.

Introduction:

[1]See H. Wolfson, Philo, i-ii, Cambridge: 1948; A. Altaner, Patrologie, Freiburg: 1938.

[2]See J. Daniélou, Origène, Paris: 1948.

[3]See H. Wolfson, The Philosophy of the Church Fathers, Cambridge: 1956; Philo, i-ii, Cambridge: 1948.

[4]See P. Merlan, From Platonism to Neoplatonism, The Hague: 1953; M. Pohlenz, Die Stoa, Freiburg: 1943.

[5]To this extent this work has as two of its paradigms J. Dillon's The Middle Platonists, Ithaca: 1977.; P. Moraux, Der Aristotelismus bei den Griechen, Berlin: 1972.

[6]According to Kant the nature of reason's activity is synthesis (KrV., 10,15 A). Synthesis is based upon the common element between the Forms of sensibility and of understanding. It completes itself in three stages: 1) sensations into perceptions; 2) perceptions into experience of the natural world of reality; and 3) the combination of judgements of experience into metaphysical knowledge. If we take Kant's model analogically, then we see Jewish and Christian philosophers using the active synthesizing forms of Platonic thought to arrange and organize their experiences of the world. They see in their Bibles, at least philosophically, a Platonic universe headed by a Platonic first principle, and deity and scripture are understood through Platonic modes of ideation. Through the Platonic conceptual system a wide range of intellectual, emotional, and moral experience finds systematic arrangement for Philo, Clement, and Origen.

[7]See Winston-Dillon, Two Treatises of Philo of Alexandria, Chico: 1983; Lilla, Clement of Alexandria, Oxford: 1972; Harl, Orgeniana, 12 (1975), 11-32; cf. de Faye, Origène, I-III, Paris: 1923-28; Koch, Pronoia und Paideusis, Berlin: 1932.; Bowersock, The Greek Sophists, Oxford: 1978.

[8]Cf. Winston-Dillon, Two Treatises of Philo, 5-180.

[9]Cf. Dorival, Origeniana, 12 (1975), 33-45; Simonetti, Rivista di filologia e d'istruzione classica, 40 (1962), 274-290; 372-392; Crouzel-Simonetti, Origene Traite des Principles, i-iv, Paris: 1978-83.

[10]It has been widely acknowledged that first Jewish and then Crhistian Platonic thought at Alexandria laid the foundation for subsequent Christian philosophical thought

in late antiquity. Recent scholarship has begun to view Rabbinic Judaism as a conceptual system based upon metaphysical principles. This research is in its infancy, but parallels have been established between the logical principles of Graeco-Roman and Rabbinic syllogistic, See, Neusner, Judaism and Scripture: The Evidence of Leviticus Rabbah, Chicago: 1985. This shows that on a fundamental level there is no disparity between the formal systems of logic in Rabbinic Judaism and late Hellenistic-Roman philosophy, cf. Berchman, "Mishnah Tractate Tohorot (M. 1:104): At Study in Formal Logic" Approaches to Ancient Judaism V, Chico: 1985. The organization of experience and the world in the Judaisms and Christianities of late antiquity is based upon common conceptual frameworks. This study examines the similarities and differences between Judaism and Christianity at Alexandria. Further studies shall focus upon the common conceptual framework which underlies Rabbinic Judaism and Judaisms and Christianities of the Graeco-Roman world of the first through seventh centuries.

Part One: Theoretic or Physics

Philo

[1] e.g., E.R. Dodds, "The Parmenides of Plato and the Origin of the Neoplatonic "One," CQ (1928) pp. 129-142; A.N.M. Rich, "The Platonic Ideas as the Thoughts of God," Mn, 7 (1954), pp. 123-133; A.H. Armstrong, Plontinus, Amsterdam: 1967, pp. 49-82; W. Theiler, Die Vorbereitung des Neuplatonismus, Berlin: 1932. These major works on the Platonism of late antiquity start from the assumption that the problem of the relation of the ideas to the intellect is the major problematic which occupies the variant strands of Platonism. It does so only if one views the history of Platonic thought from the vantage point of Plotinus backwards. Although it was a major concern for Plotinus it cannot be assumed that it was for all Platonists who precede Plotinus. While for some it was, e.g., Albinus, for others it was not, e.g., Philo, Clement, Origen. This failure to recognize the manifold problematics grappled with by Middle Platonists lies in the tendency of scholars to view the platonica minora within the context of later Neo Platonic systems. The result of this approach are the exaggeration and/or misrepresentation of Middle Platonic issues and concepts.

[2]"The Nature of God in the Quod Deus," Two Treatises of Philo of Alexandria, Chico: 1983, p. 218ff. Dillon's analysis supports my thesis concerning the categorical background to Philo's nous theology.

[3]This consequence is developed more fully by Nicostratus and Plotinus, cf. Simpl. In Cat. I. 19ff. p. 26,22ff.; Ennead VI, 1-3. For the Neo Pythagorean, Middle Platonic, and Periptetic view of the categories, see: T.A. Szlezak, Pseudo-Archytas Über die Katagorien, parallels p. 22, 31, 31.5 in Thesleff; R.E. Witt, Albinus, p. 66ff concerning Archytas' doctrine. The Neo Pythagoreans and early Middle Platonists take for granted that the categories concern only the sensible, and not the intelligible worlds. Cf. Dillon, MP., 133-135; 180.

[4]Philo's arrangement and use of the categories has a complicated background. Szlezak argues that the categories were criticized and reformulated in the earliest Middle Platonic period and one pseudo-Archytas. Working from the formal developments made by the first generaion of commentators on the Categories, including Andronicus, he asserts that the categories are applicable only to the sensible world. Furthermore, he separates the postpraedicamenta from the categories proper. Dillon notes that Philo's arrangement and definition of the function of the categories agrees with pseudo-Archytas's, cf. Dillon, MP. 180.

[5]This explanation is presented along the lines of models extant in Antiochus, cf. Seneca, Ep. 113, 16. Every individual substance, though a part of the universal substance, has a quality which individuates it and distinguishes it from every other:

> Inter cetera, propter quae mirabile divini artificis ingenium est, hoc quoque existimo, et quod in tanta copia rerum numquam in idem incidit; itiam quae similia videntur, cum contuleris, diversa sunt. Tot fecit genera foliorum: nulla non sua proprietate signatum. Tot animalia: nullius magnitudo cum altero convenit, utique aliquid interest. Exegit a se, ut quae alia erant, et dissimilia essent et inparia; virtutes omnes, ut dicitis, pares sunt.

This doctrine of the categories was also a central component of later Stoic thought, Pohlenz, J. 107 n. 3. Philo understands the physical categories Stoically. By means of the categories he defines the things of the mundus sensibilis. His procedures preclude the possibility of the physical categories being used for a definition of the intelligible world, and of God.

[6]Dexippus, In Categ. p. 31, 15 ed. Spengel.

[7]Philo calls them the duo eidopoious epi tês autês ousias amechanon sustênai, see n. 4, cf. Ae. Mun., pp. 528-529.

[8]Heres, 188; Fug., 110, 112. The Logos, collectively, is immanent in the sensible world and holds it together.

[9]This is why he is called apoios, cf. Leg. Alleg., I 47; QD 301. As the first principle he is without any of the 'marks' which distinguish derivitive entities. The mediation between God and the world is gained by distinguishing the essence from the power of God, who through his Logos creates and binds together the universe. The primal god is called the One, the Monad, the really existant (e.g., Deus, 11; Heres, 187). At times God is spoken of in even more negative terms as the entity superior to the One, the Monad, and the primal archê itself, cf. QE, II 68; Vita Con., 2.

[10]cf. De Op. Mun., 17-19; De Cher., 49. This fits a pattern common to Middle Platonic definitions of the second principle, Theiler, Vorbereitung, pp. 15-16, 18-19, 39-40; Merlan From Platonism to Neoplatonism, p. 55; Loenen, Mn. 4, 10 (1957), pp. 44-45; Lilla, Clement, pp. 199-204.

[11]Although Philo probably worked within an understanding of the categories as received in the school traditions of the platonica minora it is also clear that he, in turn, reformulated this model. Philo is in fact reacting at various points to the Pythagoreanization of the categories at the hands of pseudo-Archytas and perhaps

Eudorus. He 'improves' on these earlier formultions by redefining them in terms of his understandings of the categories. These parallel Stoic understandings cf. SVF II 449, 473, 316, 397). That each substance has distinctive qualities seems to explain his notion that ousia=hylê, and also why he moves from the categories of substance to quality, and then on to quantity, relation and so on. Each substance, i.e., a man, contains an individuating quality which differentiates him from every other man. This is a play on the Stoic notion of the duo idiôs poinoi (SVF II 397, cf. Zeller, Phil. d. Gr. III, I pp. 99-100 n. 2). Zeller explains it in this manner:

> Da der idiôs poios ein Ding von allen anderen unterscheidet, versteht es sich von selbst, dass wie Chrysippus bei Philon aetern. m. 951 b (501M.c. 9 Bern) sagt, duo eidopoious (was = idious poious) epi tês autês ousias amechanon sustênai.

Coulsen discusses the passage and states that the idios poios distinguishes a thing from every other (Philo IX LCB, Harvard: 1954, pp. 528-529). Thus, although there is one substance man, an individual man presents himself he undergoes a series of changes, i.e., qualitatively, quantitatively, relationally, and so on, to become an individual thing. This presentation by Philo is Stoic in dimensions, and reflects his Stoicized use of what originally were Peripatetic categories. This reformulation complements his Stoicized epistemology, and presents a model whereby he is able to perceive how matter is formed by explaining the process by means of the categories. cf. Leg. Alleg., III 175; De Plan., 2-3.

[12]Philo dwells on the connection between logic and metaphysics. this is usally in terms of the Logos, e.g., Fuga, 12-13.

[13]For the arithmetical aspects of Philo's first principles, see Moehring, Arithmology, pp. 191-228, esp. 215-218. e.g., De Op. Mun., 100; 102; Heres, 156.

[14]Although there is no direct evidence that he did this, statements such as Cher., 49 suggest that he worked off of the Timaeus. God is:

asomatôn ideôn asomatos chôra

and the mind of God is considered the chôra of the Ideas. In any case the Ideas are a product of the act of divine noêsis, cf. De Op. Mun., 17-19. (Plutarch and Albinus employ the same language of definition, cf. De Plac. Philos., 88, 2d; Did., p. 163, 12-13, 27-30, as does Clement, e.g., Strom., v. 16. 3.).

[15]See Wolfson, Philo, ii, 101-110; Dillon, Middle Platonists, 178-180; cf. Two Treatises of Philo, 218-221.

[16]The description of the divine logoi as dynameis, and the Logos as the sum-total fo the 'powers' or dynamis of God is an extrapolation on the Platonic notion of the ideai as dynameis. They represent the activity of God throughout the universe, cf. Migr. 182. This Logos-dynamiscomprehends the universe in itself, cf. Ling., 137. It appears that Philo understood these powers in the mathematical sense of the term, i.e. as numbers. This is alluded to in Heres 156 where God is described as employing all numbers and forms in the bringing of the world to completion. If Philo equates ideai, logoi, and dynameis then they are the formal principles which enter into the composition of things thereby

giving them form. The powers give mathematical order and harmony to the universe, e.g. Fug., 94ff. They then enter into the world, and hold it together, e.g. QE., II 68. The owers like the ideas have a transcendent as well as immanent stage. In the former they function as paradigms for the sensible world. In the latter they function as that which penetrates the sensible world giving it its structure. In the intelligible world they are defined in Neopythatorean fashion. In the sensible world they are interpreted in a Stoic fashion, cf. Diogenes Laertius, Vit., VII 147.

[17]There is evidence which suggests that this notion goes back to Antiochus, but he never expliticly states this formula. In CD VII 28 Augustine reports Varro stating that the Ideas spring from the mind of God. Since Augustine works from the testimonies of Cicero it is possible that Antiochuse knew of this doctrine.

[18]The Logos is spoken of as being filled by God with his immaterial powers (Somn., I 62), and as being the charioteer of the powers (Fug., 191). It is from the Logos that the powers go forth, not the Father (QE., II 68).

[19]Cf. Witt, Albinus, 67-68.

[20]Cf. Wolfson, Philo, ii, 101-105.

[21]Following Dillon, Middle Platonists, 180.

[22]See Heinze, Xen., 37f.

[23]See Dodds, CQ, 22 (1928), 129-142.

[24]See Dillon, Middle Platonists, 155.

[25]See Jones, CPH 21 (1926), 317-326.

[26]Cf. Theiler, VN., 15-16; 18-19; 39-40; cf. Heinze, Xenocrates, fr. 34, 171; fr. 15, 164-165; Rich, Mn., IV,7 (1954), 126.

[27]Although this notion may may go back to Xenocrates, cf. Heinze, Xenocrates, 51.

[28]See Lilla, Clement, 191-192.

[29]Although they are immaterial powers. Against Pohhenz, NGA phil.-hist. Kl. (1943), 158ff. See Pohlenz, Die Stoa i. 417-418.

[30]Cf. Lilla, C., 194-195..

[31]This was common Middle Academic and Perpatetic teaching. See Bäumker, PLM., 23 (1887) 518; Andreson, Logos and Nomos, 276-278.; Lilla, Clement, 197-198.

[32]See Lilla, C., 198 n. 2 for the background to Philo's use of the Timaeus.

[33]Following Theiler VN., 16ff.

[34]Cf. Dillon, MP., 138.

[35]For the distinction between The Stoic and Academic doctrines, See Witt, A., 71-73.

[36]See Dillon, MP., 160. Although the immediate origin is not clear this type of diairesis was introduced by Speusippus, cf. Taran, S., 64-72, and utilized by Antiochus, cf. Witt, A., 36-38.

[37]Winston-Dillon, Two Treatises of Philo, 218-219; Dillon, MP., 82.

Clement

[38]See W.H., A., 38-39.

[39]Numerous works have been written on the relation of Clement to Philo. For the best summation of their relationship, at least philosophically, See Lilla, C., 199-226.

[40]This was first noted by Dodds, CQ 22 (1928), 129-142. cf. Osborn, C., 17-18; Lilla, C., 206 n.1.

[41]On Clement's Lypostasis doctrine, See Wolfson, PCF., 208; Lilla, C., 204.

[42]This notion has its background in the Jewish-Alexandrine philosophy prior to Philo, See Lilla, C., 208-209. After Philo it appears in early second century Christian circles. On its use by Justin Martyr see Heinisch, EP., 145-148. For its use by Clement, See Lilla, C., 208-209.

[43]According to Wolfson the term "proceeds" (proelthôn) is a technical term used by the apologists to describe the generation of the Logos from the Father, cf. PCF., 208; Orbe, Ab., 100.606; Lilla, C., 204.

[44]See Lilla, C., 204-209.

[45]In opposition to Wolfson, PCF., 208ff.

[46]See Dillon, TTP., 219 n.6 on the relation of Clement to Philo and the early Neo Py Tagoreans.

[47]On the background to these notions in Clement, See Witt, A., 36, 60; Moraux, AG., 126.

[48]See Witt, A., 36.

[49]See Moraux, AG., 126.

[50]See Witt, A., 36-38. cf. 60.

[51]Following the reconstruction by Moraux, AG., 126-132. esp. 129-130.

[52]See Taran, S., 32-47 for Speusippus' diairetical theory.

[53]The claim is that Clement employs as a kindred notion of similarity to Speusippus. For Speusippus, see Taron, S., 26; 50; 53-56; 60ff.; 64-65. cf. Moraux, AG., 129-130.

[54]For the transmission of this doctrine in the New Lyceum, see Moraux, AG., 107-108; 157; 183-185; 157-160.

[55]See Owens, DB., 59.

[56]Cf. Alexander Aphrodisias, In Met., 241.9; Asclepius, In Met., 227-2-3; 231.12-15, 25. At least this was the case in the New Lyceum.

[57]For the relation of Clement to the Middle Academy and New Lyceum on this question, see Lilla, C., 189, 199.

[58]For the Middle Platonic context of Clement's proposal, see Lilla's reconstruction, 199-226.

[59]The background to this concept is traced by Heinisch, EP., 145-148.

[60]For the correspondence between Clement and Philo, See Wolfson, P., i, 210; 267; cf. 230; cf. Stählin, ii. 317.

[61]For the correspondence between Clement and Philo, see Früchtel, BPLW., 57 (1937), 591; Stählin, ii. 336.

[62]This follows from Lilla's analysis, cf. C., 205-207. God as arithmos, and the Logos as panta hen, are the measurement and center of all things.

[63]See Witt, A., 124-126.

[64]See Lilla, C., 191-192.

[65]Cf. Theiler, VN., 18f.

[66]See Lilla, C., 193ff.

[67] For the correspondence between Clement and Albinus, see Früchtel, BPLW., 57 (1937), 592; cf. Stählin ii. 385.

[68]On the Tim., 28b; cf. Andresen, LN., 280-283; Walzer Galeni Compendium Timaei Platonis, 10-11 shows that diverse figures as Gaben, Plutarch, Atticus, and Alexander held this view.

[69]Cf. Zeller, PG., ii.1 722, 727; ii.2 322 n.1.; Weiss, UJ; 30 n.3.

[70]See Lilla, C., 199-226.

Albinus

[71]See Witt, A., 125-127; 66-68; Dillon, MP., 279-285.

[72]See Koch, PP., 243-268.

[73]Cf. Weber, Zt., 27, 162; 5-6; On the conciliation of the teachings of Plato and Aristotle in the third Century, see Plotius, Bibl. Codex. 214. 172a (P6, 103. 701c 9ff.); 251.461a (P6 104. 77d 1ff.); cf. Dodds, En., V, 25; Theiler, VN., 2; Weber, Zt., 27, 160.

[74]This is in opposition to the theory proposed by Witt that the Didaskalikos is "an exposition and not a criticism of the Platonic philosophy", A., 2.

[75]See Witt, A., 126.

[76]Dillon argues the contrary, cf. MP., 284. He sets up a distinction between an unorganized and organized Soul, and the identity between the Nous, as demiurge, end this organized Soul. Loenen's reconstruction appears valid. The Soul has an intellect, and this Nous is actualized by God, cf. Mr., iv.9 (1956), 296-319.

[77]We translate noêsis as "apprehension" at Did., 164-36.

[78]See Armstrong, Er., V. 402-404.

[79]See Aristotle, Metaphys., 1080b 27-28; 1083a 21-22; 1086a 3-5; 1090a 7-9. cf. Jones, CP., 21, 317-326.; Augustine, CD., vii-28; cf. Theiler, VN., 18-19; Witt, A., 72-73.

[80]Cf. Plato, Phaedo, 75c-d, 76d-e; Rep., 596a; Parm., 132a; Sym., 211a 7-b5; Phaed., 247d6-e2; Tim., 37d-38a; 52a-e; esp. Parm., 132b-c.; Phaed., 78d; Phil., 15a-e; 16d-e; Tim., 27d-28a with 48e, 52d, esp. 51b-e.; Rep., 475e-480a.

[81]See Witt, A., 74.

[82]The doctrine is mentioned by Albinus; cf. Did., 163, 34ff.

[83]This brings him in connection with standard Middle Platonic teachings, see cf. Philo, e.g., Spec. Leg., i. 328; Clem, Strom., v. 89.6; cf. Fruchtel, BPLW, 57 (1937), 592 on Clement and Albinus.

[84]See Andresen LN; 278 on the allegorical interpretation of Tim 28b in Middle Platonism.

[85]Cf. Lilla, C., 183-196.

[86]See Witt, A., 67.

[87]Following the conclusions of Antiochus, cf. Cicero, Fin., v. 16, and Clement, Strom., viii.6 cf. Witt, A., 38; 66-67.

[88]On the connection between the Commentator and Albinus, see Dillon, MP., 279-280.

[89]Lilla draws the parallels between Philo, Clement, and Albinus too hastily, cf. Lilla, C., 199-226.

[90]Cf. books XII-XXII. begins as verbally identical, and is a close paraphrase of a section by Arius Didymus on physics. See Eusebius, PE., XI.23.2; Stobaeus, Anth., i.135.19. It is most likely a new edition of Arius' On the Doctrines of Plato. This is not to suggest it is identical but in fairness we do not know. Cf. Dillon, MP., 269.

[91]This may reflect the works pedigree if its origin is with Arius Didymus, who had close affinities to Peripatetic doctrines as a member of the Porch. cf. Diels, DG., 70ff.; 448,9.

[92]For the background to the eternal generation of matter, and the Aristotelian background of Albinus' theory, see Zeller, Vorträge und Abhandlungen., iii, 1-36; Witt, A., 120; Dillon, MP., 285-290.

[93]On the circular motion of Nous, see Did., 168, 4-5. cf. Tim., 34a; Laws, X.898a.

[94]On the correspondence with Plutarch and Philo, see Lilla, C., 212.

[95]On this see Weber, Zt., 27. 160-162; 5-6; cf. Dodds, En., V, 25; Theiler, VN., 2.

[96]See Koetschau, DePrincipiis (GCS 22), 1913, XXIII-IXXVI.

[97]ibid., CXXXVI-CXXXVII.

[98]The best example of this approach is represented by Daniélou, see Origène, Paris: 1948.

[99]On this approach, see DeFaye, Origène, Paris: 1923-28; Koch, PP., Berlin: 1932.

[100]E. Zeller, Die Philosophie der Griechen in Ihrer Geschichtlichen Entwicklung V, Leipzig: 1876-1889.

[101]These figures collected the Middle Platonic, Peripatetic, and Stoic materials to serve as an apparantum fontium for the study of Plotinus, e.g. Merlan, From Platonism to Neoplatonism, Amsterdam: 1953; Armstrong, "The Background of the Doctrine that Intelligibles are not Outside the Intellect," Les Sources de Plotin, p. 393-425; Theiler, Die Vorbereitung des Neuplatonismus, Berlin: 1932; Schwyzer, "Plotinos," in R.E. XLI (1951), col. 441-591.

[102]Andresen, Logos und Nomos, Berlin: 1955; Leonen, "Albinus' Metaphysics: An Attempt at Rehabilitation," Mn iv,9, p. 296-319; 10,35-56.; Lilla, Clement of Alexandria, Oxford: 1971; Dillon, The Middle Platonists, Ithaca: 1977; cf. Two Treatises of Philo of Alexandria, Chico: 1983; de Faye, Origène, Paris: 1928; Koch, Pronoia und Paideusis, Berlin: 1932.

[103] Merlan, From Platonism to Neoplatonism, p. 1.

[104] This was recognized by Dodd, "The Parmenides of Plato and the Origin of the Neoplatonic One," CQ (1928), p. 129-142.

[105] This was recognized and sketched by Witt, Albinus and the History of Middle Platonism, Cambridge: 1937. cf. Merlan, "Greek Philosophy from Plato to Plotinus," I The Cambridge History of Later Greek and Early Medieval Philosophy, Cambridge: 1967, p. 37-38.; Rist, Plotinus, Cambridge: 1967, III, p. 23-64.

[106] Cf. H. Koch, Pronoia und Paideusis, Berlin: 1932. For the best recent overviews of Origène's thought, see P. Nautin, Origène: Paris: 1977; J.W. Trigg, Origène, Atlanta: 1983.

[107] For the chronology of Origen's writings, see Trigg, O., 91-94; 147-165; 172-173; 201-205; 211-238.

[108] The works by Koch, Pronoia und Paideusis, Berlin: 1932 and de Faye, Origène, Paris: 1923-1928 are the exceptions.

[109] Cf. G. Bardy, Origène, Paris: 1932; J. Danièlou, Origène, Paris: 1948.

[110] Cf. For a review of the debate over the two Origens, see Trigg. O., 259-260. R. Cadiou, La Jeunesse d'Origène, Paris: 1936, p. 204-230, cf. 231-262; H. Dörrie, "Ammonius der Lehrer Plotins," Hermes 83 (1955), p. 439-477; cf. Koch, Pronoia und Paideusis, p. 291-304.

[111] e.g. H. Dörrie, "Ammonius de Lehrer Plotins," Hermes 83 (1955), p. 439-304; W. Theiler, Forschungen zum Neuplatonismus, Berlin: 1966, p. 1-45. cf. R. Cadiou, La Jeunisse d'Origène, p. 184-203.

[112] cf. Eusebius, Hist. Eccl. vi.19.5-8. cf. P. Nautin, Origène, Paris: 1977, p. 197-202.

[113] See Dodds, "The Parmenides of Plato and the Origin of the Neoplatonic "One," CQ (1928), p. 139; A.H. Armstrong, Plotinus, Amsterdam: 1967, p. 25, cf. W. Theiler, Forschungen, p. 1-45.

[114] W. Jaeger, Nemesios von Emesa, Berlin: 1914; W. Theiler, Die Vorbereitung des Neuplatonismus, Berlin: 1932; R.E. Witt, Albinus and the History of Middle Platonism, Cambridge: 1937; S. Lilla, Clement of Alexandria, Oxford: 1971; J. Dillon, The Middle Platonists, Ithaca: 1977; E. de Faye, Origène, I-III, Paris: 1923-1928; H. Koch, Pronoia und Paideusis, Berlin: 1932.

[115] Dodds was the first to warn of the naivete of too hastily conflating Middle and Neo Platonic theoretical conceptions, "The Parmenides of Plato and the Origin of the Neoplatonic One," CQ (1928), p. 129-142; cf. C. Andersen, Logos und Nomos, Berlin: 1955, p. 373-400; J. Dillon, The Middle Platonists, Ithaca: 1977, p. 155-182, 272-289.

[116] P. Merlan, From Platonism to Neoplatonism, The Hague: 1953, p. 1-7; A.H. Armstrong, Plotinus, p. 5-13; 21-28; 49-64; 65-66; 70-74; 80-81; 98-108. The primary objection is that it is an historical approach to the study of sources. All philosophic thought is a prolegomenon to the thought of Plotinus.

[117] By Nous-Henas we mean the conflation of two principle strands of Middle Platonic theological reflection, the Peripatetic and the Neopythagorean-Academic.

[118]It is plain that Origen wishes to make God a principle above all qualification, a One above the opposition of all attributes. This has a Neopythagorean origin, cf. Simpl. In Phys. Middle Platonism, Witt, Albinus, p. 66.

[119]By epekina Origen means that the Father cannot be qualified by any of the characteristics which qualify the generated and created entities. He is above substance and matter as not only nous but something above nous,; he is the One above all attributes, e.g. Philo, De Deus 52,62; Albinus, Did. p. 164,6ff; Clement, Strom. v.,12. cf. Winston-Dillon, Two Treatises of Philo of Alexandria, p. 218-221. cf. C. Cels. VI,65 p. 135, 12ff. This is Origen's interpretation of Rep. 509b; cf. C. Cels. VI,64 p. 134,23ff.: allo'oud' ousias methechei... As such he cannot be qualified, see C. Cels. VI,65 p. 135,12ff.

[120]Cf. Dodds, CQ (1928) 129-142 was the first to propose that these hypotheses underly the Middle Academy's formulation of first principles. On the relation of these hypotheses to Clement. See, Lilla, C., 205-206. Origen likely received his formulatio of the hypotheses via Clement.

[121]E.R. Dodds, CQ., 129-132. What he correctly asserts for Philo and Albinus may also be claimed for Origen. God is a superior nous, cf. p. 132 n. 1 a dn 2. When God is called a hen by Philo and Origen (this designation is wanting in Albinus) it is understood as a One above all attributes (i.e. all members of the Pythagorean table of opposites, Simp. In Phys. p. 181, 10ff. Diels).

[122]The tripartite division of being was ascribed to Plato by Aristotle (Met. I,6, 987b 15ff.; De An. I,2 404b 16ff.). In the former pericope the mathematicals mediate between the intelligibles and the sensibles, while in the latter the soul does. He also reports that Speusippus rejected the ideas in favor of the mathematicals, and separated the soul from both mathematicals and geometricals (Met. XII,1 1069a 33ff.). Iamblichus' Comm. Math. p. 15,5-18, 12 Festa, cf. Merlan, p. 86-99. In the Platonic tradition this notion was rejected, see: Xenocrates fr. 30 (Heinze). He finds no use for the mathematicals. The ideas are the only subsisting universals. This became the standard definition in Middle Platonism as well, e.g. Albinus, Did. 163, 21ff. It survived in the Peripatetic tradition, however, and it is from this source that Origen picked up the notion.

[123]Such hierarchies of being are common in second century Middle Platonism with Albinus, Numenius, Clement, See sections under these headings in Part One.

[124]This division of powers has a strong resemblance to the model proposed in Philo, e.g. QE., ii, 68; cf. Fuga, 94; 101; 109; Cher., 27ff.; Somn., i.62, and in Clement, e.g., Strom., iv.156.1-2: (ii.317.24-318.2; cf. vii.5.6: (iii. 6.3-4).

[125]Origen's model has affinities to that described a century later by Iamblichus, Theol. Arith. p. 61, 8ff. Ast.; Com. Math. p. 15,5-18, 12 Festa. From this description it is possible to see why Justinian interpreted Origen's theology as he did (EP. ad Men.=fr. 9 Koe. p. 55, 4ff.). However, as we shall see this interpretation is a mistaken one.

[126]This is generally labeled as Origen's "subordinationist" theory, Krämer, p. 288, and questioned as to its orthodoxy, cf. Daniélou, Origène, p. 250-258.

[127]C. Cels. VI, 64 p. 134, 23ff.; VI, 65 p. 135, 12ff. The Father does not participate in generated-created ousia.

[128]This aspect of Origen's thought was known to his Patristic critics and constituted the basis for the anathamas against him. cf. De Princ. p. cv-cxv.

[129]Cf. Philo, Opf., 20; Cher., 49; Clement, Strom., iv.155.2 (ii. 317.11); v.73.3: (ii.375.18-19).

[130]See, De Princ., II, 3,6 122,4; C. Cels., I, 13 66f.; II, 12, 141,1. Origen redefines the doctrine of ideas as proposed in early and middle Middle Platonism, cf. Koch, PP., 783ff.; 254 ff.

[131]Cf. Philo, e.g. Plan., 9; Clement, Strom.,v.104.4: (ii.396.16); Protr., 5.2 (i.6.7.9); Albinus, Did., 170, 3-6).

[132]Cf. Philo, e.g., Opf., 16, 17, 18, 19, 36, 129; Heres, 280; Plant., 50; Ebr., 133; Ling., 172; Clement, e.g., Strom., v.94.1 (ii.338.56-); v.16.3:(iii.336.8); Albinus, Did., 163, 10ff.; 164.29; 163, 12-13,27-30;164,27.

[133]Origen's formulation points back to Antiochus, Cicero, Ac. Post., 27ff. Cf. Dillon, MP., 67; 138-139; 167; 287.

[134]See, Koch, PP., 253.

[135]Cf. De Princ., I,3,3,50. 14ff. Origen does not follow the Aristotelian conception of matter, cf. Arist. De Caelo, 306b, 17; Phys., 191 a 8-12. This notion was inherited and developed by such figures as Moderatus and Numenius. However, he did hold that real being must contain form-in-itself, one that which is devoid of form cannot be regarded as real being (Simpl., In Phys., 231.4-5; Proclius, In Tim., 299c). Unlike Plotinus (Enn, i.8.15), Origen maintains that on original matter did not exist, cf. Armstrong, TU, 80 (1962), 127. On this point he also disagrees with Philo (Fuga, 9; Spec. Leg., i.328), and Clement (Strom., v.89.6). The reason for Origen's reformulation of the earlier doctrines of matter was that Gnostics claimed this doctrine for purposes of affirming a radical distinction between God and the world, and God and the demiurge, cf. Tertulian, Adv. Marc., i.18. This does not mean that Origen did not believe in the formation of matter. God forms matter to create a universe. However, it does not appear that God created matter out of nothing. It cannot be inferred from Origen's use of the word ktistēs that he believed in a creatio ex nihilo. Creation refers to the origin of the Logos, the Spirit, and the cosmos. It is not stated that any of them were created ex nihilo. Frankly, we are confronted with an anomaly. According to Origen there is no original matter co-eternal with God (De Princ., I,3 5), but the world is also eternal as a prefigureation of God's wisdom (De Princ., I, 4,5). The resolution can only be that God is eternally active and eternally creates all things. If Origen did hold to the doctine of an original matter, then it existed first as a pre-figuration and pre-formation in his mind, and then was created in the form of the genera and species which have for ever existed.

[136]For a summary of the rational creatures, see Trigg, O., 103-107.

[137]The Logos and Holy Spirit subsist essentialiter but exit accidentaliter. Being the same substance of the Father. They have the same characteristics. Existing differently from the Father they have the characteristics of createdness cf. Comm. in Th., II,2,17-18,20.

[138]See notes 8,9,10,12.

[139]Dillon hints at the Peripatetic source in his search back to Eudorus of Alexandria, CNPT., 22 n.11. For Origen's knowledge of Alexander see Koch, PP., 285ff.; 289; 299; 302; de Faye, O., III, 184; 272.

[140]See Merlon, PNP, 60ff., on this concept.

[141]See Moraux, AG., 151, 155.

[142]Origen's homiletical writings post-date the Periarchôn (De Principiis) some seventeen years. They were composed in Palestine while the treatise on first principles was written in Alexandria. Cf. Nautin, O., 389-409. The literary genres of these works differ as well. Because of these distinctions it has been assumed that there is little conceptual correction between Origen's Homilies and his work on first principles see Nautin Homélies sur Jérémie, Paris: 1976, 100-191. Cf. Trigg, O., 178-179. This assessment is correct, but only to a point. Origen's philosophical positions articulated in the Periarchôn (De Principiis) underly his homiletical exegesis of the Bible. Certainly the Sitz im Leben of his writings from 222 A.D. and 239-240 differ, but must we assume that the Origen of Alexandria has no connection with the Origen of Caesaria, conceptually? We propose that they do. Furthermore, we suggest that Origen's later writings help clarify some of the doctrines which are extant in the Periarchôn (De Principiis) and the Commentary on John. Hence, we use the Homilies and the Contra Celsum to shed light on Origen's philosophical doctrines. It goes without saying that what we offer in this section is merely an hypothesis of Origen's understanding of being and existence.

[143]To explain Origen's theory we will examine Aristotle and Alexander, the Metaphysica and In Metaphysica respectively.

[144]See Theiler, "Ammonius der Lehrer des Origenes," Forschungen zum Neuplatonismus, Berlin: 1966, 1-45.

[145]Cf. Cf. Ross, Metaphysics, I, 306.

[146]See De Rijk, The Place of the Categories of Being in Aristotle's Philosophy, Assen: 1952, 32ff.

[147]This was noted by Ross, Metaphysics, I, 30.

[148]Ibid., 306.

[149]See Apelt, Die Katagorienlehre, 110.

[150]The notion of ontological accident was raised by Aristotle, Top., I.8, 103b17-19, and elaborated upon by Porphyry, Isag., II, 117. Cf. Gerdt, Philosophiae Aristotelico-Thomisticae, I, nr. 163, 182.

[151]See Krämer, Geistmetaphysic, 288.

[152]See also, Arist., Metaphys., 1026b, 21-24; 1069a 20-22; 1030 a 21-23; An. Post., I.22.83a30-35. Substance is set against the praedicamenta. Owens, The Doctrine of Being in the Aristotelian Metaphysics, 66-74, and Ross, Analytics this type of symbêbekos ontological accident.

[153]See De Princ., I,3,3 50, 14ff. They are created, and this is inherent.

[154]Cf. Trendelburg, Elementa logices aristoteleae, 58; Ross, Metaphys., I, 159-160.

[155] In this sense he maintains the Platonic distinction between that which is Absolute (kath'hauto) and that which is Relative (prosti) that originates in the Old Academy with Xenocrates (fr. 12 Heinze), and the Middle Academy with Eudorus, (Simpl., In Phys., 189, 10ff).

[156] See De Princ., I,3,5 55, 4-56, 8.

[157] On Origen's doctrine of free-will, see Koch, PP., 279-291; Langerbeck, "Die Verbindung aristotelischer und christlicher Elemente inder Philosophie des Ammonius Saccas "AAWG 69 (1967) 146-166; Trigg, O., 115-120.

[158] See Comm. in Jh., I. 178; Martyr., III. The subjection to bodily existence. However, the rational creature desires to commune with God apart not only from his earthly body, but anybody. Cf. Trigg, O., 112-113.

[159] By Pros hen unity Origen means analogice as distinct from aequivoce and univoce. Their reference to God is that they proceed from God, e.g. Alexander, In Met., 241.9; cf. Syrianus, In Met., 56.18; Asclepius, In Met., 227.2-3; 231.12-15; 25. Cf. Arist. Top., I.15, 106a 19-22; b4; 8; 107a; 39; b7; Top., I.15, 106a 19-22; b4; 8; 107a; 39; b7; 16; 25; 31. God is the source from which they spring. For the background to this notion of the pros hen equivocate, see Wolfson, HRT, XXXI (1958), 151. The immediate source for Origen's theory is probably Clement.

[160] Origen follows Clement's lead on this notion of pros hen equivocals. See Clement Part 3 of this study. Origen goes one step further than Clement however. He postulates a pros hen unity between God and the universe as well. By doing this he further de-emphasizes the radical transcendence of God..

[161] Origen employs Alexander's De Anima in a variety of ways, see Koch, PP., 285 ff; 289; 299; 302. Alexander and Origen utilize similar arguments to defend psychological hypotheses. Cf. de Faye, O., III, 184; 272. In any case it is likely Origen know of Alexander's De Anima..

[162] These two kinds of equivocity were combined in the New Lyceum, e.g. Alexander, In Met., 241.9; Asclepius In Met., 227. 2-3; 231.12-15; 25. See note 159.

Part Two:

Epistemology

[1] See, A.V. Nazzaro, "Il gnôthi sauton nell'epistemologia filoniana, Annale della Facultà di lettre filosofia dell'Università de Napoli 12 (1969-1970), 49-86.

[2] This is beyond the task of this work. We only sketch the central doctrines of Philo's theory of knowledge. For a more complete analysis, see Wolfson, P., ii, 3-11.

[3] See, H. Wolfson, P., ii 11-13.

[4] For the parallel with Antiochus, see: Cicero, Ac. Post., 3off; cf. Lilla, C., 131 n.2.

[5] See Dillon, MP., 145, for the connection between Philo and the Stoic epistemology, cf. Wolfson, P., ii 3.

[6]By monotomic is meant a theory of knowledge where the knowing faculty, working from perceptions to conceptions, knows the universe. By dichotomic is meant an epistemic theory where there are two faculties of knowledge one working from an directed to sensible things, and another from and to intelligible things. Jewish and Christian Middle Platonists maintain a Stoic-Peripatetic epistemological theory, the monotomic theory.

[7]See QG., iv.140.

[8]The philosophical discussion of prophetic inspiration is uncomplete, see Wolfson, P., ii, 11-72.

[9]See Lilla, C., 118-136.

[10]See Prüm, "Glaube und Erkenntnis in zweiten Buch des Klemens von Alexandrien," S., 12 (1937), 17-57 for the connection between Clement and the Stoic epistemology., esp. pp. 23-27. On Antiochus' epistemology see Strache, EK, 7-19. Luch, NR 7 53-54; Dillon, MP., 91-96.

[11]See Lilla, C., 136 n.1.

[12]See Witt, A., 29 n.1; 34 for the similarity with Antiochus, cf. Lilla, C., 127-128.

[13]Following Lilla, C., 136 n., cf. Dillon, MP., 273-274.

[14]Früchtel notes the correspondance to Aristotelian doctrines on this point, see n. 119.27-31 in Stählin ii.524.

[15]For Lilla's excellent reconstruction, see C., 136-142.

[16]For the correlation between Clement, and Plato, Plutarch, Albinus, Justin, Maximus of Tyre, and Plotinus, see Lilla, C., 165-169.

[17]For the backgrouns and content of Albinus' epistemology see Witt, A., 47-60; Dillon, MP., 273-276; Milhaven, Aufstieg, 47-60.

[18]See Witt, A., 53f.

[19]See Dillon, MP., 274.

[20]This doctrine has been only briefly analyzed, cf. Dillon, MP., 291-292.

[21]On Albinus' dialectic and its relation to epistemology, see Witt, A., 116.9.

[22]There is no parallel between Albinus' doxastikos and epistêmonikos logos and Clement's doxastikê and epistêmonikê pistis. See Witt, A., 53 ff.; Lilla, C., 136 n.1.

[23]See Koch, PP., 83f.; 86f.; 94ff.; 183 ff.; 230 ff.; 233 ff.

[24]For the difference between Albinus and Origen see Koch, PP., 248-249.

[25]Origen illustrates this through his use of Plato's 'analogy of the line,' cf. Rep. V 509-511, the 'simile of the sun,' cf. Rep. VI 498a. In Origen's time these notions had become commonplace philosophical cliches. cf. de Faye, Origène III p. 168-178 and Koch, Pronoia und Paideusis, p. 230-235; 248-249.

[26]For a complete discussion of the epistemic assumption among Middle-platonists that scientific knowledge is the product of sense-perceptions and the activity of reason, see R. Hirzel, Untersuchungen, p. 493-524. cf. p. 141-261. For the evidence of these ideas in Clement, Origen's chief fons, S. Lilla, Clement, p. 120-131. For Clement's correlation of biblical and human pistis, see Lilla, C., 132-142.

[27]The term physikê ennoiai is of Stoic origin. However, by Origen's time it had long been a technical term in the theory of knowledge held by the Middle-Platonic school traditions to designate primary sensible impressions, of. J. Dillon, The Middle Platonists, Ithaca: 1977, see, indices under this term. The pistic dimensions of these "common perceptions" are evident in the writings of the Stoa. Diogenes Laertius reports that the Stoics held that these primary conceptions were standards to truth (Vit. VII, 54). However, strictly speaking these cannot be called the standards of truth. The real standard, whereby the truth of a perception is ascertained, consists in the power of certain perceptions, of carrying conviction to kataléptikon. The koinai ennoiai or prolêpseis are formed from a belief in the veracity of these perceptions to present valid images. These artificial perceptions then have their truth established by being subjected to a scientific process of proof.

[28]The Hellenic philosopher Galen holds this view in De Meth. Med. i.c. 5, vol. x. p. 39, 7-9 ed. Kuehn; In. Log. i, t p.4, 13-15 ed. Kalbfleisch. Origen's theory is within the mainline of Hellenistic theories of knowledge arising from the trajectory of Antiochus of Ascalon, cf. Koch, p. 230ff.

[29]Koch presents a brief discussion of Origen's notion of the ennoia in his Pronoia und Paideusis, p. 83, 248.

[30]Origen's doctrine of free-will has been widely written upon and will be passed over in this section. On this doctrine see Koch, p. 25ff., 105ff.; 113ff.; 199ff.; 279-291. cf. de Faye, III, p. 179-198.; Langerbeck, p. 146-166.

[31]Davies, "Origen's Theory of Knowledge," AJT II (1898), p. 737ff. cf. Koch, p. 86 n. 4.

[32]There is only one way to higher knowledge: the study of scripture, cf. Sel in Psalm. XII p. 190f. What scripture means is interpreted through allegorical interpretation, cf. De Princ. IV, 2-3.

[33]The general consensus has been that the Logos function as the teacher of 'divine wisdom,' cf. Koch, PP., 62-78. While this is indeed the case attention should also be directed toward the place scripture and the words of God have in Origen's theory of knowledge. The Logos functions as 'teacher' in Origen's scheme, but the final criterion of what is taught must always be tested by scripture, cf. De Princ. IV, 1,1 p. 292, 9ff.

[34]This represents Origen's attempt to present a serious philosophical explanation of the words pistis and pisteuein in the Bible. The result is a conflation of terminology. He employs the language of Hellenic epistemic theories to explain the scientific nature of scripture. He was aware of the criticisms of a Galen and Celsus who attacked the Christian and Jewish belief in the undemonstrated laws of scripture, cf. R. Walzer, Galen on Jews and Christians, p. 14-15,53. A hint of this polemic may be found in Clement's Strom. ii.8.4: ii.117-8-9, and is throughout his own C. Cels. Origen's goal is to show that the pistis of scripture is the first step on the way to truth, and it is in this sense that its priority over epistêmê is proclaimed. It contains a higher 'divine' knowledge which can be explained through rational exegesis. There is a scientific content to scripture and this constitutes its 'higher' meaning. Origen asserts that the koinai ennoiai are a source of

pistis because the sense-perceptions are enargeis, and what possesses enargeis is piston. Clement held a similar view, cf. Strom. II,9,5 (II, 118,2-4), VIII, 7,3-4 (III, 83,24-29), VIII, 14,3 (III, 88,20-21). Galen also held this view, cf. In Log. I, 5 ed. C. Kalbfleisch, De Meth. Med., I, c. 5, vol. X, p. 39,7-9 ed. C. Kühn. Although the term originated in the Peripatetic schools following Aristotle at this time it had become a standard expression within Middle-Platonic parlance as early as Antiochus of Ascalon, see R. Hirzel, Untersuchungen zu Ciceros philosophischen Schriften, III,34 Theil, Leipzig: 1883, p. 493-524 on the background to the description by Sextus Empiricus on the use of this term, e.g., Adv. Math., VII, 218,226. This term was not merely employed by Peripatetics. It also was utilized by Stoics who argued that the sense-perceptions strike the mind accompanied by a distinctive mark or enargeia. This makes it possible for us to believe them, and this aids in the guarantee of their truth. For a discussion of this term in Antiochus see, W. Theiler, Die Vorbereitung des Neuplatonismus, Berlin: 1930, p. 24-32,38ff., J. Dillon, The Middle Platonists, Ithaca: 1977, p. 53,65ff., S. Lilla, Clement of Alexandria: A Study in Christian Platonism, Oxford: 1971, p. 123-126. The question of importance is not is this term Peripatetic in origin or not, rather the focus is that the school tradition Origen and Clement drew from had accepted the Stoic epistemic model concerning sensible intellection and coupled it to certain technical terms employed originally by Peripatetics. In the development of epistemic theory among the early Middle-Platonists, such as Antiochus, there emerged the pistic dimension of intellection. By the time of Albinus, Clement, and Origen this aspect of intellection was accepted as a common-place. Among the Christian philosophers this development was utlized extensively given the many occurrences of pistis and pisteuein in their sacred writings. It permitted them to give a philosophical stature to the content of their writings, and in the case of Clement and Origen to introduce and systematically present an apodeixis euaggelikê.

[35]For the clarification of these doctrines in Aristotle and Alexander, see S. Feldman, "Gersonides on the Possibility of Conjunction with the Agent Intellect," AJSR III, (1978), 99-119.

[36]See Eusebius, H.E., vi, xix, 1-10. cf. Nautin, Origène, 197-199.

[37]See S. Feldman, AJSR, III (1978), 103-104, for the background to this generic-tree.

[38]Cf. De Princ., I, 1, 5-9 for the broad outlines of this notion.

Dialectic: Logic:

[39]This blend is well described in Bowersock, Greek Sophists, cf. ch. 5 of Winston-Dillon, Two Treatises of Philo, Chico: 1983, p. 129-180; Lilla, C., 132-136; Dillon, MP., 276-279.

[40]E.g. R. Volkmann, Die Rhetork der Griechen und Römer in systematischen bersicht, Leipzig: 1885; E. Norden, Antike Kunstprosa, Leipzig: 1909. Cf. W. Kroll, "Rhetorik," PRE vii (1940), p. 1039-1148.

[41]On the place of rhetoric in the school philosophies of this period, see I.M. Bochénski, La Log. p. 103ff; C. Prantl, Ges. d. Log. I. p. 473 ff.

[42]According to Diogenes Laertius the Stoics held rhetoric to be one of the two main subdivisions of dialectic, cf. Vit. VII, 41. This definition was accepted among Platonists as well, e.g. Cicero, De Or. i. 137-143; Plutarch, SVF II 297; cf. Quintilian, In. Or. ii.15.34. Hence, we examine logic and rhetoric together as branches of dialectic

[43]See also I. Heinemann, Philos griechische und jüdische Bildung, Breslau: 1932, p. 436ff; 519ff.

[44]The nature and origin of the Stoic term sêmeion or "signal" is difficult to ascertain. Much of the confusion rests with the difference between sêmeionta and sêmainomena, i.e., signs and significates, and the tugchanon, i.e., that which exists. According to Sextus Empiricus the Stoics connected these three things together, cf. Adv. Math., VIII,11 f. Apparently the to sêmainonta and the to tugchanon, i.e., the sign and the existent, were understood as physical objects. The ta sêmainonmena, i.e., the significate, is not a body, and is called the actual entity or to pragma, which is indicated or revealed by the sound. This sound is then apprehended in thought. In Stoic terminology the to sêmainomemon was also called the to lekton, i.e., "that which is meant." According to Sextus legein, from which lekton derived its meaning, meant "to utter a sound signifying the thought," cf. Adv. Math., VIII, 80. For another example of the distinction between these terms, see Seneca, Ep., 117.3. The fundamental difference between the physical objects and the entity is that the physical objects are only sounds or utterance, while the entity are matters of discourse, are spoken of, are lekta, cf. Diog. Vit., VII, 57.

The confusion between the distinction between these terms originates in the analysis of Stoic logic at the hands of the later Neo-Platonic-Peripatetic commenators such as the author of the Ammonian documents, In De Interp., ed. Busse, Simplicius, In Cat., ed. Kalbefleisch, Philoponus, In An Pr., ed. Wallies, and Themistius, In An Pr., ed. Wallies. These commentators were not clear whether or not the Stoics defined the sêmaionta-lekton as a thought or as a body, see B. Mates, Stoic Logic, Berkeley: 1953, p. 12-13. If we rely on a second century document rather than on fourth to sixth century testimonies we may get a better grasp of the distinctions between these terms as they were understood in Origen's time. Galen states:

> Since we have memories of things that are perceived by the senses, whenever we set these in motion they are to be called ennoiai. There are also some further notions which do not arise from sense-perception but are naturally in all of us, and when these are expressed in sound, the ancient philosophers call them by the term axiôma. The Greeks, to be sure often called notions "thoughts." In. Log., ed. Kalbfleisch, p. 7,22-8,7.

If this is coupled with the statement of Sextus that the sign (to sêmainon), as contrasted with the significate (to sêmainomenon-to lekta), is a material object, cf. Adv. Math., VIII, 11-12, then some of the confusion can be settled. On the one side is the physical aspect of speech itself, and what the speech means or signifies. In the former category are the to sêmaionton and the to tugchanon, and in the latter are the to sêmainomemon and the to lekton. The axiôma falls into the second category because the axiom is a species of Lekton.

In order to grasp what Origen means by this cacaphony of terms let us return to the epistemic model sketched by Galen. The distinction and inter-relation made between noêsis and the ennoiai is an important one. It appears that the to sêmaionton and the to tugchanon are connected to the activity of sensible intellection whereby the mind presents ennoiai, while the to sêmainomenon, to lekton-axioma are connected to the activity of intelligible intellection whereby the mind produces ta noêta. The first group are considered as physical objects because the objects of sensible intellection are material. The second group are considered non-corporeal because the objects of intelligible intellection are non-material. Although there is a distinction between the to sêmaionton-tugchanon and the to sêmainomenon-lekton-axiom it is also important to note that there is a correlation. The to sêmainon refers to one aspect of sensible intellection, and the to sêmeion to an aspect of intelligible intellection. One moves from the first to the second in the same way that one moves from aisthêsis to noêsis. When the "signal" is silent, i.e., when it has no meaning, it is an ennoiai. When the "signal" is expressed in sound, i.e., when it becomes something which "signifies" something, then it is properly noêsis.

The presentation offered by Galen is not an accurate testimony regarding the Stoic distinction between these terms, but it is a good example of a Middle-Platonic interpretation of these Stoic distinctions. When we couple Galen's testimony with that of Sextus, we receive a reliable second and third century definition of terms. This is most helpful for our analysis of Origen. It appears that Origen's understanding and use of the term sêmeion is analogous to the picture outlined above. For the use of the term sêmeion in its epistemic and ontological aspects see, G. Weltring, Das SHMEION in der aristotelischen, epikurischen und skeptischen Philosophie, Diss. Bonn: 1910.

[44]See the indices under this term and its cognates in Stählin editions of Clement's works. In the rare instances when Origen employs this term it is in connection with biblical scripture. The sêmeia of scripture initially present themselves as ta sêmainonta in the form of koinai ennoiai. The real they point toward and reveal are the ta sêmainomena-ta lekta. These present themselves in the axiomata of Scripture. For the translation of the two types of ta sêmeia into commemorative and indicative, I follow B. Mates, Stoic Logic, Berkeley: 1953, p. 13.

[46]Cf. Koch, P., 174-175.

[47]Cf. Cadiou, JD., 104.

[48]Cf. de Faye, O., i.138.

[49]Cf. Walzer, Galen on Jews and Christians, 48-55.

[50]Cf. Le Lubac, Histoire et Spirit, 92-104.

[51]According to Sextus the sêmeion has two senses, cf. Adv. Math., VIII, 143. In its common sense it serves to reveal something which has previously been observed in conjunction with it. In its special sense it reveals that which is nonevident, cf. Adv. Math., VIII, 151.

Dialectic: Rhetoric

[52]This blend is well described in Bowersock, Greek Sophists, esp. ch. 5 of Winston-Dillon, Two Treatises of Philo, Chico: 1983, p. 129-180; Barnes, Latomus, 32 (1973), 787-798.

[53]See R. Volkman, Die Rhetorik der Griechen und Roemer in systematischen Uebersicht, Liepzig: 1885; E. Norden, Antike Kunstprosa, Leipzig: 1909. cf. W. Kroll, "Rhetorik," PRE VII (1940), p. 1039-1138.

[54]On the place of rhetoric in the Peripatetic and Stoic schools: e.g. I.M. Bochénski, La Log. p. 103ff.; C. Prantl, Ges. d. Log. I. p. 473ff.

[55]According to Diogenes Laertius the Stoics held rhetoric to be one of the two main subdivisions of dialectic, cf. Vit. VII, 41. This definition was accepted among Platonists as well, e.g. Cicero, De Or. i.137-143; Plutarch, SVF II 297; cf. Quintilian, In Or. ii.15.34.

[56]Cicero, Topica, 54,56,57.

[57]Quintilian, In Or., iii.1.14.

[58]Cf. K. Barwick, "Probleme der stoischen Sprachlehre," SAW 49,3 (1957), p. 80-87.

[59]Cicero, De Inv. i.61; 8.57ff; Ad Her. ii.28ff; Quintilian, In. Or. v. 10ff. cf. Cicero, De Inv. i.44-49, 51-56; Quintilian, In. Or. v.11-14,9,1.

[60]E.g. Cicero, De In., II, 44f, 117,130; Quintilian, IO., II, 4,27, V, 10, 100. In the speeches of the Attic Ten there is ample use of the eikota sêmeia, and tekmêria. Aristotle gives a syllogistic construction for these forms (Rhet., I,2, 1357a 22b-b 25, Anal. Pr., B 27). The later scholastic activity on rhetoric filters the Attic Ten's use of these devices through the formal matrix provided by Aristotle and the pseudo-Anaximenes (Rhet. Alex., 8, 10, 13).

[61]Cf. Cicero, Top. 54; Galen, In. Log., ed. Kalbfleisch, xvi. 12.

[62]Arist. AR I,2,1355b, 1356a. cf. e.g. Quintilian, In. Or. v. 8-10, 14.

[63]On these two rationes see: J. H. McBurney, "The Place of the Enthymeme in Rhetorical Theory," Speech Monographs III (1936), p. 49-74. McBurney traces their use in rhetorical theory from Aristotle to Cicero and Quintilian.

[64]Cf. e.g. Cicero, Top. ii.8; Alex. Numenius and Neokles in Anon. Seguer. SRG I, p. 448, 23ff.

[65]Aristotle's theories reappear in Cicero and Quintilian. Cf. e.g. Cicero, De Inv. ii.5.16-12.38f; Quintilian, In. Or. v.10.53ff cf. Arist. AR I,5ff.

[66]On the theory of the genera causarum and partes orationes in Hellenistic and Roman rhetorical theory see, F. Solmsen, "The Aristotelian Tradition in Ancient Rhetoric," AJP 62 (1941), p. 169-190; K. Barwick, "Probleme der stoischen Sprachlehre und Rhetorik," SAW 49,3 (1957), p. 80-87. cf. Winston-Dillon, Two Treatises of Philo of Alexandria, p. 129-136; 171-180. These studies provide a solid insight into the rhetorical theory practiced in the New and Middle Academies.

[67] C.A.T. Keil, Opuscula academica ad Novi Testamenti interpretationem grammatico-historicam et theologiae christianae origenes partinentia, ed. J. Goldholm, Leipzig: 1821, p. 560.

[68] J. Borst, Beiträge zur sprachlich-stilistischen und rhetorischen Würdigung des Origenes, Diss. Freising: 1913.

[69] R. Cadiou, Le jeunesse d'Origène, p. 28.

[70] Ibid., p. 72, n.2.

[71] R. W. Smith, The Art of Rhetoric in Alexandria: Its Theory and Practice in the Ancient World, The Hague: 1974.

[72] At least according to the handbooks. Cf. e.g. Cicero, Top. 11.8; Alex. Numenius and Neokles in Anon. Seguer. p. I.448.23ff, SRG.

[73] The rhetorical handbooks present the speechs of the Attic ten through a rhetorical matrix. Cf. e.g. Quintilian, In. Or. v.10.20; x.5.12. These are the so-called commonplaces mentioned in a variety of other sources, cf. Cicero, de Orat. iii.27.106ff; Theon, p.II.106 SRG; Aphthonius, Progymn. 7 p. II.32 SRG.

[74] Cf. Cicero, de Orat. iii.106ff; Theon. Progymn. 12 p. II 120ff. SRG. These topics were recognized as part of rhetorical invention, e.g. Seneca, Controv. i.7.17; Cicero, Tusc. Disp. i.4.7; ii.3.9. On philosophical theses in the rhetorical schools, cf. G. Reichel, Quaestiones Progumnasmaticae, Leipzig: 1919, p. 99f; D. Winston-J. Dillon, Two Treatises of Philo of Alexandria, Chico: 1983, p. 171-178.

[75] Cf. Cicero, de Inv. ii.5.16-12.38; Quintilian, In. Or. v.10.53ff for a list and use of these topics. They were later systematized for Hermagoras, Progymn. 7. p. II.11ff SRG, but have their origin the first sophistic, cf. Arist. AR i.5; Anax. AR vii.2, 1428a17ff.

[76] Cf. Arist. Top. i.13, 105a22ff, and passim in bks. ii-vii; AR ii.xviii, xxiii. They were classified in the early Imperial era, cf. Cic. Top. i.1ff; ii.7ff; de Orat. ii.163-173; Quintilian, In. Or. v.10.53f. Minoukianos, Epich. 3 p. ix.604 WRG; Neokles, in An. Seguer. p. 448-450 SRG; Apsines, Rhet. 10 p. I.376ff SRG. For a full discussion of these topoi, see T. Conly, "Logical Hylomorphism and Aristotle's koinoi topoi," Central States Speech Journal 29 (1978), p. 92-97.

[77] On Origen's Hellenic education, see Trigg, Origen, 31-34.

[78] E.g. Cicero, de Inv. i.61.44-49; i.57ff; Ad Her. ii.28ff; Quintilian, In. Or. v.10-14; v.9.1.10,11. cf. J.H. McBurney, "The Place of the Entyhmeme in Rhetorical Theory," Speech Monographs, III (1936), p. 49-74.

[79] Aristotle, AR i.2; An. Pr. ii.27.cf. E. Havet, De la Rhetorique D'Aristote, Paris: 1843, p. 64.

[80] E.g. De Princ., I,1,6 p. 20, 24-23,14.

[81] This was a common practice in Hellenistic logic. Galen employed such a theory in converting the sayings of Hippocrates and Plato into necessary statements, cf. In. Log. xvi. 12 Kalbfleisch. Galen argues that these statements come under the force of an axiom kata dynamin. Galen's analogy of the Republic is one of his major examples of this kind of argument. On this in Galen see, J. Kieffer, Galen's Institutio Logica, Baltimore: 1964, p. 14, 27, 29-30, 59, 117, 123-128. He associates it with the Stoic practice of

undemonstrated arguments. It may have been passed on to Origen via Clement, cf. R. Walzer, Galen on Christians and Jews, p. 17, 79-86.

[82]For the difference between the two pisteis, see Arist. AR i.2, 1355b; 1356a.

[83]E.g. De Princ., I,1,8 p. 24, 22-26,14. See the rhetorical exegesis of this pericope in Part Three of this study.

[84]On the role of the implied or suppressed premise in rhetoric, see L. Bitzer, "Aristotle's Enthymeme Revisited," Quarterly Journal of Speech, 45 (1959), p. 399-408.

[85]Cf. e.g. Quintilian, In. Or. iii.3.1; Cicero, de. Inv. i.9. cf. F. Solmsen, "The Aristotelian Tradition in Ancient Rhetoric," AJP 62 (1941) p. 37ff.

[86]E.g. Cicero, de Inv. ii. 157. cf. Auctor ad Her. iii.2.10.

Part Three: The Periarchôn

[1]Cf. Paul Koetschau, GCS, 22.v, p. cxliv-cxlvii.

[2]Cf. Basilius Steidle, "Neue Untersuchungen zu Origenes Peri Archôn," ZNW 5 (1968), p. 137-155.

[3]Cf. Paul Kübel, "Zum Aufbau von Origenes 'De Principiis: (PERIARCHON)," VC, (1971), p. 31-39.

[4]Cf. Marguerite Harl, "Recherches sur le peri archôn d'Origene en vue d'une nouvelle edition," SP III (TU 78), p. 57-67. "Structure et coherence du Peri Archôn," Origeniana, p. 11-32.

[5]See Gilles Dorival, "Remarque sur la forme du Peri Archôn," Origeniana, p. 33-45.

[6]See Harl, Origeniana, p. 11-32.

[7]Cf. Henri Crouzel and Manilo Simonetti, Origène Traité des Principes, Paris: 1978-80, vol. I-IV.

[8]Ibid., p. 12-51.

[9]See R. Pfeiffer, History of Classical Scholarship, p. 213.

[10]The complementary relation of treatises (syggrammata) and commentaries (hyponêmata) is that of a polished work bearing a title, while the hyponêmata are without titles. The distinction is made by commentators who refer to Alexander's critique of the Stoic theory of mixture in both his treatise, the de mixtione, and his commentaries, cf. Themiatius, Phys. 104. 18-22, and Simplicius Phys. 530. 14-16. Genre criticism on the Periarchôn (De Principiis) has debated the question whether or not the text is a treatise or a commentary. B. Steidele, "Neue Untersuchungen zu Origenes PERIARCHON," ZNTW 40 (1941), p. 236-243, proposes that it is a hyponêmata, while M. Simonetti, "Osservazioni sulla struttura del de Principiis di Origine," Rivista di cultura classica e medioevale 6 (1964), p. 15-32, and H. Crouzel, Traité des Pincipes I, p. 19-22 propose that it is syggramma. This study follows the conclusions of G. Dorival, "Remarque sur la forme du PERIARCHON," Origeniana, I, p. 33-45 which essentially supports the Simonetti-Crouzel position with a minor correction. The work appears to be both an eisagôgê (the Praefatio) and a syggrammata (books I-IV). This is supported by the analysis of its rhetorical structure which suggests that the composition was a carefully crafted response to a series of philosophical problematics.

[11]On the polemical aspects of philosophical composition in this period, see Festugière, L'idéal religieuse, Excursus C. Cf. Todd, Alexander of Aphrodisias on Stoic Physics, 16-17.

[12]See, S. Lilla, Clement of Alexandria, p. 50-51; R. Todd, Alexander of Aphrodisias on Stoic Physics, p. 16-17. K. Mras notes in this context that the only work that Eusebius quotes of Alexander's is the de fato. It apparently complemented Christian criticisms of Stoic theories on fate, see Anz. d. Oest. Akad. d. Wiss. in Wien, Phil-Hist. Klasse, 93 (1956), p. 215.

Commentary

[13]Traité des Principes, p. 76-110.

[14]The sources primary and secondary are: L. Spengel, Aristotle Ars Rhetorica, Leipzig: 1867; Anaximene's Ars Rhetorica, Leipzig: 1847; Rhetores Graeci, Leipzig: 1854; C. Walz, rhetores Graeci, Stuttgart: 1836; E. Norden, Antike Kunstprosa, vol. ii 2nd ed., Leipzig: 1909; E.M. Cope-J. E. Sandys, The Rhetoric of Aristotle, Cambridge: 1877; G. Gebauer, De Argumenti Ex Contario Formis Quae Reperiuntur Apud Oratores Atticos, Zwikau: 1877; R.C. Jebb, The Attic Orators, London: 1876.

L. Spengel, "Über die Rhetorik des Aristoteles," ABAW 6 (1852), p. 455-513; E. M. Cope, An Introduction to Aristotle's Rhetoric, London: 1867; G. Palmer, The TOPOI of Aristotle's Rhetoric as Exemplified in the Orators, Diss. Chicago: 1934; F. Solmsen, "The Aristotelian Tradition in Ancient Rhetoric," AJP 62 (1941), p. 35-50, 169-190. Spengel's edition of the Ars Rhetorica of Aristotle presents a number of difficulties. He uses a confusing method when he cites passages from the orators which correspond to given topoi. Often his transitions from one type of citation to another have not been clearly marked. We have attempted to examine all the loci paralleli Spengel cites, and only those which fit the form of argument Aristotle describes and Origen utilizes are listed. Since my primary concern is to identify the "form" of a passage in the orators which corresponds to Aristotle's topical description, and then to employ it so as to illustrate the rhetorical dimensions of Origen's composition, the reader should not focus on the "content" of the speeches cited.

It is clear that the speeches of the Attic Ten were delivered before the appearance of Aristotle or Anaximene's Ars Rhetorica. Thus, no claim is made that these theoretical works influenced the orations of the Attic Ten. Indeed, the influence worked in the other direction, i.e. practice during the First Sophistic does permit us to identify and classify the argument forms used in Attic oratory. In the Second Sophistic at Alexandria it is clear that the speeches of the Attic Ten were evaluated through the lenses of the rhetorical handbooks which followed upon those of an Aristotle. Thus, when Origen picked up Theon's Prog. or a work akin to it, it is likely that he read these speeches through a theoretical matrix of topics, proofs, and the types and parts of speech. As such, in late antiquity, theoretical concerns preceded rhetorical practice. A good illustration of how this scholastic mentality operated clarifies itself when we examine how logical arguments were formulated. Authors were careful to form their arguments according to specific rules of logic. It can be assumed, with due caution, that rhetorical arguments were formulated in the same manner.

The analysis, which commences in the following pages, is problematic and functions as an experiment. The endeavor may turn out to be one which does not adequately provide the results it sets out to demonstrate. No claim is made that we can identify the specific speeches of the Attic Ten which were the functional models behind the Periarchôn. The primary sources would not allow such conclusions. The claim that is made is that these speeches were more than likely the formative models Origen the rhetor was trained in, and that when he composed the Periarchôn these argument forms provided models which he may have worked from. Therefore, the loci paralleli cited serve only to illustrate the types of rhetorical arguments which appealed to Origen. If the parallels are valid they are valuable because they point out the rhetorical strategy which motivated Origen in his refutation of the criticisms directed against Christianity, by those such as Celsus, or the false doctrines offered by the Christian Gnostics and Stoics.

[15]For ek kriseôs, see Arist., AR II,23,12,1398b 25ff. The procedure followed is to note the topics utilized by Origen according to the designations given them by Aristotle in the Ars Rhetorica. This simplifies the procedure of formal analysis immensely in that it allows for a single designation to be given to the topoi and loci of Hellenistic and Roman rhetoric. The names for the topics differ from author to author in late antiquity thus Aristotle's terminology is employed to anchor the analysis. Whenever loci paralleli arise from later sources these topical designations will be noted, but always in connection with the Ars Rhetorica.

[16]In Greek and Hellenistic rhetoric the palaioi martures are often the law givers such as a Solon, or one's teachers, or the gods, e.g. Arist. AR II,23,12,1398b 27ff. This definition is repeated by the Latin orators, e.g. Cicero, de In., I,30,48: Quintilian, In. Or., V,11,36-44. As Spengel notes this was also the designations favored among the Attic Ten. E.g. Solon as authority: Hyper. iii.21 et. seg., col. 10; Dem. xviii.6, p. 227; xix. 254, p. 421; Aesch. iii. 108, p. 69, where the Delphic oracle and Solon are mentioned together; Dem. XX, 93, p. 485, 102, p. 488, where the Aeropagus is the authority; e.g. the gods as authorities: Dem. xix, 298, p. 438;p xxiii. 74, p. 644; Lycurg. 97, p. 160; Isoc. iv, 31, p. 47a. Origen is following a common practice in quoting his Deity as the source for authority, or as he does later in the chapter, the so-called sophoi of his religious tradition.

[17]Scientia=epistêmê. How scripture constitutes the basis of knowledge is sketched in Part Two of this study.

[18]The enthymêma was the earlier Hellenistic designation for what was known in late antiquity as the epcheirêma. The heads of the families of enthymêma are introduced in AR II, 23, 1-29. This understanding of the topics was known in the Hellenistic and Roman period, cf. Cicero, Top., IV, 25, and utilized by Origen.

There were three kind of topoi: 1) the eidê; 2) the koinoi; and 3) the topoi entyhmêmaton. The first two comprise the topical content of the third. The specific topics are the special materials of the orators enthymemes, and are classified under the heads of the three branches of rhetoric. They are the specific topics of the genos of science to which they belong. The general topics are common to all the specific topics, and are universally applicable to the eidê as well as the genê of rhetoric. The enthymemetic topics are made up of those which are common topics, in that they are applicable to all the branches of rhetoric and to specifics. This distinction between types of topics is conflated in the later handbooks. Cicero defines the communes loci "qui communes appellati sunt proprii singularum esse debebunt," Orat. 36, 136; "quia de universa re tractari solent," de Or., III, 27, 106. Examples are illustrated in a variety of places, e.g. Cicero, de Or., III, 27, 106; Quintilian, In Or., V, 12, 15. The topics, thus, can be applied to any subject, maxim, or proposition in any field, e.g. Cicero, de Or., III, 27, 107ff; Hermogenes, Progymn., SRG II, p. 9. These topics were an integral part of the school exercises as models for arguments to be committed to memory. cf. Cicero, Brut., 12. Origen uses the topics of rhetoric and the ready made arguments of the Attic Ten, and, in common scholastic fashion, combines them to the subject at hand in the Periarchôn, which is the presentation of an apodeixis euaggelikê. The function of this procedure is to argue in a rhetorically cogent manner, which is comprehensible to the intellectual culture of his audience, for purposes of persuasion. In this pericope the topic from judgement is employed in the attempt to persuade his audience of the legitimacy of Scripture as the ground for philosophical demonstration.

[19] By agatha, at least rhetorically, what is meant is that which is aimed at by many, and that which is praised and held as something worthwhile, cf. Arist. AR I, 6, 24, 1363a 10-1363a 16ff.

[20] The topic ek kriseôs is also called an enstasis ek tôn kekrimenôn, which is an argument used in rebuttal, cf. Arist. AR II, 25, 4, 1402a 37, 1402b 9ff. See also Arist., Top., VIII, 1, 166b 20ff. This understanding of the function of the argument from authority does not undergo any significant change in later Hellenistic and Roman sources, see F. Solmsen, "The Aristotelian Tradition in Ancient Rhetoric," AJP 62 (1941), p. 35-50. Theon of Alexandria, in his Progymn., c. 7. "peri topou" (L. Spengel, Rhetores Graeci, Leipzig: 1885, II. 106, henceforth SRG), for example means topos as "headquarters" or "the place from which the enthymemes or rhetorical arguments fall or are collected," AR II, 26,1, 1403a 19ff., cf. Cicero, de Or., II, 34, 146, II, 30, 130. Aristotle and the scholastic activity in the field of rhetoric, which followed upon him, divided the topoi into two categories, the koinoi topoi and the eidê or idia topics. In AR I, 2, 21, 1358a 13ff, the specific topics are kinds of topics subordinate to and forming part of the several sciences. When the sciences come into contact with rhetoric, and thereby furnish it with propositions (protaseis) and enthymemes, the topics are used to argue for or against certain propositions. Distinguished from the specific topics are the general topics, which are universally applicable to all sciences. The eidê/idia are confined to physics or ethics and no physical enthymeme and its topic applies to ethical enthymemes and their topics. The ek kriseôs topic is one of the universal or general topics, which are applicable to all the materials of the several sciences. Another term by which topics are designated is stoicheia, e.g. AR I, 2,22 1358a 32ff, Top., IV, 1, 121b,11. What Aristotle means by this is clear from his definition of stoicheion as an ultimate element in

reasoning or proof, i.e. the syllogism, cf. Anal. Post., I, 23, 84b 22. In this sense it stands for amêsoi protaseis, propositions immediately apprehended, when the subject and predicate are apprehended simultaneously by the nous. A topos, therefore, is the genus or head of a multitude of stoicheia or elements of enthymemetic reasoning. From this it is clear what Aristotle means when he says, "to gar auto lego stoicheion kai topon. esti gar stoicheion kai topos, eis ho polla enthyêmpiptei," AR II, 26, 1, 1403a 19ff; II, 22, 12, 1396b 13ff.

<u>P 2</u>

[21] Auxêsis is a technical term in Hellenistic oratory, which denotes amplification, explication, cf. Arist. AR I, 9, 38-41, 1368a 27ff. It is common to all the genera of oratory, and functions as an aspect of the rhetorical enthymeme. This general definition was functional in the rhetoric practiced in late Hellenistic and Roman antiquity.

[22] Cf. Arist. AR II, 23, 1, 1397a 8ff. This constitutes one of the antikeimena topoi, see Cope-Sandys, Aristotle's Rhetoric, Cambridge: 1877, p. 238 n. 1 for the definition and use of this topic in Hellenistic and Roman rhetoric (Henceforth, CS:AR).

[23] Cf. Arist. AR II, 23,3 1397a 27ff. This topic is the argument from the mutual relation of terms, notions, or attributes, see CS:AR, p. 241 n.3.

[24] Cf. Arist. AR II, 23, 12, 1398b 25ff. This topic is generally associated with the antikeimena topoi in ancient rhetoric. Origen duplicates this pattern in this pericope, see CS:AR, p. 262 n. 12.

[25] E.g. Lys. xiii. 63, p. 135; Isoc. xix. 50, p. 394d; Dem. xxiv. 212ff, p. 765ff; lxi. 30, p. 1410 (Spengel). This is important to note because it suggests the possibility that Origen employed these masters as his models in the presentation of his own argument. Demosthenes and Isocrates were among the most favored of the Attic Ten copied and utilized in Hellenistic Egypt see, Pack, Greek and Latin Literary Texts from Graeco-Roman Egypt, Cambridge: 1957, p. 42; Willis, "Greek Literary Papyri from Egypt and the Classical Canon," HLB 12 (1958), p. 5-34. Given the forensic character of the Periarchôn the speeches of Demosthenes bear close attention because they may have been paradigmatic for Origen. The theoretical knowledge of the art of rhetoric was also known in the second and third centuries at this elementary level. The two texts from Platonic corpus, which are most abundant, are the dialogues which treat rhetoric, i.e. the Gorgias and the Phaedrus. This informs us to what extent the intellectual culture of Hellenistic Egypt was aware of the technê rhetorikê practiced in antiquity. From this evidence we can, with due caution, infer that Origen utilized rhetoric, and that his audience was a most sophisticated one, which could understand and appreciate the nuance of speech he practiced. For example if Origen composed his prefatory arguments with the eloquence of a Demosthenes we can assume that he would be most successful at the persuasive task he placed before himself. Although there is no indication that he argued that the scriptures were composed with oratorial eloquence, as Augustine did, cf. De Doctrina Christiana, it appears that he composed his own work with the Attic Ten in mind.

[26] Cf. Maximus Planoudes, WRG, V, 40; Minucianus, WRG, IX, p. 611.

[27]Cf. Cicero, de In., I, 30, 47; Quintilian, In. Or. X, 76-79.

[28]E.g. Dem. xlvi. 24f; Isoc. xviii. 15, p. 374c.

[29]Maximus Planoudes, WRG, V, p. 404, 3. In Apsines and Minucianus it is called topos ek tou enantiou, Apsines, WRG, IX, p. 524, 19; Minucianus, WRG, IX, p. 608, 18.

[30]Quintilian, In Or., V, 10, 73.

[31]The arousing of emotions for purposes of praising or discrediting the character of an individual or group constituted one of the manor functions of rhetoric. On the theoretical level it is not only important for rhetorical theory in antiquity, but also for ethical theory and philosophical psychology, see W.W. Fortenbaugh, "Aristotle's Rhetoric on Emotions," AGP 52 (1970), p. 40-70. Following Fortenbaugh's analysis we must be aware that a philosophical rhetorician such as Origen recognized that cognition was an essential part of emotional response, and that emotions can be reasonable, i.e. they need not be a matter of mere charms and enchantments. Furthermore, if emotions have a cognitive aspect then it is possible to distinguish emotions from bodily drives, and thus develop an adequate moreal psychology. Aristotle's Ars Rhetorica, if viewed from this perspective, offered an answer to the Academic debate concerning the relationship of emotion to cognition. Where Origen's use of emotions fit into this trajectory has yet to be ascertained, but his coupling of rhetorical and logical elements in his dialectic point toward a recognition of the cognitive dimensions of emotion. As such, while the function of the argument in this pericope is to discredit his opponents, it also raises the question of why they should be discredited, and how Origen goes about accomplishing this. Not only should their definitions be rejected because they clash with those extant in Scripture. They should be dismissed because the definitions proposed are not logically arrived at. In order to facilitate the overturning of his adversaries' position Origen rationally appeals to the emotions of his audience. The suggestion is that the definitions of the opponents arise from the emotions and unreasoned discourse, while his own are logically and cogently deduced according to reason.

[32]E.g. Dem. xliii. 65, p. 1072; Isoc. 105, p. 67. These illustrations are helpful because they center upon the notion that if one shares in the misfortunes in a certain position one should also share in the benefits. This suggests that one of the functions of this topic for Origen is to focus the attention of the audience on the "advantages" and "disadvantages" (protreponta and apotreponta) of accepting the propositions of these opponents over against the propositions of the Church.

[33]Cf. WRG, V, p. 40.

[34]Cf. WRG, IX, p. 611.

[35]Cf. Ep. ad Ammaeus, i. c. 12.

[36]Cf. de In., I, 30, 47.

[37]Cf. In Or., V, 10, 76-79.

[38]Quintilian quotes Cicero when he explains this topic, and employs the Aristotelian definition of it under antithesis or antikeimena from the Topics II, 8, 114a 13. In another passage Aristotle refers to the rhetorical topic as ek tou pros ti, see Top., V, 6, 135b. This coupling of "opposites" and "relation" is utilized by Origen to draw

inferences from knowing or knowledge, to the thing known, which are the Church's definitions, and from emotions as a sensation, to the thing seen as an object of emotions, which are the opponent's definitions. Origen sees his task as presenting the logical objections (enstaseis) ek tou pros ti against the incorrect definitions of the opposition. The rhetorical or persuasive aspect of the topic aids the logical or demonstrative aspect in that if the audience weighs advantages and disadvantages they will be likely to perceive the cogency of Origen's objections. For a discussion of this topic in Aristotle and Hellenistic and Roman theory after him, see CS:AR p. 241 n.3.

[39] The tekmêria are associated by Origen with the Apostolic tradition he draws from, and the eikota are associated with those of his opponents whose arguments are not in accord with scriptural and apostolic dogma.

The topics are thus interpreted as "lines of argument," cf. Arist. AR II, 22, 1396b. The intention is that lines of argument be correlated with causes, signs, and examples, cf. Arist. AR II, 23-24. The topic and the enthymeme are combined into a careful scientific proposition. As such the speaker goes to the general topics for his premises, and the enthymemes form the mode of demonstration. Both together constitute a ratio essendi if it combines these elements in a cogent fashion. Minimally such a logical construct is an eikos. If it combines these elements with a sêmeion, which is a tekmêrion, then together they constitute a ratio cognoscendi. The point is that the former construct constitutes a hypothetical syllogism, and the latter a categorical syllogism, if it can be formulated in the first figure of the syllogism or reduced to one of the undemonstrables. As we have seen Origen holds that the sêmeia of scripture are tekmêria. When he combines these "signs" with a type of argument which has a necessary force, he assumes that he presents a ratio cognoscendi. His opponents, on the other hand, while they may present a valid argument, at least formally, do not present a necessarily true argument. They present a ratio essendi. There are, therefore, three principal types of argument: the valid, the true, and the demonstrative. The valid is not necessarily true or demonstrative; the true is always valid, but not necessarily demonstrative; and the demonstrative is always both valid and true. The first two types of argument constitute the ratio essendi, and the third the ratio cognoscendi. Origen's task in the Periarchôn is to show that his arguments have the character of the latter, and his opponents the character of the former. If possible he would like to illustrate that the arguments of his opponents are invalid (asynaktos or aperantos), i.e. non ratio. It is difficult for Origen to argue that his Christian opponents present invalid arguments because the sêmeia they deduce their propositions from are true. Thus, he takes another tack, which is to demonstrate that they are probably arguments because they are deduced in a somatic or deficient manner. For a discussion of the three types of arguments, and what constitutes an invalid argument, see Sextus Empiricus, Adv. Math., VIII, 412ff, 424; Adv. Math., VII, 429 ff, Hyp. Pyrrh., II, 146ff, 152-153. This conflation of Peripatetic and Stoic elements probably entered the philosophical-rhetorical tradition Origen drew from in the first centuries B.C.-A.D., cf. Cicero, de In., I, 44-49; Quintilian, In. Or., V, 10-14. That they are disassociated with the Peripatetic notion of the syllogism at this time is evident from Cicero, cf. de In., I, 44. It is in the scholastic activity predating Cicero that the loci were Stoicized, see M. Wallies, De Fontibus Topic, Ciceronis, Diss. Halle: 1878. This activity may account for Origen's Stoicized understanding of sêmeia and apodeiktos.

[40]What constitutes "truth" has a number of criteria epistemic, logical, and religious. An argument is true epistemically if the data the mental faculties encounter correspond to the knowledge of the first principles of knowledge in the act of apprehension, i.e. in the knowing of particular objects as sensibles, not intelligibles. Scientific knowledge is the demonstration, which follows from these principals, or knowledge pertaining to the intelligibles. An argument is true logically if it is valid and has true premises. An argument is true religiously if the knowledge corresponds to the words to the gnôsis proclaimed by and in Jesus Christ. Truth in the first two cases is distinguished by judgement and reason, the work of the rational faculties, which are directed to the sensibles and intelligibles. This type of truth is demonstrable logically, and it is the task of the Christian to have a grasp of this logical skill for the interpretation of Scripture, for it is from scripture that the truths from the created realm are deduced. That these truths are in scripture is clear from the fact that Deity speaks to man sensibly as well as intelligibly in scripture. Truth in the third case is supra-rational, and is distinguished gnostically. It is a type of spiritual theôria. The knowledge Origen refers to in this pericope is sensible-intelligible knowledge, and its "truth" is determined by judgement and reason.

P 3

[41]Cf. Arist. AR II, 23, 21, 1399a 31ff. The argument from advantage is one of the most commonly employed topics in Hellenistic and Roman rhetoric. Advantages as well as disadvantages are generally associated with motives. This is so because the consideration of inducements and deterrents focuses upon the question of the good. For Aristotle the goods which determine advantage are coupled with eudaimonia, cf. AR I, 5, 2, 1360b 11. Syrianus and Sopater utilize many of Aristotle's criteria for determining goods, cf. WRG IV, 739; 744-45. Among the Latin orators Quintilian, in a manner similar of those listed above, refers to "bonorum adeptionem, incrementum, conservationem, usum, aut malorum evitationem, libeerationem, imminutionem, tolerantiam" as criteria for determining goods, cf. In Or., V, 10, 33. Cicero's use of this topic aids in explaining its precise use by Origen. His comparationis locus compares the greater and less good, cf. Top., XVIII, 68-71. In a similar manner Origen contrasts the greater and less good in terms of the gifts of the Spirit, i.e. the graces of language, wisdom, and knowledge. Happiness has been replaced by wisdom as the good to be procured according to Origen, and this advantage is acquired by those who receive the higher gifts. The greater good is obtainable through the exercise of the gifts of the Spirit. The lesser goods, i.e. the understanding of faith held by the dull ones, are available to all who accept Christ, but they are not on a par with the graces of wisdom, knowledge, and language. The motive for obtaining these higher goods is self-evident. Those who possess them truly know God.

[42]That is, Origen assumes that his audience knows what the necessary doctrines of the Christian faith are. He also assumes that the audience knows that these doctrines have a variety of levels of meaning, and it is the task of those who possess the higher gifts of the Spirit to discover the deepest meanings of faith and the doctrines deduced therefrom. This incomplete proof, or epicheirêma, thus constitutes the logical core of the pericope.

[43]Cf. Arist. AR II, 23, 13, 1399a 13ff. The advisory aspect of this topic is associated in Graeco-Roman rhetoric with the logical following of one argument upon another. There is an urging that the deeper meaning of Christian doctrine is being revealed, see Maximus Planoudes in WRG V, p. 405, 17, and Minucianus in WRG IX, p. 609, 14ff. for Hellenistic loci paralleli which explain the form of Origen's construct.

[44]Cf. Cicero, Top., Xii, 53 and XIII, 53. Quintilian's discussion of the topic is most informative. In it he contrasts the wise and the foolish, the necessary and the probable, while justice is coupled with right judgement, and the breach of faith is called a bad thing, see In Or., V, 10, 74. It is suggested that Origen's line of argumentation wishes to persuade his audience of the propositions that the doctrines of the Christian faith be mined for their deeper meanings because the advantages are wisdom and justice, and the disadvantages are foolishness, wrong judgement, and a breach of faith.

[45]Cf. SRG I, xvi. 10, p. 204.

P 4

[46]Cf. Arist. AR II, 23, 2, 1397a 27ff.

[47]Cf. Arist. AR II, 23, 13, 1399a 8ff.

[48]This topic appears in Aristotle's Topics as ek pros ti, cf. V, 6, 135b. Loci paralleli from the are numerous. Dionysius of Halicarnassus employs it in his letter to Ammaeus, when he discusses the relation of Demosthenes to Aristotle's Ars Rhetorica, cf. Ep. ad Amm., i. ch. 12. Maximus Planoudes, WRG V, p. 40, and Minucianus, WRG IX, p. 611, both use the topos. Both Cicero, cf. de In., I, 30, 47, and Quintilian, cf. In Or., V, 10, 76-79, know of it among the Latin orators. From the use of this topic Origen wishes to demonstrate that the definitions he is about to unpack belong to the doctrines of church. This is proved through the relation of the former to the latter.

[49]Spengel notes, cf. Arist. AR, p. 310, how Maximus uses this topic of division. The argument from authority makes a most effective line of argumentation, for Maximus Planoudes' example see, WRG V, p. 405, 7; 404, 7. For the coupling of these topics among the Attic Ten, e.g. Isocrates, 217-220, p. 103f; Demos. xviii. 24, p. 233. Another example from Demosthenes is illustrative of Origen's argumentative plan, cf. viii. 23, p. 95. In this example Demosthenes uses the topics of authority and division with past and future eikota arguments. When Origen states, "pecies vero eorum, quae per praedicationem apostolicam manifeste traduntur, istae sunt" (P4, p. 9, 12-13), he is referring to arguments past, P1-3, and those to come as the argument of the Periarchôn unfolds. Given the canonical status of the speeches of Demosthenes at Alexandria in the Imperial period it is possible that Origen was aware of this type of argument construct, and perhaps employed it in his own compositional scheme.

[50]Ek tôn pros allêla is the argument from mutual relation of terms or notions. In this pericope the stress is on the inter-relation of notions between Origen and the Apostles and teachers of the church. It is through the use of this topic that Origen attempts to legitimate his interpretation of church doctrine. That there was opposition to Origen's interpretation can be inferred from the topic itself. This topic was originally treated by Aristotle in his Topics under the head of oppositions or opposites, cf. II, 8, 114a 13. This understanding of the topos was held in the Hellenistic-Roman period. Cicero gives a good illustration of the argument from relatives: "Sin ea non modo eos ornat penes quos est, sed etiam universam republicam, cur aut discere turpe quod scire honestum est, aut quod nosse pulcherrimum est id non gloriosum docere," Orat., XLI, 142, see also Cicero, Top., XI, 49; de Inv., I, 30, 47. Quintilian provides an excellent illustration of the use of this topic as well. "Illa quoque, quae ex rebus mutuam confirmationem praestantibus ducuntur (quae proprii generis videri quidam volunt, et vocant 'ek tôn pros allela,' Cicero ex rebus sub eandem rationem ventientibus) fortiter consequentibus iunxerim si portorium Rhodiis locare honestum est et Hermocreaonti conducere; et quod discere honestum et docere," cf. In Or., V, 10, 78. The argument "If it may be said of one (of the two terms of the relation) that he has done rightly or justly, then the same terms may be applied to what the other has suffered; and similarly command implies obedience." Or, as Quintilian asserts in his example, "What is honorable to learn, is honorable to teach." If we may employ these loci paralleli to illustrate what Origen is doing in this pericope, then we can suggest that he employs this topic to persuade his audience that he has learned from the Apostles and teachers of the church, and is teaching what they taught. As such he argues that he is offering to his audience wisdom, and correct doctrine, and those who accept what he proposes will also benefit from a mutual relation with the teachings of the church. The advantages of this relationship are clear, as are the disadvantages if the hearers do not accept what Origen proposes. See, Arist. AR ed. Cope-Sandys, p. 241-244 for a complete discussion of this topic.

[51]In this brief chapter Origen presents a short outline of his philosophical theology. From (P4, p. 9, 13-15) it appears that Origen posits the essence of God, and then relates it to the second nous, Christ, and then both to spirit. Jerome states in the Ep. ad Avitum II that in the beginning of the first book of the Periarchôn Origen declared that Christ was not begotten the Son of God, but made such. (Latin factum = Greek genêton). In Rufinus' redaction what Jerome reports as Origen's testimony has been modified. This is suggested because of the topos extant even in Rufinus' version of the proposition. The division of the primal or first genus into its species is the order or line of argumentation. The Son is genêtos because, although he is not generated in the course of time, he is metaphysically dependent from an eternal cause, the Father. This is why the Son is a species of the Father. Thus, the Son is created because all things are created through the Father, cf. Comm. in Joh., II, 10. Although the Son is created he is ungenerated in the sense that he had not been generated in the course of time. This is so because the Son is not metaphysically   independent   of   the   first   cause,   but   is   eternally

dependent upon the first cause. There is a confusing use of the terms agenêtos and genêtos with Origen, but this is not uncommon with a number of Middle-Platonists, e.g. Albinus, Did., XIV 3, p. 81 (Louis); cf. F. Sassen, Geschiedenis v.d. Wijsbegeerte der Grieken en Romeinen, Antwerpen-Nijmegen: 1949, p. 157; E. Pelosi, "Een Platoonse gedachte bij Gaios, Albinos en Apuleius van Madaura," SC 15 (1939), p. 375-394 and 16 (1940), p. 226-242; J.H. Loenen, "Albinus' Metaphysics. An Attempt at Rehabilitation," Mn 9 (1956), p. 296-319. By the time of Jerome and Rufinus, however, a Christian ontology based on Neo-Platonic models had been set up, and with it a corresponding "cleaning up" of those ontological ambiguities. Jerome and Rufinus both approach Origen from the context of fifth century philosophical and theological presuppositions, and interpret and modify Origen's proposals accordingly.

Jerome attacks Origen's definition of the Holy Spirit on grounds akin to those expressed in respect to the Son, cf. Ep. ad Avitum, II. The question revolves around the issue of whether or not the Holy Spirit was created or uncreated (genêtos ê agennêtos). Rufinus modifies Origen's construct (Latin natus aut innatus=Greek gennêtos e agennêtos). It is clear from a number of pericope, e.g. Comm. in Joh., II, 10, that Origen held the notion that of the three so-called hypostases only God the Father is unbegotten. The existence of the Son and Holy Spirit presupposes a higher cause, and they find their ground in God. This construct is extant in P 4 in that the argument from division is one from the whole to its parts, genus to species. The argument of the pericope tends toward the ontological reality, that Origen wishes to proclaim.

Origen assumes one of the basic principles of dialectic, which is to examine the substance of each thing, and then its accidents. In this chapter, Substance is examined by "descending" (a priori), by the process of division and definition. This method has nothing original to Origen. It is found in Albinus, Did., V-VI, 156-160 ed. Hermann, as well as Clement, Strom., VIII, 6 (III, p. 90-93). The argument from division points toward and reveals the logical cogency of triadic Godhead.

I,1,1

[52]Cf. Arist, AR II, 23, 1, 1397a 7; also Top., II, 9, 114b 6ff.

[53]Among the Hellenistic rhetors an argument ek tôn enantiôn is well known. Apsines and Minucianus call it apo tou enantiou, cf. WRG IX, p. 524, 19; IX, p. 608, 18, while Maximus Planoudes terms the argument ek tou enantiou, cf. WRG V, 404, 3. In the Latin handbooks Quintilian translates this topic as locus ex contrariis, cf. In. Or., V, 10, 73. Cicero conflates this topic with the juxtaposition of inconsistencies, i.e. Aristotle's to ta anomologoumena skopein, AR II, 23, 1400a 15ff., which is another of the antikeimena topoi. Cicero thought that in the opposition of ideas which is characteristic of this topic was the essence of the enthymêmê, Top., XIII, 55. Quintilian concurred, In. Or., V, 10, 2. This merging of two distinct topics in Aristotle into one in the Hellenistic-Roman period is characteristic of the doxographical activity, which preceded the works listed above, but which these authors relied on for the composition of their own handbooks. In Aristotle's Ars Rhetorica it appears that ek tôn enantiôn functioned as an argument, which

highlighted the logical opposition between two hypotheses, while the topic to ta anomologoumena skopein, although pointing out contrast, focuses upon the falsity of the statements of the other side in order to bring the holder of these statements into disrepute, and to discredit the aspersions he has cast upon one's own character. Later theorists, noting the closeness of these topics, united them, cf. Gebauer, De Argumenti Ex Contrario Formis, Zwickau: 1877, pp. xxvi-xxvii. It was recognized that this topic added greatly to the force of an argument. As such Apsines described this topic as ek machês, and Minucianus as apo tou machomenou, cf. WRG IX, p. 526, 1; IX, p. 609, 12. Origen's use of this argument form reflects the later Hellenistic mixture of the topoi.

[54]Cf. Arist. Top., II, 9, 114b 6ff., III, 6, 119a 38ff, see Palmer, The TOPOI of Aristotle's Rhetoric as Exemplified in the Orators, Diss. Chicago: 1934, p. 8 n. 4. Palmer presents a solid description of the function of this topic in Aristotle, but the analysis breaks down when she discusses the adaption of these topoi in the Hellenistic and Roman sources. The expectation is that the later rhetoricians should have accurately reproduced the topical arrangement extant in Aristotle. There is no recognition that a Cicero or Apsines do not work directly from Aristotle's Rhetoric or that later theorists work, at least from their perspectives, to improve the work of their predecessors.

[55]Cf. Arist. AR ed. Cope-Sandys, p. 238-239. Cope has the passage in Aristotle's Topics in mind when he presents his explanation, cf. II, 8, 113b 27. The point to note, as Cope suggests, is that one class of demonstrative enthymemes is derived from opposites. The inference is drawn ek tôn enantiôn from the correctness or incorrectness, the truth or falsehood, between the opposites. If the audience is persuaded that your position is the correct or true one, and your opponents false, then the question of the character (ethos) of the two parties is raised. Virtue (sophrosynê) and vice (akolasia) are the predicate attributes with truth and falsehood. Origen substitutes the equivalent Christian virtues and vices. He does not need to explicitly state them. He allows his audience to assume them. Cicero and Quintilian tell us how this works when constructing an argument, cf. Top., XI, 47; In. Or., V, 10, 73.

Origen's treatment of opposites has a rhetorical as well as logical dimension. In both aspects it clearly has a reference to the art of reasoning, to the inferences affirmative and negative that may be drawn by constructive or refutative syllogisms and enthymemes.

[56]Cf. Lysias, xvi. 11 (Spengel). The form is:

Those who share in their sports are not
those whom they hate.
I am one whom they hate.
Therefore, it is provided I do not share
in their sports.

There are good examples offered from Isocrates, viii. 19. An example is also extant from one of the speeches of Demosthenes known at Alexandria in the Hellenistic-Roman period, De balsa legatione 6. This topic apparently was a favorite of Demosthenes, cf. xlvi. 24ff. This example is noteworthy because Demosthenes refers to a law in order to assume its converse. Isaeus and Lysias use the same construct, cf. x. 13; ix. 10. These loci paralleli indirectly inform us of the function, at least rhetorically, of this topic. In the case of Origen he refers to a passage in scripture, "Our God is a consuming fire" (Deut. 4:24) in order to assume its opposite, "God is Spirit..." (Jn. 4:24). This pericope offers a good example of how a Christian author forms his own literature in accordance with the rules and canon of Hellenistic rhetoric.

[57]See n. 2.

[58]Cf. Arist. AR II, 22, 15, 1396b 26ff., Apsines, WRG IX, p. 524, 19; Minucianus, WRG IX, p. 608, 18; Maximus Planoudes, V, p. 404, 3. On the whole any of the anti-keimena topic is considered primarily forensic in the Hellensitic and Roman period, see also Cicero, Top., XIII, 55, de Inv., I, 30, 46; Quintilian, In. Or., V, 10, 73. Origen employs the topic in the manner of his fellow rhetors. The pseudo-Anaximenes understands this topic as having an advisory dimension, cf. AR c. i, p. 7, 8 ed. Spengel. There are echoes of the deliberative aspect of the topic in Aristotle as well, cf. AR II, 25, 3, 1402a 35. This also appears in the examples from Hellenistic rhetors listed above. Thus, it is possible that this topic may be used for offering advice. Yet the advice is most effective once the proposition of the opponent has been demolished.

[59]Demosthenes offers an example which illustrates the inconsistencies in the story of his opponents by means of the eikota argument, cf. xlv. 35, p. 1112 (Spengel). The emphasis on this example is to discredit the character of the opponent. Origen's construct resembles the locus ex repugnantibus described by Cicero and Quintilian, cf. Top., III, 11, IV, 21; In. Or., V, 10, 74.

I,1,2

[60]Cf. Arist. AR II, 23, 12, 1398b 24ff.

[61]Cf. Ibid., II, 23, 1 1397a 7ff.

[62]Cf. Ibid., II, 23, 23, 1400a 16ff.

[63]This formal refutation of the doctrine that God is corporeal is ontologically underlined by the argument that the first principle of the universe is by definition non-corporeal, at least according to the metaphysical presuppositions Origen holds. Anything material belongs to the sensible realm, and God is not only above the sensible realm he is also above the intelligible. Origen's refutation of the corporealists' thesis in these pericopae is an attempt to demonstrate that even on their own, when examined critically, the corporealist definition proves wanting. The ground for this conclusion is formal invalidity, and non-demonstrability from scripture.

[64]Isoc. xviii. 15, p. 374c. This argument form is a type of reveral argument called by Spengel ex contrario. Lys. ix 10. Here a law is referred to in order to assume its converse. On this see also Demosthenes, xlvi, 24ff.

[65]Apsines, WRG ix, p. 524,19; Minucianus, WRG ix, p. 608,18.

[66]Cicero, Top. XIII,55; de Inv. I,30,46; Quintilian, In. Or. V,10,73. Aristotle, in his Topics, refers to the topic ek tōn enantiōn, cf. II,9,114b 6ff.; III,6,119a 38ff. In the first century B.C./A.D. these argument forms were viewed as falling under the broad heading

dialectic. It is clear from Origen's use of these topics, in conjunction with the undemonstrated argument forms, that he views the rhetorical syllogism as one of a variety of argument types applicable to scientific discourse.

[67]Aristotle states that this topic is utilized for pointing out inconsistencies in times, actions, and words, cf. AR II,23,23, 1400aff. At 1400a 15ff. he shows how useful this argument type is for pointing out the falsity of statements from one's opponents. This is exactly what Origen attempts to do in his utilization of this topic.

[68]The point being that Origen hopes to convince his audience that his own argument is a tekmêrion. It was held in antiquity that the opposition of ideas which characterize this topic was the very ground of the ehthymemâ, cf. Cicero, Top. XIII,55; Quintilian, In. Or. V,10,2. Indeed, for purposes of persuasion it was held to be one of the strongest of the argument types, cf. Apsines, WRG ix. p. 526,1; Minucianus, WRG ix. p. 609,12. Origen, apparently aware of this judgment, structures his rhetorical argument with this topic for the persuasive impact he desires.

[69]Isoc. xvii. 47; xv. 144 (Spengel).

[70]Anax. AR c. v., p. 25.2 (Spengel); c.ix.p. 33,15; ch. x. p. 33,24 (Spengel).

[71]Arist., AR II,23,23,1400a 15ff.

[72]Cicero, Top. XIII,55.

[73]Quintilian, In. Or., V,10,2.

[74]Apsines, WRG ix, p. 526,1.

[75]Minucianus, WRG ix. p. 609,12.

[76]Cf. Aristotle, AR II,23,23, 1400a 15ff. This understanding of the function of the topos, as noted, was continued in later Hellenistic and Roman rhetoric. Origen thus employs the topic within the deductive enthymeme in standard fashion.

[77]Cf. Cicero, Top. III,11; IV,21; XII,53. Quintilian, In. Or. V,10,74.

[78]Cf. Top. XIII,55.

I,1,3

[79]These topics are described in Aristotle's Ars Rhetorica, cf. AR II,23.

[80]Cf. Aristotle, AR II,23,4, 1379b 15ff.; Top. III,6,119b 17.; II,10,115a 6-14. According to Aristotle there are three divisions of the "more and less," cf. Top. II,10,114bff. Quintilian knows of this topic, cf. In. Or. V,10,87ff, although he reverses Aristotle's "less" and "more," cf. G. Palmer, The TOPOI of Aristotle's Rhetoric as Exemplified in the Orators, p. 18 n. 3. It was also known to Theon of Alexandria who called it the argument apo tês sugkriseôs, cf. WRG i. p. 225,2, and by Apsines who discusses it under apo tou elattonos and apo tou meizonos, cf. WRG ix. p. 522, 13ff.

[81]The appeal ek kriseôs is "Deus Spiritus est," cf. Jn. 4:24, posited in the previous chapters. If God is spirit, it follows, given Origen's presuppositions, that the Holy Spirit is spirit. This indirect use of an appeal from scripture is formally permissable because the first three chapters stand in a relationship to one another as a series of simple arguments compounded into a non-simple argument.

[82]Dem. xxi. 212, p. 582; vii. 44ff., p. 100.

[83]Cf. Gebauer, De Argumenti Ex Contario Formis Quae Reperiuntur Apud Oratores Atticos, see TOPOS XXII.

[84]Cf. Dem. xxi. 212, p. 582; vii. 44ff., p. 100; lxi. 4, p. 1402; li. 21ff., p. 1234. In general this is the form Origen's argumentation takes. There is the movement from question to answer in I,1,1-3.

[85]Ek tou mallon kai êtton was one of the most common types of arguments used by the Attic Ten, cf. Spengel, Dinarchus i.45; Andocides iv.15; Demosthenes liv, 63, p. 1264; Isaeus viii. 33ff.; Isocrates xiv. 52 and xv 166 in Gebauer's category of the ex contrario form; Lysias i.31, vii. 26. Gebauer's recognition that this topic falls within the antikeimena group, although not exclusively, is important to note. We know that in late antiquity the number of topics were reduced or conflated from the list presented by Aristotle. Thus, although we have only mentioned the argument "from the more and less" in this pericope, it would not be incorrect to assert that the topic has been an aspect of Origen's argumentative arsenal since the opening of the Periarchôn. The choice he gives his audience is to decide which of the two positions offered is more, and which is less. In this pericope, however, such an appeal becomes forcefully explicit. The fact that this argument form was so popular among the Attic orators is important because Origen could have utilized their speeches as formal models for his own. If he were successful at mimêsis then the effect on the audience would have been in his favor. To argue on behalf of the Holy Spirit as an intelligible entity with the force of a Demosthenes would have been Origen's ideal.

[86]In this chapter Origen's goal is to convince his audience that the materialist definition of the Holy Spirit is ek tou êtton. This then couples to the ek tou mallon construct which concludes the chapter. Loci paralleli which illustrate how this topic was used among the creators are extant in Dem. xxi. 212, p. 582; Isoc. viii. 69, p. 173ab; Lys. xxv. 17, p. 172. E.g. Dem. viii. 44ff., p. 100; Aesch. i.85, p. 11.

[87]Origen employs the mallon kai êtton argument to point out the inadequacy of his opponent's "probable" argument, and the validity and truthfulness of his own "necessary" argument.

[88]There is a strong link between this topic and ek kriseôs, e.g. Isoc. xx. 3, p. 396a; Din. ii.26, p. 108. Examples of the combination of the topics of the "more and less," "from judgement," and "from opposites" are found in Dem. xxvi. 23ff., p. 807; Aesch. i. 85, p. 26; Lycurg. 82, p. 158; 116, p. 164; 121, p. 165.

[89]Spengel's examples are: Dem. xxxix. 28, p. 102; lvii. 4, p. 1300. He also includes an example from Hyperides. This one is important because its source is late, and from Oxyrhynchus during the first centuries A.D., cf. Ox. 17, col. 8. This illustrates that the Attic Ten were copied in Hellenistic-Roman Egypt for purposes in the boulê, and as mere school exercises. The preservation of the speeches of the Attic Ten in Egypt are discussed by Brzoska, De Canone Decem Cratorum Atticorum Quaestiones, Breslau: 1883; Pack, Greek and Latin Literary Texts from Gaaeco-Roman Egypt, and Willis, "Greek Literary Papyri From Egypt and the Classical Canon," HLB 12 (1958) p. 5-34.

[90]E.g. Dem. xv. 23, p. 197; xviii. 68, p. 247; xxiii. 109, p. 656; 211 p. 690 (xxiii); xxiii. 23, p. 888; Isoc. ii. 36, p. 22a; vi. 54, p. 127bc.

[91]A contemporary with Philo, Theon of Alexandria, places ek kriseôs and ek ton mallon kai êtton together and calls the topics apo sugkriseôs, cf. WRG i. p. 225,2. It is possible that such a handbook, which conflates a number of topics, could have been used by Origen. This is suggested because in this pericope, as well as others, Origen combines topics when he argues. This combining activity is common in all the rhetorical handbooks of the Hellenistic and Roman periods.

[92]If we focus just on the topic ek tou mallon kai êtton this is evident. Aristotle discusses this topos in his Topics, II,10,115a 6-14. Quintilian also recognizes the logical aspect of this topic in his In. Or. V,10,87,88:

Adpositiva vel comparativa dicuntur, quae minora ex maioribus, maiora ex minoribus, paria ex paribus probant...

This understanding of the formal dimension of rhetoric is continued in Theon, cf. WRG i. p. 225,2; and Apsines, cf. WRG ix. p. 522,13ff.

I,1,4

[93]Cf. Arist., AR II,23,27, 1400b 6ff.

[94]Cf. Arist., AR II,23,11, 1398a 41ff. Cope's interpretation of the topic describes its function in this pericope. A case is admitted to prove a general rule from which an inference is drawn, cf. Cope-Sandys Aristotle's Ars Rhet. ii. p. 259. The argument is an induction and a resulting deduction. e.g. Isoc. 1.34, p. 9c: paradeigma poiou ta pareleluthota tôn mellontôn. See the parallel in Arist. AR I,9,40, 1368a 29ff.

[95]E.g. Dem. i.12ff., p. 12ff.; iv.3, p. 40ff., 130ff., xxiii. 141ff., p. 66ff. For further examples see Spengel's list under this topic, SRG. The orator generally employs this topic to enumerate a series of past events to show that the same thing is likely to happen in the future. In this case such temporal considerations are not considered. Origen's focus is peri logôn, and the enumeration is utilized for purposes of refuting the definition proposed by his opponents.

[96]Cf. Theon, Progymnasmata, c.vii=WRG i. p. 255,2.

[97]Cf. Arist., AR II,25,4,1402a 37, expanded 1402b 9ff.

[98]E.g. Dem., xix. 298, p. 438; xxiii. 74, p. 644; Isoc. iv.31, p. 47a.

[99]E.g. Dem. xviii. 6, p. 227; Aesch. iii. 108, p. 69. Here Solon and the Delphic oracle are coupled.

[100]E.g. Isoc., ix.51, p. 199b. As Cope cotes this is quoted by Aristotle, see AR II,23,12, 1399a 4ff. cf. Dem. xx. 93, p. 485; 102, p. 488. Here the Areopagus is the authority. At xix. 298, p. 438 the gods are the authority. e.g. Lysias, vi. 10, p. 104. In this example the sayings of a wise man is used as the basis for authoritative judgements.

[101]E.g. Element, Strom. vi.58,1 (ii.461.6-8). In this passage the beginning of St. John's gospel is used to prove the metaphysical assertion that the Logos as kosmos noêtos is the typos of the sensible things.

[102]E.g. Philo, De Op. Mun. 26-27. In this passage by quoting the beginning of Genesis Philo points out that the expression ên archê must not be understood as hinting at a determined time when the creation took place.

[103]Quintilian, In. Or. V,11,36-44 for a discussion of this topic. This argument type is one from universal consent, see Cicero, Tusc. Disp. I,12-15; especially 13,30 (of the belief in God).

I,1,5

[104]Cf. Arist. AR II,23,1,14.

[105]Cf. WRG v. p. 404,3.

[106]Cf. Arist. AR II,23,13.

[107]Ibid., II,23,9.

[108]Cf. Arist. AR II,23,15, 1399a 18ff. Cicero picks up this topic and tells us it is utilized to show 'a derivation from the right path,' cf. Orat. Partit. XXXVI, 126. Cope suggests that blaisos and hraibos valgus and varus express a deformity or divergence from the right line, or standard shape, see Arist. AR II,23,15, p. 273-274. If this interpretation of the meaning and function of the topic is correct then it tells us precisely what Origen is doing in this pericope. His goal is to point out the defect of the corporealists' definition, and thereby the correctness of his own.

I,1,6

[109]Cf. R. B. Todd, Alexander of Aphrodisias on Stoic Physics, p. 21-28.

[110]Cf. E. Bréhier, Chrysippè, p. 128-129; S. Sambursky, Physics of the Stoics, p. 15-16. The problem is in interpreting what this complex doctrine meant. There is little agreement on the specifics of this interpretation as an examination of the secondary literature will show.

[111]The theory of pneuma is one which maintains that both principles have physical properties, cf. H. J. Krämer, Platonismus und hellenistische Philosophie, p. 108 n. 3. Origen's attack seems to point this datum out.

[112]Cf. Arist. AR II,23,10, 1398a 37ff.; II,23,13, 1399a 8ff.; II,23, II,23,8, 1398a 19ff.

[113]E.g. Cicero de Or. II,164.

...si res tota quaeritur, definitione universa explicanda est, sic: si maiestas est amplitudo ac dignitas civitatis, is eam minuit qui exercitum hostibus populi Romani tradidit, non qui eum qui id fecisset populi Romani potestati tradidit.

As a method of attack it was also utilized by Maximus Planoudes, cf. WRG v. p. 405, 19.

[114]Cf. In. Or. V.10,54-58.

I,1,7

[115]This outline merely serves the purpose of framing the rhetorical argument in this chapter. For a full examination of Stoic theories of knowledge, see: E. Zeller, Die Phil. d. Gr. III,1,6, p. 507ff.; M. Pohlenz, Die Stoa, p. 47-51; E. Bréhier, Chrysippè, p. 102ff.; L. Stein, Die Erkenntnistheorie der Stoa, Berlin: 1888; J. Gould, The Philosophy of Chrysippus, p. 48-66.

[116]This is postulated on the close similarity between the argument of De Princ., I,1,7, and the theory sketched by Chalcidius. In addition, Chalcidius is a source for a number of Origen's works, cf. J.C.M. Van Winden, Calcidius on Matter of His Doctrine and Sources, p. 10-23.

[117]Cf. J. Gould, The Philosophy of Chrysippus, p. 55-59. Here this difficult question is addressed.

[118]Cf. Arist. AR II,23,3, 1397a 28ff.; Top. V,6, 135bff.

[119]Cf. Arist. Top. II,8,114a 13.

[120]This is how the topic is interpreted by Cicero and Quintilian, cf. Cic. de Or. XLI,142; Top. II,19,12; XI,49; de Inv. I,30,47; Quin. In Or. V,10,78. As these readings suggest the Greek ek tôn pros allela=Latin relata. See, Cope, Arist. AR, p. 241-242.

[121]Cic. de Inv. I,30,47; cf. Max. Plan. WRG v. p. 40; Min. WRG ix. p. 611; Quin. In Or. V,10,76-79.

[122]Ep. ad Amm. i. c. 12.

[123]Cf. Dem. xxiii. 168.

[124]Isoc. xv. 105, p. 67; Isaeus. i.39, p. 44ff.

[125]This is what the topic is called by Apsines, Minucianus, and Maximus Planoudes, cf. WRG ix. p. 524,19; ix. p. 608,18; v. p. 404,3.

[126]In the redaction offered by Rufinus the term sentire is employed to designate both the products of sensible and intelligible intellection. The reason for the use of the same term to designate two distinct, yet interrelated modes of knowing, is perhaps grounded in Origen's own use of the term theia aisthêta to characterize divine intellection in general, cf. C. Cels. VIII 20 (II, p. 238,2. For this doctrine see, H. Koch, Pronoia und Paideusis, p. 83-84. It is proposes that the Latin sentire=the Greek aisthêsis. cf. I,1,9 p. 27,8-9; C. Cels. VII 34. The Latin sensum divinum=Greek theian aisthêsin.

[127]Cf. Arist. AR II,23,21 1399a 31.

[128]Cf. Syr. WRG iv. p. 739; Sopater WRG iv. p. 744-745; Quin. In. Or. III,8,22; V,10,33. See also Cicero, Top. XVIII, 68-71 where his comparationis locus compares the greater and the less good.

[129]Arist. Ars Rhet., ed. Spengel, p. 111-113.

[130]Ibid., note on p. 1326b 34, p. 104-106.

I,1,8

[131]With Maximus the topic is employed to point out the reasonableness of an argument, cf. WRG v. p. 405,11. With Apsines the topic is useful for underscoring the authoritative bases of an argument, cf. WRG ix, p. 526,13. Apsines' corresponds to the rhetorical use of the topos as explained by Aristotle.

[132]Cf. Arist. AR II,25,4 1402a 37 and 1402b 9ff.

[133]Ibid., I,6,24, 1363a 10ff. and I,6,25 1363a 16ff.

[134]We can assume this because of the wide use of these topics for these purposes among the Attic Ten: e.g. Isoc. xix. 50, p. 394d; Dem. xxiv. 212, 765ff.; lxi. 30, p. 1410; Lys. xiii. 63, p. 135.

[135] Arist. AR II,23,1 1397a 7f.; cf. Apsines, WRG ix. p. 524,19; Minucianus, WRG ix. 608,18; Maximus Planoudes, WRG v. p. 404,3. Here the topic is called ek tou enantiou.

[136] Cf. Arist. Top. I,10, 104a 13; II,8, 113b 15 and 27; II,9, 114b 6ff.; VI,9, 147a 32; III,6, 119a 38ff. In this final citation Aristotle tells of the association between enantia and antikeimena, i.e. that of species to its genus topically. Opposites constitute one group in a three-fold division of opposition.

[137] Anaximenes, AR c. i. p. 7-8 (Spengel); Cicero, Top. XIII, 55; de Inv. I,30,46; Quintilian, In. Or. V,10,73. For Apsines, Minucianus, and Maximus see n. 3.

[138] E.g. Isoc. iv. 31, p. 47a; x. 46, p. 218b; Dem. xix. 298, p. 438; xxiii. 74, p. 644; Lysias, vi. 10, p. 104. Here the reference is to the wise men.

I,1,9

[139] The rendering of "sensum divinum invenies" is Rufinus' translation of "aisthêsin theian eurêseis," which Origen presents in C. Cels. VIII,34, p. 185,15 Koe. Rufinus repeats the translation at De Princ. IV,4,10, p. 364,8 Koe. The LXX version of this verse is: "epignosin theou eurêseis." Given Origen's epistemic assumptions it is clear why he rendered epignosin as aisthêsin theian. Cf. H. Görgemanns-H. Karpp, Origenes Vier Bücher von den Prinzipien, p. 121 n. 26.

[140] Cf. Arist. AR II,23,18, 1399b 6ff.; II,23,29, 1400b 21ff.

[141] Cf. Min. WRG ix. p. 6103ff.

[142] Cf. Max. Pl. WRG v. p. 405, 14ff.

[143] E.g. Isoc. xv. 73ff.; Dem. xxii. 46, p. 607. This loci paralleli is significant because as Demosthenes states, while employing this argument form, "the real question at stake is the future validity of the laws." This theme is certainly echoed in (1,1,9).

[144] Cf. Arist. Top. II,6,112a 32.

[145] Cf. Max. Pl. WRG v. p. 406,8ff.; Cic. Top. VIII,35; de Inv. II,9,28; Quin. In Or. V,10,30-31. The argument from the composition of a word is an aspect of this topic, cf. Arist. Top. II,6,112a 32. This notion maintains itself in the later sources. It is probable that this topic was a central one in Stoic rhetoric, cf. K. Barwick, "Probleme der stoischen Sprachlehre und Rhetorik," SAW 49 (1957), pp. 8-111. This analysis of the older Stoic dialectic and its use by Hellenistic and Roman dialecticians is important. With Origen it is quite clear that he avoids the Stoic method mostly because he does not hold propositions to be material entities which can be analyzed into their molecular components. As such he would hesitate to apply the same procedure to the analysis of names.

BIBLIOGRAPHY

Primary Sources: Editions and Translations

Albinus, Platonis dialogi secundum Thrasylli tetralogias dispositi, vol. vi., ed. C.F. Hermann, Lipsiae, 1884.

Alexander of Aphrodisias, In Analytica priora, Comment. in Arist. gr, ii.1, ed. M. Wallies, Berolini, 1883.

Alexander of Aphrosidias, In Topica, Comment. in Arist. gr., ii,2, Berolini, ed. M. Wallies, 1891.

Anecdota Graeca, ed. I. Bekker, Oxford, 1814.

Apuleius, De Philosophia Libri, ed. P. Thomas, Lipsiae, 1908.

Aristotle, Ars Rhetorica, ed. L. Spengel, Leipzig, 1867.

Aristotle, Ars Rhetorica, ed. E.M. Cope-J. E. Sandys, Cambridge, 1877.

Aristotle, Ars Rhetorica, tr. J.H. Freese, Loeb Classical Library, Cambridge-London, 1925.

Aristotle, De Caelo, ed. D.J. Allan, Oxford, 1955.

Aristotle, Fragmenta, selegit R. Walzer, Firenze, 1934.

Aristotle, Metaphysics, ed. W.D. Ross, Oxford, 1924.

Aristotle, Physics, ed. W.D. Ross, Oxford, 1936.

Aristotle, Prior and Posterior Analytics, ed. W.D. Ross, Oxford, 1949.

Aristotle, Topica et Sophista Elenchi, ed. W.D. Ross, Oxford, 1958.

Atticus, Atticos, ed. J. Baudry, Paris, 1931.

Celsus, "Der Alêthês Logos des Kelsos," Tübinger Beiträge zur Altertumswissenschaft, XXXIII, Stuttgart-Berlin, 1940.

Chalcidius, Commentary on the Timmaeus, ed. J.H. Waszink, London, 1962.

Cicero, Academica, ed. J.S. Reid, London, 1885.

Cicero, Academica, tr. H. Rackham, Loeb Classical Library, Cambridge-London, 1933.

Cicero, De Finibus bonorum et malorum, ed. J. Martha, Paris, 1928-30.

Cicero, De Inventione, tr. H.M. Hubbell, Loeb Classical Library, Cambridge-London, 1949.

Cicero, De Oratore, tr. E.W. Sutton, Loeb Classical Library, Cambridge-London, 1942.

Cicero, DeNatura Deorum, tr. H. Rackham, Loeb Classical Library, Cambridge-London, 1933.

Cicero, DePartitione Oratoria, tr. H. Rachham, Loeb Classical Library, Cambridge-London, 1942.

Cicero, Orator ad Brutum, tr. H.M. Poteat, Chicago, 1950.

Cicero, Topica, tr. H.M. Hubbell, Loeb Classical Library, Cambridge-London, 1949.

Clement of Alexandria, Extraits de Théodote, F. Sagnard, Paris, 1948.

Clement of Alexandria, ed. O. Stählin, Die griechische, christliche, Schriftsteller der ersten drei Jahrlunder, vol. i, 2e Auf., Leipzig, 1936, vol. ii., 3e Auf., Berlin, 1960, vol. iii., Leipzig, 1909.

Diogenes Laertius, Vitae Philosophorum, tr. R.D. Hicks, Loeb Classical Library, Cambridge-London, 1925.

Dozographi Graeci, ed. H. Diels, Berlin, 1879.

Epicurus, ed. C. Bailey, Oxford, 1926.

Eusebius, Historia ecclesiastica, ed. E. Schwartz (GCS), Leipzig, 1903-1908.

Eusebius, Praeparatio Evangelica, ed. K. Mras (GRS), Leipzig, 1954-56.

Galen, Claudii Galeni Opera Omnia, ed. C. Kühn, Leipzig, 1821-1833.

Galen, De Methodo Medendi, ed. C. Kühn, Leipzig, 1825.

Galen, De Placitis Hippocratis et Platonis, ed. I. von Müller, Leipzig, 1874.

Galen, De Pulsuum Differentiis, ed. C. Kühn, Leipzig, 1824.

Galen, Institutio Logica, ed. C. Kalbfleisch, Leipzig, 1896.

Irenaeus, Adversus Haereses, ed. W. Harvey, Cambridge, 1857.

Mensig, J.D., Sanctorum conciliorum nova et amplissima collecto tomus IX (texts de Justinian et du concile de Constantinople II), Paris-Leipzig, 1902.

Nichomachus, Introduction Arithmetica, ed. R. Hoche, Leipzig, 1866.

Nichomachus, Theologumena Arithmeticae, ed. V. de Falco, Leipzig, 1922.

Numenius, Numenius, ed. E. des Places, Paris, 1973.

Numenius, Numenius, ed. E.A. Leemens, Brussels, 1937.

Origen, Comm. in Joh., GCS 10, ed, Preuschen.

Origen, Contra Celsum, GCS 2 vol. i-iv, GCS 3 vol. v-viii.

Origen, Contra Celsum, tr. H. Chadwick, Cambridge, 1965.

Origen, De Martyrio, GCS 2, p. 3-47.

Origen, De Principiis, GCS 22.

Origen, De Principiis, tr. G.W. Butterworth, London, 1936. tr. M. Harl, G. Dorival, A. Le Boulleuc, Paris, 1976. tr. H. Görgemanns, H. Karpp, Darmstadt, 1976. tr. H. Crouzel, M. Simonetti, Paris, 1978-1980.

Origen, Ocellus Lucanus, ed. R. Harder, Berlin, 1926.

Origen, Pseudo-Pythagorica, ed. H. Thesleff, (The Texts of the Hellenistic Period), Abo, 1965.

Origen, the Christian, Origenes Werke, ed. P. Loetschau.

Origen, the Neoplatonist, fragments edited by K.O. Weber, "Origenes der Neuplatoniker," Zetemata 27 (1962).

Philo of Alexandria, Philo, tr. F.H. Colson, Loeb Classical Library, Cambridge-London, 1935.

Philo of Alexandria, ed. L. Cohn, P. Wendland, Philon, Berolini, 1896-1915.

Photius, Bibliotheca, Migne, PG., 103-104.

Plato, Opera, ed. J. Burnet, vol. i-v, Oxford, 1937-1945.

Plotinus, ed. E. Bréhier, Paris, 1924-28, vol. 1-vi.

Plutarch, Moralia, ed. G.N. Bernardikis, Leipzig, 1888-1896.

Porphyry, Vita Plotini, ed. E. Bréhier, Paris, 1954.

Proclus, Opera, ed. V. Cousin, Paris, 1820-1827. In Platonis Timaeum, ed. E. Diehl, vol. i-iii, Lipsiae, 1903-1906.

Quintilian, Institutio Oratoria, tr. H.E. Butler, Loeb Classical Library, Cambridge-London, 1921.

Seneca, Epistulae Morales, tr. R.M. Gummere, Loeb Classical Library, Cambridge-London, 1920.

Sextus Empiricus, Adversos Mathematicos, ed. H. Mutschman, libri, vii-xi, Leipzig, 1914.

Sextus Empiricus, Adversos Mathematicos, ed. J. Mau, libri, i-vi, Leipzig, 1954.

Sextus Empiricus, Opera, ed. H. Mutschman, Leipzig, 1912-1914.

Simplicius, In Categorias, Comment. in Arist. gr., viii, ed. C. Kalbfleisch, Berolini, 1907.

Simplicius, In Physica, Comment. in Arist. gr. ix-x, ed. H. Diels, Berolini, 1882.

Spengel, L., Rhetores Graeci, Lipsiae, 1854.

Stobaeus, Anthologium, ed. C. Wachsmuth; C. Hense, Berlin, 1884-1912, vol. i-iv.

Stoicorum Veterum Fragmenta, ed. I. von Arnim, Leipzig, 1903-1905, vol. i-iii.

Taran, L., Speusippus, Leiden, 1978.

Walz, C., Rhetores Graeci, Stuttgartiae-Tubingae, 1833.

Xenocrates, Xenocrates, ed. R. Heinze, Xenocrates, Leipzig, 1892.

I. General

Armstrong, A.H., ed., The Cambridge History of Later Greek and Early Medieval Philosophy, Cambridge: 1967.

Bigg, C., The Christian Platonists of Alexandria, 2nd ed., Oxford: 1913.

Blass, F., Die griechische Beredsamikeit, Berlin: 1865.

Chadwick, H., Early Christian Thought and the Classical Tradition, Oxford: 1966.

Cherniss, H., The Riddle of the Early Academy, Berkeley: 1945.

DeVogel, C.J., Greek Philosophy, III, 2nd ed., Leiden: 1966.

Dillon, J., The Middle Platonists, Ithaca: 1977.

Dörrie, H., Platonica Minora, München: 1976.

Entretiens Hardt, III, "Recherches sur la tradition platonicienne," Geneve: 1957.

Entretiens Hardt, V, "Les sources de Plotin," Geneve: 1960.

Jaeger, W., Early Christianity and Greek Paideia, Cammbridge: 1961.

Krämer, H.J., Der Ursprung des Geistmetaphysik, Amsterdam: 1964.

Merlan, P., From Platonism to Neoplatonism, The Hague: 1964.

Moraux, P., Der Aristotelismus bei den Griechen, Berlin: 1972.

Norden, E., Antike Kunstprosa, Leipzig: 1915.

Pohlenz, M., Die Stoa, Göttingen: 1959.

Schmekel, A., Die Philosophie der mittleren Stoa, Berlin: 1892.

Smith, R.W., The Art of Rhetoric in Alexandria, The Hague: 1974.

Theiler, W., Die Vorbereitung des Neuplatonismus, Berlin: 1930.

Uberweg, F., Praechter, K., Die Philosophie des Altertums, 13th ed., Basel: 1953.

Volkmann, R., Die Rhetorik der Grüchen und Römer, 2nd ed., Leipzig: 1885.

Zeller, E., Die Philosophie der Griechen, III.1 5th ed., Leipzig: 1923; III.2 4th ed., Leipzig: 1903.

II. Albinus

Festugière, A.J., La Révélation d'Hermes Trismégiste, IV, Paris: 1954.

Früchtel, "Klemens von Alexandria und Albinus," Berliner Philologische Wochenschrift, 57 (1937), c. 591-592.

Loenen, J.H., "Albinus' Metaphysics: An Attempt at Rehabilitation," Mnemosyne, IV, 9 (1956), 296-319; Mnemosyne, IV, 10 (1957), 35-56.

Milhaven, J.G., Der Aufsteig der Seele bei Albinus, Diss, München: 1962.

Praechter, K., "Zum Platoniker Gaios," Hermes, 57 (1922), 510-529.

Sinko, De Apulei et Albini doctrinae Platonicae adrumbratione, Krakow: 1905.

Witt, R.E., Albinus and thee History of Middle Platonism, Cambridge: 1937.

III. Antiochus, Eudorus, and Arius Didymus

Boyancé, P., "Etudes philoniennes," Révue des études grecs, 76 (1963).

Hirzel, R., Untersuchungen zu Ciceos philosophischen Schriften, Leipzig: 1883.

Luck, G., Der Akademiker Antiochus, Bern-Stuttgart: 1953.

Lüder, A., Die philosophische Persönlichkeit des Antiochus von Ascalon, Göttinger: 1940, 1909.

Sträche, H., De Arii Ditymi in morali philosophia auctoribus, Diss. Berlin:

Sträche, H., Der Eklektizismus des Antiochus von Ascalon, Berlin: 1921.

Theiler, W., "Philo von Alexandria und der Beginn des kaiserzeitlichen Platonismus," in Parusia, Frankfurt: 1965.

IV. Clement of Alexandria

Andresen, C., "Justin und mittlere Platonismus," Zeitschrift für Neutestamentalische Wissenschaft, 44 (1952/53), 157-195.

Andresen, C., Logos und Nomos, Berlin: 1955.

Bardy, G., Clément d'Alexandrie, Paris: 1926, "Aux origenes de l'école d'Alexandrie," Recherches de Science religieuse 27 (1937), 65-90.

Camelot, P., "Les idées de Clément d'Alexandrie et l'utilisation de la philosophie grecque," Recherches de science religieuse 21 (1931), 541-569.

Casey, R.P., "Clement and the Two Divine Logoi," Journal of Theological Studies 25 (1924), 43-56.

Casey, R.P., "Clement of Alexandria and the Beginning of Christian Platonism," Harvard Theological Review, 18 (1925), 39-101.

Chadwick, H., "Clement of Alexandria," The Cambridge History of Later Greek and Early Mediaeval Philosophy, Cambridge: 1966.

Chadwick, H., Early Christian Thought and the Classical Tradition, Oxford: 1966.

Clark, E.A., Clement's Use of Aristotle: The Aristotelian Contribution to Clement of Alexandria's Refutation of Gnosticism, Philadelphia 1981.

Cognat, J., Clément d'Alexandrie: sa doctrine et sa polémique, Paris: 1959.

Daskalikis, M., Die eklektischen Auschauungen des Clemens von Alexandria und seine Abhängig Keit von der griechischen Philosophie, Diss. Leipzig: 1908.

de Faye, E., "De l'originalité de la philosophie chrétienne de Clément d'Alexandrie," Annuaire de l'Ecole des Hautes Etudes, 1919, 1-20.

de Faye, E., Clément d'Alexandrie, 2nd ed., Paris: 1906.

Delatte, A., "Un fragment d'arithmologie dans Clément d'Alexandrie," Bibliothèque de l'Ecole des Hautes Etudes, 1915, 231-245.

Eibl, H., "Die Stellung des Klemens von Alexandrien zur griechischen Bildung," Zeitschrift für Philosophie und philosophische Kritik, 164 (1917), 33-59.

Festugière, A.J., La Revelation d'Hermès Tristmégiste, Paris: 1950-1954.

Früchtel, L., "Klemens von Alexandria und Albinus," Berliner Philologische Wocherschrift, 57 (1937), c. 591-592.

Gercke, A., "Eine platonische Quelle des Neuplatonismus," Rheinisches Museum für Philologie, 41 (1886), 266-291.

Görgemanns, H., "Beiträge zur Interpretation von Platons Nomor," Zetemata 25 (1960).

Hackforth, R., "Plato's Theism," Classical Quarterly, 30 (1936), 4-9.

Hébert-Duperron, V., Essai sur la polémique et la philosophie de Clément d'Alexandrie, Paris: 1855.

Hegermann, H., "Die Vorstellung von Schöpfungmittler im hellenistischen Judentum und Urchristentum," Texte und Untersuchungen zur Geschichte der altchristlichen Literatum 82 (1961).

Holte, R., "Logos spermatikos," Studia Theologica 12 (1958), 109-168.

Ivanka, von, E., Plato Christianus, Einsiedln: 1964.

Jaeger, W., Early Christianity and Greek Paideia, Cambridge: 1965.

Lilla, S.R.C., Clement of Alexandria, Oxford: 1971.

Marrou, H.I., "Humanisme et christianisme chez Clément d'Alexandrie d'après le Pedagogue, Entretiers Hardt, iii (1958), 183-200.

Merk, C., Clemens Alexandrinus in seiner Abhängigkeit von der griechischen philosophie, Diss. Leipzig: 1879.

Muckle, J.T., "Clement of Alexandria on Philosophy as a divine Testament for the Greeks," Phoenix V (1951), 79-86.

Osborn, E.F., The Philosophy of Clement of Alexandria, Cambridge: 1957.

Outler, A.C., "The Platonism of Clement of Alexandria," Journal of Religion 20 (1940), 217-240.

Pade, P.B., Logos Theos, Rome: 1939.

Pohlenz, M., "Klemens von Alexandreia und sein hellenisches Christentum," Nachrichten von der Akademie der Wissenschaften in Göttingen, phil.-list. kl (1943), 103-180.

Prümm, K., "Glaube und Erkenntnis im Zweiten Buch der Stromata des Klemens von Alexandrien, Scholastik 12 (1937), 17-57.

Sagnard, F., Clément d'Alexandrie: extraits de Théodote, Paris: 1948.

Sagnard, F., La Gnose valentinienne et le témoignage de Saint Irénée, Paris: 1947.

Scherer, W., Clemens von Alexandrien und seine Erkenntnisprinzipien, München: 1908.

Schmidt, P.J., Klemens von Alexandreien in seinem Verhältnis zur griechischen Religion und Philosophie, Diss. Wien: 1939.

Schürmann, H., Die hellenische Bildung und ihr Verhältnis zur christlichen nach der Darstullung des Clemens von Alexandrien, Münster: 1859.

Spanneut, M., Le Stoicisme des Pères de l'Eglise, Paris: 1957.

Völker, W., "Der wahre Grostiken radh Clemens Alexandrinus, Texte und Unter-Suchungen 57 (1952).

Völker, W., "Die Vollkommenleitslehre des Clemens Alexendrinus un ihren, geschichtlichen Zusammenhängen," Theologische Zeitschrift 3 (1947), 15-40.

Witt, R.E., "The Hellenism of Clement of Alexandria," Classical Quarterly 25 (1931), 195-204.

Wolfson, H.A., "Plato's Pre-existent Matter in Patristic Philosophy," The Classical Tradition, Ithaca: 1966, 409-420.

Wolfson, H.A., The Philosophy of the Church Fathers, Cambridge: 1956.

Wytzes, J., "Paideia and Pronoia in the Works of Clemens Alexandrinus," Vigiliae Christianae, 9 (1955), 148-158.

Wytzes, J., "The Twofold Way I and II," Vigiliae Christianae, 11 (1957), 226-245; 14 (1960), 129-153.

V. Three Neopythagoreans: Moderatus, Nichomachus, Numenius

D'Ooge, Nichomachus of Gerasa, Ann Arbor: 1938.

Delatte, A., "un fragment d'arithmologie dans Clément d'Alexandrie," (Etudes sur la littérature pythagoricienne) Bibliothèque de l'Ecole des Hautes Etudes, Paris: 1915.

des Places, E., Numenius, Paris: 1973.

Dodds, E.R., "Numenius and Ammonius," Entretiens Hardt, V (1960), 3-32.

Dodds, E.R., "The Parmenides of Plato and the Origin of the Neoplatonic One," Classical Quarterly, 22 (1928), 129-142.

Dörrie, H., "Die Frage nach dem Transzendenten im Mittelplatonismus," Entretiens Hardt, V. (1960), 193-223.

Leemans, E.A., "Studien over den wijsgeer Numenius van Apaméa met vitgave der Fragmenten," Mémoires de l'Académie royale de Belgique 27 (1937).

Merlan, P., "The Later Academy and Platonism," The Cambridge History of Later Greek and Early Mediaeval Philosophy, Cambridge: 1966.

Puech, H.C., "Numenius d'Apamée et les théologies orientales au second siècle," Annuaire de l'Institut de Philologie et d'Histoire orientales, 2 (1934), 745-78.

VI. Origen

The books and articles listed in this bibliography are those which pertain to Origen, and specifically those which were utilized in the analysis of the Praefatio and De Deo of the

Periarchôn. For a complete collection of the literature concerning Origen up through 1969, see H. Crouzel, Bibliographie critique d'Origène, Paris: 1969. For the years 1969-1970, see F. Farina, Bibliografia Origeniana, Roma: 1971.

Aall, A., Geschichte der Logosidee in der griechischen Philosophie, Leipzig: 1896.

Aall, A., Geschichte der Logosidee in der christlichen Literatur, Leipzig: 1896.

Achelis, H., Das Christenthum in der ersten Jahrhunderten, Leipzig: 1899.

Andresen, C., "Justin und der mittlere Plantonismus," ZNW 44 (1952-1953), p. 157-195.

Andresen, C., Logos und Nomos: Die Polemik des Kelsos wider das Christentum, Berlin: 1955.

Arnou, R., "Platonisme des Pères," DThC 12 (1932-1935), p. 2258-2392.

Bardy, G., "Le text du Peri Archon d'Origène et Justinien," Recherches de Sciences Religieuses 10 (1920), p. 224-252.

Bardy, G., "Les citations bibliques d'Origène dans le De Principiis," Revue Biblique 28 (1919), p. 106-135.

Bardy, G., "Origène et l'aristotolisme," Melanges Gustave Glotz I, Paris, 1923.

Bardy, G., "Origène," Dictionnaire de théologie catholique, XI/2 (1932), p. 1489-1565.

Bardy, G., "Recherches sur l'histoire du texts et des versions latines du De Principiis d'Origène," Mémoires et travaux des Facultés catholiques de Lille, Paris: 1923.

Barre, A. de la., "Ecole chrétienne d'Alexandrie," Dictionnaire de théologie catholique, I (Paris, 1903), p. 805-824.

Batiffol, P., L'Eglise naissante et le catholicisme, Paris: 1909.

Beutler, R., "Origenes der Neuplatoniker," RE XVIII, 1, 1939, Sp. 1033.

Bigg, C., The Christian Platonists of Alexandria, Oxford: 1886.

Blass, F., Griechische Beredsamkeit, Berlin: 1865.

Borst, J., Beiträge zur sprachlich-stilistischen und rhetorischen Würdigung des Origenes, Freising: 1913.

Cadiou, R., Introduction au système d'Origène: Histoire de l'Ecole d'Alexandrie au début du IIIe siècle, Paris: 1936.

Cadiou, R., La Jeunesse d'Origène: Histoire de l'Ecole d'Alexandrie au début du IIIe siècle (Etudes de Theologie Historique), Paris: 1936.

Capone Braga, G., "Della Dialettica," Giornale di Metafisica, 9 (1954), p. 166-171.

Chadwick, H., Early Christian Thought and the Classical Tradition: Studies in Justin, Clement, and Origen, Oxford: 1966.

Consini, E., "Commento al Vengelio di Giovanni di Origene," Classici della Filosofia, Torino: 1968.

Cornélis, H., "Les Fondements cosmologiques del'eschatologie d'Origène," Revue des Sciences Philosophiques et Théologiques 31 (1959), p. 32-80; 201-247.

Crouzel, H., "Origène et la connaissance mystique," Museum Lessianum section Theologique 56, Bruges-Paris: 1961.

Crouzel, H., "Origène et la Philosophie," Théologie 52 (Paris, 1962).

Crouzel, H., "Qu'a voulu faire Origène en composant le Traité des Principes," Bulletin le Littérature Ecclésiastique 76 (Paris, 1975), p. 161-186; 241-260.

Crouzel, H., "Théologie de l'Image de Dieu chez Origène," Theologie 34 (Paris, 1956).

Daniélou, J., "Message évangélique et culture hellénistique aux IIe et IIIe siècles. Histoire des doctrines chrétiennes avant Nicée II," Bibliotheque de Theologie (Paris, 1961).

Daniélou, J., Origène: Le Génie du Christianisme, Paris: 1948.

Davies, H., "Origen's Theory of Knowledge," The American Journal of Theology, II, 4 (1898), p. 737-762.

Denis, J., De la Philosophie d'Origène, Paris: 1884.

Diekamp, F., Die origenistischen Streitigkeiten im sechsten Jahrhundert und das fünfte allgemeine Concil, Muenster: 1899.

Dodds, E.F., "Numenius and Ammonius," Entretiens Hardt V (Geneve, 1960), p. 3-32.

Dodds, E.F., "The Parmenides of Plato and the Origin of the Neoplatonic One," Classical Quarterly 22 (1928), p. 129-142.

Dorival, G., "Remarque sur la forme du Peri Archon," Origeniana: Premier colloque international des études origéniennes (Quaderni di Vetera Christianorum), 12 (1975), p. 33-45.

Dörrie, H., "Ammonios der Lehrer Plotins," Hermes 83 (1955), p. 439-477.

Dörrie, H., "Die Frage nach dem Transzendenten im Mittelplatonismus," Entretiens Hardt V (Geneve, 1960), p. 193-223.

Dörrie, H., "Die platonische Theologie des Kelsos in ihrer Auseinandersetzung mit der christlichen Theologie auf Grund von Origenes, c. Celsum 7, 42ff.," Nachrichten der Akademie der Wissenschaften zu Göttingen, phil.-hist. Klasse 1967, 2, p. 19-55.

Dörrie, H., "Was ist spaetantiker Platonismus? Ueberlegungen zur Grenzziehung zwischen Platonisms und Christentum," Theologische Rundschau 36 (1971), p. 285-302.

Faye, E. de., Origène: Sa vie, son oeuvre, sa pensée, Paris: 1928.

Festugière, A.J., La Révélation d'Hermès Trismégiste, I-IV, Paris: 1949-1954.

Hanson, R., "Did Origen apply the word homoousios to the Son?," Epektasis, p. 293-303.

Harl, M., "Recherches sur le peri archôn d'Origène en vue d'une nouvelle Edition," Studia Patristica III (TU 78), Berlin: 1961, p. 57-67.

Harl, M., "Recherches sur l'origénisme d'Origène: la satiété de la contemplation comme motif de la chute des âmes," Studia Patristica VIII (TU 93), Berlin: 1961, p. 57-67.

Harl, M., "Structure et cohérence du Peri Archon," Origeniana 12 (1975), p. 11-32.

Harl, M., Origène et la fonction révélatrice du Verbe Incarné (Patristica Sorbonne), Paris: 1958.

Heinemann, F., "Ammonios Sakkas und der Ursprung des Neuplatonismus," Hermes 61 (1926), p. 1-27.

Hirzel, R., Untersuchungen zu Ciceros philosophischen Schriften, Leipzig: 1883.

Ivanka, E. von., Plato Christianus, Einsiedeln: 1964.

Ivanka, von, E., Hellenistisches und Christliches im frühbyzantinischen Geistesleben, Wien: 1948.

Jones, R.M., "The Ideas as the Thoughts of God," Classical Philology 21 (1926), p. 317-326.

Keil, C.A. Th., Opuscula academica ad Novi Testamenti interpretationem grammatico-historicam et Theologiae christianae origenes pertinentia, Leipzig: 1821.

Kelber, W., Die Logosides von Heraklit bis Origenes, Stuttgart: 1958.

Klostermann, E., "Origeniana," Neutestamentliche Studien 1914, p. 107-117.

Klostermann, E., "Ueberkommene Definitionen im Werke des Origenes," ZNTW 37 (1938), p. 54-61.

Koch, H., Pronoia und Paideusis, Studien über Origenes und sein Verhältnis zum Platonismus, Berlin: 1932.

Krause, W., Die Stellung der frühchristlichen Autoren zur heidnischen Literatur, Wien: 1958.

Kübel, P., "Zum Aufbau von Origenes 'De Principiis,'" Vigiliae Christianae 25 (1971), p. 31-39.

Langerbeck, H., "Die Verbindung aristotelischer und christlicher Elemente in der Philosophie des Ammonius Saccas," Abhandlung der Akademie der Wissenschaften in Göttingen, phil.-hist. Klasse 69 (1967), p. 146-166.

Le Boulleuch, A., "La Place de la polémique antignostique dans le Peri Archon," Origeniana 12 (1975), p. 47-61.

Lubac, H. de., Histoire et Spirit, L'intelligence de l'Ecriture d'après Origène (Theologie 16) Paris: 1950.

Malingrey, A-M., Etude d'un groupe de mots dans la littérature grecque des Présocratiques au IVe siecle apres J.C. (Etudes et Commentaires), Paris: 1961.

Marcus, W., Der Subordinatianismus als historiologisches Phaenomen, München: 1963.

Milhaven, J.G., Der Aufsteig der Seele bei Albinus, Diss., Munchen: 1962.

Müller, G., "Studien zu den platonischer Nomoi," Zetemata 3 (1951).

Müller, K., "Kritische Beiträge," Sitzungsberichte der deutschen Akademie der Wissenschaften zu Berlin, 1919/II, p. 616-631. (Zu den Auszügen der Hieronymus Ad Avitum aus des Origenes Peri Archon; Uber die angeblichen Auszüge Gregors von Nyssa aus Peri Archon.)

Murray, J., "Origen, Augustine, Plotinus," The Month 170 (1937), p. 107-117.

Nautin, P., Origène: Sa vie et son oeuvre, Paris: 1977.

Nemeshegy, P., La Paternité de Dieu chez Origène (Bibliotheque de Theologie), Paris-Tournai: 1960.

Norden, E., Antike Kunstprosa, Leipzig: 1915.

Orbe, A., "En los albores de la exegesis iohannea (Ioh. I,3)," (Estudios Valentinianos II): Analecta Gregoriana 65 (1955).

Orbe, A., "La teologia del Espiritu Santo," (Estudios Valentinianos IV): Analecta Gregoriana, 158 (1966).

Pépin, J., Théologie cosmique et la Théologie chrétienne, (Bibliotheque de Philosophie conteemporaine), Paris: 1964.

Redpenning, E.R., Origenes: Eine Darstellung seines Lebens und seiner Lehrer, Bonn: 1841, 1846.

Rich, A.N.M., "The Platonic Ideas as Thoughts of God," Mnemosyne IV, 7 (1954), p. 123-133.

Robinson, J.A., The Philocalia of Origen, Cambridge: 1893.

Sagnard, F., La gnose valentinienne et le témoignage de saint Irénée (Etudes de philosophie médiévale), Paris: 1947.

Schnitzer, K.F., Origenes über die Grundlehren der Glaubenswissenschaft: Widerherstellungversuch, Stuttgart: 1835.

Simonetti, M., "Due note sull'angelologia origeniana," Rivista di cultura classica et medioevale 4 (1962), p. 165-208.

Simonetti, M., "Note sulla teologia trinitaria di Origene," Vetera Christianorum 8 (1971), p. 273-307.

Simonetti, M., "Osservazioni sulla struttura dei De Principiis di Origene," Rivista di filologia e d'istruzione classica, nuova serie 40 (1962), p. 273-290; 372-392.

Simonetti, M., "Sull'interpretazione d'un passo del De Principiis di Origene (I,3,5-8)," Rivista di cultura classica e medioevale 6 (1964), p. 15-32.

Simonetti, M., I Principi di Origene (Classici della religioni, Sezione quarta), Turion: 1968.

Stange, A.M., "Celsus und Origenes. Das Gemeinsame ihrer Weltanschauung nach den acht Büchern des Origenes gegen Celsus," ZNTW Beihefte 8 (1926).

Steidle, B., "Neue Untersuchungen zu Origenes PERI ARCHON," ZNTW 40 (1941), p. 236-243.

Studer, B., "A propos des traductions d'Origène par Jérôme et Rufin," Vetera Christianorum 5 (1968), p. 137-155.

Studer, B., "Zur Frage der dogmatischen Terminologie in der lateinischen Uebersetzung von Origenes' De Principiis," Epektasis, p. 403-414.

Trigg, J.W., Origen The Bible and Philosophy in the Third Century Church, Atlanta: 1983.

Vogt, H.J., Das Kirchenverständnis des Origenes (Bonner Beitraege zur Kirchengeschichte 4), Koln-Wien: 1974.

Völker, W., Das Vollkommenheitsideal des Origenes. Eine Untersuchung zue Geschichte der Froemmigkeit und zu den Anfängen christlicher Mystik, Tuebingen: 1931.

Waszink, J.H., "Bemerkungen zum Einfluss des Platonismus im fruehen Christentum," Vigiliae Christianae 19 (1965), p. 129-162.

Waszink, J.H., "Der Platonismus und die altchristliche Gedankenwelt," Entretiens Hardt (Geneve, 1955), p. 139-178.

Weber, K.O., "Origenes der Neuplatoniker," Zetemata 27 (1962).

Wendland, P., "Die hellenistisch-römische Kultur in ihren Beziehungen zu Judentum and Christentum. Die Urchristlichen Literaturformen," Handbuch zum Neuen Testament, I,2,3, Tubingen: 1912.

Wiles, M., "Eternal Generation," Journal of Theological Studies 12 (1961), p. 284-291.

Winden, J.C.M. van, Calcidius on Matter. His Doctrine and His Sources: A Chapter in the History of Platonism, Leiden: 1959.

Wolfson, H.A., Philo, Cambridge: 1947.

Wolfson, H.A., The Philosophy of the Church Fathers, Cambridge: 1956.

VII. Philo of Alexandria

Altaner, Berthold, "Augustinus und Philo von Alexandrien. Eine quellenkritische Untersuchung," ZKT 65 (1941) 81-90; reprinted in his Kleine patristische Schriften, 181-93. Ed. Günter Glockmann (TU 83), 1967.

Andersen, C., "Erlösung," RAC 6.54-219. [Esp. 72-76.]

Argyle, A.W., "The Logos of Philo: Personal or Impersonal?" EXT 66 (1954-55) 13-14.

Arnou, Rene, "Le desire de Dieu dans la philosophie de Plotin," Deuzieme edition revue et corrige. Ed. Paul Henry. Rome, 1967. [Esp. 260-65.]

Baër, Didier, "Incomprehensibilite de Dieu et theologie negative shez Philon d'Alexandrie (I)," Presence orthodoxe 8 (1969) 38-46.

Barnes, E.J., "Petronius, Philo and Stoic Rhetoric," Latomus 32 (1973) 787-798.

Bengio, A., "La dialectique de Dieu et de l'homme chez Platon et chez Philon d'Alexandrie: une approche du concept d'chez Philon," Memoire de maitrise, University of Paris IV, 1971. [BS].

Billings, T.H., The Platonism of Philo Judaeus, Chicago: 1919.

Bormann, Karl, "Die Ideen und Logoslehre Philons von Alexandrien. Eine Auseinandersetzung mit H.A. Wolfson," Dissertation, Köln, 1955. [DHS]

Boyance, P., "Le dieue très haut chez Philon," Melanges d'histoire des religions offerts à Henri-Charles Puech, Paris: 1974.

Boyancé, Peirre, "Le dieu tres haut chez Philon," Melanges d'historie des religions, Henri-Charles Peuch, 139-49. Paris, 1974.

Bréhier, E., Les idées philosophiques et religieuses de Philon d'Alexandrie, Paris: 1925.

Bréhier, Emile. Les idées philosophiques et religieuses de Philon d'Alexandrie. Paris, 1908, ²1925; reprinted 1950.

Chadwick, H., The Cambridge History of Later Greek and Early Mediaeval Philosophy, II, Cambridge: 1967.

Chroust, Anton H., "A Fragment of Aristotle's On Philosophy in Philo of Alexandria, De opificio mundi I, 7." Divus Thomas 77 (1974) 224-35.

Chroust, Anton H., "A Fragment of Aristotle's On Philosophy. Some Remarks about Philo of Alexandria, De Aeternitate Mundi 8,41." Wiener Studien, N.F. 8 (87) (1941) 15-19.

Chroust, Anton H., "Some Comments on Philo of Alexandria, De aternitate mundi., Leval theologique et philosophique 31 (1975) 135-45.

Conley, Thomas, "General Education" in Philo of Alexandria. Center for Hermeneutical Studies in Hellenistic and Modern Culture. Protocol of the Fifteeth Colloquy: 9 March 1975. Ed. Wilhelm Wuellner (Protocol Series of the CHSHMC 15). Berkeley, 1975. [With responses by John Dillon, Alan Mendelson, David Winston and discussion by a group of participants.]

Courcelle, Pierre, Tradition neoplatonicienne et tradition chretienne des ailes de lame. In: Atti del Covegno internazionale sul tema: Plotino e il Neoplatonismo in Oriente e in Occidente, 265-325 (Problemi attuali di scienza e di cultura 198). Roma, 1974.

Daehne, A.F., Geschichtliche Darstellung der jüdisch-alexandrinischen Religionsphilosophie, Stuttgart: 1835.

Daniélou, Jean, Philon d'Alexandrie. Paris, 1958.

Dillon, J., "The Transcendence of God in Philo," Colloqey 16 (1975).

Dillon, John M., "The Transendence of God in Philo: Some Possible Sources," Center for Hermeneutical Studies in Hellenistic and Modern Culture. Protocol of the Sixteenth Colloquy: 20 April 1975. Ed. Wilhelm Wuellner (Protocol Series of the Colloquies of the CHSHMC 16). Berkeley, 1975.

Dörrie, Heinrich, Praepositionen und Metaphysik. Wechselwirkung zweier Prinzipienreihen. Museum Helveticum 26 (1969) 217-28; reprinted in his: Platonica Minora, 124-36 (Studia et Testimonia antiqua 8). München, 1976 [Esp. 130-32.]

Drummond, J., Philo Judaeus, Amsterdam: 1886.

Drummond, James, Philo Judaeus, or The Jewish-Alexandrian Philosophy in its Development and Completion. With Introductory Chapters on Greek Philosophy and the Blending of Hellenism and Judaism till the Time of Philo. With Critical Notes and Indexes of Subject and Names and of Referencs to Passages in Philo. London, 1888; reprinted, Amsterdam, 1969.

Escribano-Alberca, Ignacio, "Glaube und Gotteserkenntnis in der Schrift und Patristik" (Handbuch der Dogmengeschichte 1,2. Ed. M. Schmaus, A. Brillmeier, L. Scheffczyk). Freiburg i. B., 1974. [Esp. 7-11.]

Feibleman, James K., Religious Platonism: the Influence of Religion on Plato and the Influence of Plato on Religion. London, 1959. [Esp. 96-127, 131-34.]

Früchtel, Ursula, "Die kosmologischen Vorstellungen bei Philo von Alexandrien. Ein Beitrag zur Geschichte der Genesisexegese," (ALGHJ 2), 1968.

Gfrörer, A.F., Philo und die jüdisch-alexandrinische Philosophie, Stuttgart: 1835.

Goodenough, E.R., Introduction to Philo Judaeus, 2nd ed., Oxford: 1962.

Goodenough, Erwin R., An Introduction to Philo Judaeus. New Haven, 1940; 2d ed., Oxford, 1962.

Guillaumont, A., "Philon et les origines du monachisme," PAL 361-74.

Guttmann, Joshua. "God (in Hellenistic Literature, Philo)," EJ 7.651-54.

Harl, Marguerite, "Cosmologie grecque et representations juives dans l'oeuvre de Philon d'Alexandrie," PAL., 189-205.

Hay, David M., "Philo's Treatise on the Logos-Cutter," SP 2 (1973) 9-22.

Heinemann, I., Philons griechische und jüdische Bildung, Breslan: 1932.

Heinisch, P., Der Einfluss Philos auf die alteste christliche Exegese, Münster: 1908.

Horowitz, J., Untersuchungen über Philos und Platons Lehre von der Welt-schöpfung, Manburg: 1900.

Kretschmar, George, "Studien zur frühchristlichen Trinitätstheologie," (BHT 21), 1956.

Kuhr, F., Die Gottesprädikationen bei Philo von Alexandrien, Diss. Marburg: 1944.

Lauer, S. Philo's Concept of Time. JJS 9 (1958) 39-46.

Laurentin, A., "Le pneuma dans la doctrine de Philon," ETL 27 (1951) 390-437; reprinted Bruges, 1951.

Leisegang, Hans, "Philon," PW (Neue Bearbeitung) 39.1-50.

Leisegang, Hans, "Philons Schrift über die Ewigkeit der Welt," Philologus N.F. 46 (92) (1937) 156-76.

Lilla, Salvatore R.C., "Middle Platonism, Neoplatonism and Jewish-Alexandrine Philosophy in the Terminology of Clement of Alexandria's Ethics," Archivo italiano per la storia della pieta 3 (1962) 1-36.

Loewe, R., "Philo and Judaism in Alexandria," Jewish Philosophy and Philosophers, 20-40. Ed. R. Goldwater. London, 1962.

Mack, Burton L., "Logos und Sophia. Untersuchungen zur Weissheitstheologie im hellenistischen Judentum," (SUNT 10), 1973.

Moehring, H.R, "Arithmology as an Exegetical Tool in the Writings of Philo of Alexandria," Society for Biblical Literature Seminar Papers, 1, 1978, 191-228.

Mondin, Battista. L'universo filosofico di Filone Alessandrino. SCA 96 (1968) 371-94.

Mühl, Max, Zu Poseidonios und Philon. Weiner Studien 60 (1942) 28-36.

Nazzaro, Antonio V., Il nell' epistemologia filoniana. Annali della Faculta di lettere e filosofia del' Universita di Napoli 12 (1969-70) 49-86; republished Napoli, n.d. [E]

Nock, Arthur Darby, The exegesis of Timaeus 28 C. VC 16 (1962) 79-86. [Esp. 82.]

Pohlenz, M., "Philo von Alexandreia" Nachrichten von der Akademie der Wissenschaften in Göttingen (1943), 103-180.

Pohlenz, Max, Die Stoa. Geschichte einer geistigen Bewegung. 2 vols.

Pohlenz, Max, Göttingen, ³1964. [Esp. 1.369-78, 2.180-84.]

Pohlenz, Max, Philon von Alexandreia. Nachrichten der Akademie der Wissenschaften zu Göttingen, phil.-hist. Kl. 1942, Nr. 5, 409-87; reprinted in his Kleine Schriften 1.305-83. Ed. Heinrich Dörrie. Hildesheim, 1965.

Rahner, Hugo, Griechische Mythen in christlicher Deutung. Darmstadt, 1957.

Reister, Wolfgang, "Die Sophia im Denken Philons." In: Lang, Bernhard. Frau Weisheit. Deutung einer biblischen Gestalt, 161-74. Düsseldorf, 1975. [R]

Sandmel, Samuel. The First Christian Century in Judaism and Christianity: Certainties and Uncertainties. New York, 1969. [Esp. 107-42.]

Smith, R.W., The Art of Rhetoric at Alexandria, The Hague: 1974.

Smulders, P., A Quotation of Philo in Irenaeus. VC 12 (1958) 15-56.

Soulier, H. La Doctrine du Logos chez Philon d'Alexandre, Turin: 1876.

Theiler, Willy, "Gott und Seele im kaiserzeitlichen Denken," Recherches sur la tradition platonicienne, 65-91 (Entretiens sur l'antiquite classique 3). Vandoeuvres-Geneve, 1955. [Esp. 68-72.] Reprinted in his: Forschungen zum Neuplatonismus, 104-23. Berlin, 1966. [Esp. 106.10.]

Theiler, Willy, "Philo von Alexandria und der hellenisierte Timaeus," Philomathes: Studies and Essays in the Humanities in Memory of Philip Merlan, 25-35. Ed. Robert B. Palmer and Robert G. Hamerton-Kelly. The Hague, 1971.

Wendland, P., "Philo und Clemens Alexandrinus", Hermes, 31 (1896), 695-770.

Wendland, P., Philons Schrift über die Vorsehung, Berlin: 1892.

Wendland, Paul, Die hellenistisch-römische Kultur in ihren Beziehungen zum Judentum und Christentum. 4. Aufl. erweitert um eine Biblioghraphie von Heinrich Dörrie. Tübingen, 1972. [Esp. 203-11.]

Whittaker, J., God, Time Being, Oslo: 1971.

Whittaker, John, "God and Time in Philo of Alexandria," in his "God Time Being. Two Studies in the Transcendental Tradition in Greek Philosophy," 33-57 (Symbolae Osloenses, fasc. supplet. 23). Osloae, 1971.

Willms, H. E., Eine begriffsgeschichtliche Untersuchung zum Platonismus. 1. Teil: Philon von Alexandreia. Mit einer Einleitung über Platon und die Zwischenzeit. Münster, 1935. [DHS].

Winston, D., Dillon, J., Two Treatises of Philo of Alexandria, Chico: 1983.

Winston, David S. "Philo's Theory of Cosmogony," in Religious Syncretism in Antiquity. Essays in Conversation with Geo Widengren, 157-71. Ed. Birger A. Pearson (Series on Formative Contemporary Thinkers 1). Missoula, 1975.

Wolfson, H.A., Philo, i, ii, Cambridge: 1947.

Wolfson, H.A., Religious Philosophy, Cambridge: 1961.

Wolfson, Harry A., "Albinus and Plotinus on Divine Attributes," HTR 45 (1952) 115-30; reprinted in: Studies in the History of Philosophy and Religion, 115-30. Ed. Isadore Twersky, George H. Williams. Cambridge MA, 1973. [esp. 115-17, 126-29.]

Wolfson, Harry A., "Philosophical Implications of Arianism and Apollinarianism," Dumbarton Oaks Papers 12 (1958) 3-28; reprinted in his: Religious Philosophy. A Group of Essays, 126-47. Cambridge MA, 1961. [Esp. 137-46.]

Wolfson, Harry A., "Philo Judaeus," The Encyclopedia of Philosophy, 6.151-55. Ed. Paul Edwards. New York, 1967; reprinted, Wolfson, H.A. Studies in the History of Philosophy and Religion, 60-70. Ed. Isadore Twersky, George H. Williams. Cambridge MA, 1973.

Wolfson, Harry A., "The Philosophy that Faith Inspired. Greek Philosophy in Philo and the Church Fathers," The Crucible of Christianity, 309-16, 354. Ed. Arnold Toynbee. New York, 1969; reprinted as: Greek Philosophy in Philo and the Church Fathers. In his: Studies in the History of Philosophy and Religion, 71-97. Ed. Isadore Twersky and George H. Williams. Cabridge MA, 1973.

Wolfson, Harry A., "Two Comments Regarding the Plurality of Worlds in Jewish Sources," JQR 56 (1965-66) 245-47.

Wolfson, Harry A., Extradeical and Intradeical Interpretations of Platonic Ideas. Journal of the History of Ideas 22 (1961) 3-32; reprinted in his: Religious Philosophy. A group of Essays, 27-68. Cambridge MA, 1961.

Wolfson, Harry A., Philo: Foundations of Religious Philosophy in Judaism, Christianity, and Islam. 2 vols. (His: Structure and Growth of Philosophic Systems from Plato to Spinoza 2). Cambridge MA, 1947.

INDEX

Adrastus
17, 77
Aeschines
269
Aisthêsis
125, 169, 172, 173, 182, 183, 185,
188, 194, 196-99, 272, 282, 291, 316,
336
Aitia
157, 277
Albinus
5, 9, 11, 12, 16, 18, 58, 59, 62, 74, 75,
77, 80, 81, 83-101, 105-110, 111, 112,
115-18, 121, 122, 125-27, 129,
132-34, 136, 153, 158, 162, 163,
168-70, 173, 181-89, 201, 206, 208,
300, 302, 303, 305-309, 312, 314, 329
Alexander
17, 105, 111, 115, 116, 136, 139,
146-48, 158-61, 177, 191-99, 228,
229, 276, 304, 305, 310, 311, 314,
319, 320, 335
Alexander of Aphrodisias
111, 115, 116, 139, 146, 191, 193,
228, 320, 335
Ammonius
9, 80, 83, 99, 100, 105, 111, 112,
114-16, 139, 146, 194, 307, 310, 311
Ammonius Saccas
9, 80, 83, 99, 100, 105, 111, 114-16,
139, 146, 194, 311
Anaximenes
287, 289, 317, 331
Andresen
5, 101, 115, 305, 306
Andronicus
25, 63, 64, 77, 116, 122, 301
Antiochus
2, 9, 11, 12, 18, 23, 25-30, 33-35,
41-43, 46, 49, 50, 52, 56, 58, 64, 68,
72, 74-79, 81, 84, 85, 91, 96-98, 118,
168, 171, 172, 176, 177, 181-85, 188,
189, 206, 209, 301, 303, 306, 309,
311-14
Antiochus of Ascalon
2, 9, 23, 27, 72, 172, 182, 313, 314
Apodeixis
16, 201-204, 206-210, 212, 214, 220,
229, 230, 258, 259, 272, 293, 314, 322
Apsines
261, 263, 288, 289, 318, 324, 329-32,
334, 336, 337
Apuleius
97, 98, 133, 329
Archytas
9, 23, 25, 26, 40, 62, 106, 107, 110,
121, 161, 300, 301

Ariston
35, 77
Aristotelian
25, 33, 35, 36, 39, 40, 48, 51, 55, 56,
64, 67, 69, 73, 75, 76, 78, 80, 83, 87,
90, 91, 96, 98, 99, 107, 115-17, 121,
122, 131, 133, 136, 139, 152, 159,
192, 193, 196, 210, 228, 299, 306,
309, 310, 312, 317, 319, 320, 322, 324
Aristotle
7, 9, 34, 51, 56, 57, 62, 63, 69-71, 79,
81, 84, 88, 95, 99, 107, 115-17, 122,
136-40, 145-48, 150, 151, 154, 155,
157, 177, 191, 192, 194, 195, 198,
215-17, 220, 227, 230, 260, 263, 271,
283, 287, 289, 291, 305, 308, 310,
314, 317-34, 336, 337
Arius
29, 35, 43, 85, 88, 91, 96, 306
Arius Didymus
29, 35, 43, 88, 91, 96, 306
Armstrong
84, 87, 101, 300, 305-307, 309
Atticus
17, 84, 90, 116, 120, 305
Augustine
43, 49, 303, 305, 323
Baeumker
47
Bardy
114, 307
Barwick
317, 337
Biblikê
16, 201-203, 206, 293
Bitzer
319
Boethius
34
Bonitz
70
Borst
218, 318
Boulêsis
95, 133, 155
Bowersock
299, 314, 317
Brzoska
333
Cadiou
114, 116, 209, 210, 218, 307, 316, 318
Calcidius
120, 336
Callicratidas
33, 40
Celsus
9, 57, 210, 313, 321